Beginning Active Server Pages 2.0

Brian Francis
John Kauffman
Juan T Llibre
Dave Sussman
Chris Ullman

Wrox Press Ltd.

Beginning Active Server Pages 2.0

First Published   June 1998
Reprinted   August 1998
Reprinted   April 1999

Published by Wrox Press Ltd., Arden House,
1102 Warwick Road, Acocks Green, Birmingham B27 6BH. UK.
Printed in USA

ISBN 1-861001-34-7

Trademark Acknowledgements

Credits

Authors
Brian Francis
John Kauffman
Juan T Llibre
Dave Sussman
Chris Ullman

Development Editor
Jeremy Beacock

Editors
Andy Corsham
Ian Nutt
Chris Ullman

Technical Reviewers
Humberto Abreu
Michael Corning
Brian Francis
John Kauffman
Rick Kingslan
Andy Laken
Juan T Llibre
Larry Roof
Dave Sussman
Byron Vargas

Cover/Design/Layout
Andrew Guillaume

Index
Marilyn Rowland

About the Authors

Brian Francis

Brian is the Lead Developer for NCR's Human Interface Technology Center in Atlanta, Georgia. At the HITC, Brian is responsible for prototyping and developing advanced applications that apply superior human interfaces as developed at the Center. His tools of choice include Visual Basic, Visual C++, Java, and all of the Microsoft Internet products. Brian is focused on delivering electronic commerce systems to consumers through multiple points of presence, both in the store and through the Internet. *To my wife Kristi, who makes my life complete, I dedicate this book.*

John Kauffmann

John's early research focussed on the molecular biology of the cocoa plant and chocolate production. Subsequently he moved to East Africa and managed an assistance program. Since 1990, he has been occupied with setting-up and running software training businesses in Asia and North America; currently, his emphasis is on VB, VBA, ASP and Access, and the integration of Microsoft Products. John can be reached at KauffmanJohn@MindSpring.com. *John deeply thanks his father, John, who taught him to make a list of knowns and unknowns before starting to find a solution to an algebraic problem. He equally thanks his mother, Ruth, who for many years suffered John's pilferage of her kitchen glassware for use in his early chemistry experiments.*

Juan T Llibre

Juan T. Llibre is a Microsoft MVP (Most Valuable Professional) for Internet Development. His university degree is in Mass Communications and, as he puts it: "The Internet is the ultimate mass communications vehicle. It's just great to be able to talk to the whole world while taking in the sun at a tropical beach on the North Coast of the Dominican Republic."

Currently, he's developing Internet Applications for the Caribbean Common Market and the Dominican Republic's Central Bank. He's also researching Multilingual Web Development with a view towards making the World Wide Web intelligible to, well, the whole wide world.

David Sussman

David is a freelance developer, trainer and author, living in Buckinghamshire. He has been using Access since its first release, and now specializes in training and developing client/server solutions around Access, Visual Basic and SQL Server, and writing books for Wrox! His next project is a book on ADO 2.0, so watch this space!

Chris Ullman

Chris Ullman is a computer science graduate who has not let this handicap prevent him becoming a programmer fluent in Visual Basic, Java, SQL and Dynamic HTML. When not cutting up pictures by old masters to re-assemble them as dynamic jigsaws on his preferred browser, he's either found down his local soccer ground urging on his favorite team, Birmingham City, or at home trying to prevent his two new kittens from tearing up the house, or each other. *All my love to Kate, who's always there to give me support and a home and usually tries to look interested when I explain the latest Internet based technology.*

Beginning
Active Server
Pages 2.0

Beginning
**Active Server
Pages 2.0**

An Introduction to
Active Server Pages

Active Server Pages is the latest server-based technology from Microsoft, designed to create dynamic and interactive HTML pages for your World Wide Web site or corporate intranet. In this book, we'll start by looking at how you can get hold of ASP, and how to install it together with Personal Web Server 4.0. Then we'll show you what Active Server Pages is, and how you can use it to build really great Web sites and intranet applications.

Who is this Book For?

This is a Wrox 'Beginning' series book, so we will be aiming to teach you everything you need to know from scratch. We appreciate that most, if not all, of the web page authors and developers who take up Active Server Pages will be reasonably familiar with ordinary HTML, so we won't spend any time teaching you HTML. If you don't know HTML, then we suggest that you refer to a tutorial on HTML before attempting to learn about Active Server Pages.

There are two kinds of beginners for whom this is the ideal book:

▶ You're a **beginner to programming** and you've chosen ASP as the place to start. Great choice! Active Server Pages is easy, it's fun but it's also powerful. This book will hold your hand throughout.

▶ You can program in another language but you're a **beginner to web programming**. Again, great choice! Come in from the cold world of Visual Basic or whatever language you use, and enjoy. This book will teach you how ASP does things in terms you'll understand.

Most of all, you don't need to know anything more than the basic ins and outs of how to put your own web page together. If you've never programmed a single line of JavaScript or Visual Basic, then you have nothing to fear, this is the book for you.

What do I Need to Use this Book?

Most importantly, you'll need a copy of Active Server Pages and a web server for your platform (which must be either Windows 95 or NT 4.0). You'll also need a browser (preferably Internet Explorer 4) and a web page or text editor such as FrontPage 98, Allaire's Homepage, Visual Interdev or NotePad.

You can easily acquire both Active Server Pages and a web server for either NT 4.0 or Windows 95—they're both available as part of the NT 4.0 Option Pack, which is freely downloadable from Microsoft at `http://www.microsoft.com/ntserver/guide/whatisntop.asp`.

There are two versions of the NT 4.0 Option Pack: one for NT 4.0 and one for Windows 95. IIS 4.0 is the web server that comes with the version of the Option Pack for NT Server 4.0, while Personal Web Server 4.0 is included in the NT 4.0 Option Pack for Windows 95. Both include Active Server Pages 2.0 as standard, so there'll be no need to download anything extra. Throughout this book we will be using Personal Web Server as our vehicle of choice, since it is much less complex than IIS, and consequently much easier for the newcomer to pick up.

Nearly all of the examples use Active Server Pages and require a **web server**. You can use your own machine as a web server if necessary. As mentioned before, we recommend Microsoft Personal Web Server 4.0, but you can use a server from any other supplier that implements Active Serve Pages. There are more details about this in Chapter 1.

You may also wish to develop your pages within a specialist environment, such as Microsoft Interdev, FrontPage 98, or a similar application like HoTMetaL Pro or other web page creation software, but you'll need to edit and write the code by hand most of the time.

Lastly, there are two chapters on databases (Chapters 13 and 14). If you want to run the code in these chapters, then you'll need some database software. With a copy of Microsoft Access 97 (or alternatively, access to a copy of Microsoft SQL Server 6.5), you'll be able to take full advantage of these sections.

Where You'll Find the Sample Code

Our prominent presence on the World Wide Web provides you with assistance and support as you use our books. Our Internet-related books (including this one) have a special site: from here, you will able to execute each of the examples we demonstrate, or download the code to run on your own machine. This is at `http://rapid.wrox.co.uk`. You can also find a US-based mirror of this site at `http://www.rapid.wrox.com`. You'll also find details of any updates to the code, or to the product itself.

Our main US-based site is at `http://www.wrox.com`, and it provides details of all our books. There is also a mirror site at `http://www.wrox.co.uk` that may be more responsive if you're accessing the site from Europe.

Conventions

We have used a number of different styles of text and layout in the book to help differentiate between the different kinds of information. Here are examples of the styles we use and an explanation of what they mean:

Try It Outs – How Do They Work?

1 Each step has a number.

2 Follow the steps through.

3 Then read 'How It Works' to find out what's going on.

 Imporant bits of information that you really shouldn't ignore come in boxes like this!

> *Not-to-be-missed information looks like this*

Advice, hints and background information looks like this.

▶ **Important Words** are in a bold type font.

▶ Words that appear on the screen in menus like the <u>F</u>ile or <u>W</u>indow menu are in a similar font to what you see on screen.

▶ Keys that you press on the keyboard, like *Ctrl* and *Enter*, are in italics.

▶ Active Server Pages code has two fonts. If it's a word that we're talking about in the text, for example, when discussing the **For...Next** loop, it's in a bold font. If it's a block of code that you can type in as a program and run, then it's also in a gray box:

```
Private Sub cmdQuit_Click()
    End
End Sub
```

▶ Sometimes you'll see code in a mixture of styles, like this:

```
Private Sub cmdQuit_Click()
    End
End Sub
```

▶ In this case, we want you to consider the code with the gray background. The code with a white background is code we've already looked at, and that we don't wish to examine further.

▶ You'll also see that code in Beginning Active Server Pages is either HTML tags, client-side script or server-side script (ASP). Despite being recommended in the HTML 4.0 standard that tags should be specified in lower case, for ease of reading we have chosen to display HTML tags in upper case throughout the book and all script in lower case. Server-side script is usually surrounded by **<%** and **%>** marks. So an example might look like this:

```
<BODY>
<H1>This is some HTML </H1>
<SCRIPT LANGUAGE=VBScript>
obj1 = "This is some VBScript."
<% obj2 = "This is some ASP." %>
</SCRIPT>
</BODY>
```

These formats are designed to make sure that you know what it is you're looking at. We hope they make life easier.

Tell Us What You Think

We've worked hard on this book to make it useful. We've tried to understand what you're willing to exchange your hard-earned money for, and we've tried to make the book live up to your expectations.

Please let us know what you think about this book. Tell us what we did wrong, and what we did right. This isn't just marketing flannel: we really do huddle around the email to find out what you think. If you don't believe it, then send us a note. We'll answer, and we'll take whatever you say on board for future editions. The easiest way is to use email:

feedback@wrox.com

You can also find more details about Wrox Press on our web site. There, you'll find the code from our latest books, sneak previews of forthcoming titles, and information about the authors and editors. You can order Wrox titles directly from the site, or find out where your nearest local bookstore with Wrox titles is located.

Customer Support

If you find a mistake, please have a look at the errata page for this book on our web site first. Appendix G gives more details of how to submit an errata, if you are unsure. You'll find the errata page on our main web site, at:

```
http://www.wrox.com
```

If you can't find an answer there, tell us about the problem and we'll do everything we can to answer promptly!

Just send us an email to **support@wrox.com** or fill in the form on our web site:

```
http://www.wrox.com/Contact.stm
```

Getting Started With ASP

Active Server Pages (ASP) provides a great new way of creating dynamic web pages. Instead of using the browser to locate the page, ASP uses another machine—the **web server**—before returning the results to the user as HTML.

ASP isn't the first technology to do this, but it's undoubtedly one of the easiest and fastest. It's different from many Microsoft technologies in the following respect: while Active Server Pages has to be executed on a computer that supports it, you can actually view Active Server Pages from *any* computer, and with *any* browser. It has enabled developers to enhance their pages to a huge degree, and pages generated by ASP are fast becoming as common as those generated by HTML.

ASP was officially announced to the world by Microsoft on July 16, 1996, codenamed "Denali". It was released to beta in November 1996, and shipped on December 12, 1996. It gained much wider recognition when it was bundled with version 3 of Microsoft's *Internet Information Server Suite* in March 1997, and has been gaining popularity steadily since then. In the long run, it could prove to be one of the finest innovations to emerge on the Web, for Internet and intranet users alike.

Active Server Pages was considerably enhanced with the release of Internet Information Server 4.0 and Personal Web Server 4.0, and now offers an enriched model for managing communications between a browser and your web server. Active Server Pages allows you to create dynamic forms which can return feedback to the user; it allows you to access databases and return the sorted results on your web site; it allows you to update content on a web site without changing one jot of HTML; and it allows customization on a per-user basis, making sites more useful for each individual.

ASP is relatively simple to learn—all it involves is the learning of a scripting language, which can then be built into existing HTML pages. In short, it's the sliced bread of dynamic web sites. In this chapter, we'll be looking at:

- What ASP is, and what are the advantages of using ASP versus pure HTML
- What a web server is, and what different web servers are available
- An overview of how to install and set up ASP
- How to create your first Active Server Page
- Common errors that might prevent the page from working in the way you intended

What is ASP? And Why is it Better than HTML?

So what exactly is ASP? Perhaps it's easier to consider what it isn't. For example, unlike HTML, ASP is not a language. It's not really an application, like FrontPage 98 or Word 97, either. Instead, we'll give ASP the rather ambiguous term **technology**. ASP is a technology for building dynamic and interactive web pages.

Why do we need ASP at all? We could stick with HTML—after all, it's a tried and trusted method for building web pages; and why do we even *need* "dynamic" web pages? Surely it's much simpler to master HTML, than to learn a whole new technology?

Shortcomings of HTML

While browsing the web, you've probably noticed that the pages on many sites are composed simply of text and static images. These pages are usually composed almost entirely of HTML (with perhaps a little JavaScript code in some cases). These pages allow you to click on links or images to get to other pages, but these display much the same sort of content. Innovations, such as frames and tables, have helped to improve the presentation and usability of these sites, but they haven't made the crucial step towards making these pages truly **dynamic**.

You'll find that sites that contain ASP code are more dynamic: they're quite often tailored to the individual user, they can reflect the fact that a user has visited the site before, they can be customized easily to view preferred topics, and in general they offer the user an all round richer experience. You can see this in pages on some of the larger, more commercial sites, such as those produced by Microsoft, ABCNews.com, Dell, Compaq, Gateway 2000, ESPN SportsZone and the official NASCAR, NBA, NFL and WNBA sites. Many of these pages are easily identifiable as Active Server Pages, since they are suffixed by `.asp` (although, confusingly, you'll also find plenty of ASP-generated pages masquerading under the cover of an `.html` suffix).

However, the main difference between ASP pages and HTML pages is how the **web server** deals them.

The Importance of the Web Server

As a user of the Internet, or of your local intranet, you'll be familiar with the procedure that you go through in order to view a page: you type in the address of the page (or URL), press *Return*, and off goes your request to this mysterious faraway machine, known as a web server.

So what is a web server? It's simply a computer that provides web services on the Internet, or on a local intranet. A basic web server is designed to locate, address and send out simple HTML pages. The web server makes web pages available to all other users, who can access these pages via their local network or via the Internet.

Let's have a look at what happens when the user requests a page from the server.

What happens to HTML Pages?

When a request for a page comes from the browser, the web server performs three steps:

▶ reads the request from the browser

▶ finds the page in the server

▶ sends the page back across the Internet to the browser

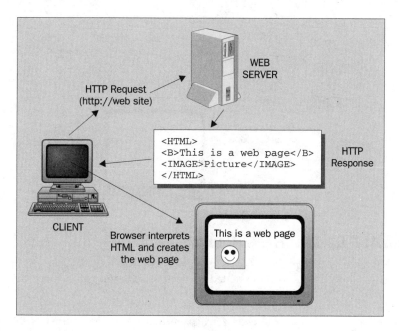

What happens to ASP pages?

In this book we will use ASP to add an additional step. Instead of throwing a static HTML page out to the user, we want the server to take some actions according to our ASP code: the ASP will make some decisions and create a page that is tailored for that particular user. Thus, when using ASP, the server actions are as follows:

▶ read the request from the browser

▶ find the page in the server

▶ perform any instructions provided in ASP to modify the page

▶ send the page back across the Internet to the browser

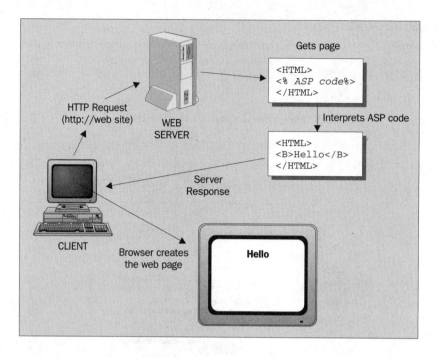

So What Can ASP Do That HTML Can't?

The crucial difference is that pure HTML is interpreted by the browser, *not* executed on the server. By writing code that is to be executed on web server, you can achieve many more things than would otherwise be possible.

For example, we may want to write code for a page that serves up notices of the Wednesday News when the page is requested on a Wednesday, then displays Thursday News on Thursday. In another example, we might want to write a page that detects the type of browser that the user is using, and then optimize the requested information for that browser. With ASP, actions of this kind will be performed by the web server in the third step of the sequence outlined above.

Here's are a few more examples of things that you can do with ASP, but that you can't do with pure HTML on its own:

   ▶ Make it easier to edit contents of a web page, by updating a text file or the contents of a database rather than the HTML code itself

   ▶ Create pages that will be customized to display only things that will be of interest to a particular user

   ▶ Display and update databases contained in the web page, and manipulate the data therein, by being able to sort the entries into any order or view a subset of them

   ▶ Create pages that rotate through a series of different graphics

   ▶ Get feedback from a user, and return information to the user based upon that feedback

And this list only scratches the surface: ASP allows you to do much more besides.

ASP and HTML

ASP is designed to be used *together* with HTML to create dynamic pages. In fact, ASP actually creates HTML code. Having said that, we really need to slow this discussion right up—because the thought of text, HTML tags and ASP code, all intermingled and intermarried in a single piece of code, gives rise to one of the main problems for beginners.

A web page that uses ASP is likely to consist of a mixture of three types of syntax. Some of the page will be constructed from simple text, part will be HTML, and part will be ASP code. The following table summarizes each of these ingredients:

Type	Purpose	Interpreter	Hallmarks
Text	Information to be shown on the page	Viewer's browser on thier PC shows the text	Simple ASCII text
HTML tags	Instructions to the browser about how to format text and display images	Viewer's browser on thier PC interprets the tags to format the text	Each tag within `< >` delimiters Usually has open and close tags, such as `<TABLE>`, `</TABLE>`
ASP statements	Instructions to the web server running ASP about how to create portions of the page to be sent out	Web site host's web server software with ASP extensions performs the instructions of the ASP code	Each ASP section contained within `<% %>` delimiters ASP statements have a flavor of Visual Basic, with the appearance of programming code with variables, decision trees, etc.

If you look at ASP/HTML code, it's not too hard to distinguish which elements are ASP and which are HTML. That's because ASP is usually denoted by opening `<%` and closing `%>` markers. Here's an example program from the Wrox book *Professional Active Server Pages 2.0* (ISBN 1-861001-26-6). The HTML code and text is shown on a white background, and the ASP code is shown on a gray background:

```
<HTML>
<HEAD>
<TITLE>Polite Web Server</TITLE>
</HEAD>
<BODY BGCOLOR="wheat">
<P>
<FONT COLOR="Teal" SIZE="3"><B>

The Polite Web Server, at <% = Time %> on <% = Date %> </B></FONT></P>

<P><B><% If Hour(Now) < 8 Then %> Don't you know what time it is? I was
still in bed! <% Else
    Randomize
```

```
    intChoice = Int(Rnd * 4)
    Select Case intChoice
        Case 0 %> So, where do you want me to go today?
<% Case 1 %> Well, look who's back visiting us again...
<% Case 2 %> Hi there, and welcome to our site.
<% Case 3 %> It's raining here, what's the weather at your end like?
<% End Select
    End If %> </B></P>
<HR>

</BODY>
</HTML>
```

Don't worry about what this program does; the main point here is to illustrate that anything that falls in between the **<%** and **%>** markers is to be executed as script code on the web server. The web server searches out these **<% ... %>** markers, executes the code contained within, converts it to HTML and sends the whole lot back to the browser. Then, the browser can display the web page: the beauty is that the browser never needs to know how to understand the ASP code, since it only ever gets to see pure HTML.

For the time being, this is all we need to know: we'll look at this process in much greater detail in Chapter 2.

Can ASP Pages be Viewed on Netscape or Internet Explorer?

Active Server Pages are executed on the server. This means that you can use any client (browser) to view the results. Hence, your Active Server Page can be viewed as easily with the Netscape Navigator browser, as with Microsoft's own Internet Explorer browser. However, you need to note that your web server *must* be capable of running ASP. We'll look at which web servers fit the bill, very shortly.

The Web—The Next Generation

ASP is one of only several technologies that can be used to create more dynamic and interactive web pages. In this section, we'll look at the historical context of ASP and at some of its competitors.

Microsoft is behind much of the drive towards the next generation of web technologies. However, Microsoft isn't the only organization pulling in the direction of interactive web sites: many of its competitors are also chipping away at the boundaries of interactive web capability.

As far as this area is concerned, the key word is **Active**. Active Server Pages forms one cornerstone of Microsoft's range of Active technologies. These technologies are intended to form the basis of the next generation of Internet application. Microsoft is quite clearly defining the next generation of web publishing; however, we need to look at what went before.

Static Publishing

The first generation was that of **static publishing**—pages that relied on HTML, static pictures and text that couldn't be positioned precisely in terms of x and y coordinates. These pages were fairly basic; in order to get genuinely impressive results from these techniques, you'd really need to be an expert in HTML—or else get a graphic designer in! Furthermore, in order to update the page, you'd need to edit the HTML by hand, or with an editor; and these pages weren't compatible with databases either. Apart from displaying text and images, there wasn't a whole lot more that they could do.

CGI

The second generation went some way to addressing this, in the form of server-side scripting. "Ah," I hear you say, "but isn't that what ASP does?" Well, yes it is: it would be a white lie to say that ASP does something that's entirely new. The Common Gateway Interface (CGI) is a mechanism for managing interaction between the web server software and the browser, and it's been around for quite a bit longer than ASP. In fact the majority of dynamically created pages on the web right now are created by CGI, in much the same way that we're trumpeting ASP.

However, CGI has some severe shortcomings. The major one is that it adds an extra level to our browser–server model of interaction: namely, it's necessary to run a CGI program to create the dynamic page, which is sent back to the server. Also, the code that CGI receives and transmits is not easily manipulated by many programming languages, so you have to use a programming language that has good facilities for manipulating text and communicating with other software. The best multi-platform programming languages for doing this are C, C++ and Perl. While they can adequately do the job for you, they're all quite complex to learn.

Active Web Sites

The new generation consists of **Active web sites**. They are built with a combination of languages and technologies—you can use any one of these alone, or any number of them together, and they're all independent (in the sense that you don't have to learn one technology before you can learn another). These technologies are namely:

- ActiveX Controls—created by Visual C++ or Visual Baisc
- Java
- Scripting languages—VBScript and JavaScript/JScript/ECMAScript
- Active Server Pages and Dynamic HTML

Let's have a quick look at each of these.

ActiveX Controls

ActiveX controls are self-contained programs, known as **components**, that are written in a language such as C++ or Visual Basic. When added to a web page, they provide a specific piece of functionality, such as bar charts and graphs, timers, client authentication, or database access. ActiveX controls are added to HTML pages via the `<OBJECT>` tag, which is now part of the HTML standard. ActiveX controls can be executed by the browser or server when they are embedded in a web page.

There is a catch. ActiveX controls were developed by Microsoft, and despite being compatible with the HTML standard, they are not supported on any Netscape browser without an ActiveX plug-in: they will only function on Internet Explorer (although some ActiveX functionality is provided for Netscape via a plug-in supplied by NCompass). Consequently, they still can't really be considered a cross-platform way of making your pages dynamic.

Java

Java (and the development tool Visual J++, which contains the Microsoft variant of Java) is a stand-alone, cross-platform language for developing applications. Despite tremendous hype and initial strong interest, the pick up of Java isn't increasing above the 8% usage among programmers that it enjoyed a couple of years ago. The main reason that Java isn't quite living up to its initial promise, is that it falls between two stools. It's simpler to learn than complex programming languages like C++ (one of its main competitors) but it doesn't offer the same speed or functionality. For the novice programmer who might be learning it in place of Visual Basic, though, it's still quite a complex language to get to grips with.

Scripting Languages

Scripting languages provide the newcomer with a more accessible gateway to programming. Client-side scripting for web use was developed to provide a dynamic alternative to static HTML. When a browser finds a scripting instruction embedded in HTML code, the browser will translate that script into pure HTML (assuming the browser understands that particular scripting language). This permits you, as a developer, to create more interactive web pages, which are far more functional than pure HTML pages.

There are two main scripting languages, namely VBScript and JavaScript (although they are not the *only* two!).

> Note that JavaScript shouldn't be confused with Java. In fact, JavaScript was originally to have been named LiveScript; at that time, Netscape intended to market the language as a completely separate programming language to Java. However, following the popularity of Java, Netscape teamed up with Sun during the development of LiveScript, changed its name to JavaScript, and borrowed several structures from Java's syntax. Hence the language shares some superficial resemblances with its namesake.

JavaScript was the first client-side scripting language. VBScript is Microsoft's scripting language, and is based on their Visual Basic programming language. Scripting has been present in Internet Explorer since version 3, and in Netscape Navigator/Communicator since version 2. Internet Explorer 4 supports both JScript (Microsoft's implementation of JavaScript) and VBScript, while Communicator 4 supports only JavaScript. VBScript may be added to Navigator with the aid of a proprietary add-in, available from `http://www.ncompasslabs.com`.

Scripting languages form the basis of ASP. ASP scripts are executed by the web server, rather than the browser. Scripting languages can be used to access the various bits and pieces that ASP provides: these are known as **objects**, and we will look at them shortly.

We've seen in the discussion so far that it's possible to execute scripting language commands on both the browser and server; furthermore, there's nothing to stop you from doing both within the course of a single program. We'll look at why you might want to do that in Chapter 2.

ASP and Dynamic HTML

ASP and Dynamic HTML can both be thought of as extensions to scripting languages and HTML; however, neither of them are programming languages in their own right. ASP takes the scripting language code and converts it into HTML on the server, before sending it back to the browser.

On the other hand, Dynamic HTML is just like scripting in that the script is interpreted by the browser level that creates a representation of the page in HTML. In fact, the only way in which Dynamic HTML differs from scripting is that it allows access to extra features such as the ability to animate pages and position graphics and text precisely by using (x, y) type coordinates. At the end of the day, the browser will be creating a page from pure HTML.

> *To reinforce the difference: ASP is a server-side technology, while Dynamic HTML is a closely related client-side technology. In this book, we will restrict our discussion to ASP.*

Over the next three chapters, we'll introduce scripting languages in detail—and since ASP uses nothing more than scripting language to access its features, we'll bring in ASP at the same time. Don't feel swamped by the multitude of new technologies: they're all interlinked and very similar in nature, and when you start to learn about one, the inevitable overlap means that the others are more accessible when you come to them.

Why Use ASP?

So, the primary difference between ASP and the other new generation technologies mentioned is that ASP must be executed on the **web server**, while the pages generated by other technologies are interpreted by the **browser** (or **client**). And the advantages that ASP enjoys over CGI and Perl are those of simplicity and speed.

At one time, the browser could do everything you needed—it interpreted your HTML page, it displayed the graphics in a certain way, and it handled errors. However, with the passing of time, browsers have had to cope with an ever-increasing list of tasks—such as handling scripts and having built in controls—and consequently, browsers have become bigger and slower.

The idea behind ASP is that we decrease the demand on browsers, by getting the server to do some of the work instead. A large central machine can be used to take some of the load, performing some of these tasks itself instead of relaying them to the browser.

The side effects offer some other significant advantages:

- minimizes network traffic by limiting the need for the browser and server to talk to each other
- makes for quicker loading time since, in the end, you're only actually downloading a page of HTML
- allows you to run programs in languages that aren't supported by your user's browser
- can provide the client with data that does not reside on the client's machine
- provides improved security measures, since you can code things which can never be viewed from the browser

The list is endless...

What do I Need to Run ASP?

By now, you'll have a good idea *why* you want to run ASP; so now you need to know what you *need* to run ASP. It's as simple as this: you need a browser and a web server.

We'll assume that you already have a browser. By 'web server', we don't mean that you need a separate machine, but simply the software to run web services on your machine. Let's get down to deciding which web server you'll need.

Which Web Server do I Choose?

There is a vast choice of web servers available. Many are available commercially (such as Netscape's web server) and some are available free (such as Apache's web server). ASP 1.0 was originally released as an **extension** that could be installed onto an existing web server. These 'extensions' are pieces of server operating system software written by Microsoft that can be installed by the systems administrator. Once the web server has the ASP extensions software loaded and running, it can then interpret pages containing ASP code. However, it isn't possible to run ASP on all servers: let's look at those servers which *do* support ASP.

Web Servers that Support ASP

There are two such available from Microsoft: namely, Internet Information Server (IIS) and Personal Web Server (PWS). The latest versions of both provide Active Server Pages 2.0 as part of their web services—so you don't need to install anything extra.

There is also a product called ChiliASP, which is available from ChiliSoft: once installed, ChiliASP enables you to run ASP on other web servers that run on Windows 95/NT, including Netscape. In addition, ChiliASP is soon to be available for UNIX web servers. For more details of this product please look at **http://www.chilisoft.com**.

The bottom line is that you can run ASP on IIS, PWS, or any web server supported by ChiliASP.

Internet Information Server (IIS)

IIS is the larger of the two web servers available from Microsoft, and in order to use it you need to be running a large machine with NT Server. IIS 3.0 was the first version of the web server to actually be bundled with ASP 1.0 (i.e. you didn't need to load it separately). The latest release of IIS (at the time of writing) is IIS 4.0, and this comes with ASP 2.0 already installed.

ASP 1.0 and 2.0 are very similar. Nearly all programs created in ASP 1.0 can be run with ASP 2.0. However, ASP 2.0 boasts some extra features which are of great use to the web page developer. Some of the programs in this book utilize new features of ASP 2.0, and are therefore incompatible with web servers running ASP 1.0.

IIS provides the ability to provide web services, not only for web pages, but also for ftp sites (ability to transfer whole files from one site to another), nntp services (newsgroups services) and video and audio services. It is also designed to integrate seamlessly with many of Microsoft's other products. It integrates with the database facilities of SQL Server, the management facilities of Site Server, and the e-mailing and messaging abilities of Exchange. If you're going to run a professional web site and you wish to use ASP, then IIS 4.0 will be among the top candidates.

However, IIS 4.0 needs to run on NT Server 4.0, which in turn needs to be run on a large machine. Therefore, for the purposes of this book, we are going to skate past it and move on to PWS.

Personal Web Server (PWS)

PWS is Microsoft's slimmed-down web server, which provides a basis on which to develop corporate networked applications. There have been two versions of PWS to date. The first one was Personal Web Server for Windows 95 (also known as 1.0). This didn't come with ASP bundled, but at the time of its release, you could download ASP 1.0 separately as an extension from Microsoft and install it on PWS.

ASP 1.0 is no longer available as a separate extension from Microsoft. You can obtain ASP 2.0 as part of a bundled package with the latest releases of IIS and PWS—presumably to encourage people to use the up-to-date versions. The latest version of PWS, version 4.0, can be run on any home machine that runs Windows 95, Windows 98 or Windows NT Workstation. Just like IIS 4.0, PWS 4.0 comes with ASP 2.0 as standard. With PWS 4.0, you can create ASP programs and test them as though you were an external user, running on the same machine.

PWS 4.0 runs on Windows 95, Windows 98 and NT Workstation, and since most home users will be using one of these platforms, we'll be using PWS 4.0 throughout this book as the web server of choice, and we'll use it to test all the examples. Since it ships with ASP as standard, and is much simpler than IIS 4.0, it is our favored web server on which to learn ASP.

As we've mentioned, earlier versions of PWS support only the early verson of ASP (namely ASP 1.0); this version will not support a number of the examples in this book.

Finally, if you own either FrontPage 97 or FrontPage 98, you'll find that a cut-down version of PWS is included. However, with this version of PWS, it isn't possible to run Active Server Pages at all (even with the ASP extensions). If you try executing an Active Server Page on this, then you will most likely see your ASP code printed on the screen exactly as you typed it.

Where do I Get IIS or PWS?

IIS and PWS come in two different versions of the NT 4 Option Pack for the different Windows platforms, one for NT and one for 95/98 and NT Workstation. We recommend downloading the NT 4 Option Pack for Windows 95/NT Workstation without further ado (if you haven't already), so that you can follow the examples in the book. It's downloadable, for free, from Microsoft at `http://www.microsoft.com/ntserver/guide/whatisntop.asp`.

Installing Personal Web Server 4.0

Once you've obtained the NT 4 Option Pack from Microsoft's web site, it's a simple matter to install Personal Web Server 4.0. First, you'll need to install Internet Explorer 4.01 (which also comes in the NT 4 Option Pack)—if you don't do this, the PWS installation wizard won't let you install PWS. Once IE 4.01 has been installed, the installation wizard guides you through the steps and makes most of the crucial decisions for you, so you don't even have to worry about setting it up. We'll look at how to do it right now.

Try It Out – Installing Personal Web Server

1 You need to start the installation process by running `setup.exe` (if you're running it from CD, the `.exe` will auto-run and you need to click on Install). You'll be greeted by the startup screen. Click Next.

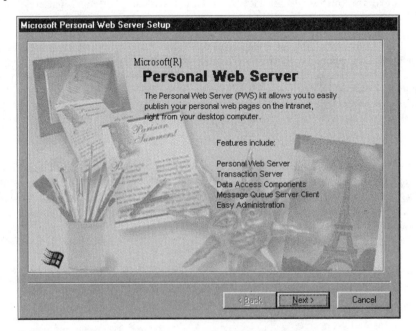

2 Having Accepted the license, we need to decide whether to pursue a Minimum, Typical or Custom installation (the Minimum installation provides all the components we'll use in the book). It's easier to click on Minimum or Typical; if you choose Minimum you won't get the vast array of ASP documentation. If you choose Typical, you'll get the basic documentation. If you want to install the full documentation, you'll need an extra 60MB of hard disk space. I've chosen Typical here.

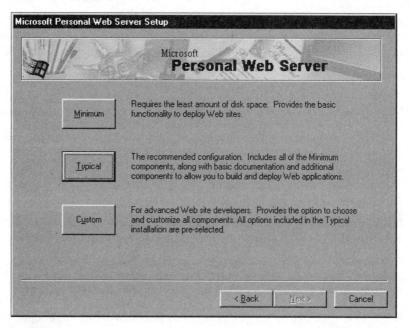

3 Personal Web Server will then install with the minimum of fuss, and will set up default web services. Unless you've got any particular objections to where it proposes to set up your **default web directory** (explained shortly), click on Next to accept the default `C:\InetPub\wwwroot`.

The options in the bottom two panels are not enabled, since they are IIS-only features.

4 Click Finish to end the setup process.

How It Works

When Personal Web Server installs, you may notice that it also installs bits of Microsoft Transaction Server (MTS) and some Front Page Server extensions. Once it has finished loading, it will automatically start web services running for you.

You'll find that Personal Web Server installs most of its bits and pieces on your hard drive under the `InetPub` directory. If you expand this directory, you'll find that it contains four subdirectories:

> ▶ `IISsamples`: You'll find two directories under here. The first is `default`: this holds a default home page, which is where you'll be directed if you type in the name of your web server as a URL (more on that in a moment). The second is `homepage`: this contains some example ASP pages.

> ▶ `Scripts`: This is an empty directory, which is a useful place to store any ASP scripts you might create.

> ▶ `WebPub`: This is also empty. This is a 'special' virtual directory, used for publishing files via the Publish wizard.

> ▶ `WWWroot`: This is the top of the tree for your web site. This should be your default web directory. It contains links to the other three directories mentioned here. It also contains a lot of subdirectories which contain various bits and pieces of Personal Web Server. This is where you should create any physical directories on your web site.

Personal Web Server starts automatically when you boot up Windows, so you won't need to run any `.exe` files in the way that you would with Word or Excel (although `PWS.exe` is located in `C:\Windows\System\Inetsrv`). So, if PWS doesn't run, it's likely that there's a problem with the installation not functioning correctly: in this case it's usually wise to try and reinstall.

Finding your Way Around Personal Web Server

Once installed, Personal Web Server runs as a small icon in your task tray. On my machine, it's the icon just to the left of the clock.

If you float your cursor above this icon, you should see a message which informs you that PWS is running.

By double clicking on this icon, you will start an application called Personal Web Manager, which you can use to administer your web pages.

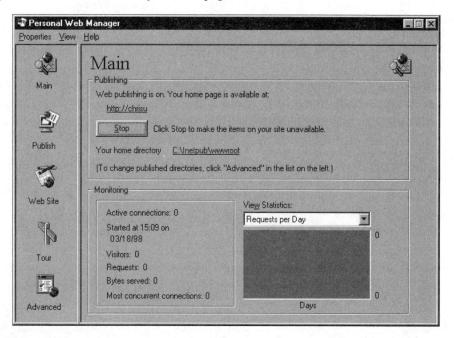

Enabling Web Services

To ensure that any pages you create are visible to anybody else with access to machine on the Internet or local intranet, all you need to do is press the Start button. This starts web services up, and makes all of the specified pages under the **wwwroot** folder available to the outside world (as long as you're not behind a firewall, proxy server or some other security device). Once running, the Start button becomes a Stop button, so that the Personal Web Manager looks like the screen shown above.

Naming your Server

By default, Personal Web Server will take the name of your web server from the name of your computer. You can change it by changing the name of your machine. When you first run Personal Web Manager, you should find that your web server is already named. The name will appear on the Publishing panel of Personal Web Manager. In my case, as you can see in the above screenshot, the server has assumed my computer name, which is chrisu.

If your machine hasn't been named, then the machine will probably adopt the name localhost. Throughout this book, in the examples that require a web server name, we'll put the following in the code: **my_server_name**. This means you should substitute your own server name for **my_server_name**, rather than typing this in literally.

Directories on your Web Server

When the user executes a web page on the server, the position of the page on the server—that is, which directory or folder it's in—comes into play. You have to set up permissions that will allow a browser to view or execute the pages. Permissions are set on a directory-wide basis, and you can control how these are allocated through Personal Web Manager's **Advanced** icon:

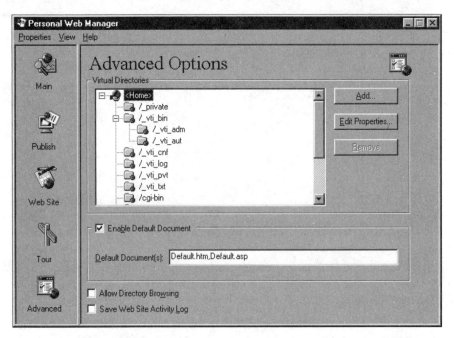

 FYI If you've installed PWS, then you can view these screens now. We'll go through a complete application, and explain exactly how to use these screens, later in the chapter.

Directory Browsing

If you don't want to allow people to view the contents of the directory, then you can prevent them from doing this by unchecking the **Allow Directory Browsing** option on the **Advanced** screen of the Perswonal Web Manager. If someone tries to view the contents of a directory that is not read-enabled (for example, as in the screenshot below), then they'll receive the following message:

Virtual Directories

When you add a directory, you must first specify the directory path; you must also add an alias, which is known as a **virtual directory**. Virtual directories are used as aliases for directory paths on the server. Virtual directories also enable you to construct your web site independently of the directory structure on your hard drive, and hence disconnect the layout of your site from the physical layout of the file system. This allows you to move files on your disk between different folders, drives, or even servers, without having to change the structure of your web pages.

Virtual directories also provide a very useful way of protecting the users of your site from the necessity of typing an extremely long URL each time they want to access a particular page on your site. For example, consider the following URL:

```
http://mycoolsite/onedirectory/anotherdirectoryanextremelylongdirectoryname
/asppage/default.asp
```

You can see that it's laborious to type, and consequently quite error-prone too. Instead, by setting up a simple `/asppage` alias, the user can simply type:

```
http://mycoolsite/asppage/default.asp
```

to refer to exactly the same page as above. We'll set up an alias of our own, very shortly.

Permissions

Permissions can be assigned to a new directory when it is created; alternatively you can use the Edit Properties button, in Personal Web Manager, to amend an existing one. When you click on the Edit Properties button you get the following dialog:

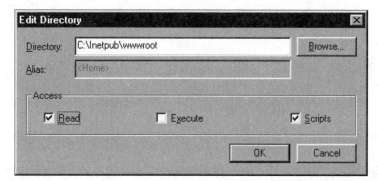

As you can see, for the given directory there are three types of access, which dictate the permissions of the files contained within that directory. Let's have a look at what each of them means.

Read enables browsers to read or download files stored in a home directory or a virtual directory. If the browser requests a file from a directory that doesn't have the Read permission enabled, then the web server will simply return an error message (such as the one shown below). Generally, directories containing information that you want to publish (HTML files, for example) should have the Read permission enabled.

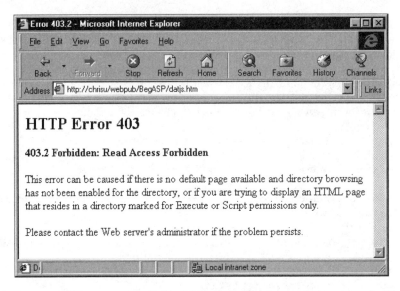

However, ASPs can still be run even if the folder has Read permission turned off.

Execute enables any application in a directory to run, including script engines. For security reasons, your content folders shouldn't have the Execute permission enabled.

Scripts enables a script engine to run in a directory, without the need for the Execute permission to be set. You should use Scripts permissions for directories that contain ASP scripts. It's a lot safer to use than Execute, because you can limit the applications in the directory that can be run. If a client sends a request to run a script in a folder that does not have Scripts permission, the Web server returns an error. By default, all directories created during setup have Scripts permission enabled.

 FYI   We'll learn more about what what a script engine is, and what it does, in Chapter 2.

Now we're ready to have a crack at setting up our own aliases and permissions.

Try It Out – Creating a Virtual Directory and Setting Up Permissions

Let's take a quick look now at how you can create your own virtual directory. We'll use it to store the examples that we'll create during the course of this book.

1 Start Windows Explorer and create a new directory named BegASP under the Inetpub\wwwroot directory created by PWS on your hard drive.

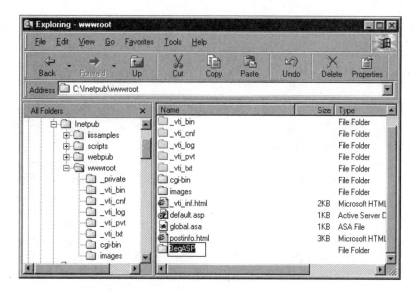

2 Next start up Personal Web Manager and click on the **Advanced** icon.

3 Select the directory <Home>.

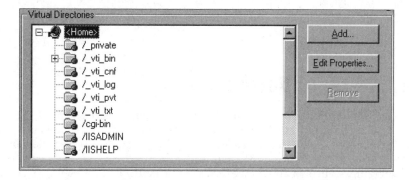

4 Click on the **Add** button, and click on the **Browse** button and select the directory \Inetpub\wwwroot\BegASP that you created in step 1. Add the name **BegASP** to the **Alias** box.

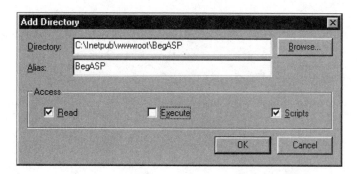

5 Make sure that the Read and Scripts checkboxes are checked, and that the Execute checkbox is empty.

6 Click on OK—the BegASP directory will appear on the tree.

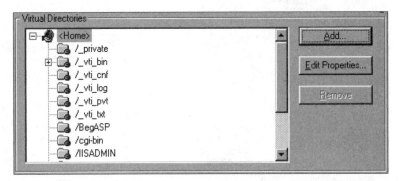

You've now created a directory in which to store all of the examples, and one which can be accessed via a URL on Personal Web Server, using the URL `http://my_server_name/BegASP`.

> *Note that the URL uses the alias* `/BegASP`—*PWS knows that this stands for the directory path* `C:\Inetpub\wwwroot\BegASP`. *When executing ASPs, the URL must call the page via the alias: if you try to use the directory structure as part of the URL, you won't be able to call the web page.*

Getting ASP Up and Running

So by now, you should understand a little about what ASP is, and where to get it and how to get your web server installed and started. As we mentioned earlier, in previous incarnations it was necessary to install Active Server Pages separately on the web server. Now, however, if you've got IIS 4.0 or PWS 4.0 installed, then ASP is complete and ready to go. You can start at once by banging up your own rough and ready-made ASPs. First, though, we need to consider the tools that will aid the creation of your first ASP script.

Checking it's all Working Fine

OK, if Personal Web Server is up and running, it's time to check to see if ASP is functioning correctly. We'll create a simple web page in HTML, view it and then add a line of ASP script and view that to see if everything's OK.

The Punctual Web Server Example

We'll start with a simple enough example, in which the web server that you are running returns the current time.

Try It Out – The Punctual Web Server

1   We'll discuss code editors later in the chapter, but for now we'll use NotePad. Crank it up, and type in the following program:

```
<HTML>
<HEAD>
<TITLE> Punctual Web Server Example</TITLE>
</HEAD>

<BODY>
<FONT COLOR=Blue SIZE=5>
Hello, the time is exactly <% = Time %> in web server land
</FONT>
</BODY>

</HTML>
```

If you don't wish to type in the examples, then you can run them directly from the Wrox web site at `http://www.wrox.com,` **or you can download them and run them on your own machine. This goes for all of the examples in the book.**

2   Save the document as **punctual.asp** in the `C:\Inetpub\wwwroot\BegASP` directory. Be sure that your new file has the correct suffix, **.asp**: your editor may not set this as the default! You must do this, since the **.asp** suffix is the only way your web server will be able to recognize you file as being an ASP file.

3   Kickstart your browser of choice and enter the URL **http://*my_server_name*/BegASP/ punctual.asp**

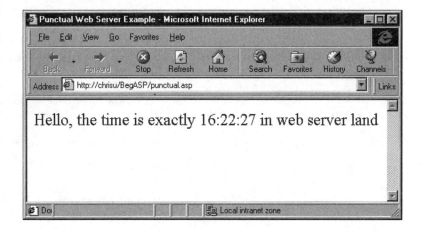

4 Click on the Refresh button: the displayed time will change. In effect, you're now viewing a different web page.

5 Now select the View Source option: you will see that the time is actually now part of the HTML and that there is no ASP script to be seen. This is because, just as we promised, the ASP script has been converted to HTML code.

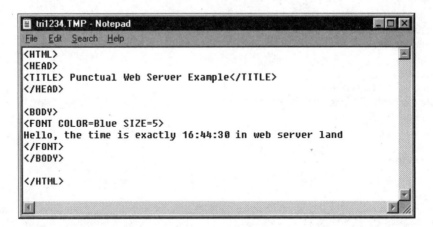

Easy wasn't it? (If you didn't get it to work first time, then have a little look at the next section, "Common Pitfalls and Errors with ASP".) Now let's take a look at the ASP that makes this application tick.

How It Works

Of course, there is only one line of ASP in the whole program:

```
Hello, the time is exactly <% = Time %> in web server land
```

This line tells the web server to go off and run the VBScript function, **Time**, *on the web server*—this returns the current time *of the web server*. If you were accessing a web server in another time zone or country, then the time that the web server returns would be different to the time you'd have on your own computer.

The **Time** function isn't unique to ASP: indeed, it's just a VBScript function that's being run on the server.

This example isn't wildly interactive or dynamic, but it's a neat illustration of the principle of getting the web server to go off and do something for you, and then return the answer within the context of an HTML page. Of course, if you extrapolate this step a lot further, you can see how this might be used with forms and so on, to build a more informative interface with the user.

Common Errors and Pitfalls with ASP

If you had difficulty with the example above, then perhaps you fell into one of the simple traps that commonly snare new ASP programmers—but that can be easily rectified. In this section we'll look at a few common errors; if you did have problems, maybe this section will help you to identify the problem.

The first and most obvious check is to confirm that you're actually *running* your ASP page (rather than just viewing it). To execute an ASP, you need to reference the server in the URL, like this:

`http://chrisu/default.asp`

You'll have problems if you try to view the page as a local file on your hard drive, like this:

`C:\InetPub\wwwroot\default.asp`

or if you click on the file in Windows Explorer. In each of these cases, you're not actually running the page, because the ASP page hasn't been submitted to the server. How can you detect that the page is not actually being run? That depends on which browser you're using.

The Internet Explorer 4 browser can recognize whether you're trying to view an ASP as a local file, and will prevent access to the file.

However, older versions of Internet Explorer, and all versions of Netscape Navigator, will attempt to download the file:

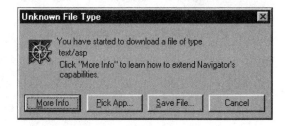

This won't help you to run the program, so simply cancel out of the operation and make sure that you are running the `http://` version of the URL on the browser.

> *If you've loaded FrontPage 98 on your machine then you won't get either of the above messages. It doesn't matter then which browser you're running; FrontPage 98 will always start up whenever you try to view an ASP on IE4 and Navigator 4 because it has been associated with ASP files. When FrontPage 98 installs, it automatically allocates the `.asp` extension to itself.*

Let's move on to the second common pitfall. If you attempt to execute an ASP page that hasn't got the PWS **Scripts** permission enabled, then you'll be refused permission to execute the page. You'll receive an HTTP error 403.1, which looks like this:

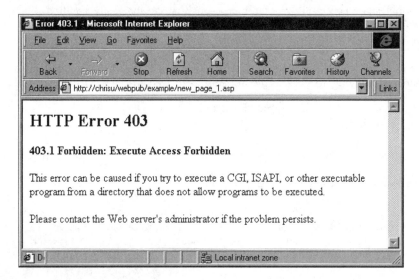

To get around this problem, start Personal Web Manager, click on the **Advanced** icon and select the appropriate alias. Then click on **Edit Properties** and make sure that the **Scripts** box is enabled.

The third common pitfall is simply that you have incorrectly typed the URL into the browser prompt. You'll get this problem, for example, if you

> Make a simple typing error in the URL—e.g. `http://chrisu/BegASP/puntual.asp`

> Include a directory separator (/) after the file name—e.g. `http://chrisu/BegASP/punctual.asp/`

> Use the directory path in the URL, rather than using the alias—e.g. `http://chrisu/Inetpub/wwwroot/BegASP/punctual.asp`

In this case, the browser simply can't find the file you've requested. You'll receive an HTTP error 404 message, which looks something like this:

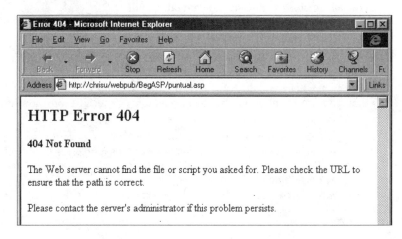

The simple solution to this is to check your URL and retype it.

Finally, if you see nothing in your browser then you haven't remembered to save, FTP or refresh the browser, or (if you get an error such as **Expected statement**) then you probably left out the closing **%>** tag on your code.

If your problem isn't covered by this description, it's worth testing some of the sample ASPs that are supplied with PWS and found in the **InetPub/IISSamples** directory. These should help you to check that PWS has actually installed properly; you can always reinstall if necessary.

By now, you should have successfully downloaded, set up and installed PWS, created your first application in ASP, and been able to get it up and running. Let's look at some of the more popular editors with which you can create and edit ASP scripts.

Creating and Editing ASP Scripts

There are a variety of different editors and applications with which you can create and edit ASPs. However, we'll only look at the four most common. Three are available commercially, while one comes free with Windows. The three commercially available tools are Visual Interdev, FrontPage 98 and Allaire's Homesite. If you own one of these products, we recommend using them to edit ASP.

Visual Interdev 1.0

Visual Interdev comes as part of Microsoft's suite of professional programming tools, Visual Studio, and is a tool for designing dynamic web applications. It is, in effect, just a development environment and collection of useful tools and utilities. Visual Interdev is the tool that Microsoft are promoting as their favored ASP editing tool. One simple but very useful feature of Visual Interdev is the fact that it highlights all ASP code in yellow, which makes it stand out from the HTML and normal client-side script. If you load any of the ASP files that come with Personal Web Server into Visual Interdev, you'll get a view that looks something like the following:

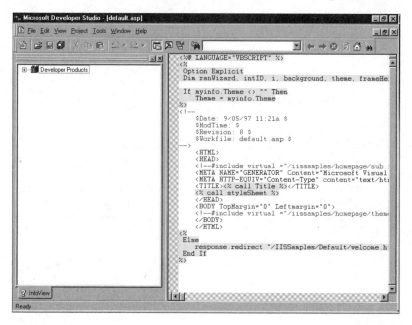

In addition, Visual Interdev boasts strong links with SQL Server, which makes it very easy to set up databases combining ASP and SQL Server. It also provides several useful web-based tools which can check links, highlight the broken ones on your site, and allow you to drag and drop pages from one location to another. Visual Interdev 6.0 (not out at the time of writing) looks likely to increase the featureset 10-fold.

FrontPage 98

FrontPage 98 is Microsoft's tool for creating and designing web pages, and it lets you do this without actually having to program the HTML. It allows you to create web pages in the same way that you would create documents in Word, or spreadsheets in Excel. It generates the HTML 'underneath the covers' without you having to raise a finger. One particular application of the FrontPage 98 editor is its ability to create and edit ASPs. We've just loaded a default ASP page that comes with Personal Web Server to demonstrate:

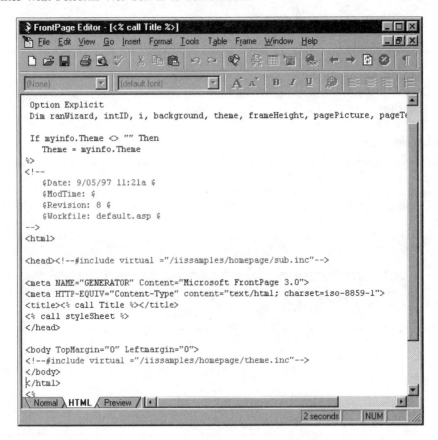

There are three tabs on FrontPage 98, which correspond to three possible views of your web page. The first is Normal. In this view you can put together a web page, in the same way you'd type up a Word document. You can insert pictures, links and sounds without having to write a single line of HTML.

The second view is HTML. If you go to this view, you'll see all of the HTML that has been generated by any work you might have done in Normal view. Even if the Normal view of the page is blank, you'll find there is a certain amount of HTML code under the covers. This is because the action of displaying a blank page on the web still requires some HTML code.

The final tab, Preview, lets you preview HTML pages. However, this is limited to previewing HTML-only pages. So, while it can't give you a complete preview of an ASP page, it'll give you some idea of what the final ASP page will look like—it simply won't execute the ASP code. In other words, FrontPage 98 will display what the HTML tags do, but won't translate any of the ASP to HTML.

Another quirk of FrontPage is that it likes to 'improve' your HTML and ASP. Be careful to check the true HTML after saving your page, to ensure that it hasn't been changed in this way. This 'window dressing' can change your code and even affect the intended function of the code.

You can prevent FrontPage from performing these modifications to your ASP code. Using the FrontPage Editor Menu, select Insert | FrontPageComponent | InsertHTML option to place `<!-- webbot bot="HTMLMarkup" startspan -->` and `<!--webbot bot="HTMLMarkup" endspan -->` tags around your ASP code, so that is not modified by FrontPage.

Allaire's Homesite

One of the best third party web page editors is Allaire's Homesite. The evaluation copy of version 3.0.1 is currently available from their web site at `http://www.allaire.com`. The evaluation copy allows you run the program 50 times or for 30 days—whichever elapses sooner. It has special features which allow you to edit and preview ASP scripts on another machine. This is something that neither FrontPage 98 or NotePad are capable of. It also features an extremely easy to use interface, which allows you to keep track of your files and folders at the same time as your file contents:

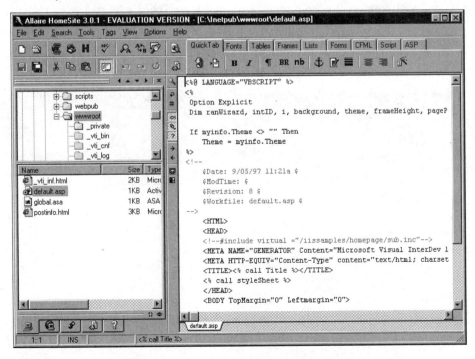

Homesite, like Visual Interdev, makes your ASP script easy to identify, by color-coding it. It's also used in producing `microsoft.com`. In short, Homesite is a very powerful editor, and well worth a look.

There are several other editors, such as NetObjects, HotDog, HotMetal and Adobe's PageMill. They all feature varying degrees of ASP support, and are all useful tools with which to create ASP scripts.

NotePad

NotePad is a time-honored text editor. No matter how much Microsoft promote Visual Interdev, there will always be people who will use NotePad as their editor of choice. It doesn't highlight the ASP in anyway, but because it's so simple and doesn't generate any extra code, it's still a very popular choice.

> *It doesn't really matter which editor you use in this book and, provided you watch for 'improvements', won't affect how you run the examples. We're not going to provide a tutorial on how to use any of these editorial tools since this is beyond the scope of the book.*

Viewing ASPs

You've probably noticed that, when browsing the web, you can view HTML code directly using your browser. (For example, of your browsing with IE4 then you can do this by choosing View | Source from the toolbar; if your browsing with Netscape Navigator, then choose View | Page Source.) When you do this, you are in fact viewing a document *client-side*—you have already downloaded the HTML code in order to view the web page, and now you're viewing that HTML source. By contrast, it's not possible for the client to view ASP code directly: instead, you have to view it on the server by using a web page editor such as Visual Interdev or NotePad.

If the user tries to view the source code on the browser, what does he see? For example, in the following screenshot the user (browsing with IE4) has encountered an ASP error:

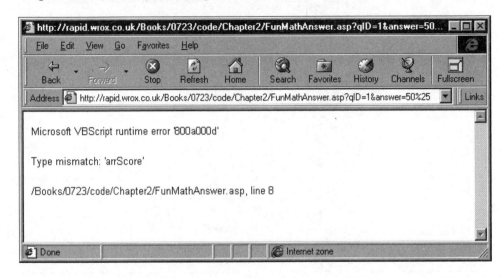

If the user now tries to view the code, he simply finds a rendering of the error message in HTML. The screenshot above would be rendered as:

```
<FONT FACE="Arial" size=2>
<p>Microsoft VBScript runtime </FONT> <FONT FACE="Arial" SIZE=2>error
'800a000d'</FONT>
<p>
<FONT FACE="Arial" SIZE=2>Type mismatch: 'arrScore'</FONT>
<p>
<FONT FACE="Arial" SIZE=2>/Books/0723/code/Chapter2/FunMathAnswer.asp</
FONT><FONT FACE="Arial" SIZE=2>, line 8</FONT>
```

This is because, as mentioned previously, when the ASP script is executed, the server actually returns it to the browser as HTML. When the user views the source code of the page, he actually views the HTML that was created by the ASP.

If it's an error message, as in this case, then he won't be able to see the ASP code that created the error—he'll only be able to see the HTML version of the error message. When the user views the source code, they simply see the final result of the ASP code, *after* it has been executed on the server.

This also has the advantage that your code isn't available for everybody to view. This makes ASP much more secure than HTML. This means that things like sensitive database queries and proprietary formulas are kept from prying eyes.

So, What is ASP, Again?

Let's have another go at defining ASP. ASP is actually an extension to your web server that allows server-side scripting. At the same time it also provides a compendium of objects and components which manage interaction between the web server and the browser. These 'objects' can be manipulated by scripting languages. Take a look at the following diagram:

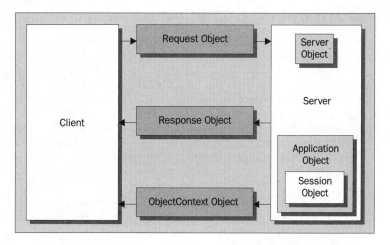

ASP neatly divides up into objects which manage their own part of the interaction between client and server. We'll now take a quick tour through all of the different objects and components that come as part of ASP.

Active Server Objects

There are six Active Server objects, each of which deals with a specific aspect of interactivity. We'll look at them in much more detail over the forthcoming chapters, but for now we'll just go through them briefly. Here's a list of the six Active Server objects:

- `Request`
- `Response`
- `Server`
- `Application`
- `Session`
- `ObjectContext`

The `Request` and `Response` objects are perhaps the most self-explanatory. The `Request` object is used to deal with a request that a user might make of a site or application. The 'request' might be made in the form of input from an HTML form. The `Response` object is used to deal with the server's response back to the browser.

The `Server` object is used to provide several commonly-used functions, such as creating new objects, setting timeout properties for scripts and converting text into HTML or URLs. The `Application` and `Session` objects are used to manage information about the application that is currently running and the unique instances (versions) of the application, which individual users run, known as sessions. The `ObjectContext` object is used with Microsoft Transaction Server, which is beyond the scope of this book: we're not going to cover this object in our book.

Active Server Components

Active Server components are ActiveX controls that come with ASP. They have a wide range of purposes: for example, they are capable of determining the abilities of the browser. We mentioned ActiveX controls earlier in this chapter, and you may have come across them in your travels across the web. The main difference is that a lot of ActiveX controls are visually oriented, while Active Server Components are generally invisible and non-interactive.

There are five components provided with Personal Web Server 4.0 (if we count the Database Access component), but many more are available from third parties. We'll be looking at the most important ones in more detail in Chapter 10. Here's a brief summary of the components and what they do:

- **Ad Rotator component**: this does exactly what you might surmise—it rotates ads on each page load. More specifically, you supply this component with a list of images, and it displays each one in rotation for a set proportion of the total cycle time, before moving on to the next one. It also allows you to associate each image with a separate hyperlink, which takes the user straight to the associated site by clicking.

- **Browser Capabilities component**: this references a file `browscap.ini`, which details every version of every Microsoft and Netscape browser ever created and can determine whether or not the browser currently used supports frames, tables, and so on.

▶ **Content Linking component**: this provides a list of links from an ASP page to a series of text files. It allows the administrator to provide extra information about each link on a web page and keeps the links in an orderly list so that they can be easily maintained.

Database Access Component

In addition to what we've already seen, there is a special component that comes as part of ASP, and is known as the **Database Access Component**. This in turn contains several objects known collectively as the **ActiveX Data Objects** (ADO) as well as several components that are essential to the viewing of databases on different platforms. The ActiveX Data objects enable database access and allow databases to viewed, manipulated and updated via web pages. We look at these in detail in Chapters 13 and 14.

Active Server Pages Scripting Objects

Finally, there are three objects provided in a separate library file known as **Microsoft Scripting Runtime**. These objects are the `Dictionary`, `FileSystemObject` and `TextStream` objects—we won't go into these now, since we cover them in detail in Chapter 11.

Summary

In this chapter we've mentioned some of the different ways in which you can bring interactivity to your web pages. We outlined the changing technologies that are coming to the Web and revolutionizing Web capability. This book focuses on ASP, so we have looked at some of the main advantages that ASP offers over HTML, and why you'd want it to use ASP to enhance your web pages.

We have looked at the different components that you need to run ASP, and where you can find them. In our opinion, Personal Web Server 4.0 forms the most suitable foundation for learning ASP—and since it's free and requires the least processor power, it's also the most cost-effective. We've covered how to set up Personal Web Server 4.0, and how to set up a directory in which to place of all of the examples from this book.

We created our first ASP page, and viewed it; we looked at some of the common pitfalls that you might encounter when checking that your ASP example is correctly set up.

In order to provide a *general* overview of why you'd want use ASP, we've avoided detailed explanation of ASP code, and how it's inserted into your web pages. In the next chapter we'll take a closer look at the differences between running your programs on the server and running them on the client; and we'll investigate why we choose one of these in preference to the other.

Client-Side Scripting and Server-Side Scripting

In the first chapter we introduced Active Server Pages and the associated technologies for making your web pages more dynamic. The main difference between ASP and the other technologies is that ASP code must be executed on the web server, while languages such as HTML, Java or Dynamic HTML are interpreted by the browser. We learned that ASP programs are composed of a mixture of HTML and script. We also learned that the ASP engine runs on the server and processes instructions that are coded in scripts and included in `.asp` files that are stored at the server.

What we haven't done is discuss the difference between a script file that's executed on the server, and one that's executed on the browser. Both IE4 and Navigator 4 are capable of executing JavaScript, and this raises the following question: "Why are some scripts sent to the server for execution, while others are executed on the browser?" We'll also need to resolve the question of how your computer knows which bits of your program are to be executed server-side, and which bits client-side. It's now time to consider these questions, since they are crucial to understanding ASP.

In this chapter we'll look at:

- What client/server architecture is, and why it's useful
- How to insert scripts into HTML pages
- Using VBScript or JScript
- The difference between server-side and client-side scripting
- Using `<RUNAT=SERVER>` tags, and using `<% ...%>` tags
- The ASP order of execution

We'll start with a little history lesson.

Client/Server Architecture: What's the Fuss?

You might well be thinking, "What is a **client/server architecture**?" Let's start with the most obvious example of a client/server architecture, namely the World Wide Web. It might sound complex, but client/server simply refers to the fact that browsers (henceforth known as **clients**) are used to retrieve documents from a web server. The web server could be located on your own local network, or it might be halfway around the world, thanks to the wonder of the Internet.

You can think of it in a 'fast food restaurant' kind of way. You are the client: to make an order, you tell the cashier (the server) what you want, hand over your money, wait a bit and then take away your food. It's the same with the web: you type in the address of a desired web page on your browser, and this gets sent to the server. After a little wait, the server returns the page you wanted.

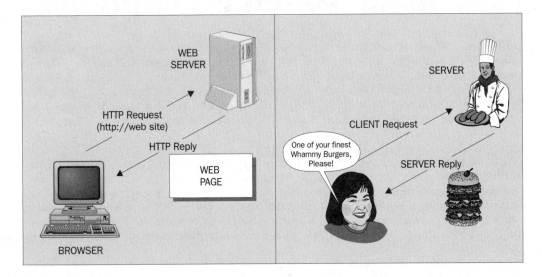

Client/server is a big 'buzz concept' these days, and companies and consultants make huge amounts of money from what is really a very simple idea. In a nutshell, it is the distribution of tasks between a *server* (which stores and processes data, like the cashier taking the money and putting together your order), and the *clients* which access the server (like the customers buying their food), in order to achieve maximum efficiency for the network on which they are connected.

The earliest web browsers were only able to handle text. If you wanted to send any information, then you typed in your details into an HTML form and sent it off (submitted it) to the web server. Nowadays, browsers can support a whole lot more, such as video, animation, sound and images. Furthermore, scripting languages, Java applets and ActiveX Controls can also be added to web pages. These are all interpreted and executed by the client (browser).

In the Bad Old Days

From the description above, you may be able to see that the more your browser (client) is capable of, the bigger the browser becomes, the slower it operates, and the more memory it will gobble up. So why don't we get the web server to do *all* of the work for us? Well, cast your mind back to the 1970s...

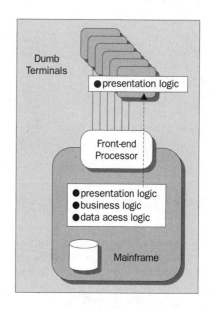

In the early days of Network Computing this is exactly what happened. All of the programs—and the data associated with them—were stored on one huge machine, known as a **mainframe**. The mainframe acted as a server and the clients took the form of 'dumb' terminals, which in many in businesses were scattered all around the building, and had no computing power of their own. They were simply connections to the mainframe. These terminals were used to execute the programs on the mainframe and display results.

This networking system quickly proved insufficient, as the demands of the users expanded to take in more than just simple word processors; users began to demand computing power of their own. Client/server grew from an effort to eliminate or reduce the presence of the mainframe. The idea was to separate out the 'functions' of the processing of the mainframe to cheaper-to-buy, cheaper-to-maintain systems.

Separating the Tasks

The answer to those problems was the client/server architecture. Client/server architectures separated complex, centralized applications into smaller, more manageable tasks or application logic. These tasks/application logic were split up into three layers:

- **Presentation** logic, which handled user interaction
- **Business** logic, which handled the business rules
- **Data Access** logic, which managed the storage and retrieval of data, and which ensured data integrity

The first attempt at client/server applications saw the centralized mainframe being replaced by a Relational Database Management System (RDBMS). RDBMSs provided fast transaction rates and substantial cost economies by moving the presentation and business logic to the client, and by enabling multiple clients to safely update the same set of data. This architecture is known as **two-tier** client/server architecture because it divided the processing of the data between the workstation and the server.

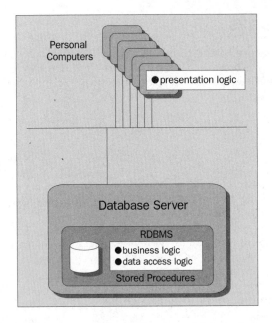

However, placing the business logic on clients led to very high maintenance costs, primarily as a result of deploying any changes to the logic. Updating software on clients became the new nightmare, and two-tier client/server architecture was replaced by a **three-tier** client/server model. In the three-tier computing model, an application server is used to manage the business logic, a database server handles the data access logic, and the client manages only the presentation logic.

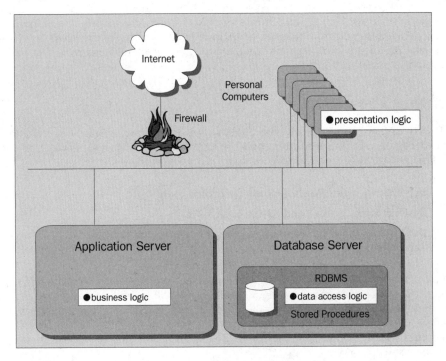

The biggest advantage gained from this model is that the business layer can be updated **once** for all clients: this makes for large savings in deployment costs. Additionally, it's relatively easy to add new business and database layers to construct **multi-tier** (or **n-tier**) systems. This makes it possible, for example, to provide local services—keeping slow long distance network communications to a minimum. At the same time it's possible to continue to provide data for enterprise-wide computing needs.

Web Client/Server Architectures

The Internet has given a new twist to client/server architecture. Network clients can now, given proper authorization, economically access any Internet-enabled network from anywhere in the world without having to be physically connected to the network via coaxial cable or long-distance telephone service. The Web didn't really take off in business circles until the introduction of **intranets**. While the Internet is global and publicly accessible, an intranet is closed and accessible only to those people who have permission to use it—for example, the employees of a company. Intranets operate in just the same way as the Internet, using browsers to provide employees and other valid users with access to corporate information and processes.

Intranets provide applications that are server-based, and this means that there's far less maintenance required, because (with the exception of the operating system and Web browser) it's not necessary to configure each individual machine, or go through the process of loading software many times over. Users can navigate to an internal web site on an intranet and have easy access to the application without any setting up or configuration required. If any application is changed, perhaps due to a bug fix or enhancement, updates can be made on the server, instantly upgrading *all* desktops. This dynamic application distribution can produce considerable savings to organizations which have many hundreds of desktops distributed throughout their enterprise.

Pretty soon, however, using HTML to display the information wasn't enough. Business demanded more than just the ability to view text and graphics. People wanted to summarize and display their sales figures in the form of graphs; to store and order their customer information in databases; and to display this information as web pages. HTML doesn't suffice for provision of interactive data on the Internet. Hence, ASP was developed as a way of providing interactive content efficiently. However, ASP is an adaptation of an already existing technology. To program the Active Server, we actually use a mixture of scripting languages and HTML.

Scripting Languages

In order to add depth to the capability provided by the HTML language, we can sprinkle our HTML code with commands that don't strictly belong to HTML at all. Instead, these commands are written in one of a number of **scripting languages** that are available. We distinguish these 'foreign' commands, embedded within the HTML code, by referring to them as **scripts**. HTML allows us to include scripts at (almost) any point in our HTML code: it does this by providing us with legal ways of inserting scripts, which we'll come to shortly.

Subsequently, when the page is viewed by the browser, each script is sent to a **script host** (an application that can run a program in another language), where it is interpreted by a **script engine**. Each scripting language needs its own interpreter to interpret it, so a VBScript program must be sent to a VBScript interpreter, and a JavaScript program to a JavaScript interpreter. Internet Explorer 4 contains both interpreters for VBScript and for JScript (Microsoft's version of JavaScript), while Netscape Navigator 4 only contains a JavaScript interpreter. Active Server Pages supplies interpreters (script engines) for both VBScript and JScript.

Client-Side or Server-Side Scripts?

So for the most part, our model of the browser making a connection, sending a request, receiving a reply and then getting the browser to interpret the subsequent HTML to construct a web page still holds true. The only bit that differs is that when the browser comes across something within script tags, it is submitted to the appropriate script engine for interpretation and execution. However (and here's the important bit), the script host containing the script engine doesn't have to be resident on the browser: it can be resident on either client-side, or server-side. The essential difference is as follows:

▶ A script that is interpreted by the *browser* is called a **client-side script**. A client-side script is an instruction set that is processed by the client, without contacting a server.

▶ A script that is interpreted by the *web server* is called a **server-side script**. A server-side script is an instruction set that is processed by the server, and the resulting data is sent to a client.

As we'll see, there are advantages to each. We'll have a look at client- and server-side scripts in more depth, and later in this chapter you'll see an example of how client-side and server-side scripts can interact. First, we'll put ASP and server-side scripting to one side for a moment, and take a look at client-side scripting.

Client-Side Scripts

Client-side scripting involves the execution of the scripting language by the browser that interprets the web page. The main disadvantage of client-side scripting is that exactly how the script works is dependent on the type of browser that executes the script. In other words, client-side scripting is **browser specific**.

Client-side scripting also means that your code is visible to the user—they can use the View | Source option on IE4, or the View | Page Source option on Netscape Navigator, for example—so it isn't very secure.

If you're using Microsoft's Internet Explorer 4, you'll find that it supports both JScript and VBScript. Alternatively, if you're using Netscape Communicator 4, you'll find that this browser only supports JavaScript. If you try to view a VBScript page with Netscape Navigator, then at best it won't look quite as intended, and at worst it'll cause an error message. If you want to view the results of VBScript scripting with Netscape browsers, then you'll need to use a third party add-in.

Consequently, you'll find that JScript/JavaScript tends to be the popular language of choice on the web in client-side code. This has been further reinforced by the adoption of JavaScript as a standard, maintained by ECMA (European Computer Manufacturer's Standards) and known as ECMAScript—which sets a bottom line that both can adhere to.

Adding Client-Side Scripts to HTML Pages

As we now know, in order to view a web page, the browser interprets the HTML itself, and sends any non-HTML code—that is, scripts—to the appropriate script host in the browser for interpretation. In order to do this, the browser must be able to distinguish between the HTML code and the script code. In client-side script, this is achieved by using HTML **script tags**.

You're probably already familiar with tags in HTML, so you'll know that there are two types of tags: **opening tags** and **closing tags**. In this sense, script tags work in much the same way as other HTML tags: within the code, a script (or block of scripts) is preceded by the opening tag, `<SCRIPT>`, and terminated by the closing tag, `</SCRIPT>`. Note that the browser receives the client-side script; the browser then interprets its instructions, and then either writes the appropriate HTML or performs a function such as displaying an alert box, or calculating and updating the fields in a form.

In order to illustrate this, we need a few samples. The following snippets are fragments of HTML source files. Here's the first sample:

```
...
<SCRIPT LANGUAGE=VBSCRIPT>
   ... VBScript code goes here
</SCRIPT>
...
```

This first snippet shows how we'd write a script in the VBScript scripting language. When the browser views the web page, it recognizes the script tags, and sends the script to the client for interpretation.

The next sample looks rather similar:

```
...
<SCRIPT LANGUAGE=JAVASCRIPT>
   ... JavaScript code goes here
</SCRIPT>
...
```

The processes involved are similar to those for the first sample. Notice that the script tag identifies the scripting language in which the enclosed scripts are written. You can have both JScript and VBScript within the same page, as long as they have their own tags. A `<SCRIPT>` section can be placed almost anywhere in the page. You'll often find scripts at the end of the HTML document, so that the rest of the page can be loaded and rendered by the browser before the interpreter loads and runs the code. In this way, the whole of the page can be loaded first—rather than alternate chunks of HTML and script. However, if we are using the code to insert something into the page, like the time and date, we need to place the `<SCRIPT>` section in the appropriate position in relation to the HTML within the HTML source:

```
...
The date and time is
<SCRIPT LANGUAGE=VBSCRIPT> Document.Write(Now)</SCRIPT> have a nice day!
<P>
...
```

In this snippet, the browser must execute the **Now** function (which is a VBScript function) and pass the result to the **Write** method of the **Document** object. (Don't worry, you're not expected to know about methods and objects just yet! We'll look at them in more detail later in this chapter, and consider the whole topic of objects and methods within Chapter 6.) The **Write** method writes the information into that page at the point where it's called, so the result is something like this:

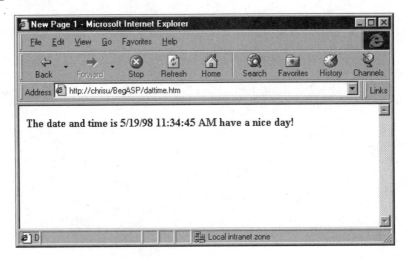

Don't worry about typing this example in just yet, we'll give you full working one very shortly.

Comment Tags

As we've mentioned, successful execution of a chunk of script is dependent on whether your browser supports the requisite scripting language. What happens if you're using an older version of Navigator or Internet Explorer to browse a web page that contains script? The script will simply be displayed as text on the web page, which is all very messy and not at all what you'd want to happen.

So, the traditional way to prevent the code from being displayed by the browser is to enclose the contents of the **<SCRIPT>** section within a **comment tag**. Any non-script enabled browsers will ignore code contained within comment tags, while browsers that *do* support scripting will still be able to interpret and execute the script (unless of course they only support JavaScript, in which case any VBScript will be ignored). Here's how we'd add comment tags to the above code fragment:

```
...
The date and time is
<SCRIPT LANGUAGE=VBSCRIPT>
<!-- hide from older browsers
Document.Write(Now)
//-->
</SCRIPT> have a nice day!
<P>
...
```

Notice the positioning of the comment tags `<!--...//-->`. Placing the tags on the same line as the script results in some browsers being unable to interpret the enclosed script. If both tags appear on the same line then the whole of that line acts as a comment; if the tags appear on two separate lines, the lines containing the `<!--` and `//-->` tags are considered as comment lines.

Of course, most browsers will be able to deal with a script like this, since support for a scripting language is pretty much a prerequisite anyway. However, it doesn't hurt to hide the scripting in case the page is loaded by an older browser.

Don't make the mistake of using --> (which is sometimes used in IE as the closing comment tag) because when faced with a valid JavaScript script in Navigator, this will cause a syntax error.

Creating Script Routines that Don't Execute as the Page Loads

In each of the examples above, the script is executed as the page is loaded by the browser. However, we don't always want this to happen. Sometimes we might want certain parts of the script to be executed before other parts. To prevent the script from being executed as the page is loaded, we can use a technique that creates separate code routines in a page that are *not* executed as the page is loading.

To prevent VBScript code being executed as the page loads, we place it inside a **subroutine**, or inside a **function**. Here's an example in which a VBScript subroutine and a VBScript function are embedded into HTML code:

```
<SCRIPT LANGUAGE=VBSCRIPT>
<!--
Sub MyNewRoutine()
   ... VBScript code goes here
End Sub

Function GetAnyNumber()
   ... VBScript code goes here, including setting the return value
   GetAnyNumber = 42
End Function
//-->
</SCRIPT>
```

This example illustrates the differences between a subroutine and function. The first (very obvious) difference is in the way that each is defined within the script tags. The second difference is that a function produces a value, that gets passed back to the code that called it. As far as this book is concerned, we'll mainly be using subroutines. These routines will only run when we call them from code elsewhere, or an event occurs in the browser that calls them automatically.

To attempt the same thing using JScript/JavaScript scripts requires a slightly different approach, because JScript/JavaScript doesn't support subroutines. We also have to write the code a little differently:

```
<SCRIPT LANGUAGE=JAVASCRIPT>
<!--
function MyNewRoutine()
{
    ... JScript code goes here;
}

function GetAnyNumber()
{
    ... JScript code goes here, including setting the return value;
    return 42;
}
//-->
</SCRIPT>
```

JScript/JavaScript requires the code in a routine to be enclosed in curly braces, and each line within a function to be separated by a semicolon. JScript/JavaScript is also case sensitive. So, for example, it would treat **now** and **Now** differently. **Now** will function correctly, while JavaScript will claim that it's never heard of **now**, and will hiccup errors at you.

However, this still doesn't cover every situation in which you might wish to use scripting.

Events and Scripts

Much of the dynamic nature of modern web pages is down to script code that reacts to **events** occurring within the browser. You can also place scripts in your code, which will only execute if a certain event takes place, such as a mouse being clicked, or a key being pressed. These are examples of **events**. We will look at events in detail in Chapter 6. In the meantime, just consider the following; to get VBScript to respond to an event, you'd add code as follows:

```
<SCRIPT LANGUAGE=VBSCRIPT>
<!--
Sub Mouse_OnClick()
    .. VBScript code goes here
End Sub
//-->
</SCRIPT>
```

This code would only be executed in the event of the user clicking on the mouse. If the user then clicked on the mouse again, the code would be run again. The browser would stop nearly everything else (apart from execution of another script) just to execute this code. The code to do the same thing in JavaScript/JScript is very similar:

```
<SCRIPT LANGUAGE=JSCRIPT>
<!--
function Mouse_OnClick()
{
    .. JScript code goes here ;
```

```
}
//-->
</SCRIPT>
```

Now we're finally ready to take a look at a very simple example of how to insert a client-side script into HTML.

Try It Out - A Client-Side Script Using VBScript

For our first scripting example, we'll spare you the usual "Hello, World". Instead, we will use script instructions to 'write' the current date to an HTML document.

1 Open your HTML editor, create a new file, and type the following:

```
<HTML>
<HEAD>
<TITLE>Writing the Current Date to a Document with VBScript</TITLE>
</HEAD>

<BODY BGCOLOR=WHITE>
<P>This is your first script example. Today's date is
<SCRIPT LANGUAGE=VBSCRIPT>
<!--
Document.Write(Date)
//-->
</SCRIPT>
.
</BODY>

</HTML>
```

> *Please don't miss out the period in these examples, we'll be using it to illustrate a point later in this chapter.*

2 Save the file as **datevbs.htm**, in your **Inetpub/wwwroot/BegASP** directory.

3 Open Internet Explorer 4, and type the address **http://my_server_name/BegASP/datevbs.htm** into the address line:

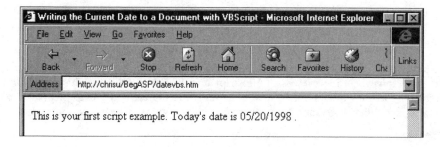

The HTML output will show a single sentence containing the current date. The date is generated by the VBScript script, and is formatted in the default date format used by the client computer.

How It Works

The first thing to notice is that client-side scripts are saved with the `.htm` or `.html` extension. This is because both the HTML and the script are interpreted and executed by the browser—in this sense, a page containing client-side script can be treated in just the same way as a page containing only HTML. When the browser comes across a `<SCRIPT>` tag, it knows to send the code to the appropriate script engine. In this example the `<SCRIPT>` tag contains the **LANGUAGE** attribute:

```
<SCRIPT LANGUAGE=VBSCRIPT>
```

indicating that the scripting language is VBScript.

If you tried to run this example on a browser that does not support VBScript—such as Netscape Navigator 4.0—you would see something like this:

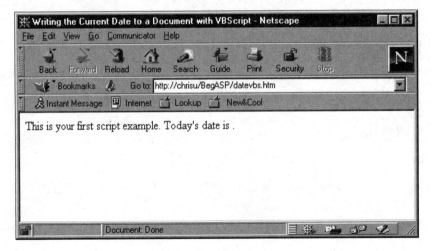

There would be no error message, but at the same time, the output of the program would not be what we wanted.

The next part of the program is the VBScript itself:

```
Document.Write(Date)
```

This tells an entity, known as the **Document** object, to use its **Write** method to display an interpreted script function. In this example, we're using it to display the value returned by the built-in VBScript function, **Date**.

Notice that we've enclosed the **Date** function in parentheses. We could have omitted the parentheses; however, the syntaxes of VBScript and JScript overlap on this point, and consequently JScript would be able to understand this line of code. One great rule of thumb in scripting is this: when two languages share the same syntax, use the common syntax at all times.

Now let's take a look at the mysterious **Document**. The **Document** in question is, quite literally, a representation of the HTML document or web page that is being currently displayed. The line **Document.Write(Date)** simply tells the **Document** (the current web page) to use its **Write** method to display the contents of the **Date** function. However, the **Document** object isn't part of ASP: it's something that exists only on the client side (i.e. it's part of the browser).

> *You can also use the **Document** object to get information about the document; to analyze and modify the HTML elements and text in the document; and to process events. We'll discuss the concept of objects in general, more fully, at the beginning of Chapter 6. We won't be looking at the browser objects in any detail, since they aren't part of ASP.*

That's all we need to know about VBScript scripts for now. Next, we'll have a look at how to insert a JScript/JavaScript script into our code.

Try It Out – Client-Side Script Using JavaScript

We're going to cheat slightly, in that we're not going to construct a wholly new program: we're simply going to go back to our VBScript example and replace the VBScript with JavaScript.

1 Open the file you have just created, **datevbs.htm,** with your favored HTML editor, and change the lines that have been highlighted:

```
<HTML>
<HEAD>
<TITLE>Writing the Current Date to a Document with JavaScript</TITLE>
</HEAD>

<BODY BGCOLOR=WHITE>
<P>This is your first script example. Today's date is
<SCRIPT LANGUAGE=JAVASCRIPT>
<!--
d = new Date();
document.write(d);
//-->
</SCRIPT>
.
</BODY>

</HTML>
```

> *Make sure that you type all of the cases correctly in this example. JavaScript is case sensitive and will treat **date** and **Date** differently.*

2 Save the file as **datejs.htm**.

3 Open either of your browsers, and type the address `http://my_server_name/BegASP/` `datejs.htm` into the address line:

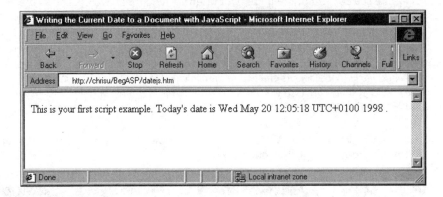

This is your first script example. Today's date is Wed May 20 12:05:18 UTC+0100 1998.

How It Works

It works in exactly the same way as the VBScript example:

```
d = new Date();
document.write(d);
```

This all looks rather frightening, doesn't it? The first line in this short two-line program uses the built-in JavaScript object, `Date` which is found on the client-side, in the browser—to generate the current date. It reads it into something known as a **variable**, which we're not going to explain here, as variables are covered in Chapter 4. The second line displays the contents of the variable. Phew! You can take a breath now.

Indeed, JavaScript can be more difficult than VBScript for the novice programmer to master, and consequently we're not going to cover JavaScript in this book. There's a choice of two languages to learn in your early days of ASP study, and to cut down the time and confusion, we're only going to be looking at one, VBScript.

In fact, there's a more significant reason for avoiding JavaScript in the remainder of this book. It is that, while JavaScript is the more popular language on the client side, ASP works entirely on the server side, where the default language and language of choice is VBScript.

FYI Consequently, we won't go into the detail of the above code in any more detail than we have already. All you need to know is that JScript/JavaScript code is inserted into your script in the same way as VBScript code.

This book is oriented towards ASP, primarily as a server-side platform. However, there are many ways in which client-side script can help to ease your server's load. We will return to client-side scripts, and show you some uses for them, later on. Next, though, we'll have a look at what server-side scripts are, and what they do.

Server-Side Scripts

So as you've probably gathered by now, ASP uses server-side scripting. So what differentiates a client-side script from an ASP script? An ASP script is very much like an HTML file. It includes HTML tags, text, and **server-side** scripts, and can also include **client-side** scripts. It can also, optionally, create ASP **objects**—you'll learn about those in Chapter 6 onwards.

The first difference is that an ASP script must have an `.asp` extension, to differentiate it from other files on the server. When an HTTP request is made for an `.asp` file, the filename suffix informs the web server that the contents of the file are to processed *on the server* before being returned to the client. The `.asp` file contains a mixture of HTML code and ASP script. This server-side script is read by the server, which interprets the ASP instructions and translates them into appropriate HTML code. The server then returns the whole file as pure HTML (although this can contain client-side script and ActiveX controls), which is then interpreted by the browser.

Inserting Server-Side Scripts

There are two ways to identify your server-side scripts within the HTML code, so that the server can interpret them correctly:

- Include the `RUNAT=SERVER` attribute in the `<SCRIPT>` tag
- Use `<%` ... `%>` server script delimiters

So let's look at a sample using `RUNAT=SERVER` first:

```
...
<SCRIPT LANGUAGE=VBSCRIPT RUNAT=SERVER>
 ... ASP Script code goes here
</SCRIPT>
...
```

It looks very similar to our first two snippets of script that we encountered at the beginning of this chapter, doesn't it? The `<SCRIPT>` tag again specifies the scripting language, but in addition it also specifies the target script host—the web server. By default, a script will always be sent to the client for execution, unless you specify otherwise. So by specifying the attribute of `RUNAT` as `SERVER`, we're making sure that it's sent to the server. However, that is all that's different from the method we used for inserting client-side scripts.

You can still use subroutines and functions on the server side:

```
...
<SCRIPT LANGUAGE=VBSCRIPT RUNAT=SERVER>
<!--
Sub MyNewRoutine()
 .. ASPScript code goes here
End Sub

Function GetAnyNumber()
 .. ASP Script code goes here, including setting the return value
  GetAnyNumber = 42
End Function
```

```
</SCRIPT>
...
```

The second method doesn't involve the `<SCRIPT>` tag at all, but uses the `<%` and `%>` tags in place of them. These are generally more popular, because they are a lot less cumbersome and make the code easier to read:

```
...
<%
   ... ASP Script code goes here
%>
...
```

You might be wondering how you can specify the `LANGUAGE` attribute within the `<%` and `%>` tags. This is done using a special notation:

```
<% @ LANGUAGE = VBSCRIPT %>
```

Now we've looked at all the possible permutations and combinations for inserting scripts, it's time to try out an example.

Try It Out – Inserting a Server-Side (ASP) Script

We'll take the example we've done in VBScript and JavaScript, and we'll adapt it for ASP script.

1 Open the file `datevbs.htm` with your preferred HTML editor, and change the lines that have been highlighted:

```
<HTML>
<HEAD>
<TITLE>Writing the Current Date to a Document with ASP Script</TITLE>
</HEAD>

<BODY BGCOLOR=WHITE>
<P>This is your first script example. Today's date is
<SCRIPT LANGUAGE=VBSCRIPT RUNAT=SERVER>
Response.Write(Date)
</SCRIPT>

</BODY>

</HTML>
```

2 Save the file as `dateasp.asp` in your `Inetpub\wwwroot\BegASP` directory.

3 Open your browser, and type the address `http://my_server_name/BegASP/dateasp.asp` into the address line:

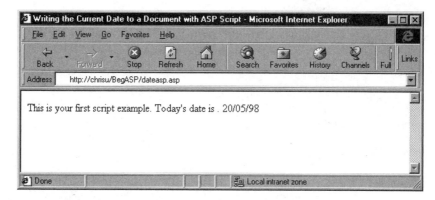

As you can see it works, but not quite as we expected it to. The date comes *after* the period!

4 Now go back to `dateasp.asp` and change the lines that have been highlighted:

```
<HTML>
<HEAD>
<TITLE>Writing the Current Date to a Document with ASP Script</TITLE>
</HEAD>

<BODY BGCOLOR=WHITE>
<P>This is your first script example. Today's date is
<%Response.Write(Date)%>.
</BODY>

</HTML>
```

5 Save it as `dateasp2.asp` and run the example again. You should get a similar result, but this time it'll be correctly formatted as well:

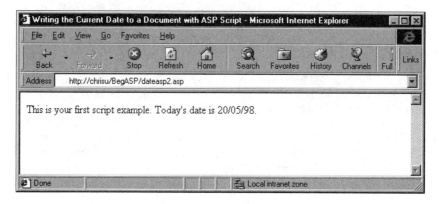

Well, what's that all about then?

How It Works

First, you'll notice that we've changed the file extension to `.asp`, to indicate to the server that this isn't just an HTML file, and therefore needs special processing. This is our first clue as to what might have happened.

Second, we've changed the line that used to read:

```
Document.Write(Date)
```

so that now it reads:

```
Response.Write(Date)
```

This is because the **Document** object is something that exists only on the client side. So if you tried running that line on the server, you'd just get an error. Its equivalent on the server is the **Response** object. We'll be looking at it more closely in the next chapter. For now, you'll have to trust me that in this example, it's performing the same function as the **Document** object did earlier.

If you consider how ASP changes the order in which things are done, you should remember that ASP is translated into equivalent HTML *before* the HTML page is sent back to the client. It becomes obvious that execution of the code in `<%  ...  %>` tags happens *before* execution of the code in `<SCRIPT  ...  RUNAT=SERVER>` tags.

So which server-side tag format should you use? The answer depends on the **order of execution** you need. We'll look at that in more depth later, but before we do, we need to examine how the server handles ASP code.

How Does ASP Work?

In Chapter 1 we talked about the sequence of events involved when a user requests and acquires a web page; we also explained the basics of where ASP fits into this sequence. What we didn't do was go into the details of what actually happens to the ASP. The ASP file contains sets of instructions for the server. Each set of instructions is called an **ASP script**. When an ASP script is requested via HTTP, it is **interpreted** by the Active Server Pages engine, which is the file `asp.dll`.

You can find the file `asp.dll` on your hard drive, at C:\Windows\System\InetSrv. If you can't see it, make sure you've turned the Show Hidden Files option on in Windows Explorer. Be careful that you don't alter the file in any way!

This file does all the work in ASP. `asp.dll` is an Internet Services Application Programming Interface (ISAPI) extension to PWS and IIS, and is compiled as a Windows dynamic link library (DLL). Though this sounds daunting, it simply means that you can access your web server's functions directly, via the `asp.dll`, using code in ASP scripts.

The process of interpreting ASP scripts is as follows:

▶ A client (browser) requests an ASP page from the web server.

▶ The server passes the request to **asp.dll**, which checks to see if another file (named **global.asa**) has been executed. If **global.asa** hasn't been executed, then ASP executes it.

> *The file* global.asa *is a text file that contains details about an ASP application, such as when it should begin and end. You will learn more about* global.asa *and ASP applications in Chapter 9.*

▶ ASP includes any files: these are dealt with *before* the scripting engines take over—so you can't have conditional includes.

▶ Any objects that were requested by the ASP script are created by the scripting language and then script instructions are sent to the appropriate scripting engine(s).

▶ The scripting engine(s) process the scripting instructions and send the feedback to ASP.

▶ ASP translates the feedback from the scripting engine(s), into HTML code.

▶ The interpreted contents are sent to the browser as an HTML data stream, which the browser displays.

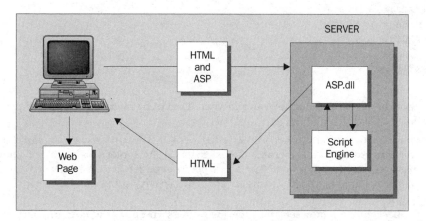

This process is fundamental to the internal workings of ASP; you may want to revisit this list from time to time as you work through this book. Don't worry too much if you don't understand some of these terms right now; the concepts will become increasing clear as you make progress through the book.

Now we know the fundamental process that ASP follows, we can use an example to explore the mysterious 'order of execution' a little further.

Try It Out - Testing the Order of Execution

For our next ASP script example, let's test the order of execution sequence. We will create a script which writes a number sequence to the document; this will give us a chance to exercise the **RUNAT=SERVER** attribute and the **<% ... %>** tags, side by side, as well as a little pure HTML code.

1 Open your HTML editor, create a new file, and type the following code:

```
<HTML>
<HEAD>
<TITLE>Testing the Order of Execution</TITLE>
</HEAD>

<BODY BGCOLOR=WHITE>
 One <%="Two"%> Three
<SCRIPT RUNAT=SERVER LANGUAGE=VBSCRIPT>
     Response.Write "Four"
</SCRIPT>
 Five <%="Six"%> Seven
<SCRIPT RUNAT=SERVER LANGUAGE=VBSCRIPT>
     Response.Write "Eight"
</SCRIPT>
 Nine <%="Ten"%>
</BODY>

</HTML>
```

2 Save the file as **execorder.asp** in your **Inetpub/wwwroot/BegASP** directory.

Since, by definition, server-side scripting does involve the server, we **must** use a file with an **.asp** extension. The **.asp** file extension is the server's *only* way of knowing that it must process the file as an ASP script before sending it to the browser. By contrast, files with the **.htm** or **.html** extension are sent directly to the browser.

3 Go back to your browser and type the address **http://*my_server_name*/BegASP/ execorder.asp** into the address line.

If you follow these instructions you should get something that looks like this:

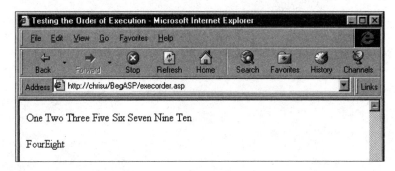

If you use Internet Explorer 3, you'll get a similar result; however, all of the output will be displayed upon one line.

Perhaps this is not exactly what you expected—after all, the strings `"One"` through `"Ten"` *were* written into the script in numerical order—but the 'order of execution' is all-important. Let's see what's happening.

How It Works

This ASP script exercises two ways in which the server can write data to documents:

```
Response.Write

<%="string"%>
```

In fact, these notations are equivalent. `Write` is a method of the `Response` object. The equal sign, `=`, as used here after the server script delimiter (like this: `<%=`), performs exactly the same function as `Response.Write`. Put simply, ASP's `Response` object allows the server to perform several types of duties. We will explain ASP objects thoroughly in Chapters 7 through 9.

From the resulting output, we can see that the web server *first* processes the HTML together with any instructions that are delimited with `<% ... %>`, **then** processes any server-side code enclosed in `<SCRIPT>` tags. The `<%` and `%>` tags are executed immediately within the HTML code, but the code in the `<SCRIPT RUNAT=SERVER>` section isn't executed until after the HTML code has been wholly interpreted.

The conclusion of all this is that the order of rendering of the text in your ASP code is not as it may seem at face value—you must also consider the methods that you are using to output the text.

One last thing: how is the order of execution affected if we try adding some JScript scripts? Let's try it out by making a small change to the example above.

Try It Out – Test the Order of Execution Using JScript

1 Amend the file `execorder.asp` above by replacing the following shaded lines:

```
<HTML>
<HEAD>
<TITLE>Testing VBScript and JScript Order of Execution</TITLE>
</HEAD>

<BODY BGCOLOR=WHITE>
 One <%="Two"%> Three
<SCRIPT RUNAT=SERVER LANGUAGE=VBSCRIPT>
      Response.Write "Four"
</SCRIPT>
 Five <%="Six"%> Seven
<SCRIPT RUNAT=SERVER LANGUAGE=JSCRIPT>
      Response.Write ("Eight");
```

```
</SCRIPT>
 Nine <%="Ten"%>
</BODY>

</HTML>
```

2 Save the file, and view it on your browser by clicking on the **Refresh** button. The result is:

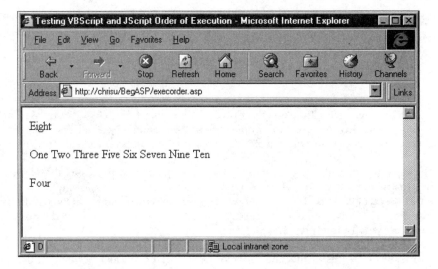

As you can see, the JScript script is rendered first. The next to be rendered are the HTML code and code within **<% ... %>** delimiters; and finally, the VBScript code in **<SCRIPT RUNAT=SERVER>** is rendered last.

We can summarize the order of execution as follows:

- **global.asa**
- Server-side includes
- JScript scripts tagged within **<SCRIPT>** tags
- HTML together with Scripts tagged within **<% ... %>** delimiters
- VBScript scripts tagged within **<SCRIPT>** tags

Don't worry that we haven't touched upon **global.asa** and server-side includes—we'll be looking at both of these later in the book. For now, just think of them as special exceptions to the normal 'order of execution' rules. This concludes our little foray into the world of client/server.

Summary

So now, you should have a strong idea of the differences between the client and the server, client-side scripting and server-side scripting, and JavaScript/VBScript and ASP. We haven't actually shown you how to program in any way—but it's far more important, before you start programming, to know *when* you need to program on the client side and when to use ASP.

Briefly, we have learned that the browser is referred to as the client and that it submits requests to the web server using HTTP, in the form of URLs. The web server fetches the web page that matches the request: if there is any ASP script present, the web server will identify and translate it into equivalent HTML and create a new HTML file. These new web pages are returned to the server as HTML, which the browser then interprets and executes to create the web page.

We learned that, rather confusingly, the default language on the client side is JavaScript while the default server-side language is VBScript. We also saw that the way the server treats them is slightly different. Since JavaScript is the more complex language, and since it isn't practical to learn two languages at once, we will be using VBScript exclusively throughout the rest of the book.

Finally we learned that there is an 'order of execution'. The execution sequence of the program depends on the method used to insert the script, and the scripting language used: by using different methods we can produce different results on the screen display.

In the next chapter we'll start looking at how you can code some simple ASP programs.

Basic ASP Techniques

When I first started to study Chinese my tutor, Lao Wang, gave me a Chinese-English dictionary, a Chinese grammar book and a primer. But he placed all of these books in a basket and said that they were not to be used until the next week. In the first week he instructed me just to listen and memorize some phrases. Before beginning a rigorous and orderly study he wanted me to learn how to repeat a few phrases. "Excuse me, where is a restaurant?" "Please sir, may I have some rice?" "How much does this cost?" That week, I had to accept on faith the content, sentence structure, pronunciation and grammar. But by Friday I could at least walk into a Chinese restaurant, order a bowl of rice and pay for it. Those first few phrases, without theory or explanation, gave me enough grammar and vocabulary.

We will take the same approach in this book. After this chapter you will get an in-depth study of the syntax and techniques of ASP, but to start, we want to give you three basic techniques. Here we won't explain the theory, exceptions or intricacies; those will come later. But at the end of this chapter you will be able to:

▶ Create a web page that asks the user a question, and returns the answer to another ASP page

▶ Instruct ASP to retain the information supplied by the user

▶ Use ASP code to write a line of text back to the user

So without further ado, let's get started.

Getting Information From the User

In the first chapter of this book, we discussed what ASP can do and how to indicate to the web server exactly which sections of your HTML page are ASP code. Our first example in that chapter just demonstrated how ASP works on your server. That simple text and HTML tags plus ASP code that you wrote, with the help of ASP on the server, generated an appropriate page which returned the current time on the server. Two visitors requesting the page at different times on the same day will actually get two different pages back.

Now let's consider some real situations in the business world:

▶ We would like to ask the user what product they are interested in and then have ASP generate a page specific to that interest.

▶ We want to ask a visitor if they are a member of the organization. If they are, then they get a page with the organization's calendar. If not, they get a form to fill out and join the club.

▶ We have a page that uses advanced HTML techniques (e.g. formatting) which do not show up well in some browsers. We would like to establish which browser this visitor is using, and then send out a page of information formatted appropriately for that browser.

▶ We want to give the visitor a tour of pages displaying this week's featured items. The user will proceed through the site by clicking on **Next** buttons. However, since the pages change week by week, we want ASP to check our current list of pages featuring items and insert hyperlinks for those pages into the **Next** buttons at the moment the page goes to the user.

In each of these cases, we want to do something beyond simply serving a page. We'll either need to make a decision about what page to serve, or we'll need to create a customized page for that particular request.

In order to make our decision we need to get some information from the user. In the first case, we need to know what product the user wants to see. In the second case we need to know if they are members or not. In the programming world this kind of information is considered as **input**. ASP needs input from the user in order to make its decisions.

Suppose that our web site has a 'Page 1' that asks if the user wants retail or wholesale information; how do we get that information from 'Page 1' into the ASP of the second page in a connectionless system? The simplest technique is to use a feature of HTML called the **form**. Forms perform four tasks:

▶ `<FORM>` tags can ask the user for information and provide a space (called a *field*) in which to receive the answer

▶ The form has a button to submit information back to the server

▶ The submission has instructions to open a new page (usually an ASP page)

▶ The submission also carries the information that the user typed into the fields—which is to be used by the ASP code of the new page

We use forms to provide a means for users to input data to the server, the information that we need to make decisions in ASP.

Using Forms to Obtain Information from the User

Here is the first set of tags needed to set up the structure of a form (we will add the spaces for input in the next example). You begin and end the form section of the page with the `<FORM>` tags. Here's an example:

```
<P>Please fill in the following form:</P>
<FORM ACTION="Calendar.asp" METHOD=POST>
</FORM>
```

The opening **<FORM>** tag here has two attributes. The first, **ACTION**, gives the name of the ASP file that should be opened next—this file will use the information that we gather in the form. The second attribute, **METHOD**, determines which of two ways (**POST** or **GET**) that the browser will use to send the information to the server. In this chapter, we will always use **POST**, we will explain **GET** in chapter 7.

The **ACTION** attribute of the **<FORM>** tag tells the browser what page is going to be opened when the submit button is pressed. After the user has submitted the data, the browser automatically requests this file. It is good practice to put the name of the file in double quotes, although it doesn't have to be.

Within the **<FORM>** tags, you generally need to put at least three sets of tags. Two of them are the **submit** and **reset** buttons. Their tags are similar:

```
<P>Please fill in the following form:</P>
<FORM ACTION="Calendar.asp" METHOD=POST>
<P><INPUT TYPE="SUBMIT" VALUE="Submit"></P>
<P><INPUT TYPE="RESET" VALUE="Reset"></P>
</FORM>
```

The code above will produce the following page on the browser:

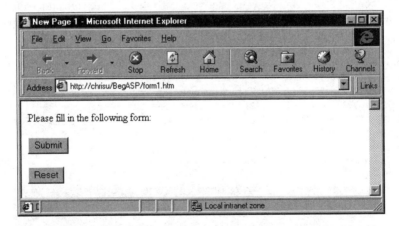

The Submit and Reset button tags generally have two attributes. The first declares the type of button and the second the value, that is the word to display on the button. Note that both of these attributes should be enclosed in quotes. The type must be either **"SUBMIT"** or **"RESET"**; those are keywords to the browser so you should not try to rename them.

The **VALUE** will appear to the user and thus can be anything you like, as long as you type it in quotes. For example, consider the following form:

```
<FORM ACTION="Calendar.asp" METHOD=POST>
<P><INPUT TYPE="SUBMIT" VALUE="Click here to submit this information"></
P>
<P><INPUT TYPE="RESET" VALUE="Whoa, man. I need to start over."></P>
</FORM>
```

This code produces a web page that looks something like this:

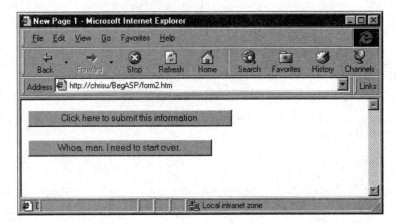

OK, that's enough to give us the framework of a form: but now we need the item of real interest—a place for the user to input data. The input spaces on a form are called fields and are created with the **<INPUT>** tag. Now we need to get the field set up, into which the user will actually enter information. One such field is a text box as added in the code in the shaded lines:

```
<FORM ACTION="Calendar.asp" METHOD=POST>
<P>Please type your name in the space below</P>
<P><INPUT TYPE="TEXT" NAME="LastName"></P>
<P><INPUT TYPE="SUBMIT" VALUE="Click here to Submit"></P>
<P><INPUT TYPE="RESET" VALUE="Whoa, man. I need to start over."></P>
</FORM>
```

This new line changes the browser page to the following:

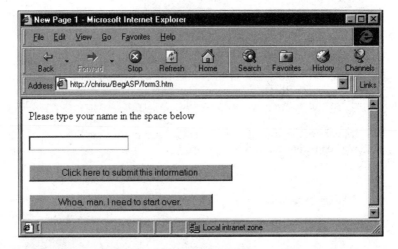

The new input line has two attributes, **TYPE** and **NAME**. In this case, we have specified **TYPE="TEXT"**: this gives us an input box.

The second attribute, **NAME**, is the more important: every input field must have a **NAME**. The data (entered by the user) will be joined to the name of its field: this will be passed on to the ASP page specified by the **ACTION** attribute.

For example, suppose we have a page, containing a form—and that the form has three fields that ask the user for his first name, middle name and last name as follows (of course, the form also has two fields presenting the Submit and Reset buttons).

```
<P><INPUT TYPE="TEXT" NAME="FirstName"></P>
<P><INPUT TYPE="TEXT" NAME="MiddleName"></P>
<P><INPUT TYPE="TEXT" NAME="LastName"></P>
<P><INPUT TYPE="SUBMIT"></P>
<P><INPUT TYPE="RESET"></P>
```

When the user clicks of the Submit button, a second page (usually with an **.asp** suffix) will be called: this page will have the information from these three fields available, in a format such as **FirstName="Alexander"**, **MiddleName="The"** and **LastName="Great"**. If the **INPUT** tag didn't contain a **NAME** attribute, then in the **INPUT** tag there would be no way to know which information was from which field.

We can now put this together into a few practice forms. You won't be able to do anything with the information that you gather just yet, but it's important to get the forms working first.

Try It Out – Form to Get Department Affiliation

Your boss wants to register employees for an upcoming Spring Retreat. Each department will meet on a different weekend, so they need to get each employee's department affiliation when an employee first visits the site. We'll now make a form page asking for the user's department affiliation.

1 Open your preferred page editor and type in the following code for the form page:

```
<HTML>
<HEAD>
<TITLE>Spring Retreat - Get Department Form</TITLE>
</HEAD>

<BODY>
<IMG SRC="tulip1.jpg" WIDTH="221" HEIGHT="120">
<H1>Spring Retreat Logistics</H1>
<H2>Each department will meet at a different time and place.<BR>
Please provide the name of your department<BR></H2>

<FORM ACTION="SpringRetreatNotice.asp" METHOD=POST>
Please type your department here:
```

```
<P><INPUT TYPE="TEXT" NAME="Department"></P>
<P><INPUT TYPE="RESET" VALUE="Reset data"></P>
<P><INPUT TYPE="SUBMIT" VALUE="Click here to send this information"></P>
</FORM>
</BODY>

</HTML>
```

FYI This page contains a reference to `tulip1.jpg`. You can download this file and any other images used in this chapter from the Wrox Web site at `http://rapid.wrox.co.uk/books/1347`. Alternatively, you can substitute your own image—you'll need to adjust the `WIDTH` and `HEIGHT` attributes!

2 Save this page as `SpringRetreatDepartForm.asp`.

3 Create a new page, which should contain the following code:

```
<HTML>
<HEAD>
<TITLE>Spring Retreat Notice</TITLE>
</HEAD>

<BODY>
<H1>Spring Retreat</H1>
<H2>Thank you for registering your department</H2>
</BODY>

</HTML>
```

4 Save this as `SpringRetreatNotice.asp`.

5 Open your browser and run the page `SpringRetreatDepartForm.asp`, which will produce the following:

6 Type in the name of the department (for argument's sake, type *Sales*) and click on the Click here to send this information button. The following page should be displayed:

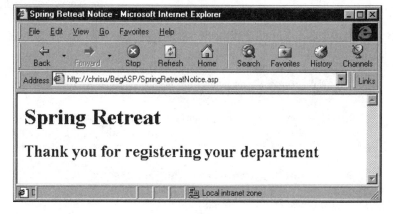

In this chapter all of the files have the extension .asp. The form files that do not have ASP code are not required to have the .asp extension, they would work fine with .htm or .html. However, as your site grows in complexity and you expand your repertoire of ASP skills, you will want to include ASP code on almost every page. Naming all of your files with the .asp extension from the start overcomes the problems of changing the extension to .asp at the time you add code.

How It Works

The first few lines of `SpringRetreatDepartForm.asp` are the standard lines of the header. The first line of the body creates the image and then we have five lines that format and display some opening text. The excitement starts with the opening `<FORM>` tag:

```
<FORM ACTION="SpringRetreatNotice.asp" METHOD=POST>
```

Within that tag we have two attributes. `ACTION` tells the browser which page to call when the user clicks on the Submit button. The `METHOD` tag tells the browser how to send the data the user types to the server.

 At this point in your study, always use the POST **method.**

Within the `<FORM>` and `</FORM>` tags we have one text line and three input lines:

```
Please type your department here:
<P><INPUT TYPE="TEXT" NAME="Department"></P>
<P><INPUT TYPE="RESET" VALUE="Reset data"></P>
<P><INPUT TYPE="SUBMIT" VALUE="Click here to send this information"></P>
```

Let's have a quick look at these four lines. The first line simply displays text so that the user knows what to type in the field. The second line actually creates the box in which the user will type. Note the two attributes: `TYPE="TEXT"` tells the browser this should be a text box, as opposed to a check box or options buttons. `NAME="Department"` gives the identifier, `Department`, that is attached to the data that the user will type.

> *Never leave the* NAME *attribute out of an* <INPUT TYPE="TEXT"> *tag; without it, the data can never be used by ASP.*

The other two input lines provide the standard Submit and Reset buttons. In this case we have used the `VALUE` attributes to change the words on the buttons from the default values, so that the buttons contain text which is customized for our situation.

Then we close the form section with the `</FORM>` tag:

```
</FORM>
```

When the user sees this page, they can enter information in the box. If the user isn't happy with what they've entered, they can click on Reset data and enter different information in the text box.

So, what happens when the user clicks on the Click here to send this information button? First, the browser takes the information in the text box (this might be "Sales", if that's what you wrote in the text box) and assigns it to the input box name to make `Department="Sales"`. Then, the browser sends this to the server, along with a request for the page called `SpringRetreatNotice.asp`. When the server gets an `.asp` page, it will run it through the ASP DLL and will have available the information that the user typed into

`SpringRetreatDepartForm.asp`.

 FYI In the next few pages we will learn how to use that information.

This code then displays the contents of the `SpringRetreatNotice.asp` in the browser.

At this point, we have not used the information from the visitor; however, we have demonstrated how the `<FORM ACTION="page.asp">` is activated by the Submit button to send a request to the server for the next page. Now, let's create a form that gets several items of information back from the user.

Try It Out – Forms: Get Jacket Information

For the upcoming corporate retreat, your Department of Employee Spiritual Growth plans to provide jackets with the company logo. You have been asked to create a page for employees to visit and register information for ordering their jacket. You need to know their preferences in size (Small, Medium, Large or Extra Large), gender (Male or Female) and color (Argent or Azure).

1 You're probably getting used to the procedure by now: open up your preferred page editor and type in the following code:

```
<HTML>
<HEAD>
<TITLE>Form for Spring Retreat Jacket</TITLE>
</HEAD>

<BODY>
<H1>Company Spring Retreat<BR>
Jacket Order Form</H1>
<H3>Please fill in this form and click on Save My Preferences</H3>

<FORM ACTION="SpringRetreatJacketConfirmation.asp" METHOD=POST>
<P>Please type your gender</P>
<P>("male" or "female"):
<INPUT TYPE="TEXT" NAME="gender"></P>
<P>Please type your preference of size</P>
<P>"S"   "M"   "L"   "XL":
<INPUT TYPE="TEXT" NAME="size"></P>
<P>Please type your preference of color</P>
<P>"Argent" or "Azure":
<INPUT TYPE="TEXT" NAME="Color"></P>
<P><INPUT TYPE="RESET" VALUE="Start Over on This Page">
<INPUT TYPE="SUBMIT" VALUE="Save my Preferences"></P>
</FORM>
</BODY>

</HTML>
```

2 Save the page as `SpringRetreatJacketForm.asp`. This is the page that will ask for the jacket information.

3 Keep your editor open and type in a new page:

```
<HTML>
<HEAD>
<TITLE>Spring Retreat Jacket Confirmation</TITLE>
</HEAD>

<BODY>
<H1>Company Spring Retreat<BR>
Jacket Order</H1>
<BR>
<H1>Confirmation</H1>
</BODY>

</HTML>
```

4 Save this as `SpringRetreatJacketConfirmation.asp`. This is a confirmation page to which the form information will be transferred.

5 Now start up your browser and run the page `SpringRetreatJacketForm.asp`, which will produce the following:

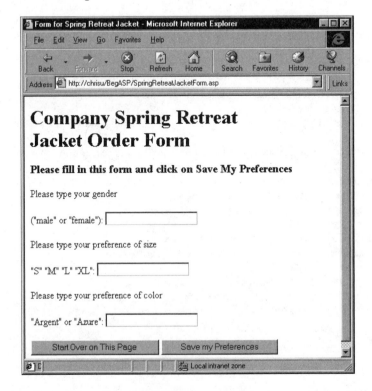

6 Enter some details, and click on the Save my Preferences button to send the information to the server. The page called `SpringRetreatJacketConfirmation.asp` is then opened up automatically by the browser:

How It Works

This code is similar to the last except that we are now working with three fields of data instead of one. The first few lines are the page header. Within the body we first present three lines of simple HTML text giving the user some instructions for the page.

```
<HTML>
<HEAD>
<TITLE>Form for Spring Retreat Jacket</TITLE>
</HEAD>

<BODY>
<H1>Company Spring Retreat<BR>
Jacket Order Form</H1>
<H3>Please fill in this form and click on Save My Preferences</H3>
```

Then we begin the important part with the `<FORM>`. The `<FORM>` tag must contain the attribute to tell the browser what page to call when the Submit button is pressed. In this case that is the `ACTION=SpringRetreatJacketConfirmation.asp`. At this point in your study we are also always using the `METHOD=POST` attribute.

```
<FORM ACTION="SpringRetreatJacketConfirmation.asp" METHOD=POST>
```

The next section alternates between plain HTML text and input fields of the text type. The first field is named "gender," followed by text and a field for "size" and then "color".

```
<P>Please type your gender</P> ("male" or "female"):
<INPUT TYPE="text" NAME="gender"></P>
<P>Please type your preference of size</P>
<P>"S"   "M"   "L"   "XL":
<INPUT TYPE="text" NAME="size"></P>
```

```
<P>Please type your preference of color</P>
<P>"Argent" or "Azure":
<INPUT TYPE="Text" NAME="Color"></P>
```

As always, we add Submit and Reset buttons and close off the form as follows.

```
<INPUT TYPE="reset" VALUE="Start Over on This Page">
<INPUT TYPE="submit" VALUE="Save my Preferences">
</FORM>
```

Here are some take home messages for forms. HTML has tags to create forms to gather information from users. This input will be used by our ASP pages in their decision-making. Remember that:

- The `<FORM>` tag needs two attributes: `ACTION=` and `METHOD=`
- The action equals the page (usually .ASP) that will use the information gathered by the user
- For now always use `METHOD=POST`
- Every input needs a name
- Every form must have a submit button and should have a reset button
- Don't forget to close off your forms with `</FORM>`

Holding Information Obtained From the User

Forms do a fine job of gathering information from the user and passing it to ASP along with a request for a new ASP page. But how can the new ASP page use that information? We need to place that information in a holding tank and then have a way to use it in our ASP code. Like all programming, ASP solves this problem with tools called **variables** which temporarily store information.

Chapter 4 explains the subtleties of variable types and duration, but for now I will show you the quick and dirty technique. Recall that on the first Try-it-out for forms we asked the user for their department using an input box named Department, it's the third line below.

```
<FORM ACTION="SpringRetreatNotice.asp" method=post>
Please type your department here:
<P><INPUT TYPE="Text" NAME="Department"> </P>
<INPUT TYPE="Reset" VALUE="Reset data">
<INPUT TYPE="Submit" VALUE="Click here to send this information">
</FORM>
```

When the user types their name and clicks on the Submit button the browser sends two pieces of information to the server. First is that the server should get the file named `SpringRetreatNotice.asp`. Second is a list of the data the user typed in to the field, in this case the word "sales" was typed into the field named "Department."

Within `SpringRetreatNotice.asp` we can then do as follows.

```
<%
Dim strLastName
strLastName = Request.Form("Department")
%>
```

The first line tells the server to begin a section of ASP code. The second line creates a variable called `strLastName`. Then in the third line we set the contents of `strLastName` to a value ASP has requested from the server - the piece of information we returned from the form. Once that information is saved in a variable, you can use it in any way needed in your ASP code. We will see this used in our next Try It Out.

The key here is to get the syntax correct. You must start with a line that creates the variable using the command `Dim`. For now, keep your variable names very simple by only using letters, no numbers or symbols. Variable names can never contain spaces. To make it easier for you in this chapter we begin all variables with the letters `str` since we are working with text.

Having been created with the `Dim` keyword, the variable must now be filled with some information. The line which stuffs the variable must begin with the name of a variable. The variable name is followed by a space and the equals sign then another space. On the right of the equals we must use the exact words `Request.Form` then open parenthesis, a double quote and the name of the input field from the page. Finish the line with another double quote and close the parenthesis.

You can create more than one variable at a time using one `Dim` and then commas.

```
Dim strLastName, strMiddleName, strFirstName
```

We will be using this technique in our next few Try It Outs, but that will be after we add another idea. The most common errors are typos. If variable assignments don't work you should check:

- Exact spelling of the name that you gave to the input tag, and it is a good habit to make them the same case as well, since in some servers a *Rose* is different from a *rose* is different from a *ROSE* (contrary to Shakespeare).

- Exact typing of the keywords: `Request.Form`.

- Keep your variable names very simple for starters: all letters, no symbols. Never use spaces in variable names.

- Field name must be in double quotes and that within parenthesis.

- Be sure to put the variable name first (left of equals sign) and the source of data second (right of equals sign).

- The assignment of the variable must be within ASP code (between `<%` and `%>`).

- Be sure that in your form page you added the attribute `METHOD=POST` in the `<FORM>` tag.

In our second Try It Out for forms, the request for information on the jackets, we would use the following code in the action page:

```
<%
Dim strGender, strSize, strColor
strGender = Request.Form("gender")
strSize = Request.Form("size")
strColor = Request.Form("color")
%>
```

The variables **strGender**, **strSize** and **strColor** would now be created on line two and then filled with the data typed by the user into those fields. Let us learn one more idea before we do the next Try It Out.

Output to the User

If we want the words *Autumn Sweaters* to appear to the viewer of a simple HTML page we merely have to type it into the page. We don't even need a tag. However, if we want ASP to show those words to the user we must specifically tell ASP to write the words out to the page in HTML. A statement, or command, is needed to direct ASP to do that writing. If we just typed the words *Autumn Sweaters* in ASP code - that is between **<%** and **%>** - ASP would look in its index for the command statement key word *Autumn* using the parameter *Sweaters*. After not finding such a command ASP would send an error message page to the requesting user.

The technique to tell ASP to write information to the HTML page is called **Response.Write**. The command says get the **Response** object to display a message on the screen. (All the **Response** object is, basically, is a representation of the HTML page that is about to be sent by the web server to the browser.) The syntax is simple:

```
<%
Response.Write "Autumn Sweaters"
%>
```

When ASP interprets this code it inserts the words Autumn Sweaters into the HTML page the same as if you had put in the following simple HTML text:

```
Autumn Sweaters
```

These techniques and a potential error are summarized in the following table.

Region of code on page:	Type in	Result in Browser
HTML	Autumn Sweaters	Autumn Sweaters
ASP	Response.Write "Autumn Sweaters"	Autumn Sweaters
ASP	Autumn Sweaters	*Error*

`Response.Write` also works to write tags into the HTML page. For example, to have ASP add a horizontal line to the page we can use `Response.Write` to put the `<HR>` tag into the HTML page as follows.

```
<%
Response.Write "<HR>"
%>
```

ASP also works well for putting the contents of a variable into a page's source HTML. Let's say we have asked the user, in a form, for the name of his item of interest. We could write the name of that item with the following code.

```
<%
Dim strItem
strItem = Request.Form("ItemChoice")
Response.Write strItem
%>
```

The first line starts the ASP code. Then we create a variable called **strItem**. The third line takes the data that the user typed into the form field called **ItemChoice** and it moves that data into the variable called **strItem**. This line makes the user's input available for ASP. The third line writes the contents of **strItem** onto the HTML page and then the fourth line closes off the ASP section.

Do not underestimate the power of what we have just done. The text that will be written on the page going out of the server will be different for each user. Whereas with static HTML we can only send the exact same page to every visitor, with ASP we can customize this page to reflect the exact needs of the requestor.

Make a note that the `Response.Write` syntax for variables is slightly different than for text or tags. For `Response.Write` a variable should not be in double quotes, only text and tags should be in double quotes. Also note that you can have problems if you put the user information directly into a `Response.Write`. It is better to stuff the information into a variable first and then the variable can be used as the source of characters for the `Response.Write`.

Remember that your ASP code will be mixed in with HTML tags and text that goes directly onto the page. So we can have words appear on the page two ways. They can come directly from the HTML sections of the page or they can be written onto the page from ASP commands. And these two techniques can be mixed, for example:

```
Next week's featured item:
<%
Dim strItem
strItem = Request.Form("ItemChoice")
Response.Write strItem
%>
```

In the above example the first line is straight text and HTML tags, the same as if you had never heard of ASP. The second line starts ASP and then we create **strItem**. The fourth line stuffs the user's information into the variable. Then the fifth line directs ASP to write the contents of **strItem** onto the HTML page.

If the user had typed into the `ItemChoice` field *Autumn Sweaters* then the result of the above code would be a page in the browser as shown below.

This intermingling of HTML and ASP-written text applies to the tags as well. If we want to make some words bold (using the `<B>` and `</B>` tags) we can insert the tag from HTML like this:

```
<P>Next week's featured item<P>
<P><B>
<%
Response.Write "Autumn Sweaters"
%>
</B></P>
```

In the above example the paragraph starts before the ASP code begins. ASP writes its two words into the space that will be bold. Then ASP finishes and the HTML page adds the bold off `</B>` tag. The result is the same as if you had just written straight HTML as follows:

```
<P>Next week's featured item <B>Autumn Sweaters</B></P>
```

Alternatively we can insert it those bold tags from the ASP like this:

```
<P>Next week's featured item
<P>
<%
Response.Write "<B>"
Response.Write "Autumn Sweaters"
Response.Write "</B>"
</P>
%>
```

The above code writes to the page the first line from the HTML. The third line begins ASP and then the next three lines put in code and text. The ASP `Response.Write` command doesn't care if it is writing text, tags or a mix. You can put text plus one or more tags in a single `Response.Write`. Therefore the above code can be distilled down to the following code:

```
<P>Next week's featured item
<P>
<%
Response.Write "<B>Autumn Sweaters</B>"
%>
</P>
```

To see another example, let us say the boss wants the form data (Autumn Sweaters) on a second line. We need to have a `<BR>` tag in the HTML page. This can be done several ways, again some inside ASP and some from outside the ASP code. Compare the location of the `<BR>` code in the following three solutions.

Solution One

```
<P>Next week's featured item <BR>
<%
Response.Write "Autumn Sweaters"
%>
```

Solution Two

```
<P>Next week's featured item
<%
Response.Write "<BR>"
Response.Write "Autumn Sweaters"
%>
```

Solution Three

```
<P>Next week's featured item
<%
Response.Write "<BR>Autumn Sweaters"
%>
```

All three solutions produce the following result in the browser:

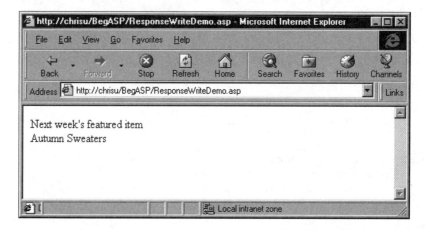

You may have been thinking that this works, and you understand it, but it isn't very impressive. Why not just write text on the page itself rather than having ASP use **Response.Write** to put it onto the page? The power comes from being able to write the contents of variables onto a page. For example if we use a form to get a visitor's product of interest, we can stuff that information into a variable named **strProductInterest**. Now we can use **Response.Write** to put that information onto the page. In later chapters you will learn how to use the contents of that variable to actually make decisions about which page to show.

The syntax to put the contents of a variable onto the page follows:

```
<% strProductInterest=Request.Form("Product") %>
<P>Next week's featured item
<% Response.Write strProductInterest %>
</P>
```

Notice how in the third line we did not ask ASP to print *Autumn Sweaters*, but rather whatever data the user had typed into the Product field of the form.

Now let us finish with a shortcut. Since **Response.Write** is used so often to put the contents of a variable on the page an abbreviated form was created. By simply using **<%=strName%>** you can put onto the page the contents of the variable **strName**. For example, we may have asked the user for the product of their interest on a form and we stored that in a variable named **strProductInterest**. In the past we have used:

```
<%strProductInterest=Request.Form("Product")%>
Next week's featured item
<%Response.Write strProductInterest%>
```

With this shortcut we can write the third line more quickly with:

```
<%strProductInterest=Request.Form("Product")%>
Next week's featured item
<%= strProductInterest%>
```

Note that this technique doesn't work within other ASP code. In the sample below, line four will fail.

```
<%
strProductInterest=Request.Form("Product")
Response.Write "Next week's featured "
=strProductInterest
%>
```

However, it will work fine within a line of HTML text:

```
<%strProductInterest=Request.Form("Product")%>
Next week's featured item<%=strProductInterest%>
```

Take-home points for this section

In this section we have talked about how to direct ASP to write characters to the HTML page before it goes out to the user.

- ▶ These characters can be of three types: text, HTML tags, or the contents of an ASP variable

- ▶ The command for ASP to write characters to the HTML page is **Response.Write**

- ▶ The syntax for text is: **Response.Write "text goes here"**

- ▶ The syntax for variables is **Response.Write strName**

- ▶ We also covered a shortcut to put the contents of a variable into a line of HTML text using the equals sign

Lets now improve the confirmation page that we return in our example after asking the user for their department.

Try It Out – Registration of Department Reply

In our form **SpringRetreatDepartForm.asp**, the **<FORM>** tag has the attribute **ACTION=SpringRetreatNotice.asp**. However the reply isn't exactly informative, "Thank you for registering your department", you don't know if you've even registered the correct department.

So let's now amend this second page to show text that not only confirms the visitor's registration, but also confirms which department they have registered. Keep in mind that it won't be until later in the book that you will learn how to actually make a registration in a database. But for now, we will just focus on returning a message to the user.

1 This solution needs you to change and add the highlighted lines to **SpringRetreatNotice.asp**.

```
<HTML>
<HEAD>
<TITLE>Spring Retreat Notice</TITLE>
</HEAD>

<BODY>
<H1>Spring Retreat</H1>
<H2>Thank you for registering as a member of the
<%
Dim strDepartment
strDepartment = Request.Form("Department")
Response.Write strDepartment
%>
Department.</H2>
</BODY>
</HTML>
```

2 Save the page with the same name as previously.

3 Now, if you run the page on the browser, the page is sent back to the user, together with the information the user entered. For example, if the visitor typed Sales into the field they would get back the page below.

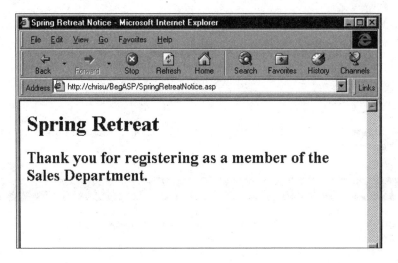

How It Works

This code starts the same head information as when we left it in first Try-It-Out for forms.

```
<HTML>
<HEAD>
<TITLE>Spring Retreat Notice</TITLE>
</HEAD>

<BODY>
<H1>Spring Retreat</H1>
<H2>Thank you for registering as a member of the
```

But now we kick in ASP with a <% and our first statement creates a variable named **strDepartment**. Into that variable ASP sets the data sent from the browser labeled as "Department" which in this case is the word *Sales*. The third ASP statement prints the contents of the variable **strDepartment** onto the page. Then ASP is closed.

```
<%
Dim strDepartment
strDepartment = Request.Form("Department")
Response.Write strDepartment
%>
```

In order to make the page look neater add one line of simple HTML text **Department**. That finishes of both the body and the page as a whole.

Our jacket registration form has sent three fields of data to the server. And as we now know how to put that information into variables, it's time to produce a confirmation page that reads this information back to the user.

Try It Out – Jacket Order Confirmation

1 Open the form `SpringRetreatJacketConfirmation.asp` once again, and replace all of the code between the `<BODY>` tags with the following:

```
<BODY>
<%
Dim strGender, strSize, strColor
strGender = Request.Form("gender")
strSize = Request.Form("size")
strColor = Request.Form("color")
%>
<H1>Company Spring Retreat<BR>
Jacket Order<BR>
Confirmation<BR>
</H1>
We will order for you a
<%Response.Write strGender%>
<BR>jacket in size
<%Response.Write strSize%>
and the
<%Response.Write strColor%>
 color.
</BODY>
```

2 If you open `SpringRetreatJacketForm.asp` in a browser, and fill in the details female, M and Argent and submit this to the server, you will see the following:

How It Works

The first few lines create the variables, then pick up the data the user typed and put that information into variables named **strGender**, **strSize**, and **strColor**.

```
<BODY>
<%
Dim strGender, strSize, strColor
strGender = Request.Form("gender")
strSize = Request.Form("size")
strColor = Request.Form("color")
%>
```

Then we shift out of ASP and into HTML to put some text on the page

```
<H1>Compamy Spring Retreat<BR>
Jacket Order<H1><BR>
<H1> Confirmation</H1>
<BR>
We will order for you a
```

The next line instructs ASP to write on the HTML page the contents of the variable named **strGender**.

```
<%Response.Write strGender%>
```

We shift out of ASP again to put in a line break **
** and some text, then shift back into ASP to put on the page the user's input for Size. The ASP statement is **Response.Write**, that is to write onto the HTML page, the contents of the variable **strSize**. That variable was filled earlier in the statement **strSize = Request.Form("Size")** with the data returned from the user.

```
<BR>
jacket in size
<%Response.Write strSize%>
```

Then we repeat the same shift, write some simple HTML text and then use **Response.Write** for the last variable:

```
and the
<%Response.Write strColor%>
 color.
</BODY>
```

Alternative Solutions to Our Problem

Lets look at a second solution that uses less shifting between HTML and ASP. We can write both the boiler-plate text and the contents of the variables using **Response.Write** as follows.

```
<BODY>
<%
Dim strGender, strSize, strColor
strGender = Request.Form("gender")
```

```
    strSize = Request.Form("size")
    strColor = Request.Form("color")
    Response.Write "<H1>Compamy Spring Retreat<BR>"
    Response.Write "Jacket Order Confirmation</H1>"
    Response.Write "<BR>"
    Response.Write "We will order for you a "
    Response.Write strGender
    Response.Write "<BR>jacket in size "
    Response.Write strSize
    Response.Write " and the"
    Response.Write strColor
    Response.Write " color."
    %>
    </BODY>
```

This solution gives you less shifting since the whole body section is ASP code. However, there are more **Response.Write** statements.

A third - and I believe *best* - solution is the opposite: start with a few lines of ASP to stuff the variables, then stay mainly in HTML and just plunk in the contents of variables as needed using the equals shortcut.

```
    <BODY>
    <%
    Dim strGender, strSize, strColor
    strGender = Request.Form("gender")
    strSize = Request.Form("size")
    strColor = Request.Form("color")
    %>

    <H1>Compamy Spring Retreat<BR>
    Jacket Order Confirmation</H1>
    <BR>
    We will order for you a <%=strGender%><BR>
    jacket in size <%=strSize%>
    and the <%=strColor%> color.
    </BODY>
```

All three of these solutions produce the same page.

Exercises Utilizing these Basic ASP Techniques

Before we head on to the in-depth discussions in the rest of the book I suggest you give these first techniques a few tries. Here are two business situations. The solution for each requires two files, the first is a form and the second is a response page, which utilizes the data the user entered to return a customized page to the user. Once you are comfortable with these simple ASP projects you will be able to incorporate the scores of improvements that the rest of this book presents.

Try It Out – Tax Page Example

Imagine the following, as an international accountant you have set up a Web site. You would like to ask your visitors what country they reside in, then give them some tax rules for their country. Your boss needs you to ask the user for the country where they live for tax purposes. Then you will give the user a new page that has a line at the top of the page stating "Tax Regulations for " and then the name of the country. (The techniques to add the actual selection of appropriate tips you will learn to do later.)

1 Open your favored web page editor and type in the following:

```
<HTML>

<HEAD>
<TITLE>Query user for country of residence</TITLE>
</HEAD>

<BODY>
<P>Entry Form for Country of Domicile</P>
<FORM ACTION="TaxRules.asp" METHOD=post>
Please enter your country of domicile
<P><INPUT TYPE="text" NAME="Country"></P>
<INPUT TYPE="submit" VALUE="Submit Query">
<INPUT TYPE="reset" VALUE="Reset">
</FORM>

</BODY>
</HTML>
```

2 Save this page as `TaxGetResidenceForm.asp`

3 Close that down and create another file, and this time type in:

```
<HTML>

<HEAD>
<TITLE>Tax Rules Entry Form for Country </TITLE>
</HEAD>

<BODY>
<P>The tax rules for the country of
<%
Dim strCountryDomicile
strCountryDomicile = Request.Form("Country")
Response.Write strCountryDomicile
%>
</BODY>

</HTML>
```

4 Save the file as `TaxRules.asp`

5 Open up your favorite browser and run `TaxGetResidenceForm.asp`:

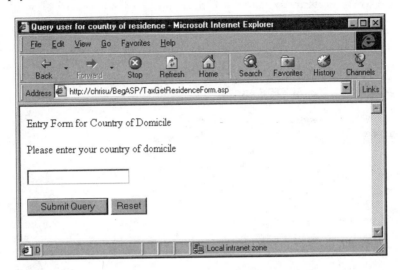

6 If you were to type in *Canada* and submit your query the results would be:

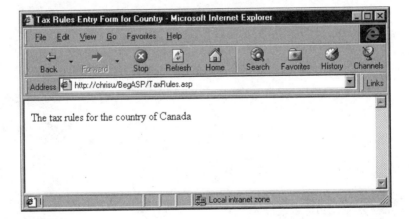

How It Works

The first file starts off with the usual HTML tags for the header and title of the page. Then the page asks the user for their country of domicile by using an HTML Form. There is no ASP code on this page (in fact it would work without the `.asp` file extension).

```
<HTML>
<HEAD>
<TITLE>Query user for country of residence</TITLE>
</HEAD>
<BODY>
<P>Entry Form for Country of Domicile</P>
```

Let us look at the form tags below to review a few ideas The open form tag `<FORM>` must have the attribute of `ACTION=`*`filename`*`.asp`. The value for that attribute should be the ASP file which will be opened when the form is submitted, in this case `TaxRules.asp`. The next line displays a half dozen words of simple HTML text to explain to the user what to do in this text box. Then the form contains three fields, the first is a text type, which is where the user types the name of their country. It is important to name this field so we can identify it for use in the page that is called by the Action. The second and third fields are the simple and standard Submit and Reset buttons. Remember that when the Submit button is hit the browser will gather the data typed into the input field and give it an identifying label which is the name of that input field. That data and label are sent to the web server with a request to open the page indicated by the `ACTION` attribute of the `<FORM>` tag.

```
<FORM ACTION="TaxRules.asp" METHOD=post>
Please enter your country of domicile
<INPUT TYPE="text" NAME="Country"></P>
<INPUT TYPE="submit" VALUE="Submit Query">
<INPUT TYPE="reset" VALUE="Reset">
</FORM>
```

Now we can analyze the second file, the one that is opened after the user clicks the submit button. The server calls up the page asked for in the `ACTION=`, in this case `TaxRules.asp` shown below, and checks if it has an `.asp` file extension. It does, so it gets sent over to the ASP DLL for interpretation.

```
<HTML>

<HEAD>
<TITLE>Tax Rules Entry Form for Country</TITLE>
</HEAD>

<BODY>
<P>The tax rules for the country of
```

The first few lines are usually head junk, then a line of text *The tax rules for the country of* goes onto the page as simple HTML text. Then the ASP DLL spots the <% and starts interpreting.

```
<%
Dim strCountryDomicile
strCountryDomicile = Request.Form("Country")
Response.Write strCountryDomicile
%>
</BODY>
</HTML>
```

The first line creates the variable, then ASP asks for the data labeled Country in the line sent from the form. The ASP server checks and sees `Country="Canada"` so it takes the word `Canada` and uses it to stuff the variable named `strCountryDomicile`. Then on the next line the word in the variable `strCountryDomicile` is written onto the page using `Response.Write`. ASP stops at the `%>` and turns the result back over to the web server. The server adds addressing lines and sends the page out over the Internet.

Alternative Versions of the Code

An alternative to the `TaxRules.asp` file is to generate the words *The tax rules for the country of* from the ASP as well as the name of the country. Here is what just the body would look like.

```
<BODY>
<%
Dim strCountryDomicile
Response.Write "<P>The tax rules for the country of "
strCountryDomicile = Request.Form("Country")
Response.Write strCountryDomicile
%>
</BODY>
```

An improvement on the above idea would be to stuff the variable one line earlier so that chore is taken care of at the outset.

```
<BODY>
<%
Dim strCountryDomicile
strCountryDomicile = Request.Form("Country")
Response.Write "<P>The tax rules for the country of "
Response.Write strCountryDomicile
%>
</BODY>
```

Finally, we could tighten up the code a bit more by moving the text out into HTML and using the equals sign shortcut to splice in the contents of the variable.

```
<BODY>
<% Dim strCountryDomicile
strCountryDomicile = Request.Form("Country") %>
<P>The tax rules for the country of <%=strCountryDomicile%>
</BODY>
```

Let's try another example.

Try It Out – Sign-In Sheet Example

You travel to various offices around the world giving your colleagues seminars on the features of new products your company is about to introduce. Paris in April, Tokyo in September; it is a very glamorous job. But you do have some paperwork. At each seminar you have to make a sign-in sheet with the company logo, date, etc. and lines for people to sign when they attend the seminar. You would like to make up a template of the sign-in sheet on your web site. Then, wherever you are in the world, you want to be able to type in the location and date of the seminar, and have the web server put that at the top of the sheet and return it to your browser. Then you can just print the page and have a beautiful sign-in sheet. For this example, pick any piece of clipart for your company logo.

1 You've guessed it...crank up your trusty web page editor and type in the following:

```
<HTML>

<HEAD>
<TITLE>Where Am I form for sign-in sheets</TITLE>
</HEAD>

<BODY>
<H1>Type the information to make a sign-in sheet for the New Products
seminar.</H1>
<BR>

<FORM ACTION="SignInSheet.asp" METHOD=POST
  <P><INPUT TYPE="text" VALUE="name of city" Name="City"></P>
  <P><INPUT TYPE="text" VALUE="date of seminar" Name="Date"></P>
  <P><INPUT TYPE="submit" VALUE="Click here to submit the information"></
P>
  <P><INPUT TYPE="reset" VALUE="Click here to start over"></P>
</FORM>

</BODY>
</HTML>
```

2 Save this as `WhereAmI.asp`.

3 Close this page down and start another one by typing in the following:

```
<HTML>

<HEAD>
<TITLE>Sign In Sheet for New Products Seminar</TITLE>
</HEAD>

<BODY>
<H1>On-Line Clothiers <IMG SRC="Bizrun.jpg" WIDTH="105" HEIGHT="111"></
H1>
<H1>Welcome to the New Products Seminar</H1>
Held in
<%
Dim strCity
strCity = Request.Form("City")
Response.Write strCity
%>
 on
<%
Dim strDate
strDate = Request.Form("Date")
Response.Write strDate
%>
```

```
<P ALIGN="left">please sign in by printing your name</P>
<HR>

<P ALIGN="left">please sign in by printing your name</P>
<HR>

<P ALIGN="left">please sign in by printing your name</P>
<HR>

</BODY>
</HTML>
```

4 Save this file as `SignInSheet.asp`

5 Open the `WhereAmI.asp` page in your normal browser and type in a city and date and click on the Submit button.

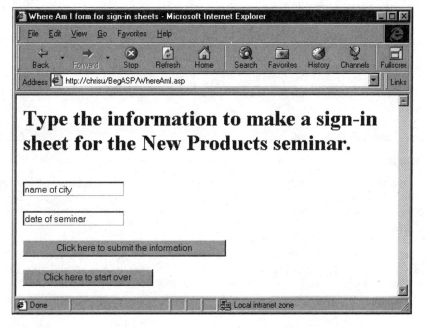

6 If you submitted the name Myerstown and the date 09 May 1999, then you'd see the following:

How It Works

As before, the solution is contained in two pages, the first is a page that doesn't contain ASP but does contain a form with input fields for the user to submit data. That submission calls an ASP page and makes the user's typing available to be written at appropriate points in the second page.

The form page (code for the body shown below) is similar to the last exercise. The **<FORM>** tag must always have the action attribute, in this case pointing to the second file, the one named **SignInSheet.asp**. There are two input fields in this form which makes the Name attribute of each input tag very important, so that in the second **.asp** page we can differentiate the two data.

```
<H1>Type the information to make a sign-in sheet for the New Products
seminar.</H1>
<BR>

<FORM ACTION="SignInSheet.asp" METHOD=POST
  <P><INPUT TYPE="text" VALUE="name of city" Name="City"></P>
  <P><INPUT TYPE="text" VALUE="date of seminar" Name="Date"></P>
  <P><INPUT TYPE="submit" VALUE="Click here to submit the information"></
P>
  <P><INPUT TYPE="reset" VALUE="Click here to start over"></P>
</FORM>
```

The second page is the `.asp` page, which is where the action happens. The objective of this page is to take the sign-in sheet template and add in the city and date for this particular seminar as was entered in the first page. You can then print it to put at the registration table. After the normal `<HEAD>` material, the `<BODY>` begins. A heading level one line splashes the company name and logo across the top of the page, followed by another heading level one that writes the Welcome… line. Then some text starts the line of interest with the words *Held In* presented with normal HTML text.

```
<HTML>
<HEAD>
<TITLE>Sign In Sheet for New Products Seminar</TITLE>
</HEAD>
<BODY>
<H1>On-Line Clothiers <IMG SRC="Bizrun.jpg" WIDTH="105" HEIGHT="111"></
H1>
<H1>Welcome to the New Products Seminar</H1>
```

In the next line we use <% to shift gears into ASP. The first ASP line creates a variable named `strCity` and stuffs into it the text sent back by the form with the name "City." Then the ASP code immediately ends. The next line is very short, we just want to write using HTML text the word *on*.

```
Held in
<%
Dim strCity
strCity = Request.Form("City")
Response.Write strCity
%>
  on
```

Then ASP kicks back in to create the variable `strDate` and stuff it with the date information sent in with the request. Having stuffed that information into a variable we can write the variable contents to the page using `Response.Write`. Remember that you can't write directly to the page from the `Request.Form`. You must put the information into a variable first. ASP closes with the %>.

```
<%
Dim strDate
strDate = Request.Form("Date")
Response.Write strDate
%>
```

The page is finished by repeating three lines of HTML tags that put the actual sign-in lines on the page.

```
<P ALIGN="left">please sign in by printing your name</P>
<HR>

<P ALIGN="left">please sign in by printing your name</P>
<HR>
```

```
<P ALIGN="left">please sign in by printing your name</P>
<HR>

</BODY>
</HTML>
```

Alternative Versions of The Code

There is an alternative to the above `SignInSheet.asp` file. Rather than shift out of ASP and into HTML to put the one word *on* into the page we could stay in ASP and use `Response.Write` to put the text on the HTML page.

```
Held in
<%
Dim strCity, strDate
strCity = Request.Form("City")
Response.Write strCity
Response.Write " on "
strDate = Request.Form("Date")
Response.Write strDate
%>
```

It is not a bad idea to get all the variable stuffing done first, for reasons that you learn later. So a better solution would have some lines re-arranged from above to be more like:

```
Held in
<%
Dim strCity, strDate
strCity = Request.Form("City")
strDate = Request.Form("Date")
Response.Write strCity
Response.Write " on "
Response.Write strDate
%>
</P>
```

And if you recall the equal sign short cut you can even reduce down to:

```
<%
Dim strCity, strDate
strCity = Request.Form("City")
strDate = Request.Form("Date")
%>
Held in <%=strCity%> on <%= strDate%>
```

This finishes our basic ASP examples. You might not have understood all of the working behind the code, but you should at least have an idea of how to send information in a form and display it on a separate page.

Summary

In this chapter we first covered forms and then practiced making forms, including the importance if the **ACTION** attribute in the **<FORM>** tag and the **NAME** attribute in the **<INPUT>** tag. When the browser submits the user's information to the server, you now know how to grab that information and stuff it into a variable using **strName=Request.Form ("field name")**. The last idea was the use of **Response.Write "text"** to get ASP code to put text onto an HTML page headed out to the browser. If we want to put the contents of a variable onto the page we use **Response.Write strname** or **<%=strName%>**.

Now, as my professor of Chinese told me, you are ready to begin your study. I haven't gone into detail about the theory, logic or exceptions to these ASP techniques; that will come in the remaining chapters. But at least you have some basic tools to create an ASP page, get information from the user, store it in a variable and then put it back out on a subsequent ASP page.

Variables

One of the most important facilities in any programming language is the ability to store information. Suppose the user is required to input their name: where do you store this information so that it can be used later? How do you store other types of data, such as numbers and dates? And what if several users have all provided similar pieces of data: how does the computer know how to match up the information provided with the user who provided it? This is all done via the use of **variables**.

Your programming language gives you the power to create variables, to assign values to them, and to reuse them in your program. They will enable you to perform mathematical functions, calculate new dates, dissemble text, count the length of sentences, and so on. Variables are fundamental to programming—they'll form the foundations of nearly everything you'll come to program.

In this chapter we'll look at:

▶ What a variable is

▶ What a variant is

▶ Different subtypes in VBScript

▶ How to declare a variable

▶ How to perform calculations with variables

▶ What 'scope' is

▶ What an array is and how it can be used to store information about several related data items

We'll start by establishing exactly what a variable is.

What is a Variable?

A **variable** is a section of memory that is allocated a name by the programmer. These sections of memory can be used to store pieces of information that will be used in the program. Think of variables as you might think of boxes. They're simply containers for information that you wish to store. For example, here are three variables—they contain a string of text, a numerical value and a date respectively:

```
CapitalCityOfUnitedKingdom = "London"
NumberOfStates = 50
IndependenceDay = 7/4/1776
```

Any variable is empty until you put information into it. You can then look at the information inside the variable, get the information out, or replace the information with new data. In fact, variables are essential for storing data in any computer language; in this book, we'll discuss variables in the context of VBScript and ASP.

Naming Variables

As we go, we'll look at the different types of variables, how to assign values to them, and how to use them in expressions. We'll also talk about the kinds of names that you should give to your variables. For example, while the variable names above reflect their contents in a fairly self-explanatory way, the meanings of the variables in the following expressions are less obvious:

```
a=1*x+73
objBoolean=true
```

They're not particularly helpful, are they? It's really up to the programmer to find a suitable name for his variable when he creates it. Ideally, you should find a name that is meaningful to a developer who subsequently reads your code. At the same time, excessively long variable names are unwieldy and easy to mistype, so you should avoid these too. If the variable names are well-chosen, then the thinking behind the apparent gobbledygook in expressions like those above will become clearer. It's a good idea to make variable names descriptive even if this means making them longer.

In most languages, the name of a variable can be almost anything you choose, but there are usually a few restrictions:

▶ There's usually a practical limit to the length of your variable names. In VBScript, the limit is 255 characters—this should be more than ample for most people!

▶ There are usually restrictions on which characters you can use in your variable names. In VBScript:

  ▶ all variable names must begin with an alphabetical character

  ▶ variable names must not contain an embedded period/full-stop

▶ Case-sensitivity is another important issue. VBScript is case-insensitive, which means that you can use upper- and lower-case characters to refer to exactly the same variable. For example, VBScript will interpret **counter** and **COUNTER** as one and the same. On the other hand JScript/JavaScript is case sensitive and would interpret **counter** and **COUNTER** as two entirely different entities.

We'll say a little more about variable names later in this chapter.

Data Types in VBScript, or One Type For All

Variables come in many different shapes and sizes, and it's primarily the **data type** that defines what sort of information is stored inside the variable. Most programming languages have a list of the different types of data they can accommodate, although VBScript is slightly different.

There are many different data types you can use, such as numerical types, text types and date types, and VBScript can accommodate each of these different data types. However, as you'll see, VBScript actually treats each of these different data types as though they were all of just one type. VBScript doesn't have explicit data types.

In most programming languages, it is common to specify a data type for a variable, so that your system knows what type of variable it's dealing with. However, these days this is no longer the case. In VBScript, all of the variables with seemingly different data types are actually only one type. This is the **variant**. A variant is a special type of variable, which can store a value of any type. This means that you don't have to specify a data type for a variant when you declare it. (In fact, you can't specify a data type in VBScript—you'll get an error.) Hence, you could declare a variable like this:

```
Dim LengthOfAPieceOfString
```

Then you could assign an **integer** value to it:

```
LengthOfAPieceOfString = 5
```

Later on, you might decide that you want to replace this value with a **string** value:

```
LengthOfAPieceOfString = "Not very long"
```

This means that we need a mechanism for keeping track of the type of data that is being stored in each variant. VBScript assigns a **subtype** to the variant, that reminds the variant of the type of data being stored. Basically, a subtype can be any of the following:

Numeric Subtypes

You can assign almost any number to a variable. We can assign whole numbers, fractions, and even negative floating pointing numbers:

```
IntegerNumber1 = 76
DecimalNumber2 = 2.5356
FloatingPointNumber3 = -1.4E06
```

You should know about floating point numbers from your math classes, and they're really not hard. Basically we use floating point numbers to represent very small or very large decimals more simply: for example, instead of writing 0.00000123, you can represent the same number as 1.23E-6 (which is equivalent to 1.23×10^{-6}).

In VBScript, there are five different numeric subtypes, which are outlined below.

Integer

Integers are simply whole numbers. Examples of integers are 3, 12 and -5127. The integer data type can handle whole numbers within the range -32,768 to 32,767. If you wish to use anything outside this range then you'll need to use the long type, which we'll see shortly.

Byte

Bytes are integers within the range 0 to 255. They're used for very basic arithmetic. It's a useful type, because the method in which data is made available means that a variable can be easily stored by the computer within a single byte, which is the computer's basic storage unit.

Long

The long type is very similar to the integer type, but supports a much larger range. A long variable can contain a value in the range -2,147,483,648 to 2,147,483,647.

Single

The single type can hold single precision floating point numbers, within the range -3.402823E38 to -1.401298E-45 (for negative values), and 1.401298E-45 to 3.402823E38 (for positive values).

Double

The double type holds double precision floating point numbers. This means that it will support a much larger range than the single type. In reality, this range is -1.79769313486232E308 to -4.94065645841247E-324 (for negative values), and 4.94065645841247E-324 to 1.79769313486232E308 (for positive values).

String Subtype

Variants with the string subtype can hold any type of textual information. We can use string variants to store pure text, or a mixture of text and numerical data, and even date information. For example, the following code creates a variant called `CarType`, with the value `"Buick"`; a variant called `CarEngineSize`, with the value `"2.0L"`; and a variant called `DatePurchased`, with the value `"March 29, 1998"`:

```
CarType = "Buick"
CarEngineSize = "2.0L"
DatePurchased = "March 29, 1998"
```

String values are usually put into quotation marks, so that they can be differentiated from numerical values. Note that you can't perform mathematical functions on strings, even if the content of the strings involved are purely numerical. Hence, if you try to add the two strings `"12"` and `"14"` together, as shown in the following example, you won't get the result `"26"` that you might have anticipated:

```
Number1 = "12"
Number2 = "14"
Number3 = Number2 + Number1 'Will produce "1412"
```

This is because the string subtype itself can hold different types of data, but it only holds *textual* representations of other types, such as Integer or Date. VBScript does provide a number of special functions that you can manipulate strings with. These functions allow you to measure the length of a string, truncate a string at the beginning or end, or return certain characters from a given string. We'll look at these string manipulation functions later in this chapter.

Date Subtype

VBScript also supports a subtype, date, that can be used to hold dates and times. Variants of this subtype use a predefined format. The same subtype is used to record both date and time. For example, we can use the variant `DateTime` to store a given date:

```
DateTime = #12/15/97#
```

A date must be surrounded by the `#` symbol: otherwise it will be evaluated as a numeric expression. Later in the same program, we could use the same variant to store a given time:

```
DateTime = #11.03#
```

The predefined format of the date type prevents 'regular' numerical arithmetic from being carried out on variants of subtype date. Once the computer is aware of their special format, it's possible to carry out simple numerical arithmetic on them. For example, if you subtracted July 20, 1998 from the July 24, 1998, you'd get the answer 4. (However, you wouldn't be able to multiply two dates together.)

Boolean Subtype

Boolean variants can be set to one of two values, namely TRUE or FALSE. In VBScript, these values are represented by −1 and 0 respectively. They can be used to record the state of the variable, in that if a variable isn't TRUE then it must be FALSE. They can be set when a user performs a certain action, i.e. runs a certain form, and they can then be used to determine a certain course of action:

```
blnVariant = FALSE
If blnVariant = FALSE Then do this
...
Else do that
...
```

Also you can specify a condition such as:

```
If (colorOfSky = Blue) Then do Part A
...
Else do Part B
...
```

Here, a Boolean value has been returned by the expression within brackets, which is evaluated by the VBScript interpreter: a value TRUE or FALSE is returned, depending on the status of the expression. In this example, if the value is TRUE then the engine will execute Part A, if not it will execute Part B.

Booleans are an integral part of structures such as the `If ... Else` structure shown in this example. We'll be looking at `If ... Else`, and other control structures, in the next chapter.

Special Subtypes

There are three other subtypes that we should briefly outline here.

Empty

Empty variants are variants that have yet to be assigned a value. Note that you shouldn't confuse these variants with variants that have been assigned the value 0 (zero)! This is because 0 is a valid value (which also implies that the variable is likely to be a numeric type), while an empty variant has no value at all (because no value has yet been assigned to it).

NULL

`NULL` is an unusual subtype, that is used in conjunction with databases. It is again used to refer to sets that are empty, or when it is not known whether or not a value exists. We'll be using `NULL` in Chapter 15.

Object

The object subtype refers to special Microsoft objects; don't worry about what these are just yet. We'll be taking a closer look at them in Chapter 6.

Determining Subtypes with TypeName()

So, if VBScript treats all these different subtypes as basically the same type, how does it keep track of which variant is of which subtype? It does this by using the VBScript function `TypeName()`. If you feed a variant into the `TypeName()` function, as follows:

```
LengthOfAPieceOfString = 5
WhatTypeOfVar = TypeName(LengthOfAPieceOfString)
```

then one of the following variant types is returned:

Empty	Date
Null	String
Integer	OLE object
Long Integer	Error
Single	Boolean
Double	Data Access object
Currency	Byte
	Array

If some of these variant sub types are unfamiliar to you, don't worry: we'll be looking at arrays later in this chapter, objects in Chapter 6 and Data Access objects in Chapters 13 and 14.

We'll now take a quick look at how you can use `TypeName()` to return the subtype that VBScript is storing for a particular variant.

Try It Out – Using TypeName to return a Variant Subtype

1 Start up your favorite ASP editor and type in the following:

```
<HTML>

<HEAD>
<TITLE>Using TypeName</TITLE>
</HEAD>

<BODY BGCOLOR="white">

<%
Dim dblPi, whatIsPi, datToday, whatIsDate, strText, whatIsText
dblPi = 3.142
whatIsPi = TypeName(dblPi)

datToday = Date
whatIsDate = TypeName(datToday)

strText = "Hello World"
whatIsText = TypeName(strText)

Dim emp
emptyVar = TypeName(emp)
%>

<P><B>dblPi returns <% = whatIsPi %> </P>
<P>datToday returns <% = whatIsDate %> </P>
<P>strText returns <% = whatIsText %> </P>
<P>emp returns <% = emptyVar %></B></P>

</BODY>
</HTML>
```

2 Save it as `TypeName.asp`

3 Run this in your preferred browser.

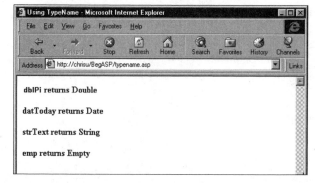

103

How It Works

This example is very simple. We assign four variants values with different subtypes, and four corresponding variants to record the subtypes of the variables. We start by declaring all of the variants we're going to use, and then we allocate the value of *pi*, 3.142, to the variant `dblPi`. Then we create a variant `whatIsPi`, which contains the `TypeName` value of this variant:

```
<%Dim dblPi, whatIsPi, datToday, whatIsDate, strText, whatIsText
dblPi = 3.142
whatIsPi = TypeName(dblPi)
```

We then assign a variable `datToday` with today's date (provided by the VBScript `Date` function), and assign `TypeName(datToday)` to the variant `whatIsDate`:

```
datToday = Date
whatIsDate = TypeName(datToday)
```

We assign a string value to the variant `strText`, and then assign `TypeName(strText)` to the variant `whatIsText`:

```
strText = "Hello World"
whatIsText = TypeName(strText)
```

We then declare a variant `emp`, but we don't actually assign it a value:

```
Dim emp
emptyVar = TypeName(emp) %>
```

Finally we return the four `TypeName` values in the ASP:

```
<P><B>dblPi returns <% = whatIsPi %> </P>
<P>datToday returns <% = whatIsDate %> </P>
<P>strText returns <% = whatIsText %> </P>
<P>emp returns <% = emptyVar %></B></P>
```

When passed to the function `TypeName`, `dblPi` returns Double, `datToday` returns Date, `strText` returns String and `emp` returns Empty. This confirms the fact that when you allocate data to a variable, VBScript also assigns a subtype to the variant. The subtype of the variant can be determined by using the VBScript `TypeName` function.

Arithmetic and Comparison Operators

Of course variants aren't much use unless you can manipulate them in some way. In the descriptions above, we have already seen one or two examples of basic data manipulation, but in this section we'll introduce the concepts more formally.

Assignment Operator

The familiar 'equal' sign (=) is probably the most common operator in computing. You've already seen it used several times to **assign** values to our variants. The variant **name** goes on the left, the variant **value** goes on the right:

```
Number1 = 2
```

Mathematical Impossibilties

You can also use the assignment operator to increase (or decrease) the value of variants using the following, mathematically unsound, formula:

```
Number1 = 2
Number1 = Number1 + 1
```

Mathematicians will be scratching their head, wondering how `Number1` can be equal to `Number1` plus 1: it's equivalent to saying 2 = 2 +1, which is impossible. The answer is, of course, that it can't. In programming, the equality operator is used to assign a new value to `Number1`. It's a way of saying "whatever the old value of `Number1` is, take that and add it to 1"—this value comprises the new value of `Number1`.

Comparison Operators

The comparison operators are used slightly differently. The comparison operators available in VBScript are:

Equality	=	Inequality	<>
Less than	<	Greater than	>
Less than or equal to	<=	Greater than or equal to	>=

We've just seen the 'equal' sign (=) in its guise as the assignment operator. In this case, the 'equal' sign is used as the equality operator, to test for equality:

```
If Number1 = 2 Then
```

This statement says, "If the value inside `Number1` is already equal to 2 then (perform a certain operation)". It depends upon the context in which the equals sign is used. If it's used on its own, then it assigns one value to a variant, if it's used as part of an `If ... Then` statement, then it's being used as a comparison operator. You can also use these operators to compare the values of two operands—such as variants or expressions. The result of the comparison is a Boolean value—that is, either TRUE or FALSE.

We'll be looking at exactly how the `If ... Then` structure works in the next chapter.

Logical Operators

There's also a set of logical operators you can use:

AND

OR

NOT

Actually there are more than three logical operators, but they're only required in specialist situations, so we won't be using them in this book. The logical operators are used in the same way as comparison operators and also return a Boolean value:

```
If (Number1=1 AND Number2=2) Then
```

They are used to determine a particular course of action. The parentheses indicate that the expression inside them should be evaluated first. When using AND, both of these conditions have to be TRUE for the condition to be fulfilled. This differs from OR where either one of two conditions has to be TRUE for the condition to be fulfilled.

```
If (Number1=1 OR Number2=2) Then
```

The third logical operator NOT, simply implies the reverse of the condition. If `Number1` isn't equal to 1 then the condition is fulfilled:

```
If (NOT Number1=1) Then
```

Arithmetic Calculations

The arithmetic operations available in VBScript are:

Addition	+	Exponentiation	^
Subtraction	–	Negation	–
Multiplication	*	Modulus	`MOD` or \
Division	/		

Here is a very simple example: we'll assign values to the variants `Number1` and `Number2` before adding them together, and assigning the result to a third variant, `Number3`:

```
Number1 = 14
Number2 = 12
Number3 = Number1 + Number2
```

As a result of this, `Number3` will contain the value 26.

You can also use brackets to influence the order in which a calculation is performed. For example, in the following code we divide the variant `Number2` by 6 and add the result to the variant `Number1`:

```
Number1 = 14
Number2 = 18
Number3 = Number1 + (Number2/6)
```

First, the computer evaluates the contents of the brackets, following normal mathematical procedure: **Number2** divided by 6 yields the result 3. This is added to the value of **Number1**, and the result of this—17—is assigned to the variant **Number3**.

Concatenating Variants

It makes sense to add integers together, using expressions such as **2 + 3**, or **Number1 + Number2** (as we showed above). But what happens if you wish to 'add' strings together? It doesn't make much sense to add them in the arithmetic sense—**"Beans"** plus **"Rice"** doesn't have a tangible meaning. However, VBScript allows us to 'add' strings together in a different sense—using a process known as **concatenation**.

When two strings are concatenated, the second string is attached at the end of the first string, creating a new string. In order to concatenate two strings we use the ampersand operator (**&**), although you can also use the + operator. Let's run through a few examples. We can concatenate the strings **"Helter"** and **"Skelter"**, as follows:

```
strConcatenate = "Helter" & "Skelter"
```

Here, the result of the concatenation is the string **"HelterSkelter"**, which will be assigned to the variant **strConcatenate**, of type string. You can also concatenate a number of strings within the same expression. Here, we'll concatenate three strings, one of which is a space:

```
strConcatenate = "Helter" & " " & "Skelter"
```

Now, **strConcatenate** will contain the string **"Helter Skelter"**. You can concatenate as many string variants as you like (within reason):

```
strFirst = "Never "
strLearline = strFirst & strFirst & strFirst & strFirst & strFirst
```

Then **strLearLine** will contain the line "**Never Never Never Never Never**   ".

Declaring Variants

We've got descriptions of the subtypes, and examples of how variants are used, but we missed an important step: how to declare a variant. Variants should be declared *before* they are used within a program. A variant declaration is made with the keyword **Dim**, which is short for 'dimension'. This rather odd-looking incantation tells the computer that you're setting up a new variant.

For example, the first line here declares a variant with the name **CarType**; the second line assigns a string value to that variant:

```
Dim CarType
CarType = "Buick"
```

107

Declaring a variant in this way is known as **explicit** declaration, because we are explicitly telling the computer what the name of our variant is, before we use it.

Many programming languages require you declare your variables explicitly, before you can use them. This isn't strictly necessary in VBScript: indeed, you can just as easily assign a value to a variant without having first declared it. This process is known as **implicit** declaration of variables. As an example of implicit declaration, we can create another variant, `CarType2`, and assign the value to it, without using the `Dim` command:

```
CarType2 = "Pontiac"
```

It's generally good practice to explicitly declare a variable before you use it. This will allow you to keep track of all of the variants in VBScript that you've created. It should help you to avoid creating unnecessary variants, as you won't be creating them on the off chance that you might need them later in the program. Further, you can use explicit declaration together with the keywords `Option Explicit` to help debug your programs.

Using Option Explicit

`Option Explicit` is very simple. You simply add this line to your programs (preferably at the beginning): if you do this, it means that every variable in the program must be explicitly declared in the code before it's used. If an implicitly declared variable is used, then `Option Explicit` ensures that an error is generated, highlighting the particular omission.

Here's an example of how `Option Explicit` is useful in keeping errors down. Consider the following program:

```
<SCRIPT LANGUAGE=VBSCRIPT>
Option Explicit
Dim intHeight, intWidth, intTotal
intHeight = 150
intWidth = 140
intTotal = (intHeight * (intWidth +40))/(intHeigth+intWidth)
</SCRIPT>
```

In such a short code fragment, you can probably spot pretty quickly that we've misspelled `intHeight` in the second usage on the last line. However, imagine that this fragment of code is buried in a list of 100 variables, about 50 lines into the page. Would you be able to spot it so quickly then?

With the `Option Explicit` line, this error would be detected immediately as an illegal implicit declaration. Without `Option Explicit`, the implicit declaration is entirely legal, so your page would execute without an error. In fact, the only clue to the error is the value assigned to `intTotal`, which is calculated with the value of `intHeigth` (i.e. 0) instead of `intHeight` (i.e. 150). Indeed, if you didn't know what value to expect for `intTotal`, then you might not even notice the mistake at all!

There's one important catch though: when using `Option  Explicit` in Internet Explorer 4, it must always be included on the first line of script. So in a script such as this:

```
<SCRIPT LANGUAGE=VBSCRIPT>
Dim intHeight, intWidth, intTotal
Option Explicit
intHeight = 150
intWidth = 140
intTotal = (intHeight * (intWidth +40))/(intHeigth+intWidth)
</SCRIPT>
```

the position of **Option Explicit** in this script will actually cause a syntax error. And on the server-side, in ASP, **Option Explicit** must come even before the first line of HTML:

```
<%Option Explicit%>
<HTML>
...
```

When you think about it, where else could it go? Scripts are run from top to bottom. If you want it to check for **Dim** statements, you better tell it to do that before it starts reading the script. In ASP, the ASP script is processed before the HTML, so it has to come before the HTML. However, *why* Microsoft have chosen to make this line cause an error if positioned anywhere else in the program is a still a bit of mystery, so be warned.

Try It Out – Using Variants to Perform a Simple Calculation

OK, we've seen lots of theory, so now it's time to try out an example. We're going to perform a simple calculation of tax. To do this we need to declare three variants: one for the earnings, one for the tax percentage and one for the total. We're going to deduct the earnings by whatever percentage the tax rate is set at and display the final income in an ASP page.

1 Type the following program into your ASP editor:

```
<HTML>

<HEAD>
<TITLE>Declaring Variants</TITLE>
</HEAD>

<BODY BGCOLOR="white">
<%
Dim intEarn, intTax, intTotal
intEarn = 150
intTax = 20
intTotal = intEarn - ((intEarn/100)*intTax)
%>

<B><P>Your total earnings after tax are $<% = intTotal %> </P></B>
</BODY>
</HTML>
```

2 Save it as `taxcalc.asp`

3 Now start your browser and run `taxcalc.asp`.

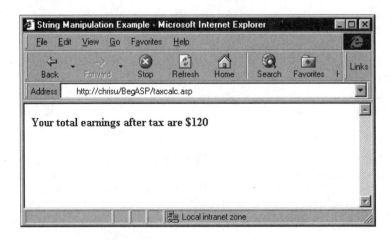

Please note that all of the Try-It-Outs in this chapter are available on our web site at ***http://rapid.wrox.co.uk/books/1347***. *You can either execute the examples directly or download them from here, whichever you prefer.*

How It Works

There are only five lines of ASP code in this program. The first declares three variants, `intEarn` for the earnings, `intTax` for the tax rate and `intTotal` for our final amount:

```
Dim intEarn, intTax, intTotal
```

In the next line we set the value of the earnings to 150, and the tax rate to 20:

```
intEarn = 150
intTax = 20
```

The `intTotal` variant is where the calculation is performed. To gain our percentage, we first have to calculate what 20% of the earnings are: this is done by dividing the earnings by 100 and multiplying the result by the tax rate. Brackets are used to indicate the order of calculation within this expression:

```
intTotal = intEarn - ((intEarn/100)*intTax)
```

Finally, we return the value of `intTotal`, embedded in normal HTML code:

```
<B><P>Your total earnings after tax are $<% = intTotal %> </P></B>
```

You could calculate tax deductions for any percentage rate and any earnings, by altering the values of variants `intEarn` and `intTax`.

Conversions

As we now know, when you assign a value to a variant, a subtype is also automatically assigned. Sometimes, however, the assigned subtype is not the one that you intend, and in such cases a little force is required to explicitly convert the value into the type you actually wanted. VBScript provides plenty of functions to do this for you. In fact, it provides so many of these functions that you'll probably never use many of them. In a moment we'll exercise some of these functions in an example. First, here's a complete list of them:

Function	Description
Abs	Returns the absolute value of number.
Asc, AscB, AscW	Returns the ANSI character code of the first letter in a string. AscB is used on byte data while AscW is used on 32-bit platforms that use UNICODE data (a format that falls outside the scope of this book).
Chr, ChrB, ChrW	This is the opposite of Asc, and returns the character code of a specific character. ChrB is used on byte data contained in a string while ChrW is used on 32-bit platforms that use UNICODE data.
CBool	Returns the variable that has been converted into a variant with the subtype Boolean.
CByte	Returns the variable that has been converted into a variant with the subtype Byte.
CCur	Returns the variable that has been converted into a variant with the subtype Currency.
CDate	Returns the variable that has been converted into a variant with the subtype Date.
CDbl	Returns the variable that has been converted into a variant with the subtype Double.
CInt	Returns the variable that has been converted into a variant with the subtype Integer.
CLng	Returns the variable that has been converted into a variant with the subtype Long.
CSng	Returns the variable that has been converted into a variant with the subtype Single.
CStr	Returns the variable that has been converted into a variant with the subtype String.
DateSerial	Returns the variable that has been converted into a variant with the subtype Date for given year, month, day.
DateValue	Returns a value representing a variant of subtype Date.
Hex	Returns a string containing the hexadecimal value of a number.
Oct	Returns a string containing the octal value of a number.
Fix	Returns the integer portion of a number.
Int	Also returns the integer portion of a number.

Function	Description
`Sgn`	Returns the sign of a number, i.e. positive or negative.
`TimeSerial`	Returns the variable that has been converted into a variant with the subtype Date for given hour, minute, second.
`TimeValue`	Returns a value representing a variant of subtype Date.

> *If you assign a fraction or decimal value to an integer, normally the integer is rounded up or down to the next closest whole number. This process is known as an implicit conversion.*

These functions all work in much the same way. As a demonstration, we'll have a look at how to use a couple of them now.

Try It Out – Converting a Variant

In this example we're going to take the value of *pi*=3.142, read it in as a string, convert to a single data type, convert it into an integer and then finally convert it back to a string. We're also going to display the value and subtype of each variant after the conversion.

1 Type the following program into your favorite editor:

```
<HTML>

<HEAD>
<TITLE>Converting Variants</TITLE>
</HEAD>

<BODY BGCOLOR="white">
<%Dim strPi, dblPi, intPi,strPi2, whatisPi1, whatisPi2, whatisPi3,
whatisPi4
strPi = "3.142"
whatIsPi1 = TypeName(strPi)
dblPi = CSng(strPi)
whatIsPi2 = TypeName(dblPi)
intPi = CInt(dblPi)
whatIsPi3 = TypeName(intPi)
strPi2 = CStr(intPi)
whatIsPi4 = TypeName(strPi2) %>

<P><B>Pi is a <% = whatIsPi1 %> and Pi returns <% = strPi %> </B></P>
<P><B>Pi is a <% = whatIsPi2 %> and Pi returns <% = dblPi %> </B></P>
<P><B>Pi is a <% = whatIsPi3 %> and Pi returns <% = intPi %> </B></P>
<P><B>Pi is a <% = whatIsPi4 %> and Pi returns <% = strPi2 %> </B></P>
</BODY>
</HTML>
```

2 Save it as `convert.asp`.

3 Run the page on your preferred browser.

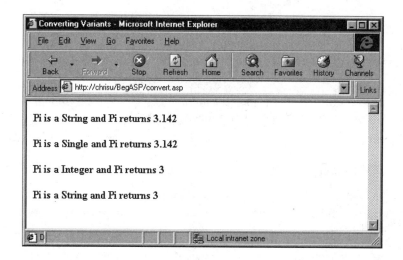

How It Works

This program explicitly declares all of the variants we will use and then assigns the variant `strPi` a value of 3.142. It then reads the subtype of this variant into another variant, `whatIsPi1`:

```
<%Dim strPi, dblPi, intPi,strPi2, whatisPi1, whatisPi2, whatisPi3,
whatisPi4
strPi = "3.142"
whatIsPi1 = TypeName(strPi)
```

Next, we declare three more variants; the value assigned to each is generated by converting the subtype of the preceding one. Hence, the value assigned to `dblPi` is the conversion of `strPi` from subtype string to subtype single. Also, the `TypeName` of the variant `dblPi` is assigned to `whatIsPi2`:

```
dblPi = CSng(strPi)
whatIsPi2 = TypeName(dblPi)
```

The value assigned to `intPi` is the conversion of `dblPi` from subtype single to subtype integer. The `TypeName` of `intPi` is assigned to `whatIsPi3`:

```
intPi = CInt(dblPi)
whatIsPi3 = TypeName(intPi)
```

Last, the value assigned to `strPi2` is the conversion of `intPi` back to subtype string. The `TypeName` of `intPi` is assigned to `whatIsPi4`:

```
strPi2 = CStr(intPi)
whatIsPi4 = TypeName(strPi2) %>
```

The final lines simply display the subtype and value of each of these variants:

```
<P><B>Pi is a <% = whatIsPi1 %> and Pi returns <% = strPi %> </B></P>
<P><B>Pi is a <% = whatIsPi2 %> and Pi returns <% = dblPi %> </B></P>
<P><B>Pi is a <% = whatIsPi3 %> and Pi returns <% = intPi %> </B></P>
<P><B>Pi is a <% = whatIsPi4 %> and Pi returns <% = strPi2 %> </B></P>
```

Notice that as a result of the conversion from subtype single to subtype integer, the fractional part of the value of *pi* is lost. Further, when you convert back to subtype string, you don't regain the information! (This is because the final conversion is from type integer to subtype string: the value to be converted is 3, not 3.142.) It's easy to lose information in this way, so you should be sure to control your conversions carefully. Don't be put off, though: data conversions are a useful tool to have, and they're not difficult to use.

Naming Conventions

You've probably noticed by now that in the examples we've looked at so far, some of our variants have rather odd prefixes such as **str** and **int**. If you were wondering why, you're going to find out now.

If we have lots of variants in a program, we need a way to keep track of which variants contain which subtype. The fact that we can convert variants from one type to another makes this 'tracking' even more important. The sensible answer is to use a good naming convention. By doing so, you can tell at a glance whether you're using an integer, a string, or date, and can manipulate it in a consistent way.

Naming conventions aren't compulsory and can't be enforced, and generally it's up to the programmer as to which convention to apply, but a sensible rule is to use the first three letters of a variant's name to distinguish the sub type. The fourth letter of the variant is then typed in upper case, to indicate that this is where the actual variant name starts.

Here's our suggested naming convention: we'll be using it in our applications throughout the rest of the book:

Data Type	Prefix	Example
Boolean	bln	blnBoolean
Byte	byt	bytByte
Date / Time	dat	datDate
Double	dbl	dblDouble
Error	err	errError
Integer	int	intInteger
Long	lng	lngLong
Object	obj	objObject
Single	sng	sngSingle
String	str	strString

Constants

There will be occasions when you want a value assigned to a variable to remain constant throughout the execution of the code. **Constants** are like variables except that, once they have been assigned a value, they don't change. Many programming languages provide an explicit facility for constants, by allowing the programmer to assign an initial value to the constant, and subsequently forbidding any alteration of that value.

VBScript supports constants and uses the `Const` keyword to define them. By convention, constants are quite commonly written in upper case:

```
Const ABSOLUTEZERO = -273
```

If you tried then to assign another value to `ABSOLUTEZERO`, such as:

```
ABSOLUTEZERO = 0
```

then VBScript would stop you from changing this, and produce an error message.

VBScript Constants

VBScript also presents a list of its own constants, with values that you can use but will be unable to change. These constants correspond to the list of subtypes that we looked at earlier:

Constant	Value	Constant	Value
VbEmpty	0	VbString	8
VbNull	1	VbObject	9
VbInteger	2	VbError	10
VbLong	3	VbBoolean	11
VbSingle	4	VbVariant	12
VbDouble	5	VbDataObject	13
VbCurrency	6	VbByte	17
VbDate	7	VbArray	8192

You can use these constants in the same way that you use variants; each of them represents the particular constant value indicated, and you cannot alter their values in any way.

String Manipulation

String manipulation is a whole new ball game, that allows you to glean information from text. For example, if a user's full home address was stored in a string, how would you go about extracting just the house number and street name from the string, while removing all the other extraneous information? Have no fear: VBScript provides a set of functions that allow you to chop, prune and order strings in any way you like. There are several functions provided; we'll only look at the major ones.

These are:

        Len

        Left

        Right

        Mid

        InStr

        LTrim, Rtrim and Trim

Returning the Length of a String

The **Len** function is used to return the length of a string—that is, the number of characters. You can use it in the following way:

Len(*string*)

This function only takes one argument, namely the string that you are measuring:

```
intHowLong = Len("HowLongIsAPieceOfString?")
```

In this example, there are 24 characters in this string, and so **intHowLong** is assigned the value 24. Any symbols, punctuation and spaces within the string are valid characters, and therefore they are counted in the length of the string. You can also supply a variant name to the **Len** function; in this case it will measure the contents of the named variant:

```
strText = "HowLongIsAPieceOfString?"
intHowLong = Len(strText)
```

In this example, the **Len** function would again return the value 24. Later on, we'll use this function in an example that loops through a string, character by character—the function is used to tell us when we've reached the end of the string.

Pruning the Beginning or End of a String

The **Left** and **Right** Functions can be used to extract a given number of characters from the beginning or end of a string. They don't actually 'remove' the characters per se; instead they act like the 'Copy' function of a word processor and copy the selected section into the new variant. Each of these functions takes two parameters:

Left(*string, number_of_characters*)

and

Right(*string, number_of_characters*)

The **Left** function's second parameter, *number_of_characters* specifies how many characters to extract from the beginning (left-hand side) of the string:

116

```
strLeftChars = Left("HowLongIsAPieceOfString?",3)
```

StrLeftChars would contain the string **"How"**. Again, you can also supply a variant name to the **Left** function, which will extract the appropriate substring from the string contained by this variant. For example:

```
strText = "HowLongIsAPieceOfString?"
strLeftChars = Left(strText,7)
```

This would assign the string **"HowLong"** to the variant **strLeftChars**.

The **Right** function works in the same way, except that it extracts characters from the (right-hand) end of the string:

```
strRightChars = Right("HowLongIsAPieceOfString?",7)
```

Here, the variant **strRightChars** is assigned the string **"String?"**. Again, this function supports the option of extracting characters from a string variant; and once again, symbols, spaces and punctuation count as valid characters.

Removing the Middle of a String

Of course, that leaves the problem of extracting a section from the middle of a string. To do this, VBScript provides another function, **Mid**. The function **Mid** works along the same principles as **Right** and **Left**, but it takes an extra parameter:

Mid(*string*, *where_in_the_string*, *number_of_characters_to_be_extracted*)

Once again, the first parameter is the source string itself. The second parameter is the position of the first character in the substring that you want to extract, and the third is the number of characters in the substring. In our little example, we can isolate the word **"Piece"** by setting the second parameter to 11 (corresponding to the letter **"P"**) and the third parameter to 5 (indicating the number of characters in the desired substring). The following example extracts the word **"Piece"** from our original string, and assigns it to the variant **strMiddleChars**:

```
strText = "HowLongIsAPieceOfString?"
strMiddleChars = Mid(strText,11,5)
```

Finding a Particular Word

Of course, they'll be times when you want to find a particular word within a string and where it occurs. The function that will do this for you is **InStr**. This function takes the string itself and the text to be located:

InStr(*string*, *text_to_be_located*)

In our example we can use it isolate a particular word and return its position in a string.

```
strText = "HowLongIsAPieceOfString?"
intwhere = InStr(strText,"Long")
```

This example would return the number 4, as the word "Long" starts on the fourth character. However, **InStr** is also case-sensitive, so if you searched for "long" instead of "Long", you wouldn't find it at all. In this case **InStr** returns the value 0.

Giving it a Quick Trim

Finally in this section, we'll have a look at the functions **Trim**, **LTrim** and **RTrim**. These three related functions give us three different ways to remove extraneous space characters from a string. They're particularly useful when dealing with user input. Each function takes a single parameter—a string—and they are written as follows:

```
Trim(string)
LTrim(string)
RTrim(string)
```

The function **LTrim** removes spaces from the left-hand side of a string, while **RTrim** (you guessed it) removes spaces from the right-hand side of the string. The **Trim** function combines the two, by removing all of the spaces from the beginning and end of the string.

As an example, let's consider the following string, which has three spaces at each end:

```
strSpace="   feeling kinda spaced out   "
```

Then the code:

```
<% =Ltrim(strSpace) %>
```

would return the string "**feeling kinda spaced out   **". Meanwhile,

```
<% =Rtrim(strSpace) %>
```

would return the string "   **feeling kinda spaced out**"; and of course,

```
<% =Trim(strSpace) %>
```

would return the string "**feeling kinda spaced out**". OK, we're ready to exercise nearly all of these functions in an example.

Try It Out – String Manipulation

This is quite a complex example. We're going to take a sentence, in the form of a string, and return each of the words separately to the screen. We'll do this by assigning the sentence to a variant, and then detecting the spaces in the sentence. We will go through the sentence, character by character, and chop off everything that runs from the previous space to the current space, i.e. a whole word and put this into a separate variant, which we will display on the screen. Don't worry: it's not as difficult as it sounds!

1 Start your ASP page editor and type in the following code:

```
<HTML>

<HEAD>
<TITLE>String Manipulation Example</TITLE>
</HEAD>

<BODY BGCOLOR="white">
<%
Dim strText, intSpace, strWord, intCounter
intSpace = 1
strText ="the quick brown fox jumped over the lazy dog"
For intCounter = 1 To len(strText)+1
If mid(strText,intCounter,1) = " " Or intCounter = len(strText)+1 Then
strWord = mid(strText,intSpace,intCounter-intSpace)
intSpace = intCounter
strWord = trim(strWord)
%>

<P><B><% =strWord %>
<%End If
Next
%>
</B></P>
</BODY>
</HTML>
```

2 Save the file as `string.asp`.

3 Execute the file on your normal browser.

4 This program is very flexible, and will perform this operation on any sentence you feed in. So go back to the source code and amend the line that assigns a sentence to the variant `strText` to:

```
intSpace = 1
strText ="the hyena munches on the overripe banana"
For intCounter = 1 To len(strText)+1
```

5 Now run the program again.

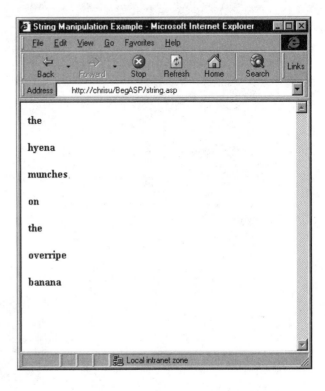

How It Works

Take a deep breath before we look at this one: there's a lot to absorb. The first line defines the four variants we'll need:

```
Dim strText, intSpace, strWord, intCounter
```

`strText` will be used to store the whole sentence, while `strWord` will be used to store each word in turn. `intSpace` will be used to store the position of the previous space in the sentence and `intCounter` will be used to store the 'current' position in the sentence.

We assign the value 1 to the variant holding the location of the previous space. This is to let the computer know where the first word begins, which (logically enough) is with the first character of the sentence.

```
intSpace = 1
```

Next we read in the sentence to our **strText** variant:

```
strText ="the quick brown fox jumped over the lazy dog"
```

Next, we start a loop: the loop control is the variant **intCounter**, whose first value is 1 (for the first character in the string); the value of **intCounter** increments by 1 with each iteration of the loop, until it reaches the value of **len(strText)** (for the *last* character in the string):

```
For intCounter = 1 To len(strText)+1
```

Don't worry too much about the **For** loop and the **If ... Then** structure for the moment. We'll give a little information about what's happening in a moment, but we'll explain them in detail in the next chapter.

The next line is really the crux of the program: it's a conditional statement which is used to detect whether we've encountered a space character, or the end of the sentence (denoted by the value, length of the string + 1), in our string:

```
If mid(strText,intCounter,1) = " " Or intCounter = len(strText)+1 Then
```

This says, "If the current character we're at in the sentence is a space, or if we've reached the end of the sentence, then go on to the next part of the program; otherwise jump to the **End If** statement".

> *In this statement, remember that the parameter **intCounter** indicates our current position within the sentence, and the parameter **1** indicates that we want to examine just a single character. In the first iteration of the loop, the character encountered is the letter ' **t** ': the program will just jump to the **End If** statement. From there, the next line is the end of the loop, so that the value of **intCounter** is incremented by 1 before the loop begins again.*

If we encounter a space character or the end of the sentence, then we can run the code within the **If-End If** keywords. In this section of code we examine our sentence and extract a word. The word is defined as being the series of characters between the previous space in the string (or the beginning of the sentence) and the current space. The position of the previous space is stored in **intSpace**. The clever bit is finding out how many characters are in the word. Well, if we've encountered a space and we know where the last space is, the total amount of characters must be the current position in the sentence, minus the position of the previous space. We feed this into our variant, **strWord**:

```
strWord = mid(strText,intSpace,intCounter-intSpace)
```

The next time we traverse the loop, we will need our 'current' space character to take the role of the 'previous' space: therefore, we save the current space position into the variant **intSpace**:

```
intSpace = intCounter
```

Just in case some bright spark has entered multiple spaces between consecutive words in our string, we will trim any extra space characters around the word:

```
strWord = trim(strWord)
```

Now we can display our word on the screen:

```
<P><B><% =strWord %>
```

That's the end of our condition, and this is marked by the **End If**. Then we move on to the next character in the loop:

```
<%End If
Next
%>
```

The program continues, displaying each word in turn on the screen, until we reach the end of the sentence—as I mentioned, this is determined by the loop running out of characters to test.

String manipulation functions are among some of the most useful features of VBScript. In order to apply them properly, they can take a little thought. However, they can be put to some very practical uses, such as identifying items of information within an address or a form, and being able to save only the pieces that we want, while discarding the rest.

Next we'll be taking a look at why variables don't always contain the values you might expect.

Variable Scope

When we mentioned some of the restrictions on naming variables at the beginning of this chapter, we neglected to mention one rather odd requirement that you might have taken for granted. That requirement is the following: that when you name a variable, it should have a *unique* name.

The reasons for avoiding this in the early stages of this chapter are the complications that arise when a piece of code contains two variables of the same name—because under certain circumstances it *is* allowed. It all depends on a rather glib sounding concept known as **scope**.

Local Variables

On the surface it seems to defy logical explanation, but I promise you that there is logic here: let's look at it more closely. Consider two variables, both with the name **strDifferent**. We'll try and assign different values to these two variables:

```
strDifferent = "Hello I'm variable one"
strDifferent = "Hello I'm variable two"
```

If you return the value of **strDifferent**, you'd find that is contains the string **"Hello I'm variable two"**, thus overwriting the first value assigned to **strDifferent**. That's because we haven't created two variables at all; we simply created one variable, **strDifferent**, and then changed its value.

However, if you defined **strDifferent** twice *within two different procedures* (which we came across in the last chapter) then you'd be on the right track:

```
Sub Procedure_Number_1
strDifferent = "Hello I'm variable one"
End Proc

Sub Procedure_Number_2
strDifferent = "Hello I'm variable two"
End Proc
```

If you return the value of **strDifferent** in **Procedure_Number_1**, then you'd get **"Hello I'm variable one"**. If you return the value of **strDifferent** in **Procedure_Number_2**, you'd get **"Hello I'm variable two"**. However, if you *then* go back and run **Procedure_Number_1** again, you'd get **"Hello I'm variable one"** again. They are effectively two different variables, although they share the same name.

These variables are known as **local** variables (in the Microsoft documentation, they're called **procedure level** variables), because they are local to the procedure that created them. Outside the procedure, the local variable has no value: this is because the **lifetime** of the variable ends when the procedure ends. When a local variable is created, it only exists while the procedure that invokes it is running; once the program exits the procedure, the variable's lifetime is over.

Now, let's take a look at how two local variables, sharing the same name, can be used within an ASP program.

Try It Out – Creating Local Variables

1 Start your favorite editor and hammer out the following program:

```
<HTML>

<HEAD>
<TITLE>Using TypeName</TITLE>
</HEAD>
<BODY bgcolor="white">

<% Sub Procedure_1()
strDifferent = "Hi I'm strDifferent in Procedure 1"%>
<%=strdifferent%>
<%End Sub%>

<%Sub Procedure_2()
strDifferent = "Hi I'm strDifferent in Procedure 2"%>
<%=strdifferent%>
<%End Sub%>

<P>Calling Procedure 1...<I><%Procedure_1()%></I></P>
<P>Calling Procedure 2...<I><%Procedure_2()%></I></P>
<P>Calling Procedure 1...<I><%Procedure_1()%></I></P>
</BODY>
</HTML>
```

2 Save the program as `local.asp`

3 Execute it in your browser of choice:

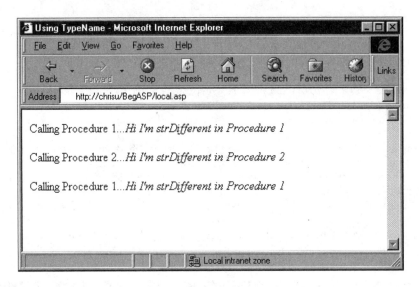

How It Works

This program contains two almost identical procedures:

```
<% Sub Procedure_1()
strDifferent = "Hi I'm strDifferent in Procedure 1"%>
<%=strdifferent%>
<%End Sub%>

<%Sub Procedure_2()
strDifferent = "Hi I'm strDifferent in Procedure 2"%>
<%=strdifferent%>
<%End Sub%>
```

However, each of the variables called **strDifferent** is defined within the confines of its respective procedure, and so doesn't exist outside the context of the procedure. If you asked the ASP program to print the value of **strDifferent** from *outside* either of these procedures, it would in fact return no value at all.

Global Variables

So, if variables created in procedures are local to the procedure that created them, how do you ensure that the value of one variable persists from one procedure to the next when you need it to? In other words, how do you extend the lifetimes of your variables? The answer comes in the form of **global** variables (in the Microsoft documentation, these are called **script level** variables), which are variables that are declared outside procedures.

The lifetime of a global variable begins at the start of the script and ends at the end of the script, and spans any procedures created within the script. In comparison, local variables contained within a procedure are destroyed when the procedure is exited, and hence the memory space is saved. It's a good idea to use local variables where possible.

Now let's see how we can amend our previous program to include a global variable:

Try It Out – Using Global Variables

We're going to simply add a new global variable to this program and then display it from inside and outside the procedures.

1 Load up the previous program, `local.asp`, in your preferred ASP editor and add the highlighted lines:

```
<HTML>

<HEAD>
<TITLE>Using Global Variables</TITLE>
</HEAD>

<BODY BGCOLOR="white">
<% strGlobal = "I'm a persistent script-level variable"%>
<% =strGlobal %>
<%Sub Procedure_1()
strDifferent = "Hi I'm strDifferent in Procedure 1"%>
<%=strdifferent%>
<P><%=strGlobal%> </P>
<%End Sub%>
<%Sub Procedure_2()
strDifferent = "Hi I'm strDifferent in Procedure 2"%>
<%=strdifferent%>
<P><%=strGlobal%> </P>
<%End Sub%>

<P>Calling Procedure 1 ...<I><%Procedure_1()%></I></P>
<P>Calling Procedure 2 ...<I><%Procedure_2()%></I></P>
<P>Calling Procedure 1 ...<I><%Procedure_1()%></I></P>
</BODY>
</HTML>
```

2 Save it this time as `global.asp`

3 Run this program on your browser.

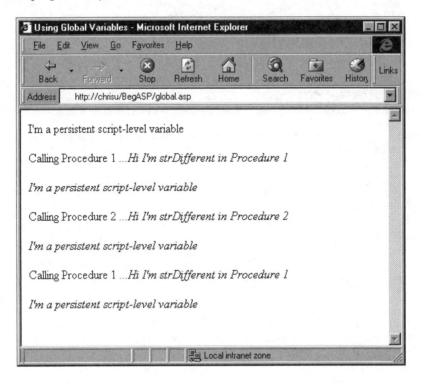

How It Works

We've not changed our original program much, other than to add a global variable, `strGlobal`. This variable is assigned the text "I'm a persistent script-level variable" and is then called at various points in the program:

```
<% strGlobal = "I'm a persistent script-level variable"%>
```

We first display this string from outside both procedures; the second time, from within `Procedure 1`; the third time from within `Procedure 2`; and the final time from within `Procedure 1` again. Each time, the variable is displayed using the following code, so there's no trickery of any sort:

```
<% =strGlobal %>
```

The output shows how global variables and local variables can be used side by side in any ASP program.

In Public and in Private

Of course, sometimes an ASP program consists of more than one script. So what happens to global (i.e. script level) variables in this case? There are a couple of keywords that you can use when declaring global variables: the keyword `Private` indicates a global variable which is available only within the script in which it is declared, and the keyword `Public` indicates a global variable that holds its value in all scripts.

You can create a global variable that is local to just one script by declaring it with the keyword **Private** instead of the keyword **Dim**:

```
Private strGlobal
```

Alternatively, to declare a global variable that can be used within all scripts, declare it with the keyword **Public** instead of the keyword **Dim**:

```
Public strGlobal
```

You can even have **Public** or **Private** constants.

```
Public Const ABSOLUTEZERO = -273
```

However, these are rare occurrences, and most of the time you'll just want to declare your variables using the keyword **Dim** and your constants with **Const**.

There is one last use of the keyword **Dim** that we've yet to consider, and we'll take a look at that now.

Arrays

Variables are fine for storing individual items of data. However, they're not so good if you wish to store items of similar information. In this case you'll need to use an array. Arrays are used to store a series of related data items, which are related by an index number at the end. You could use them to store the names of the Marx brothers, for instance:

```
strMarx(1) = "Groucho"
strMarx(2) = "Harpo"
strMarx(3) = "Chico"
strMarx(4) = "Zeppo"
strMarx(5) = "Gummo"
strMarx(6) = "Karl"
```

However, you don't have to store something in each item of the array, and you don't even have to store it sequentially:

```
strMonths(28) = "Feb"
strMonths(30) = "Apr, Jun, Sep, Nov"
strMonths(31) = "Jan, Mar, May, Jul, Aug, Oct, Dec"
```

Arrays are particularly useful if you want to manipulate a whole set of data items as though they were all one item. For example, if you want to adjust the pay rates for a set of five employees, then the difficult way is the following:

```
intExtraPay = 10
intEmployeePay(1) = intEmployeePay(1) + intExtraPay
intEmployeePay(2) = intEmployeePay(2) + intExtraPay
intEmployeePay(3) = intEmployeePay(3) + intExtraPay
intEmployeePay(4) = intEmployeePay(4) + intExtraPay
intEmployeePay(5) = intEmployeePay(5) + intExtraPay
```

The following "much simpler" code utilizes your array structure, and has exactly the same effect:

```
intExtraPay = 10
For intLoop = 1 to 5
intEmployeePay(intLoop) = intEmployeePay(intLoop) + intExtraPay
Next
```

Arrays are much more versatile than regular plain variables.

Declaring Arrays

Arrays are declared in the same way as variables, using the `Dim` keyword. However, an array declaration needs an extra parameter at the end, which is used to specify the size of the array. We could set up an array to have 50 entries for each of the states in the US, with the following statement:

```
Dim StatesInUS(49)
```

The index number 49 isn't a mistake. It's just that arrays count up from zero in VbScript, rather than one. So in this case the 50 states are indexed by the 50 different parameter values 0, 1, ..., 49. This type of array is known as a **fixed-size array**, because you fix the maximum number of items that the array can contain. If you don't know the number of items there are to be in your array, or don't wish to specify, you can create a **dynamic array** instead:

```
Dim BritishOscarWinners()
```

You can then go back and specify how many items there should be at a later point, using the keyword `Redim` (short for re-dimension):

```
Redim BritishOscarWinners(0)
```

There was only one (sniff)...

Redeclaring Arrays

Sometimes there are situations when you've already specified the number of items in a dynamic array, but then you have to amend that amount. If, for example, you'd estimated the number of items but found that you'd needed a larger array than first envisaged, you could use the `Redim` keyword once again, to set up the array with the new amount:

```
Dim amoeba()
Redim amoeba(2)
amoeba(1) = "Geronimo"
amoeba(2) = "Geronimee"
amoebas divide...
Redim amoeba(4)
```

However, you'd lose the information held in the already existing array, so you'd have to replace the information. Fortunately help is at hand, in the form of another keyword, `Preserve`, which can be used, together with `Redim`, to ensure that the existing contents of your array are not irretrievably lost:

```
Redim Preserve amoeba(4)
```

Now we're ready to a look a small example utilizing some of these concepts.

Try It Out – Setting Up An Array

In this example, we're going to set up a dynamic array, add some contents and then display the contents. Then we're going to resize the array, add an extra item, and redisplay it just to prove that we haven't destroyed the original contents.

1 Give your ASP editor a poke in the ribs to wake it up, and then type in the following:

```
<HTML>

<HEAD>
<TITLE>Using Arrays</TITLE>
</HEAD>

<BODY BGCOLOR="white">

<P>Here are the Marx Brothers: </P>
<%
Dim strMarx()
Redim strMarx(4)
strMarx(0) = "Groucho"
strMarx(1) = "Harpo"
strMarx(2) = "Chico"
strMarx(3) = "Zeppo"
strMarx(4) = "Gummo"
%>
<P><B>
<%For intCounter = 0 to 4 %>
<% =strMarx(intCounter) %>...
<% Next %>
</B></P>

<P>Whoops! Nearly forgot the bearded leftish one... </P>
<%
Redim Preserve strMarx(5)
strMarx(5) = "Karl"
%>
<P><B>
<%For intCounter = 0 to 5 %>
<% =strMarx(intCounter) %>...
<% Next %>
</B></P>
</BODY>
</HTML>
```

2 Save it as `array.asp` and close it down.

3 Get your browser up and ready and run this program on it:

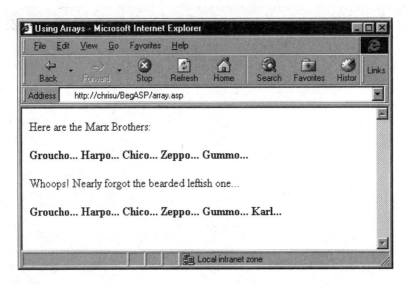

How It Works

This program starts by setting up a dynamic array **strMarx**, and then declaring that it contains five items:

```
<%
Dim strMarx()
Redim strMarx(4)
```

We then populate our array with five values, the names of the Marx Brothers:

```
strMarx(0) = "Groucho"
strMarx(1) = "Harpo"
strMarx(2) = "Chico"
strMarx(3) = "Zeppo"
strMarx(4) = "Gummo"
%>
```

To display the contents of our array, rather than printing out each one individually, we define a loop with the variant **intCounter** to go through each item in our array. We close the ASP code block here, since we need to display some text using HTML:

```
<%For intCounter = 0 to 4 %>
```

The loop goes through five values, 0, 1, 2, 3 and 4 and substitutes the value in **intCounter** on each pass of the loop:

```
<% =strMarx(intCounter) %>...
<% Next %>
```

The first item in the array, `strMarx(0)`, contains the string `"Groucho"`, and this is displayed on the screen. The next statement tells the loop to go back and add another 1 to the value of `intCounter`. This time `strMarx(1)` is displayed, which contains the string `"Harpo"`, that we assigned earlier. It's repeated for `strMarx(2)` and `strMarx(3)`, and on the final iteration of the loop, the value of 4 is assigned to `intCounter` which enables the contents of the variant `strMarx(4)` to be displayed.

However, the program doesn't end there. Next we display some more HTML, before going back into ASP and resizing the array so that it can hold six items. The keyword `Preserve` ensures that none of the original items are lost:

```
<P>Whoops! Nearly forgot the bearded leftish one... </P>
<%
Redim Preserve strMarx(5)
```

We set up a value for the new item in our dynamic array:

```
strMarx(5) = "Karl"
%>
```

Then we go around the loop again, outputting the contents of the array, except that this time the loop is iterated six times, not five:

```
<%For intCounter = 0 to 5 %>
<% =strMarx(intCounter) %>...
<% Next %>
```

If we were to omit the keyword `Preserve` when resizing the dynamic array, we would lose the names of the five original Marx brothers, so the array would be empty again before adding their political namesake. Try running the program again without the word `Preserve`, just to see.

Multi-Dimensional Arrays

If you need to keep information of a two-dimensional nature, then you can do it by declaring a two-dimensional array. For instance, if you wanted to store a set of related (x,y) map coordinates, a normal array would probably be unsuitable. Instead, you achieve it by adding another parameter to your array declaration. Thus:

```
Dim str2Darray(3,3)
```

would set up a two-dimensional array of size 4 by 4, which could hold a total of 16 values. You can assign values to a multi-dimensional array by referencing each element of the array through its two-value index. For example, you could use such an array to reference areas on a map:

```
str2Darray(0,0) = "The mountains"
str2Darray(0,1) = "The lake"
str2Darray(0,2) = "The road"
str2Darray(0,3) = "The forest"
```

In fact, VBScript is not limited to arrays of one or two dimensions; you can declare an array with up to 60 dimensions, should you so require. This takes us as far as we need to go with arrays and variables for the next few chapters.

Summary

In this chapter we have considered how we can go about storing the data collected by the computer, both from the user and from its own calculations. We looked at what a variable is and saw that VBScript treats each of the different subtypes of data as just one type, the variant. We looked at how you would go about declaring variants and how the `Option Explicit` commands can be used to lessen the chance of making a typing mistake in the variant name. We then looked at various functions that VBScript provides to manipulate variants.

We looked at how variables are only effective within certain scopes. Also, we saw that while some variables keep their value throughout the whole script, others keep their values only within the procedures that created them.

Finally, we looked at how you could store a series of related data items with an array, and refer to the elements of the array using an index. We looked at how you can size and populate arrays, and we finished off by looking briefly at how you could make them multi-dimensional.

In the next chapter, we'll expand on a number of very useful programming tools, the **control structures**.

ASP Control Constructs

In the first several chapters of this book you have been writing simple ASP code. Up until now your code has been read and executed in a very simple order: line 1 first, then line 2, then line 3 and so on until the last line. But in the real world ASP can operate in a more complicated way than that: given certain conditions, it can skip or repeat lines—or groups of lines. This chapter will teach you ways to change the order in which the lines of your ASP code are executed.

This chapter covers the three ways that you can use ASP to sequence the execution of your lines of code. Respectively, these are:

> Deciding which of two or more sections of code to run.

> Repeating a section of code as many times as needed.

> Jumping out of the code sequence and executing sections of code in another part of your ASP program.

Before we look at these processes in detail, let's step back and think in more general terms for a moment.

An Example in Plain English

Before we begin to look at ASP code let us think about these ideas in simple English for a business situation that you can easily picture in your mind. Let's consider the type of instructions a mechanic might be given by their boss. The code you have written so far is similar to the mechanic's boss telling them to:

> Take truck number one to the fuel pump.

> Fill up the tank with gasoline.

> Bring the truck back to its parking spot.

Although these instructions are very clear and easy to follow in order of line one, line two, line three, they do not cover some possible problems. What if the truck is already full of gasoline? What if the truck needs oil? What about providing service for the other trucks?

In order to get the job done the boss needs to provide a more complex set of instructions, for example:

1. Check if truck number one needs gasoline.
2. If truck number one needs gasoline, then take it to the fuel pump and fill it.
3. If the truck does not need gasoline then skip the filling and go to the next step.
4. Check if truck number one needs oil.
5. If truck number one needs oil then get out the truck's manual and follow the instructions for adding oil. After you are done adding oil come back and finish these instructions.
6. If the truck does not need oil then skip the oil step and go to the next step.
7. When truck one is full of gas and full of oil, bring it back to its parking spot.
8. When you are done with truck one, repeat the above steps for the rest of the trucks.

The second set of orders will work better for three reasons. First, it covers a range of possibilities regarding the need for gasoline and/or oil. Second, it takes advantage of existing instructions—the truck manual's pages for how to add oil. And third, it gives sufficient instructions to get the job done on the whole fleet of trucks.

This simple example illustrates the three types of constructs that you will use as an ASP programmer:

▶ **Branching statements** such as lines 2 and 3: If the truck needs gasoline then fill it up, but if it does not need gasoline then skip the filling up step.

▶ **Jumping statements** such as line 5: if you need oil, then stop executing these instructions and instead go follow the instructions for adding oil. When you are done following those adding oil instructions, then come back and continue with these instructions.

▶ **Looping statements** such as line 8: when you are done with truck one, go back and repeat these same steps for truck two, then truck three and so on until all of the trucks have been serviced.

There are Two Kinds of ASP Statements

Note that all of the lines of your code can be divided into two types:

▶ **Action statements** carry out a task, such as showing the price of an item on a web page.
▶ **Control statements** have the task of *directing* the execution of the action statements.

In our motorpool example, instructions such as "Fill the tank with gasoline" and "Fill the oil" are **action** statements. The rest are **control** statements, such as "If the truck needs gasoline then..." or "Repeat the above steps for the next truck."

This idea of controlling which lines of code execute in what order, and how often, has several names. Some people refer to these techniques as **flow control** or **execution order**, and the sets of code that we use to control the flow of execution are called, logically enough, **Control Structures**.

Definitions

There are several new terms introduced in this chapter. Be particularly careful since some of these are interchangeable: for example, most programmers consider the terms **line**, **code** and **statement** to mean just about the same thing—that is, *one* line of instructions to ASP. Here's a summary list of the terms we'll be using regularly:

- **Statement**: A single instruction to ASP, usually on a single line
- **Code**: One or more instructions to ASP
- **Line**: A single instruction to ASP
- **Command**: A single instruction to ASP, usually on a single line

In general use, these terms can often be used interchangeably.

- **Flow**: The order in which statements are executed by ASP. The flow may be designed to repeat or skip some statements
- **Execution**: The process of ASP carrying out the instruction in a statement

And remember, there are two types of statements in ASP:

- **Actions statements:** Statements that perform an activity, such as the creation of a part of a page, a change to a variable, a redirection to another page, or changing a setting on the server.
- **Control statements:** Statements that give ASP instructions on which statements to execute, and in what order.

The ASP statements can be organized into larger groups:

- **Code structures:** Several lines of code that work together to achieve a task. For example, five lines of code may work to put data into a table.
- **Control structures:** A set of control statements that collectively govern the order of execution.

Types of Control Statements

When programming ASP or any other computer language, we have three types of structures (groups of statements) to control the order in which the lines of code are executed. These are: **branching structures**, **looping controls**, and **jumping controls**. We'll now look at each of these in more detail.

Branching Structures

Branching Controls perform some type of test. Based on the test results a set of code will be executed and other sets of code will be skipped. From our Motorpool example, this is like testing if the gasoline tank is full. If it is not full then we perform the steps to fill it. If the tank *is* full then we skip the filling steps and move on to the next lines of code. In our example in Chapter 3—where we asked people to order their 'Spring Retreat' jackets—we could test the variable holding the user's answer to our "Confirm by Telephone, Fax or E-mail?" question: if the variable holds the answer "E-mail" then we run the code that sets up an E-mail, and skip the code that writes a fax or finds the telephone number.

There are two types of branching structures.

▶ `If...Then...Else` is generally used to select one of two sets of lines to execute. A simple example would be in a page announcing a meeting: we could have one of two different meeting room numbers shown depending on whether the addressee was in the Sales or R&D department.   `If...Then` is also the tool of choice for complicated comparisons, such as expressions using the terms *and, or, not.*

▶ `Select...Case` is generally used to select one set of lines to execute from *many* possibilities. For example, in a page announcing a meeting we could have the room number of one of five different meeting rooms shown, depending on whether the addressee was in the Sales, R&D, Distribution, Personnel or Accounting department.

Looping Controls

Looping controls allow the same block of code to be run a number of times. Instead of skipping code—which is what the branching technique does—we *repeat* code. In the example of the mechanic, the idea of completing all the steps for the first truck, and then going back and repeating those same steps for the rest of the trucks demonstrates looping. In our clothing example we may want to generate a page with each item ordered listed on a line. The construction of those lines (print the description, print the quantity, print the price, put in a line break) would be looped to produce one line for each item ordered.

▶ `For...Next` is used to repeat line(s) when, at the beginning of the repetitions, we know exactly how many repetitions we want. For example, if we know there are five reviewers we could repeat five times the set of steps that adds and formats a comment form.

▶ `Do...While` is used to repeat line(s) when we *don't* know how many repetitions we want. `Do...While` will repeat lines as long as a specified condition is true.

Jumping Controls

Jumping controls allow the programmer to pause the execution of the current code and jump to *another* named block of code. For example, we may have written a block of code called `ShowOrder` that produces lines that show the customer the goods that they ordered. When we want ASP to show those lines we don't have to re-write or copy all of that code. Instead we just have ASP jump out of our current code, perform `ShowOrder` and then come back and continue executing our original bit of code.

There are three types of jumping controls:

▶ `Call` starts a subprocedure, runs it, and then returns to the main procedure.

▶ `Functions` can be used to perform some statements and return an answer to the main body of code.

▶ `Exit`, a third type of jumping statement, is outside the scope of this book.

Examples of Control Structures

With these three classes of controls—branching, jumping and looping—we can solve virtually any programming objective in ASP. In the table below we've listed several situations we might want to program for, and suggested which class of controls will help us achieve them.

Situation	Solution	Why?
I want ASP to show page A or page B.	Branching	We want to perform only one of two possible events.
I want ASP to generate a sign-in box for each member of the club. The boxes are essentially the same: only the member's name and photo change.	Looping	We will be performing the same set of code (create a box) many times (once for each member).
I want to build a table.	Looping	We will perform the same code (make a row for a table) again and again until we have built all of the rows needed.
I need to calculate prices in several places on each page. The prices will be set according to input from a user form.	Call	We will pause building the page, execute code to calculate the price of an item, then return to building the page. Since we will calculate many prices it is best to write the formula once and have it called when needed.
I need to show the user which of several meetings they should attend. The meeting displayed is based on which department they belong to.	Branching	We want to write to the page only *one* out of several possible meeting locations.
After every item that I describe in a catalog page, I want to put in a few lines of information about 'How to Order'.	Call	We want to pause the main code and perform several lines of *another* set of code that describes 'How to Order'. Then we want to resume the main code. Since the 'How to Order' set of code will be performed at various times across the page, it is best to write it once and call that one piece of code as needed.

Let's recap on what we've discussed so far. There are three kinds of statements that control the flow of our code's execution:

- **Branching statements** that perform a test and then execute some lines of code but not others
- **Jumping statements** that pause the execution of the current code, jump over to another set of code, and then return
- **Looping statements** that execute a set of code again and again

Now let's have a closer look at branching statements, and what we can do with them.

Branching Statements

ASP offers two techniques for branching. **If...Then** is used when there are only two choices of outcome. **Select Case** is used when there are *more* than two outcomes. For example, if you are asking the user "Do you want a confirmation by telephone?" the outcome is either Yes (True) or No (False), so you would perform the branch using **If...Then**. But if you ask the user "Do you want confirmation by telephone, FedEx or E-mail?" then there are more than two outcomes and it is better to use **Select Case**. We will start with **If...Then**.

If...Then Control Structure

The **If...Then** statement has four parts:

- An **expression**: that is, a test that gives a true or false answer
- An "**if true**" section of code
- An "**if false**" section of code
- An **ending** statement

The first part is the **expression**, which we looked at in the last chapter. It must answer either true or false. If the test answers true, then the lines of code in the "if true" section are executed. If the test answers false, then the lines of code in the "if false" section are executed. After one of these two sections has been executed, the execution jumps down to the ending statement and continues with the next line of code. There is never a situation where both the true *and* the false sections would be used in a given case.

There are three ways of building **If...Then** statements. To select the proper syntax you must answer two questions:

- Do I want to do anything if the test is false?
- Do I want to execute more than one statement if the test is true?

The first and most simple way is used if you only have one statement to perform in the case of a 'true' test. You want to execute no statements at all if the test is false. For example, if **varFaxConfirm** contains the value **"Yes"** then you want to print the fax number. If the expression reads **"No"** then you don't want to do anything. In this most simple case you can use the one-line syntax:

```
<%
If varFaxConfirm = "Yes" then Response.Write "Please enter your fax
number."
%>
```

The next, more complex level, is where you want to perform more than one statement in the case of truth, but still nothing if the test is false. For example, if **varFaxConfirm** contains the value **"Yes"**, then ask for the fax number and jump over to the fax entry page. In this case we must write the **If...Then** with two changes from case one: each statement must go on its own line, contrasting with the simple **If...Then** example above. And, since there is now more than one line for the **If...Then** code, we must use a closing line of **End If**:

```
<%
If varFaxConfirm = "Yes" then
Response.Write ("Please click below and provide your fax number.")
Response.Write  "<A HREF=>http://www.On-LineClothier.com/FaxForm</A>"
End If
%>
```

The third level deals with the case when you want to perform more than one statement in the case of 'true', and also one or more lines of code if the test is false. For example, if **varFaxConfirm** contains the value **"Yes"** then ask for the fax number and jump over to the fax entry page. If **varFaxConfirm** is anything other than **"Yes"** then show a line that says that a fax will not be sent. In this situation we must write the **If...Then** with a line called **Else** to separate the code that is run in the true case from the code that will run in the false case.

```
<%
If varFaxConfirm = "Yes" then
Response.Write "Please enter your fax number."
Else
Response.Write "No fax confirmation will be sent."
End If
%>
```

Three kinds of If...Then Control Structures

Situation	Syntax	Example	Notes for use

If the test is true
 	
do one statement
 	
otherwise do nothing
	If test **Then** statement	`If strAge < 18 Then`
		`Response.Write "You`
		`must be 18 or`
		`older to order by`
		`credit card."`
			If you want nothing to happen in the False case
			And
			You only want *one* statement to run in the True case

If the test is true
 	
do two or
more statements
 	
If the test is false do nothing
	If test **Then**
	
	True code line 1
	True code line 2
	
	End If
		`If strAge <18 Then`
		`Response.Write "You`
		`must be 18 or older`
		`to order by credit`
		`card."`
		`Display graphic`
		`End If`	

If the test is true
 	
do one or more
statements
 	
If the test is false
 	
do a different set of
one or more
statements
	If test **Then**
	
	True code line 1
	True code line 2
	
	Else
	
	False code line 1
	False code line 2
	
	End If
		`If strAge <18 Then`
		`Response.Write "You`
		`are eligible for the`
		`student rate of $49."`
		
		`Else`
		
		`Response.Write "The`
		`fee for this service`
		`is $59."`
		`End If`	

So let's now look at an example where you're responsible for notifying your colleagues of the date and location for the Corporate Spring Retreats that we introduced in Chapter 3. There will be four meetings: two on March 15th running in Malibu, California and Myerstown, Pennsylvania, and two on April 16th in the same two cities. Your goal is to design a form that gathers user preferences for month and location, and then provide a response that confirms the date and city.

Try It Out – If...Then

1 We'll start by creating the form to gather user information. Open your web page editor and type in the following:

```
<HTML>
<HEAD>
<TITLE>Spring Retreat Form</TITLE>
</HEAD>
<BODY>
<H1>Corporate Retreat Registration</H1>
<H3>To get the logistics information
for your meeting please answer these two questions.</H3>
<FORM ACTION="TioIfThenOneResponse.asp" METHOD="post">
Please type your preference in month, either March or April:<BR>
<INPUT TYPE="text" NAME="MonthPref"><P>
Please type your preference in location, either East or West:<BR>
<INPUT TYPE="text" NAME="Location">
<BR><BR>
<INPUT TYPE="submit"> <INPUT TYPE="reset">

</BODY></HTML>
```

2 Save this page as `TioIfThenOneForm.asp`.

3 Close that page down. Next, we'll create the response page:

```
<HTML>
<HEAD>
<TITLE>Spring Retreat Response</TITLE>
</HEAD>
<BODY>
<%
varMonthPref = Request.Form("MonthPref")
varLocation = Request.Form("Location")

Response.Write "<H1>Corporate Retreat Registration <BR>Your Details</H1>"

If varMonthPref="March" Then
Response.Write "Your meeting will be held on March 15th "
Else
Response.Write "Your meeting will be held on April 16th "
End If

If varLocation="East" Then
Response.Write "in Myerstown, Pennsylvania"
Else
Response.Write "in Malibu, California"
End If
%>
</BODY>
</HTML>
```

143

4 Save this as `TioIfThenOneResponse.asp`.

5 Open up the page `TioIfThenOneForm.asp` in your web browser:

6 If you type in March and West and submit your query, you'd come up with the following:

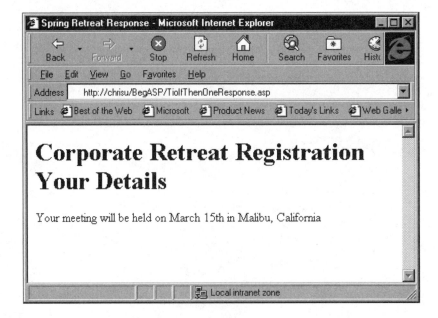

How It Works

The form simply follows the guidelines of Chapter 3.

```
<FORM ACTION="TioIfThenOneResponse.asp" METHOD="post">
Please type your preference in month, either March or April:<BR>
<INPUT TYPE="text" name="MonthPref"><P>
Please type your preference in location, either East or West:<BR>
<INPUT TYPE="text" name="Location">
<BR><BR><INPUT TYPE="submit"> <INPUT TYPE="reset">
```

The important points to remember in the code are:

▶ The Action attribute of the `<FORM>` tag must equal the URL of the page the server will return when the submit button is pressed

▶ Also in the `<FORM>` tag use `METHOD=Post`

▶ Always include inputs of type "submit" and "reset"

▶ Each input must have a name, in this case `MonthPref` and `Location`

The response page is where we use the control structure `If`...`Then`. The page starts with the basic `<HEAD>` tags, then immediately starts ASP. The first job is to pass the information typed by the user into variables named `varMonthPref` and `varLocation` using the technique covered in the last chapter.

```
<%
varMonthPref = Request.Form("MonthPref")
varLocation = Request.Form("Location")
```

Then we use `Response.Write` to get some text on the page.

```
Response.Write "<H1>Corporate Retreat Registration <BR>Your Details</H1>"
```

The first control structure checks the contents of `varMonthPref` to see if it contains the word "March". We must check for several possible ways that the user may have typed the word since the comparison is case-sensitive. Since that is a proper expression, it can be answered with a true or false. If it is true then two things happen:

▶ The true section of code is executed to put " ...March 15th" onto the HTML page

▶ ASP skips the false line of code ("...April16th") and jumps down to after the `End If`

If the expression is false (if the value entered isn't "March" we assume it to be "April") then ASP will do the following:

▶ Skip the true section of code ("...March15th")

▶ Perform the false section of code ("...April16th") and continue on down through the `End If`

```
If varMonthPref="March" Then
Response.Write "Your meeting will be held on March 15th "
Else
Response.Write "Your meeting will be held on April 16th "
End If
```

The second **If...Then** works the same way. If it is *true* that **varLocation** is "East" then ASP executes the writing of the city—Pennsylvania—and then jumps down to the line after **End If**. If **VarLocation="East"** is *false* we assume that the user typed "West" and so we skip the Myerstown line and go to the Malibu line.

```
If varLocation="East" Then
Response.Write "in Myerstown, Pennsylvania"
Else
Response.Write "in Malibu, California"
End If
```

Common Errors of the If...Then Statement

There are several common errors that we can make when creating an **If...Then** statement:

- ▶ Make a test that does not resolve to True or False
- ▶ Try to put more than one statement on the line of the one-line version of **If...Then**
- ▶ Leave out the **End If**
- ▶ Leave out the **Else**
- ▶ Code **End If** as **EndIf**
- ▶ Stuff the user response into variables in one set of ASP code, then close that code, and expect to access those variables in another set of ASP code

Basic Rules of If...Then

- ▶ You can only evaluate one expression (do one test) in an **If...Then** structure
- ▶ There are only two possible results from the expression: True or False
- ▶ You can only use one statement in the one-line version of **If...Then**
- ▶ If there is more than one line of action statements then you *must* use the **End If**
- ▶ If you want action in the case of a false result then you must use an **Else** line

Select Case

After working with **If...Then** for a few minutes you might become frustrated with its major limitation: **If...Then** never allows you to have more than two outcomes because it is based on a test that can only answer True or False. What if you want to show a different page to visitors from each of five departments? What if you want to do a calculation based on the user providing one of twelve salary grades? What if you have different procedures for confirming an order by telephone, fax or E-mail? **Select Case** is the control structure for handling branching that caters for these situations: anytime you need to make a choice among several answers (more than just True and False) then use **Select Case**.

The syntax for `Select Case` has four parts:

- State which variable to test
- State a possible answer and what to do if that answer is correct
- Repeat for as many possible answers as you want to handle
- End the `Select Case` control structure

The first example, below, carries out one of three actions depending on what is contained in the variable `varConfirmation`.

```
<%
Select Case varConfirmation
Case "Fax"
        Response.Redirect ("www.On-LineClothier.com/FaxConfirmation.asp")
Case "Telephone"
        Response.Redirect ("www.On-LineCLothier.com/telephone.asp")
Case "EMail"
        Response.Redirect ("www.On-LineClothier.com/EMail.asp")
End Select
%>
```

ASP will know from the first line that you want to compare values to the variable `varConfirmation`. Next, ASP will begin testing the contents of the variable against the values shown in the `Case` lines. When ASP finds a match it will execute the following code up to the next `Case` line, and will then jump down to the first line after the `End Select` statement. You may have noticed in the last Try It Out that if the user typed "March" in lower case then the program failed: it displayed April on the Spring Retreat Response page. This was because we only coded for the possibility of the user typing "March", and printed April in all other cases. This next Try It Out will solve the problem by deciding between several possible answers including *March, march, Mar* or *mar*.

Try It Out – Select Case

The form page is the same as the one we used in the last Try It Out. The response will have be changed.

1 Open up the page `TioIfThenOneResponse.asp` and change the following highlighted lines:

```
<HTML>
<HEAD>
<TITLE>Corporate Retreat Response</TITLE>
</HEAD>
<BODY>
<%
varMonthPref = Request.Form("MonthPref")
varLocation = Request.Form("Location")
Response.Write "<H1>Corporate Retreat Registration <BR> Your Details</
H1>"
```

```
Select Case varMonthPref
Case "march"
        Response.Write "Your meeting will be held on March 15th "
Case "March"
        Response.Write "Your meeting will be held on March 15th "
Case "april"
        Response.Write "Your meeting will be held on April 16th "
Case "April"
        Response.Write "Your meeting will be held on April 16th "
End Select

If varLocation="East" then
Response.Write "in Myerstown, Pennsylvania"
Else
Response.Write "in Malibu, California"
End If
%>
</BODY>
</HTML>
```

2 Now if you open the form page in your browser and try it again, you'll find that the example works for both "march" and "March".

How It Works

The essential change is the replacement of an `If...Then` structure with a `Select Case` structure. When ASP reads the `Select Case` it knows that ensuing tests will be against `varMonthPref`. The first possible answer it tries is "march" and if that *is* a match then it does the first `Response.Write` line. If "march" is not a match then it drops down to the next Case line and tries "March" and so on.

> *Easy mistakes: Since this form and response are similar to the last Try It Out be careful not to accidentally call the wrong one up in you browser when testing. If you copied the last Try It Out response page and modified it here, be sure you changed the <form> action attribute.*

Common Errors of the Select Case Structure

▶ Put a comparison (= or < or >) on the `Select Case` line. The first line says which variable to compare to, but it is NOT an expression.

▶ Putting more than one variable on the `Select Case` line. For example, ASP will not accept: `Select Case varNameFirst, varNameLast`.

▶ Not making the possible answers mutually exclusive.

▶ Not including `Case Else` (`Case Else` is not required, but good programming practice, see below).

▶ Each `Case` line should have a possible answer. That possible answer must be in quotes if it is text.

▶ Type `Select Case` or `End Select` as one word.

▶ Forgeting the **End Case** line

▶ Finishing the structure with **End Case** instead of **End Select**

▶ Trying to use "Where" or "Is" on a **Case** line (these comparitors are only available in other embodiments of VB).

▶ Using **Select Case** to check only two outcomes. For just two outcomes **If...Then** is faster.

Improving your Select Case Structures

The most common problem is that even though you test several cases, none of them match. Perhaps the user has typed the word "Tiger Beetle" instead of "March" or "April"? Obviously you can't test for every word in the dictionary, so ASP allows you to write a special test called **Case Else** which will kick in some lines of code if all of the other **Case** tests fail. For example, in the code below we provide an error message:

```
Select Case varMonthPref
Case "march"
      Response.Write "Your meeting will be held on March 15th "
Case "March"
      Response.Write "Your meeting will be held on March 15th "
Case "april"
      Response.Write "Your meeting will be held on April 16th "
Case "April"
      Response.Write "Your meeting will be held on April 16th "
Case else
      Response.Write "your request for " & varMonthPref
      Response.Write " is not recognized."
      Response.Write "Please strike the back button on your browser "
      Response.Write "and reset then refill the form again.<BR>"
End Select
```

Another improvement is to have ASP test more than one possible answer on one case line. As an example, for both **"march"** and **"March"** we would do the same action (**Response.Write** **"...March 15th"**). This syntax is simple, just line up the possible answers separated by commas as demonstrated in the text below:

```
Select Case varMonthPref
Case "march", "March", "mar", "Mar", "MAR"
      Response.Write "Your meeting will be held on March 15th "
Case "april", "April", "apr", "Apr", "APR"
      Response.Write "Your meeting will be held on April 16th "
Case Else
      Response.Write "your request for " & varMonthPref
      Response.Write " is not recognized."
      Response.Write "Please strike the back button on your browser "
      Response.Write "and reset then refill the form again.<BR>"
End Select
```

ASP also offers a completely different way to solve the case problem. If you change all input text to uppercase before testing you can reduce the number of tests needed. The **Ucase()** function will convert a string to all uppercase as follows:

```
Select Case Ucase(varMonthPref)
Case "MARCH", "MAR"
        Response.Write "Your meeting will be held on March 15th "
Case "APRIL", "APR"
        Response.Write "Your meeting will be held on April 16th "
Case Else
        Response.Write "your request for " & varMonthPref
        Response.Write " is not recognized."
        Response.Write "Please strike the back button on your browser "
        Response.Write "and reset then refill the form again.<BR>"
End Select
```

Basic Rules of Select Case

▶ Use **Select Case** for taking action for more than two possibilities.

▶ The first line states the variable to compare to, but does not define the comparison.

▶ Case lines give a value and comparitor to check against the variable.

▶ ASP will execute the code after the first match.

▶ It is always best to use **Case Else** to cover unexpected circumstances

We've covered a lot of ground so far in looking at branching controls. We'll now take a look at our next type of controls: **looping controls**.

Looping Controls

ASP has two types of looping structures: **Do While** and **For...Next**. Which of these structures you use depends on whether you know in advance how many loops you want to do. If you *do* know the number of loops and have it stored in a variable, then use **For...Next**. If you do *not* know ahead of time how many loops you want to do and will have to decide after each loop whether to continue, then I suggest using the **Do While**.

For...Next

The **For...Next** structure has three parts. The first is a line that describes how many times to repeat the loop. Second come a set of lines with action statements that carry out the task you want repeated. Last is a line that indicates the end of the action statements and tells ASP to go back and repeat the action statements again.

Here is a simple case to get started: imagine that we have salesman on the road who wants to print a sign-in sheet for attendees to seminars. The salesman would like to log in to the company's web site, get the sign-in sheet and print it. In this first case we know that the seminars always have five attendees:

```
<%
Response.Write "Sign-In sheet for Attendees"
Response.Write "On-Line Clothing Store - Fashions of Spring<BR><BR>"
For varCounter = 1 to 5
Response.Write "Attendee Name _____    <BR><BR>"
Response.Write "Attendee EMail _____    <BR><BR><HR><BR>"
```

```
Next
%>
```

ASP will execute the first two lines to display a heading for the sheet—this part is not inside the loop. On the third line ASP begins the process of doing the loop five times. In order to keep count we provide ASP with a variable. The lines that will be repeated five times are all of the lines in between (but not including) the **For**... line and the **Next** line. In this case it is the two **Response.Write** statements that create a line for an attendee to write their name and Email address.

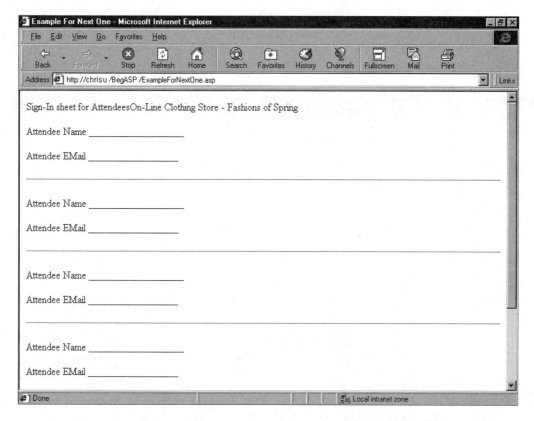

That simple first example assumed that we would always have five attendees. What if that number varies? We would like to have a first web page that asks for the number of attendees, and then use that number to determine how many lines to print.

If we assume that the text field called **NumberAttendees** contains the number of attendees input by the user, then the responding page (below) can grab the user's data from the field named **NumberAttendees** and stuff the data into the variable named **varNumber**. Then we can begin the **For**...**Next** loop. But this time we don't go up through exactly five cycles. Rather, we go through the number of cycles specified in the **varNumber**. Our sign-in sheet is now usable for your seminar, no matter how many attendees there are:

```
<HTML>
<HEAD>
<TITLE>Example For Next Two Response</TITLE>
```

```
</HEAD>
<BODY>
<H2>Welcome to the Seminar<BR>Please Sign in below</H2><BR>
<%
varNumber=Request.Form("NumberAttendees")
For varLineCounter = 1 to varNumber
Response.Write "Attendee Name _____    <BR><BR>"
Response.Write "Attendee EMail _____    <BR><BR><HR><BR>"
Next
%>
</BODY>
</HTML>
```

Now we're about ready to try an example.

Try It Out – For...Next

Your boss asks you to turn in a sheet about once a week that lists the clients you have visited. Since you travel a lot, you want to make a web page that is a form: the form asks you how many people you have visited in total, and then responds with a page that you can print and enter the client's names on.

1 Open your web page editor and type in the following code:

```
<HTML>
<HEAD>
<TITLE>TIO For Next One Form</TITLE>
</HEAD>
<BODY>
<H2>Weekly Client Contacts</H2><BR>
<FORM ACTION=TioForNextOneResponse.asp METHOD = post>
<P>Please enter the first day of the week in the form mm/dd/yy such as
09/20/98 <BR>
<INPUT TYPE=text NAME="start">
<P>Please enter the last day of the week in the same form<BR>
<INPUT TYPE=text NAME="end"><BR>
<INPUT TYPE=submit>
<INPUT TYPE=reset>
</BODY>
</HTML>
```

2 Save this form as `TioForNextOneForm.asp`.

3 Close the form down and create a new file, and this time type in the following code.

```
<HTML>
<HEAD>
<TITLE>TIO ForNext One Response</TITLE>
</HEAD>

<BODY>
<H2>Weekly Client Contacts for George Washington</H2><BR>
<%
varStart=Request.Form("start")
varEnd=Request.Form("end")
varStart = cdate(varStart)
varEnd = cdate(varEnd)

varNumberDays=(varEnd-varStart)

For varLineCounter = 0 to varNumberDays
Response.Write "Clients: _____"
Response.Write "<BR ><BR><BR>"
Next
%>
signed _____
George Washington
</BODY>
</HTML>
```

4 Save this page as `TioForNextOneResponse.asp`.

5 Open up the form page `TioForNextOneForm.asp` in your web browser and fill in any two close dates:

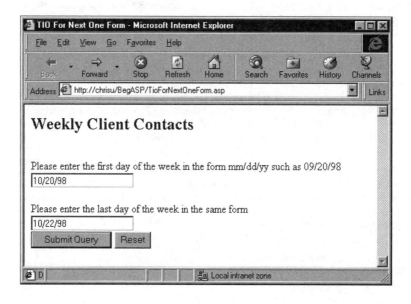

6 Click on **Submit** and you will see an entry on the **Response** page for each day:

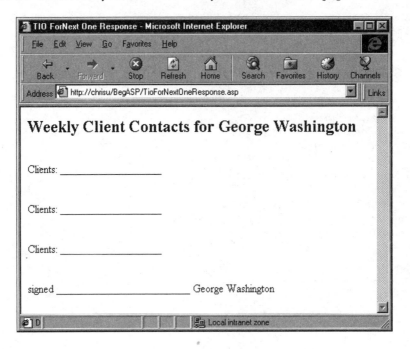

How It Works

The form page is nothing new to you, but we have started slimming the code down to fewer lines so that you get used to seeing some good ASP coding practices.

> *Note that we have specified the **action=TioForNextOneResponse.asp**. If you are copying pages from earlier Try It Outs be sure you update this line.*

We have two pieces of user data going back to the server: the first and last dates of the week we're interested in. This data is used to stuff the variables that ASP will use to determine how many times to loop.

The response page actually uses the **For...Next** loop. The first few lines receive the first and last data from the browser. The data coming from a form's **text** input type will always be text, but we want to work with *dates*. So we convert the text by saying that the new value of **varStart** will become equal to the result of doing a **cdate** conversion on the old value. This means ASP will read the contents of **varStart,** take that text and convert it into a real date, then use that real date to replace the text in **varStart**. The initial loading of the variables is on the first two lines below, and the conversion from text to true dates is on the next two lines:

```
varStart=Request.Form("start")
varEnd=Request.Form("end")

varStart = cdate(varStart)
varEnd = cdate(varEnd)
```

Then we calculate the number of days by subtracting the start date from the end date as below.

```
varNumberDays=(varEnd-varStart)
```

Then we can begin our loop. We need a counter which we called **varLineCounter**, and we say "run the loop starting with the counter set at one, and stop when the counter gets to the number of days". The lines of code to be performed on each cycle are simple: write the word **Clients**, a few underscores, and then some line breaks. The last line, **Next**, indicates to ASP when to go back and repeat the cycle.

```
For varLineCounter = 0 to varNumberDays
Response.Write "Clients: _____"
Response.Write "<BR><BR><BR>"
Next
```

A Few Improvements

We can tighten the first four lines by putting the conversion of text to dates in two commands as follows:

```
varStart=cdate(Request.Form("start"))
varEnd=cdate(Request.Form("end"))
```

A further improvement would be to number the days by printing the value of **varLineCounter**:

```
For varLineCounter = 0 to varNumberDays
Response.Write "Day " & varLineCounter
Response.Write " Clients: _____"
Response.Write "<BR><BR><BR>"
Next
```

In fact, it would be more useful to print the actual date (such as *09/22/98*) at the beginning of the line. In the code below we add a line to the loop which creates a new variable called **varDateThisLine**. Into that variable we stuff the result of a calculation which takes the start date and adds to it the number of the **varLineCounter**, that is, the number of the cycle we are on.

```
For varLineCounter = 0 to varNumberDays
varDateThisLine = varstart + varLineCounter
Response.Write varDateThisLine
Response.Write " Clients: _____"
Response.Write "<BR><BR><BR>"
Next
```

Common Errors of the For...Next Structure

- ▶ Leave out a counter variable
- ▶ Forget the '=' symbol or the word "to" on the first line
- ▶ Leave out the statement **Next**
- ▶ Forget to put appropriate formatting (like a line break) within the repeated section

> Accidentally include a statement in the repeating section so that it is executed many times instead of only once. It's possible that such a line should be above or below the **For**...**Next** structure

> Accidentally leave out a statement from the repeating section so that it is executed once instead of many times. That line should have been *within* the **For**...**Next** structure

Basic Rules of For...Next

> Line one must have: counter variable, equal sign, start number and end number

> All lines within the **For** and **Next** will be repeated until the counter variable gets up to the end value

> You can use the counter variable within the loop

> Last line of control structure is **Next**

For Each...Next

A common cousin of the **For**...**Next** statement is **For Each**...**Next**, which works in an identical way to the **For**...**Next** statement, except that it's used for each element inside an array or collection. If you remember, in Chapter 4 we looked at arrays, and mentioned that they could be populated using a **For**...**Next** statement: well, **For Each**...**Next** makes that task even simpler. Here's an example bit of code:

```
<%
Dim strCities(2)                    'Declare an array
strCities(1) = "London"     'Populate it
strCities(2) = "Paris"

For Each Item In strCities
 Response.Write Item & "<BR>"       'List the contents of each item
Next
%>
```

It looks almost identical to **For**...**Next** doesn't it? The only difference is that you don't have to specify the number of items you want to loop through, just that you want to apply a certain condition to every item. So if there were one hundred cities in our array, each one would be displayed by this loop. The **For Each**...**Next** statement is used to obtain the contents of collections of ASP objects in the next four or five chapters, and we'll be looking at it in greater detail then. For the moment, we'll take a closer look at another looping control: the **Do While** loop.

Do...While

We briefly mentioned the **Do While** loop earlier in the chapter: remember that it's used to repeat a loop *while a specified condition exists*. The **Do While** loops and **For**...**Next** loops has one significant difference in syntax.

For...**Next** has a variable for counting, a start point, and an end point. **Do While** has an **expression test**: at the beginning of each loop ASP checks the expression and if it is true then it runs the loop. If the expression is *false*, then the loop is not run and ASP jumps down in the code to the line after **Loop**.

For...Next technique to stop looping	Do...While technique to stop looping
`For  varCounter  1  to  5`	`Do  While  varEnough<varTooBig` … (Here, one line of code would be incrementing **varEnough** during each cycle of the loop).

There is a serious trap that every beginning programmer falls into: if you start a loop and do not provide a means for it to stop then it will continue forever as an **infinite loop**. Most servers will eventually cut off a given ASP page, since the server needs to attend to other visitors and tries to optimize its resources, but it's still good practice to avoid generating infinite loops.

The **Do While** form of looping is ideal if we have to make a row in a table for each month of the year up to the present month. However, we don't know—at the time of writing our ASP code—in which month the user will be viewing the page. In May, the fifth month, we would like five rows. We can find the number of the current month (May = 5) using the code `month(now())`.

```
<HTML>
<HEAD>
<TITLE>Example Do While</TITLE>
</HEAD>
<BODY>
<H1>Year To Date: Monthly Sales Calls</H1><BR>
<%
varMonthCount = 0
varMonthNow = Month(now())
Do While varMonthCount<=varMonthNow
 Response.Write "number of clients met: _____  <BR>"
 varMonthCount = varMonthCount+1
Loop
%>
<BR>Signed _____ George Washington
</BODY>
</HTML>
```

The first line takes care of 'administrative' HTML matters, then in the body of the code we have a line to write a heading. Next the ASP script begins and we establish two variables: `varMonthCount` will track where we have got to in creating the rows (it starts with a value of zero since we have no rows printed so far). The second variable is `varMonthNow`, which we will use to hold the current month. This is obtained by running the `month(now())` trick I mentioned earlier.

Now we can begin the `Do While` loop. The trick is to ensure that the expression that stops the loop is correct. In this case we will test at the beginning of each loop whether `varMonthCount` is still less than or equal to the current month. For example, suppose we run this in May. The first loop will be executed, provided the `varMonthCount` (currently=1) is less than the `MonthNow` (5). This is true, so ASP does one loop. Next in the loop we have the expected line to print the text. The next line takes the old value of `varMonthCount` and replaces it with a new value exactly one increment higher. Now ASP loops back up and tests again. Since `varMonthCount` (now=2) is *still* less then `MonthNow` (=5) the loop runs again: and this will happen five times. After the fifth loop `varMonthCount` will equal 6 and when ASP tests for the `Do While` condition the answer is *false*. ASP immediately jumps down to the first line following the `Loop` statement and prints the signature line.

Try It Out – Do While...Loop

Your boss likes the sheet you made in the last Try It Out that lists the clients you met each day. But now your job will change. You will meet clients during the first half of the month, then in the second half you will be at the office performing other duties. So the 'meeting clients' sheet will cover from the first day of the month up to the day you return to the office. But your boss's definition of the first half of the month is flexible. Sometimes you have twelve days of visits, sometimes twenty. You need a form that looks at today's date and gives you enough lines for enough days of client visits: that is, one line for each day from the beginning of the month until today, whichever day of the month that is.

1 Open up your preferred web page editor and type in the following code.

```
<HTML>
<HEAD>
<TITLE>TIO Do While</TITLE>
</HEAD>
<BODY>
<H1>Sales Calls for This Month</H1><BR>
<%
varRowCount = 0
varTodayDate = day(now())

Do While varRowCount<=varTodayDate
 Response.Write "For _____ "
 Response.Write "number of clients met was _____<BR>"
 varRowCount = varRowCount + 1
 Loop
%>
</BODY>
</HTML>
```

2   Save this as `TioDoWhile.asp`.

3   Open up your browser and run this page. When run on May 4th, this produces the following page.

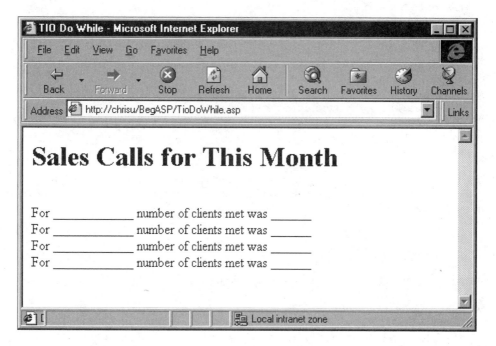

How It Works

This code starts by setting up two variables. The first is the counter, which we set at zero. The second holds today's date which we get from the function `day()` applied to the function `now()`. The result of these functions is to provide the text "5" when this page is requested on the fifth day of the month.

Then the loop begins, with ASP testing whether the **varRowCount** is still less than or equal to today's date. If that expression is true then ASP goes through the cycle. There are two steps in the cycle: the first simply puts the text and HTML on the page. The second line takes the old value of **varRowCount**, adds one to it and uses that new number as a replacement for the old contents of **varRowCount**. This is one of the key ideas of loops. We need to change some condition on each cycle of the loop so we can, at some point, return a 'false' value for the **Do...While** expression and end the loop.

Improvements

Since we are getting and using the actual date it would improve the product if we put the date on each line.

```
<%
varRowCount = 0
varTodayDate = day(now())
varTodayMonth = MonthName(month(date()))

Response.Write "<H2>Report for " & varTodayMonth & "</H2>"
Do While varRowCount<=varTodayDate
 Response.Write "For " & varTodayMonth & " " & varRowCount
 Response.Write ": number of clients met was _____<BR>"
 varRowCount = varRowCount + 1
Loop
%>
```

This gives us a nice result, but with one problem: the code creates an extra line for the zero day of the month. We can solve that below by starting the counter named **varRowCount** at *one* instead of *zero*.

```
<%
varRowCount = 1
varTodayDate = day(now())
varTodayMonth = MonthName(month(date()))

Response.Write "<H2>Report for " & varTodayMonth & "</H2>"
Do While varRowCount<=varTodayDate
 Response.Write "For " & varTodayMonth & " " & varRowCount
 Response.Write ": number of clients met was _____<BR>"
 varRowCount = varRowCount + 1
Loop
%>
```

When requested on the May 4th this will produce:

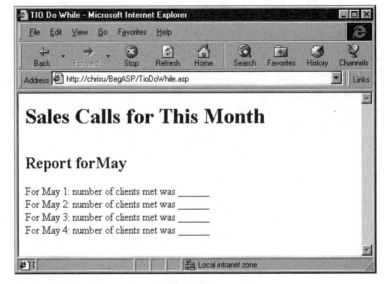

160

Common Errors of the Do While Structure

▶ Using **Next** instead of **Loop** for the closing statement.

▶ Not having the variable of the expression change during the execution of each cycle. This results in the expression *never* becoming false and thus the loop never stops.

▶ Performing one too many or one too few cycles.

▶ Putting code that should be done once *inside* the loop by mistake.

▶ Putting code that should be repeated *outside* the code by mistake.

Basic Rules of Do While

▶ The opening statement uses the key words **Do While**, followed by an expression.

▶ The expression, like all expressions, must resolve to true or false.

▶ There is usually a variable in the expression that will change with each cycle of the loop.

▶ The code to run in the loop is ended with the keyword **Loop**.

We've spent a lot of time looking at the important **looping controls**. Next, we'll turn our attention to the equally important **jumping structures**.

Jumping Structures and the Art of Reusing Code

As you write more ASP code you'll find that you want to use the same code in more than one place. ASP allows you to write some code once, then run it as many times as needed to support the main body of code. These mini-programs are called **procedures** or **functions**. We will want ASP to jump away from execution of the main body of code, run through the commands of a procedure or function, then return to executing the main body.

For example, you may have a few lines of code that insert some lines of text explaining how to contact the sales department. You would like to display this text in various places on the page, but you want to avoid having to rewrite the code separately each time. The solution is to put the lines of code into a procedure (sometimes called a **Sub Procedure** or a **Sub**). Then, at every place that you want that code to run, you can invoke the **Sub** rather than rewrite the code.

A second example is to calculate the delivery date of a shipment. You may have to do this several times for different items on a page. In this case you want to start with information such as the ship date, and from that calculate the delivery date. There may be some branching in the **Sub** to accommodate the fact that there is no delivery on Sunday.

There are two types of procedures:

▶ **Subprocedures** carry out an action. For example, a **Sub** would be used to carry out the actions of putting text onto a page.

▶ **Functions** carry out action statements and *return an answer* to your code. A function would be used to calculate a delivery date and return that answer to your main program.

Procedures

Procedures are easy to write—they have just three parts. First is the **name**, second is the **code** that the procedure should execute, and last is an **ending statement**. In addition you will have to direct your main body of code to *run* the procedure.

In our first example we may want a procedure to put the contact information for the sales department on the web page. That would be done with the following code:

```
Response.Write "Price quotes for this product are available from "
Response.Write "Joe at 201/555-1212.<BR>"
```

In order to avoid writing this same code in many places throughout the page we can put it into a subprocedure:

```
Sub SalesContactInfo
Response.Write "Price quotes for this product are available from "
Response.Write "Joe at 201/555-1212.<BR>"
End Sub
```

This first line must start with the key word **Sub**, then a space and the name of the subroutine. The name should start with a letter and contain only letters and numbers—no spaces or symbols. The following lines hold the ASP code to be performed in the sub. The last line must be the command **End Sub**.

This subprocedure can then be called from your code whenever needed, by using the statement **Call** followed by the name of the procedure, as in the following example:

```
many lines about sweaters
Call SalesContactInfo
...
many lines about vests
Call SalesContactInfo
...
many lines about hats
Call SalesContactInfo
```

The sub does not have to be in the same set of ASP code as the calling statement. The following two sets of code both work fine.

Sub in **separate** section of ASP from calling code:

```
<%
Sub SalesContactInfo
Response.Write "Call Joe at 201/555-1212."
End Sub
%>
<H3>Sweaters For Autumn<//H3>
Warmest, woolliest sweaters now in stock.
New colors for autumn including Orange/Black and
an Autumn Medley.
<%call SalesContactInfo%>
```

Sub in **same** section of
ASP as calling statement:

```
<%
Sub SalesContactInfo
Response.Write  "Call  Joe  at  201/555-1212."
End  Sub
Response.Write  "<H3>Sweaters  For  Autumn</H3>"
Response.Write  "Warmest,  woolliest  sweaters  now
in  stock."
Response.Write  "New  colors  for  autumn  including
Orange/Black  and  an  Autumn  Medley."
Call  SalesContactInfo
%>
```

You can improve your subroutine by having more than one possible outcome. The result will depend on variables sent from your main code over into the subroutine. A datum passed to a subroutine is called an **argument** and is transferred by placing it in parentheses *after* the name of the subroutine. For example, let's say you have four sales specialists, each covering a different region, and you want to display the appropriate sales representative for a given user. Let us also assume that you have picked up from the user their region and stuffed it into **varRegion** by a simple form. You may have created a subroutine that writes the name of the appropriate sales representative. The **varRegion** can be stuffed into a variable and then passed from your main form over to the procedure by putting the name of the variable in parenthesis as an argument. The calling code would now look like:

```
<HTML>
<HEAD>
<TITLE>Example Procedures Two</TITLE>
</HEAD>
<BODY>
<%
varRegion=Request.Form("region")
Sub SalesContactInfo(region)
Response.Write "Price quotes for this product are available from "
Select Case Region
Case "North"
        Response.Write "Brian at 201/555-1212."
Case "South"
        Response.Write "Rob at 719/555-1212."
Case "East"
        Response.Write "Pat at 604/555-1212."
Case "West"
        Response.Write "John at 312/555-1212."
End Select
End Sub
%>

<H2 align="center">On-Line Clothier<BR>
New Items for September, 1998</H2>
<H3>Sweaters</H3>
<P>New selections of warm and woolly Autumn Sweaters<SMALL>.</SMALL>
Special line of
  colors for fall festivities including Black/Orange and our new
Autumn Medley.
```

```
<%call SalesContactInfo(varRegion)%>
<H3>Vests</H3>
<P>Get ready to dance around the MayPole in this season's brightest
selection of Flowered
Vests. We're in swing with the retro look featuring flowers from the
50's, 60's and 70's.
<%call SalesContactInfo(varRegion)%>
<H3>Ties</H3>
<P>No reason to look uncomfortable just because you are wearing a noose!
We have a new
line of ElastoTies<EM>&#153;</EM> with lots of bungee in the middle to
allow you to <EM>Expand
under Pressure</EM><SMALL>®</SMALL>.
<%call SalesContactInfo(varRegion)%>
</BODY>
</HTML>
```

It would display the following:

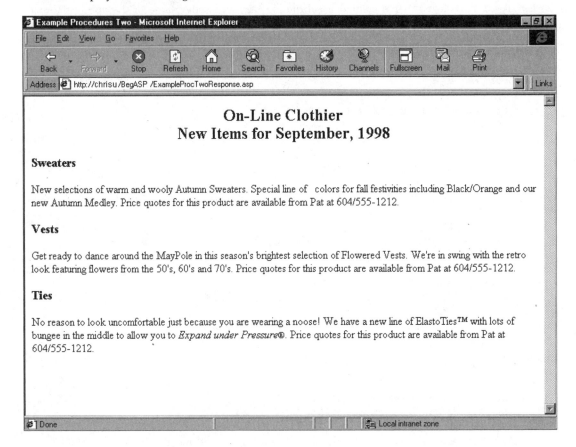

The above routine will put the appropriate `SalesRep` info into your code. There are three changes from our last example. The most obvious change is that inside the `Sub` where we used to have `Response.Write "Joe at...`, we now have a `Select Case` structure that determines which sales representative we should write onto the page.

Also notice two slight differences in the syntax. First is in the line that calls the `Sub`:

```
call SalesContactInfo(varRegion)
```

In order for the subroutine to decide which sales rep to use it must know the regional location of the user. This information is passed over to the subroutine by enclosing it in parenthesis after the name of the subroutine.

Second, the subroutine has a change in the first line. After the name of the subroutine there are parenthesis which specify the data that is being sent over from the main body of code.

```
Sub SalesContactInfo(region)
```

Many new programmers get confused by the idea that we have the same piece of information (in this case it could be the word *North*) being transferred and held by variables of several different names. The table below sketches out where some example data is set, and the references that it must be consistent with:

Location	Purpose	First Established	Must Match
Field of **FORM** Page	Gives name to data so it can be sent from browser back to server	Set in *name=attribute* of the **INPUT** tag	In response page must match the text in parenthesis of **Request.Form** (`"text"`) statement
Variable in main body of code	Holds information for use by ASP	When receiving the data from the form	The text in parenthesis after the name of a **Sub** when the **Sub** is called
In parenthesis after **Sub** name in a **Call**	Send data over to the **Sub**	(already established)	The name given to the variable when stuffed from the **Request.Form**
Input of Proc	Hold information for manipulation within the Proc	Text within parenthesis at end of the proc name	Any use of that data within the ·proc *must* use this name

A confusing point arises here on our definition of subprocedures and functions. Both subprocedures *and* functions can receive information from the main code. They can both take action on that information. But only the function can *return* a value to the main code. Notice that the subprocedure performs its action (**Response.Write** a line on the page) without sending anything back up to the main code. In a function there can be some information (such as the result of a calculation) sent back for the main code to use.

We discussed the use of subprocedures as a way of saving you from re-typing code in several places. There is a second—and very important—use for **Sub**s: the clarification and readability of your programs. ASP code can easily run on for several pages. When you or a colleague need to maintain or modify that code, it can be difficult to see the organization of the whole page. This can be solved by breaking your code into several blocks and making each of them a subroutine. Then the beginning of your ASP code calls each of these blocks. When a programmer looks at the beginning of the code they can immediately see the general idea of what is going on, and then jump to the appropriate subroutine to perform the editing. In the code below you can see how easy it would be to rearrange the order of the subs or to substitute a new model of sweaters.

The first three lines after the **<%** tell ASP to perform the steps of the three subroutines. The subs are spelled out over the following lines. Note that ASP skips the lines of sub procs unless they are specifically called. Therefore after ASP performs the last **Call** on line 4 (**Call TieNum333**) it sees nothing but subs below and so skips over the rest of the code. You can understand procedures better when you understand that they are executed when (and if) called, *not* based on their position in the code.

```
<HTML>
<HEAD>
<TITLE>Example Procedures Three</TITLE>
</HEAD>
<BODY>
<H2 ALIGN="center">On-Line Clothier <BR>
New Items for September, 1998</H2>
<%
Call Sweater98Autumn
Call Vest98Autumn
Call Tie98Autumn

Sub Sweater98Autumn
Response.Write"<P>New selections of warm and wooly Autumn
Sweaters<SMALL>.</SMALL>"
Response.Write "Special line of colors for fall festivities "
Response.Write "including Black/Orange and our new Autumn Medley. "
End Sub

Sub Vest98Autumn
Response.Write "<P>Get ready to dance around the MayPole in "
Response.Write "this season's brightest selection of Flowered Vests. "
Response.Write "We're in swing with the retro look featuring "
Response.Write "flowers from the 50's, 60's and 70's. "
End Sub
```

```
Sub Tie98Autumn
Response.Write"<P>No reason to be uncomfortable because you wear a noose!
"
Response.Write "We have a new line of ElastoTies<EM>&#153;</EM> "
Response.Write "with lots of bungee in the middle to allow you to
<EM>Expand "
Response.Write "under Pressure</EM><SMALL>®</SMALL>."
End Sub
%>
</BODY>
</HTML>
```

Basic Rules of Procedures

To review, procedures have a name and contain some lines of code. Whenever you `Call` a procedure its lines of code are run. Procedures are perfect for `Response.Write` or other actions, but what if you want to have some lines of code that give you back an answer? For example you may frequently calculate a 5% commission on a wholesale price. Or you may want to find out the due date of a library book. Note that these questions require lines of code to generate an answer that you will use in the main body of your code. **Functions** fill this niche by accepting some information from your code, performing calculations or decisions, then returning an answer to your code.

Functions

Functions are written in a similar way to procedures, but with several special characteristics that handle the returning of information. There are five ideas that you should master when writing and using functions.

First, when you write a function you use `Function` (instead of `Sub`) on the first line and `End Function` (instead of `End Sub`) on the last line. The naming rules of functions are the same as for procedures: start with a letter, no spaces, and avoid symbols.

In the next few paragraphs we will build a function to calculate the due date of a library book (two weeks after the check-out date). The start and end of the function will look like this:

```
<%
Function FindDueDate()

...
lines of code
...

End Function
%>
```

Back to those five ideas. Second, the function usually receives some information from your main code. ASP passes this information in the variable that you have named in the parenthesis following the function's name. You do not have to declare this variable using `dim`—it is available for use automatically. For example, in our due date function we would expect to receive the check-out date from the main body of the code—this would give the due date function the starting point for its calculations.

```
<%
Function FindDueDate(varCheckOutDate)

...
lines of code, some of which can use the variable varCheckOutDate

...
End Function
%>
```

Once the function has done its calculation it has to report the result back to the main ASP code. ASP sends back whatever value is assigned to the name of the function. This is a little tricky for most beginners. Not only do you have available the variable which passed the data (**varCheckOutDate**); there is also a variable (usable only within this function) that is automatically created with the name of the function, in this case **FindDueDate**. Whatever value is stuffed into that variable is sent back to the main ASP code when the function is finished.

```
<%
Function FindDueDate(varCheckOutDate)
 FindDueDate = varCheckOutDate + 14
End Function
%>
```

The fourth concept is easy: how to use a function. Instead of the **Call** that we used in procedures, for function we just type the named function followed by parentheses:

```
<%
varOut=Date()
varDueDate = FindDueDate()
Response.Write "Your books are due on " &  varDueDate
%>
```

The last idea is how to send the information from your main body of code to the function. We put whatever we want to send to the function *in the parentheses*. For example:

```
<%
checkoutDate = date()
varDueDate = FindDueDate(checkoutDate)
Response.Write "Your books are due on " &  varDueDate
%>
```

And so we get the final product; ASP code that creates a function, and then some code that uses the function.

```
<HTML>
<HEAD>
<TITLE>Sample Function Page</TITLE>
</HEAD>
<BODY>
<%
function FindDueDate(varCheckOutDate)
FindDueDate = varCheckOutDate + 14
```

```
    End Function
    %>
    <H2>Thank you<BR>
    for using the On-Line Library.</H2>
    <%
    checkoutDate = date()
    varDueDate = FindDueDate(checkoutDate)
    Response.Write "Your books are checked OUT on "  & checkoutdate
    Response.Write "<BR>Your books are due on "  &  varDueDate
    %>

    </BODY>
    </HTML>
```

Common Errors when Writing Functions

▶ Functions can only return one answer.

▶ When using a function you must pass it the data it *expects* to receive. Sending a date when the function expects a price would cause an error.

▶ The answer that the function will provide the main code must be assigned to a variable that is named the same as the function name.

So now we're ready to look at an example.

Try It Out – Function to Calculate Expenses

Your colleagues regularly come to hear a seminar that you provide once per month. They can attend for two, four or six days. They need a rough idea of how much they will be charged for travel, and per diem. Some people like to stay in the city (hotel is $175) while others prefer to stay in the suburbs ($85/night). Everyone gets $75 a day for food. If they stay in the city it costs $85 for transport to and from the airport. If they stay in the suburbs they rent a car for $45 per day. Your task is to design a form that asks for the visitor's preference (a hotel in the city or in a suburb) and then creates a response page that gives them an estimate of their trip cost if they stay for two, four or six days of the seminar.

1 Rouse your web page editor from its slumber and type in the following:

```
<HTML>
<HEAD>
<TITLE>TIO Function Form</TITLE>
</HEAD>
<BODY>
<H2>Cost Calculator for<BR>
Attendance at Corporate Conference</H2>
Please provide the following information so we can estimate your
local costs while attending the conference
<FORM ACTION="TioFunctionResponse.asp" METHOD=post>
Please type your preference in location, either city or suburb:
```

```
<INPUT TYPE=text NAME="location"><BR>
<INPUT TYPE=submit>
<INPUT TYPE=reset>
</BODY>
</HTML>
```

2 Save it as `TioFunctionForm.asp` in your `BegASP` directory.

3 Close this down and create a new web page with the following code:

```
<HTML>
<HEAD>
<TITLE>TIO Function Response</TITLE>
</HEAD>
<BODY>
<%
Function CityCost(NumberDays)
varHotelTotal = NumberDays*175
varMealsTotal = NumberDays*75
varAirportTransport = 85
CityCost = varHotelTotal+varMealsTotal+varAirportTransport
End Function

Function SuburbCost(NumberDays)
varHotelTotal = NumberDays*85
varCarTotal = NumberDays*45
varMealsTotal = NumberDays*75
SuburbCost = varHotelTotal+varMealsTotal
End Function

varLocation=Request.Form("location")
%>
<H3>Your have chosen the hotel in the <%=varlocation%>.<BR>
your estimated costs for this seminar will be:</H3>
<%
Select Case varLocation
case "city","City","CITY"
varCost = CityCost(2)
Response.Write "The two day course will cost $" & varCost & "<br>"
varCost = CityCost(4)
Response.Write "The four day course will cost $" & varCost & "<br>"
varCost = CityCost(6)
Response.Write "The six day course will cost $" & varCost & "<br>"
case "suburb","Suburb","SUBURB"
varCost = SuburbCost(2)
Response.Write "The two day course will cost $" & varCost & "<br>"
varCost = SuburbCost(4)
Response.Write "The four day course will cost $" & varCost & "<br>"
varCost = SuburbCost(6)
Response.Write "The six day course will cost $" & varCost & "<br>"
```

```
case else
Response.Write "error"
end select
%>
</BODY>
</HTML>
```

4 Save it as `TioFunctionResponse.asp` in the usual directory.

5 If you start up your web browser and run the `TioFunctionForm.asp` form page, you'll see the following.

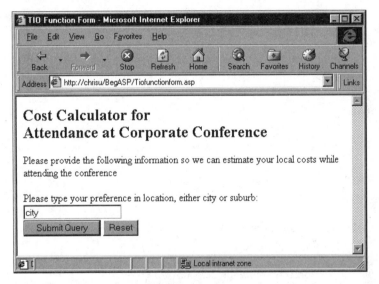

6 If you type in city and press Submit Query, you'll see the following information.

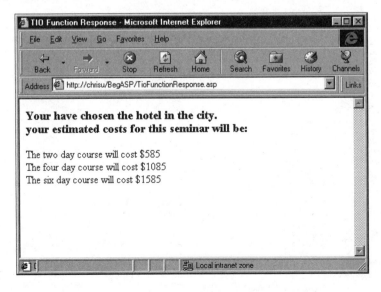

The same result can be obtained by using the function directly, without the intermediate variable. The longer way we used is shown below first:

```
Select Case varLocation
case "city","City","CITY"
varCost = CityCost(2)
Response.Write "The two day course will cost $" & varCost & "<BR>"
```

A faster technique is to directly write the function into the concatenation:

```
Select Case varLocation
case "city","City","CITY"
Response.Write "The two day course will cost $" & CityCost(2) & "<br>"
```

Summary of Reusing Code

Remember that subroutines are used to meet one of two needs:

- Reusing sections of code
- Organizing your code into blocks

Remember that both subroutines and functions can:

- Carry out actions
- Receive data in order to perform calculations or perform one of several actions

The difference between a procedure and a function lies in whether they send data back to the main code:

- Procedures perform actions, but give no reply
- Functions perform action and can also give a reply

Summary

The real power of programming comes from the ability to control and direct the order of execution of statements. In this chapter we looked at three families of control structures:

- Branching, where only one of several possible sets of code is executed
- Looping, where a set of code is performed over and over
- Jumping, where ASP stops execution of the main code, jumps over and executes other code, and then comes back to resume the execution of the main code.

Each of these techniques has two ways of being implemented in ASP:

When **branching** between just two choices we use the `If`...`Then` statement that makes its decision based on an expression which evaluates to true or false. If we have more than one outcome then we use the `Select Case` structure.

When we write a **loop** we must consider how many cycles we want ASP to run through. If we know the number of cycles before starting the loop we generally use the `For`...`Next` structure. If we *don't* know then we use the `Do While` structure.

When writing **jumping** structures we must ask if we expect ASP to return some kind of answer from the code that we jump to. If yes, then we write the other code as a *function*. If we expect the other code only to perform actions then it is written as a subprocedure.

With these tools we can now orchestrate the order in which our lines of code are executed. In some cases we may skip over lines while other times we may repeat code. Each of these control construction techniques will provide a supporting role in the use of the ASP objects and components that you will learn to use in the next several chapters.

Objects, Properties, Methods and Events

In this chapter, we will be looking at objects. A number of readers of this book will have heard about things like "object oriented programming", "object models" and the like. In order to understand what these terms mean, we first need to look at the word found at the core of each of them: **object**.

In our study of objects, we will find that an object features properties (that describe the object), methods (that allow the object to do things for you), and events (ways of communicating with the object).

Once we have looked at what an object is, we'll then be able to look at how objects are useful to us in developing ASP applications. Developing web applications requires us to deal with both client-side and server-side programming, and therefore we'll take a look at how objects can be used on both sides of the wire.

Before we get started, here is what we will cover in this chapter:

- What is an object?
- What exactly are properties, methods and events?
- How can we change the characteristics of an object?
- How do we know when the object tells us something?
- What is an object model?
- How do we use the object model in Active Server Pages?

So, we'll begin by taking a look at what an object is.

What is an Object?

In the real world, we already know what objects are. They're the things we look at, pick up, and use every day—things like our chairs, our telephones, and our computers. All these are solid, tangible entities.

However, if we want to describe a telephone to somebody in abstract terms, we can do this by talking about it in terms of its essential characteristics—what properties it has, what it can do, and how we can interact with it. All telephones have these characteristics, and we can use them to establish exactly how one telephone differs from the next.

So, for our telephone's physical properties, we could say that it has a microphone, a speaker, and a dialing pad. We could also say that it lets us do things, such as call someone and talk to them. Our telephone will also tell us when certain events are happening: for example, if a friend is trying to call you, your telephone will ring to let you know. This ringing will prompt you to take some action, like picking up the handset and talking to your friend. As an abstract object, our telephone has:

> Certain properties that define and describe it

> A set of things that it lets us do

> The ability to prompt action when events occur

By learning about what an object is, we can then look at how to use them in a way known as **object-oriented programming**. In the object-oriented way of programming, the application is broken down into a set of objects. In doing this, you can build the application as the relationships and interactions between objects. Later in this chapter, we will see how the objects of Active Server Pages relate and interact with each other and allow us to build our applications.

Our Telephone in Detail

Here is our telephone. To look at this as an object, let's put down some information about it. We will be classifying the information into three categories:

> Things that describe the telephone

> Things that we can do with the phone

> Things that the telephone tells us

Let's look at each of these aspects in turn:

Describe the telephone	The telephone is gray
	The telephone is made of plastic
	The handset weighs 6.5 ounces
	The telephone has 12 keys
	The telephone number is (714) 555-1523
	The telephone is connected to the wall

What can we do with it?	We can place an outgoing call
	We can answer an incoming call
	We can hang up the current call
	We can enter our calling card number
	We can disconnect it from the wall
What can it tell us?	Someone is trying to call us
	The person we are calling is busy
	Another person is calling while we are talking

How It Works

The three categories that we have created in the left-hand column can be applied to any object. In fact, the best way to describe an object is to break down its characteristics into these three categories, and put information about your object into these categories. Any information that you have about a particular object can be included in one of these categories.

If you have another telephone that features all these characteristics, except that its color is blue, then we can describe your telephone by changing that one part of the description above. Moreover, this technique works for any type of object.

Object Terms

So far, we have used verbose English terms to describe our three categories. In the world of objects, we need terms that concisely describe each of these three categories. These terms are **properties**, **methods** and **events**. In addition to these terms, we need to look at the term **instance** as it relates to objects. In this section, we'll look more carefully at what each of these means in abstract terms.

Instance

When we are talking about a unique object, we can use the term **instance** to say that we are dealing with a particular telephone object—*your* telephone for example—that has a specific set of properties and values. When we want to talk about another telephone, we will then use a different instance of the telephone object. In this way, both you and I can have instances of the telephone object. Both individual objects are real instances of the object 'telephone'. For example, my telephone (my *instance* of a telephone object) is gray and comes with special answerphone facilities, your telephone (your *instance* of a telephone object) may be red, blue or whatever. These *instances* represent completely different physical objects. But since they are both instances of the same object, they share the same types of characteristics, such as properties, events and methods.

Properties

When talking about those characteristics that describe an object, we are talking about the **properties** of the object. Each property describes a particular aspect of the object. The property is actually described as a **name/value pair**. This means that for every **named** property, there is a single unique **value** that describes that property for a particular instance of the object. If we go back to our telephone example, we can create a table that lists each of the property names and the value of each property.

Property Name	Property Value
Color	Grey
Material	Plastic
Weight	6.5 ounces
NumberOfKeys	12
TelephoneNumber	(714) 555-1523
Connected	Yes

We now have a set of properties that describe this instance. The properties of an object are used to represent a value associated with the object. A new instance of the object may have different property values, but it has the same property *name*.

Color	Grey	Blue
Material	Plastic	Thermoplastic
Weight	6.5 ounces	22 ounces
NumberOfKeys	12	12
TelephoneNumber	(714) 555-123	(615) 555-8329
Connected	Yes	Yes

Even with different property values, these two telephones are instances of the same object. Since we know that all telephone objects have a 'Color' property, we can determine the color of each of the phones by examining its 'Color' property value.

Now that we have a way of describing the telephone object, let's take a look at what we can do with it.

Methods

Another characteristic of objects is that they can perform functions for us. Well, at least *most* objects can. A chair object allows you to sit in it, so you could say that it is functioning to support your body. But objects can also perform tasks that are more 'functional'. The tasks that an object can perform are called **methods**.

A method is defined as an action that an object can take. A method usually manifests itself by a **function call**, or **method call**. When we have an instance of an object, we can tell it to perform a certain task calling one of its methods.

Let's illustrate this using the telephone example. Our telephone object can carry out five methods. Each of these methods will cause the telephone object to perform an action. Here is a list of functions that will perform the methods of the telephone object:

Method Name	Description
PlaceCall	Place an outgoing call
Answer	Answer an incoming call
HangUp	Hang up the current call
SendCardNumber	Enter our calling card number
Disconnect	Disconnect the phone from the wall

These methods are used when we want our telephone object to perform a certain function: all we need to do is tell it to execute the corresponding method.

Parameters

You may have noticed that some of the methods can be executed directly, while others look like they will need additional information. To contrast these ideas, consider the following examples:

▶ Suppose that our telephone took an incoming call (in the next section, we'll see how we can tell that this is happening). All we need to do to answer the call is to invoke the 'Answer' method of our telephone object.

▶ Suppose that we want to place a call. Simply calling the 'PlaceCall' method isn't enough in this case: we need to supply more information (i.e. the telephone number!) in order to complete the action.

Let's look more closely at the second of these examples. The telephone object has a 'TelephoneNumber' property, and this is used to identify our telephone's *own* telephone number (i.e. the number that other people use to call us). So, the 'TelephoneNumber' property of our phone isn't going to help us to make outgoing telephone calls.

So how do we tell the phone which number we want to call? It's possible, I guess, for the telephone object to have another property, called 'OutgoingTelephoneNumber', that would identify the desired number; but that would be too cumbersome, because every time we wanted to make a call we would have to:

▶ Set the 'OutgoingTelephoneNumber' property value to the desired phone number
▶ Execute the 'Call' method of the telephone object to place the call

As you know, telephones just don't work that way. It would be much more elegant (and intuitive) to have some way of passing the outgoing phone number to the 'Call' method, so that we can place an outgoing call in a single step. This is done by passing a **parameter** to the 'Call' method. With this in place, we can place an outgoing call by simply executing the 'Call' method and telling it which number we want to call, like this:

▶ Execute the 'Call' method of the telephone object, passing the outgoing telephone number as a parameter

If we look again at the methods of the telephone object, we can identify those methods that require parameters, and what the values of those parameters mean to the object:

Method Name	Parameters
PlaceCall	Outgoing telephone number
Answer	No Parameters
HangUp	No Parameters
SendCardNumber	Calling card number, PIN
Disconnect	No Parameters

You can see that a method can have none, one, or more than one parameter. The 'SendCardNumber' method actually requires two parameters. You are required to pass in both the calling card number and the personal identification number (PIN) for the method to execute properly. By defining the information that a method needs to execute as parameters of the method, you can ensure that the method will only execute if all parameters are supplied.

Return Values

In addition to passing parameters to a method, the method can also return information to us. The value returned by a method is (rather conveniently) called a **return value**. If a method has a return value, then it will pass information back to us. This information could have a number of purposes. For example, the return value might be an indication of whether or not the method completed successfully. Alternatively, the method could also pass back the results of some processing that it did for us.

As the user of an object, we can decide whether we want to do anything with the return value. If the information is pertinent to what we are doing, then we can capture the return value and do something with it later. If we do not care what the return value is, we can just ignore it and continue with our work.

Just as the methods of the telephone object can have parameters, we can identify those methods that pass return values, and what those values mean.

Method Name	Return Value
PlaceCall	True (if call completed successfully) False (if call failed)
Answer	No Return Value
HangUp	True (if telephone was hung up successfully) False (if not)
SendCardNumber	True (if card was accepted) False (if card was not accepted)
Disconnect	No Return Value

Encapsulation

A description of methods would not be complete without a discussion of **encapsulation**. The concept of encapsulation means that a user of an object need not be concerned with the inner workings of the object. For example, when you use a telephone to answer an incoming call, all you need to do is pick up the handset. This is the equivalent of executing the 'Answer' method. You do not need to know how the telephone interacts with the phone company to connect your phone with the person at the other end of the call—that's all encapsulated within the 'Answer' method. This is an example of encapsulation.

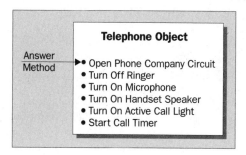

One advantage of encapsulating the workings of an object within a method is that the implementation of the method can be changed without having to adjust the client.

For example, suppose the phone company decides to change the way that an incoming call is answered. Without encapsulation, all of the users of the telephone object would have to be adjusted to support this new way of answering the phone. Instead, by encapsulating these new steps within the 'Answer' method, the actions of the client never need to be changed: with either system, all the client needs to do is execute the 'Answer' method. Not only does encapsulation make the telephone user's life easier; it allows the developer of the telephone object to change the implementation at any time.

Events

We have now looked at two of the three characteristics of an object. The properties and methods of an object are ways that the user of the object can communicate with the object. Now, what if the object needs to communicate with the program?

As an example, consider what happens when our telephone receives an incoming call. The fact is that it needs some way of telling us to answer the call. How will the telephone communicate this information to us?

Again, it's possible for the telephone object to have a property (called 'IncomingCall', perhaps) that was set to 'True' whenever an incoming call was present. However, there are two disadvantages to this. First, it would require the user of the telephone object to check this property on a regular basis. Second, the user would require a great deal of knowledge of the inner workings of the object—so it doesn't fit in with our ideal of encapsulation.

What is needed is a way for the object to tell the user that something has happened. The mechanism for this is called an **event**. An object generates an event whenever something of interest happens. In our telephone example, when the telephone receives an incoming call, it tells us so in the form of an event—we'll call it the 'IncomingCall' event. (On most telephones, this particular event takes the form of the telephone ringing.)

The telephone object would generate an 'IncomingCall' event every time an incoming call is received. In a physical phone, the ringing sound is the phone notifying you of the 'IncomingCall' event. When the user receives this event, they can execute the 'Answer' method (pick up the handset), and begin the call. This frees the user from having to check regularly for incoming calls: the event is designed to notify the user just at the appropriate moment.

Just like methods, events can have parameters. These parameters can hold specific information about the event. For example, if our telephone supports *CallerID*—a feature that reveals the identity of the incoming caller—then the 'IncomingCall' event could include a parameter that contains the telephone number of the incoming caller.

Here is a list of the events that our telephone object will generate, along with their associated parameters:

Event Name	Parameters
IncomingCall	Incoming CallerID information
LineBusy	No Parameters

There are a couple of useful pieces of terminology that are often used in this context. When an object generates an event, the object can be said to **fire** the event. When the object has fired the event, we say that the user must **handle** the event.

Synchronous vs Asynchronous

One of the advantages of working with objects and events is that it awakens us to the concept of asynchronous programming. First off, let's look at the definitions of synchronous and asynchronous.

These terms refer to how two separate actions are related to each other. If the first action must be completed before the second one begins, then these two actions are said to be **synchronous**. If the second action can begin at any time, no matter what the status of the first action, then these two actions are said to be **asynchronous**.

We've already discussed what it would be like if our objects didn't support events. For example, to detect an incoming call, you would need to constantly check the value of some property to see whether an incoming call was waiting. While you're performing these frequent, regular checks, you would be unable to perform any other tasks. This is an example of synchronous activity. All other activity would grind to a halt, while you wait for that incoming call property to become true.

With events, we can have asynchronous activity. By having an event handler that is called when the object fires the 'IncomingCall' event, we can perform other tasks without having to devote any effort to monitoring the incoming call status. Our event handler code will be dormant until such a time as it detects the 'IncomingCall' event, and then sets about dealing with the incoming call.

This is not to say that all synchronous is bad and all asynchronous is good. We will see many instances where it makes sense to use a synchronous activity to perform a certain type of processing. Likewise, we will also see instances where an asynchronous activity is not an optimal way of dealing with an event.

Moving On to Programming

Now that we have a basic understanding of what an object is, we can move on to look at how programming concepts can be changed by using objects. When working with objects in software development, we will create objects that have properties, events and methods. We can use these three attributes to describe physical objects and abstract concepts. Either way, the programmatic object will allow us to interact with it through its properties, events and methods.

Programming with Objects

To begin our look at programming with objects, let's use our trusty telephone object again. Being a technophile and always needing to have the latest and greatest, you have even hooked up your telephone to your computer. Now you want to be able to do something with it. If we want the computer to interact with the telephone, we need a programmatic object that will allow us to control the physical telephone.

It is this **representation** of a physical object that gives programmatic objects their power. If you remember, in the last section we talked about encapsulation, where we interact with an object through its properties, methods and events—its **interfaces.** How the object connects these interfaces to something that actually performs actions is hidden from us. That is, the internal workings of the object are encapsulated.

When the user interacts with the programmatic telephone object (the representation of the telephone and its actions in code) the interface (the 'exposed' methods or properties not hidden by encapsulation) translates the user's instructions into something that can interact with the physical interface of the physical phone. So, in the real world, when you enter a telephone number into your interface, the programmatic object must tell the physical phone to perform the actions necessary to make a telephone call. It's simple, as the actual physical workings of what goes on underneath are hidden from you.

We are therefore using encapsulation in our programmatic object. In this case, the interfaces of the programmatic object will know how to connect from the programmatic interfaces to the physical interfaces. We don't have to know how this works. These physical interfaces encapsulate the actual working functionality.

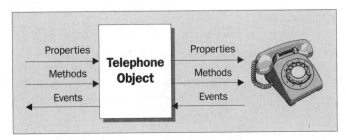

So what we need is a programmatic object that will allow us to access the physical object. This book will not cover how to create the object itself: rather, we will take a look at the programmatic object, and then look at how we can interact with the properties, methods and events of the object.

The Telephone Object

The properties of the telephone object are:

Property Name
Color
Material
Weight
NumberOfKeys
TelephoneNumber
Connected

As you can see, we have used the same names that we used when discussing the physical telephone object. The methods of the telephone object are the same as well. In this case, the methods that have parameters will have the same parameters as well.

Method Name	Parameters
PlaceCall	NumOutgoing
Answer	No Parameters
HangUp	No Parameters
SendCardNumber	NumCCN, NumPIN
Disconnect	No Parameters

Finally—as you will expect by now—events that the object will support are the same events that are supported by the physical telephone object.

Event Name	Parameters
IncomingCall	NumIncoming
LineBusy	No Parameters
CallWaiting	NumIncoming

Now that we have defined the interfaces of our telephone object, we can take a look at some code examples that will show you how to use these interfaces. For these examples, we will be using VBScript, which is the language that is being used throughout the book. Since there are three types of interfaces, we will look at three code samples—one for each type.

Altering the Properties of an Object

So, we have a telephone object, which defines the characteristics of any telephone. For a particular instance of the object—that is, a real physical telephone—values are associated with the properties that describe the characteristics of that one telephone.

A program that uses the instance can then retrieve the values associated with these properties. Alternatively, they can be used by a method or event to perform some action. The programmer working with the instance of the telephone object is responsible for setting the values of many properties; other properties will be set based on the results of methods being called.

Setting a Property

First, let's look at how to set a property. The four properties that we'll use here to describe our instance of the telephone object are:

- ▶ `Color`
- ▶ `Material`
- ▶ `Weight`
- ▶ `NumberOfKeys`

When the instance of our object is created, these values are left blank or set to default values. It is up to the program that creates the object to set the specific values that we want.

Try It Out – Setting Property Values

In this example, we will be configuring the properties of our object so that it represents this telephone:

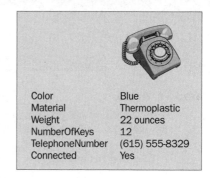

Color	Blue
Material	Thermoplastic
Weight	22 ounces
NumberOfKeys	12
TelephoneNumber	(615) 555-8329
Connected	Yes

1 Download the `MyTelephone.exe` file from the WROX web site.

2 Once the file has been downloaded, you can run it to expand all of the files into a temporary directory.

3 Go to that temporary directory and run `setup.exe` to install the `MyTelephone` object. You can choose to install it into any directory, or accept the default.

4 Using your editor of choice, enter the following source code:

```
<%
Dim objTelephone
Set objTelephone = Server.CreateObject("MyTelephone.Telephone")

objTelephone.Color = "Blue"
objTelephone.Material = "Thermoplastic"
objTelephone.Weight = 22
objTelephone.NumberOfKeys = 12

Response.Write "Done"
%>
```

5 Save this file, with the name **SetProperties.asp**, to your **BegASP** directory.

6 View the file in your web browser. If everything worked properly, then the browser will display the word Done.

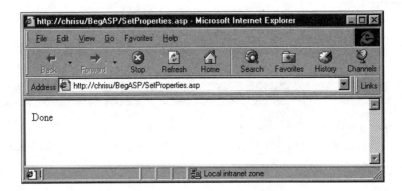

How It Works

The first step in obtaining a reference to an object is to allocate a variable to hold the reference. The variable is allocated using the **Dim** statement:

```
Dim objTelephone
```

You'll recall from Chapter 4 that the variables in VBScript are in fact variants.

The next step actually creates the object:

```
Set objTelephone = Server.CreateObject("MyTelephone.Telephone")
```

This is done using the **Server.CreateObject** method. The **Server** object is one of the built-in ASP objects. We will cover it in more detail in Chapter 10. One of its methods is **CreateObject**. This method has one parameter—the name of the object you want to create. The method also has a return value—it's a reference to an instance of the object.

Since the value returned by the **CreateObject** method is a reference to an instance of the Telephone object, we must use the **Set** statement to assign its reference to our variable. The **Set** statement is a VBScript statement that lets us store object references in variables. Since the return value is a reference to the object, and not the object itself, we have to use the **Set** method to store its value for later use.

Now that we have our reference to the instance of the telephone object, we can go about setting the properties. To do this, we simply use the *object.property* notation and set the property to the value that we desire:

```
objTelephone.Color = "Blue"
objTelephone.Material = "Thermoplastic"
objTelephone.Weight = 22
objTelephone.NumberOfKeys = 12
```

As you can see, the general syntax for this is:

```
object.property =   value
```

Now that we have set some property values in our telephone object, we can look at how to retrieve these values.

Retrieving a Property

The last section showed how to set the values of properties of an object. Now that information is stored there, we can retrieve this information at a later time. This idea is called **data hiding**.

In essence, we have an instance of an object that has some data stored in its properties. All we need to refer to this instance is the reference to the object's instance. All of the data that the object has stored inside of it comes along with the object. Since we don't have to worry about this data until we need it, this is referred to as data hiding.

Read-Only Properties

In addition to the data that we have explicitly stored in the object, there is information that the object uses to describe its state. In our telephone object, there is a property called **Connected**, that describes whether or not a telephone is connected to the wall. In order to change the connection state of the phone, we would use a method.

You may wonder why we would not just change the property by hand? This is another example of encapsulation. There is more to disconnecting a phone than just changing a value of a property: the object needs to perform some actions, which the user of the object does not need to be concerned about. This functionality is encapsulated in a method, and the method is responsible for updating the value of the **Connected** property. This makes the **Connected** property a **read-only property**, which means that we cannot set its value, only retrieve it.

Try It Out – Retrieving Property Values

In this example, we will be retrieving the values of some of the properties of the object, and storing them in local variables.

1 Using NotePad or your editor of choice, adapt the program `SetProperties.asp`, from the previous exercise, as follows:

```
<%
Dim objTelephone
Set objTelephone = Server.CreateObject("MyTelephone.Telephone")

objTelephone.Color = "Blue"
objTelephone.Material = "Thermoplastic"
objTelephone.Weight = 22
objTelephone.NumberOfKeys = 12

Dim strColor
Dim strMaterial
Dim intNumKeys
Dim intWeight
Dim blnConnected

strColor = objTelephone.Color
strMaterial = objTelephone.Material
intNumKeys = objTelephone.NumberOfKeys
intWeight = objTelephone.Weight
blnConnected = objTelephone.IsConnected

Response.Write "objTelephone.Color = " & strColor & "<BR>"
Response.Write "objTelephone.Material = " & strMaterial & "<BR>"
Response.Write "objTelephone.NumberOfKeys = " & intNumKeys & "<BR>"
Response.Write "objTelephone.Weight = " & intWeight & "<BR>"
Response.Write "objTelephone.IsConnected = " & blnConnected & "<BR>"
%>
```

2 Save this code in the file `RetrieveProperties.asp`, in the `BegASP` directory.

3 View the page in your browser.

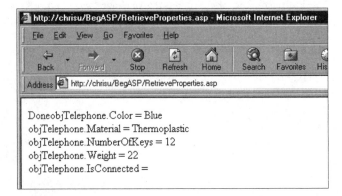

```
http://chrisu/BegASP/RetrieveProperties.asp - Microsoft Internet Explorer
File   Edit   View   Go   Favorites   Help
Back   Forward   Stop   Refresh   Home   Search   Favorites   His
Address   http://chrisu/BegASP/RetrieveProperties.asp

DoneobjTelephone.Color = Blue
objTelephone.Material = Thermoplastic
objTelephone.NumberOfKeys = 12
objTelephone.Weight = 22
objTelephone.IsConnected =
```

How It Works

First, we set the `Color`, `Material`, `NumberOfKeys` and `Weight` properties of our telephone, just as we did in the previous example. Next, we allocate some variables that will hold the values of the properties of our telephone object, using the `Dim` statement. We allocate one variable for each property that we are storing:

```
Dim strColor
Dim strMaterial
Dim intNumKeys
Dim intWeight
Dim blnConnected
```

Next, we set about retrieving the property values. To do this, we use the *object.property* notation again—this time to retrieve the property, and then we store the property in the appropriate variable. Here's the code that does this for the `Color` property:

```
strColor = objTelephone.Color
```

As you can see, the general syntax for this is:

myVariable = *object.property*

Then we output the results. Here's the line that does this for the `Color` property:

```
Response.Write "objTelephone.Color = " & strColor & "<BR>"
```

If the value of the property is a reference to an object, then you will need to use the `Set` statement to assign the property value to our local variable:

Set *myVariable* = *object.property*

We have now seen how to put information into the properties of an object and retrieve that information. Next, we will be getting our object to do some work for us. To tell it to do some work, we will be calling its methods.

Calling Methods of an Object

Calling the method of an object is very similar to setting or retrieving a property value. There are two points that we need to be concerned about:

- If the method requires parameters, that they are passed correctly.
- If the method has a return value we are interested in, that it is properly captured.

Try It Out – Calling a Basic Method

To make this first example a simple one, we will be calling a method that has no parameters. Also, in this example, we are not interested in its return value. We will be using the same `objTelephone` instance of our telephone object that we have been using in the previous examples in this chapter.

1 Using your editor of choice, enter the following source code:

```
<%
Dim objTelephone
Set objTelephone = Server.CreateObject("MyTelephone.Telephone")

Response.Write "Answering the phone...<BR>"
objTelephone.Answer()

dim blnIsConnected
blnIsConnected = objTelephone.IsConnected
Response.Write "The IsConnected property is " & blnIsConnected & "<P>"

Response.Write "Hanging up the phone...<BR>"
objTelephone.HangUp()
Response.Write "The IsConnected property is " & objTelephone.IsConnected
& "<P>"
%>
```

2 Save this file, with the name `MethodsExample.asp`, to your `BegASP` directory.

3 View the file in your web browser.

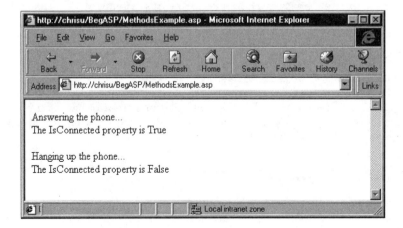

How It Works

In this example, we are using two of the methods that the `Telephone` object supports. We will also be checking one of the properties after calling the methods to see if they had any effect.

```
<%
Dim objTelephone
Set objTelephone = Server.CreateObject("MyTelephone.Telephone")
```

The first step, as we have done in the previous examples, is to create an instance of the `Telephone` object using the `Server.CreateObject` method. The reference that this method returns will be stored in a local variable. Remember that since we are storing a reference, we have to use the `Set` statement.

```
Response.Write "Answering the phone...<BR>"
objTelephone.Answer()
```

The next step is to call the `Answer` method of the `Telephone` object. We will use the reference to the instance that we created to call the method. The preceding `Response.Write` line is being used to provide a visual indication that the method is being called.

```
dim blnIsConnected
blnIsConnected = objTelephone.IsConnected
Response.Write "The IsConnected property is " & blnIsConnected & "<P>"
```

Next, we will want to check the status of the `IsConnected` property. This property indicates if the phone is in use or not. Since we have just answered the phone, we would assume that this property would be set to true. We will store its value in a local variable, then use that local variable in a `Response.Write` method to display its value.

```
Response.Write "Hanging up the phone...<BR>"
objTelephone.HangUp()
Response.Write "The IsConnected property is " & objTelephone.IsConnected
& "<P>"
%>
```

Finally, we will hang up the phone by calling the `HangUp` method of the `Telephone` object. Once that has completed, we will check the value of the `IsConnected` property again. This time, instead of storing the value of the property to a local variable before displaying it, we will directly display the value of the property. Both alternatives work exactly the same way.

Next, we will look at a variation of this example and see how to call a method that has a parameter.

Try It Out – Calling a Method with Parameters

In this example, we will be calling a method that has parameters—we're still not interested in the return value, just yet. Again, we will be using the `objTelephone` instance of our telephone object that we have been using in all the previous examples.

1 Using or your editor of choice, enter the following source code:

```
<%
Dim objTelephone
Set objTelephone = Server.CreateObject("MyTelephone.Telephone")

Dim strPhoneNumber
strPhoneNumber = "615-555-8329"
Response.Write "Calling " & strPhoneNumber & "...<P>"
objTelephone.PlaceCall(strPhoneNumber)
```

```
   Dim blnIsConnected
   blnIsConnected = objTelephone.IsConnected
   Response.Write "The IsConnected property is " & blnIsConnected & "<P>"
   %>
```

2 Save this file, with the name `ParameterExample.asp`, to your `BegASP` directory.

3 View the file in your web browser.

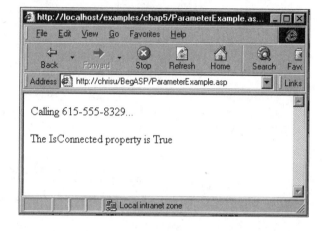

How It Works

Now we're telling the telephone to execute the `PlaceCall` method. As we know, the `PlaceCall` method doesn't work alone: we need to tell the telephone who to call! We do this by specifying the telephone number as a parameter to the `PlaceCall` method.

```
<%
Dim objTelephone
Set objTelephone = Server.CreateObject("MyTelephone.Telephone")
```

First, as we have done in the previous examples, we will create an instance of the `Telephone` object. The reference to this instance is then stored in a local variable.

```
Dim strPhoneNumber
strPhoneNumber = "615-555-8329"
Response.Write "Calling " & strPhoneNumber & "...<P>"
objTelephone.PlaceCall(strPhoneNumber)
```

The telephone number that we will be calling is stored as a string. In this example, the number is hard coded. We could have just as easily used a FORM to supply the value. We then will display a message indicating the number that will be called. We can then pass this value to the `PlaceCall` method. The parameter that we supply to the `PlaceCall` method is included within the method's parentheses. The contents of the parentheses are known as the **parameter list**. The entries in the parameter list could be variables or explicit values.

> *One thing that you need to be careful with is the order of the parameters in the parameter list. If we were calling a method which requires multiple parameters, then the order of the parameters in the parameter list must **exactly** match the order that the method is expecting. So, for example, if you call the SendCardNumber method, then you must specify two parameters: the first must be the value of the NumCCN parameter, and the second must be the value of the NumPIN parameter.*

```
Dim blnIsConnected
blnIsConnected = objTelephone.IsConnected
Response.Write "The IsConnected property is " & blnIsConnected & "<P>"
%>
```

Finally, we will check the value of the **IsConnected** property and display its value to the user.

We have now seen how to program with the properties and methods of objects. In our examples, we have been using an object that represents a physical entity. The remainder of this chapter will be devoted to looking at a set of objects that represent an application environment in Active Server Pages. These objects comprise the Active Server Pages **object model**.

What is the Active Server Pages Object Model?

In this chapter, we have looked at how a physical object can be represented by a programmatic object. This programmatic object has all of the interfaces of the physical object, and it can be used as an interface between an application and the physical object itself. But what about objects that don't have a physical counterpart?

In the Active Server Pages programming model, there is a wide range of functionality that is accessible to the programmer. ASP allows us to track the state of a user, dynamically generate HTML output, and take data from forms to be inserted into a database. All of this functionality makes ASP a rather complex beast. Microsoft was tasked with finding the best compromise between offering a simple programming model and providing access to all of the power that ASP provides. To do this, the functionality was grouped into a set of objects. These objects were then related together into what is known as an **object model**.

An object model is a representation of a set of objects and their relationships to one another. These relationships can take the form of containment, where one object is embedded inside of another. Or, they can take the form of a parent–child relationship, where one object has a set of child objects associated with it.

We will not be examining the various methods for grouping objects together in this book. What is important to us is what the objects that make up Active Server Pages are, and how they are related to each other.

Object Model Structure

Six objects make up the core of Active Server Pages. These are known as the **built-in objects**. These objects form a hierarchy. The objects are:

- **Server** object
- **Application** object
- **Session** object
- **Request** object
- **Response** object
- **ObjectContext** object

Each of these objects interacts with a different part of the ASP system. This chart shows how they are related to each other, and how they are related to the client and to the server.

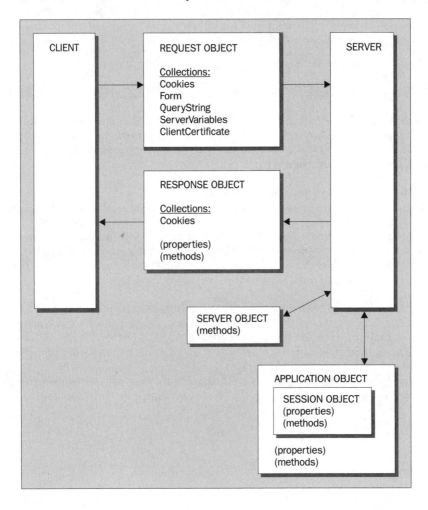

The following chapters in the book will go into each of these objects in greater detail. They will also provide a series of basic examples that will quickly show you how to use these objects to create ASP scripts. But for now, we will just take a quick look at what each object is for.

Server Object

The `Server` object is a low-level object that provides some basic properties and methods that can be used in almost every Active Server Page. This object will allow you to do things such as:

▶ Set the amount of time a script can run before an error occurs

▶ Take a user-supplied string and encode it into HTML format

▶ Convert a virtual path to a physical path on the server

▶ Take a user-supplied string and encode it into the proper format for a Uniform Resource Locator (URL) string

▶ Create an instance of an ActiveX component. You saw this earlier in the chapter with the `CreateObject` method of the `Server` object.

These methods and properties are provided as utility functions for you to use in your pages. They are not used to affect the display of the page, but they still provide valuable support in creating Active Server Pages. Chapter 10 will cover this object in greater detail.

Application Level Objects

As the web is moving from just serving up pages to providing access to dynamic information from a wide range of systems, the sites that a user may access begins to look more like a traditional desktop application. In ASP, each virtual directory (excluding the root in some cases) on the server is an application. All of the pages in that directory, whether static or dynamically generated, are part of that application.

Application Object

Since these pages are functioning together as an application, naturally the developer would want some control over the application as a whole. This is the responsibility of the `Application` object. This object will be covered in detail in Chapter 9, but let's just introduce a few things that it can do.

With this object, you can:

▶ Be notified when an application is first started, so that you can perform some startup processing.

▶ Be notified when an application is ending, so that you have the opportunity to perform functions so that the application closes down cleanly.

▶ Store information that can be accessed by all clients accessing the application.

There is one instance of the `Application` object for each application running on the web server. There may be many clients accessing the same application. They each can get a reference to the same `Application` object. Next, we will look at an object that is unique to each client of an application.

Session Object

There is one **Application** object for each application on the web server. Every client accessing that application can get a reference to it. Each of these clients is called a **Session**. Therefore, each of them has a reference to a unique **Session** object. This object will be covered in Chapter 9, but here is a little of what it can do. The **Session** object will allow you to:

▶ Be notified when a user session begins, so that you can take appropriate actions for a new client.

▶ Be notified when a client has ended their session. This can either be caused by a timeout or an explicit method called **Abandon**.

▶ Store information that can be accessed by the client throughout the session.

The **Session** object is the most powerful object for creating applications using Active Server Pages. One of the problems that have existed in creating web-based applications is that the connection between the client and the server is **stateless**. The web server itself has no mechanism for tying a request for a page by a client back to a previous request for a page by the same client. This means that each request that one client makes of a web server is treated independently from the rest. While this allows for a very efficient and fast web server, it makes writing applications nearly impossible.

Think of it this way. If you are writing an application using a standard web server, then every request to the server must carry along with it *everything* that you have done related to the application up to this point. Since the web server has no way of storing and retrieving that information, it is up to you to provide it *every time* you make a request of the server. Sounds pretty cumbersome? Well, with the **Session** object, Active Server Pages takes care of that for you. Nevertheless, this is just to whet your appetite. Stay tuned for Chapter 9 when the **Session** object will be explored in detail.

Page Level Objects

As we traverse our way through the object model, we now move from the Session level down to the individual page level. In working at the page level of the application, we need to look at the basic function of a web server.

Basically, a web server operates by receiving a request from a client and then sending a response back to it. This request could be for an HTML page, or it could be the data from a Form submission that the user has made. To make our pages dynamic in ASP, we need to take the information that has been submitted and craft a response to send back to the client. Active Server Pages provides two objects that allow you to interact at the page level. The information that is sent from the client to the server is hidden, or encapsulated, in the **Request** object. The information that the server prepares to send back to client is encapsulated in the **Response** object.

Request Object

When a web browser or other client application asks for a page from a web server, this is called **making a request**. Along with the actual page that the client wants, it can send a great deal of information to the server as well. The **Request** object is responsible for packaging up that information to make it easily accessible to the ASP application.

The client asks the server to provide a page with a `.asp` suffix. When the server sees this request, it interprets this type of page as an Active Server Page. All of the information that the client is sending along with the request is then packaged into the **Request** object. This information is then accessible to the actual ASP script that is used to construct the page. The information is categorized into five sets of information. Since each set of information can include multiple individual pieces of information, the data is stored as a **collection**. In a collection, each piece of information is stored as a name/value pair. We talked about name/value pairs earlier when we introduced object properties.

The collections in the **Request** object will be explained in detail in Chapter 7, but we will quickly introduce them here. The collections hold information about:

> The values that are provided in the URL that are sent by the client. In the URL, the client can include name-value pairs of information after the file name. This information is stored in the collection called **QueryString**.

> If the client is sending a Form request, then the values of the form elements are stored in another collection.

> The web server itself has a great deal of information about the request. These are called the **HTTP Server Variables**. This information is made available as a collection as well.

> If the client is sending any cookies along with the request, these are included in their own collection.

> In addition, if the client is sending any security certificates to the server, then these are included in their own collection.

By using the information that is included with the request, along with the script code in the Active Server Pages script file, the server can dynamically generate a page for the client to display. In order for the client to display the information, the server needs a mechanism to relay the data back to the client. This is the job of the **Response** object.

Response Object

The primary feature of Active Server Pages is the ability to dynamically create web pages. The basic task needed to execute this feature is the ability to tell the client what information to display. There are a number of different ways to shape what the client will be displayed. To provide an efficient interface to control the output to the client, the **Response** object exists.

The **Response** object provides the ASP script with a set of interfaces that allow the script to control what information is being sent back to the client. The details of the **Response** object will be covered in Chapter 8. For now, we will just touch on some of functions that the **Response** object provides.

With the **Response** object, the ASP script can:

> Insert information into the page being sent back to the client.

> Send cookies back to the client.

> Send the client to another page via a redirection.

> Control whether the page is sent as it is created, or whether it is completely built and then sent at one time.

> Control the various properties of the page, such as the HTML headers or the type of content.

These interfaces give the designer of the script the ultimate flexibility to decide how the information is presented back to the client.

ObjectContext Object

The `ObjectContext` object is used in conjunction with Microsoft Transaction Server (MTS). This advanced tool is part of IIS 4.0. It allows you to develop scalable applications out of components. This object allows you to access the MTS system from within an ASP page, and it is well beyond the scope of this book. For a detailed look at this object, as well as how to build applications using Microsoft Transaction Server, check out 'Professional Active Server Pages 2.0' (ISBN 1-861001-26-6) from Wrox Press.

Next, we will look at how to use the object model as a road map to developing an ASP application.

Using the Object Model as a Road Map

While being able to create a page dynamically is a nice feature, the real power of Active Server Pages comes from its ability to create web-based applications. These applications allow the user to perform tasks that are beyond simply requesting pages. The logic and structure to create these applications are laid out in the object model.

We can use the object model as a road map that lays out:

> Where information should be stored in our applications

> How information specific to a single user can be tracked

> How to set up client pages to send the appropriate information to the server for it to dynamically build a page

> How to dynamically build a page, using all of the features that ASP provides, and then send that page back to the client

In the next few chapters, we will be walking through this landscape in detail and building up the expertise needed to put together an application using Active Server Pages.

Summary

In this chapter, we have introduced the concept of objects. For our purposes, an object is a programmatic concept that enables us to access a physical item, or a set of associated data. An object is described by its interfaces. These interfaces are broken into three categories:

▶ Properties are pieces of data that describes an attribute of the object

▶ Methods are used to have the object perform some task for us

▶ Events let the object notify us that something has happened

In learning how to develop with objects, we have seen how to:

▶ Set and retrieve information from the object's properties

▶ Call the methods of an object

▶ Write an event handler to deal with an event that an object may fire

With the concepts of objects well in hand, we introduced the Active Server Pages object model. These five objects encapsulate the functionality offered by the ASP server.

▶ The **Server** object provides basic functionality across the web server.

▶ The **Application** and **Session** objects provide the application functionality that is not present in a basic web server.

▶ The **Request** and **Response** objects are used to interpret the information sent by the client and then construct the HTML page that will be sent back in response.

By understanding the relationships of these objects to one another, we can start to build true applications by using the power of Active Server Pages. The next few chapters will begin to show us how.

The Request Object

We'll now delve into the Active Server Pages object model, and examine each of the objects in turn. This chapter will consider the **Request** object, which handles communications from the browser to the server. This is one of the central objects in the Active Server Pages object model, and is vital for controlling how the user sends information to the server—via forms, for example. Using the **Request** object, the server can obtain information about what the user wants: this information can then be manipulated within ASP.

In the next chapter we'll begin to consider how to return information to the client from the server, via the **Request** object's *alter ego*, the **Response** object. After that, we'll be able to look at how to go about sending and retrieving more complex data. However, the **Request** object comes first, and so in this chapter we'll look in detail at:

▶ What the **Request** object does

▶ The **QueryString** collection

▶ The **Form** collection

▶ The **ServerVariables** collection

▶ The **ClientCertificate** collection

▶ The **Cookies** collection

▶ **Request** object properties and methods

First, then, what is the **Request** object, and what does it do?

The Request Object

When a web browser or other client application asks for a page from a web server, we say that the client is making a **request**. In order to make a request from the server, the client must supply the specific page using an address (usually a URL); in addition, the client can send a whole host of other information to the server. The **Request** object is responsible for packaging all this information, and making it easily accessible to the ASP application.

When the client asks the server to provide a page with a `.asp` suffix, this suffix tells the server to access an Active Server Page. All of the information that the client sends along with the request is then packaged into the `Request` object. This information is then accessible to the ASP script that is used to dynamically construct the page that the user has requested.

The information supplied by the client is categorized, in the ASP model, into groups of items called **collections**. In a collection, each piece of information is stored as a **name/value pair**. We talked about name/value pairs in the previous chapter, when we introduced object properties. In ASP, a collection is simply a set of these name/value pairs, specific to this `Request` object. More particularly, a collection lists added items and their properties, each of which has a unique value that describes the property.

Request Object Collections

The `Request` object has five collections. We'll explain these in detail later in this chapter, but we will quickly introduce them here:

- ▶ `QueryString`: When sending the request the client can include name/value pairs of information within the URL, after the file name. This collection stores any values that are provided in the URL.

- ▶ `Form`: If the client sends a Form request, then the values of the form elements are stored in this collection.

- ▶ `ServerVariables`: The web server itself has a great deal of information about the request, contained in **HTTP server variables**. This information is made available as a collection.

- ▶ `Cookies`: If the client is sending any cookies along with the request, then they are included in this collection.

- ▶ `ClientCertificate`: If the client sends any security certificates to the server, then they are stored in this collection.

By using the information included with the request, along with the scripting logic in the ASP script file, the server can dynamically generate a page for the client to display. In order for the client to display the information, the server needs a mechanism to relay the data back to the client. This is the job of the `Response` object, which is the subject of the next chapter. Let's now take a look at each of the collections in the `Request` object.

The QueryString Collection

A **querystring** is extra query information that is passed to the server in the form of a name/value pair. A querystring could contain the client's username, or an e-mail address, or personal information. A querystring is appended to a URL with a question mark, '?'. A typical querystring might look like this:

```
?name=DaddyKool
```

A querystring's name/value pair is composed of two strings—the name and the value. These two strings are separated by an equal sign, '='. If the request generates more than one querystring name/value pair, then subsequent name/value pairs are separated from each other by an ampersand, '&':

```
?name=DaddyKool&email=DaddyKool@kool.com
```

When this information is appended to a URL, it looks something like this:

```
http://chrisu/BegASP/demo.asp?name=DaddyKool&email=DaddyKool@kool.com
```

The `QueryString` collection retrieves the values of the variables that are given in the HTTP query string. The `QueryString` collection returns exactly the same information as the `Query_String` variable in the same format. So, `<%=request.querystring%>` returns:

```
name=DaddyKool&email=DaddyKool@kool.com
```

and `<%=request.servervariables("QUERY_STRING")%>` also returns:

```
name=DaddyKool&email=DaddyKool@kool.com
```

How are Querystrings Generated?

There are three situations in which a querystring can be generated. The first is by clicking on an anchor tag, `<A>`, which already has an in-built querystring:

```
<A HREF="somepage.ext?name=value">a querystring example</A>
```

This anchor tag, when clicked, generates a querystring variable named `"name"`, with the value `"value"`.

The second situation is when a form is sent to the server by the `GET` method. Take a look at the following code:

```
<FORM NAME=logging ACTION="RequestQuery.asp" METHOD ="GET">
Type your first name:   <INPUT TYPE="TEXT" NAME="FIRST"> <BR>
Type your last name:   <INPUT TYPE="TEXT" NAME="LAST"> <BR>
<INPUT TYPE="SUBMIT" VALUE="Login">
```

When the browser displays an ASP page containing this code, it might look something like this:

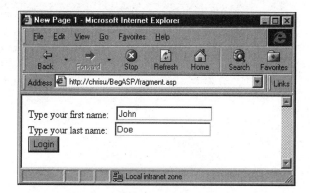

When the user enters his username and password, and clicks on the Login button, two querystring name/value pairs are generated. They correspond to the names of the form's input textboxes and their respective values. Hence, the URL requested by these actions might look like this:

```
http://chrisu/begASP/RequestQuery.asp?first=john&last=doe
```

It's important to note that the POST form method won't allow you to retrieve querystring name/value pairs. We'll look into the POST form method shortly.

The main difference between POST and GET is that POST sends the information as part of the HTTP headers, while GET sends information by appending it to the Uniform Resource Locator, commonly abbreviated as URL. There's another important difference: when sending by URL, the length of the URL should be less (although doesn't have to be) than 255 characters, because some older client or proxy implementations may not properly support these lengths.

The final method is, very simply, via a user-typed HTTP address:

When the *Enter* key is pressed, two name/value pairs are generated, namely `first=john` and `last=doe`.

Retrieving a QueryString

You can retrieve a querystring from the server in several different ways. In its simplest form, you could retrieve it with just the following statement:

```
<%=Request.QueryString%>
```

This will return *all* of the querystring name/value pairs. Thus, if the name/value pair was equal to `name=DaddyKool  pass=ChangeMe` then this command would return `"name=DaddyKool&pass=ChangeMe"`. In fact, it's more common to use the following:

```
<%=Request.QueryString("property_name")%>
```

This will return a specific name/value pair, as specified by *property_name*, provided it holds a single value. The pair is returned in the form `"property_name=property_value"`. Thus, you can retrieve information for the string variable name using the following code:

```
<%=Request.QueryString("name")%>
```

In the example above, the result `"DaddyKool"` is returned.

The Keyword Count

If another value is subsequently assigned to **name**, then (unlike variables) the original value persists, and the second value is appended to the name/value pair. For example, by assigning the value **"Junior"** to the name property, the name/value pair would be extended to **"name=DaddyKool,Junior"**. If more than one value exists for the same name, the values are returned separated by commas, thus: **"name=x,y,z"**.

In such a situation, you might need more than just a name/value pair to keep track of your data. Help is at hand in the form of the keyword **Count**, which is used to track the number of querystring name/value pairs. Let's see an example of this:

```
<%= Request.QueryString("name").Count %>
```

This line of code will return the number of querystring name/value pairs that have the name **"name"**. So if the name/value pair was **name=DaddyKool**, then this code would return the value 1. If the name/value pair was **name=DaddyKool,Junior** then the code would return 2; and so on.

How can we use this to get hold of one specific value from a set of values? The answer is to use an **index**. An index enables you to retrieve one of a number of values for a given property name. The value of an index can be any integer that lies in the range 1 to **Request.QueryString("*property_name*").Count**.

To use an index for the property **name** would require code with the following format:

```
<%=Request.QueryString("name")(index_val)%>
```

Of course, *index_val* is an integer value between 1 and the value held in **Count**. If the value of *index_val* doesn't correspond to a valid index value (that is, *index_val* doesn't fall between 1 and **Count**), then ASP returns an error similar to the following:

Request object error 'ASP 0105 : 80004005'
Index out of range
/directory/somefile.asp, line xxx
An array index is out of range

The good news is that we can account for the possibility of an invalid index value within the code, and hence prevent such an error from occurring:

```
<%
if not isempty (Request.QueryString("name")) then
%>
name=  <%=Request.QueryString("name")(1)%>
<% else %>
<% end if %>
```

This code translates to the following:

If there is *any* value in the querystring, then take the first element of the querystring and display it. Otherwise, do nothing.

By using this, we can guarantee that our code won't break, since if the querystring is empty we fill it with the first value in our index.

Let's now build a complete example using all of the concepts we have looked at so far.

Try it Out – Using Request.QueryString

In this example, we'll request three items of information from the user: first name, last name and password. We'll then place these values in a querystring and display the values, along with some complementary information, on the web page.

1 Open your HTML editor, create a new file, and type in the following:

```
<HTML>
<HEAD>
<TITLE>Request QueryString</TITLE>
</HEAD>

<BODY BGCOLOR="white">
<P>

<FORM NAME=QueryString ACTION="RequestQuery.asp" METHOD="GET">
Type your first name:  <INPUT TYPE="TEXT" NAME="name">
<BR>
Type your last name:  <INPUT TYPE="TEXT" NAME="name">
<BR>
Type your password:  <INPUT TYPE="TEXT" NAME="pass">
<BR>
<INPUT TYPE="SUBMIT" VALUE="Login">
</FORM>

<BR>
<HR>
<P>
The information received from the QueryString object was:
<P>
Name =  <%=Request.QueryString("name")%>
<BR>
Password =  <%=Request.QueryString("pass")%>
<BR>
The 'name' property's count is: <%=
Request.QueryString("name").Count %>
<BR>

<%
if not isempty (Request.QueryString("name")) then
%>
```

```
First name =  <%=Request.QueryString("name")(1)%>
<BR>
Last name =  <%=Request.QueryString("name")(2)%>
<BR>
<% end if %>


<P>
<%=Request.QueryString%>
<BR>
<%=Request.ServerVariables("QUERY_STRING")%>
<BR>
</BODY>
</HTML>
```

2 Save the file as **RequestQuery.asp** in your **BegASP** directory.

3 Start your browser and open the file **RequestQuery.asp**. The resulting HTML output for this script is:

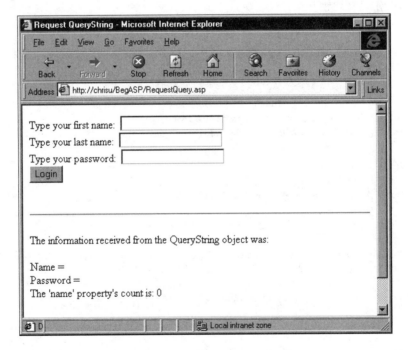

As you can see, the querystring variables are empty, the script error was avoided, and the value of **Count** for the property **"name"** is zero.

4 Now fill in your first name, your last name, and some alphanumeric password in the appropriate boxes and click the Login button. The result is:

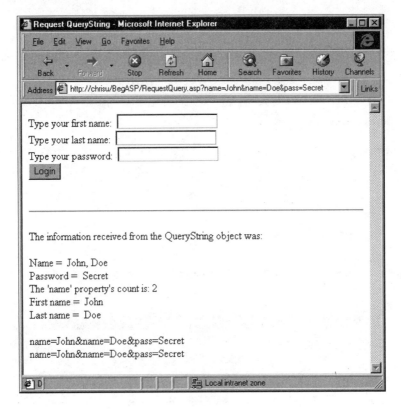

The full URL is `http://my_server_name/BegASP`
`RequestQuery.asp?name=John&name=Doe&pass=secret`

How It Works

We'll take a look at how the ASP code works, and what is contained in the querystring. We ask the server for the contents of the property **name**:

```
Name =  <%=Request.QueryString("name")%>
```

In this example above, the values **"John"**, **"Doe"** are held—this will be different if you entered different names. We then ask the server for the contents of the variable **pass**:

```
Password =  <%=Request.QueryString("pass")%>
```

This holds the value **"secret"**. We then query the property **name** for the number of values it holds:

```
The "Name" property's count is: <%=
Request.QueryString("name").Count %>
```

The property name stores two names, so the value of **Request.QueryString("name").Count** is 2. Next, use an index to query the **name** property: these queries allow us access to each of the values within **name**, separately. The first element is accessed by the line:

```
Name =  <%= Request.QueryString("name")(1)%>
```

Here, `Request.QueryString("name")(1)` holds the value `"John"`. The second value us accessed using:

```
Last name =  <%=Request.QueryString("name")(2)%>
```

where `Request.QueryString("name")(2)` holds the value `"Doe"`. Finally we access the whole value contained within the querystring:

```
<%=Request.QueryString%>
```

This holds the complete querystring collection, which is shown on the resulting output: `"Name=John&Name=Doe&Pass=secret"`. The final line of the script does exactly the same thing:

```
<%=Request.ServerVariables("QUERY_STRING")%>
```

Hence, this holds the exact same value as `Request.QueryString`, the complete querystring collection: `"Name=John&name=Doe&Pass=secret"`.

Amending Our Program

We can amend the script above, so that it displays a list of all the name/value pairs in the querystring collection. To do this, you can use a 'shorthand' code that involves the `For Each...Next` VBScript statement. Add the following highlighted lines to the end of the above code:

```
<P>
<%=Request.QueryString%>
<BR>
<%=Request.ServerVariables("QUERY_STRING")%>
<BR>
<% For Each key in Request.QueryString %>
The name "<%= key %>" has the value "<%= Request.QueryString(key) %>".
<BR>
<% Next %>
</BODY>
</HTML>
```

The `For Each...Next` statement repeats a group of statements for each element in an array or collection.

With this additional code, the browser displays the following lines at the end of the page:

The name "Name" has the value "John, Doe".
The name "Pass" has the value "secret".

Now that we've covered every facet of the `QueryString` collection, we'll move on to a related collection, `Form`.

The Form Collection

The **Form** collection holds the values of form elements sent to the HTTP request body via the POST method. In other words, when you fill in the text boxes on a form and press the Submit button, all of the values you have typed in can be stored in the **Form** collection. Again, this collection can be used together with the keyword **Count**, which enables the calculation of the number of values in a given name/value pair; also, the **Form** collection can use an index to access the individual values within a set of multiple values.

Items in the **Form** collection are also, like the **QueryString** collection, composed of name/value pairs. To construct items in a **Form** collection we follow a similar procedure to that used when creating items in the **QueryString** collection—that is, with two strings separated by an equal sign, "**=**". The first string is the form element's name, and the second string is the element's value. Again, multiple form name/value pairs in the form collection are separated by an ampersand, "**&**".

The main difference between a **QueryString** collection and a **Form** collection is that while the **QueryString** collection gets appended to a URL (with a question mark), the **Form** collection is sent as part of the HTTP request body. Note, also, that there's only one way to generate a form collection—by POSTing a form.

The best way to understand the **Form** collection is to dive in and take a look at another example.

Try It Out – Using Request.Form

In this example we're going to do exactly the same thing as we did in the **QueryString** example—except that we'll be storing our values in the form collection.

1   Open your HTML editor, create a new file, and type in the following:

```
<HTML>
<HEAD>
<TITLE>Request Form</TITLE>
</HEAD>

<BODY BGCOLOR="white">
<P>

<FORM NAME=RequestForm ACTION="RequestForm.asp" METHOD="POST">
Type your first name:  <INPUT TYPE="TEXT" NAME="Name">
<BR>
Type your last name:  <INPUT TYPE="TEXT" NAME="Name">
<BR>
Type your password:  <INPUT TYPE="TEXT" NAME="Pass">
<BR>
<INPUT TYPE="SUBMIT" VALUE="Login">
</FORM>
```

```
<BR>
<HR>
<P>
The information received from the Form object was:
<P>
Name =  <%=Request.Form("name")%>
<BR>
Password =  <%=Request.Form("pass")%>
<BR>
The 'name' property's count is :  <%= Request.Form("name").Count %>
<BR>

<%
if not isempty (Request.Form("name")) then
%>

First name =  <%=request.Form("name")(1)%>
<BR>
Last name =  <%=request.Form("name")(2)%>
<BR>
<% end if %>

<P>
<%=Request.Form%>
</P>

</BODY>
</HTML>
```

2   Save the file as **RequestForm.asp** in your **BegASP** directory.

3   Start your browser and type in the following URL into the address line:
http://*my_server_name***/BegASP/requestform.asp**

The HTML output of
that script is:

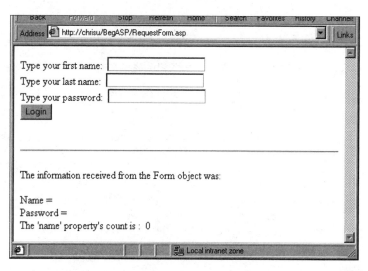

4 As in the first example, fill in your first name, last name, and some combination of alphanumeric characters into the appropriate boxes, then click the Login button. The result is:

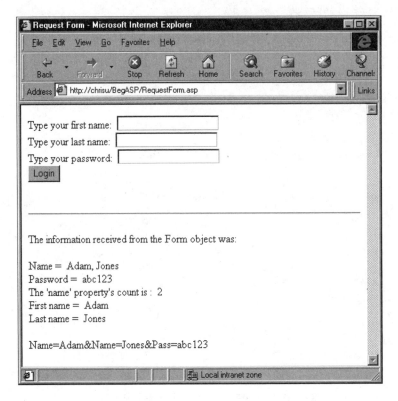

How It Works

The program looks the same, and it runs in the same way; it even returns the same answers. So what's different? The answer is, very little. All we've done is changed every occurrence of `Request.QueryString` to read `Request.Form`:

```
<P>
Name =  <%=Request.Form("Name")%>
<BR>
Password =  <%=Request.Form("Pass")%>
<BR>
The 'name' property's count is :  <%= Request.Form("Name").Count %>
<BR>
```

The only noticeable difference in the whole program is that the information is no longer passed to the server as part of the URL.

Amending The Program

Again, we can display a simple list of all the name/value pairs in the form collection, by using the `For Each...Next` VBScript statement as 'shorthand' code. Try adding these lines at the end of the script above, just before the HTML end `<\BODY>` tag:

```
<% for each key in Request.Form %>
The name "<%= key %>" has the value "<%= Request.Form(key) %>".
<BR>
<% next %>
```

As expected (just like in the querystring example), that code displays:

The Name "name" has the value "Adam, Jones".
The Name "pass" has the value "abc123".

Checkboxes

You can also add **checkboxes** to a form—these require special attention. Checkboxes are special because they don't actually store the information, but they denote one of two values, such as on/off, true/false or yes/no. Let's take a look at our example again and see how it can be altered to include a checkbox and how the values can be stored in the **Form** collection.

Try It Out – Adding a Checkbox to your Form

1 Go back to **RequestForm.asp** and add the following code, just above the code for the Login button:

```
Type your password:  <INPUT TYPE="TEXT" NAME="pass">
<BR>
Do you want to receive further information from us?  
<INPUT TYPE="CHECKBOX" NAME="chkspam">
<BR>
<INPUT TYPE="SUBMIT" VALUE="Login">
```

Notice that the new **<INPUT>** HTML tag doesn't include a default **VALUE**.

2 Save the amendment; return to your browser and refresh the web page:

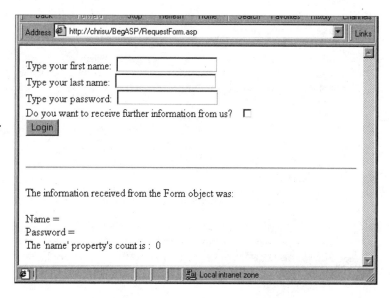

How It Works

If you *don't* check the box before clicking the Login button, then:

- `chkspam` (and its value) will not be returned by the `For Each` statement
- `chkspam` will be returned, with a blank value, if requested by element name
- The `chkspam` *count* will be returned

Alternatively, if you *do* check the box before clicking the Login button, then:

- `chkspam` (and its value) *will* be returned by the `For Each` statement
- `chkspam` will be returned, **with a default value of** `"on"`, if requested by element name
- The `chkspam` *count* will be returned

Additionally, you can include a default value for `chkspam`, by writing the `<INPUT>` tag as follows:

```
<INPUT TYPE="CHECKBOX" NAME="chkspam" VALUE="whatever">
```

In this case, `chkspam` will be returned—although only if checked and with the specific value written in—if requested by the element name.

Multiple Checkboxes

If you wish to use more than one check box, and you want to obtain separate values, then you need to make sure the checkboxes have distinct names:

```
Do you want to receive further information about?
 Games<INPUT TYPE="CHECKBOX" NAME="chkspam1" VALUE="Games">
 Money<INPUT TYPE="CHECKBOX" NAME="chkspam2" VALUE="Money">
```

If you don't need separate values, and can manage with comma-delimited returned values, you can use the same name:

```
Do you want to receive further information about?
 Games<INPUT TYPE="CHECKBOX" NAME="chkspam1" VALUE="Games">
 Money<INPUT TYPE="CHECKBOX" NAME="chkspam1" VALUE="Money">
```

The difference between these two methods is that if you use the same `NAME` for the checkboxes, "`Games,Money`" will be returned (the values are separated by a comma). If you use different names, each value will be returned individually: "`Games`" and "`Money`".

Radio Buttons

You can also use radio buttons to send information via `Request.Form`:

```
Do you want to receive further information from us?
 Yes<INPUT TYPE="RADIO" NAME="grpspam" VALUE="Yes">
 No<INPUT TYPE="RADIO" NAME="grpspam" VALUE="No">
 Maybe<INPUT TYPE="RADIO" NAME="grpspam" VALUE="Maybe">
```

This returns the selected value. Note that the radio group's **Name** property must be the same for each radio button in the group. When using multiple radio buttons, you need to ensure that each one has a distinct Radio Button Group **Name**.

The ServerVariables Collection

The **ServerVariables** collection holds all of the **HTTP headers** and also additional items of information about the server. HTTP headers are sent (either by the browser or by the server) along with a request for a web page, and contain extra information, usually about the contents of the request. These headers contain a wide array of information, from the type of browser being used to the name of the page that referred the user to your own page. Some of these headers originate at the client, some originate at the server. Every time an ASP application is executed the web server creates a set of headers and server variables to accompany that application. These server variables can be interrogated and manipulated using ASP.

It's probably best to start with a list of all the **ServerVariables** available, but rather than list them all in the book, you'll learn more by physically retrieving the contents of the **ServerVariables** collection in an example.

Try It Out – Retrieving the Request.ServerVariables Collection

In this example we'll list all of the variables contained in the **ServerVariables** collection in a two column table. The left-hand column lists the variables' names and the right-hand column their values.

1 Open your HTML editor, create a new file, and key in the following:

```
<HTML>
<HEAD>
<TITLE>The HTTP Server Variables Collection</TITLE>
</HEAD>

<BODY BGCOLOR=white>
<CENTER>
<H2>The HTTP Server Variables Collection</H2>
</CENTER>

<TABLE BORDER=1>
<TR><TD><B>Variable Name</B></TD> <TD><B>Value</B></TD></TR>
<% for each key in Request.ServerVariables %>
<TR>
<TD><% = key %></TD>
<TD>
<%if Request.ServerVariables(key) = "" then
      Response.Write " "
else
      Response.Write Request.ServerVariables(key)
end if
```

```
Response.Write "</TD>"%>
</TR>
<% next %>
</TABLE>
</BODY>
</HTML>
```

2 Save the file as **servvars.asp** in your **BegASP** directory.

3 Start your browser and open the file: **http://*my_server_name*/BegASP/servvars.asp**

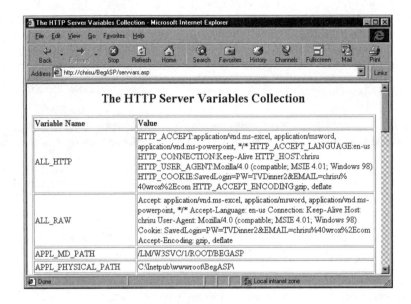

How It Works

The **ServerVariables** collection holds all HTTP header variables, plus the **QUERY_STRING** variables. For the querystring values to show, a form must be submitted, and the form's method must be "GET".

To retrieve individual variables in the collection, the syntax is:

```
<%=Request.ServerVariables("variablename") %>
```

In our example, to retrieve every **ServerVariable** within the collection, we use a **For Each...Next** loop to iterate through each of the items in the collection. However, instead of the normal use of a loop (which increments the loop variable at each iteration of the loop), we use the following line:

```
<% For Each key in Request.ServerVariables %>
```

In this case, the variable **key** is used to store each different ServerVariable name in the collection—so for the first iteration, the value in **key** is **ALL_HTTP**, in the second iteration it's **ALL_RAW**, and so on. For each unique value of **key** this loop will execute the following lines:

```
<%if Request.ServerVariables(key) = "" then
      Response.Write " "
else
      Response.Write Request.ServerVariables(key)
end if
Response.Write "</TD>"%>
```

If the variable **key** is empty then this displays a space; otherwise it displays the value stored within the ServerVariable contained by **key**.

What do ServerVariables do?

Some **ServerVariables** are merely informative. **SERVER_SOFTWARE**, for example, tells you the name of the Server's software. For IIS 4.0 or PWS 4.0, it returns "Microsoft-IIS/4.0". Other informative **ServerVariables** are **SERVER_PROTOCOL** and **GATEWAY_INTERFACE**.

On the other hand, some variables in the **ServerVariables** collection are very useful. One of the most useful is **HTTP_USER_AGENT**. By retrieving the **HTTP_USER_AGENT**, you can determine which browser is viewing your pages, allowing you to **customize** the page's content to take advantage of specific browser features, or to prevent scripting errors if a browser supports a different scripting engine from the one you usually script for.

If you've already read past this part of the book, you might ask, "Doesn't the ASP BrowserType do this for me already?" The answer is yes, provided that your **browscap.ini** has an entry for the browser viewing the page.

> *browscap.ini is a file found in C:\Windows\InetServ. It provides a list of all the different browser types available, along with their capabilities, such as do they support frames or JavaScript? With every new browser, this file will need updating. A company called Cyscape, Inc. maintains a list of browscap.ini files, you can find a copy of the most up to date one at http://www.cyscape.com/browscap.*

If there isn't an entry for a particular browser, **BrowserType** returns *unknown* or *default*, which will disregard the true features the browser might have. If **BrowserType** is to return correct information, it needs an up-to-date **browscap.ini** file to access.

On the other hand, parsing **HTTP_USER_AGENT** returns the correct information *no matter which browser is viewing the detecting page*. Our next example shows you can use **HTTP_USER_AGENT** to return information and also illustrates how server-side and client-side scripts interact.

Try It Out – Detecting Browser and OS with Request.ServerVariables

In this example we examine which browser the user is viewing the page with, and display information detailing which browser, which browser version, and which operating system the user is using. It's quite a long example, but it's really very simple, as you will see.

1 Open your HTML editor, create a new file, and type the following:

```
<%
Response.Expires=0
Dim Var
Set Var = Request.ServerVariables

Dim ua, os
ua = Var("HTTP_USER_AGENT")
os = Var("HTTP_UA_OS")

Dim AnyIE, IE5, IE4, IE3, IE302, AnyNetscape, Netscape3, Netscape4
AnyIE = False
IE5 = False
IE4 = False
IE3 = False
IE302 = False
AnyNetscape = False
Netscape4 = False
Netscape3 = False

Dim Win95, Win98, WinNT, Mac, PPC, Mac68K, Unix, Win31_WinNT351
Win95 = False
Win98 = False
WinNT = False
Mac = False
PPC = False
Mac68K = False
Unix = False
Win31_WinNT351 = False

if Instr (ua, "MSIE") then
    AnyIE = True
    if Instr(ua, "MSIE 5.") then
       IE5 = True
    elseif Instr(ua, "MSIE 4.") then
       IE4 = True
    elseif Instr(ua, "MSIE 3.") then
       IE3 = True
       if Instr(ua, "MSIE 3.02") then
          IE302 = True
       end if
    end if
elseif Instr(ua, "Mozilla") and Instr(ua, "compatible") = 0 then
    AnyNetscape = True
    if Instr(ua, "Mozilla/4") then
       Netscape4 = True
    elseif Instr(ua, "Mozilla/3") then
       Netscape3 = True
    end if
end if

if InStr(ua, "Windows 95") or InStr(ua, "Win95") then
    Win95 = True
```

```
   elseif InStr(ua, "Windows 98") or InStr(ua, "Win98") then
      Win98 = True
   elseif InStr(ua, "Windows 3.1") or InStr(os, "Win16") then
      Win31_WinNT351 = True
   elseif InStr(ua, "NT") or InStr(os, "NT") then
      WinNT = True
   elseif InStr(ua, "Mac") then
      Mac = True
      if InStr(ua, "PowerPC") or InStr(ua, "PPC") then
         PPC = True
      elseif InStr(ua, "68000") or InStr(ua, "68K") then
         Mac68K = True
      end if
   elseif InStr(ua, "X11") then
      Unix = true
   end if

%>

<HTML>
<HEAD>
<TITLE>Detecting most browsers and OSs in ASP</TITLE>
</HEAD>

<BODY>

<HR>
<DIV align=center>
<FONT size="3">
<B>Detecting browsers and operating systems<BR>
with interacting server-side VBScript<BR>
and client-side JavaScript.</B></FONT></DIV>
<BR>
<HR>
<BR>
<SCRIPT LANGUAGE="JavaScript">
<!--
{
document.writeln ("You're browsing this page with: ")
<%
if AnyIE then
Response.Write "document.writeln (""Internet Explorer,"");"& VbCrLf
%>
<%
elseif AnyNetscape then
Response.Write "document.writeln (""Netscape,"");"& VbCrLf
%>
<%
else
Response.Write "document.writeln (""Browser Not detected,"");"& VbCrLf
%>
<%end if%>
```

219

```
<%
if IE5 then
Response.Write "document.writeln ("""Version 5.x, running on "");"& VbCrLf
%>
<%
elseif IE4 Or Netscape4 then
Response.Write "document.writeln ("""Version 4.x, running on "");"& VbCrLf
%>
<%
elseif IE3 Or Netscape3 then
Response.Write "document.writeln ("""Version 3.x, running on "");"& VbCrLf
%>
<%
else
Response.Write "document.writeln ("""Version not detected, running on:
"");"& VbCrLf
%>
<%end if%>


<%
if Win95 then
Response.Write "document.writeln ("""Windows 95."");"
%>
<%
elseif Win98 then%>
Response.Write "document.writeln ("""Windows 98."");"
%>
<%
elseif Win31_WinNT351 then
Response.Write "document.writeln ("""Windows 3.1 or Windows 3.51."");"
%>
<%
elseif WinNT then
Response.Write "document.writeln ("""Windows NT."");"
%>
<%
elseif Mac then
Response.Write "document.writeln ("""Macintosh."");"
%>
<%
elseif Unix then
Response.Write "document.writeln ("""Unix."");"
%>
<%
else
Response.Write "document.writeln ("""OS not detected."");"
%>
<%end if%>
}
// -->
</SCRIPT>
</BODY>
</HTML>
```

2 Save the file as **browser-os.asp** in your **BegASP** directory.

3 Start your browser and open the file

```
http://my_server_name/BegASP/browser-os.asp
```

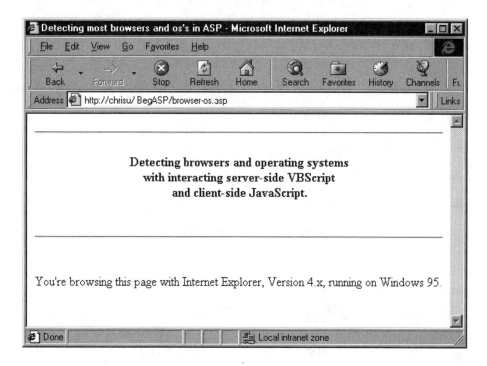

How It Works

The code of this program falls roughly into three parts. The first part declares and initializes the variables that we will need to identify the browser, browser version and OS. The second part attempts to identify these properties, and consequently sets the values of our variables according to what it finds. The third part outputs the findings to the web page. Let's look more closely at the code.

The first line ensures that the page is not cached:

```
Response.Expires=0
```

Since **Request.ServerVariables** is an ASP object which can hold many properties, we have to **set** its variable's value, so we can refer to its properties via the variable's name.

```
Dim Var
Set Var = Request.ServerVariables
```

We then declare and initialize two variables, the UserAgent and OS value requests:

```
Dim ua, os
ua  = Var("HTTP_USER_AGENT")
os  = Var("HTTP_UA_OS")
```

As a result of these lines, the variables **ua** and **os** will contain strings, which describe the user agent, and the OS that the user is employing to view the page. We'll get information from these in a moment, and use it to write these details onto the web page.

We declare a number of variables, which describe various browser types:

```
Dim AnyIE, IE5, IE4, IE3, IE302, AnyNetscape, Netscape4, Netscape3
```

To begin with, we'll set each of these to **False**:

```
AnyIE = False
...
Netscape3 = False
```

We also declare a second set of variables, that describe various OS types:

```
Dim Win95, Win98, WinNT, Mac, PPC, Mac68K, Unix, Win31_WinNT351
```

We'll also set these to false, to begin with, and we'll use them later in the program:

```
Win95 = False
...
Win31_WinNT351 = False
```

With all of our variables declared and initialized, that's the end of the first part of the code.

In the second part, we compare the values of ua and os with recognized strings, in order to identify the browser and OS being used by the client. The code to establish these pieces of information comes in the form of a couple of **If...End If** blocks. The first of these blocks attempts to find out which browser is being used:

```
If Instr (ua, "MSIE") then
    AnyIE = True
    if Instr(ua, "MSIE 5.") then
        IE5 = True
    elseif Instr(ua, "MSIE 4.") then
        IE4 = True
    elseif Instr(ua, "MSIE 3.") then
        IE3 = True
        if Instr(ua, "MSIE 3.02") then
            IE302 = True
        end if
    end if
Elseif Instr(ua, "Mozilla") and Instr(ua, "compatible") = 0 then
    AnyNetscape = True
```

```
      if Instr(ua, "Mozilla/4") then
         Netscape4 = True
      elseif Instr(ua, "Mozilla/3") then
         Netscape3 = True
      end if
   End if
```

In the code above, the function `InStr()` is used first to search for the substring `"MSIE"` in the contents of the variable `ua`. If the substring is found, then we conclude that the browser is a Microsoft Internet Explorer (IE) browser: the variable `AnyIE` (which was initialized to `False`) is set to `True`, and the code continues to try and establish which version of IE is being used (identifed by `"MSIE5."`, `"MSIE4."`, `"MSIE3."` or `"MSIE3.02"`)—if the browser version is identified then the appropriate variable is set to `True`.

If the substring `"MSIE"` is not found, then we conclude that the client-side browser is not a Microsoft IE browser. Execution jumps to the `elseif` line (about two-thirds through the block above), where the code uses the search substring `"Mozilla"` to find out whether the user is using a Netscape compatible browser. The code uses the function `Instr()`, in exactly the same way as we've just described. If this search is positive, then `AnyNetscape` is set to `True`, and the search goes on to find the browser version (identified by the string `"Mozilla/4"` or `"Mozilla/3"`).

If the browser is neither a Microsoft IE or Netscape browser, then the user agent variables shall all remain set to `False`.

In the second `If...Else` block, a very similar tactic is used to determine which operating system is being used:

```
If InStr(ua, "Windows 95") Or InStr(ua, "Win95") Then
   Win95 = True
ElseIf InStr(ua, "Windows 98") Or InStr(ua, "Win98") Then
   Win98 = True
ElseIf InStr(ua, "X11") Then
   Unix = true
End If
```

And that's about it for the second part of the code. Let's move on to the third part, where the fruits of all this work are brought to bear.

The client-side script begins with the `<SCRIPT>` tag:

```
<SCRIPT LANGUAGE="JavaScript">
<!—
{
```

This script is written by combining pre-written script and server side variables into a complete client side script. The script first writes an initial, non-changing, HTML string to the document:

```
document.writeln ("You're browsing this page with: ")
```

The remainder of the client-side script consists of three `If...Else/End If` blocks, that will complete the output by displaying the appropriate browser and OS details that we established in the earlier parts of the code.

Let's have a look at the first of these blocks:

```
<%
If AnyIE Then
Response.Write "document.writeln (""Internet Explorer,"");"& VbCrLf
%>
<%
elseif AnyNetscape then
Response.Write "document.writeln (""Netscape,"");"& VbCrLf
%>
<%
Else
Response.Write "document.writeln (""Browser Not detected,"");"& VbCrLf
%>
<%End If%>
```

Understanding the `If...Elseif...End If` logic is easy. If the variable `AnyIE` is `True`, then this means that the browser is a Microsoft IE browser—we worked this out in the second part of the code. In this case, the first `Response.Write` command is executed.

If `AnyIE` is `False`, then we move on. If `AnyNetscape` is `True`, then the client-side browser is a Netscape browser, so the second `Response.Write` statement is executed. Otherwise, the browser is not identified, and the third `Response.Write` statement is executed. Remember that the ASP script (server-side) runs first, which means that it can create the client-side script.

Now, let's look closely at the output statements and see what's happening. As we mentioned, of `AnyIE` is `True` then the following line of ASP script is executed:

```
Response.Write "document.writeln (""Internet Explorer,"");"& VbCrLf
```

The syntax used for writing a client-side script based on server-side variables is tricky, so let's analyze this line a step at a time:

- `Response.Write " ... "`—This results in the contents of the inverted commas being written to the client by the `Response` object. We'll see more of the `Response` object in the next chapter.

- `document.writeln (""Internet Explorer,"");`—JavaScript requires that the `document.writeln` command's string parameter be enclosed in parentheses, and that the string be enclosed in double quotes between the parentheses. To get one double quote written **inside** a JavaScript script, you must use two double quotes. The JavaScript command is terminated with the semicolon.

- `&VbCrLf`—This inserts a carriage-return/line-feed combo, so that JavaScript syntax is adhered to.

The other two **If...Elseif...End If** blocks use much the same logic. The second block outputs the browser version, and the third block outputs information on the OS, based on the information that was established in the second part of the script. If we failed to identify either the browser version or the OS, then the output reflects this.

The JavaScript that results from this code is composed from server-side variables. You can see this resulting script by viewing the source code after you've displayed the page on your browser. It should look something like this (where *browser*, *number* and *operating_system* will be substituted by their actual values):

```
<SCRIPT LANGUAGE="JavaScript">
<!—
{
document.writeln ("You're browsing this page with: ")
document.writeln ("browser,");
document.writeln ("Version number, running on ");
document.writeln ("operating_system.");
}
// —>

</SCRIPT>
```

So in this example, we have learned not only how to detect client browsers using the **HTTP_USER_AGENT** variable, but also how to build a client-side script based on server-side variables.

The Cookies Collection

Before we discuss the type of information stored in this collection, we need to be clear what a **cookie** is, and why they are needed. Cookies were designed to overcome a specific problem, which is that web pages are based on an **anonymous protocol** system. This means that when a browser looks at a web page, it's impossible for the web site to determine whether that visitor has been there before, which parts of the site they might be interested in, and so on. A web site might have had a thousand visitors, but for all the web site coordinator could know, every visit might have been made by the same visitor! Cookies were introduced as a method of identifying and marking each different visitor to a web site.

Cookies are text files that reside on the user's computer. They store information about the user, and are used by a particular server *that the user has visited previously* to personalize web pages, determine where a user has been before, and keep users up to date with relevant information. Each web server, when a user accesses it, can *send* a cookie, which the user must *accept* if the server is to utilize the cookie on the user's machine during future visits. If the user doesn't accept the cookie, it can't be used by the server in future.

There are all sorts of cookie myths on the Internet. Mostly they revolve around the notion that a smart programmer can get unauthorized information from a user, violating the user's "right to privacy". Let's set the record straight. A cookie can **only** store information which the user sends **voluntarily** or selects on a page and that can only happen if the "accept cookies" option is turned on by the user. No one can get your e-mail address or your home address if you don't voluntarily send the information by filling and submitting a form.

Individual cookies are limited to 4kb of data. The maximum number of cookies allowed is 300. Once this limit is reached, the oldest cookie will be deleted to make room for the newest one. This means that the maximum disk space which cookies can occupy is 1.2Mb. In practice, though, the actual disk space used by cookies is far less than that, since most cookies are around 100 to 200 bytes in size.

The cookies collection holds information from all the cookies set by any one application: that is, when a client establishes a session with the server, the *values* that the server reads from the cookies on the client's machine are held in the cookies collection. This means that they are available for easy access by the server. We look at these concepts in much more detail in Chapter 9.

Unlike the `Form` and `Querystring` collections, the cookie collection does not have a `Count` property but, like the `Form` collection, it can hold multiple values for the same cookie name. When this happens, the cookie is said to have **keys**, and each key holds a separate value.

FYI The cookie collection is implemented much like the `Dictionary` object, which you'll be meeting soon. For now, just remember that when a cookie has multiple values stored under the same cookie name, the values are stored as a `Dictionary` object. You'll learn how to set cookies with multiple values in the next chapter, where we look at the `Response` **object.**

Applications and servers can **only** read cookies that they themselves have set. If server X writes a cookie, then server Y **cannot** read it. If application `http://Myapp` sets a cookie, then application `http://MyApp2` cannot read the cookies set by `MyApp`, and vice versa. When requested, cookies are read-only. You can set the value for a cookie using the `Response` object, which you will learn about in the next chapter.

The general syntax for retrieving cookies is:

```
Request.Cookies("cookie")[("key")].attribute
```

To determine whether a cookie holds multiple values, we use the `HasKeys` property:

```
<%
if Request.Cookies("theCookie").HasKeys then
...
%>
```

If the cookie `theCookie` has keys, this statement returns `True`, otherwise it returns `False`.

To iterate through the individual values for cookies with keys, use this model script:

```
<% for each cookie in Request.Cookies
if Request.Cookies(Cookie).HasKeys then
for each CookieKey in Request.Cookies.Cookie %>
<%=Cookie %>.<%=CookieKey%>=<%=Request.Cookies(Cookie)(CookieKey) %>
<% next %>
<% else %>
```

```
<%=Cookie %> = <%=Request.Cookies(Cookie)%><BR>
<% end if %>
<% next %>
```

We'll be coming back to cookies in Chapter 9. For the moment, just remember that cookies can be useful for storing information that allows the server and the client to communicate more effectively.

FYI   You will learn how to set and retrieve cookies in Chapter 9, when we discuss the `Application` **object.**

The ClientCertificate Collection

Client Certificates are sent by the browser. They allow a server to identify the user, so that the server can send sensitive information to a certified user via secure transmission methods. A **client certificate** is an encrypted number that is stored in a file on the user's computer. The browser sends the number along with a request for an ASP page.

In order to do that, the **secure sockets layer** (SSL) protocol must be used. The latest version of the SSL protocol is SSL3.0/PCT1. The acronym PCT stands for **Private Communication Technology**.

Using SSL/PCT allows server and client authentication, encryption, and the use of data integrity methods. **Authentication** ensures that the data is being sent from an 'approved' client to the correct server. **Encryption** ensures that the data can only be read by the server it is intended for. **Data Integrity** ensures that the information sent arrives unaltered, exactly as it was sent. When the SSL protocol is used, URLs are prefixed by `https://` (instead of `http://`).

Before you can use the `ClientCertificate` collection, you must configure the Web server so it can request client certificates, otherwise the `ClientCertificate` collection will be empty. MS Certificate Server (CS) will not run on PWS/Win95 or Win98 because Windows95/98 cannot provide a secure environment. CS *will* run on NT and NT Workstation.

> *Once the web server is enabled and configured, only SSL-enabled clients will be able to communicate with the SSL-enabled WWW folders. By default, IIS4.0 and PWS for NT Workstation do not request certificates. You can set up IIS and PWS/NTWKS to request certificates for virtual directories. The process of enabling certificate requests is beyond this book's scope, but for more information, read:*
>
> `http://support.microsoft.com/support/kb/articles/q171/0/84.asp`
>
> `http://support.microsoft.com/support/kb/articles/q172/0/23.asp`
>
> `http://support.microsoft.com/support/kb/articles/q142/8/49.asp`

There are two constants that need to be declared when working with the `ClientCertificate` collection:

```
Const ceCertPresent = 1
Const ceUnrecognizedIssuer = 2
```

As with all **Request** object collections, you can iterate through the **ClientCertificate** collection's values:

```
<%
For Each key in Request.ClientCertificate
   Response.Write( key & ": " & Request.ClientCertificate(key) & "<BR>")
Next
%>
```

To retrieve an individual value, use the following syntax:

```
Request.ClientCertificate( key[SubField] )
```

Here, **key** specifies the name of the certification field to retrieve. A client certificate may have these fields:

Key	Meaning
Certificate	A string containing the binary stream of the entire certificate content in ASN.1 format.
Flags	A set of flags that provide additional client certificate information. **CeCertPresent** - A client certificate is present. **CeUnrecognizedIssuer** - The last certification in this chain is from an unknown issuer.
Issuer	A string that contains a list of subfield values containing information about the issuer of the certificate. If this value is specified without a **SubField**, the **ClientCertificate** collection returns a comma-separated list of subfields. For example, C=US, O=Verisign, etc.
SerialNumber	A string that contains the certification serial number as an ASCII representation of hexadecimal bytes separated by hyphens (-). For example, 04-67-F3-02.
Subject	A string that contains a list of subfield values which contain information about the subject of the certificate. If this value is specified without a **SubField**, the **ClientCertificate** collection returns a comma-separated list of subfields. For example, C=US, W=Wrox, and so on.
ValidFrom	A date specifying when the certificate becomes valid. This date follows VBScript format and varies with international settings. For example, in the U.S., it could be : 6/31/98 11:59:59 PM.
ValidUntil	A date specifying when the certificate expires.

SubField is an optional parameter you can use to a retrieve an individual field in either the **Subject** or **Issuer** keys, or both. This parameter is added to the **Key** parameter as a suffix. For example, IssuerC, SubjectCN, SubjectS, SubjectL, etc.

This table lists some **SubField** values:

Value	Meaning
C	The name of the country of origin.
CN	The common name of the user. (This subfield is only used with the Subject key.)
GN	A given name.
I	A set of initials.
L	A locality.
O	The company or organization name.
OU	The name of the organizational unit.
S	A state or province.
T	The title of the person or organization.

The following script examples display all the fields of a client certificate:

```
Issuing organization : <%=Request.ClientCertificate("IssuerO")%><br>
```

```
Subject Name : <%=Request.ClientCertificate("SubjectCN")%><br>
```

```
Valid from : <%=Request.ClientCertificate("ValidFrom")%><br>
```

```
Valid until : <%=Request.ClientCertificate("ValidUntil")%><br>
```

```
Serial Number : <%=Request.ClientCertificate("SerialNumber")%><br>
```

```
Issuer : <%=Request.ClientCertificate("Issuer")%><br>
```

```
Subject : <%=Request.ClientCertificate("Subject")%><br>
```

```
<%TheCompleteCertificate=Request.ClientCertificate("Certificate")%>

Certificate Raw Data: <%=TheCompleteCertificate %><BR>
Certificate Length: <%=len(TheCompleteCertificate)%><BR>

Certificate Hex Data :
<%for x=1 to 100%>
<%=hex(asc(mid(TheCompleteCertificate,x,1)))%>
  <%next%>
```

Further discussion of this collection is beyond the scope of this book. For further information on the `ClientCertificate` collection, we suggest you consult Professional Active Server Pages 2.0 (ISBN 1-861001-26-6), available from Wrox Press.

Properties and Methods of the Request Object

The **Request** object also has a single property and a single method. We'll look at these very briefly now.

The TotalBytes Property

The **TotalBytes** property holds the total number of bytes the client sent in the **Request** object:

```
This Request's size is : <%=Request.TotalBytes%>  Bytes.
```

The BinaryRead Method

The **BinaryRead** method retrieves data sent to the server from the client as part of a POST request and stores it in a **SafeArray**. A **SafeArray** is an array that contains information about the number of dimensions and the bounds of its dimensions.

Once you have called **BinaryRead**, referring to any variable in the **Request.Form** collection will cause an error. Once you have referred to a variable in the **Request.Form** collection, calling **BinaryWrite** will cause an error:

```
<%
Dim bread, bytecnt
bytecnt = Request.TotalBytes
bread = Request.BinaryRead(bytecnt)
%>
```

Summary

The **Request** object is a conduit for information between the client and the server: it encapsulates the information that the user sends, and packages it for storage and use on the server. In this chapter we've looked at the attributes of the **Request** object in some detail. It contains five **collections** that store information about the user's request. Briefly, they were:

- **QueryString**—this contains the values that are provided in the URL that is sent by the client.

- **Form**—this contains the values sent by the client in a form request.

- **ServerVariables**—this contains information about the request and about the server, stored in the form of ServerVariables. These are created for a specific ASP application when that application is executed

- **Cookies**—this stores details of any cookies sent with the request

- **ClientCertificate**—this stores details of any security certificates included with the request

We also looked at the **TotalBytes** property and the **BinaryRead** method of the **Request** object.

Using the **Request** object is a critical operation, but it really only handles one side of the client/server interaction. What happens when you want to send information back from the server to the client machine? That's the subject of our next chapter, the **Response** object.

The Response Object

In the previous chapter, we saw how to use the **Request** object. The **Request** object allows ASP to deal with all of the information that is sent to it from the client. This information can include form data, querystring data, and even cookies. With access to all of this information, we can now use the scripting power of ASP to create an interesting and useful page for the user. Once that page is created, we need a way to get the page *back* to the user's browser, and to do this, we use the **Response** object. While the **Request** object dealt with everything being sent from the client to the web server, the **Response** object will allow us to deal with everything being sent from the web server to the client.

The topics we'll look at in this chapter are:

▶ Sending information back to the client

▶ Controlling how information is returned

▶ Controlling what the browser does

▶ Additional information that can be sent

▶ An example that uses both the Request and Response objects

We'll begin by considering the **Response** object itself.

The Response Object

As we have briefly mentioned earlier in the book, the **Response** object is used to send the server's output to the client. In this sense, the **Response** object is the counterpart to the **Request** object: the **Request** object gathers information from both the client and the server, and the **Response** object sends, or resends, the information to the client by writing to the outgoing page.

With the **Response** object, the ASP script can:

▶ Send information back to the client

▶ Control *when* to send information back to the client

➡ Tell the browser how long—or until when—to cache the contents of the page

➡ Tell the browser to go fetch another page

➡ Perform other functions with the information that's being sent back to the browser

These features allow you to use ASP scripts to flexibly control how information is presented to the client.

Sending Information back to the Client

The primary function of the **Response** object is to send information to the client. Usually, this is a direct result of the client making a request of the server. It is the responsibility of the server-side script to come up with a response that will be understood by the client. Once this valid response information has been created, the **Response** object can be used to transmit the information.

There are two main ways that your can use the **Response** object to send information back to the client. One way is by using the **Write** method of the **Response** object. The other way is through the use of a shortcut notation.

The Write Method

The **Write** method will be the most-used method of the **Response** object. When the method is called, the **Response** object will take the information that the user has supplied and add it to the HTML output stream.

HTML Output Stream

Let's step back a bit and take a look at what the HTML output stream is. If you go back to our initial definition of what ASP is supposed to do, then you know that its primary job is to create an HTML page that can be displayed by a client. Although an ASP script can do much more than static HTML, whatever we want to put on the client's screen has to be displayed through the creation of an HTML page. ASP dynamically builds HTML pages to be displayed on the client's browser.

When an ASP script begins, it also creates an empty HTML output stream. This stream can be thought of as a holding bin, where the web server builds a dynamic HTML page, and then the stream is sent down to the client. The most common method that ASP scripts use to add information to the output stream is using the **Response** object to set the HTML headers. We will cover that later in the chapter. First, let's talk about the HTML output stream in general terms.

At the simplest level, the HTML output stream is always built in the same way: the stream starts off as empty, and when new information is added to it, it can only be added to the *end*. This means that if we send some custom HTML headers to the output stream, which have to be at the top of the HTML page, the header information has to be written to the stream first.

Once the headers have been sent to the output stream, we can start to send the contents of the page to the output stream. The easiest way to do this is with native HTML in the ASP script file. Any HTML that is not encompassed by the **<%...%>** tags will be added to the HTML output stream. The **Response** object provides two ways to add information to the output stream: the **Write** method and the 'shortcut' technique.

The **Write** method of the **Response** object allows you to add information to the end of the HTML output stream. This information can be the contents of a server-side variable, the return value from a function, or a string constant. No matter what the information, the syntax of the method is consistent:

```
Response.Write value
```

The contents of *value* can contain any valid information that can be output in an HTML file. In other words, it is up to the developer to make sure that whatever data is contained in *value* can be properly displayed on a client browser. We'll be seeing lots of examples of how to use **Response.Write** throughout this chapter.

Using Shortcuts

You can use shortcuts for outputting information to the HTML output stream using a special form of the standard ASP script delimiters. When adding ASP script to a HTML page, you use the <%....%> to indicate what is script and what is HTML. The shortcut method allows you to use a modified version of the script delimiter, <%= ... %> as a shortcut reference to **Response.Write**. For example, to use the shortcut method to write the contents of the variable value as we did above, you would write:

```
<%= value %>
```

This would result in exactly the same information being written to the HTML output stream as we would get with this statement:

```
<% Response.Write value %>
```

Now, the question is, "When should I use which method?"

When to Use each Method

We have just seen two ways to output information to the HTML output stream. There are some very simple rules that you can follow to help choose which of the two methods you should use.

The **shortcut method** is best used when you have a block of HTML code into which you want to insert a single piece of dynamic code. As you can see in these two examples that do the same thing, the shortcut method really reduces the amount of code that you have to write:

```
<BODY>
The time is now:
<%
Response.Write Now
%>
</BODY>
```

Now, if you were to rewrite this using the shortcut method, you can see the savings in code that you would gain:

```
<BODY>
The time is now: <%= Now %>
</BODY>
```

But the shortcut method is not always the most efficient. If you have a big block of ASP script code and want to output information to the HTML output stream, then using the `Response.Write` method directly would be the way to go. It doesn't change the performance of the page, but it *does* improve the readability. And that will make it easier to remember what you were doing when you look at the page two months later.

Try It Out – Writing to the Output Stream

In this example, we will be looking at the two ways that you can send dynamic information back to the client by using the two methods of the `Response` object.

1 Using your editor of choice, create the `OutputTest.asp` file with the following source code:

```
<HTML>
<HEAD>
<TITLE>Testing the Write Method</TITLE>
</HEAD>
<BODY>
Here is some plain HTML being added to the HTML output stream<P>
<%
Response.Write ("Here is a string being output using
Response.Write<P>")
%>
<%= "Here is a string being output using the shortcut method<P>" %>
<HR>Now let's try some dynamic text<P>
<%
Response.Write ("With Response.Write, the time is now: ")
Response.Write Now
Response.Write ("<P>")
%>
With the shortcut method, the time is now: <%= Now %><P>
</BODY>
</HTML>
```

2 Save the file to your usual `BegASP` directory.

3 View the page in your web browser.

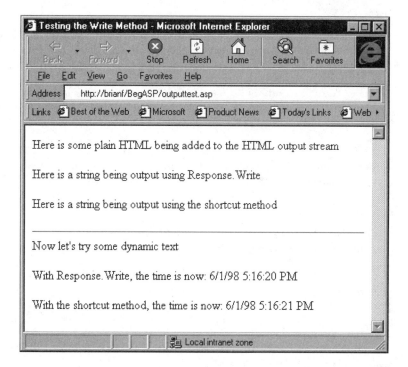

How It Works

The use of these two methods is pretty self-explanatory. Basically, whatever information you pass as the parameter to the method call will be added to the HTML output stream. This information can be a string constant, a variable, or the value of a built-in function. Anything goes, as long as the output is something that the browser will understand.

You can also see in this example that while you can use both the `Response.Write` method *and* the shortcut method to output information to the output stream, the context in which you output the information should determine what method you would use. Given a choice like this, most developers will choose the method that is the easiest to read and also requires the fewest keystrokes. None of us likes typing, but it goes along with the job!

Controlling How Information is Returned

Now that we know how to send information back to the client, we can turn and look at how we can *control* that process. To begin this discussion, let's look at how the information is normally returned.

In the previous section, we talked about the HTML output stream. This is where the ASP scripts put all of the information that it is being sent back to the client. This output stream starts out as empty when the script begins. As the script is run, information that is destined for the client is placed in the output stream. The order in which information is placed in the stream is the same order that it will be sent to the browser. Once all of the ASP scripts have been processed, then the HTML output stream is sent to the browser in one fell swoop.

This is fine for most pages, but what if your ASP script is going to take a long time to process? For example, maybe you are trying to access information from a remote system. Since the HTML output stream will not be sent to the client until the script has completed, the browser will just appear to be spinning its wheels waiting for the server to respond.

In this case, we may want to send some information to the client, to let the user know that the script is processing. Then once the processing has completed, we can send all of the information back to the client.

To do this, we will be manually controlling the way that ASP buffers the HTML output stream. There is one property and three methods that will allow us to control when the output stream is sent to the client. These are: **Buffer**, **Flush**, **Clear**, and **End**. We'll look at each in turn.

Buffer

The **Buffer** property of the **Response** object is used to tell ASP that we will be manually controlling when the HTML output stream is sent back to the browser. Buffering is, by default, turned **off**. To turn it on, we would need to set the value of the property to **true**:

```
Response.Buffer = true
```

Response.Buffer has to be inserted after the language declaration (if one is used), but before any HTML is written:

```
<%@ LANGUAGE="scriptinglanguage"%>
<% Response.Buffer = true %>
<HTML>
...
```

If you try and set the buffer property *before* the language declaration, you'll generate an error.

Flush

The **Flush** method sends any previously buffered output to the client immediately, but continues processing the script. This can be useful for displaying partial results before your script finishes processing so that your user does not get impatient while waiting for the full result of a long query.

To call this method, simply use:

```
<% Response.Flush %>
```

Flush causes a run-time error if the **Response.Buffer** property has not been set to **true**.

Clear

The **Response.Clear** method erases any already-buffered HTML. However, it only erases the response body and does not erase response headers. It will only erase information that has been added to the HTML output stream since the last call to **Response.Flush**. If you have not called **Response.Flush**, then it will erase all of the information that has been added since the beginning of the page, except the headers.

To call this method, simply use:

```
<% Response.Clear %>
```

`Clear` will cause a run-time error if `Response.Buffer` has not been set to `true`.

End

The `End` method causes the server to stop processing the script and send the buffered output. Any further script instructions are not processed. Calling `Response.End` flushes the buffer, if `Response.Buffer` has been set to `true`.

To call this method, simply use:

```
<% Response.End %>
```

Try It Out – Controlling the Output Buffer

In this example, we will take a look at how you can use the buffer control in an ASP script to control when—and if—information is sent back to the browser.

1 Using NotePad or your editor of choice, create the `BufferOutput.asp` file with the following source code.

```
<%@ LANGUAGE="VBSCRIPT"%>
<% Response.Buffer = true %>
<HTML>
<HEAD>
<TITLE>Testing the Response Buffer</TITLE>
</HEAD>

<BODY>
Let's send some text to the HTML output stream.<P>
It is waiting to be sent - Let's send it.<P>
<% Response.Flush %>
Now we want to send this to client<P>
Oops, we just changed our minds - let's clear it<P>
<% Response.Clear %>
<%
Response.Write "We can control the output of Response.Write method
too<P>"
Response.Flush
%>
I think we are finished - let's end it.<P>
<% Response.End %>
Wait a minute - I wanted to say this, but it is too late!
</BODY>
</HTML>
```

2 Save the `BufferOutput.asp` file in your `BegASP` directory

3 View the page in your web browser - you should see something like this:

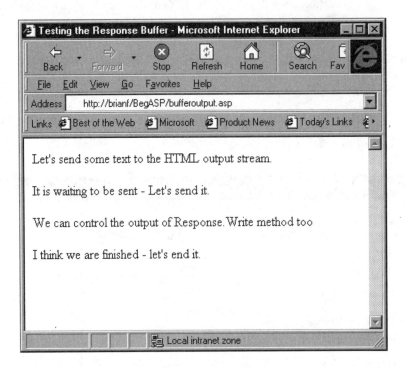

4 View the source of the ASP file so that you can see exactly where the `Response.End` was called.

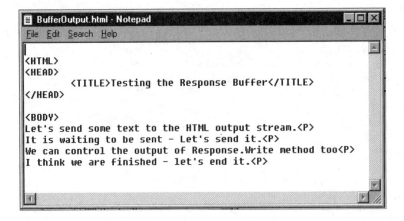

How It Works

The first step in taking control over how the HTML output stream is sent back to the browser is to turn buffering on.

```
<%@ LANGUAGE="VBSCRIPT"%>
<% Response.Buffer = true %>
<HTML>
```

By setting the **Buffer** property of the **Response** object to **true**, we are telling ASP that we will be controlling when information should be sent to the browser. This statement needs to be before any statements that may cause information to be written to the HTML output stream. In this example, the first line, with the **LANGUAGE** directive, does not affect what is sent to the browser. This means that we can still put in the line to control the buffer, even though it is not the first line in the file.

```
Let's send some text to the HTML output stream.<P>
It is waiting to be sent - Let's send it.<P>
<% Response.Flush %>
```

Now we want to output some HTML text to the browser. We are doing this by putting native HTML code inside the ASP script, but outside of the <%...%> tags. Even though we are not using one of the **Response** object's methods to send information back to the client, this HTML is still being written to the HTML output stream.

Once we have written some text, we want to send it immediately to the browser. This is done by calling **Response.Flush**. When ASP encounters this statement, it will immediately send whatever information is in the HTML output stream to the client, before clearing that information from the stream.

```
Now we want to send this to client<P>
Oops, we just changed our minds - let's clear it<P>
<% Response.Clear %>
```

Next, we want to output some more text to the browser. But this time, after adding the text to the HTML output stream, we decide that we really didn't want that text after all. There is no way to selectively remove it from the output stream, but we can erase everything that is already in the stream. To do this, we will call the **Clear** method of the **Response** object. If you look at what the browser is displaying, or even the source HTML for what the browser is displaying, you won't find these two lines of text there.

```
<%
Response.Write "We can control the output of Response.Write method
too<P>"
Response.Flush
%>
```

All of the information that is sent to the HTML output stream, whether from a method of the **Response** object, such as **Write**, or from native HTML, is under our control when we have enabled buffering. In this step, we are adding information to the output stream by using the **Response.Write** method. After outputting the line of text, we will send it to the client by again using the **Flush** method.

```
I think we are finished - let's end it.<P>
<% Response.End %>
Wait a minute - I wanted to say this, but it is too late!
</BODY>
</HTML>
```

We then want to send some final information to the browser. Once we have added it to the output stream, we call the **End** method of the **Response** object. This tells ASP that we have sent all of the information that we want to the client. Its job is to send the remaining contents of the HTML output stream to the browser, then stop processing any more script.

If you look at the source HTML for the page that ASP generated, you will see that the last line of code is the line just prior to the call to **Response.End**. None of the other information that was in the ASP script, including the terminating **</BODY>** and **</HTML>** tags, has been sent to the client. So in this case, calling **End** really does mean the end.

Controlling what the browser does

In addition to sending HTML code back to the client, the **Response** object can be used to control some of the things that the browser itself does.

▶ If the browser requested a certain page, but you really think that it should be displaying another page, you can use the **Response** object to tell the browser to go get another page. This could be used if you have moved a page in your site, but still want people with links to the original page to be able to get to the information.

▶ If you want the browser to cache the page that you are creating until a certain date, or for a certain length of time, you can use the **Response** object to pass the browser this information.

The use of these methods is a bit more complex than just sending information back to the browser. They provide us with increased flexibility, and are worth discussing a little further here.

Content Expiration

As you are surfing the web using your web browser, you are downloading pages and images and other types of content to your computer so that the browser can display them. Since most people tend to visit the same sites regularly, browsers have been developed with a **cache** that exists on the client's computer. The browser will fill this cache up with the information that is downloaded from various web sites. Later, if the user returns to a site they had already been to, the browser can check to see if the page that the user is requesting is in its cache. If it is, then the page can be displayed immediately, rather than having to wait for it to download from the server.

Web site developers can use this cache to their advantage as well. HTML pages are not the only items that are cached. All JPG and GIF images are also cached. Knowing this, web site developers can reuse graphics in their site, so that the only time they have to be downloaded is for the first page that uses them.

When the browser is asked to display a page that it already has in cache, it will check that cached page to see if it has expired. A web page developer can set the expiration date of a page so that they can ensure that the person viewing the page is always seeing the latest content, but not forcing them to download the page every time.

As an ASP developer, we have a bit of a dilemma. Our pages are dynamically created, so they are really different pages every time. Even if the underlying data that generated the page hasn't changed, a new page is always freshly created to send to the browser. There are many cases where the page will only change on a periodic basis. We would like the clients viewing the page to be able to take advantage of the caching that their browser offers.

There are two properties of the **Response** object that we can use to control the expiration of the page that is generated. These properties are **Expires** and **ExpiresAbsolute**.

Expires

The **Expires** property specifies the number of minutes before a page cached on a browser expires. If the user returns to the same page before the specified number of minutes have elapsed, the cached version is displayed.

To set this property, you would use:

```
<% Response.Expires = minutes %>
```

In this example, **minutes** represent the number of minutes before this page will expire. Setting **minutes** to 0 causes the page to be refreshed with each access.

ExpiresAbsolute

The **ExpiresAbsolute** property sets the date and/or time at which a page cached on a browser expires. If the user returns to the page before the specified date and/or time, the cached version is displayed. If no time is set, the page expires at midnight of that day. If a time *is* set, the page expires at the specified time on the day that the script is run.

To set this property, you would use:

```
<% Response.ExpiresAbsolute = #DateTime# %>
```

The value of **DateTime** must be a valid date or time combination. The value must be enclosed within the **#** signs. If you set this value to a date in the past, this is the same as setting the **Expires** property to 0.

Redirection

When a client requests a specific ASP page from the server, the script for that page is processed. As that page is being processed, we may determine that there is a different ASP page that the browser should actually be displaying. For example, we could have a page that validates a user's login. Based on the results of that validation, the user could be shown a guest page or a registered user's page.

We could have the code to create both pages within the same script, but that would make for a very complicated script file. It would also make it more difficult for another developer to look at the page at a later time and understand what we were doing. It would be much easier if we could check the user's login and, based on what the results were, send the user to a completely different page.

To do this, we can use the **Redirect** method of the **Response** object. This method will tell the browser that it needs to go and fetch a different page. This page could be on the same site, or it could be on a completely different web site.

To call this method, you would use:

```
<% Response.Redirect = destinationPage %>
```

The value of **destinationPage** would need to be a string value, and hold a valid URL that the browser would then be told to retrieve. The destination page should be formatted just as a hyperlink would. If the URL is on the same site, then a relative reference can be used. If it is on a different site, then you need to include a full **http://** reference.

There are a few things that you need to be careful with when using the **Redirect** method. A browser is told to fetch a different page through the use of a custom HTML header. This means that for the browser to recognize this, it can't receive any other information along with it. If the ASP script has output the HTML headers, or has added any information to the HTML output stream, then calling the **Redirect** method will cause an error.

Earlier in this chapter, we learned how to control the contents of the HTML output stream by using the **Buffer** property. The use of this property goes hand in hand with using the **Redirect** method. By buffering the HTML output, we can call **Redirect** almost anywhere, as long as we clear out the buffer by calling the **Clear** method before redirecting the browser.

> *Remember, if you are going to use the* Redirect *method, be sure to set the* Buffer *property to* true *at the beginning of the page.*

Try It Out – Redirecting the Browser

In this example we will show how you can create a page that processes some information and makes a decision on which page the browser should display. Once it has made that decision, it will use the **Redirect** method to tell the browser to load that page.

1 Using your favored editor, create the **PageChoice.html** file with the following source code and save it in your **BegASP** directory:

```
<!DOCTYPE HTML PUBLIC "-//W3C//DTD HTML 3.2 Final//EN">
<BASEFONT FACE="Tahoma">
<HTML>
<HEAD>
  <TITLE>Redirection Example</TITLE>
</HEAD>
<BODY>
<H2>Choose which page you wish to display</H2>
<FORM ACTION="choosePage.asp" METHOD="POST">
```

```
<INPUT TYPE="Radio" NAME="PageChoice" VALUE="Page1" CHECKED>Page Number
1<BR>
<INPUT TYPE="Radio" NAME="PageChoice" VALUE="Page2">Page Number 2<P>
<INPUT TYPE="Submit" VALUE="Choose Page">   <INPUT
TYPE="RESET">
</FORM>
</BODY>
</HTML>
```

2 Create another file and save it as `choosePage.asp` in the `BegASP` directory. This file should contain the following code:

```
<%
Option Explicit
dim     strChoice

strChoice = Request.Form("PageChoice")

if strChoice = "Page1" then
      Response.Redirect "page1.html"
else
      Response.Redirect "page2.html"
end if
%>
```

3 Next, create and save a file called `Page1.html` with the following source code:

```
<!DOCTYPE HTML PUBLIC "-//W3C//DTD HTML 3.2 Final//EN">
<HTML>
<HEAD>
      <TITLE>Page 1</TITLE>
</HEAD>
<BODY>
      <H1>This is Page Number 1</H1>
</BODY>
</HTML>
```

4 Create the `Page2.html` file with the following source code:

```
<!DOCTYPE HTML PUBLIC "-//W3C//DTD HTML 3.2 Final//EN">
<HTML>
<HEAD>
      <TITLE>Page 2</TITLE>
</HEAD>
<BODY>
      <H1>This is Page Number 2</H1>
</BODY>
</HTML>
```

5 Make sure all these files are stored in you `BegASP` directory

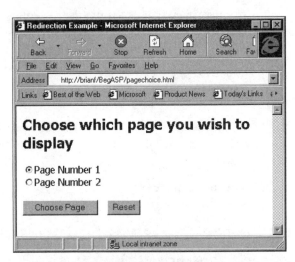

6 View the `PageChoice.html` file via your web browser

7 Select Page Number 1 and press the Choose Page button. This should produce:

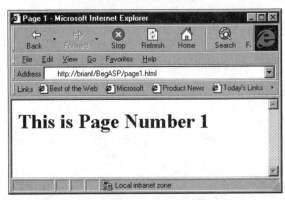

8 Go back to the `PageChoice.html` page and choose the other option.

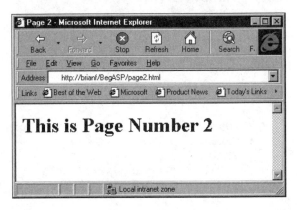

How It Works

The first page we create is a straightforward static HTML page. The job of this page is to present a standard HTML form that will allow the user to select which page they wish to display.

```
<FORM ACTION="ChoosePage.asp" METHOD="POST">
<INPUT TYPE="Radio" NAME="PageChoice" VALUE="Page1" CHECKED>Page Number
1<BR>
<INPUT TYPE="Radio" NAME="PageChoice" VALUE="Page2">Page Number 2<P>
<INPUT TYPE="Submit" VALUE="Choose Page">  <INPUT
TYPE="RESET">
</FORM>
```

The form displays two radio buttons, which allow the user to select which page to display. The results of the form are going to be sent to the **choosePage.asp** file for processing.

```
<%
Option Explicit
dim    strChoice

strChoice = Request.Form("PageChoice")
```

The first thing we want to do when processing the form is to grab the selection that the user made in the previous page. Before we do that, we are going to follow good programming practice and add the **Option Explicit** statement to help ensure that we build up the good habit of always declaring in advance the variables that we will be using.

Once we have declared the variable to hold the user's selection, we will retrieve it from the **Form** collection of the **Request** object. In our HTML form, we had two radio buttons with the same name, **PageChoice**, but with different values. Depending on which button the user selected before submitting the form, the value for that button will added the **Form** collection.

```
if strChoice = "Page1" then
      Response.Redirect "page1.html"
else
      Response.Redirect "page2.html"
end if
%>
```

We can then compare the value that was passed from the form with the *possible* values. Based on that comparison, we can choose to send the browser to either **page1.html** or to **page2.html**. You will notice that there are no **Response.Write** statements, or any HTML text outside of the <%...%> block. This ASP file is designed to produce no output to send to the browser: it is simply designed to evaluate some data that is passed to it, and based on that evaluation, to send the browser making the request to another page. In this case, both of the possible destination pages are static HTML files. They could have just as easily been ASP scripts, or could have been pages on a completely different web server. If that were the case, then we would need to use the complete URL as the parameter to the **Redirect** method. For example:

```
Response.Redirect "http://www.wrox.co.uk"
```

The critical thing to remember from this example is that when you are using the **Redirect** method, make sure that you are not sending any information to the HTML output stream. If you are, then make sure that you turn buffering on, and clear the output stream before calling redirect.

Other Information to Send

The **Response** object gives you very fine control over the information that is returned to the client. In most cases, you will only need the broad-brush strokes that methods like **Write** and **Redirect** provide you. But for limitless flexibility, there are other functions that the **Response** object provides you with.

Some of these functions include:

▶ Changing the content type of the response so that not only HTML can be sent back to the client.

▶ Detecting if the client making the request is still connected to the server. This allows you to abandon any processing if the browser has moved on to another page.

▶ Adding additional information to the log file entry that is made in the web server's log file.

▶ And being able to write binary information, as well as text information, back to the client.

These functions are defined in Appendix B. They are really beyond the scope of this book, but you can find more information about them in *Professional Active Server Pages 2e, ISBN 1-861000-26-6*, available from Wrox Press.

Using the Request and Response Object

Now that we have reached the end of the two-chapter arc on the **Request** and **Response** object, we will take a look at one example that combines most of the topics from the two chapters. Of course, sending information to the server can only be of some use if you going to get information returned. We've not yet really looked at how the two objects work in tandem, but in the real world, you're rarely going to use one without other. It's time to look at how the **Request** and **Response** objects work together to create dynamic pages.

Try It Out – Big Form Example

So far in this chapter we have seen a few form handling examples, but now we will look at one that combines all of the form types, as well as dealing with the **QueryString** too.

1 Using your usual editor, create the following **FormExample.html** file in your BegASP directory.

```
<!DOCTYPE HTML PUBLIC "-//W3C//DTD HTML 3.2 Final//EN">
<BASEFONT FACE="Tahoma">
<HTML>
<HEAD>
        <TITLE>Big Example</TITLE>
</HEAD>
<BODY>
        <H4>Here is the first form example</H4>
        <FORM ACTION="FormExample.asp?WhichForm=1" METHOD="POST">
                <INPUT TYPE="Text" NAME="MyTextField" VALUE="Type your
info here" SIZE="30" MAXLENGTH="75"><BR>
                <INPUT TYPE="Password" NAME="MyPWField" SIZE="30"
VALUE="password"><BR>
                <TEXTAREA NAME="MyTextArea" COLS="30" ROWS="3"
WRAP="VIRTUAL">
This is the text area you can type in...
                </TEXTAREA><P>
                <INPUT TYPE="Submit" VALUE="Submit this
Form">  <INPUT TYPE="RESET">
        </FORM>
<HR>
        <H4>Here is the next form example</H4>
        <FORM ACTION="FormExample.asp?WhichForm=2" METHOD="POST">
        <TABLE BORDER = 0>
        <TR><TD><INPUT TYPE="Radio" NAME="MyRadio" VALUE="Choice1"
CHECKED>Radio Choice 1<BR>
                <INPUT TYPE="Radio" NAME="MyRadio" VALUE="Choice2">Radio
Choice 2<BR>
                <INPUT TYPE="Radio" NAME="MyRadio" VALUE="Choice3">Radio
Choice 3
        </TD><TD width=30> </TD><TD><INPUT TYPE="Checkbox"
NAME="MyCheckBox" VALUE="Check1">Check Box 1<BR>
                <INPUT TYPE="Checkbox" NAME="MyCheckBox"
VALUE="Check2">Check Box 2<BR>
                <INPUT TYPE="Checkbox" NAME="MyCheckBox"
VALUE="Check3">Check Box 3</TD>
        </TR>
        </TABLE><BR>
        <INPUT TYPE="Submit" VALUE="Submit this Form">  <INPUT
TYPE="RESET">

        </FORM>
<HR>
        <H4>Here is another form example</H4>
        <FORM ACTION="FormExample.asp" METHOD="GET">
                <INPUT TYPE="Hidden" NAME="WhichForm" VALUE="3">
                <SELECT NAME="MyDropList" SIZE="1">
                        <OPTION VALUE="ListChoice1">List Choice 1
                        <OPTION VALUE="ListChoice2">List Choice 2
                        <OPTION VALUE="ListChoice3">List Choice 3
                </SELECT>
```

```
                    <SELECT NAME="MyListBox" SIZE="3" MULTIPLE>
                            <OPTION VALUE="ListBox1">MultiSelect List Box 1
                            <OPTION VALUE="ListBox2">MultiSelect List Box 2
                            <OPTION VALUE="ListBox3">MultiSelect List Box 3
                    </SELECT><P>
                    <INPUT TYPE="Submit" VALUE="Submit this
Form">  <INPUT TYPE="RESET">
            </FORM>
</BODY>
</HTML>
```

2 Next, create the `FormExample.asp` file with the following source code:

```
<!DOCTYPE HTML PUBLIC "-//W3C//DTD HTML 3.2 Final//EN">
<BASEFONT FACE="Tahoma">
<HTML>
<HEAD>
        <TITLE>Big Example Results</TITLE>
</HEAD>
<BODY>
<%
dim iFormChoice
iFormChoice = Request.QueryString("WhichForm")

Select Case iFormChoice
        Case 1
%>
This will show the results of the text input form fields<P>
<TABLE BORDER=1 CELLPADDING=5 width=75%>
<TR><TD>My TextField Input Field</TD><TD><B><%=
Request.Form("MyTextField") %></B></TD></TR>
<TR><TD>My Passsword Input Field</TD><TD><B><%=
Request.Form("MyPWField") %></B></TD></TR>
<TR><TD>My TextArea Input Field</TD><TD><B><%=
Request.Form("MyTextArea") %></B></TD></TR>
</TABLE>
<HR>
<%
        Case 2
%>
This will show the results of the radio and checkbox form fields<P>
<TABLE BORDER=1 CELLPADDING=5 width=25%>
<TR><TD>Radio Button Selected</TD><TD><B><%= Request.Form("MyRadio")
%></B></TD></TR>
<TR><TD>Check Boxes Checked</TD><TD><B><%
dim strCheck
for each strCheck in Request.Form("MyCheckBox")
        Response.Write strCheck & "<BR>"
next
%></B></TD></TR>
```

```
</TABLE>
<HR>
<%
        Case 3
%>
This will show the results of the selection form fields<P>
<TABLE BORDER=1 CELLPADDING=5 width=35%>
<TR><TD>List Choice Selected</TD><TD><B><%= Request("MyDropList") %></
B></TD></TR>
<TR><TD>MultiSelect Choices Selected</TD><TD><B><%
 for each strCheck in Request("MyListBox")
        Response.Write strCheck & "<BR>"
 next
 %></B></TD></TR>
</TABLE>
<HR>
<%
End Select
%>
```

3 Make sure these files are both stored in your regular **BegASP** directory.

4 Open up your web browser and view the **FormExample.html** file:

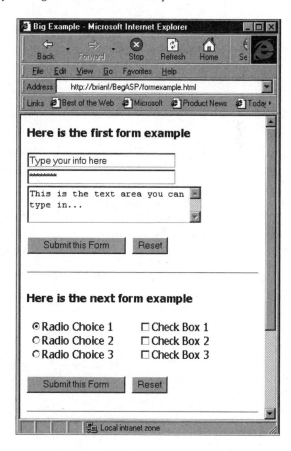

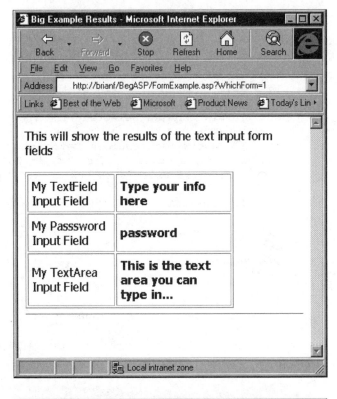

5 Enter some information into the first form example, and press Submit this Form.

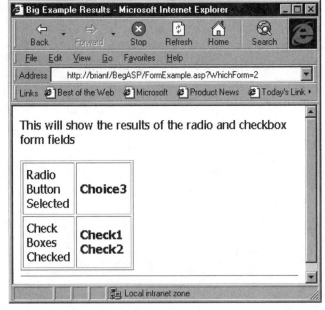

6 Press the Back button to return to the Big Example page. Enter some information into the next form example, and press Submit this Form. This will produce something like:

7 Press the Back button to return to the Big Example page. Enter some information into the last form example, and press Submit this Form.

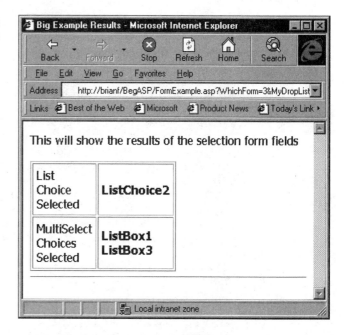

How It Works

In this example, we will be looking at the different types of form fields, and how those fields should be handled in an ASP script. The `FormExample.html` file contains three sections, each with different types of form fields.

```
<FORM ACTION="FormExample.asp?WhichForm=1" METHOD="POST">
<INPUT TYPE="Text" NAME="MyTextField" VALUE="Type your info here"
SIZE="30" MAXLENGTH="75"><BR>
<INPUT TYPE="Password" NAME="MyPWField" SIZE="30"
VALUE="password"><BR>
<TEXTAREA NAME="MyTextArea" COLS="30" ROWS="3" WRAP="VIRTUAL">
This is the text area you can type in...
</TEXTAREA><P>
<INPUT TYPE="Submit" VALUE="Submit this Form">  <INPUT
TYPE="RESET">
</FORM>
```

In the first example, we are using two types of input fields along with a **TEXTAREA** field. The action of this form is to call the **FormExample.asp** file. We will be passing a **Query String** parameter called **WhichForm** along with the form information. You will see how this is used when we look at the ASP script that receives the information from the form.

```
<TR><TD><INPUT TYPE="Radio" NAME="MyRadio" VALUE="Choice1" CHECKED>Radio
Choice 1<BR>
<INPUT TYPE="Radio" NAME="MyRadio" VALUE="Choice2">Radio Choice 2<BR>
<INPUT TYPE="Radio" NAME="MyRadio" VALUE="Choice3">Radio Choice 3
</TD><TD width=30> </TD><TD><INPUT TYPE="Checkbox"
NAME="MyCheckBox" VALUE="Check1">Check Box 1<BR>
<INPUT TYPE="Checkbox" NAME="MyCheckBox" VALUE="Check2">Check Box 2<BR>
<INPUT TYPE="Checkbox" NAME="MyCheckBox" VALUE="Check3">Check Box 3</TD>
```

The next section will display a form that contains both radio buttons and check boxes. We have used a table so that the presentation will be nicely formatted. By having the same **NAME** parameter for all of the radio buttons, the browser will group those buttons together—allowing you to select only one button.

```
<FORM ACTION="FormExample.asp" METHOD="GET">
<INPUT TYPE="Hidden" NAME="WhichForm" VALUE="3">
<SELECT NAME="MyDropList" SIZE="1">
        <OPTION VALUE="ListChoice1">List Choice 1
        <OPTION VALUE="ListChoice2">List Choice 2
        <OPTION VALUE="ListChoice3">List Choice 3
</SELECT>
<SELECT NAME="MyListBox" SIZE="3" MULTIPLE>
        <OPTION VALUE="ListBox1">MultiSelect List Box 1
        <OPTION VALUE="ListBox2">MultiSelect List Box 2
        <OPTION VALUE="ListBox3">MultiSelect List Box 3
</SELECT><P>
<INPUT TYPE="Submit" VALUE="Submit this Form">  <INPUT
TYPE="RESET">
</FORM>
```

The final form on the page will be used to show the list-type form elements. We will also be using the **GET** method to submit the form, rather than the **PUT** method we used earlier. This means that the information from the form will be passed as part of the query string. Since we had been using the query string in the earlier examples to identify which form was being submitted, we need to pass this information in another way. To do this, we will be using an **INPUT** field of type **HIDDEN**. This field will pass its **VALUE** to the processing script, but it will not display anything for the user to see or edit.

```
<HEAD>
        <TITLE>Big Example Results</TITLE>
</HEAD>
<BODY>
<%
dim iFormChoice
iFormChoice = Request.QueryString("WhichForm")

Select Case iFormChoice
```

We now need a file to receive the information from the form, and display some results for the user. We have three separate forms that are all submitting their information from the same page. While all of these forms are from the same page, they could just have easily been from *different* pages. To identify which form is actually being submitted, we included a **QueryString** value called **WhichForm**. To decide how to process the submitted form, we will check the value of this **QueryString** property, and use it to decide how to process the request.

```
        Case 1
%>
This will show the results of the text input form fields<P>
<TABLE BORDER=1 CELLPADDING=5 width=75%>
<TR><TD>My TextField Input Field</TD><TD><B><%=
```

```
Request.Form("MyTextField") %></B></TD></TR>
<TR><TD>My Passsword Input Field</TD><TD><B><%=
Request.Form("MyPWField") %></B></TD></TR>
<TR><TD>My TextArea Input Field</TD><TD><B><%=
Request.Form("MyTextArea") %></B></TD></TR>
</TABLE>
<HR>
```

In the first case, we will be displaying the value of the three text fields that were submitted. To retrieve this information, we will first look for the data we want inside of the **Form** collection of the **Request** object. We use the name of the field as the key to the collection to retrieve the information that we want. This information is then displayed on the browser by using the **Write** method shortcut of `<%=`.

```
<%
        Case 2
%>
This will show the results of the radio and checkbox form fields<P>
<TABLE BORDER=1 CELLPADDING=5 width=25%>
<TR><TD>Radio Button Selected</TD><TD><B><%= Request.Form("MyRadio")
%></B></TD></TR>
<TR><TD>Check Boxes Checked</TD><TD><B><%
dim strCheck
for each strCheck in Request.Form("MyCheckBox")
        Response.Write strCheck & "<BR>"
next
 %></B></TD></TR>
</TABLE>
<HR>
```

In the second case, we will be displaying the results from the form that contained both radio buttons and check boxes. While each of the radio buttons had the same **NAME** parameter, they each had a different **VALUE** parameter. The value of this parameter will be passed into the Form collection. We can then retrieve it and display it using the **Write** shortcut method.

The check boxes are a bit different from the radio buttons. Since a user can select multiple check boxes, we have to approach the display of the ones that the user selected a bit differently. We can access the multiple values that the user selected as a collection, but since we don't necessarily know how many items are in the collection, we can just use the **For Each** statement. This loop statement will allow us to retrieve each value from the collection. This value is stored in the **strCheck** local variable. Once we have this value, we can then display it for the user. Since we are inside of a VBScript code block, it makes more sense to use the **Response.Write** method to output information rather than the shortcut method.

```
<%
        Case 3
%>
This will show the results of the selection form fields<P>
<TABLE BORDER=1 CELLPADDING=5 width=35%>
<TR><TD>List Choice Selected</TD><TD><B><%= Request("MyDropList") %></
B></TD></TR>
```

In this final case, we will be displaying the information from the two list elements. Since the drop-down list allows for the selection of only one item, we can simply retrieve the user's selection from the **Form** collection. But remember, for this form we used the **GET** method rather than the **PUT** method. Because of this, we need to get the information from the **QueryString** collection. But what this does is make our ASP code dependent on the method that was used for submitting the form.

A way around this is to use the whole **Request** object as a collection. In addition to providing collection for **QueryString**, **Form**, **Cookies**, etc., the **Request** object can also combine all of these collections together. This allows you to access a piece of information without knowing exactly where it came from. It comes in very handy when processing forms, since you are not dependent on the method used to submit the form.

One thing to be careful with is to understand the order in which ASP organizes the information in the **Request** collection. This becomes important if you have a query string variable with the same name as a form field or cookie. ASP will search through the collections in the following order:

> **QueryString**

> **Form**

> **Cookies**

> **ClientCertificate**

> **ServerVariables**

So if you have a cookie with the same name as a form field, the value in the **Request** collection will be the value from the form field.

```
<TR><TD>MultiSelect Choices Selected</TD><TD><B><%
for each strCheck in Request("MyListBox")
      Response.Write strCheck & "<BR>"
next
 %></B></TD></TR>
</TABLE>
<HR>
```

The multi-select list box is just like the check boxes. The user can select more than one value. So we will need to use the **For...Each** statement here as well. We will be reusing the **strCheck** local variable to store the information before it is output using the **Response.Write** method.

```
<%
End Select
%>
```

Now that we have finished handling each of the forms, we need to end our **Select Case** statement block.

In this example, we have seen how to retrieve information from the various types of form fields. Since some of these fields can return multiple pieces of information, we can use the **For...Each** statement to step through each piece individually. Finally, if we are not sure which collection the information is in, we can search the **Request** collection, which contains all of the information submitted to the server. We hope that you can use this example as a reference point for building your own form processing scripts. For whatever type of form field you are using, you can refer back to this example to see how it should be handled.

Summary

In this chapter we've looked in some detail at the **Response** object, and discussed its critical role in handling ASP's transmission of data from the server to the client. In particular, we saw:

▶ How to use the **Write** method and the shortcut method to send information back to the client

▶ How to use the buffering methods to control when that information is sent back to the client

▶ How the **Expires** and **ExpiresAbsolute** properties can tell the browser how long or until when to cache the contents of the page

▶ How the **Redirect** method can be used to tell the browser to go fetch another page

▶ And some of the other functions that can affect the information being sent back to the browser

In the next chapter we'll move on to look at two objects that help the server organize Active Server Pages and track the interaction between the server and the clients: the **Application** and **Session** objects.

Applications, Sessions and Cookies

In our travels through the world of Active Server Pages, we have been dealing with how information can be sent from the client to the server, and how the server can dynamically create a page that is returned to the client. In all of these interactions, the request and the response existed by themselves. We haven't introduced a mechanism that allows you to tie two pages, or a set of pages, together.

Until recently, existing web technologies meant that if you wanted to pass information from one page to another, you had to use cookies or hidden form fields. Active Server Pages gives you a much more robust and flexible way to do this: the **Application** and **Session** objects.

In this chapter, we will look at these objects and the power and flexibility they add to ASP. In fact, we will now be able to start referring to our web sites as applications, rather than just a group of pages. Specifically, we will be examining:

▶ The **Application** object, which allows us to tie together all of the pages on a single web site into a consistent web application.

▶ The **Session** object, which allows us to treat a user's interaction with the web site as a continuous action, rather than just a disconnected series of page requests.

▶ How to use **cookies** to store information at the client's computer, and what cookies should be used for.

To get us started, let's look at what makes up a web application.

A Web Application

As the web is moving from just serving up pages to providing access to dynamic information from a wide range of systems, the sites that a user may access begin to look more like a traditional application, such as one written in Visual Basic or Powerbuilder. In ASP, each virtual directory on the server, which we first saw in Chapter 1, is an application. All of the pages in that directory, whether static or dynamically generated, are part of that application. Since these pages are functioning together as an application, naturally the developer would want some control over the application as a whole. This is the responsibility of the `Application` object. With this object, you can:

▶ Be notified when an application is first *started*, so that you can perform some startup processing.

▶ Be notified when an application is *ending*, so that you have the opportunity to perform processes that close the application cleanly.

▶ *Store information* that can be used by all clients accessing the application.

There is one instance of the `Application` object for each application running on the web server, but there may be many clients accessing the same application. They can each get a reference to the same `Application` object. We'll now take a closer look at the `Application` object.

The Application Object

To understand what the `Application` object is, and what it can do, keep in mind that an Application is defined as all the files contained in a virtual directory and its subdirectories.

A PWS Server can host any number of Applications, and each application has its own `Application` Object. This object stores variables and objects for **application-scope** usage. Application-scope means that variables (and objects) can be accessed from any ASP page that is part of the application. Since any page that is in the virtual directory is part of the application, this means that any page in the directory can access an application-scope variable. The `Application` Object also holds information about the Sessions active within a particular Application.

The diagram that follows shows the relationship between Applications, `Application` Objects and `Session` Objects:

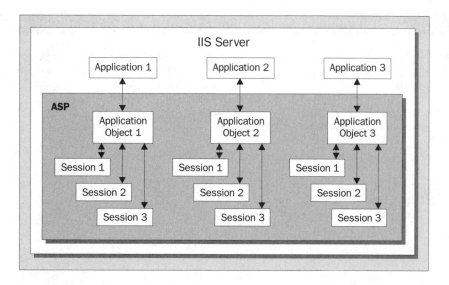

In the diagram, The **Applications** at the top refer to the collections of web pages and objects defined on the server as virtual directories. The **Application Objects** are the ASP objects that control access to the Application. The **Sessions** represent individual client sessions with the application—we'll discuss sessions in detail later. For the moment, remember that the first time a client asks for a page with the `.asp` suffix from your server, a session is established for that client. Any number of Sessions can be hosted by any one Application, limited only by the memory resources of your server. But suffice it to say, the number is quite large.

Application Variables

One of the features of an application is that you can store information that is available to all clients that are accessing the application. This information is stored in what is known as an `application-scope` variable.

In ASP scripts, if you have not added the `Option Explicit` statement to the file, you can create new variables just by naming them for use. For application-level variables, it is absolutely essential that you explicitly declare them *before* they are used.

To initialize variables in the `Application` Object, you store the information about them in a text file named `global.asa`. Each Application can have only one `global.asa`, and it's placed in the virtual directory's root. We will cover the items that can be placed in `global.asa` later in this chapter, but we will introduce what we need here to get us started on application-level variables.

Try It Out – Your First global.asa

In this example, we will create a very basic `global.asa` file so that we can declare some application-level variables. Later in this section, we will access these variables from an ASP page in our application.

1 Create a new file, and write the following:

```
<SCRIPT LANGUAGE="VBScript" RUNAT="Server">

Sub Application_OnStart
Application("myAppVariable") = ""
Application("anotherAppVariable") = 0
End Sub

</SCRIPT>
```

2 Save the file as `global.asa` in your `BegASP` virtual directory.

What It Does

In our first `global.asa` file, we are declaring some application-level variables that we will use later in our examples. The first thing that you will notice about this file is that there are no `<%...%>` blocks. As you have seen before, these `<%` and `%>` tags are used to indicate ASP script within a file. In the `global.asa` file, we will be using the following syntax instead:

```
<SCRIPT LANGUAGE="VBScript" RUNAT="Server">
```

The procedures that are part of `global.asa` are defined within a script block. The language that we are using for scripts is VBScript. Since these scripts will be run at the server, as opposed to the client, we have included the **RUNAT** parameter, and passed it a value of **Server**. If you include script that is not enclosed by `<SCRIPT>` tags, the server returns an error.

```
Sub Application_OnStart
Application("myAppVariable") = ""
Application("anotherAppVariable") = "0"
End Sub
```

There are four possible events that can be handled in `global.asa`:

- ▶ `Application_OnStart`
- ▶ `Application_OnEnd`
- ▶ `Session_OnStart`
- ▶ `Session_OnEnd`

The first one we will look at is `Application_OnStart`. This event will be fired when the first visitor hits the page. So, an application is 'started' the first time one of its pages is accessed by a user.

Inside of this event handler, we are initializing two application-level variables. Application-level variables are actually elements of the **Application** object. We set and retrieve their values in the same way that we set and retrieve the values in a collection. In this example, we have created two application-level variables:

▶ `myAppVariable`

▶ `anotherAppVariable`

The **myAppVariable** variable has been initialized to an empty string. The **anotherAppVariable** variable has been initialized to a string containing 0. Once that is complete, the event handler is finished, and we can complete the **global.asa** file with a closing **</SCRIPT>** tag.

Application Object Collections

The Application Object has two Collections:

▶ The **Contents** collection contains all variables that have been added to the Application via scripts in **global.asa**. Though you can only *add* application-scope variables by using names from **global.asa**, you can retrieve and change the variables' values from any ASP page.

▶ The **StaticObjects** collection contains the names of all objects added via the **<OBJECT>** tag in **global.asa**. Objects that are added to **global.asa** can be either application-scoped objects or session-scoped objects.

The Contents Collection

You use the **Contents** collection to get a list of items with application scope or to set a value for a particular Application-level variable.

The general syntax for retrieving a variable's value in the **Application.Contents** collection is:

```
Application.Contents("Key")
```

where **Key** specifies the name of the key to retrieve.

You can iterate through the **Contents** collection the same way you would for any collection, with a **For...Each** statement. An example of this is:

```
<%
For Each Key in Application.Contents
  Response.Write (Key)
Next
%>
```

Just as with a normal collection, you can retrieve the number of elements in the collection by using the **Count** property.

```
<%=Application.Contents.Count%>
```

The StaticObjects Collection

The `StaticObjects` collection contains all the objects created with the `<OBJECT>` tags in the `Application` Object's scope. Use the `StaticObjects` collection to determine the value of a property for an object, or to iterate through, and retrieve, properties for all static objects. We will see how to create static objects when we take a deeper look at the `global.asa` file.

Application Object Methods

The Application object has two methods:

▶ `Lock`

▶ `UnLock`

Lock Method

The `Lock` method prevents clients—other than the one currently accessing it—from modifying the variables stored in the `Application` object.

UnLock Method

This method removes the lock from variables stored in the `Application` object, freeing them up after the `Application` object has been locked previously using the `Application.Lock` method.

Try It Out – Working with Application-Level Variables

In this example, we will take a look at an ASP script that will demonstrate how to interact with the application-level variables that were created in the `global.asa` file we looked at earlier.

1 Create a new file, and enter the following:

```
<!DOCTYPE HTML PUBLIC "-//W3C//DTD HTML 3.2 Final//EN">

<HTML>
<HEAD>
<TITLE>Application Variable Test</TITLE>
</HEAD>

<BODY>
Let's retrieve the values of the Application Variables:<P>
myAppVariable = <%= Application("myAppVariable") %><BR>
anotherAppVariable = <%= Application("anotherAppVariable") %><HR>

Now, let's set the variables:<HR>
<%
Application.Lock
Application("myAppVariable") = Now
Application("anotherAppVariable") =
```

```
CStr(CInt(Application("anotherAppVariable")) + 1)
 Application.UnLock
%>
Variables set - <A HREF="appVarTest.asp">click here</A> to reload the
page to view

</BODY>
</HTML>
```

2 Save the file as `appVarTest.asp` to the `BegASP` directory.

3 View the file in your web browser. The first time you view the page the variables will be blank. Click on **Refresh** to view the contents.

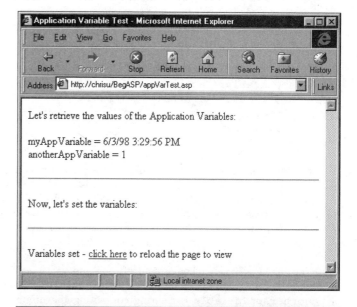

4 Open another browser instance and view the file again.

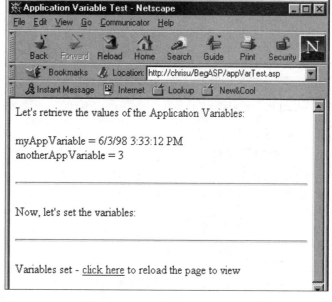

How It Works

In this example, we are using the application-level variables that were created in the `global.asa` example we ran earlier.

```
<BODY>
Let's retrieve the values of the Application Variables:<P>
myAppVariable = <%= Application("myAppVariable") %><BR>
anotherAppVariable = <%= Application("anotherAppVariable") %><HR>
```

First, we will retrieve the values that are currently stored in the two application-level variables that we have declared. Since all we are doing is reading the values stored in the variables, there is no need to call the `Lock` method.

```
Now, let's set the variables:<HR>
<%
Application.Lock
Application("myAppVariable") = Now
Application("anotherAppVariable") =
CStr(CInt(Application("anotherAppVariable")) + 1)
Application.Unlock
%>
```

The next step is to reset the values of the two application-level variables. In order to give this script exclusive control over the variables, we first need to call the `Lock` method of the `Application` object. This will give total control of all application-level variables to this script until the corresponding call to `UnLock` is made. Since there can be multiple users accessing a web site at the same time, and possibly accessing the same page, we need to take these precautions to ensure that the data is updated properly.

Now that we have exclusive control over the variables, we can update their values. The value of the `myAppVariable` variable is set to the current date and time. The value that is stored in `anotherAppVariable` is a string containing the number of times this page has been accessed. Here, we want to increment this count by one. We could rely on VBScript's automatic type conversion, but to make our code more readable by someone trying to learn what it is doing, we will explicitly convert the variable's type.

The first step is to convert the string value that is stored in the application-level variable to an integer value. This is done using the `CInt` function. Now that we have an integer value, we can add 1 to it to get the new count. Finally, to store the value back into the application-level variable, we will convert the new count back to a string using the `CStr` function.

With all of the changes successfully made, we will release our hold on the application-level variables by calling the `UnLock` method of the `Application` object.

Now that we have learned some of the basics of the `Application` object, let's take a more in-depth look at the `global.asa` file.

Global.asa

Since we can now store objects and variables in an application-level scope, we need to have a file to store these declarations in. This file is called **global.asa**. Each Application can have only one **global.asa**, and it's placed in the virtual directory's root. In **global.asa**, you can include event handler scripts and declare objects that will have Session or Application scope. You can also store application-level variables and objects used by the application. The file has no display component, as it is not displayed to users.

Understanding the Structure of global.asa

If you are using VBScript, **global.asa** can contain only four event handling subroutines:

- **Application_OnStart**
- **Application_OnEnd**
- **Session_OnStart**
- **Session_OnEnd**

An example of the most basic **global.asa** file would be:

```
<SCRIPT LANGUAGE="VBScript" RUNAT="Server">

Sub Application_OnStart
'...your VBScript code here
End Sub

Sub Application_OnEnd
'...your VBScript code here
End Sub

Sub Session_OnStart
'...your VBScript code here
End Sub

Sub Session_OnEnd
'...your VBScript code here
End Sub
</SCRIPT>
```

Notice that we have to use the **<SCRIPT>** tag at the top of the page. Also, as previously mentioned, there are no **<%...%>** blocks in the file, because in the **global.asa** file all of the ASP script needs be enclosed in the **<SCRIPT>** block. All four of the event handling scripts have to be defined within this **<SCRIPT>** block. Since these scripts will be running on the server rather than on the client's machine, we have also included the **RUNAT** directive inside of the **SCRIPT** element.

Application_OnStart

This event handler is run **once**, when the Application starts. The Application starts when the first visitor to the Application calls the first .asp page. In this procedure, you should put any application initialization steps that need to be run before anyone can access the application. For example, you could store the database login information, which you will see in Chapter 13, in an application-level variable, so that all pages have easy access to it.

If you want to initialize an Application-scoped variable in **Application_OnStart**, you'd use:

```
Sub Application_OnStart
Application("YourVariable") = "SomeValue"
End Sub
```

Once this event handler is complete, **Session_OnStart** runs.

Application_OnEnd

This event handler runs when the server is stopped. You can use the Personal Web Manager application to do this. From this screen, you can press the Stop button to stop the server.

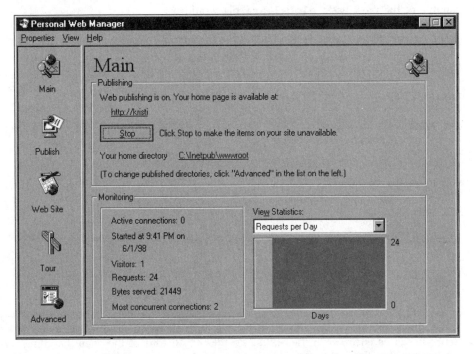

Application_OnEnd scripts are used for "cleaning up" settings after the Application stops. For example, you might want to insert code to delete unnecessary database records or write information you want to keep to text files.

Declaring Objects in global.asa

You can declare Application-scoped Objects in `global.asa`. This will allow you to create one instance of an object and then use it on any page and in every session that accesses your web application. To declare an object in `global.asa`:

```
<OBJECT RUNAT=Server SCOPE=Scope ID=Application PROGID="progID">
</OBJECT>
```

Or if you are using the `CLASSID` of the object:

```
<OBJECT RUNAT=Server SCOPE=Scope ID=Application CLASSID="ClassID">
</OBJECT>
```

Some Warnings on Declaring Objects in global.asa

You should be careful about creating components in Application scope: some components are not designed to be given application scope. If you are not sure if an object can be used in Application-scope, then you should err on the side of caution and find another place to store the object.

Objects declared in `global.asa` are not created until the server processes a script that calls the object. This saves resources by only creating objects that are actually used.

The use of Objects in Application or Session scope is really an advanced topic that is beyond the scope of this book. There are advantages that can be gained by using them, but along with those advantages comes a host of possible problems. For a more detailed look at how to use objects in `global.asa`, take a look at Professional Active Server Pages 2.0, available from Wrox Press, ISBN 1-861001-26-6.

Next, we'll have a look at ASP's link between the Application and the client—the **Session**.

What is a Session?

In addition to providing support for applications across the web, Active Server Pages also supports sessions within an application. We have just looked at how applications are created and at some of the things that you can do with them. To begin our look at sessions, we first need to define what a session *is*.

If you are using a traditional desktop application, say Microsoft Word for example, you start up the application and open a file to edit. You can continue to make changes to the file until you save and close it. Each change you make is recorded into the file, whether you are adding new text or deleting existing text. The time period during which you are editing this file can be thought of as a session.

There is a connection between you—the user—and the file. All of your edits go to that file (that is, unless you switch to a different file). You do not have to tell Microsoft Word which file you are editing each time that you make a change, because the application maintains information about your current editing session.

Things are different on the web. In contrast to the way that traditional applications work, on the web the relationship between the client and the server is said to be **connectionless**. In a connectionless environment, the server does not track a client from request to request. Each request that comes in from a client is treated as if the server knows nothing about the client. There is no connection between the client and server.

For serving up standard web pages, this is an ideal situation. The server can just concern itself with providing pages as fast as possible. It does not have to worry about what a client did previously before it sends a page. Unfortunately, this makes writing applications very difficult.

If traditional applications like Word operated like this, then each time you made an edit on a file, you would also have to send all of the instructions that Word needs to do the following: open the file, get to its proper place in the edit, and close the file once the edit has completed. This would have serious performance consequences, and would probably render the program unusable.

Applications like Word are designed to get around this clumsy processing method, and we want our web programs to allow the creation of robust web applications: ASP gives us this ability. ASP allows the developer to track a user from page to page in an application through the use of a **session**. A user's Session begins when any user without a current session opens any `.asp` page within an ASP Application. The user's Session will continue as they navigate from page to page in the site.

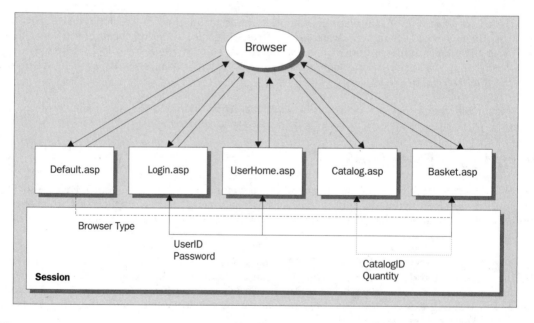

There are two ways that a Session can be terminated. If the user stops interacting with the application, then the session will end after a certain period of time has elapsed. The default value for this time period is 20 minutes. The **Abandon** statement in an ASP script can also explicitly end the session.

The Session can be used to store pieces of information that will be available to every page in the application. This can be used to track things like the contents of a user's shopping basket, or a flag indicating that this user has been properly authenticated with the system. In addition, just as there are event handlers in **global.asa** for the beginning and end of an Application, you can also write an event handler that will be called when a session is started and when it is ended.

To interact with the session itself, you will be using the **Session** object.

The Session Object

There is one **Application** object for each application on the web server. Every client accessing that application can get a reference to it. Each client's unique set of interactions with the application is called a Session. For ASP to manage these processes, each client has a reference to a unique **Session** object.

The **Session** object will allow you to:

▶ Be notified when a user session begins, so that you can take appropriate actions for a new client.

▶ Be notified when a client has ended their session. This can either be caused by a timeout or the explicit **Abandon** method.

▶ Store information that can be accessed by the client throughout the session.

The **Session** object is the most powerful object for creating applications using Active Server Pages. With the session object, ASP can maintain an active session for a client which lets your application keep track of each client, and maintains all the variables that they have set and used.

Session Object Collections

Like the **Application** Object, the **Session** Object has two collections:

▶ **Contents** collection
▶ **StaticObjects** collection

Contents Collection

The **Contents** collection contains all the variables established for a session without using the `<OBJECT>` tag. The **Contents** collection is used to determine the value of a specific session item, or to iterate through the collection and retrieve a list of all items in the session.

```
Session.Contents("Key")
```

Where *"Key"* stands for a specific variable's name.

For example:

```
<%=Session.Contents("VisitorID")%>
```

For single session variables, this is usually shortened to:

```
<%=Session("VisitorID")%>
```

Both code lines will produce the same result.

You can iterate through the `Session.Contents` collection with the following code:

```
<%
Dim SessProp
For Each SessProp in Session.Contents
Response.Write("Session " & SessProp & " = " & Session.Contents(SessProp)
& "<BR>")
Next
%>
```

This code will produce a list of all the **Session** variables' names and values. The **For   Each** statement will iterate through each of the elements in the **Contents** collection. Each of these elements will be a key into the collection. You can then display this key, as well as the element in the collection associated with that key. The **Next** statement will take you to the next key in the collection, or if you are at the end, it will take you to the next line in the script.

StaticObjects Collection

The Session **StaticObjects** collection contains all the objects created with the **<OBJECT>** tag within session scope. The **StaticObjects** collection is used to retrieve the value for an object's specific property, or to iterate through the collection and retrieve all properties for all objects.

Session Object Properties

The Session Object has four properties

- **SessionID**
- **Timeout**
- **CodePage**
- **LCID**

SessionID Property

The **SessionID** property is a read-only property that returns the session identification number for each user. Each session has a unique identifier, generated by the server when the session is created.

To retrieve the current user's **SessionID**, use:

```
<%=Session.SessionID %>
```

Within the same server cycle, all SessionID's have unique values. If the Web server is stopped and restarted, some SessionID values may be the same as values generated before the server was stopped. For that reason, you should not use the SessionID property to generate primary key values for a database application. You could use it as a way of tracking all of the currently active users in an application-level variable such as an array.

Timeout Property

The **Timeout** property sets the timeout period assigned to the **Session** object for any application, in minutes. If the user does not request or refresh a page before the timeout period expires, the session ends.

You can set the **Timeout** value by:

```
<% Session.Timeout = 30 %>
```

This will cause the session to timeout in 30 minutes if there is no activity. If you want to retrieve the value of the **Timeout** property, you can use this:

```
<%= Session.Timeout %>
```

You should exercise caution when setting **Timeout** values. If you set **Timeout** to too short a duration, the server will terminate user sessions too quickly. If you rely on session variables to process user data and the user has not been able to complete the processing of a identification form, for example, the loss of session variables will cause all sorts of problems.

Setting **Session Timeout** to too long a duration also has its problems. All **Session** variables are stored in the server's memory. Since the server has no way to determine if the user is still viewing your site's pages (other than the **IsClientConnected** property, which is cumbersome to use in *every* **.asp** page), you are probably going to have quite a few user sessions eating up server memory resources if sessions last for too long a time. This is particularly critical if you store database query results in Session arrays. These results can hold a lot of data sometimes, and having multiple unused sessions still open, with large amounts of data stored in them, could hamper your server's capacity to operate speedily.

The best strategy is to analyze each application, by conducting average user browsing time tests, and then set the session timeout to a more appropriate value where needed. Generally though, the 20 minute timeout is a good compromise for most applications. So use that as a starting point, and begin tweaking from there.

CodePage Property

The **CodePage** property determines the code page that will be used to display content. A code page is used to map between the characters that are displayed on the screen and an internal table. Unless you are developing sites that use non-Roman alphabets, such as Russian or Japanese, you will not have to worry about setting this property.

In order to be able to set the session's code page you must have first enabled code page support with:

```
<%@ CODEPAGE = CodePage %>
```

Then, to set the code page to the Roman alphabet, use:

```
<% Session.CodePage=1252 %>
```

The LCID Property

A locale identifier determines time-zone and language rules for the system. The `LCID` property specifies the system's **location identifier,** which will be used to display content. `LCID` uniquely identifies one of the installed system-defined locales. There are two predefined `LCID` values: `LOCALE_SYSTEM_DEFAULT`, the system default locale, and `LOCALE_USER_DEFAULT`, the current user's locale. If a location identifier has not been installed, it cannot be set.

To set the `LCID` to U.S. English, use:

```
<% Session.LCID = 1033 %>
```

This also happens to be the default value for the `LCID` property for servers installed in the US, meaning you don't need to explicitly set it. The various `LCID` values are usually defined in the documentation as hexadecimal values. You must convert these values to a decimal value to use when setting the `LCID` property.

> *There's a "gotcha" in that you can only use the* `<%@...%>` *statement ONCE per page. So, if you set @CODEPAGE, you can't set @LCID and vice-versa.*

Session Object Methods

The `Session` object has just one method.

The Abandon Method

The `Abandon` method destroys all the objects stored in a `Session` object and releases the server resources they were occupying. If you do not call the `Abandon` method in a script, the server destroys the session objects when the session times out.

To call this method, you would use:

```
<% Session.Abandon %>
```

If you know that when a user finishes browsing a certain page they don't need any more session variables, you can call the `Abandon` method to release server memory resources associated with that session. Bear in mind that if you set certain useful session variable values, like `UserName`, all the values will be lost. On the other hand, if you are programming web games, which use server memory resources heavily, you might be better off explicitly ending the session and having the user log in for another game.

One use of the `Abandon` method is during development when testing `Session` variables. If you create a page named `abandon.asp`, as described below, you can call it when needed.

```
<%
Session.Abandon
Response.Redirect "default.asp"
%>
```

In this page, we first call the `Abandon` method of the `Session` object. This releases all of the session-level variables. Next, the `Redirect` method of the `Response` object is used to send the browser to the starting page of the application. In this example, that page is named `default.asp`.

Now we'll look at example of making variables persist across different ASP pages.

Try It Out – Passing Data from Page to Page

In this example, we will see how the `Session` object can be used to pass information from page to page within a particular user session. A good rule of thumb to remember is that session-level variables work best to pass information between the pages of a single user's session. Application-level variables are used to store information that can be retrieved at any time by any user accessing the system.

1 Create a new file, and key in the following:

```
<!DOCTYPE HTML PUBLIC "-//W3C//DTD HTML 3.2 Final//EN">

<HTML>
<HEAD>
<TITLE>Session Variable test</TITLE>
</HEAD>

<BODY>
<%
dim tAccessTime
tAccessTime = Session("LastAccessTime")

If tAccessTime = "" Then
        Response.Write ("This is the first time this page has been
accessed!<P>")
Else
        Response.Write ("This page was last accessed at " & tAccessTime &
"<P>")
End If
%>
<HR>Writing current access time to the Session object<P>
<% Session("LastAccessTime") = Now %>
```

```
<A HREF="sessVarTest.asp">Click here</A> to refresh the page.<P>
<A HREF="abandon.asp?dest=sessVarTest.asp">Click here</A> to abandon the
session.<P>

</BODY>
</HTML>
```

2 Save the file as **sessVarTest.asp** in your **BegASP** directory.

3 Create another new file, and enter the following:

```
<%
Session.Abandon
Response.Redirect Request("dest")
%>
```

4 Save the file as **abandon.asp** in your **BegASP** directory.

5 View the file **sessVarTest.asp** in your web browser.

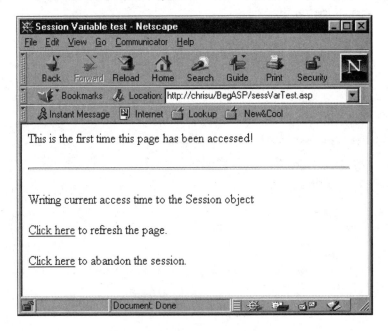

6   Open another instance of the browser and view the page again.

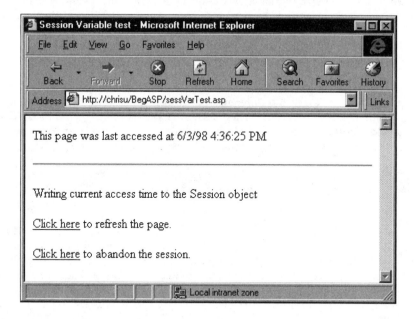

How It Works

In this example, we are using a session-level variable to store the date and time that this page was last accessed. If there is a value present, then it will be displayed for the user. If there is no value present, then the user will be shown a message telling them this.

```
<%
dim tAccessTime
tAccessTime = Session("LastAccessTime")
```

This first thing that we will need to do when processing this page is to retrieve the value stored in the session-level variable. We will be storing it in a local variable, which we can use throughout this page. This is very efficient way of working with session-level variables. It's important to remember that since the act of retrieving the session-level variable tends to consume a good deal of processor time, it is better to store the data locally, and then work with the local variable.

```
If tAccessTime = "" Then
        Response.Write ("This is the first time this page has been
accessed!<P>")
Else
        Response.Write ("This page was last accessed at " & tAccessTime &
"<P>")
End If
```

Next, we check to see if there is a value in the variable that we just retrieved. If no value has been set, then the contents of the variable will be an empty string. This will be the case if the session has not been created before, if the session timed out, or if this is the first time a user has been to this page. This may seem a bit strange to some people who are familiar with other languages in which a variable must have a value before it can be accessed. But in ASP, you can check to see if a session-level variable exists simply by trying to access it. If the variable does not exist, then a blank string will be returned. If there is a value there, then we will display it.

```
<HR>Writing current access time to the Session object<P>
<% Session("LastAccessTime") = Now %>
```

We will then update the value of the session-level variable called `LastAccessTime` with the current date and time. Notice the difference between interacting with a session-level variable, and an application-level variable. Since the session is user-specific, there are no `Lock` and `UnLock` methods for the `Session` object as there are for the `Application` object. To set a value in a session-level variable, nothing special has to be done beforehand.

```
<A HREF="sessVarTest.asp">Click here</A> to refresh the page.
<A HREF="abandon.asp?dest=sessVarTest.asp">Click here</A> to abandon the
session.<P>
```

We then provide two hyperlinks to allow the user to navigate from this page. The first hyperlink will reload the current page. This will cause the value that was just stored in the session-level variable to be displayed, and a new time stored there. The second hyperlink will call the `abandon.asp` file, which will abandon the current session. The `abandon.asp` file needs to know where to send the browser once the session has been abandoned, and this page name is passed as the `dest` query string variable.

```
<%
Session.Abandon
Response.Redirect Request("dest")
%>
```

The `abandon.asp` file will perform two functions. First, it will explicitly end the current session by calling the `Abandon` method. This will free any session-level variables and reset their values. Next, the script will redirect the browser to the page that the user supplied. Notice that we have used the short cut to retrieving the value of a query string variable, whereby we don't tell ASP which collection the information resides in. ASP will search each of the collections looking for the supplied key. When and if it finds it, it will return the value to the script.

Sessions and global.asa

Earlier in this chapter, we saw how the `global.asa` file can be used to process the startup and the shutdown of web applications. The file can also be used to handle events fired by the startup and shutdown of user sessions within a specific web application. Just as there are two event handlers for the `Application` object, there are two for the `Session` object as well.

Session_OnStart

`Session_OnStart` is called every time a new user begins a session with the web site. If you want to initialize a Session-scoped variable in `Session_OnStart`, you'd use:

```
Sub Session_OnStart
Session("YourVariable") = "SomeValue"
End Sub
```

A basic difference between application-level and session-level variables is that you can create session-level variables any time, whether in `global.asa` or from any ASP page, whereas you can only initialize Application variables in `global.asa`, though you can *change* application-level variable values from any ASP page. The reason for this is that `Application_OnStart` only runs *once*—when the Application starts—so you can't add any variables unless you stop and restart the Application.

For example, let's say you want to track the number of visitors currently accessing your site. This is different from a traditional counter that tracks total numbers of visitors. To do this, you would have an application-level variable that tracked the current number of users that were accessing the site. This is the same number of sessions that are currently active. Every time that a new session was started, we would want to add one to that number, and that can be done in the `Session_OnStart` routine.

Session_OnEnd

`Session_OnEnd` is called whenever a session terminates. This can happen if the session times out, or if it is explicitly abandoned. In `Session_OnEnd`, you might want to transfer temporary session variables to databases, or set application-level variables to another value: for example, if you are tracking the number of users currently visiting a site in an application-level variable, then you would subtract one from this number every time `Session_OnEnd` was run.

```
SUB Session_OnEnd
Application.Lock
Application("Active")= Application("Active") - 1
Application.Unlock
END SUB
```

Declaring Session Objects in global.asa

You can also declare session-scoped objects in `global.asa`:

```
<OBJECT RUNAT=Server SCOPE=Scope ID=Session PROGID="progID">
</OBJECT>
```

```
<OBJECT RUNAT=Server SCOPE=Scope ID=Session CLASSID="ClassID">
</OBJECT>
```

You can use either `ProgID` or `ClassID`, but not both.

As with application objects, session-level objects declared in `global.asa` are not created until the server processes a script that calls the object. Again, this saves resources by only creating objects that are actually used.

Try It Out – Visitor Tracking Using global.asa

In this example, we will take what we've learned and construct a `global.asa` file that will allow us to track the number of current visitors to the application, as well as the total that have visited since the application was started.

1 Create a new file, and key in the following:

```
<SCRIPT LANGUAGE=VBScript RUNAT=Server>
Sub Application_OnStart
Application("visits") = 0
Application("Active")= 0
End Sub

Sub Application_OnEnd

End Sub

Sub Session_OnStart
Session.Timeout = 1
Session("Start")=Now
Application.lock
        Application("visits")= Application("visits") + 1
        intTotal_visitors = Application("visits")
Application.unlock
Session("VisitorID") = intTotal_visitors

Application.lock
        Application("Active")= Application("Active") + 1
Application.unlock
End Sub

Sub Session_OnEnd
Application.lock
        Application("Active")= Application("Active") - 1
Application.unlock
End Sub
</SCRIPT>
```

2 Save this file as `global.asa`. For this example, you need to store your `global.asa` file in a different directory. We suggest that you store it in your Scripts directory, found under C:\InetPub\Scripts.

3 Create a new file, and key the following:

```
<!DOCTYPE HTML PUBLIC "-//W3C//DTD HTML 3.2 Final//EN">

<HTML>
<HEAD>
```

```
<TITLE>Retrieving Variables Set in Global.asa</TITLE>
</HEAD>

<BODY>
<P>
There have been <B><%=Session("VisitorID")%></B> total visits to this
site.
<BR>You are one of <B> <%=Application("Active")%></B> active visitors.
<BR>Your session started at <%= Session("Start") %>

</BODY>
</HTML>
```

4 Save this file as **VisitorCount.asp**. You will need to save it to the same virtual directory as **global.asa**, which in this case is Scripts.

5 View the file in your browser.

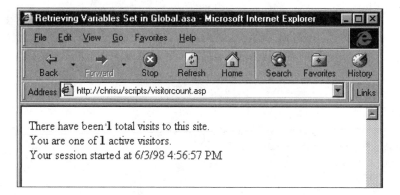

6 View the file in another browser.

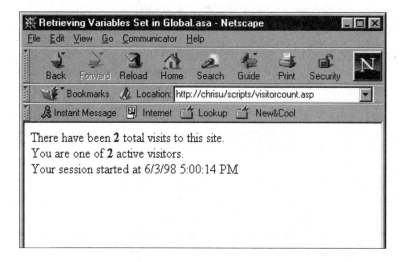

7 Close down the second browser and press Refresh on the first.

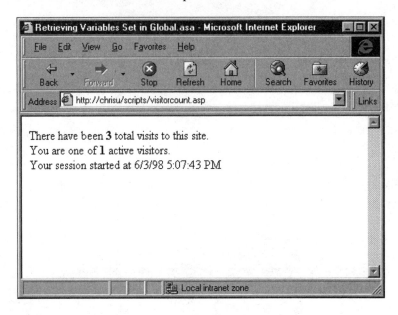

How It Works

In this application, we are using application-level variables to track the number of users that are currently looking at a site, as well as the total number that have accessed it.

```
<SCRIPT LANGUAGE=VBScript RUNAT=Server>
Sub Application_OnStart
Application("visits") = 0
Application("Active")= 0
End Sub
```

In the first event handler of the `global.asa` file, we will be working with the `OnStart` method that is called whenever the application is started.

> *This doesn't happen if you didn't put the example in its own virtual directory along with* `global.asa`. *This is because* `global.asa` *has to be in its own virtual directory, otherwise it won't be picked up correctly by ASP, and you can end up viewing the HTML text without the ASP added numbers.*

There are two variables that we will need to maintain throughout the life of the application. The `visits` variable will hold the total number of visits since the application was started. The `Active` variable will hold the number of current user sessions in the application.

```
Sub Application_OnEnd

End Sub
```

We will not be doing any processing when the application is ended, so we are just adding this event handler as a placeholder.

```
Sub Session_OnStart
Session.Timeout = 1
Session("Start")=Now
```

When a session is started, we will perform some processing in the **Session_OnStart** event handler. To make our example work faster, we set the **Timeout** value of the **Session** object to 1 minute. In a real application, you would very rarely have your **Timeout** value set so low. We will also store the starting date and time for this session in a session-level variable.

```
Application.Lock
        Application("visits")= Application("visits") + 1
        intTotal_visitors = Application("visits")
Application.Unlock
Session("VisitorID") = intTotal_visitors
```

Next, we will need to find out the total number of visitors to the site since the application was started. This information is stored in an application-level variable. In order to change an application-level variable, we need to first **Lock** the **Application** object. We can then increment the value stored in the **visits** variable by one. This new value will represent the total number of visitors, including the one currently starting. The incremented value is stored back into the same application-level variable it came from. Once we have made all the changes that we need to at this point, we will call **Unlock** to free up the **Application** object.

```
Application.Lock
        Application("Active")= Application("Active") + 1
Application.Unlock
```

Finally, we will update the current number of active users by one. This information is stored in another application-level variable.

```
Sub Session_OnEnd
Application.Lock
        Application("Active")= Application("Active") - 1
Application.Unlock
End Sub
```

When the user leaves the site and their session times out, this event handler will be called. The important thing that needs to happen in this file is for the number of active users to be decremented by one. Since this information is stored at the application-level, you will need to **Lock** the **Application** object when making the change, and **Unlock** the object as quickly as possible.

```
There have been <B><%=Session("VisitorID")%></B> total visits to this
site.
<BR>You are one of <b> <%=Application("Active")%></B> active visitors.
<BR>Your session started at <%= Session("Start") %>
```

In our test page, we will be displaying the total number of visits to this site since the application was started. We will also be showing the number of active visitors, as well as the time at which the current session began. Even though we are interacting with an application-level variable, we do not need to **Lock** and **Unlock** the **Application** object if we only want to *read* the data.

As you can see from the screen shots, once a session times out, the `Session_OnEnd` really is called. This can be seen by the change in number of active users as we look at each of the browser snapshots.

We've completed our discussions on how to preserve data from page to page using the `Session` object. Also, we have covered how to keep information from session to session in an application using the `Application` object. Next, we will turn our attention towards a mechanism that will allow you to store information about the client that will persist between their visits to your web site—the cookie.

Using Cookies

As we discussed in Chapter 7, the cookies collection stores values from any cookies that are sent by the client to the server. As well as reading information supplied by a client's cookies, the server needs to be able to *write* information to cookies on the client's machine. ASP uses the `Response` object's features to set cookies' values.

Before the advent of Active Server Pages, cookies were one way that data could be transferred between different pages on a site, as a user moved between them. As we saw earlier in this chapter, the `Session` object gives us a very powerful mechanism that allows you to do just that. So what is the role for cookies now?

Cookies play a vital role behind the scenes in ASP. They serve as the mechanism that tells each page that a user accesses during a session what session that request belongs to. ASP can take this cookie and retrieve all of the session information that is stored on the server. But cookies can still play a role in storing information between sessions. While a session has a timeout value, of usually 20 minutes, after which all of its information is deleted, a cookie can persist for a much longer period of time. So cookies can still play an important part in storing information during the times when the user is off visiting other sites, or is not even using their browser at all.

Creating Cookies

Until ASP was released, the most common way to set cookies was to use JavaScript. The syntax for doing this with JavaScript is fairly complex—even daunting—if you're not over-familiar with JavaScript. ASP provides a one-line instruction method to set and retrieve cookies.

The syntax for writing cookies in ASP is:

```
<% Response.Cookies("cookie") = value %>
```

If *value* is a string, it must be enclosed in quotes.

```
<% Response.Cookies("cookie")("key") = value %>
```

If you add a *key* value, then you can access this cookie like a collection. This means that one cookie can have multiple values stored with it.

If you use this method to set a cookie, the following HTTP header is generated:

```
Set-Cookie:YOURCOOKIENAME=somevalue
```

You can see that the **Response.Cookies** method is simply a way of sending the Set-Cookie HTTP header without resorting to complicated code.

Using Keys

If a cookie is used to store more than one value we have specify which of these multiple values we want to set. To do this, we refer to it via its *key* value. The key value is similar to a variable name. The general syntax for writing cookies with keys is:

```
Response.Cookies("thesameCookieName")("somekey") = "SomeValue"
Response.Cookies("thesameCookieName")("anotherkey") = "AnotherValue"
```

If you issue another cookie with the same name but without specifying the key, you will overwrite all cookie values for that cookie's name.

ASP uses the **HasKeys** property to determine whether or not a cookie holds multiple values. To check if a cookie holds multiple values, we interrogate the **HasKeys** property:

```
Request.Cookies("theCookie").HasKeys
```

If the cookie named **theCookie** has keys, then this value will be true. If not, then it will be false.

Making your Cookie Persist

A cookie set with the basic syntax will persist for as long as the browser is open, or until the session expires. As soon as the browser is closed, the cookie's value will disappear. To make a cookie persist, i.e., for the cookie to be written to the client browser's hard disk (the "cookie jar"), you have to set an expiration date for the cookie. The general syntax for doing this is:

```
Response.Cookies("Cook").Expires = "July 4, 1999"
```

A Better Way to Set a Cookie's Expiration Date

Though setting the cookie's expiration date as "July 4, 1999" works, a better way to set the expiration date is to use *relative* date values. Since **Date** is a built-in VBScript function, you could set the expiration date as **Date** + X, where X stands for the number of days you want the cookie to "live":

```
Response.Cookies("Cook").Expires = Date + 1
```

This will set the expiration date to 1 day from today.

Deleting a Cookie

To delete a cookie, set its **Expires** property to any date prior to today. The easiest way to do this is to use relative date values, as shown in this example:

```
Response.Cookies("Cook").Expires = Date - 1
```

Try It Out – Using Cookies in ASP

There are many sites on the web that will ask you to register in order to get some level of enhanced access. Once you have registered, you are given a user name and password. The next time you visit the site, you are asked to enter these before being granted access. Some sites will give you the option of saving your username and password as a cookie, so that you will automatically be logged in next time you visit. In this example, we will look at how to do this.

1 Open your favorite HTML editor, and create the following file:

```
<!DOCTYPE HTML PUBLIC "-//W3C//DTD HTML 3.2 Final//EN">
<HTML>
<HEAD>
<TITLE>Cookie Test - Login</TITLE>
</HEAD>
Please enter your e-mail address and password to login to the system.
<FORM ACTION="CheckLogin.asp" METHOD="POST">
E-Mail Address:      <INPUT TYPE="Text" NAME="email" SIZE="40"><BR>
Password: <INPUT TYPE="Password" NAME="Password" SIZE="40"><P>
<INPUT TYPE="Checkbox" NAME="SaveLogin"> Save Login as a Cookie?<P>
<INPUT TYPE="Submit" VALUE="Login">  <INPUT TYPE="RESET">
</FORM>
</BODY>
</HTML>
```

2 Save the file as **login.asp** in the **BegASP** virtual directory of your web server.

3 Create another new file, and enter the following:

```
<%
dim bLoginSaved
If Request.Form("SaveLogin") = "on" Then
        Response.Cookies("SavedLogin")("EMail") = Request.Form("email")
        Response.Cookies("SavedLogin")("pw") = Request.Form("Password")
        Response.Cookies("SavedLogin").Expires = Date + 30
        bLoginSaved = True
Else
        bLoginSaved = False
End If
%>
```

```
<HTML>
<HEAD>
<TITLE>Cookie Test - Check Login</TITLE>
</HEAD>
<BODY>
<% If bLoginSaved then %>
        Saving Login information to a cookie<HR>
<% End If %>
Thank you for logging into the system.<P>
E-Mail address confirmation: <%= Request.Form("email") %>
</BODY>
</HTML>
```

4 Save the file as **checkLogin.asp** in the same directory.

5 Load the **login.asp** page into your browser.

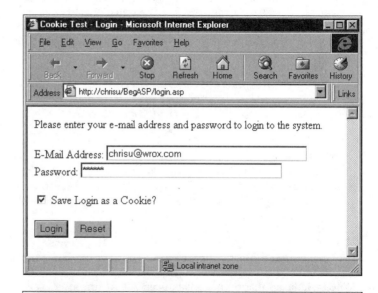

6 Enter an e-mail address and password. You should also check the Save Login as a Cookie button to save your login. The press the Login button. Note: we will not be validating the e-mail and password against anything, so feel free to enter whatever you want.

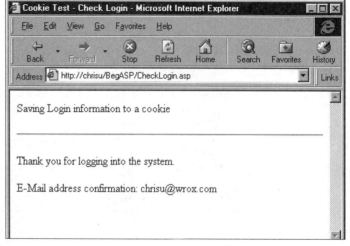

How It Works

In this example, we are using two ASP files. The first one will display the login screen for the user. They are asked to enter their e-mail address and password. They can also click on a checkbox that will have their login information saved as a cookie.

If you look at the code for `login.asp`, you will see no Active Server Pages code. So you may be wondering why this file is an ASP and not a plain HTML. In the next example, we will be adding some server-side script to this file, so we went ahead and gave it the `.asp` name. Once the FORM is submitted, the `checkLogin.asp` page will handle the results.

```
<%
dim bLoginSaved
If Request.Form("SaveLogin") = "on" Then
```

When the FORM information is passed to the `checkLogin.asp` page, the first thing that we want to do is see if the user has requested that their login information be saved in a cookie. We are declaring a variable called `bLoginSaved`. This boolean variable will be set to true if the user wants a cookie set. It will be false if they do not. This will allow us to display a notification later in the page.

```
Response.Cookies("SavedLogin")("EMail") = Request.Form("email")
Response.Cookies("SavedLogin")("pw") = Request.Form("password")
Response.Cookies("SavedLogin").Expires = Date + 30
bLoginSaved = True
```

We will be creating one cookie with two keys. The name of the cookie we are creating is `SavedLogin`. It will contain two keys of information. These keys will hold the e-mail address and password of the user. The values for these keys will come from the `Form` collection of the `Request` object. The information that the user entered in the fields on the `login.asp` page will be stored in this collection.

We will be setting this cookie to expire 30 days from today. As you saw earlier, you can use the VBScript `Date` function to determine the current date, and then add the desired lifetime of the cookie in days to that value. The last step is to set the flag that we declared earlier to true. This is to indicate that a cookie has been set for the user.

```
Else
        bLoginSaved = False
End If
%>
```

In the case where the user did not request that a cookie be set, we will set the flag to false. We have now reached the end of our ASP script block, so we terminate it with the `%>` statement.

```
<BODY>
<% If bLoginSaved Then %>
        Saving Login information to a cookie<HR>
<% End If %>
Thank you for logging into the system.<P>
```

Now that we have done all of the cookie processing, we can turn to what the user sees. First, we want to inform the user that a cookie was saved to their machine. Since we set a boolean flag earlier in the page, we can check its value. If it is set to true, then we will display a message for the user. If not, then we will just go on displaying the rest of the page.

```
E-Mail address confirmation: <%= Request.Form("email") %>
</BODY>
</HTML>
```

Finally, we want to display the user's e-mail address that was just entered. This is done primarily as a validation that the correct information was entered. To display the e-mail address, we will retrieve it from the **Form** collection of the **Request** object.

Now that we have seen how to set the cookies, let's take a look at another example that will show how we can use the cookies in our login page.

Try It Out – Using Cookies in ASP Part 2

In this example, we will modify the two ASP scripts from the previous example so that the login page will check for the existence of a cookie. The login check page will inform the user if their login was entered via a cookie, or by direct input.

1 Using your favorite HTML editor, open the **login.asp** file, and make the following changes.

```
<%
If Request.Cookies("SavedLogin").HasKeys Then
        Response.Redirect "CheckLogin.asp?cookie=1"
End If
%>
<!DOCTYPE HTML PUBLIC "-//W3C//DTD HTML 3.2 Final//EN">
<HTML>
<HEAD>
<TITLE>Cookie Test - Login</TITLE>
</HEAD>
Please enter your e-mail address and password to login to the system.
<FORM ACTION="CheckLogin.asp" METHOD="POST">
E-Mail Address:        <INPUT TYPE="Text" NAME="email" SIZE="40"><BR>
Password: <INPUT TYPE="Password" NAME="Password" SIZE="40"><P>
<INPUT TYPE="Checkbox" NAME="SaveLogin"> Save Login as a Cookie?<P>
<INPUT TYPE="Submit" VALUE="Login">  <INPUT TYPE="RESET">
</FORM>

</BODY>
</HTML>
```

2 Close and save the file.

3 Open the `checkLogin.asp` file and make the following changes.

```
<%
dim strEmail
If Request.QueryString("cookie") = 1 Then
        strEMail = Request.Cookies("SavedLogin")("Email")
Else
        strEMail = Request.Form("email")
End If
```

```
dim bLoginSaved
If Request.Form("SaveLogin") = "on" Then
        Response.Cookies("SavedLogin")("EMail") = Request.Form("email")
        Response.Cookies("SavedLogin")("pw") = Request.Form("password")
        Response.Cookies("SavedLogin").Expires = Date + 30
        bLoginSaved = True
Else
        bLoginSaved = False
End If
%>
<HTML>
<HEAD>
<TITLE>Cookie Test - Check Login</TITLE>
</HEAD>
<BODY>
<% If bLoginSaved Then %>
        Saving Login information to a cookie<HR>
<% End If %>
Thank you for logging into the system.<P>
<% If Request.QueryString("cookie") = 1 Then %>
Login submitted via cookie<P>
<% End If %>
E-Mail address confirmation: <%= strEMail %>
</BODY>
</HTML>
```

4 View the `login.asp` page in your browser.

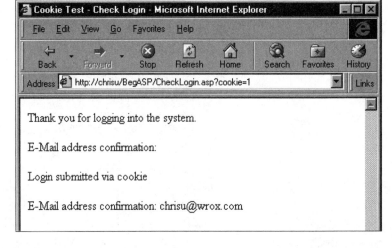

How It Works

In this example, we have made changes to both the **login.asp** file and the **checkLogin.asp** file. The changes to **login.asp** will be used to detect if a cookie has been set to save the login information.

```
<%
If Request.Cookies("SavedLogin").HasKeys Then
        Response.Redirect "CheckLogin.asp?cookie=1"
End If
%>
```

This section of ASP code that has been added to the top of the **login.asp** page will check to see if a cookie has been set. If you recall from the previous example, the cookie that is set actually contains two keys: one for the e-mail and one for the password. We can determine if the correct cookie has been set by checking to see if the cookie named **SavedLogin** has keys. This is why we named the file **login.asp** earlier.

If the correct cookie has been set, then we will use the **Redirect** method of the **Response** object to send the browser to the **checkLogin.asp** page. To notify this page that the request is due to the result of a cookie being read, we will set a query string parameter. We will then be able to check for this value when we are processing the **checkLogin.asp** page.

```
<%
dim strEmail
If Request.QueryString("cookie") = 1 Then
        strEMail = Request.Cookies("SavedLogin")("Email")
Else
        strEMail = Request.Form("email")
End If
```

In the **checkLogin.asp** page, we will first add some code that will determine if the page was requested by the redirection from the **login.asp** page. We set a query string parameter called **cookie** when we redirected the browser to this page. By checking to see if its value is set to 1, we will know if this page was called due to a cookie login.

There are two possible places that the user's e-mail address can come from. If they have selected to save their logon information in a cookie, then their e-mail address can be retrieved from that cookie. If they have entered their e-mail address directly, then we can recover it from the **Form** collection of the **Request** object. In either case, we want to save its value into a local variable. This will allow us to use it later in the page, without having to check which method it was supplied by again.

```
<% If Request.QueryString("cookie") = 1 Then %>
Login submitted via cookie<P>
<% End If %>
E-Mail address confirmation: <%= strEMail %>
```

We want to display an indication to the user that their login information was supplied via a cookie. The query string parameter **cookie** being set to 1 indicates this. If this is the case, then we will display a message. We also need to change the **Response.Write** shortcut that displays the e-mail address that the user logged on with. Earlier in the page, we stored the value in the **strEmail** local variable. We will now display the contents of that variable here.

All that would be left to do is add the proper user authentication code, and you would have a workable user login system for your web site. Later in the book, we will take a look at how to insert and retrieve information from databases. You can then tie this method of user login with the databases and have yourself a very robust authentication system.

Summary

The world of web-based applications is made possible by Active Server Pages and the `Application` and `Session` object. These powerful objects allow you transform a web site from a series of linked pages to an actual application by creating a means to hold user information from page to page. In this chapter, we have looked at:

▶ How the `Application` object can be used to store information that can be accessed by all users accessing a web site.

▶ The powerful `Session` object, which allows us to treat a user's interaction with the web site as a continuous action, rather than just a disconnected series of page requests.

▶ What the `global.asa` file is used for and how it helps us interact with the beginning and the end of sessions and applications.

▶ How **cookies** can help us store information over a long period of time, and even after the user has left our site.

▶ When and how to use cookies to store information at the client's computer.

Now that we are on our way towards building web-based applications, we will look at how we can enhance the functionality of our ASP scripts. To do this we will need to become familiar with Active Server Components, which are the subject of our next chapter.

Active Server Pages Components

With the multitude of web site programmers today employed doing very similar jobs, you'll find that many of them will share similar goals. For example, many developers would consider the following features among those that they would like to include on their sites:

- A technique to navigate through their web site
- A way to manage advertisements on the site
- A method to customize your pages to the capabilities of the browser viewing them

Rather than allowing all these people to waste thousands of programmer hours, as each site develops and troubleshoots the same tools, Microsoft has created a set that are available to programmers. These are grouped together, and called the **Installable Components for ASP**.

There a lot of Server components that come with ASP, as we saw in Chapter 1, but rather than swamp you with details on every one of them, we've decided to concentrate on three of the main components you might use on a web site. Once you've mastered these, you should find that working with other components, such as the MyInfo Component, is relatively simple.

In this chapter we will cover:

- The `Server` Object
- How to use Server Components.
- The Advertisement Rotator Component.
- Using the Content Linker component to direct users through a set of pages
- Using the Content Linker to produce a Table of Contents
- The Browser Capabilities component

But first we need to understand how we can use the `Server` Object to create Server Components for us...

The Server Object

The tools that Microsoft provides are organized into several groups, according to good programming practice as defined in the ASP object model. In the object model, the software designer (in this case, Microsoft) creates an object which can hold information and can carry out certain tasks, called **methods**. We covered objects and methods in Chapter 6. As part of that discussion we noted that each object has its own methods: and this is an important point. For example, an object that directs a user through the site has a method whose job is to 'provide the next URL'.

As we discussed in Chapter 6, ASP has 6 objects: they are the `Server`, `Application`, `Request`, `Response`, `Session` and `ObjectContext` objects. These are the built-in objects of the ASP object model. This section consists of an overview of how to use the `Server` object. Although there are several methods within the `Server` Object, one stands out in its usefulness. `CreateObject` allows the programmer to make instances of components that are running on the server. These can use the Common Object Model to make connections to ActiveX objects. Microsoft has provided about a dozen components that contain the ability to add powerful features to your site. We will look at three of those components in this chapter.

Creating an Instance of a Component Object

When you want to use a Server component, the first step is to create an **instance** of the Server object from the object model.

You'll recall our discussion of the relationship between objects and instances from Chapter 6. Essentially, the object is the template; and an instance is a particular copy which is created in the shape of that template. This action is similar to cookies coming out of a cookie cutter.

In ASP, we create an instance of an object in the `Set` statement with the `Server.CreateObject` method and the location and name of the object. The instance must be assigned to a variable name—this allows you to refer to the instance, later on in your code. Although you can use any name, many programmers prefix the name of their object, by appending the letters `obj` before it. For example, if you were using an instance of the Next Linker (also called the Content Linker), then you might want to give it a variable name like `objNextLink` or `objNL`.

Since the name that you give to an instance of an object is effectively just a variable name, then the same naming rules apply. You may recall that we discussed naming conventions and rules in Chapter 4.

A typical instantiation might look something like the following piece of code:

```
<%
Set objNL = Server.CreateObject("MSWC.NextLink")
    These lines can contain code that uses objNL
%>
```

FYI

Instantiation **is the name we give to the process of creating an instance of an object. For example, in thise piece of code we have** instantiated objNL, **which is an instance of the** Server **object.**

As you can see, we have used the **Set** statement, followed by the name that we have chosen for our instance. On the right of the equals sign is the code that we use to create an instance of the **Server** object's **NextLink** component.

The general syntax for establishing a reference to a component of the **Server** object is as follows:

```
<%
Set objInstanceName = Server.CreateObject("ClassName.ComponentName")
%>
```

Don't forget to include the keyword **Set**, and the equals sign. Once you've used the **Set** statement, and the **CreateObject** method in this way, the instance of the object will be ready to use. Subsequently, you use the instance by referring to it using the name you gave in within the **Set** statement.

> *One important point with this syntax is that the ComponentName referred to within the parentheses can have two parts separated by a period. They could be either in the form of ("ProjectName.ClassName") or ("ClassName.Method").*

In this chapter, we will be performing two instantiations. We instantiate the Advertisement Rotator component by using the following code:

```
<%
Set objAd=Server.CreateObject("MSWC.AdRotator")
%>
```

Later, we'll use the code below to instantiate the Content Linker component:

```
<%
Set objNL=Server.CreateObject("MSWC.NextLink")
%>
```

Now, we'll look at three components, namely the Ad Rotator, Content Linker and Browser Capabilities components.

The Ad Rotator Component

To date, one of the most successful sources of revenue on the World Wide Web has been the sale of advertising space. An **ad** is a graphic—often it's a `.gif` file, in a banner format of about 400 pixels wide by 60 pixels high. Since viewers will pay little attention to the same ad again and again, site designers will rotate a collection of ads in the hope of giving each visit a fresh and interesting look. ASP includes a component, the **Ad Rotator** component, that is designed to perform and manage just such a task.

The Ad Rotator component utilizes a **scheduler file**: this file is used to keep track of which ads should be displayed, and how frequently to display them. A scheduler file is a simple ASCII text file with two sections. The first section sets the general parameters for displaying all ads. The second section sets specific parameters for each ad in the rotation. These two sections appear in a single text file, where they are separated by a single asterisk.

In the first section, there are four general parameters that can be set:

▶ The width of the borders

▶ The height of the ad as it will appear on the page

▶ The width of the ad as it will appear on the page

▶ The URL of a file that can provide redirections when the user clicks on the ads

If you leave any of these parameters out, then ASP will provide a default. Remember that this section must end with a single line, containing an asterisk and nothing else as follows:

```
border   4
height   50
width 400
*
```

In the second section we write four lines for each ad in the rotation:

▶ The name of the ad file (for example, `WroxBooks.gif`)

▶ The URL of the hyperlink to be executed if the user clicks on the ad. If no hyperlink is required—that is, the user's click causes 'no action'—then we use a single hyphen (with no spaces) in place of any URL

▶ A text description of the ad, which will be shown in browsers without graphics in the same way as the HTML `<ALT>` tag

▶ The frequency with which the ad should be displayed

> *Note that we do not type double quotes for any of the parameters, in either of the two sections of the scheduler file.*

Let's illustrate the parameters, as we've described them. A typical scheduler file would might look like the one shown below:

```
border   4
height   50
width 400
*
Airplane90.gif
www.AirManCo.com
Airplane Manufacturing Company provides you with easier-to-build planes.
20
RedTrain88.gif
www.LocosRus.com
Call Locos-R-Us for great discounts on 22 and 26 wheeled Locomotives.
40
Auto57.gif
www.HomeCars.com
Stand out in a crowd: Drive your own Home-built Auto.
40
```

That's enough theory for now. Let's get to grips with a real example.

Try It Out – The Ad Rotator Component

We'll create a page that gives a tip for programming students. Each time the page is viewed, it will also feature display of three ads.

1 Download the three graphic files **stonebroom.gif**, **TechTools.gif** and **worldofatl.gif** from the Wrox Press web site (at **http://rapid.wrox.co.uk/books/1347**), and save them into the **BegASP** directory.

2 Open up your editor of choice, and insert the following code:

```
border 4
height 50
width 400
*
stonebroom.gif
http://www.stonebroom.com
Stone Broom Software - Tomorrow's Technology Today.
20
TechTools.gif
-
Tech Tools for programmers in High Efficiency mode
40
WorldOfATL.gif
http://www.worldofatl.com
World of ATL: It's a wonderful world.
40
```

You can download all of these examples from the Wrox web site at
http://rapid.wrox.co.uk/books/1347.

3 In your **BegASP** directory, save this code as **AdSchedule.txt**.

4 Once you've saved the code above, clear your editor and now type the following code:

```
<% Option Explicit %>
<HTML>
<HEAD>
<TITLE>Example Ad One</TITLE>
</HEAD>

<BODY>
<H1>Programming Student's Tip Sheet</H1>
<%
Dim varAd, objAd
Set objAd = Server.CreateObject("MSWC.AdRotator")
varAd = objAd.GetAdvertisement("AdSchedule.txt")
Response.Write varAd
%>

<BR>
<H2>Tip #456: When writing Do While loops</H2>
Always double check that tasks to be performed once are outside the loop
and
<BR>tasks to be performed multiple times are inside the loop.
</BODY>

</HTML>
```

5 In your **BegASP** directory, save this code as **Ad.asp**.

6 Open up your browser of choice. At the address line, type in the URL **http://my_server_name/ BegASP/ad.asp**.

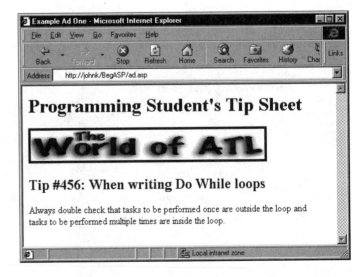

7 Try viewing the page a number of times by pressing the Refresh/Reload button. You should get the same information every time, but a different ad appearing.

How It Works

We have set up an ad rotation scheme featuring the ads of a number of different institutions. First, we decided the physical dimensions of our advertising space, and they are specified in the first section of the file `AdSchedule.txt`:

```
border 4
height 50
width 400
*
```

Next, we code the details of the three institutions that wish to advertise on our web page:

```
stonebroom.gif
http://www.stonebroom.com
Stone Broom Software - Tomorrow's Technology Today.
20
TechTools.gif
-
Tech Tools for programmers in High Efficiency mode
40
WorldOfATL.gif
http://www.worldofatl.com
World of ATL: It's a wonderful world.
40
```

We must ensure that this section contains exactly four rows for each ad. These rows contain the name of the ad file; the hyperlink URL; a comment that the browser associates with the graphic; and the relative frequency with which the ad should be shown.

Note that the Tech Tools Software Co does not have a URL to create a hyperlink, and thus we've typed a hyphen instead. There must be only a hyphen on that line: don't type any spaces, tabs or other characters.

Each institution has supplied a `.gif` file, that we display on our site. While HiTech and ATL each pay for 40% of the fee for this advertising space, Stonebroom pays only 20%. These proportions are indicated on the fourth, eighth and twelfth lines above, which control the frequency with which each ad is shown.

You need to create the scheduler file before you test the ASP file, otherwise it won't work. You should also be sure to save the scheduler file as an ASCII text file.

FYI You'll also notice that, in this example, the graphic files are contained in the same directory as the scheduler file, namely `Inetpub\wwwroot\BegASP`. If a graphic is in a different folder, then you must provide the relative path from the scheduler file to the graphic file.

The code to place the ads in the page is contained within the file **Ad.asp**. First, we create an instance of the Ad Rotator component, called **objAd**:

```
Set objAd = Server.CreateObject("MSWC.AdRotator")
```

Then, we use the **GetAdvertisement** method of **objAd** to return the information needed to display a graphic in HTML:

```
varAd = objAd.GetAdvertisement("AdSchedule.txt")
```

This information is stuffed into the variable named **varAd**.

FYI Again, in this example, the scheduler file is contained in the same directory as the .asp file. If the scheduler file is in a different folder, then you must provide the relative path from the .asp file to the scheduler file.

Next, we **Response.Write** the ad information to the page:

```
Response.Write varAd
```

FYI The frequency value for each ad can be confusing. ASP divides each individual frequency by the total of all the frequencies, in order to get a ratio. The number is not a *percentage* unless the total comes to 100. Some site designers prefer to make the numbers add to a round number like 10 or 100. Other designers sell their ads at the same price, and give each a frequency of 1 so that all ads will be shown an equal number of times. If an advertiser wants more exposure, they can pay twice as much for the privilege of having an ad frequency of 2.

The Content Linker Component

A well-designed web site will provide the visitor with tools and guidance, to navigate the site. This guidance can be at a number of levels of sophistication. At the simplest level are the **hyperlinks**—for example, a web page displays a piece of underlined text, and the user clicks there to request the corresponding link: Click here to see our new sweaters. The next level of sophistication displays a **frame**, listing the contents of the site. More sophisticated site designers can also include a **search engine**, such as the FrontPage WebBot, to assist visitors in finding desired content.

ASP allows you to create even more sophisticated guidance tools by using the **Content Linker**. This object helps you to create a list of pages in a specific order, that you want to establish as a path through the site. On any given page in this path, the user can click on the Next or Previous buttons, and display the appropriate page in the path. The Content Linker even allows you to display the URL of the current page, and a description of the next/previous pages. Finally, some features of the Content Linker allow you to program sophisticated jumps or loops.

The content linker is commonly used to support the following types of web page:

- Tutorial
- Five-minute tour
- Review of new products (we'll use this as the example in this chapter)
- Multi-page forms

In this section of the chapter, we'll start with a very simple example. After explaining the example you can test yourself on the technique by doing the Try-It-Out. Then we'll improve on the example in step by step manner (with Try-It-Outs for you) until you have a very sophisticated set of navigation tools.

Structure of the Content Linker

The content linker has two parts:

- **The index file**. This holds a list of `.asp` pages, in the order that they should be presented to the viewer. The index file can easily be changed, for example, if we want to reflect new pages added to the list, a revision in the order of pages, or the substitution of new pages for older pages.
- **The ASP pages**. Each `.asp` file contains two parts. The first part consists of the normal content of the page, such as the text and graphics. The second part is the ASP code that uses the Content Linker to give the user options for moving through the list of pages. These options are typically hyperlinks for the Next Page, Previous Page, First Page and Last Page.

Although most people refer to this component as the Content Linker component, it's actually referred to within the ASP program in IIS4 as **NextLink**. For our purposes, the two terms will be used interchangeably.

Before we get to view any pages, we first need to construct the index file. Then, with our index file in hand, we'll briefly discuss the motivation and advantages of Content Linker over other forms of navigation. With all this on board, we'll then get down to using our index file in a real example.

Content Linker Index File

The index file is a simple ASCII text file that takes only a few minutes to write. The best way to describe one is to create one, so we'll do that now: we'll be using this file in our examples.

Try It Out – Creating an Index File

We're going to be exercising the Content Linker by creating a number of pages detailing new products featured by an on-line clothier. Here's the index file that we'll use.

1 Start Notepad and create a file with one line for each URL that will be in the tour of pages:

```
hat501.asp        This Week's Hat       Run for September 01-08 1999
sweater304.asp    This Week's Sweater   Run for September 01-08 1999
tie784.asp        This Week's Tie       Run for September 01-08 1999
trouser422.asp    This Week's Trousers  Run for September 01-08 1999
vest562.asp       This Week's Vest      Run for September 01-08 1999
```

 It's important to format this file correctly, so separate the entries on each line with a *Tab*—nothing else—and press *Enter* at the end of each line, to start the new line. Hence, each line should be formatted as: *URL Tab Description Tab Comments Enter*. The URL does not need to be prefixed with `http://`, provided the page will is stored in the same folder as the other pages—in this case, we'll be creating the .asp files and placing them in the same folder as the index file.

2 Save this file in your `BegASP` folder, giving it the name `NewProductsTour.txt`.

What It Does

In the lines of the index file, we have created three columns:

- URL column
- Description column
- Comments column

The URLs are the files that are contained in our tour of pages: we must list them in the order in which we want them to appear in the tour. The contents of the Description column will be used later, to give information to the user. The contents of the Comments column will only ever be seen by the site designers, when they look at the index file. The Comments column is optional. You can add various comment lines such as a title for the file, comments or a revision date.

It's important that this file is typed correctly, therefore you should be careful to avoid the following pitfalls:

- Adding more than one tab between the columns
- Using spaces between columns rather than the required tab
- Forgetting to save the file in ASCII text format
- Forgetting to put the `.asp` extension on the file names in the first column

Motivation for Using Content Linker

Over the next few pages we will build several examples, increasing in complexity. However, let's start here by looking at an example that doesn't even use ASP.

Consider the HTML page shown below, which displays information about the first item on our tour of new products—hat model #501. We'll refer to this at `hat501.htm`.

```
<HTML>
<HEAD>
<TITLE>Hat501</TITLE>
</HEAD>

<BODY>
<P>Hat of the Week:</P>
<P>You can be both fine and dandy with this number just in from Dave's
Hattery of Venezia.</P>
<A HREF="sweaters304.asp">Click here for next item</A>
</BODY>

</HTML>
```

At the top of the page, the user will see text that describes this hat; at the bottom of the page, there is a hyperlink which, when clicked, takes the user to the next item on the tour of products (in this case, the page describing sweater #304).

In this context, what we're really interested in is the site navigation technique. Here's the line that should jump to our attention:

```
<A HREF="sweaters304.asp">Click here for next item</A>
```

The text Click here for next item is shown on the screen: when the user clicks on this, they activate the hyperlink to the next page. In this first case the HREF to the next page is hard-wired: that is, it's typed in raw HTML. Note that the target of the HREF attribute must be in double quotes. Provided you've already created the target page `sweaters304.asp`, then the user will have no problem with this.

However, when it is time for the web master to make changes to the order of the pages, he will have to dig through every page and find each of these Next hyperlinks and write in the new HREF. It's a laborious task (believe me, I've done it); and it's also very confusing, since there is no stage at which the web master ever sees the whole list of pages on the tour.

This can become a huge headache for the web master. However, this problem can be neatly overcome by using a simple form of the content linker—as we have already seen, the index file contains the full list of the tour, making management of the tour significantly easier.

ASP Pages that Use Content Linker to Hyperlink to the Next Page

Now, we've got the motivation, we've got the index file, so let's write some ASP pages and create our first working model. Our first example will use the Content Linker simply to show us the next URL based on what ASP finds in the index file. This example uses the Index File introduced earlier in this chapter, which is named `NewProductsTour.txt` and is located in the same folder as these ASP pages.

Try It Out – A Simple Content Linker Example

This example uses the index file, `NewProductsTour.txt`, that we created earlier, and also requires five ASP files. This looks like a lot of code, but the five ASP files are all very similar.

1 Open your editor of choice, and type in the following:

```asp
<% Option Explicit %>
<HTML>
<HEAD>
<TITLE>Hat501</TITLE>
</HEAD>

<BODY>
<P>Hat of the Week:</P>
<P>You can be both fine and dandy with this number just in from
<EM>Dave's Hattery</EM> of Venezia</P>

<%
Dim MyPageNext
Dim objNL

Set objNL = Server.Createobject("MSWC.NextLink")
MyPageNext = objNL.GetNextURL("NewProductsTour.txt")
%>
<A HREF="<% =MyPageNext %>"> Click here for next item </A>

</BODY>
</HTML>
```

2 In your `BegASP` folder, save this code as `hat501.asp`.

3 Now we need to make very similar pages for the next four items of clothing that we sell. To make life easier we will just change a few lines in the `Hat501.asp` page and use **SaveAs** to make that our Sweater page. So after you have saved the above file, use the editor to change it to the following:

```
<% Option Explicit %>
<HTML>
<HEAD>
<TITLE>Sweater304</TITLE>
</HEAD>

<BODY>
<P>Beautiful Blue Cardigan Sweater</P>

<%
Dim MyPagePrev
Dim MyPageNext
Dim objNL

Set objNL = Server.Createobject("MSWC.NextLink")
MyPagePrev = objNL.GetPreviousURL("NewProductsTour.txt")
MyPageNext = objNL.GetNextURL("NewProductsTour.txt")
%>
<A HREF="<% =MyPagePrev %>"> Click here for previous item</A><BR>
<A HREF="<% =MyPageNext %>"> Click here for next item </A>

</BODY>
</HTML>
```

4 Use **SaveAs** to store this file in the same directory, as **sweater304.asp**.

5 Once you have safely saved the sweater file, change the highlighted code to create the following page.

```
<% Option Explicit %>
<HTML>
<HEAD>
<TITLE>Tie784</TITLE>
</HEAD>

<BODY>
<P>Ridiculous Colored Tie</P>

<%
Dim MyPagePrev
Dim MyPageNext
Dim objNL

Set objNL = Server.Createobject("MSWC.NextLink")
MyPagePrev = objNL.GetPreviousURL("NewProductsTour.txt")
MyPageNext = objNL.GetNextURL("NewProductsTour.txt")
%>
<A HREF="<% =MyPagePrev %>"> Click here for previous item</A><BR>
<A HREF="<% =MyPageNext %>"> Click here for next item </A>

</BODY>
</HTML>
```

6 Save this as `tie784.asp`.

7 After saving the ties page change the code to:

```
<% Option Explicit %>
<HTML>
<HEAD>
<TITLE>Trouser422</TITLE>
</HEAD>

<BODY>
<P>Red Plaid Pants</P>

<%
Dim MyPagePrev
Dim MyPageNext
Dim objNL

Set objNL = Server.Createobject("MSWC.NextLink")
MyPagePrev = objNL.GetPreviousURL("NewProductsTour.txt")
MyPageNext = objNL.GetNextURL("NewProductsTour.txt")
%>
<A HREF="<% =MyPagePrev %>"> Click here for previous item</A><BR>
<A HREF="<% =MyPageNext %>"> Click here for next item </A>

</BODY>
</HTML>
```

8 Save this as `trouser422.asp`.

9 Finally, modify the page to create a page for our last item of clothing and save it as `vest562.asp`.

```
<% Option Explicit %>
<HTML>
<HEAD>
<TITLE>Vest562</TITLE>
</HEAD>

<BODY>
<P>Flowery Vest</P>

<%
Dim MyPagePrev
Dim objNL

Set objNL = Server.Createobject("MSWC.NextLink")
MyPagePrev = objNL.GetPreviousURL("NewProductsTour.txt")
%>
<A HREF="<% =MyPagePrev %>"> Click here for previous item</A>
```

```
</BODY>
</HTML>
```

10 Open up your browser of choice. At the address line, type in the URL
`http://my_server_name/BegASP/hat501.asp`. Click on the Next and Previous
hyperlinks, to move back and forward through the tour.

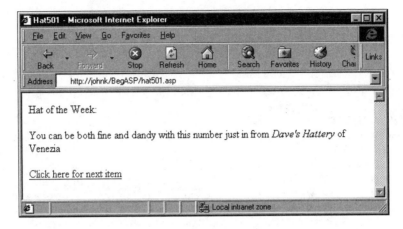

How It Works

Let's look at the file **hat501.asp** first. In fact, it looks very similar to the HTML file
hat501.htm that we saw in the file HTML file earlier in this chapter, when considering the
benefits of using Content Linker. However, we have also inserted the following ASP code:

```
<%
Option Explicit
Dim MyPageNext

Set objNL = Server.Createobject("MSWC.NextLink")
MyPageNext = objNL.GetNextURL("NewProductsTour.txt")
%>
<A HREF="<% =MyPageNext %>"> Click here for next item </A>
```

  Carefully note the use of double-quotes within parentheses.

So what's happening here? The **Set** statement creates an instance of the **NextLink** component,
named **objNL**. Then, we ask **objNL** to use a method called **GetNextURL**: this method, when
invoked by the single ASP statement, will perform four steps:

▶ Open the index file, **NewProductsTour.txt**

▶ Find the line of the index file that shows the URL of the current page

▶ Move down one line, to the *next* URL line in the index file

▶ Return the URL listed on that line

Once these four steps are complete, the variable **MyPageNext** will contain the URL of the page that follows the current page, in our grand tour.

The last line of this block of code looks very similar to the **<A>** tag that was contained in our first HTML example, **hat501.htm**:

```
<A HREF="sweaters304.htm">Click here for next item</A>
```

The difference is that, before, the **HREF** names the hyperlink directly as **sweaters.asp**. Now, with our added ASP code, it's much smarter. Let's look at that line again:

```
<A HREF="<% =MyPageNext %>"> Click here for next item </A>
```

This line is a little tricky, because there is a mixture of two types of syntax: we have to carefully interleave HTML and ASP. Let me explain each character so that you have a good grounding for future elaborations. This first section opens the **<A>** tag and states the attribute name of **HREF**. The attribute must be followed by an equal sign and then the value must be in quotes.

Now the two versions start to differ. In the non-ASP version (**hat501.htm**) we type in the URL. In the enlightened ASP version (**hat501.asp**) we start an ASP script, with **<%**, then use the shortcut for **Response.Write**, which is the equal sign. We want **Response.Write** to write the contents of the variable **MyPageNext**, that contains the URL of the next page on the tour—we covered that at the start of this explanation. We must then immediately end the ASP script and hard-wire the closing double quotes and the closing **>** of the **<A>** tag. After ASP executes its code the result will be the same as if we had typed the URL.

FYI **There's a common confusion here, which is caused by the fact that we must supply two variable names. The first variable name identifies the instance of the NextLink object—in this case, we used** objNL. **The second name is for the variable which will hold the URL found by the** objNL.GetNextURL **method—here, we used** MyPageNext.

And that pretty well covers how the ASP controls the hyperlink from **hat501.asp** to the next page in the tour, **sweater304.asp**.

As we've mentioned, the file **sweater304.asp** is very similar to **hat501.asp**, and it works in much the same way as we have already described, with one difference. The ASP within that file is as follows:

```
<%
Dim MyPagePrev
Dim MyPageNext
Set objNL = Server.Createobject("MSWC.NextLink")
MyPagePrev = objNL.GetPreviousURL("NewProductsTour.txt")
MyPageNext = objNL.GetNextURL("NewProductsTour.txt")
%>
<A HREF="<% =MyPagePrev %>"> Click here for previous item</A><BR>
<A HREF="<% =MyPageNext %>"> Click here for next item </A>
```

The additional lines are shaded. Having created an instance of **NextLink** (which we call **objNL**), we now have two variables instead of one: **MyPagePrev** uses the method **objNL.GetPreviousURL** to acquire the URL of the previous page in the tour, from the index file. The **<A>** tag provides us with a hyperlink for that page. The remainder of the ASP code works in exactly the way we have described above.

Note that we *don't* need to create two Content Linker objects here. We have only created a single Content Linker object, namely objNL. Having created this object, we can use it over and over to refer back to the index file.

The files **tie784.asp** and **trousers422.asp** have exactly the same structure as **sweater304.asp**. The final file in the tour, **vest562.asp**, supports a link to the previous page, but not to the next page (since it's the last page on the tour). The ASP code within **vest562.asp** is:

```
<%
Set objNL = Server.Createobject("MSWC.NextLink")
MyPagePrev = objNL.GetPreviousURL("NewProductsTour.txt")
%>
<A HREF="<% =MyPagePrev %>"> Click here for previous item</A>
```

Some folks get confused about which page we mean by 'current', 'next' and 'previous'. Recall that the ASP code is written within a page. That ASP code will be executed on the server in the process of the server building a page to send to the browser. So the server considers the *current* page to be the one which it is now building. If your user clicks on next, this sends an <A HREF> for the next page to the server, and as that page is being built, its URL becomes the *current* page for the ASP Content Linker methods finding the next and previous pages.

ASP Pages that Use the Content Linker to Display Descriptions

When we created the index file, we saw that it was organized into three columns of data with a row for each URL in the progression. The first column contains the name of the URL, the second column contains a description, and the third column holds comments about the page.

We can adapt the previous example, so that the user can click on text that is more descriptive than Previous or Next. To do this, we make use of user the descriptions contained in the index file: we can show these descriptions to the user. In fact we will even embellish that description with some hard-wired text to give us a dynamic hyperlink label. Hence, when the user clicks on the hyperlink text, they know exactly what they are going to learn about in advance.

Try It Out – Using Content Linker with Descriptions

We'll have to make similar changes to all of the `.asp` files in the last example.

1 With your editor of choice, open up `hat501.asp` and make the following changes:

```
<% Option Explicit %>
<HTML>
<HEAD>
<TITLE>Hat501</TITLE>
</HEAD>

<BODY>
<P>Hat of the Week:</P>
<P>You can be both fine and dandy with this number just in from
<EM>Dave's Hattery</EM> of Venezia</P>

<%
Dim MyPageNext
Dim MyDescriptNext
Dim objNL

Set objNL = Server.Createobject("MSWC.NextLink")
MyPageNext = objNL.GetNextURL("NewProductsTour.txt")
MyDescriptNext = objNL.GetNextDescription("NewProductsTour.txt")
%>
<A HREF="<% =MyPageNext %>"> <% =myDescriptNext %></A>

</BODY>
</HTML>
```

2 Save the new code.

3 Open the file `sweaters304.asp`, and make the following changes:

```
<% Option Explicit %>
<HTML>
<HEAD>
<TITLE>Sweater304</TITLE>
</HEAD>

<BODY>
<P>Beautiful Blue Cardigan Sweater</P>

<%
Dim MyPageNext
Dim MyDescriptNext
Dim MyPagePrev
```

```
Dim MyDescriptPrev
Dim objNL

Set objNL = Server.Createobject("MSWC.NextLink")
MyPagePrev = objNL.GetPreviousURL("NewProductsTour.txt")
MyDescriptPrev = objNL.GetPreviousDescription("NewProductsTour.txt")
MyPageNext = objNL.GetNextURL("NewProductsTour.txt")
MyDescriptNext = objNL.GetNextDescription("NewProductsTour.txt")
%>
<A HREF="<% =MyPagePrev %>"> <% =myDescriptPrev %></A><BR>
<A HREF="<% =MyPageNext %>"> <% =myDescriptNext %></A>

</BODY>
</HTML>
```

4 Save the new code.

5 Repeat steps 3 and 4 for the files `tie784.asp` and `trousers422.asp`.

6 Open the file `vest562.asp`, and make the following changes:

```
<% Option Explicit %>
<HTML>
<HEAD>
<TITLE>Vest562</TITLE>
</HEAD>

<BODY>
<P>Flowery Vest</P>

<%
Dim MyPagePrev
Dim MyDescriptPrev
Dim objNL

Set objNL = Server.Createobject("MSWC.NextLink")
MyPagePrev = objNL.GetPreviousURL("NewProductsTour.txt")
MyDescriptPrev = objNL.GetPreviousDescription("NewProductsTour.txt")
%>
<A HREF="<% =MyPagePrev %>"> <% =myDescriptPrev %></A><BR>
</BODY>
</HTML>
```

7 Save the new code.

8 Open up your browser of choice. At the address line, type in the URL `http://my_server_name/BegASP/hat501.asp`. Click on the hyperlinks, to move back and forward through the tour.

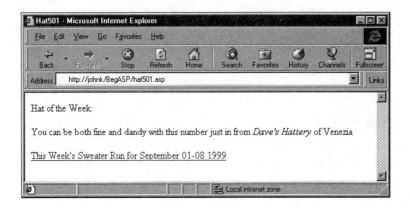

How It Works

In this example we have added to each `.asp` file a line that utilizes a new method—one which can get the description of a page. Note that even though we have an additional method, we can still use the same instance of the `NextLink` object. In other words, there's no need for a second `CreateObject` statement. Here's the statement, for a given page, that calls the description of the next page in the tour:

```
MyDescriptNext = objNL.GetNextDescription("NewProductsTour.txt")
```

The description is contained in the variable `MyDescriptNext`. Then we use this to make the hyperlink even more complex, as follows:

```
<A HREF="<% =MyPageNext %>"> <% =myDescriptNext %></A>
```

Hold on to your hats—we actually bounce in and out of ASP twice in this one line, so it is important to understand the syntax. This first bit is the same as before, starting the `<A>` and setting the `HREF` attribute to the value returned by the `MyPageNext` variable:

```
<A HREF="<% =MyPageNext %>">
```

But then, instead of typing the message Click here for next page, we now jump back into ASP with `<%`; then an equals sign acts as the `Response.Write` shortcut, which then outputs the contents of the variable `myDescriptNext`. We immediately end the ASP script with the `%>` and then finish off the hyperlinked text with the `</A>` closer. In summary, the first ASP code supplies the target of the hyperlink, the second ASP code supplies the text which can be clicked to fire off the hyperlink. Thus the full line is:

```
<A HREF="<% =MyPageNext %>"> <% =myDescriptNext %></A>
```

 Keep in mind that the URL of the HREF needs double quotes, but the hyperlinked text does not.

The first four pages in the tour all contain the lines described above, so that each of these pages contains a hyperlink describing the contents of the next page. The last four pages in the tour (that is, all except `hat501.asp`) also contain a line that obtains a description of the previous page in the tour:

```
MyDescriptPrev = objNL.GetPreviousDescription("NewProductsTour.txt")
```

and then creates a hyperlink to that page, using the following line:

```
<A HREF="<% =MyPagePrev %>"> <% =myDescriptPrev %></A>
```

Using the Content Linker and Control Structures to Display Only Appropriate Links

By now your hyperlinks for touring the on-line clothier are efficient for several reasons:

- ▶ The user is guided through the pages of the tour in the order of your design.
- ▶ The viewer gets a description of the next and previous pages, which assist his or her orientation.
- ▶ The first page in your tour doesn't contain a 'previous page' link; and similarly, the final page doesn't contain a 'next page' link.

But there remain some rough edges. For example, what happens when the webmaster wants to change the order of the pages on the tour? The order of the pages is controlled by the index file; however, amending the tour by adding pages, removing pages or switching the order will cause headaches.

Let's see what we mean. Suppose, for example, that the webmaster decides to amend the tour by adding an extra page to the end of the tour. He does this by writing the code for the new page, saving it, and amending the index file to include details of the new page. However, the previous end-of-tour page, `vest562.asp`, contains no link to a 'next page', and that means that the webmaster must *also* find `vest562.asp` and amend its code to add the link.

Similar problems will occur if we remove certain pages from the tour, or switch them around. Suppose that the on-line clothier discontinues his hat product. The webmaster can remove the page `hat501.asp` from the tour, but the result is the new 'first page' of the tour will have a link to a 'previous page'—and that's not what we want.

The fact is that in its current state, the tour is not easy for the webmaster to modify. Every time he modifies the index file, he must also trawl through the `.asp` files and amend the links. However, there is a smarter solution. There are two major advantages to it:

- ▶ The webmaster is free to switch the order of the pages, simply by editing the index file
- ▶ He can also add new pages by using an existing page as a template—the ASP code in all of the pages is exactly the same.

1 Open the file `hat501.asp` and amend it to the following:

```
<% Option Explicit %>
<HTML>
<HEAD>
<TITLE>Hat501</TITLE>
</HEAD>

<BODY>
<P>Hat of the Week:</P>
<P>You can be both fine and dandy with this number just in from
<EM>Dave's Hattery</EM> of Venezia</P>
```

```
<%
Option Explicit
Dim MyPagePrev
Dim MyDescriptPrev
Dim MyPageNext
Dim MyDescriptNext
Dim myListIndex
Dim myListCount
Dim objNL

Set objNL = Server.Createobject("MSWC.NextLink")
MyPagePrev = objNL.GetPreviousURL("NewProductsTour.txt")
MyDescriptPrev = objNL.GetPreviousDescription("NewProductsTour.txt")
MyPageNext = objNL.GetNextURL("NewProductsTour.txt")
MyDescriptNext = objNL.GetNextDescription("NewProductsTour.txt")
myListIndex = objNL.GetListIndex("NewProductsTour.txt")
myListCount = objNL.GetListCount("NewProductsTour.txt")
%>

<%If myListIndex >1 Then %>
<A HREF="<% =MyPagePrev %>"> Click here to move back to <%
=myDescriptPrev %> </A><BR>
<%End If %>

<%If myListIndex <> myListCount Then %>
<A HREF="<% =MyPageNext %>"> Click here to move ahead to <%
=myDescriptNext %> </A>
<%End If %>
```

```
</BODY>
</HTML>
```

2 Save the code.

3 Using the above code, recreate the file `sweater304.asp` by amending the title and text lines only, as follows:

```
<% Option Explicit %>
<HTML>
<HEAD>
<TITLE>Sweater304</TITLE>
</HEAD>

<BODY>
<P>Beautiful Blue Cardigan Sweater</P>

<%
Dim MyPagePrev
Dim MyDescriptPrev
Dim MyPageNext
Dim MyDescriptNext
Dim myListIndex
Dim myListCount
Dim objNL

Set objNL = Server.Createobject("MSWC.NextLink")
MyPagePrev = objNL.GetPreviousURL("NewProductsTour.txt")
MyDescriptPrev = objNL.GetPreviousDescription("NewProductsTour.txt")
MyPageNext = objNL.GetNextURL("NewProductsTour.txt")
MyDescriptNext = objNL.GetNextDescription("NewProductsTour.txt")
myListIndex = objNL.GetListIndex("NewProductsTour.txt")
myListCount = objNL.GetListCount("NewProductsTour.txt")
%>

<%If myListIndex >1 Then %>
<A HREF="<% =MyPagePrev %>"> Click here to move back to <%
=myDescriptPrev %> </A><BR>
<%End If %>

<%If myListIndex <> myListCount Then %>
<A HREF="<% =MyPageNext %>"> Click here to move ahead to <%
=myDescriptNext %> </A>
<%End If %>

</BODY>
</HTML>
```

4 Repeat step 3 for the files `tie784.asp`, `trousers422.asp` and `vest562.asp`.

5 Open up your browser of choice. At the address line, type in the URL `http://my_server_name/BegASP/hat501.asp`. Click on the hyperlinks, to move back and forward through the tour.

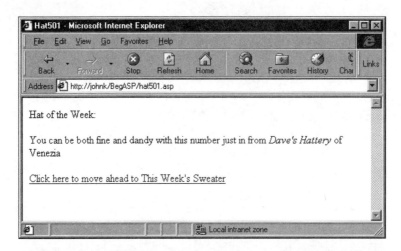

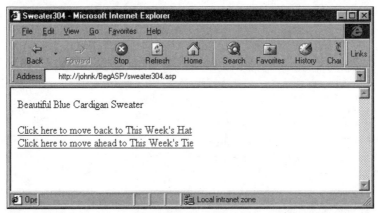

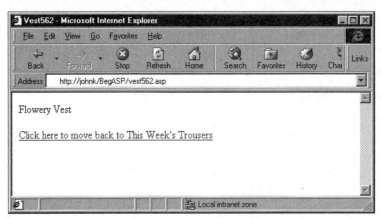

How It Works

The whole thing works because we are able to use our **NextList** object to obtain the following information from the index file:

▶ The number of URL lines in the index file

▶ The number of the URL that is currently shown

The two files methods that supply this information are, respectively, **objNL.GetListIndex** and **objNL.GetListCount**. First, **objNL.GetListIndex** returns a number that ASP obtains by counting the lines in the URL index file:

```
myListIndex = objNL.GetListIndex("NewProductsTour.txt")
```

ASP cleverly skips the comment lines—those that begin with three hyphens. For example, from the file **tie784.asp**, this line refers to the index file, **NewProductsTour.txt**, and returns the value 5 (because there are five pages in the tour: this line gives the same result when called from any of our **.asp** files).

Then, **objNL.GetListCount** returns the number of the URL line for the current page:

```
myListCount = objNL.GetListCount("NewProductsTour.txt")
```

For example, in the file **tie784.asp**, this line refers to the index file, **NewProductsTour.txt**, and returns the value 3 (because **tie784.asp** is the third on the list).

Then, armed with these values we can use logic to say that, provided we are not on URL number 1 (that is, **myListIndex** is greater than 1), then we are not at the beginning and therefore we should show a 'Previous' hyperlink:

```
<%If myListIndex >1 Then %>
<A HREF="<% =MyPagePrev %>"> Click here to move back to <%
=myDescriptPrev %> </A><BR>
<%End If %>
```

We can also say that, provided our current URL number is not equal to the total number of URLs (that is, **myListIndex** is not equal to **myListCount**), then we should show a 'Next' hyperlink:

```
<%If myListIndex <> myListCount Then %>
<A HREF="<% =MyPageNext %>"> Click here to move ahead to <%
=myDescriptNext %> </A>
<%End If %>
```

If the webmaster changed the order of these pages in the index file the pages would automatically compensate their Next/Prev appearance and descriptions, all from the magic of the Content Rotator.

Using the Content Linker with Home and End Hyperlinks

Most modern computer users are accustomed to the idea of having options for Home and End when in a series of steps. This probably comes from Microsoft Wizards, as much as from well-designed web pages. The Content Linker gives you clean options for providing these features.

Jumping to the last page can be coded using two more methods, `GetNthURL` and `GetNthDescription`. In these methods, `Nth` is the programmer's way of implying that a page number is to be determined. We will be particularly concerned with two page numbers, the first and the last. The first page number is easy: in that case, `N=1`. But since our webmaster is inclined to adding and removing pages from the index file, we will never be sure what the last page number will be. However, we can ask ASP to count them at the moment it builds the page by using the method `GetIndexCount` again. As you recall from the previous example, this is done with the following line:

```
myListCount = objNL.GetListCount("NewProductsTour.txt")
```

We can then get the last page, since we recognize that in that case, `N` is equal to the current value of `myListCount`.

To use the `GetNthURL` method, we need to know how to tell the method the number that we want. This transfer of information is done in a way similar to the way we pass the name of the index file to the method. Previously, when giving the index file name to a method, we have placed it in parentheses after the name of the method, like this:

```
MyPageNext = objNL.GetNextURL("NewProductsTour.txt")
```

However, in this case we want to pass *two* parameters: the name of the index file and the number of the page to return information. We do this by listing the two parameters separated by a comma. For example, to get the URL of the first page we use:

```
MyFirstPage = objNL.GetNthURL("NewProductsTour.txt", 1)
```

And to get the URL of the last page we use our a variable as the second parameter:

```
MyEndPage = objNL.GetNthURL("NewProductsTour.txt", myIndexCount)
```

Let's test this out. There are only a few changes to make.

Try It Out – Adding Home and End Links

1 Open your file `hat501.asp` and add the following lines:

```
<% Option Explicit %>
<HTML>
<HEAD>
<TITLE>Hat501</TITLE>
</HEAD>
```

```
<BODY>
<P>Hat of the Week:</P>
<P>You can be both fine and dandy with this number just in from
<EM>Dave's Hattery</EM> of Venezia</P>

<%
Dim MyPagePrev
Dim MyDescriptPrev
Dim MyPageNext
Dim MyDescriptNext
Dim myListIndex
Dim myListCount
Dim MyFirstPage
Dim MyEndPage
Dim MyIndexCount
Dim objNL

Set objNL = Server.Createobject("MSWC.NextLink")
MyPagePrev = objNL.GetPreviousURL("NewProductsTour.txt")
MyDescriptPrev = objNL.GetPreviousDescription("NewProductsTour.txt")
MyPageNext = objNL.GetNextURL("NewProductsTour.txt")
MyDescriptNext = objNL.GetNextDescription("NewProductsTour.txt")
myListIndex = objNL.GetListIndex("NewProductsTour.txt")
myListCount = objNL.GetListCount("NewProductsTour.txt")
myFirstPage = objNL.GetNthURL("NewProductsTour.txt", 1)
myEndPage = objNL.GetNthURL("NewProductsTour.txt", myIndexCount)
%>

<%If myListIndex >1 Then %>
<A HREF="<% =MyPagePrev %>"> Click here to move back to <%
=myDescriptPrev %> </A><BR>
<%End If %>

<%If myListIndex <> myListCount Then %>
<A HREF="<% =MyPageNext %>"> Click here to move ahead to <%
=myDescriptNext %> </A><BR>
<%End If %>

<A HREF="<% =myFirstPage %>"> Click here to move to New Products Home</
A><BR>
<A HREF="<% =myEndPage %>"> Click here to move to New Products End</A>
</BODY>
</HTML>
```

2 Repeat step 1 for the files **sweaters304.asp**, **tie784.asp**, **trousers422.asp** and **vest562.asp**.

3 Open up your browser of choice. At the address line, type in the URL **http://*my_server_name*/BegASP/hat501.asp**. Click on the hyperlinks, to move back and forward through the tour.

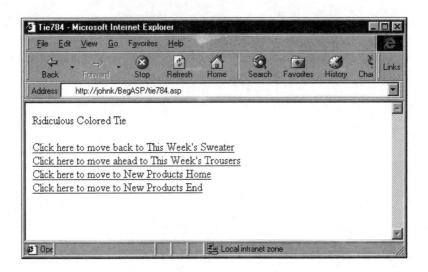

ASP Content Linker to Generate a Table of Contents

Now we have some very clever hyperlinks for jumping to the next and previous pages, as well as to the first and last pages. Best of all, we will never have to go into the HTML to revise the pages which are ordered as *Next* or *Previous* to which those hyperlinks point. All we have to do is open the index file in NotePad and reorder, delete or add pages. If you are writing ASP pages on contract you can charge your clients more for writing such programmer-friendly code. And if you write ASP as part of a salaried job you can ask your boss for a raise. But wait, let's cover another trick so you can ask your boss for a double increase in salary grade.

As long as we have the index file made up, what else can we do with it? Well, we could use that information to make a table of contents for the tour of new products. We will create a loop that reads the first URL out of the index file and writes it on the page, then puts in a `<BR>` (line break) tag, and then repeats these steps for each URL in the index file.

When we discussed loops, back in Chapter 5, we noted two types. The first option is the `For...Next` loop, that we use when we know ahead of time how many loops we want to do. The second option is the `Do While` loop, that allows you to make a test as you go and stop when the test is satisfied. Since we can easily find out how many URL lines exist in the `IndexFile` with the `GetListCount`, we will use the `For...Next` here.

A Solution for a Table of Contents Based on an Index File

We don't need to make any further changes to our existing `.asp` files, in order to create an table of contents page. Here's how it's done.

Try It Out – A Basic Table of Contents Page

1 Open your editor, and type in the following code:

```
<% Option Explicit %>
<HTML>
<HEAD>
<TITLE>Tour of Products TOC</TITLE>
</HEAD>

<BODY>
<P>Tour of New Products  - Table of Contents</P>
<P>
<%
Dim MyCurrentURL
Dim MyListCount
Dim objNL
Dim URLCounter

Set objNL=Server.CreateObject("MSWC.NextLink")
myListCount = objNL.GetListCount("NewProductsTour.txt")

For URLcounter=1 To myListCount
mycurrentURL = objNL.GetNthURL("NewProductsTour.txt", URLcounter)
Response.Write mycurrentURL
Response.Write "<BR>"
Next
%>
</BODY>

</HTML>
```

2 Save this code in the **BegASP** folder, with the file name **toc.asp**.

3 Fire up your browser, and at the address line type the URL
http://*my_server_name*/BegASP/toc.asp.

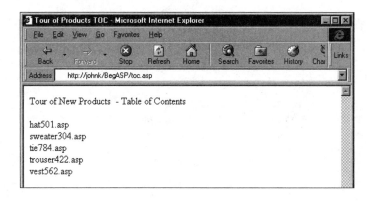

323

How It Works

First, we must set up an instance of the Content Linker:

```
Set objNL=Server.CreateObject("MSWC.NextLink")
myLastCount = objNL.GetListCount("NewProductsTour.txt")
```

The instance is called **objNL**. We then create a variable **myLastCount**, which will contain the total number of URL lines in the index file:

```
myLastCount = objNL.GetListCount("NewProductsTour.txt")
```

Now we are ready to loop. Our loop will iterate once for each of the values between 1 and **myLastCount** inclusive:

```
For URLcounter=1 To myLastCount
```

Within each iteration of the loop, we'll take the value of **URLcounter**, and use the method **getNthURL** to acquire the URL corresponding to the value of **URLcounter**. That URL is placed in the variable **myCurrentURL**:

```
mycurrentURL = objNL.GetNthURL("NewProductsTour.txt", URLcounter)
```

Then, we **Response.Write** this URL to the page. In order to give each URL its own line, we also need a **
** tag:

```
Response.Write mycurrentURL
Response.Write "<BR>"
```

Remember that we are in the middle of ASP code here, not HTML. Therefore, we need to have ASP actually write out the four characters"
" to the page which HTML will send out to the browser. As you can see, we do that using the ResponseWrite method.

Finally, we close off the loop:

```
Next
```

Try It Out – Table of Contents by Description

It's easy to adjust the code above, so that the table of contents lists the descriptions of each page rather than just the URL.

1 Open up the file **toc.asp**, and amend the following lines:

```
<% Option Explicit %>
<HTML>
<HEAD>
```

```
<TITLE>Tour of Products TOC</TITLE>
</HEAD>

<BODY>
<P>Tour of New Products  - Table of Contents</P>
<P>
<%
Dim myCurrentDescription
Dim myListCount
Dim objNL
Dim URLCounter

Set objNL=Server.CreateObject("MSWC.NextLink")
myListCount = objNL.GetListCount("NewProductsTour.txt")

For URLcounter=1 To myListCount
myCurrentDescription=objNL.GetNthDescription("NewProductsTour.txt",URLcounter)
Response.Write mycurrentDescription
Response.Write "<BR>"
Next
%>
</BODY>

</HTML>
```

2 Save this code in the **BegASP** folder, with the file name **tocByDescription.asp**.

3 Fire up your browser, and at the address line type the URL
http://*my_server_name*/BegASP/toc.asp.

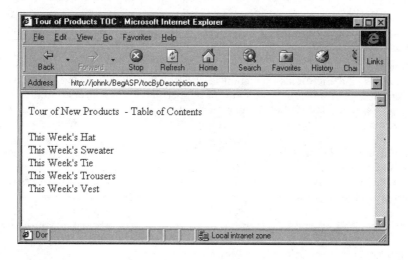

How It Works

The changes here are similar to our study of creating the Next/Prev hyperlinks. In this Table of Contents we ask our instance of the Content Linker, `objNL`, to give us the description of the current URL on each loop. This method is activated with `objNL.GetNthDescription`.

The Browser Capabilities Component

One of the problems we face when creating all kinds of web pages, not just dynamic ones that use Active Server Pages, is deciding which of the range of tags and techniques we should take advantage of. While it's great to be able to use all the latest features, such as Java applets, ActiveX controls, and the most recent HTML tags, we need to be aware that some visitors will be using browsers that don't support these. All they might see of our carefully crafted pages is a jumble of text, images, and—even worse—the code that makes them work.

We mentioned in Chapter 7 that you can use a Server variable, `HTTP_USER_AGENT`, to help detect which type of browser is viewing your page. However, life can be made much easier by using a special server component called the Browser Capabilities component. This component can determine which of a whole range of features a browser supports, at the point when it actually references one of our pages.

When a user requests a page from the server, the details of `HTTP_USER_AGENT` are effectively mapped to the Browser Capabilities component, which then adopts a range of properties equivalent to the user's browser features. Hence, at any time while the page is being executed, the Browser Capabilities component can provide details of which individual features are—or are not—supported. You can create an instance of the Browser Capabilities component as follows:

```
Set objBCap = Server.CreateObject("MSWC.BrowserType")
```

Then not only will we have a Browser Capabilities component for the specific browser that views the page, but it will have a series of properties dependent on what is held in the `browscap.ini` file.

The Browscap.ini File

The `Browscap.ini` file is the bit that does the work. It contains the information about each known browser, and there's also a default section of the file which is used when the browser details don't match any of the ones more fully specified in the file. So adding new information about browsers, or updating the existing information, is as easy as editing the `Browscap.ini` file. The `Browscap.ini` file is normally found in `C:\Windows\System\InetServ`.

We'll look at the format of this file first. All of the entries in `Browscap.ini` are optional, but it's important that we always include the default section. If the browser in use doesn't match any in the `Browscap.ini` file, and no default browser settings have been specified, all the properties are set to `"UNKNOWN"`.

```
; we can add comments anywhere, prefaced by a semicolon like this

; entry for a specific browser
[HTTPUserAgentHeader]
parent = browserDefinition
property1 = value1
```

```
property2 = value2
...


[Default Browser Capability Settings]
defaultProperty1 = defaultValue1
defaultProperty1 = defaultValue1
...
```

The `[HTTPUserAgentHeader]` line defines the start of a section for a particular browser, and the **parent** line indicates that another definition contains more information for that browser as well. Each subsquent line defines a property that we want to make available through the Browser Capabilities component, and sets its value for this particular browser. The **Default** section lists the properties and values that are used if the particular browser in use isn't listed in its own section, or if it is listed but not all the properties are supplied.

For example, we may have a section for Internet Explorer 4.0. This has no **parent** line, and so the only properties it will have (other than those defined in the default section) are those we define explicitly:

```
[IE 4.0]
browser=IE
Version=4.0
majorver=4
minorver=0
frames=TRUE
tables=TRUE
cookies=TRUE
backgroundsounds=TRUE
vbscript=TRUE
javascript=TRUE
javaapplets=TRUE
ActiveXControls=TRUE
Win16=False
beta=False
AK=False
SK=False
AOL=False
crawler=False
cdf=True
...
```

Each of its abilities are listed precisely and so when a browser is identified, you can determine its individual abilities exactly and customize the page as necessary. So when you view a page using Internet Explorer 4.0, ASP will look it up and go to the above section in **browscap.ini**.

A company called cyScape, Inc. **maintains a list of** browscap.ini **files, which is sometimes more up-to-date than even the Microsoft web site. You can find the newest one at their web site,** http://www.cyscape.com/browscap.

Try It Out – Using the Browser Capabilities Component

Having grasped how the `Browscap.ini` file can provide customizable properties containing information about a particular browser, it's time to actually see the Browser Capabilities component in use. This example checks to see whether or not the browser supports VBScript, and displays the appropriate message. This example can be modified to direct the user to different pages, depending on the response given by the browser.

1 Open up your favorite editor and type in the following code.

```
<% Option Explicit %>
<HTML>

<HEAD>
<TITLE> Browser Capabilities Component Example </TITLE>
</HEAD>

<BODY>
<%
Dim objBCap,blnVBScriptOK
Set objBCap = Server.CreateObject("MSWC.BrowserType")
blnVBScriptOK = objBCap.vbscript   'save the value in a variable
If blnVBScriptOK Then
Response.Write "This browser supports VBScript"
Else
Response.Write "This browser doesn't support VBScript"
End If
%>
</BODY>
</HTML>
```

2 Save this page as `BrowserCap.asp`.

3 Open up this page in Internet Explorer 4.0.

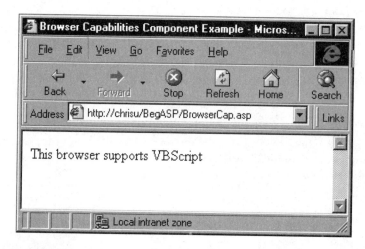

4 Now view the same page in Netscape 4.0.

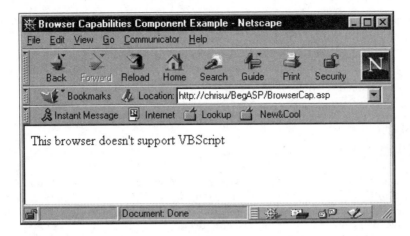

How It Works

This example is very simple. We first set up two variables:

```
Dim objBCap,blnVBScriptOK
```

The first is used to create an instance of the object:

```
Set objBCap = Server.CreateObject("MSWC.BrowserType")
```

The second variable we create is used to store the **vbscript** property:

```
blnVBScriptOK = objBCap.vbscript   'save the value in a variable
```

If the **vbscript** property holds the value *yes* in **browscap.ini**, then we can assume that this browser supports VBScript:

```
If blnVBScriptOK Then
Response.Write "This browser supports VBScript"
```

Otherwise we can assume the browser doesn't.

```
Else
Response.Write "This browser doesn't support VBScript"
End If
```

And that's all there is to it. Of course, we can use the properties to do other things. One of the favorite techniques is to load a different index page for a site, depending on what features the browser supports. If our site has a set of pages using frames, and a different set using only simple text, we can check the browser's ability to display frames when it first hits our site, and redirect it to the appropriate index page.

Other Components

PWS 4.0 currently provides a total of five different components with the NT 4 Option Pack. These are as follows:

- Ad Rotator component
- Content Linking component
- Browser Capabilities component
- MyInfo component
- Database Access component (ADO)

The Page Counter and Content Rotator Components, which are covered in the PWS documentation and which were previously available with PWS, are no longer available as part of the current NT 4 Option Pack. They can be downloaded separately from Microsoft at `http://www.backoffice.microsoft.com/downtrial/moreinfo/iissamples.asp`. You can also get hold of the Status, Tools and Counters components here, which also work with PWS. For third party components we suggest you look at Appendix E, where we provide some useful URLs which will point you in the right direction.

Summary

Web site developers that have preceded you have found that almost everyone shares a need for some types of code, such as rotating ads. Microsoft has written code to perform these tasks and made it available as Server Components. To use a component you must first create an instance of the component using `Server.CreateObject(MWSC.ComponentName")`. Then you can use that server with *myComponent.method*.

To direct users through a set of pages on a site we can use the Content Linker component. Once we make a list of pages we can get the URL and description of the next and previous pages from the Content Linker.

A second component rotates advertisements on a page without making any changes directly on the page. The number and source of ads can be changed in a scheduler file. In that same file we can also change the frequency of appearance for each ad.

Finally, we looked at the Browser Capabilities component, which allows you to customize your page to the abilities of the browser viewing it.

There is a multitude of components available from Microsoft, and also from a number of other third parties. As long as you download them fron the requisite web page, you will be able to integrate them into your pages using the `Server.CreateObject` method. They can be used to enhance your web pages in all kinds of ways.

The Scripting Objects

In the last five chapters, we have been looking at all of the different objects that can be used with Active Server Pages. Some of them, such as the **Application** and **Session** objects, are built-in to Active Server Pages. Other objects like the **AdRot** and **ContentLink** objects are not part of ASP itself, but are included with the NT 4 Option Pack by Microsoft. Still others can be created by you or other third parties for use in your application.

There is one final type of object we will be looking at. These objects do not directly deal with the communication between the client and the web server, as the built-in objects do. These objects provide additional functionality to the scripting language itself. This is why they are known as the **Scripting Objects**.

In this chapter we'll look at:

▶ The **Dictionary** object

▶ The **FileSystemObject** object

▶ Collections of the **FileSystemObject** object

▶ Server-side includes

▶ The **TextStream** object

But first what exactly are the scripting objects...?

What are Scripting Objects?

One of the "Active" technologies that Microsoft has developed is called **Active Scripting**. This technology provides a common interface for scripting languages to communicate with an application. Active Scripting is what allows you to write ASP code using VBScript, JavaScript, or any other Active Scripting compliant-language. In fact, you can use both VBScript and JavaScript within the same ASP script file itself.

The VBScript library that provides the scripting language support to both ASP and Internet Explorer also provides a number of objects that a developer can use to enhance their application. These objects are known as the **Scripting Objects**.

> *Even though these objects are part of the VBScript library, they can be accessed from other scripting languages, such as JScript. In this book, we are creating most of our examples in VBScript, so you will need to refer to the Microsoft documentation of JScript if you want to see how to use Scripting Objects with JScript. This documentation, along with the latest and greatest information on all Microsoft scripting technologies, can be found at*
> **http://www.microsoft.com/scripting.**

There are three scripting objects that a developer can use from within their scripts. The `Dictionary` object allows you to store information in a single data structure for easy retrieval. It is similar to an array, and it is also similar to a collection. The `FileSystemObject` object provides access from an Active Server Pages script to the hard disk file system of the server. This object will allow you to work with files, as well as directories and sub-directories.

The `TextStream` object allows you to deal with the contents of a file that you have got information about using the `FileSystemObject` object. You can read information from the file and write data *to* it.

Since dealing with data is very important to a lot of web applications, let's take a look at how the `Dictionary` object allows you to manipulate sets of data very easily.

The Dictionary Object

When you pick up a copy of Webster's dictionary, you have the ability to find out information about a particular word. In this case, the information is the definition of the word. All of the words are organized in a particular order. In a dictionary, this order is alphabetical. Associated with every word in the dictionary is its definition. This could also very easily be a synonym for the word, or a picture of what the word represents. The key concept is that for each word, there is a piece of information.

The `Dictionary` object can be thought of as a Webster's for your application. You can store information in it and attach a key word to each piece of information. Later, when you want to retrieve the information, all you do is provide the dictionary with the key word, and it will return the information you have stored there.

Try It Out – Simple Dictionary Example

To start becoming familiar with the `Dictionary` object, let's take a look at a very simple example that shows you how to store and retrieve information from a `Dictionary` object.

1 Use your editor of choice to create the `SimpleDictionary.asp` file with the following source code.

```
<%
dim objDictionary
Set objDictionary = CreateObject("Scripting.Dictionary")
objDictionary.Add "Apple", "Red"
objDictionary.Add "Lemon", "Yellow"
```

```
dim strKey
dim strValue
strKey = "Cherry"
strValue = "Red"
objDictionary.Add strKey, strValue

Response.Write "<P>All Data Stored in the Dictionary"
Response.Write "<P>Let's retrieve"
Response.Write "<HR>"
Response.Write "<P>Retrieving Data..."
strValue = objDictionary.Item("Apple")
Response.Write "<P>Value stored with key of 'Apple' is " & strValue

strKey = "Lemon"
strValue = objDictionary.Item(strKey)
Response.Write "<P>Value stored with key of '" & strKey & "' is " &
strValue
Response.Write "<HR>"
Response.Write "<P>Let's store for later use"
Set Session("MyDictionary") = objDictionary
Session("MyDictionaryStored") = True
Response.Write "<P>Dictionary information stored in your session object."

%>
```

2 Make sure this file is stored in a directory that is shared by your web server.

3 View the page in your web browser.

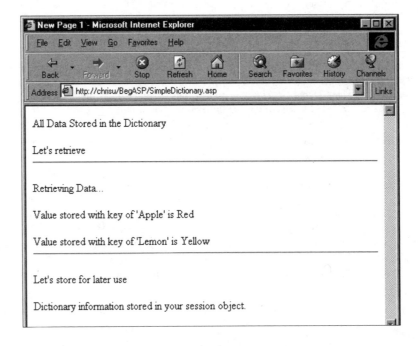

How It Works

Using the `Dictionary` object is actually quite easy. The first step is to create an instance of the `Dictionary` object. Earlier, we talked about how the Scripting Objects are part of the VBScript library, so they are a bit different in the way you create an instance of the objects. With the standard ASP objects, you would use:

```
Set objNewObj = Server.CreateObject("ObjectName")
```

to create the object. This version of the `CreateObject` method is actually a method of the `Server` object. Since the Scripting objects are objects that are part of VBScript, it makes sense that we would use a method of VBScript to create the instance of the object. The name of this method is also `CreateObject`, but since it is part of VBScript, we don't need to call it using the `object.method` syntax. All we need to do is:

```
Set objNewDictionaryObj = CreateObject("Scripting.Dictionary")
```

Once we have created an instance of the `Dictionary` object, we are ready to add data to it. The data that is stored in the dictionary is stored as a name/value pair. The name part of the pair is known as the key. When you add an item to the dictionary, you will use the `Add` method. This method takes the key and the value associated with the key and adds it to the `Dictionary`.

```
objDictionary.Add key, value
```

You can either pass the explicit values of the key and value parameters, or you can pass variables that hold the data that you want for either parameter.

After we have stored items in the `Dictionary` object, the next logical step is to retrieve the information. To access information in a `Dictionary`, you need to supply the key. Given that key, the `Dictionary` object will return the value associated with it. This returned value can either be stored in a variable, or used immediately in another method. As with the `Add` method, you can either pass an explicit reference to the key's name, or you can pass a variable that contains the name of the key.

> *Since in VBScript all variables are treated as variants, you don't need to worry about what the data type of the data that is stored in the `Dictionary` object is. Except in one case, that is. If you have stored a reference to an object as a value in your dictionary, you need to use the `Set` statement to assign the reference to another variable.*

To access the information for a specific key, you will use the `Item` method of the `Dictionary` object.

```
value = objDictionary.Item(key)
```

The last step is to store the reference to the dictionary object so that we can use it again in another page. In Chapter 9, we learned about the `Session` object. The `Session` object provides a storage space for information that can span multiple pages during a user's session. We will be storing two Session-level variables. The first will be a reference to our `Dictionary` object. This will be called `MyDictionary`. Since we are storing a reference, we need to use the `Set` statement to perform the assignment.

```
Set Session("MyDictionary") = objDictionary
Session("MyDictionaryStored") = True
```

The second value we are storing will be used to identify that we have created and stored a valid **Dictionary** object in the current user's session. This will allow us, in subsequent pages, a quick check to see if there is a **Dictionary** available to store information, or to retrieve information from. It can also help us take steps to avoid losing any data that may have been previously stored.

Now that we have loaded information into the **Dictionary** object and successfully retrieved it, the next step is to look at how to change the value of an entry in the **Dictionary**.

Try it Out – Changing Items in the Dictionary

1 Using your favorite ASP editor, enter the source code for **ChangeValueDictionary.asp**.

```
<%
dim bDictionaryExists
bDictionaryExists = Session("MyDictionaryStored")

if bDictionaryExists <> True then
        Response.Redirect "SimpleDictionary.asp"
else
        dim objDictionary
        Set objDictionary = Session("MyDictionary")

        if objDictionary.Exists("Apple") then
                objDictionary.Item("Apple") = "Green"
                Response.Write "<P>Changed the value of Apple to Green"
                Response.Write "<HR>"
                Response.Write "<P>Value stored with key of 'Apple' is " & 
                        objDictionary.Item("Apple")
                Response.Write "<HR>"
        end if

        if objDictionary.Exists("Lemon") then
                objDictionary.Key("Lemon") = "Banana"
                Response.Write "<P>Changed the key of Lemon to Banana"
                Response.Write "<HR>"
                Response.Write "<P>Value stored with key of 'Banana' is "& 
                        objDictionary.Item("Banana")
        end if
end if

%>
```

2 Make sure the file is saved in a directory that your web server can access. Make sure that that directory has scripting permissions enabled.

3 View the `ChangeValueDictionary.asp` file in your web browser.

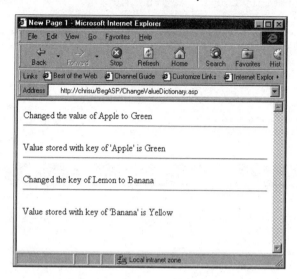

How It Works

In the first example, we stored a reference to the `Dictionary` object that held our information inside of a session-level variable. We also stored a Boolean flag to indicate that we stored a valid `Dictionary` object. Our first step is to check to see if this Boolean flag is set.

If the value contained in this session-level variable is not set to `True`, then we know that we do not have a valid `Dictionary` object to work with. This could have happened for two reasons. First, if the user had not previously viewed the `SimpleDictionary.asp` file, then the `Dictionary` object would never have been created and loaded. Second, as we discussed in previous chapters when we looked at the `Session` object, if the user had let their session time-out, then any values in the session-level variables would have been lost. If there is no `Dictionary` object to work with, then the browser will be redirected using the `Response.Redirect` method to the `SimpleDictionary.asp` so that the `Dictionary` object can be created and loaded.

Once we have determined that the dictionary exists and is valid, then we can retrieve the reference to it and store that in a local variable. Our next step is to see if the key we are interested in is available.

If we try to access a value for a key that does not exist, then an error will occur. To prevent this from happening, we can first check to see if the key exists before trying to retrieve its associated value. To do this, we will use the `Exists` method of the `Dictionary` object.

```
boolKeyExists = objDictionary.Exists(keyValue)
```

This method will return a `True` if the key supplied as a parameter exists. If the key does not exist, then the method will return a `False`. Once we have determined that the key is valid, we can now change the value associated with it.

In the previous example, you saw that the `Item` method could be used to access the value. This method can also be used as the left side of an assignment statement to set the value for a particular key.

```
objDictionary.Item(keyValue) = newValue
```

Along with changing the value for a particular key, we can also change a key itself. While this technically makes sense, from a real-world usage perspective it may not be a wise thing to do. If you are familiar with relational databases, then you know that each record in a table must have a unique key, and you cannot change the identity of that key. Changing the key itself in a `Dictionary` object is a very similar operation. So, a word of warning: be very sure you know why you are doing this before you start.

Now that all the disclaimers are out of the way, we can get to down to seeing how this is done. It is very similar to the way the `Item` method was just used. The method to change the key itself is the `Key` method of the `Dictionary` object.

```
objDictionary.Item (key) = newKey
```

Again, you should check to see if the original key exists before trying to change it.

These examples have shown you how to retrieve values from the `Dictionary` object by knowing the keys themselves. But what if you want to access information without knowing the keys? This next example will show you how to do this.

Try it Out – Getting Everything at Once

1 Using your favorite ASP editor, enter the source code for `GetAllValuesDictionary.asp`.

```
<%
dim bDictionaryExists
bDictionaryExists = Session("MyDictionaryStored")

if bDictionaryExists <> True then
      Response.Redirect "SimpleDictionary.asp"
else
      dim objDictionary
      Set objDictionary = Session("MyDictionary")

      Response.Write "<P>Retrieve list of keys"
      dim arKeys, i
      arKeys = objDictionary.keys
      for i = 0 to objDictionary.Count - 1
            Response.Write "<P>Key = " & arKeys(i) & "  --  Value = " &
objDictionary.Item(arKeys(i))
      next

      Response.Write "<HR>Retrieve list of values"
      dim arItems
```

```
        arItems = objDictionary.items
        for i = 0 to objDictionary.Count - 1
                Response.Write "<P>Value = " & arItems(i)
        next

  end if

%>
```

2 Make sure the file is saved in a directory that your web server can access. Make sure that that directory has Scripting permissions enabled.

3 View the `GetAllValuesDictionary.asp` file in your web browser.

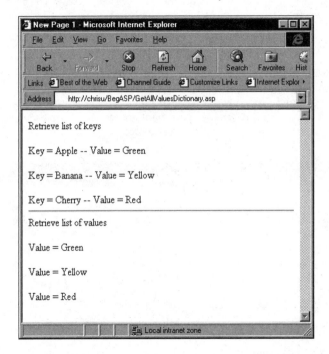

How It Works

In this example, we are looking for a way to retrieve all of the keys or items in the `Dictionary` object at once. There are many practical applications of this. For example, you could have multiple pages all dumping information into a `Dictionary` object. Another page could quickly access all of the information without having to know all of the keys that have been added.

There are two sets of information that can be retrieved from a `Dictionary` object:

▶ A list of all keys in the Dictionary
▶ A list of all values for the keys in the Dictionary

There are different uses for both of these sets of information. If you retrieve all of the keys from a **Dictionary** object, then you can use the **Item** method to retrieve each corresponding value. Unfortunately, if you retrieve all of the items in the **Dictionary** object, there is no way to tie each item back to its key.

The first step is to check to see if we have a valid **Dictionary** object stored in a session-level variable. As with our other examples, if a valid **Dictionary** object cannot be found, then the browser will be redirected to the first example page where the **Dictionary** object is created. The first way that we will retrieve information in bulk from the **Dictionary** object is with the **Keys** method. This method will return an array, where each element contains one key. Once we have this array, we can loop through the array and display each of the keys on the client.

In order to loop through the array, we need to know how many items there are in it. To do this, we will use the **Count** property of the **Dictionary** object. This property will tell us how many items are in the **Dictionary** object. Since the **Keys** method returns all of the keys, and each item must have a key, then the **Count** property will also tell us the size of the array.

Counting in an Array

There is an important issue involved in looping through the array. While the **Count** property will tell us how many items are in the array, this does not mean that there is a valid entry at **arKeys(Count)**. All arrays in VBScript are zero-based. This means that if an array has 5 items, then these statements will return valid information:

- **arKeys(0)**
- **arKeys(1)**
- **arKeys(2)**
- **arKeys(3)**
- **arKeys(4)**

There is no valid value at **arKeys(5)**. In fact, if you try to access this value, you will get an error. A **zero-based array** means that the first element's index will be 0, and if there are **n** elements in the array, then the last valid index will be **n-1**. What all this means is that to loop through all the elements in an array with **n** elements, you would use this loop statement:

```
For i = 0 to n-1
… Process element i here
next
```

As we loop through each element in our array of keys, we will display the key to client using the **Response.Write** method. To provide a bit more information to the user, we will also display the value for the key by using the **objDictionary.Item(arKeys(i))** technique.

The other type of information that we can retrieve in bulk from a **Dictionary** object is all of the values in the **Dictionary**. This is done using the **Items** method. This method will return an array that contains all of the item values from the **Dictionary** object. With this array, we can iterate through it and display each of the values to the client. As we stated before, we have no way of retrieving the corresponding key for each item. So all we can do is display the value on the client.

We have now covered the various ways that the **Dictionary** object can be used. Later in the book, we will be using the **Dictionary** object to store detailed information about the current user in a web application that we are going to develop. Next, we will take a look at a pair of objects that will allow you access to the file system and files of your web server. These objects will allow you to manipulate the files and directories on your server, as well as manipulate the contents of the individual files themselves.

The FileSystemObject Object

When our ASP server is handling requests from its clients, there are two types of pages it can return. As we have seen in this book, we can use the scripting power of ASP to dynamically create pages on-the-fly and send them back to the client. We can also serve static pages that are stored on the web server itself. But up until this point, we as web application developers had to know which files were stored in what place on what drive.

With the **FileSystemObject** object we can now use our code to access the file system of the web server itself. This will allow us to:

▶ Get and manipulate information about all of the drives in the server. These can be physical drives or remote drives that the web server is connected to

▶ Get and manipulate information about all of the folders and sub-folders on a drive

▶ Get and manipulate information about all of the files inside of a folder

▶ With this information, there is a very broad range of things that we can do with the file system. Aside from setting security information, basically anything that you can do with the file system using Windows Explorer or File Manager can be done using the **FileSystemObject** object

The FileSystemObject Object and its Object Model

In a previous chapter, we talked about what an object model was. This is a group of related objects that are working together to provide access to a certain group of functions on the server. The **FileSystemObject** object has an object model associated with it as well. This object model follows this hierarchy:

▶ **FileSystemObject** object
▶ **Drives** collection
▶ **Drive** object
▶ **Folders** collection
▶ **Folder** object
▶ **Files** collection
▶ **File** object

Let's take a look at each of the objects in the object model and briefly describe what they are used for. Then, our examples will show different ways to use the **FileSystemObject** object in real-life web applications.

Drive Object

Each of the **Drive** objects that form part of the **Drives** collection contains a wealth of information about a drive in the web server. This information includes:

- ▶ Free space available
- ▶ The Volume name of the drive
- ▶ An indication of whether or not the drive is ready
- ▶ The type of file system that exists on the drive
- ▶ The physical type of drive it is
- ▶ A reference to the root folder on the drive

Most of the information contained in the **Drive** object is read-only. You can't change the amount of free space available that a drive has. However, you can change the Volume name of a drive, if it can physically be changed.

Drives Collection

This collection contains one **Drive** object for each of the drives on the system. This includes all of the local drives, both fixed and removable, as well as any currently connected network drives.

Folder Object

The **Folder** object allows you to access all of the properties of a folder. These properties include the name of the folder, the collection of files within it, the size of the folder in bytes, and what its attributes are. In addition, if there are subfolders within this folder, then it will contain a reference to a collection of folder objects that represent its subfolders. With the folder object, you can also copy, delete, and move folders within the file system.

Folders Collection

A **Folders** collection contains a set of **Folder** objects. This collection is a bit different from the others in that you will usually find a **Folder** collection as a property of a **Folder** object. If you think about how these objects map to the physical world, then it begins to make sense. With Personal Web Server we have **wwwroot** as our root folder, and then underneath we have **BegASP** as a subfolder. The **Folders** collection also provides a way for you to add a folder object to it. This is like adding a sub-folder to an existing folder.

File Object

The lowest level object in the **FileSystemObject** object model is the **File** object. The **File** object allows access to all of the properties of an individual file in the file system. These properties include the file name, the path to the file, a reference to the folder object where the file exists, and the size of the file. With the **File** object, you can also copy, delete, and move files in the file system. Another method allows you to open the file itself, and read it as a text stream. In the next part of this chapter, we will be looking at the **TextStream** object and how it can be used to manipulate the actual contents of a file.

Files Collection

The `Files` collection contains all of the `File` objects within a folder. Each `Files` collection corresponds to a particular folder or sub-folder in the file system. By iterating through a `Files` collection, you can examine in turn each of the files within a particular folder.

Now, let's take a look at a few examples that show you the different ways that you can use the `FileSystemObject` object.

Try It Out – Display a Directory

When displaying content from a web page, we can either display static information that is retrieved from a file stored on the web server, or we can dynamically create information to be displayed. One thing that we may want to do is combine these two choices. We may want to be able to display a list of the files stored on the web server.

Now, with PWS, we have the ability to enable directory browsing. This can be done from the Advanced Options selection of the Personal Web Manager.

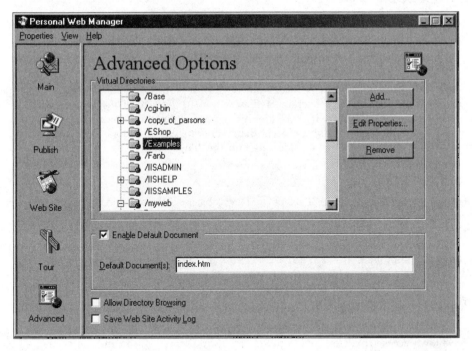

By checking the Allow Directory Browsing checkbox, then the client is able to view the contents of the selected directory. However, this method has some drawbacks. If there is a default document, such as `index.htm` in this example, then there is no way to display the directory. Also, if the directory is displayed, then there is no way to control the fact that each file in the directory is also an active link. This has many implications, especially in the area of security. This setting will allow unauthorized individuals to see hidden files and URLs. This is why most commercial sites disable directory browsing.

This first example will show how to use the `FileSystemObject` object to display a listing of the files in the current directory.

1 Using your editor of choice, create the `DisplayDirectory.asp` file with the following source code.

```
<!DOCTYPE HTML PUBLIC "-//W3C//DTD HTML 3.2 Final//EN">

<HTML>
<HEAD>
<TITLE>Chapter 11 Example - Display Directory</TITLE>
</HEAD>
<BODY>
<%
Dim strPathInfo, strPhysicalPath
strPathInfo = Request.ServerVariables("PATH_INFO")
strPhysicalPath = Server.MapPath(strPathInfo)

    Dim objFSO, objFile, objFileItem, objFolder, objFolderContents
Set objFSO = CreateObject("Scripting.FileSystemObject")

Set objFile = objFSO.GetFile(strPhysicalPath)

Set objFolder = objFile.ParentFolder

Set objFolderContents = objFolder.Files
%>
<TABLE cellpadding=5>
<TR align=center><TH align=left>File Name</TH><TH>File Size</TH><TH>Last
Modified</TH></TR>
<%
For Each objFileItem in objFolderContents
        Response.Write "<TR><TD align=left>"
        Response.Write objFileItem.Name
        Response.Write "</TD><TD align=right>"
        Response.Write objFileItem.Size
        Response.Write "</TD><TD align=right>"
        Response.Write objFileItem.DateLastModified
        Response.Write "</TD></TR>"
Next
%>
</TABLE>
</BODY>
</HTML>
```

2 Make sure this file is stored in a directory that is shared by your web server.

3 View the page in
your web browser.

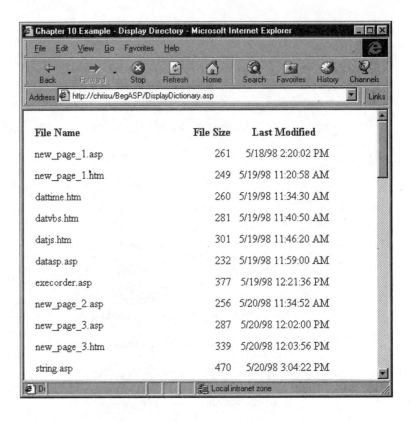

How It Works

After putting all of the requisite header stuff at the top of the page, the first thing that we need to do is determine the physical path to the current file. Our ASP page will display a list of the files in the directory that the file resides in. The URL that is used to display this file is a **virtual path**. This means that the path is defined by the web server's configuration. The virtual path does not necessarily correspond to the file's location in the drive's local directory tree. It's also very important to remember that, for the **FileScriptingObject** objects to work, they need the *physical* path and not the virtual path.

To get the physical path to the current file, we need to start with the virtual path to the file. This information can be found in the HTTP variable **PATH_INFO**. In our example program, this variable contains:

```
/BegASP/displayDirectory.asp
```

If this looks familiar, it is the part of the URL that follows the name of the server. To retrieve this value, we will use the **Server** object's **ServerVariables** collection.

Now that we have this value, we need to translate it to the physical path. There is a **Server** object method that will allow you to do this. The **MapPath** method will take a virtual path and convert it to a physical path. After we convert our virtual path to a physical path, we have:

```
C:\InetPub\wwwroot\BegASP\displayDirectory.asp
```

Note: A physical path will always relate to a drive letter, and not a UNC name for the path.

This is the data that we need to use with the `FileScriptingObject` objects. In this example, the virtual path looks very similar to the physical path. This is a just a coincidence of the way that this particular web server is configured. In other cases, only the file name could be similar.

To start working with the `FileSystemObject` object, we will need to create an instance of it.

Since this object is part of the Scripting Objects Library, we will not have to use the `Server.CreateObject` method to create it. We create the object and save its reference in the `objFSO` variable. Before we dive into how the code itself works, let's look at the strategy we will use to generate the directory.

We are starting with the physical path to the file. This file is in the directory that we want the contents for. So, we need to find a way to relate this file to the directory that it is in. Fortunately, one of the `FileSystemObject` objects provides this type of functionality. To get started, we need to get a `File` object that corresponds to the file that we have the path for. If you remember, the `File` object allows you to get information about a particular file. The `FileSystemObject` object itself provides a method called `GetFile` that will take a physical path to a file and return a reference to a `File` object that represents that file.

Now that we are armed with a `File` object representing a file in the directory we are interested in, we can use a property of the `File` object to get a reference to the folder that it is in.

> *We have been using the words directory and folder interchangeably. For those of us who came from the DOS world, our files have always been arranged in directories. With the advent of Windows 95 and the addition of Windows Explorer, the folder term has become more prevalent. But, they still both refer to the same thing.*

One of the properties of the `File` object is the `ParentFolder` property. Given a valid file object, this will return a reference to a `Folder` object that represents the folder that the file resides in. If you have a `File` object in the root folder, the `ParentFolder` property will be null (not known or missing). We have now reached our objective of having an object that represents the directory we are interested in.

Now it is time to look at the files that are in this directory. To do this, we will use the `Files` collection that is stored as a property of the `Folder` object. This collection is a set of `File` objects; one object for each file in the directory.

To display the files, we will be using a `<TABLE>` for formatting. There will be three columns in the table, we will display the file name, the size of the file in bytes, and the date and time the file was last modified. The easiest way to go through all of the items in a collection is to use the `For Each` loop statement.

```
For Each objFileItem in objFolderContents
```

This statement will set up a loop structure that will be called one time for each object in the `objFolderContents` collection. Each time through the loop, the reference to the current object will be available using the `objFileItem` variable. The information that we are interested in displaying is available in three properties of the `File` object:

- **objFileItem.Name**—returns the name of the file
- **objFileItem.Size**—returns the size of the file in bytes
- **objFileItem.DateLastModified**—returns the date and time of the last modification of the file

Each of these pieces of information will be stored in their own table cell. Before moving to the next item in the collection, we will need to end the current row in the table. Once we have reached the end of the collection, we can end the table, then finish the page and send it back to the client to be displayed.

The next example will enhance the directory viewer page that we have just completed. While displaying a list of files is nice, we may want to be able to interact with the files in the list. This will make the directory an interactive directory similar to the directory provided by the web server, but with you, the developer, in control of the way the information is presented. If we enable the web server to allow directory browsing, then the contents of the directory we are working in would look like this:

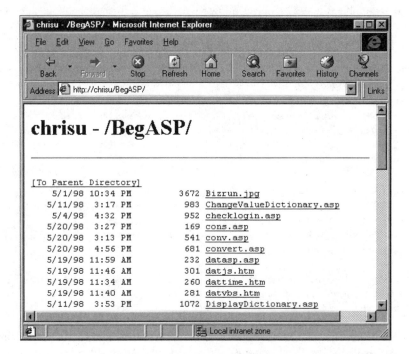

Since this page is generated by the server itself, there is no way that we can change the way that page looks. So let's take a look at how to use the **FileSystemObject** objects to obtain the same information and, using the power of ASP, create a different presentation of the data.

Try It Out – Make the Directory Interactive

1 Copy the `DisplayDirectory.asp` file from the last chapter to a new file and name it `InteractiveDirectory.asp`.

2 Using your favorite editor, make the following additions and changes to the `InteractiveDirectory.asp` file:

```
<!DOCTYPE HTML PUBLIC "-//W3C//DTD HTML 3.2 Final//EN">

<HTML>
<HEAD>
<TITLE>Chapter 11 Example - Display Directory</TITLE>
</HEAD>
<BODY>
<%
dim strPathInfo, strPhysicalPath
strPathInfo = Request.ServerVariables("PATH_INFO")

strPhysicalPath = Server.MapPath(strPathInfo)

    Dim objFSO, objFile, objFileItem, objFolder, objFolderContents
Set objFSO = CreateObject("Scripting.FileSystemObject")

set objFile = objFSO.GetFile(strPhysicalPath)

set objFolder = objFile.ParentFolder

set objFolderContents = objFolder.Files
%>
<TABLE cellpadding=5>
  <TR align=center><TH align=left>File Name</TH><TH>Type</TH><TH>File
Size</TH><TH>Last Modified</TH></TR>
  <%
  For Each objFileItem in objFolderContents
  %>
        <TR><TD align=left>
        <A HREF="<%= objFileItem.Name %>"><FONT FACE="Verdana"
SIZE="3"><%= objFileItem.Name %></A></FONT></TD>
        <TD align=right><FONT FACE="Tahoma" SIZE="2" COLOR="DarkGreen"><%=
objFileItem.type %></FONT></TD>
        <TD align=right><FONT FACE="Tahoma" SIZE="2" COLOR="DarkGreen"><%=
objFileItem.size %></FONT></TD>
        <TD align=right><FONT FACE="Tahoma" SIZE="2" COLOR="DarkGreen"><%=
objFileItem.DateLastModified %></FONT></TD>
        </TR>
  <%
  Next
  %>
```

```
</TABLE>
</BODY>
</HTML>
```

3 Make sure this file is stored in a directory that is shared by your web server.

4 View the page in your web browser.

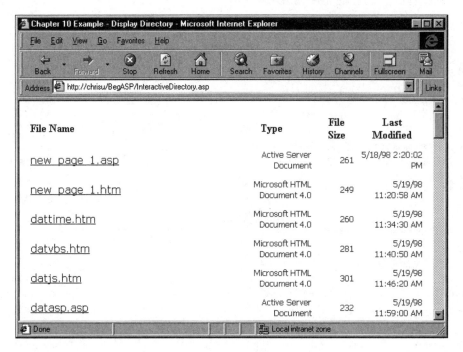

How It Works

We have made three major changes to the previous example to arrive at this new interactive directory display.

First, we have added some text formatting to the file information. There are two text styles that we will be using. One will be for the display of the file name itself in the directory listing. The other will be for the display of the other pieces of information about each file. To make the file names stand out, and to lessen the appearance of the file data, we have put the file names in a different font at a larger font size.

> *Note that while we set the color for the file data information, we did not set a color for the file name. This is because the file name will be an active link to the file. This means that the color of this text will be controlled by the settings in the user's browser. If we were to change the colors, then we run the risk of confusing the user as to which files they may have already visited.*

Second, we added a `<A HREF>` tag to the name of the file itself. This is to replicate the functionality that is in the standard directory browsing display. All files in that display have a link associated with them. This will allow the user to click on the name of the file to navigate to it. To support this functionality in our page, we need to wrap the name of the file with a `<A HREF>` tag. The value of the `HREF` will need to be the same as the virtual path and name of the file, so that when the user clicks on the link they will be taken to that file.

> *Even though the user may be able to navigate to any file in the directory, there may be files present that when clicked on will not return any valid information. Other files may actually include information that you don't want the user to be able to see. So while the ability to list files in a directory may be powerful, you need to exercise some care when using it.*

Finally, we have added another column to our directory display. This column will display the file type for each file. This information is retrieved from the registry of the web server. This is the same file type that would be displayed for the file when viewed using Windows Explorer. To display this information, we retrieve it from the `Type` property of the `File` object.

Displaying directories is a nice feature, but let's look at some of the other things we can do with the `FileSystemObject` objects. One thing that you see on a lot of web pages is some small text at the bottom of the page that identifies certain properties about the page. Some of these properties include:

▶ File Name

▶ Size

▶ Creation Date

▶ Last Modification Date

▶ Last Accessed Date

For a person viewing the page, this information can be helpful in determining the accuracy of the information on the page. Or it can be useful for debugging purposes. Whatever it is used for, there should be an easy way to add it to each page. We'll now look at another method that can be used in ASP to further enhance our directory display example.

Server-Side Includes

Server-side includes (SSIs) are a very useful way to make your site easier to manage, and for providing extra information. The important point to note is that the 'including' is done *before* the Active Server Pages interpreter gets to see the page. So it isn't possible to use code to decide *which* SSI `#include` directives we want to put into action. They will all be included automatically. There are five basic types of SSI we can use. We can:

▶ Include text files in our pages, as they are loaded

▶ Retrieve the size and last modification date of a file

▶ Define how variables and error messages are displayed

▶ Insert the values of HTTP variables in the page sent back to the browser

◗   Execute other programs or scripts, such as CGI and ISAPI applications

Only the first of these is directly applicable to Active Server Pages. SSIs are normally used in a separate file, which can be referenced and loaded from an ASP file.

Including Text Files in a Page with #include

One of the most useful techniques with SSI is to insert pre-built blocks of text into a page. As an example, we created a function for our calendar page that calculated the last day of any month. We can save this as a text file called, say, `GetLastDay.txt`. Then, anytime that we want to use the function, we just add an include statement to the page, and call the function:

```
<!-- #include file="GetLastDay.txt" -->
...
intLastDayAugust = GetLastDay(datAugust)    'call our included function
...
```

The only point to watch out for is that, if you want to include script from another file, this file must contain complete script sections. In other words, it has to have opening and closing `<SCRIPT>` or `<%...%>` tags—we can't place part of the code section in an included file, and the rest in the main page. However, we could include half of, say, an `If...Then` construct in the file, and the rest in the main page, as long as each part was enclosed in the `<%...%>` tags. This isn't likely to produce code that is easy to read or debug later, though!

Of course, the text we include doesn't have to be VBScript or JScript code. We can quite easily use it to include HTML or just plain text. If your site uses pages with standard footers for your copyright notice, or a standard `<STYLE>` tag to set up the text and page styles, these can equally well be stored as a separate file, and referenced with a `#include` statement.

Virtual and Physical File Addresses

The `#include` directive allows us to specify a file using either its **physical** or **virtual** path. For example, the file `MyFile.txt` could be in the directory `C:\TextFiles`. If this directory also had an alias (virtual path) of `/Texts` set up as we saw earlier in this chapter, we could then reference it using either method:

```
<!-- #include file="C:\TextFiles\MyFile.txt" -->      'physical path
<!-- #include virtual="/Texts/MyFile.txt"    -->      'virtual path
```

We can also, as you've already seen, use relative paths. If the file is in the same folder, we just use the file name. If it's in the `Projects` subdirectory, we can use:

```
<!-- #include file="Projects\MyFile.txt" -->          'physical path
```

One point to note is that if you place the included file *outside* a virtual root directory on the server, then make changes to the file, these changes are *not* available to Active Server Pages until the web server is next restarted.

In this example, we will actually be building an SSI that can be added to any Active Server Page.

Try It Out – Enhanced File Info Display

The SSI in this example will display information about the current file to the client.

1 Use NotePad to create the `FileDetails.inc` file with the following source code.

```
<%
Dim strFDPathInfo, strFDPhysicalPath
strFDPathInfo = Request.ServerVariables("PATH_INFO")
strFDPhysicalPath = Server.MapPath (strFDPathInfo)

    Dim objFDFSO, objFDFile
Set objFDFSO = CreateObject("Scripting.FileSystemObject")

Set objFDFile = objFDFSO.GetFile(strFDPhysicalPath)
%>
<P><HR>
<DIV STYLE="font-size:11; font-family: Verdana; ">
File Name: <B><%= objFDFile.Name %></B><BR>
Server Path: <B><%= strFDPathInfo %></B><BR>
Physical Path: <B><%= objFDFile.Path %></B><BR>
File Size: <B><%= objFDFile.size %> bytes</B><BR>
Date Created: <B><%= objFDFile.DateCreated %></B><BR>
Date Last Modified: <B><%= objFDFile.DateLastModified %></B><BR>
Date Last Accessed: <B><%= objFDFile.DateLastAccessed %></B><BR>
</DIV>
```

2 Make sure this file is stored in a directory that is shared by your web server.

3 This example is of a sever-side include file. This means that we will need to add it to an existing ASP file. For this example, let's pick the `InteractiveDirectory.asp` file from the previous example. Open this file in your favorite editor and add this entry near the bottom.

```
        <TD align=right><SPAN CLASS=FileData><%= objFileItem.size %></
SPAN></TD>
        <TD align=right><SPAN CLASS=FileData><%=
objFileItem.DateLastModified %></SPAN></TD>
        </TR>
<%
Next
%>
</TABLE>
<!-- #include file="FileDetails.inc" -->
</BODY>
</HTML>
```

4 View the page in your web browser.

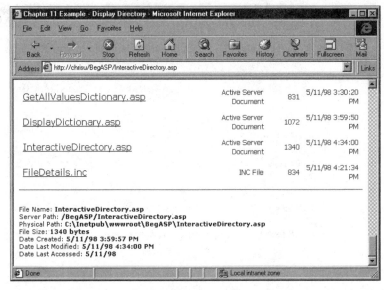

How It Works

This server-side include file has two primary functions. First, it needs to obtain a `File` object for the file that it is included in. Then, using that `File` object, we can display the information about the file itself.

If we were to just load this file directly from the server, then it would display information about itself. This would not be the type of information we are looking for. The nice part about making it a server-side include file is that even though it is a separate file, when the server includes it into the other file, it acts as if it were part of that file. This means that when we get the `File` object that corresponds to the current file, we get the file that we are really interested in.

In the previous examples, we have shown how to get a `File` object that corresponds to the current file. In those examples, we went a step further and used that `File` object's `ParentFolder` property to get a reference to the current folder. In this server-side include file, we will stop once we get the reference to the `File` object.

One change that we have made from the earlier examples is that we are going to use different variable names. In the earlier examples, the variable names were both easy to read and corresponded closely to the data the variable contained. In a server-side include file, you need to be careful about the naming of any variables. Since this file is actually treated as part of the file that it is included in, you need to ensure that the variable names do not conflict. In our example, since we are leveraging code from the `InteractiveDirectory.asp` example, our variables would have been named

- `strPathInfo`
- `strPhysicalPath`
- `objFSO`
- `objFile`

If this server-side include file is then included into the `InteractiveDirectory.asp` file itself, then there would be two statements that each declared a variable with each of these names. This would cause a script error when the page was processed. To get around this, we have changed the names of the variables in the hope that they will be unique. Since this server-side include file provides additional file data, we have added a *FD* to each variable name. This results in variables named

- `strFDPathInfo`
- `strFDPhysicalPath`
- `obFDjFSO`
- `objFDFile`

With our `File` object referencing the file we are interested, we can now turn to the display of the information. The information will be visually separated from the rest of the page with a horizontal line generated by the `<HR>` tag. To set the formatting for all of the information, we have created a `<DIV>` section and set the text format properties for that container element. All of the information that is displayed is retrieved from a property of the `File` object except one. Since the `FileSystemObject` objects deal with files in their physical space, the `File` object has no information about the virtual path to the file as seen by the web server. Since we want to display that information on the client, we will need to retrieve that information from the HTTP Server Variables that are passed with each request to the server. The `strFDPathInfo` variable will contain the virtual path that points to the file we are currently viewing.

Up until now, we have been using the `FileSystemObject` objects to access information about the properties of folders and files in the physical file system. They also provide one other function with respect to files. With a valid `File` object, you can open the file itself as a text file and deal with the data contained inside of it. To do this, you will interact with the file's data using the `TextStream` object.

The Text Stream Object

The `TextStream` object allows you access the contents of a file as a text file. This does not mean that the file has to have a `.txt` extension. Rather, its contents have to be in text readable form. Naturally, `.txt` files work fine. But, you can also open `.html` files, `.asp` files, and event `.log` files. Once you have access to the text contents of a file, you can read information from it and write information to it.

There are three ways that you can get a `TextStream` object. With a valid `File` object, you can use the `OpenAsTextStream` method. This will return a `TextStream` object that you can then use to manipulate the contents of the file. If you know the physical file name of the file, and don't want to worry about creating a `File` object for it, then the `FileSystemObject` object's `OpenTextFile` method will open the file in the same way. Lastly, if you want to create a brand new file and add text to it, you can use the `CreateTextFile` method of the `FileSystemObject` object and pass it the name of the file you want to create. This method will return a `TextStream` object, which you can use to add text to the file.

Try It Out – ASP Source Code Viewer

Our first example will look at just accessing the information contained in a file. One of the best ways to learn how to program on the web is to look at people's source code. You can learn many HTML tricks by looking at the source code of pages you like. But how can you use this same approach to learning the insides of ASP? With ASP, the source is interpreted on the server, and all the client sees is the completed HTML.

In this example, we will create an Active Server Pages script that will display the source of any of the ASP files on your server. The file name will be passed in as a URL parameter. We will also show how to link it to an existing ASP page.

1 Using your editor of choice, create the `DisplaySource.asp` file with the following source code:

```
<!DOCTYPE HTML PUBLIC "-//W3C//DTD HTML 3.2 Final//EN">
<%
Const ForReading = 1, ForWriting = 2, ForAppending = 3
    Const TristateUseDefault = -2, TristateTrue = -1, TristateFalse = 0
Dim strPathInfo, strPhysicalPath
strPathInfo = Request.QueryString("FileName")
strPhysicalPath = Server.MapPath(strPathInfo)


    Dim objFSO, objFile
Set objFSO = CreateObject("Scripting.FileSystemObject")
set objFile = objFSO.GetFile(strPhysicalPath)
%>

<HTML>
<HEAD>
<TITLE><%= objFile.Name %> Source Code</TITLE>
</HEAD>
<BODY>
Source code for <%= objFile.Name %><HR><P>
<FONT FACE=Courier SIZE=2>
<%
Dim objFileTextStream
Set objFileTextStream = objFile.OpenAsTextStream(ForReading,
TristateUseDefault)

Dim strLine
Do While objFileTextStream.AtEndOfStream <> True
        strLine = Server.HTMLEncode(objFileTextStream.ReadLine)
        strLine = Replace (strLine, Chr(9), "    ")
        Response.Write strLine
        Response.Write "<BR>" + vbCrLf
    Loop
objFileTextStream.Close
%>
</FONT>
```

```
<P>
<HR>
<A HREF="<%= strPathInfo %>">Return to Displayed File</A>
</BODY>
</HTML>
```

2 Make sure this file is stored in a directory that is shared by your web server.

3 To link to this file, add this source code to the `InteractiveDirectory.asp` file from a previous example:

```
</TABLE>
<!-- #include file="FileDetails.inc" -->
<HR>
<A HREF="DisplaySource.asp?FileName=<%=
Server.URLEncode(Request.ServerVariables("PATH_INFO")) %>">Click here to
see ASP source</A>
</BODY>
</HTML>
```

4 View the page `InteractiveDirectory.asp` in your web browser.

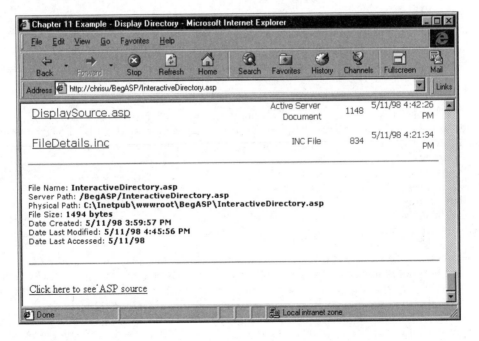

5 When you click on the hyperlink at the bottom of the page, you will then see this in your browser.

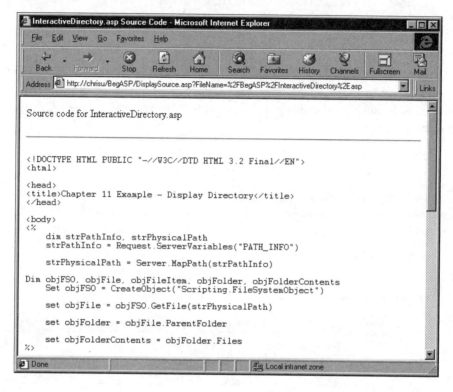

How It Works

For this application to work, we need to build on what we did in the previous examples. In order to create a `TextStream` object, we need to start with a valid `File` object for the file we are interested in. To get this, we will use the tried and true method that we have used in the previous examples.

The difference in this case is that the virtual path to the file we are interested in is passed in as a query string variable. So, to begin our steps to getting a `File` object, we need to use that passed in value to compute the physical file path, instead of using a server variable as we did in the other examples.

Once we have the valid `File` object, the next step is to open that file as a text file. To do this, we will use the `OpenAsTextStream` method of the `File` object. This method will return a reference to a `TextStream` object that contains the contents of the file. The `OpenAsTextStream` method takes two parameters:

The first parameter is used to determine the state the file is opened in. There are three possible states for opening the file. To make the code more readable, we have defined constants at the top of the source file for these three states.

The possible values are:

- **ForReading**—The file is read-only. You cannot write any information to this file.
- **ForWriting**—You are able to write to the file. If there is any data that was already in the file, it will be overwritten as soon as you open it in this mode.
- **ForAppending**—You are able to read the file, as well as add text to the end of it. You cannot change any of the text that was originally there.

The second parameter indicates in what file format the file should be opened. The possible values are:

- **TristateTrue**—This will open the file in UNICODE format.
- **TristateFalse**—This will open the file in ASCII format.
- **TristateUseDefault**—This will use the default setting for the web server.

To be safe, you should usually open the file in the default mode, unless you are absolutely sure that the contents are not of the default type.

Once the file is open, we can begin reading the information from the file. There are a number of ways information can be read from the file. It can be read all at once, using the **ReadAll** method. This will return all of the text in the file in one big chunk. While this is the easiest to implement, it does not work very well at all for large files. Rather than reading the file all at once, it can be read in pieces. There are two different size chunks that can be read from a file. The **Read** method can be used to read a certain number of characters from the file into a string. This number of characters is determined by a parameter passed to the **Read** method.

Alternatively, the file can be read one line at a time using the **ReadLine** method. This method will return all of the text starting at the current location in the file up to the first line break. When you have a file open for reading, the **TextStream** object maintains a pointer in the file indicating where you last read text. When you first open the file, this pointer is pointing at the beginning of the file. When you read text from the file using either the **Read** or **ReadLine** methods, the object moves this pointer to a point just after where you finished reading. In the case of the **ReadLine** method, the pointer will be pointing at the first character *after* the line break.

As you are reading the file piece by piece, you will need some indication as to when you have run out of file to read. The **TextStream** object provides a property that is very simple to access which will tell you when you are at the end of the file. The **AtEndOfStream** property will return True when you have reached the end of the file.

In our example, we will be reading the file one line at a time. To do this, we will be using the **ReadLine** method. Since we want to read the entire file, we will need to call the **ReadLine** method over and over again until we have read the entire file. This can be easily done using a loop. The condition that we are checking every time we go through the loop is based on the **AtEndOfStream** property. As long as this property's value is not true, we still have more data to read, so we can grab the next chunk using the **ReadLine** method.

Once we have the line stored in a string, there is one more procedure that we need to perform on it. Since we will be displaying primarily the source code for Active Server Pages files, we need to take care of how special characters in the file are handled.

If we were to just spit the contents of the file back to the client using a `Response.Write` method, we will probably not get the desired results. Since a large part of an ASP source file is HTML, when this is sent back to the client, it will just display it as if it were regular HTML. This will not give us the display that we are interested in.

In order to display the HTML as source, we need to change the way the HTML tags are presented. When the client is displaying an HTML page, it is looking for HTML tags that are bounded by `<` `>`. When it finds one of these, it will use it as formatting instructions, and not as text to be displayed. In order for the browser to display the HTML source as text, we need to change the `<` `>` to a character that will look the same, but will be interpreted differently.

To do this, we need to look through the string and wherever we find a `<` or `>` we need to replace it with a `&lt;` or `&gt;` respectively. When the client sees this set of characters, it will display a `<`, but it will not treat what is inside as an HTML tag. This is exactly what we need for our source code viewer. Lucky for us, there is a very convenient `Server` object method called `HTMLEncode`. It does exactly what we need. Given a string, it will search for characters that would be interpreted as HTML by a browser, when we really want it to display as text.

The last bit of formatting that we need to do concerns the area of indented text. Many ASP source files use indented sections to make the code more readable. These indents are usually made using tab characters. Unfortunately, when a web client is told to display a tab character, it will just ignore it. We want our source code display to retain the formatting that the developer added. To do this, we will use the `Replace` method to look for tab characters. The tab character is one of those **non-printable characters**. This means that there is no visible character that represents it. But we need a tab character as input to the `Replace` method. VBScript also provides us with a `Chr` function. This function will convert a number into its equivalent ASCII character. After consulting our ASCII character chart, we know that the ASCII code for the Tab character is 9. So we will be using `Chr(9)` as our search sub-string in the `Replace` method. We will be replacing each of the tab characters with four non-breaking space characters. These are represented as ` ` and when the client encounters one of these, it adds an explicit space character to the output.

Now that the whole line is properly formatted, we can output it to the client using the `Response.Write` method. Since the client will ignore any carriage returns in the text file, we need to add our own line break to the displayed source code. To do this, we add the `<BR>` tag to the end of the line. Having finished all of the processing on this line, we start our loop all over again with the next line. When we run out of lines to process, we close the `TextStream` and send the completed page back to the client.

In order to launch this page, we need to add a few lines of code to an existing ASP file. We will be using one of the examples from earlier in this chapter. At the bottom of the page, we will add a hyperlink that will request the `DisplaySource.asp` file. The name of the file that we are displaying the source for is passed as a URL parameter. Before we pass the file name as a query string variable, we need to make sure that all of the characters in the file name are valid URL characters. The easiest way to do this is to use the `Server.URLEncode` method. This method will replace any invalid characters in a URL string with their corresponding URL representations. This will ensure that the file name is properly passed to the

`DisplaySource.asp` file, regardless of the characters in the file name. So now, when the user clicks on this link, the source code of the ASP file that generated the page will be displayed for the user.

This example has shown us how to read information from a text file on the server and display it on the client. Next, we will take a look at how to write information to a text file. There are many instances in web applications where you want more detail than is available in the standard server logs, yet you don't want to have a database to write the information to. This example will show how to create an application log file routine that can be packaged into a server-side include and dropped into any ASP file.

Try It Out – Application Log File

In this example, we will be creating a server-side include file that can be added to any of your Active Server Pages script files. This file will provide your script with a method that can be called to write information to a log file. All that your script will need to do is add this include file and then call the method to write the information to the file.

1 Using NotePad, create the `WriteLog.inc` file with the following source code:

```
<%
Const ForAppending = 8

dim strLogFileName
strLogFileName = "c:\AppLogFile.log"

dim objLogFileFSO
set objLogFileFSO = CreateObject("Scripting.FileSystemObject")

dim objLogFileTS
if objLogFileFSO.FileExists(strLogFileName) then
        set objLogFileTS = objLogFileFSO.OpenTextFile(strLogFileName,
ForAppending)
else
        set objLogFileTS = objLogFileFSO.CreateTextFile(strLogFileName)
end if

sub WriteToLog (strNewEntry)
        dim strLogEntry

        strLogEntry = FormatDateTime(Now) & " - "
        strLogEntry = strLogEntry & strNewEntry
        objLogFileTS.WriteLine strLogEntry
end sub

sub CloseLog()
        objLogFileTS.Close
end sub
%>
```

2 Save this file to the directory where your other ASP files are located.

3 Next, add the include statement to your ASP file. For this example, we will be using the `DisplayDirectory.asp` file that we looked at earlier.

```
set objFolderContents = objFolder.Files
%>
<!-- #include file="WriteLog.inc" -->

<TABLE cellpadding=5>
```

4 We'll add a line which will call the `WriteToLog` method to write information to the log file.

```
        Response.Write objFileItem.DateLastModified
        Response.Write "</TD></TR>"
        WriteToLog "Directory Entry for " + objFileItem.Name
Next
%>
```

5 At the end of the ASP file, add a call to the `CloseLog` method to close the log file.

```
        Response.Write objFileItem.DateLastModified
        Response.Write "</TD></TR>"
        WriteToLog "Directory Entry for " + objFileItem.Name
Next
CloseLog
%>
```

6 View the `DisplayDirectory.asp` file in your web browser. This will cause the server to generate the page, which will write the information to the log file. The contents of the log file which will be called `AppLogFile.log` can be found under the `C:\` folder on your hard drive and can be viewed using any editor, we're using Notepad. The contents will look something like this:

```
AppLogFile.log - Notepad
File  Edit  Search  Help
5/11/98 4:59:47 PM - Directory Entry for new_page_1.asp
5/11/98 4:59:47 PM - Directory Entry for new_page_1.htm
5/11/98 4:59:47 PM - Directory Entry for dattime.htm
5/11/98 4:59:47 PM - Directory Entry for datvbs.htm
5/11/98 4:59:47 PM - Directory Entry for datjs.htm
5/11/98 4:59:47 PM - Directory Entry for datasp.asp
5/11/98 4:59:47 PM - Directory Entry for execorder.asp
5/11/98 4:59:47 PM - Directory Entry for new_page_2.asp
5/11/98 4:59:47 PM - Directory Entry for new_page_3.asp
5/11/98 4:59:47 PM - Directory Entry for new_page_3.htm
5/11/98 4:59:47 PM - Directory Entry for string.asp
5/11/98 4:59:47 PM - Directory Entry for conv.asp
5/11/98 4:59:47 PM - Directory Entry for cons.asp
5/11/98 4:59:47 PM - Directory Entry for typename.asp
5/11/98 4:59:47 PM - Directory Entry for convert.asp
5/11/98 4:59:47 PM - Directory Entry for where.asp
5/11/98 4:59:47 PM - Directory Entry for TioIfThenOneForm.asp
5/11/98 4:59:47 PM - Directory Entry for TioIfThenOneResponse.asp
```

How It Works

This server-side include file will need to perform two functions. First, it will need to get the **TextStream** object that represents our log file properly prepared to accept information written to it. Secondly, it will need to provide an easy mechanism for the file that includes it to write information to the log file.

In our example, we have defined the name of the log file. This could have just as easily been stored in a variable and retrieved by the include file. Once we have this file name, which is already a physical file name, we can then prepare the **TextStream** object to accept information written to it.

```
dim objLogFileTS
if objLogFileFSO.FileExists(strLogFileName) then
        set objLogFileTS = objLogFileFSO.OpenTextFile(strLogFileName,
ForAppending)
else
        set objLogFileTS = objLogFileFSO.CreateTextFile(strLogFileName)
end if
```

There are two states that we need to work with when preparing the **TextStream** object. The first state is when there is no log file present. In this case, we need to create the log file and then open it with write permissions enabled. To check to see if the file is present, we will be using the **FileExists** method of the **FileSystemObject** object. This method takes the name of a physical file and returns true if the file exists and false if it does not.

If this method returns True, then we know that our log file exists and all we need to do is open it. To open it, we will use the **OpenTextFile** method of the **FileSystemObject** object. This method will return a **TextStream** object that represents the file. There are two parameters that we will pass to this method. The first is the name of the physical log file. This is stored in the **strLogFileName** variable. The second parameter is used to tell the **FileSystemObject** object what we want to do with this file once we have opened it.

There are two possible values for this parameter. If we just want to read information from the file, then we can set this parameter's value to **ForReading**. This value will cause the file to be opened as read-only, meaning we can only read information from the file. Since our task here is to create a file that we can write information to, we need to supply the other value for the parameter. The value of **ForAppending** means that we will be able to both write information to the file, as well as read information from it. To define the actual value for this parameter, we have included a **Const** statement to set the value of **ForAppending** to 8.

If the **FileExists** method returns False, then we know that we have to create the log file so that we can write to it. This is done using the **CreateTextFile** method of the **FileSystemObject**. For this method, we will be supplying one parameter. We will pass in the physical name of the file that we want to create. This method will return a **TextStream** object that represents our new physical file. This **TextStream** object will be set up so that information can be written to the file.

The steps involved in opening or creating the file are the first steps in our server side include file. These steps need to be executed as soon as the server reads them from the source file. The other step in the log file is writing information to the log file itself. We need to be able to call this step from anywhere in the source file. In order to do this, we have created a **subroutine**.

```
Sub WriteToLog (strNewEntry)
      dim strLogEntry

      strLogEntry = FormatDateTime(Now) & " - "
      strLogEntry = strLogEntry & strNewEntry
      objLogFileTS.WriteLine strLogEntry
End sub
```

This subroutine is a feature of the server-side include file. It will accept one parameter and then perform some processing. The parameter will be the text information that is written to the log file. When the method receives this information, it will add a date and time stamp to the beginning of it, then write the information to the log file. To write the information to the log file, we will be using the **WriteLine** method of the **TextStream** object. This method will add the text contained in its one parameter to the file associated with the instance of the **TextStream** object. It will also add a line break at the end of the text that it adds to the file.

Now that we have created our server-side include file, we need to add the logging functionality to another ASP file. For this example, we will be adding it to the **DisplayDirectory.asp** file that we looked at earlier in this chapter.

```
set objFolderContents = objFolder.Files
%>
<!-- #include file="WriteLog.inc" -->
```

There are three steps to adding the logging capabilities to this file. First, we will need to include the **WriteLog.inc** file that we just created. This will be done using the **#include** directive in the **DisplayDirectory.asp** file. This statement needs to be included prior to any calls to the **WriteToLog** method, so that the method can be properly defined before it is called.

```
            Response.Write objFileItem.DateLastModified
            Response.Write "</TD></TR>"
            WriteToLog "Directory Entry for " + objFileItem.Name
      Next
%>
```

The next step will be to call the **WriteToLog** method whenever we want to add information to the log file. For this example, we will be writing the name of each file that is read in the current directory to the log file. When you view the log file in Notepad, you can see that the date and time that the entry was made has been added to the beginning of each entry in the log.

```
            Response.Write objFileItem.DateLastModified
            Response.Write "</TD></TR>"
            WriteToLog "Directory Entry for " + objFileItem.Name
      Next
CloseLog
%>
```

The final step is to call the **CloseLog** subroutine, which will close the log file on the server.

While logging this type of information may not be very useful on a production basis, there are a number of occasions where a method like this can come in useful. This method can be used to output information to a log file as you are developing a page. If a problem occurs, it is very easy to go back to the log file to see what processing actually took place, and thereby determine what the error was.

Summary

In this chapter, we have looked at the Scripting Objects and how they can be used inside of Active Server Pages. The Scripting Objects are part of the VBScript library, and are useful as a set of helper routines for developing web applications.

The Scripting Objects consist of:

- The **Dictionary** object, which lets you store and retrieve information in a flexible data structure. In a **Dictionary**, each piece of information that you store is associated with a key. At a later time, that information can be retrieved simply by producing the key.

- The **FileSystemObject** object, which provides access to the physical file system of the web server. With this object, you can view and manipulate the directories and files that make up the server's file system.

- And the **TextStream** object, which gives you access to the contents of text files stored on the web server. This object allows you to read text from the file as well as write information to the file.

By using these objects, you can extend the reach of your web applications beyond what exists inside of the six built-in ASP objects. They allow you to categorize and store information more efficiently, as well as manipulate the physical file system of the server itself.

In the next chapter, we will look at a subject that we just briefly touched on in our last example. We will look at the different ways to debug your ASP applications.

Debugging ASP

Despite the effort that went into this chapter it would be nice if we never needed it. In fact, it would be great if we could just skip onto the next chapter now; unfortunately, it's a fact of life that debugging is a necessity. No matter how hard we try, it really is very difficult to write error-free software. We are inherently fallible. That's not to say it's impossible to write perfect software; it's just very hard, and takes effort, practice, diligence and lots of experience. Let's face facts, we all make mistakes occasionally.

So, given we make these mistakes, how to we go about tracking them down? Most of the popular programming languages are supported by a rich set of development tools, and these tools usually include a debugger. However, it's a sad fact that web developers have often had to rely on the WYSINWYI or WYSIAAMEM approach to debugging—that's "What You See Is Not What You Intended," or "What You See Is An Arcane Microsoft Error Message".

In this chapter we are going to look at debugging and how we apply it to our ASP environment. In particular we will be looking at:

- How to start debugging your ASP code
- The difference between debugging client-side script and server-side script
- The `Err` object
- Tips on how to reduce errors
- The Microsoft Script debugger

Of course, none of these will make you a perfect programmer, but that's really a false goal anyway. The best that you can do is to understand your code, recognize where it might break, and be sure to handle possible error conditions. Making a mistake is acceptable, as long as you find out what the problem is quickly, and then learn from it.

Arrgh! I Goofed Again!

We've already said that it is acceptable to make mistakes. If you're a manager reading this, don't rip this chapter out before giving it to your programmers. The fact is that 'trial and error' is often a good way to learn a new technology—once you've crashed the server for the third time in 20 minutes, you will probably have worked out what it is you're doing wrong. OK, if you're writing monitoring software for a hospital intensive care unit, your quality goals might be a little stricter, but on your own, while learning, you will make mistakes. Guaranteed. You will learn from them; you won't make them again, and you'll go on to write books that tell people how to debug applications.

So what this chapter is really about is how to track down those errors quickly and efficiently. How to get to the root of the problem. How to fix it, and how to find sources of information when the error still mystifies you.

One important thing to note is that this chapter veers away from the Windows 95 version of Personal Web Server in places. Some of the things we are going to talk about are only available under NT, but we've included them here for two reasons. The first is that you might already be running PWS or IIS under NT, and the second is that some time in the future you might be. The debugging facilities between the two are different, so it's useful to know what is available on which platform. We've marked which sections of the chapter are applicable only to NT.

Where am I?

To help answer this question we're going to have a brief look at the ASP architecture again, because it's important to know where the error is occurring. This is partly revision from earlier chapters, but we're looking at it again here so you see its importance to debugging. Let's have a look at a request for an ASP page.

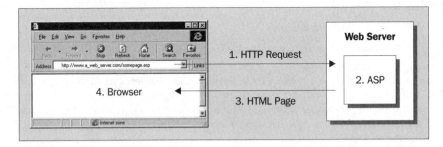

This shows a typical situation. In step 1, the user selects a URL for an ASP page, and the request is forwarded to the web server. Step 2 shows ASP processing the ASP script code on the server. The processed HTML is then sent back to the client, in step 3. And finally, in step 4, the web browser displays the HTML and executes any client-side script. Pretty obvious, but also very important, as you must be aware of where certain actions are processed.

The thing to remember is the difference between server-side script and client-side script. Server-side script is enclosed in the following tags:

```
<%
    ' server-side script here
%>
```

Alternatively, server-side script can be denoted by using the standard script tag and the **RUNAT** property:

```
<SCRIPT LANGUAGE=VBScript RUNAT=Server>
    ' server-side script here
</SCRIPT>
```

Client-side script is enclosed in the standard script tag:

```
<SCRIPT LANGUAGE=VBScript>
    ' client-side script here
</SCRIPT>
```

You might already be used to this by now, but it's surprising how often you forget where the script code is being executed, especially if your ASP page has both server-side and client-side script.

What Am I Doing Here?

Having decided where your script code is executing it's also important not to do the wrong thing in the wrong place, and knowing where you are means you won't try and use objects that aren't appropriate to your current location. Try using Guatemalan Quetzals to pay for souvenirs of your trip to France, and you'll get the idea.

What's all this leading to? Well, there are distinct sets of objects. Some are server-side objects, such as the **Response** object, and some are client-side, such as the **Document** object.

For example, consider this client-side script:

```
<HTML>
    . . . ' some HTML tags

<SCRIPT LANGUAGE=VBScript>
Sub Window_onLoad()
    Response.Write "Hello"
End Sub
</SCRIPT>

</HTML>
```

Try running that and you'll get the following error:

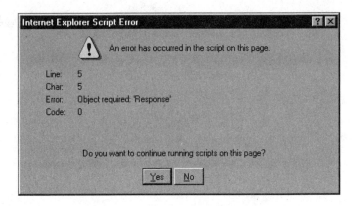

This is because the **Response** object is only available as part of ASP, that is, in server-side scripting. Thus this is a client-side error, not an ASP one.

Likewise, trying this code:

```
<HTML>
<BODY>
<A ID=FieldName>Some text</A>

<%
    Dim objField
    Set objField = Document.All("FieldName")
%>

</BODY>
</HTML>
```

gives the following error:

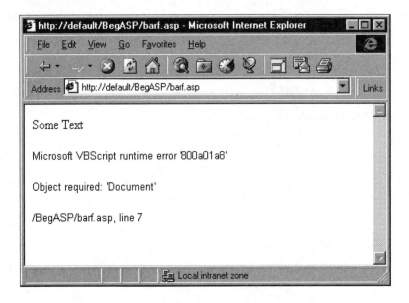

This is because the **Document** object is only available at the client, that is, in the web browser.

Also notice the difference between how the two error messages are displayed. The first example generated an error on the client, so it popped up an error dialog. The second example generated an error in ASP, so the error was returned as HTML code, which subsequently made up the web page. ASP can't display error dialogs because it is running on the server—any dialog would appear on the screen of the web server, which isn't much good if you're five thousand miles away. We'll be looking at the difference between client and server debugging a little later.

The Lack of Good ASP Debuggers

Now to the nitty gritty, and how to actually do this debugging. If you flick back to the diagram at the beginning of this chapter then you might have an idea of why the debugging process has been so difficult for ASP developers. As a developer all you are doing is creating HTML and script code as a text file. Even in Visual InterDev, you haven't a fully-fledged development tool. However good it is, it's still just a glorified text editor. Once the ASP file is created you have to instruct PWS to load it, and it's PWS that executes the script. So the development tool has no way to run ASP script code, because it has to be run on the server, under PWS, and the results are shown in a web browser, whose purpose is just to view the results.

As neither the development tool nor the web browser has the capability to track the program as it runs, how do you go about debugging ASP script? If you're running NT then lucky you, as a separate tool is available, which hooks into IIS to monitor the script as it's being processed. Although not a perfect solution, it's quite effective, and extremely useful. Although it's an NT only tool, we'll have quite a good look at it because it really is extremely useful. But before we do look at it, let's look at some general rules and techniques for debugging ASP script that will work on Windows 95, as well as NT.

Debugging ASP Script

One of the first difficulties you might encounter is finding out exactly where the error is occurring. Remember the first ASP error we showed you, where we tried to access the **Document** object from within ASP:

```
Microsoft VBScript runtime error '800a01a8'
Object required: 'Document'
/BegAsp/Debug.asp, line 5
```

That's pretty easy to follow, since there are only a few lines in the page, but imagine a large ASP page with mixed HTML tags and script, and the error occurs on line 45. Not too bad if you're using Visual InterDev, but what about Notepad, which doesn't have line numbers. It gets a bit tedious constantly moving the cursor down trying to keep count. Unfortunately there's no quick and simple way to track this down, no tool to tell you where the problem is. However, let's look at some tips you can use to make your errors easier to find.

Use Option Explicit

Back in Chapter 4 we mentioned this, and it really is worth using, especially if your typing is as bad as mine. If you remember it just forces you to declare all of your variables before you use them, and it will force an error to be generated if you use a variable that hasn't been declared. As a refresher it's simple to use.

For server-side script, just put the following line at the very beginning of your ASP file:

```
<% Option Explicit %>
```

For client-side script you can add it at the beginning of the script:

```
<SCRIPT LANGUAGE=VBScript>
    Option Explicit
    . . .
</SCRIPT>
```

That's all there is to it, and saves a lot of time hunting for those little typing mistakes.

Use Response.Write

This is one of the oldest methods of debugging, and involves putting in lots of trace statements that indicate where you are in a particular script. If you remember **Response.Write** writes a line of text into the output stream, so this will be seen as text when the page is viewed. For example, consider the following ASP script that expects some details from a Form on the previous ASP page.

```
<%
    Dim strName
    Dim strEmail

    strName = Request.Form("Name")
    strEmail = Request.Form("Email")

    ' do some complex processing with the form details

    ' do more processing
%>
```

Let's suppose an error occurs in the 'complex processing', and you have little idea what it is doing. Changing the script can help track down the problem:

```
<%
    Dim strName
    Dim strEmail

    strName = Request.Form("Name")
    strEmail = Request.Form("Email")
```

```
        Response.Write "Debug: Name=" & strName & "<BR>"
        Response.Write "Debug: Email=" & strEmail & "<BR>"
        Response.Write "Debug: Now entering complex processing<BR>"

    ' do some complex processing with the form details

    Response.Write "Debug: Complex processing finished<BR>"

    ' do more processing

    Response.Write "Debug: More processing finished<BR>"
    %>
```

Now when you run this script you'll see the name and email address displayed before the processing starts, and can tell you whether they are correct or not. If the last message does not appear, then you know that the error occurred before it got to this line.

Although a very simple idea it's extremely valuable, and is a technique I still use to debug complex ASP pages.

Use Subprocedures

We've mentioned the use of procedures, but you might not realize that this is quite a good debugging technique too. As you start writing more and more ASP code you'll find that you're using lots of similar routines in many of your pages, and maybe several times in the same page. Instead of repeating this code you can put it into a sub-procedure and then just call this procedure:

```
<%
    ' get the Form details

    Call ProcessFormDetails (strName, strEmail)

    ' some processing

    Call ProcessFormDetails(strName, strEmail)


Sub ProcessFormDetails (strN, strE)
    ' do some processing here
End Sub

%>
```

Now the processing of the form details is only done in one place, and if anything is wrong you only need to look for errors in one place. You can combine this quite easily with the trace statements too:

```
Sub ProcessFormDetails (strN, strE)
    Response.Write "Debug: ProcessFormDetails Started<BR>"
```

```
    ' do some processing here

        Response.Write "Debug: ProcessFormDetails Ended<BR>"
    End Sub
```

This allows you to see when a sub-procedure started and ended. You could even take this one step further and create some debugging and tracing routines:

```
    Sub Trace (strString)

        Response.Write "Debug: " & strString & "<BR>"

    End Sub
```

Your procedure to process the form details would now look like this:

```
    Sub ProcessFormDetails (strN, strE)
        Trace "ProcessFormDetails Started"

        ' do some processing here

        Trace "ProcessFormDetails Ended"
    End Sub
```

This makes it even easier to see what's going on.

Use Include Files

Using include files is just one step up from using procedures, as you can make your procedures available to many ASP files. You'll see one really good example of this in one of the database chapters, where we have an include file that automatically creates an HTML table from data in a database. This file can be included in any ASP script and is run with only one command.

The one thing you have to watch when using include files, is the possibility of changes affecting more than one ASP script. If you have taken out a set of routines and put them into an include file, and then made them available to other ASP developers in your organization, you must be careful not to suddenly change the functionality of those procedures. This could reek havoc amongst other programs, so be careful when using this method in a shared development environment.

Conditional Tracing

Conditional tracing can be quite useful during the development of an ASP application, especially if it is quite large. This simply involves having a variable that tells you whether or not tracing is in action. So our tracing routine could look like this:

```
    Sub Trace (strString)

        If intTracing Then
            Response.Write "Debug: " & strString & "<BR>"
```

```
      End If

  End Sub
```

you can now scatter **Trace** statements amongst your code, and you can simply turn tracing on or off by setting **intTracing** to **True** or **False**.

You might think that all of these techniques are a bit cumbersome, but let's have a look at combining them all together into a set of tracing routines that can be included in any ASP script.

Try It Out – Debugging Tips and Tricks

1 Create a new file called **Tracing.html**. This will be our HTML form.

2 Add the following code

```
<HTML>
<HEAD>
<TITLE>Tracing Form</TITLE>
</HEAD>
Enter your name and email address here:

<FORM NAME=Tracing ACTION="DoTracing.asp" METHOD="POST">
Name: <INPUT TYPE=TEXT NAME="Name"><BR>
Email: <INPUT TYPE=TEXT NAME="Email"><BR>
<INPUT TYPE=SUBMIT VALUE="Process">
<INPUT TYPE=RESET VALUE="Clear">
</FORM>

</HTML>
```

This code can be found on our web site at ***http://rapid.wrox.co.uk/books/1347*** *along with the rest of the examples in this book.*

3 Save this file, and create a new one called **DoTracing.asp**. This is the ASP file into which we have put the tracing statements.

4 Add the following code to this new file.

```
<% Option Explicit %>
<HTML>
<!-- #INCLUDE FILE="Trace.asp" -->
<HEAD>
<TITLE>Tracing Example</TITLE>
</HEAD>
<BODY>
```

```
Tracing is on for this bit<BR>
<%
    Dim strName
    Dim strEmail

    TraceStart

    Trace "Getting form details"

    strName = Request.Form("Name")
    strEmail = Request.Form("Email")

    ProcessFormDetails strName, strEmail

    TraceStop

    ProcessFormDetails strName, strEmail

Sub ProcessFormDetails (strN, strE)

    TraceProcedureStart "ProcessFormDetails"

    ' some form of processing goes here
    Response.Write "We are doing some processing here<BR>"

    Trace "Name=" & strName
    Trace "Email=" & strEmail

    TraceProcedureEnd "ProcessFormDetails"

End Sub

%>

</BODY>
</HTML>
```

5 Save this file, and create a new one called **Trace.asp**. This will be our include file.

6 Add the following code.

```
<%

Dim intTracing

Sub TraceStart()

    intTracing = True
    Trace "Tracing started"
```

```
    End Sub

Sub TraceStop()

    Trace "Tracing stopped"
    intTracing = False

End Sub

Sub Trace (strString)

    If intTracing Then
        Response.Write "Debug: " & strString & "<BR>"
    End If

End Sub

Sub TraceProcedureStart (strProcedure)

    Trace strProcedure & " started"

End Sub

Sub TraceProcedureEnd (strProcedure)

    Trace strProcedure & " ended"

End Sub

%>
```

7 Save this file, and open the first file, `Tracing.html`, in your browser:

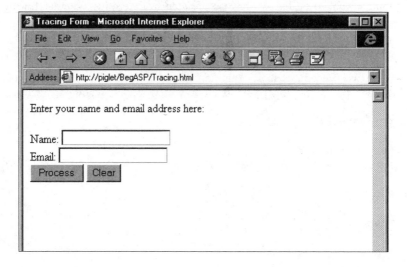

8 Enter some details and press the Process button.

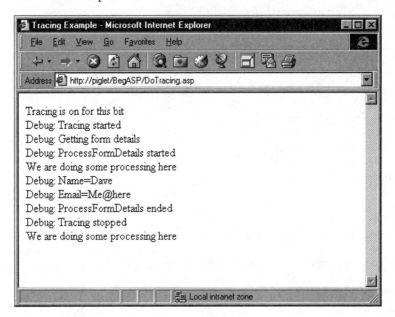

You can see that all of our trace lines start with Debug. You can also see that the processing procedure that outputs We are doing some processing here is run twice, but that the second time it is run tracing has been turned off.

How it Works

We don't need to look at the HTML file, since this is just a standard file with a form on it, whose purpose is to call the ASP page. Before we look at this ASP page, let's first look at the actual tracing code.

The first thing to notice is that we have a variable to determine whether tracing is enabled or not.

```
Dim intTracing
```

We then have two procedures to set this flag. We also have a trace message telling us that tracing has been turned on and off—this stops you worrying whether you have set it or not.

```
Sub TraceStart()

    intTracing = True
    Trace "Tracing started"

End Sub

Sub TraceStop()

    Trace "Tracing stopped"
```

```
        intTracing = False

    End Sub
```

We then have the actual trace procedure. This accepts a single string as an argument, and it writes this to the output stream if the trace flag is true. This way you can still call the **Trace** statement even if tracing is disabled.

```
Sub Trace (strString)

    If intTracing Then
        Response.Write "Debug: " & strString & "<BR>"
    End If

End Sub
```

Lastly we have two procedures that can be called at the start and end of procedures, just so you can see when procedures are called.

```
Sub TraceProcedureStart (strProcedure)

    Trace strProcedure & " started"

End Sub

Sub TraceProcedureEnd (strProcedure)

    Trace strProcedure & " ended"

End Sub
```

This gives you five procedures:

- **TraceStart** to turn on tracing.
- **TraceEnd** to turn off tracing.
- **TraceProcedureStart** to indicate the start of a procedure. The argument should be the procedure name.
- **TraceProcedureEnd** to indicate the end of a procedure. The argument should be the procedure name.
- **Trace** to indicate a trace message. The argument should be the string to be displayed.

Let's now see how they were used in the ASP script in **DoTracing.asp**.

After declaring the script variables, the first thing to do is turn on tracing.

```
<%
    Dim strName
    Dim strEmail

    TraceStart
```

Now tracing is enabled, we write a message indicating that we are about to get the form details.

```
    Trace "Getting form details"

strName = Request.Form("Name")
strEmail = Request.Form("Email")
```

Once we have the form details in variables we pass them to our processing routine.

```
    ProcessFormDetails strName, strEmail
```

We then turn off tracing, and call our processing routine again.

```
    TraceStop

    ProcessFormDetails strName, strEmail
```

Now onto the processing routine. It doesn't actually do any processing in this case, but simply displays a string. The first thing done is to trace the start of the procedure.

```
Sub ProcessFormDetails (strN, strE)

    TraceProcedureStart "ProcessFormDetails"
```

We then display our processing string, and display the name and email address using the **Trace** statement.

```
    ' some form of processing goes here
    Response.Write "We are doing some processing here<BR>"

    Trace "Name=" & strName
    Trace "Email=" & strEmail
```

Lastly we display the end of the procedure.

```
    TraceProcedureEnd "ProcessFormDetails"

End Sub

%>
```

So all we have done is used a few simple routines to see exactly where in the ASP code we are. You can see that we can include tracing in routines, and then turn off tracing without worrying about them, because the tracing routine detects whether tracing is in action or not. This allows you to turn on tracing to see what's happening, and then turn it off with a single statement without having to remove the tracing code.

So you can see we have achieved our objectives here:

- We have reusable subroutines.
- We have those reusable routines in an include file so it can be used in other ASP scripts.
- We have conditional tracing so it can be turned on and off at will.

Although this include file won't stop errors, it will allow you to start debugging them quicker. In large ASP projects you might like to include this file in all of your ASP scripts and place tracing statements throughout your code. Should you encounter problems you can simply turn tracing on. Once the ASP page is ready for the real world you can strip the tracing statements out so that execution isn't slowed down at all.

The Err Object

You might not have heard much about the **Err** object, because it's a part of VBScript, and not ASP, and you probably won't be surprised to learn that it contains information about run-time errors. It's an extremely simple object, so let's have a look at what it contains before we give it a try. It's only got five properties:

- **Description** is the descriptive text of the error.
- **Number** is the error number.
- **Source** identifies the object or application that originally generated the error.
- **HelpFile** identifies the help file associated with the error.
- **HelpContext** identifies the Context ID in the help file for a particular error.

And it's only got two methods:

- **Raise**, to raise an error of your own.
- **Clear**, to clear the properties.

That's all there is to it, and it's just as easy to use.

Try It Out – The Err Object

1 Create a new asp file, called **Err.asp**.

2 Enter the following code:

```
<HTML>
<HEAD>
<TITLE>The Err Object</TITLE>
</HEAD>
<BODY>
```

```
<%
    On Error Resume Next

    Response.Write "10 / 0 = " & 10/0

    Response.Write "<BR>Err.Description = " & Err.Description
    Response.Write "<BR>Err.Number = " & Err.Number
    Response.Write "<BR>Err.Source = " & Err.Source
    Response.Write "<BR>Err.HelpFile = " & Err.HelpFile
    Response.Write "<BR>Err.HelpContext = " & Err.HelpContext

%>

</BODY>
</HTML>
```

3 Now save the file and open it your browser.

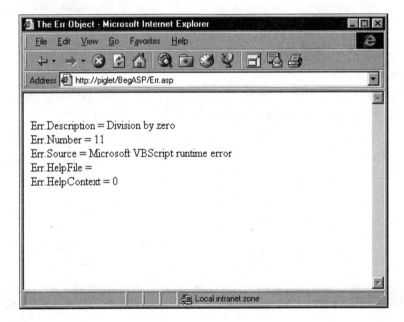

Well not very exciting really, and perhaps no great surprise, but this does give you the ability to detect errors and act on them before they throw up one of those arcane error messages.

How It Works

Despite its simplicity let's look at the code in detail. The first thing to notice is the line to enable error handling.

```
    On Error Resume Next
```

If you've used other programming languages you can usually have a central error routine, and using **On Error** you can identify this routine. Unfortunately that's not possible with VBScript, as all you've got is the **Resume Next** statement, which tells VBScript to continue with the next line if an error occurs.

Once error handling is turned on we generate an error, with the oft-used division by zero.

```
Response.Write "10 / 0 = " & 10/0
```

This error causes script processing to just move onto the next line, where we simply display the error details.

```
Response.Write "<BR>Err.Description = " & Err.Description
Response.Write "<BR>Err.Number = " & Err.Number
Response.Write "<BR>Err.Source = " & Err.Source
Response.Write "<BR>Err.HelpFile = " & Err.HelpFile
Response.Write "<BR>Err.HelpContext = " & Err.HelpContext
```

You might think that only being able to continue to the next line doesn't make this a useful procedure, but you'd be wrong. It just makes it a bit verbose to use, but you can still centralize your error handling by putting it all in a separate procedure. For example:

```
Sub CheckError()

    Select Case Err.Number
    Case 11
        Response.Write "Help, help, panic. Division by zero."
    Case 6
        Response.Write "No panic. Just an overflow error."
    . . .
    End Select

End Sub
```

You could then simply call **CheckError** whenever you needed to. This is very powerful as it allows you to deal with errors yourself, and rather than having your application fall over every time a user puts in an unexpected value. You can avoid having error dialogs appear during the program and instead circumvent the error with your own code.

> *Error codes 11 and 6 are the VBScript error codes for a division by zero and a numeric overflow. For more information, see Appendix A.*

The Error Source

We mentioned that the **Source** property identifies where the error originally came from, but this might not seem very useful. Its real use comes when you start using other objects from within script code, because this can identify the object where the error occurred. For example, imagine calling a **Server** object that someone had created in Visual Basic, and this object called two other objects. If an error occurred the **Source** property would identify which of the three objects the error came from.

Raising Errors

As well as detecting errors, you can raise your own in VBScript, using the **Raise** method. For example, instead of actually generating a division by zero error, we could have simulated it like so:

```
Err.Raise 11
```

We can add the **Source** and **Description** to this as well:

```
Err.Raise 11, "My Routine", "Oh no - you divided a number by zero!"
```

You don't have to use **Err.Raise** in connection with **On Error**. In fact, using **Err.Raise** while not trapping errors is a useful way of using the built-in error handling but with your own errors. For example, using the above line as an ASP script gives the following:

```
My Routine error '800a000b'
Oh no - you divided a number by zero!
/BegASP/RaiseErr.asp, line 10
```

The Script Debugger

To debug ASP script code under NT you can use the Microsoft Script Debugger. Microsoft Script Debugger is a separate application that comes with Personal Web Server for NT Workstation and IIS for NT Server. Although it seems quite basic, don't be fooled as it is actually quite powerful. Before you can debug ASP script code you need to mark your virtual directory as an **application** and enable the server-side debugging option within IIS or PWS for NT Workstation.

 Remember, this feature isn't available with PWS under Windows 95

Enabling Debugging in IIS and PWS for NT Workstation

An application is a virtual directory, with a few more features. As well as allowing debugging, it also allows ASP to know where your **Global.asa** file is.

You can tell whether a virtual directory is an application or not by looking at the icon in the Management Console. Normal virtual directories are shown as a folder with a tiny blue world, such as SCRIPTS and msadc, and applications are shown as a little open box, such as IISSAMPLES and Wrox.

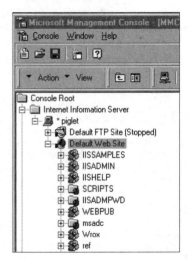

You can create an application from a virtual directory by clicking the **Create** button when viewing the properties for a directory in the Management Console.

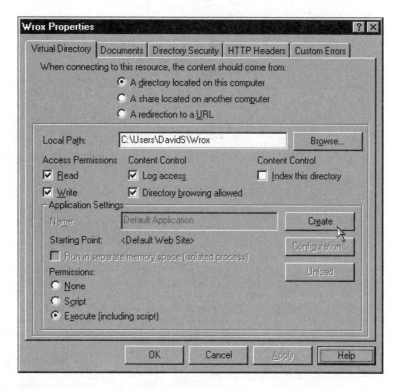

This will create the application and allow you to enter a name in the **Name** box:

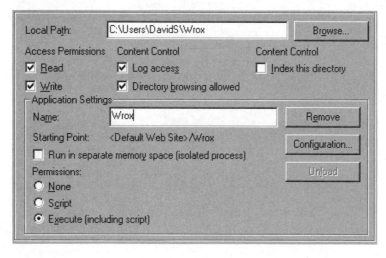

You can then click the **Configuration** button to access the application details.

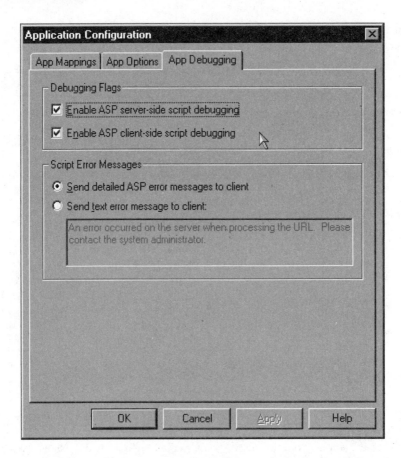

The **App Debugging** tab is the one you are interested in, specifically the **Debugging Flags**. The first is the most important as checking this allows the Script Debugger to be used for ASP script code. The client side script debugging option is reserved for future use and is unused in this version (4.0) of IIS, so it doesn't matter whether this is checked or cleared.

One really important thing to note is that when you have enabled script debugging for an application, error messages are not returned to the client as part of the page, but raised on the server, where the debugger can intercept them. You should therefore only use the script debugger when you can work on the server itself.

The Script Debugger

Before we start debugging let's look at the various windows in the script debugger:

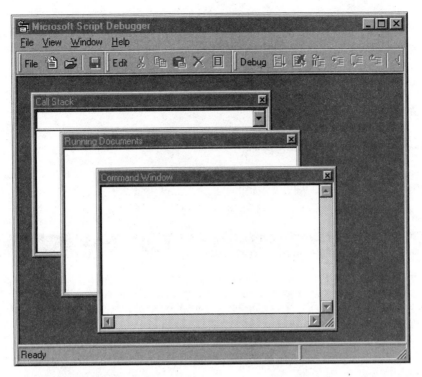

The Call Stack window displays a list of active procedure calls. The combo box at the top of this window display the current threads, and is generally only used if you are debugging Java applets.

The Running Documents window displays a list of applications, along with their documents, that are hosting scripting.

The Command Window allows you to inspect and modify variables during the executing of the script code.

Starting the Debugger

So you've set the application up for debugging, and we've shown you what the debugger windows look like. Now, how do you actually start the debugger? The debugger is actually located on the server-side, but can be run in one of four ways:

- The first is the most obvious, by selecting it from the Programs menu.
- You can also use the Script Debugger option from the View menu in Internet Explorer.
- You can force the debugger to start by placing a `Stop` statement (or `debugger` in JScript) in your script code.
- Lastly you can respond to an error. Remember the ASP error shown earlier, where a dialog popped up and asked us whether we wanted to debug the current page— selecting Yes will start the debugger.

It's important to remember that to debug server-side ASP script the debugger needs to be open on the web server. So if you access an ASP page with an error from a client machine, then the debugger dialog will appear on the web server. Your client page will be blank, and will suspend operation until the error dialog is cleared or the page reaches its timeout value.

Now you know how to set up debugging and how to start the debugger it's about time to see how it all works.

Using the Script Debugger

The best way to learn how to debug scripts is to actually try it, so we'll jump straight in now. What we're going to do is create a script with some known errors and then you'll see exactly how this works.

Try It Out – Debugging Scripts

During this Try It Out, don't worry if your browser displays a Timeout error message, stating it can't contact the server. It's lying. It can, and has contacted the server, but we'll be using breakpoints, so the script may not complete before the time allocated for a timeout. You can just close the error dialog and continue.

1 Create a new asp file, calling it **Debug.asp**.

2 Add the following code. Note, copy this code exactly. There are deliberate errors in it, so don't correct them as you type it in.

```
<HTML>
<HEAD>
<TITLE>ASP Debugging with the Script Debugger</TITLE>
</HEAD>
<BODY>

<%
    strVar = Request.ServerVariables("HTTP_USER_AGEN") & "<P>"
    Response.Write "HTTP_USER_AGENT=" & strVsr

    ShowVariables

Sub ShowVariables

    For Each strVar In Request.ServerVariables
        Response.Write strVae & "<BR>"
    Next

End Sub
%>
</BODY>
</HTML>
```

3 Run the file from your browser, and you should see this:

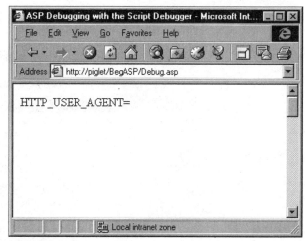

Now it doesn't work, but then you knew that already. So where are the errors, and how do you find them using the Script Debugger?

4 Start the Script Debugger, and from the View menu select Running Documents:

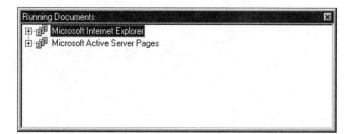

5 Expand both the Microsoft Internet Explorer and the Microsoft Active Server Pages levels, by clicking on the small plus signs. You might have to keep expanding these items if there are more under the ASP branch:

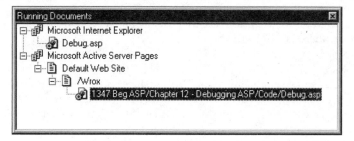

This shows that the script debugger is now attached to both IE and IIS, and it shows the current documents. Two copies of **Debug.asp** are shown because this shows the two places where scripting can take place—at the client, shown under Microsoft Internet Explorer, and at the server, shown under Microsoft Active Server Pages.

6 We are interested in ASP script so double click on the `Debug.asp` under Microsoft Active Server Pages. This will open the ASP page:

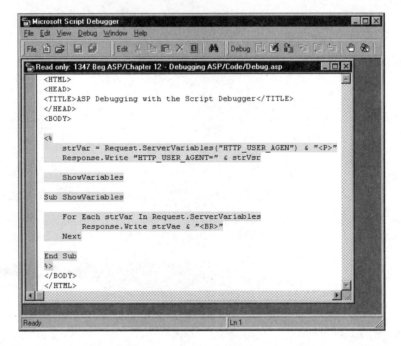

Notice that the title states this is read only. This is because the Script Debugger only allows us to follow the script through and not actively change it. We can change variable contents though, as you'll see soon.

7 Place the cursor on the first **Response.Write** line and press *F9* to toggle a break point. Notice that the line is highlighted in red, with a large dot to show a breakpoint.

8 Switch back to your browser and press the Refresh button. Notice how you are automatically switched into the Script Debugger, with the current highlighted line the one on which there is a breakpoint.

9 From your first run of this script you noticed that nothing was printed for **strVar**, but why? Well, you've probably spotted that the second time we use the variable we've spelt it incorrectly, putting **strVsr** instead of **strVar**. Because the script debugger only gives us read only access to the script we can't change the variable name, but we can check that **strVar** is correct.

10 From the <u>V</u>iew menu select Co<u>m</u>mand Window.

11 Type **?strVar**, pressing the enter key after you have typed this in:

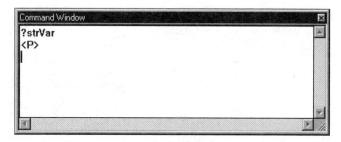

The question mark is how we tell the debugger that we want to print out (in the command window) the value of a variable. Now look at what the value is. Not what was really expected, but that's because we've also made another spelling mistake, in the name of the server variable we wanted to look out—there's a **T** missing from the end.

 FYI **You don't need to use the question mark to print out values when you are debugging Jscript—you can just type the variable name.**

12 Once again we can't modify the script, but we can modify the contents of the variable, so type this in—note there's no question mark here. Don't forget to hit the *Enter* key after you've typed it in:

```
strVar = Request.ServerVariables("HTTP_USER_AGENT")
```

This assigns **strVar** to the value of the server variable, using exactly the same syntax as if you were typing the script in. In fact, you type using the syntax of the current script language—in our case this is VBScript. Now examine **strVar** again:

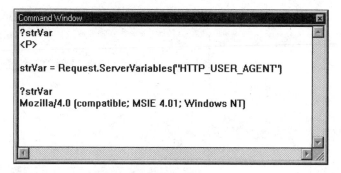

That's better—much more like we expected. You can also update **strVsr**, just so that the variable is returned to the browser, by typing:

```
strVsr = strVar
```

13 Now you've updated this variable, click back into the main script window and press F8 to step onto the next line.

14 Move the cursor to the second **Response.Write** line and press *F9* to set another breakpoint. Now press *F5*—this continues executing script until it finds another breakpoint, or it finishes the script.

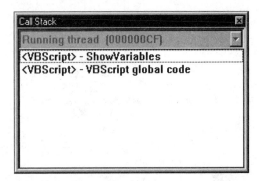

15 As the script has stopped at the second breakpoint we are now in a function, so it's a good time to look at the call stack. From the View menu select Call Stack.

This shows where we are in the code, with the most recent procedure at the top. You can see we started in a set of global code, with no procedure, and then moved into the **ShowVariables** procedure. You can double-click on an item to get the main script window to show you exactly where you are in the code. For example, if **ShowVariables** was called several times, but you'd lost track of which time it was, you could double-click on the VBScript global code line to show which call it was:

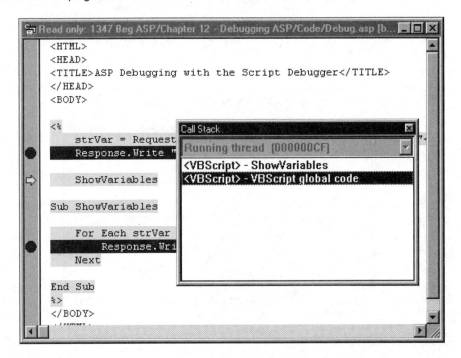

Notice the arrow in the margin, pointing to the calling routine. This doesn't change the currently executing line, so pressing *F8* will switch you back into the **ShowVariables** routine and continue executing, one line at a time.

16 You'll also notice there is a spelling mistake on this **Response.Write** line, but because this is in a loop, it's not really practical to change this every time. At this stage you are best served by either continuing, even with the error, or stopping the script by selecting Stop Debugging from the Debug menu. These sort of spelling errors are much more easily caught by using **Option Explicit**, to force all variable names to be declared, and any variable not declared generates a run-time error.

That's really all there is to using the Script Debugger. You can see that's it's quite a simple tool, but very effective, allowing you almost everything you could expect from a more high powered tool. If you make syntax errors in your script code, then the Script Debugger will be launched automatically, showing you the line with the problem.

Client-side versus Server-side debugging

There's really no difference between client and server-side debugging. If you remember the Running Documents window, you have a chance to decide where you want your debugging to occur.

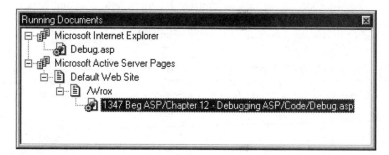

Remember that we double-clicked on the bottom instance of **Debug.asp** to open the main window, and then set break points in this window. But what happens if you do the same with the first instance of **Debug.asp**? Why not give it a try—you'll be rewarded with a window that might not make sense. You might like to clear any breakpoints in the ASP script (*Ctrl-Shift-F9*) and then refresh your browser window first.

```
Read only: Debug.asp
<HTML>
<HEAD>
<TITLE>ASP Debugging with the Script Debugger</TITLE>
</HEAD>
<BODY>

HTTP_USER_AGENT=<BR><BR><BR><BR><BR><BR><BR><BR><BR><BR><BR><B

</BODY>
</HTML>
```

This is the HTML page as returned by ASP. Remember when we are debugging the client-side, all of our ASP script has been executed, so all we see here is the HTML tags and any client-side script. Now this file doesn't have any client-side script, so it's not shown, but if it did have script you follow exactly the same methods as debugging server-side script.

Summary

You can clearly see that debugging in the ASP world is not fraught with the problems that you might have thought and that with a little careful planning and a simple set of rules to follow it can be made easier. There are some simple rules to follow:

▶ Use `Option Explicit`. This saves huge amounts of time looking for typing mistakes.

▶ Reuse code where possible, by use of sub-routines and include files.

▶ Don't get confused between client-side and server-side script.

▶ Use sensible variable names, as this stops you getting confused as to what the variable is for.

▶ Comment your code. A lot of experienced programmers joke that if it was difficult to write, then it should be difficult to read. That's just an excuse for laziness. Remember you might not be the one who has to maintain the code.

If you've done any programming before, you've probably realized that ASP programming is not that different from any other type and that you need the same range of skills. You need to plan ahead and be prepared to think laterally when errors occur, as the problem isn't often where you think it is.

Databases with ASP

Even when web pages consisted of plain old HTML, there was still a great demand for pages to be as accurate and up-to-date as possible. Most companies have databases of one sort or another, and it seemed sensible to create the web pages from this data. In fact, a company's databases weren't necessarily its only sources of data: web designers could tap such sources as mail systems and legacy mainframes, whose stores of information could also benefit from being published on the web.

There's no point in storing huge amounts of information if you're not going to tell anyone about it. It's also sensible if you can create the web page from the most up-to-date data, at the time the user requests the page—and this is the significance of the word 'Active' in 'Active Server Pages'.

You've already seen how to put active scripting into an ASP page; now we'll look at how you can use this scripting to access databases. In this chapter we are going to look at:

- What we mean by a data store
- How ADO fits in
- What ODBC is
- What OLE-DB is
- Exactly what a database connection is
- How to use the ASP Connection object

In this chapter, we will really concentrate on the database and how to connect to one. The chapter is (very) loosely like a shampoo advert. In a shampoo ad, they first explain what the product is; then a gorgeous model flicks her hair in a seductive manner so we can see how good the product is; then a smooth voice-over expert tells us the technical details.

Apart from the product (oh, and the model), we have a similar plan. First we're going to have a brief introduction to some concepts, and then we'll delve straight into a working example in which we return some data from a database (that's the sexy, hair-flicking bit—you might have to stretch your imagination a little for this). Then we'll look at some of the more technical issues in more detail.

What is a Data Store?

Since this is the very first section of the chapter, I'm going to stop referring to databases and start using the term **data store**. "Why introduce another name to confuse us?" I hear you ask. And I shall explain.

A database is an example of a data store. Another example of a data store is a mail system, with its mail messages. Other examples include spreadsheets, and word processing documents. Do you get the picture? What I am getting at is this: there is no reason why you should just limit yourself to databases to store and retrieve information. A data store is *any* store of information.

So what does a data store have to do with ASP? Well, maybe not a great deal initially, but it may do soon. What you'll be learning in the next couple of chapters will teach you the techniques that will enable you to get data from any data store. Although your first introduction to data access within ASP will be a database, the potential is there to use any source of data—and this is a point that I wanted to get across early on. I'll be using the term 'data store' when referring to a source of data.

What is a Connection?

This might seem pretty obvious, but a **connection** is what links your ASP script code to the data store. Cast your mind back to when you were young, and your Mom fixed a piece of string to your gloves and threaded it through the arms of your coat, to stop you losing the gloves. Connections are just like that—instead of using a piece of string and a coat to connect you to your gloves, we'll be using a connection to connect you to a data store. That's all it is—a way to tie us to the data store.

> *Unlike the gloves, we can actually untie from one data store and retie to another, or even tie ourselves to several data stores at once.*

Once we have a way of connecting to a data store, we really need to know how to identify the data store. We can't get our Mom to stitch the name in, but we can use other information to identify them, and this information will depend upon what you are connecting to, and how. For example, an Access database is just identified by the `.mdb` file. SQL Server, on the other hand, is designed to handle more (and larger) databases, and there is often more than one machine running SQL Server—so in order to uniquely identify a database, you have to use the name of the server as well as the name of the database.

Every data store that you connect to will have some form of connection. Sometimes you might create the connection yourself; other times you might allow the system to create it for you. Either way, you're using a connection.

Before we can connect to a data store, we need some way of knowing *what* it is and *where* it is. For this you can use a data source name.

What is a Data Source Name?

You can think of a **data source name** (**DSN**) as the name tag for your pair of gloves. More accurately, perhaps, you should think of it as a name tag for the piece of string, because the DSN is the name of the connection. It's just a simple way to bring together all of the pieces of information that we know about a data store.

Later on in this chapter, we'll show you how to use connections *without* a DSN. But that's all in the future: first, let's see how to create one.

Creating a DSN

You can see a list of data source names from the ODBC (or 32bit ODBC) icon from the Control Panel, which is the one that looks something like this:

ODBC

 We'll explain ODBC in more detail, later in this chapter.

Double-click on this icon. You are presented with the following screen:

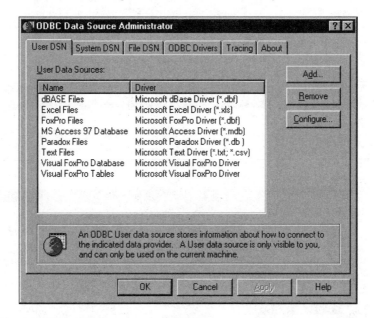

Yours may look slightly different from this, depending upon whether or not you have any data sources set up. The drivers shown above (and also SQL Server, which isn't shown) are supplied with a variety of Microsoft products, such as Office and the NT Option Pack.

The User DSN tab shows all data sources for the user who is currently logged on. This allows you to have data sources that are only available for selected people who log onto the machine. This is no good for ASP, since ASP can only use System DSNs. So let's have a look at the System DSN tab:

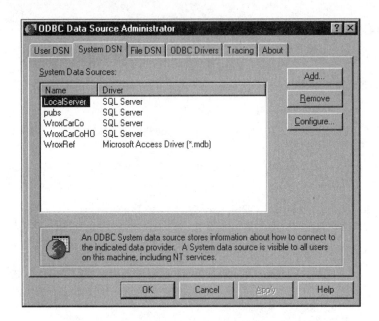

A data source that appears in this tab is available to anyone who logs onto the local machine, including ASP. As you can see, this machine has four SQL Server data sources and one Access data source.

Most of the samples in this chapter are fairly interchangeable between Access and SQL Server. We are going to concentrate on Access in this chapter, but we've included instructions for creating a DSN for SQL Server too. The sample Access database can be downloaded from the Wrox Press web site at **http://www.wrox.com**. There's also a SQL Server script to create the Contact table and insert some sample data if you wish to use SQL Server instead.

Try It Out – Creating an Access Data Source Name

1 To create a new data source for an Access database, you click the Add... button, which will give you a list of available drivers. The **driver** is the underlying code that handles the connection for you, but you don't need to know anything about it except its name.

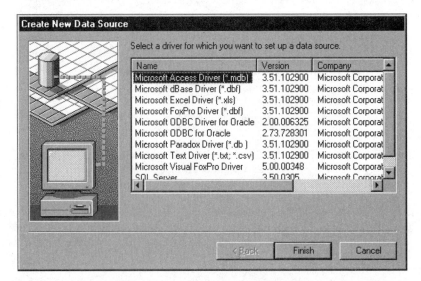

2 Select the Microsoft Access Driver (*.mdb) and then click the Finish button. This presents you with another dialog, in which you can name the data source and pick the **.mdb** file to use:

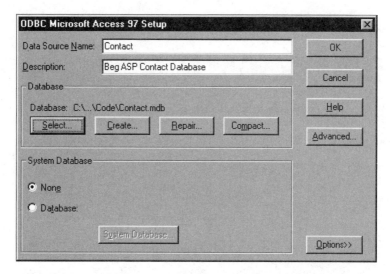

You can click the Select button to get the standard file open dialog, which will allow you to find an existing **.mdb** file, or you can click the Create button to create a new database. The picture above shows a DSN called Contact, which points to the `Contact.mdb` database.

For this example, I placed my `Contact.mdb` **file in the following directory:** `Inetpub\wwwroot\BegASP\code.`

3 If you now click OK you'll see that your new data source has been added to the list.

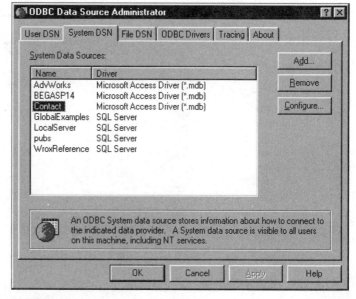

OK, if you've done that then you can skip past the next Try It Out and get straight on to using a data store.

Alternatively, if you're feeling ambitious, or you're particularly interested in using SQL Server, then you can create a SQL Server data source name by following the next set of instructions.

Try It Out – Creating a SQL Server Data Source Name

1 For a SQL Server data source the method is much the same, although there are more options that need to be filled in. The first part is the same as for Access: click the A<u>d</u>d button, but then you pick the SQL Server driver from the list:

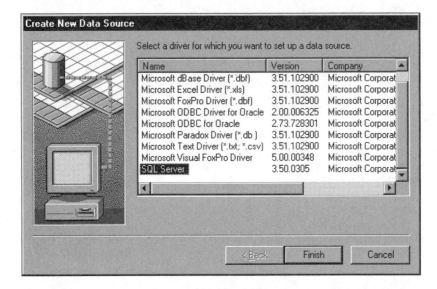

The remaining steps are very different from the Access data source name setup procedure.

2 Click the Finish button, which allows you to continue to the first page of the SQL Server details. Enter the data source name and description, and the name of the SQL Server.

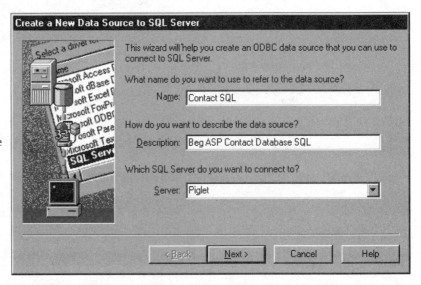

3 Press Next to get to the security settings screen, which is where you can enter how the connection is going to be made to SQL Server.

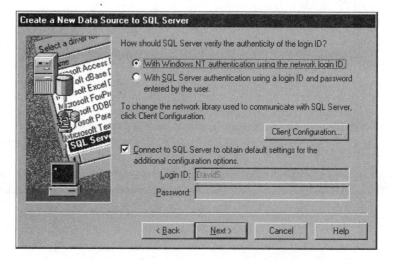

The first option will log you into SQL Server using your current network login name, and the second will require the user name and password to be supplied. The options at the bottom of this screen allow the connection to query the SQL Server for some default information. This only happens during this setup, and does not apply when you actually use the data source. You'll notice that the Login ID and Password fields are grayed out here, because NT authentication is selected, and my network login has already been filled in. If you pick the SQL Server authentication option then you can enter a name and password.

4 There are three further pages of options, allowing you to configure various aspects of the data source, but we're not going to show them here, as for most cases you can leave all of the settings at their default values. So just press the Next button each time.

5 You'll finally get to the end screen; this summarizes the data source details.

And that's it, so pressing OK will add this data source to the list.

Using a Data Store

Now that you have a DSN, you can get data from your data store, so let's have a look at this. We're not going to waste any more time explaining details, and some of the code you'll see won't be explained until the next chapter, but this short section of code shows how simple it is to get data from a data store. After all, that's what you're really interest in isn't it?

You might like to set up a virtual root to the directory you're going to put your ASP files into, so that you'll have to do less typing when you wish to view the pages.

Try It Out - Connecting to a Data Store

1 Using your favorite ASP editor, type the following lines of code:

```
<HTML>
<HEAD>
<TITLE>Contact information</TITLE>
</HEAD>
<BODY>

<%
    Dim objConn
    Dim objRec

    Set objConn = Server.CreateObject ("ADODB.Connection")
    Set objRec = Server.CreateObject ("ADODB.Recordset")

    objConn.Open "DSN=Contact"

    objRec.Open "Contact", objConn, 0, 1, 2

    While Not objRec.EOF
        Response.Write objRec("Name") & "<BR>"
        objRec.MoveNext
    Wend

    objRec.Close
    objConn.Close
    Set objRec = Nothing
    Set objConn = Nothing

%>

</BODY>
</HTML>
```

2 Save the code in a new file, called `Contact.asp`.

3 Now save the file, and type the URL to it into your browser:

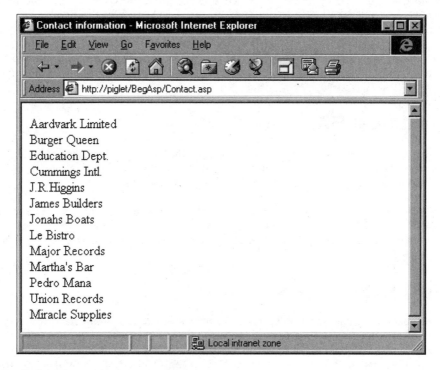

Pretty easy, huh? Who told you ASP database programming was hard?!

How It Works

We're not going to explain everything about the code sample you've just seen. Some points will be explained later in this chapter, and others in the next chapter, but there are a few points to get your teeth into now.

This is the first piece of completely new code. This line creates a connection object, that is stored in the variable `objConn`:

```
Set objConn = Server.CreateObject ("ADODB.Connection")
```

Remember our gloves and piece of string? At this stage, `objConn` is a piece of string, but it's not attached to the gloves. To attach a connection to a data store we **Open** the connection:

```
objConn.Open "DSN=Contact"
```

This line does just that. It uses the **Open** method of the connection, and tells that method that we want to use the DSN called `Contact`—this was the one we set up earlier. When we have finished with the connection, we can **Close** it:

```
objConn.Close
```

At it's very simplest that's all there is to connecting to a data store. We put in some extra lines of code to get some data from the Access table (since just connecting to and disconnecting from the data store is not particularly exciting on it's own). That's really the domain of the next chapter, so we'll skip explaining how that works.

So if it's that simple, how come we've a whole chapter devoted to it? We'll like most things there's a lot more to the `Connection` object than meets the eye, so let's look at those now.

The Technical Bit

This is the technical bit, where we explain some of the underlying principles behind connecting to data stores. We've left it to the latter portion of the chapter because, although you don't really *need* to know all this in order to get data from a data store, it is quite important.

We are going to look at why this connection stuff all came about, and why it's such a good thing. We'll then look at DSN-less connections, where we access data stores without using a DSN, and we'll look at the `Connection` object in more detail, examining some of its properties and methods.

What is ODBC?

If you've done any database programming in the past, then you might have heard of ODBC. It stands for **Open DataBase Connectivity**, and was designed to allow a common set of routines to be used to access data stores, although it was primarily aimed at relational databases. This allowed a programmer to connect to a data store using ODBC and manipulate the data, without worrying exactly where the data was stored, or what particular database was storing it. For example, when looking at databases it allowed the user to use the same routines to connect to an Access database, or SQL Server, or Oracle:

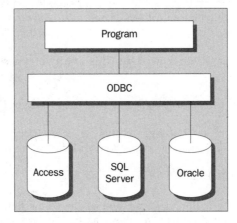

This gave the programmer freedom to concentrate on the functionality of the application without worrying too much about the underlying data, or even how to access it.

What is OLE-DB?

OLE-DB is the next step in the evolution of the anonymous data store. Microsoft have done a great deal of work to ensure that OLE-DB is faster and easier to use than ODBC, and eventually it may well replace ODBC, although that won't be for a long time yet.

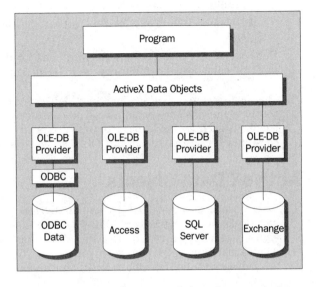

As you can see, it's a very similar idea to ODBC, but in fact it has a much broader range of data stores. In fact, you'll notice that OLE-DB can sit on top of ODBC, meaning that you can keep your existing ODBC connections *and* use the new OLE-DB drivers.

OLE-DB introduces two new terms: **data providers** and **data consumers**. You'll probably be able to guess that a data provider is something that provides data, and the data consumer is something that uses that data. In the real world, you might have several data providers, each for a different data store. At the time of writing, the only available data providers are the Microsoft data providers for ODBC—namely Microsoft Index Server and Microsoft Active Directory Services—although a whole new suite of providers are due. Microsoft will be shipping some in the new version of Visual Studio, as well as making them available in other products. These will include:

▶ Microsoft Access

▶ Microsoft SQL Server

▶ Oracle

▶ Microsoft Exchange Server

▶ AS/400 and VSAM

Other external OLE-DB providers will be shipped by other companies. These will include:

▶ ASNA—Acceller8-DB, DataGate/400

▶ IBM—AS/400

▶ ISG—Oracle, Sybase, RDB, Informix, Inres, D_ISAM, C_ISAM, RMS, Adabas C, VSAM, DB2, IMS/DB

▶ Intersolv—Notes, MAPI

- MetaWise—DP/400, DP/VSAM
- SAS—SAS datasets, SAS/SHARE server
- Sequiter—Codebase, FoxPro, dBase, Clipper

Don't worry if you're not familiar with some of these names. The point to take from all this is that, although this is a fairly new technology, it's got a lot of industry support.

The data consumer is just something that uses data. In this book, your ASP page is the data consumer; In another context, the data consumer could well be an application written in another language, such as Visual Basic or Visual C++. In fact, ActiveX Data Objects (ADO) is the actual consumer, because ADO talks to OLE-DB, and we talk to ADO. So what's ADO?

ActiveX Data Objects

ActiveX Data Objects (ADO) is the friendly face of OLE-DB. This means that you don't actually have to know anything about OLE-DB, since ADO will hide all of the complexity from you, giving you a simple way of accessing data from any data store. ADO is the way we actually get data to and from a data store, as you've already seen; and ADO allows us, among other things, to read records, find specific records, and update data.

In database-speak, a record is a collection of data containing information from each field, relating to a specific entry. For example, suppose your database was an address book, in the form of a table consisting of the columns (or fields) "Name", "Address", "Phone Number". Then each row of your table is referred to as a record.

If you've done any database programming in Access or Visual Basic then you'll have come across Data Access Objects (DAO) or Remote Data Objects (RDO). Well don't worry, because ADO is a superset of DAO and RDO, and is much easier to understand. You'll be using ADO in the next couple of chapters to access data stores.

Before we start looking in detail at the various parts of data access, let's have a quick look at the object model of ADO— this tells us how it all links together. We won't go into each object in detail here, because we'll be covering that in these two chapters, but this will give you a good overall picture.

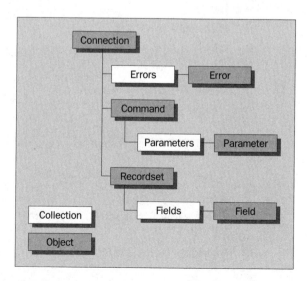

It's important to note that just because the `Connection` object is at the top, that doesn't necessarily mean you have to *have* a `Connection` object. You can work directly with a `Command` or `Recordset` without having first created a separate `Connection`. Having said that, we're going to start with the connection object, because if you understand how it works, you'll find the rest of the database work easier.

The Connection String

Earlier in the chapter we looked at DSNs, and how they are used, but now we need to look at what a connection string is. The **connection string** is just a combination of all of the information needed to connect to a source of data.

First of all we need some key pieces of information:

- ▶ **Provider**, which is the type of OLE-DB provider. If you omit this then the default OLE-DB provider for ODBC is used
- ▶ **Driver**, to identify the ODBC driver (such as Access or SQL Server)
- ▶ **Server**, to specify which server to connect to
- ▶ **DSN**, which is the name of the data source, as we created earlier
- ▶ **Database/DBQ**, to identify the actual database name
- ▶ **UID**, to specify the user name to connect to the database
- ▶ **PWD**, for the user's password

If you've set up a DSN, as in either of the 'Try It Out's earlier in the chapter, then you might have already provided some of this information. For example, when setting up a data source, you specify the driver and the database. To get a connection string you just join the various pieces of information together, so for a connection string that uses a DSN you might use this:

```
DSN=Contact
```

which assumes that you have filled in the `Database` and user details in the `DSN` called `Contact`. You can also add more details if needed:

```
Provider=MSDASQL; DSN=Contact; UID=DavidS; PWD=
```

This just adds the `Provider` and the user name and password. So this means that you can set up a DSN to hold just the bare minimum, and then add other information in your ASP script at a later date. This is particularly useful when setting up the user details, since you may want to ask the user for them, rather than storing them in the DSN. If you're using the OLE-DB driver for ODBC you can leave out the `Provider`, since this is the default, but you must add it for other providers.

DSN-Less Connection Strings

You can also create DSN-less connection strings, which don't use a DSN, but you must include the information that would have been stored in the DSN. So for example, an Access database would have a connection string like this:

```
Driver={Microsoft Access Driver (*.mdb)};
DBQ=C:\Inetpub\wwwroot\BegASP\Code\Contact.mdb
```

For a SQL Server database, it is slightly different:

```
Driver={SQL Server}; Server=Piglet; Database=GlobalExamples; UID=DavidS;
PWD=
```

If you flick back to the diagrams showing the creation of a DSN for SQL Server, you'll see that this is exactly the same information you entered there. The database name used here is `GlobalExamples`, the sample database installed with SQL Server.

OLE-DB versus ODBC

OK, so we have two methods for connecting to data stores. Which should you use, given that they both seem to achieve the same thing?

Having just shown you how to create an ODBC data source, it seems odd to say OLE-DB, but that's really the future now. However, as we've already mentioned, the only available database driver at the moment is the OLE-DB driver for ODBC, so you're still using ODBC anyway.

If you look back to the picture showing OLE-DB and ODBC together, you'll see that OLE-DB sits on top of ODBC: so what it's doing is translating between the two different connection methods. Moving to a straight OLE-DB driver will remove this extra layer, and will therefore be faster.

The good thing about the current approach is that you can write all of your code to support OLE-DB, and as soon as the new driver is available you can switch over, with minimal change, or in most cases, no change at all. In fact you can switch between the providers fairly simply too, a fact shown by the samples which mostly work with both Access and SQL Server. This is extremely useful, because it allows you to learn and prototype ASP applications and pages using Access; then if you need to scale to a larger database, you can switch to SQL Server (or another database) with very little change.

So if we're sure that OLE-DB is the way to go, should the questions really be 'DSN or DSN-less?' One of the things to think about when making this decision is setup and support. Since this is an ASP book, the code you'll be writing will run from within ASP pages, and this will be called from IIS, running on a server. So you only have to create the DSN once, therefore configuration of lots of DSNs on lots of machines isn't an issue. But what happens if you move your web server to another machine? You'll have to reconfigure your DSNs, thus a DSN-less approach can be useful.

You might think that without a DSN you'll have to put the connection string into each ASP page, and that would be a real maintenance nightmare, but there's a really simple way around this: **include files**.

> *Include files are a way of having one file included within another. When ASP sees the* **#INCLUDE** *command, it yanks the file pointed to by the* **FILE** *argument into the current file (see the example below). The contents of the included file behave as though they were typed directly into the first file.*

Using this technique, you put a DSN-less connection string in a separate file and include it in each ASP page, thus making sure it's declared only once. For example, suppose you have an include file called `DataStore.inc`, with the following contents:

```
<%
strConnect = " Driver={Microsoft Access Driver (*.mdb);
DBQ=C:\Inetpub\wwwroot\BegASP\Code\Contact.mdb"
%>
```

You can then include this in each ASP page using the following line:

```
<!-- #INCLUDE FILE="DataStore.inc" -->
```

Now you have a central file with your connection in it. If the connection details change you can just change the include file, `DataStore.inc`, and since it will be re-read every time an ASP page is requested you don't have to modify any other pages. You can also easily change the provider from the generic one for ODBC to a native driver when it becomes available. And if you should ever need to move the web site, you only need to move the files (this include file being one of them)—no configuring of the new server is required.

The Connection Object

The `Connection` object is what ADO uses to store our information about the data store connection. In fact, it actually represents a unique session with the data store, and there is nothing to stop us having different connections to different data stores, at the same time. Given that you can use a connection for different data stores, it is implied that the connections can also have different providers. So you could have one connection to SQL Server and another to Access. That may seem obvious, but you must remember that when dealing with different providers, the same functionality might not be available in each provider. In fact, when dealing with the ODBC provider the functionality might differ between data stored by different providers. For example, Access doesn't provide the same functionality as SQL Server.

This probably won't be a problem for you, especially in your early stages of ASP and ADO development, but it is something you should be aware of for the future.

Creating a Connection to a Database

We've spent an awful lot of time explaining what this connection business is about, and it's about time we started looking at the real coding issues. To create a `Connection` object in ASP code you use the following:

```
Dim objConn
Set objConn = Server.CreateObject ("ADODB.Connection")
```

This might look a bit complex, but it's actually quite simple. We need to create an object, so we use the `CreateObject` method to do this. `CreateObject` is a method of the `Server` object, which creates an object for us. The object we want to create is a `Connection`, which is part of the `ADODB` object model.

ADODB is the actual name given to ADO, and all ADO objects that we create will be done in this way.

So that actually creates a **Connection** object, but nothing has been done with it yet. It's important to realize that, just because you have a **Connection** object, it doesn't mean to say that you are connected to the database. To do that you need to **Open** the connection:

```
objConn.Open strConnect
```

This calls the **Open** method of the **Connection** object, and uses the string **strConnect** as the connection string. There are two *optional* arguments to the **Open** method, that allow you to specify the user and password as you open the connection:

```
objConn.Open strConnect, "DavidS", ""
```

> *Interestingly, the ADO documentation states that if you pass the user and password both in the connection string and in the arguments above, then the results are unpredictable. It doesn't explain what unpredictable means in this case, but it's probably best to just stick to one method or the other.*

The above examples have assumed that **strConnect** is the connection string we set in our include file, but you could equally well just put the actual string in instead:

```
objConn.Open "Driver={Microsoft Access Driver (*.mdb);
DBQ=C:\Inetpub\wwwroot\BegASP\Code\Contact.MDB"
```

You can also do this another way by using the **ConnectionString** property before opening the connection:

```
objConn.ConnectionString = strConnect
objConn.Open
```

Once you have finished with a connection, you should **Close** it and free any associated system resources:

```
objConn.Close
```

This doesn't actually remove the object from memory; so you can **Open** it again if you need to. To completely free the memory for the object you should set it to **Nothing**:

```
Set objConn = Nothing
```

You should be sure to Close the connection before you free the memory for the object, or you'll create a memory leak.

The Properties Collection

You've seen one of the properties, the `ConnectionString`, in action above, but you might not know what the names of the properties are. If this is the case you can use the `Properties` collection to look through them all. The `Properties` collection contains a `Property` object for each property that the connection supports.

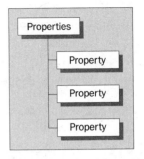

Since a collection is much like an array (we covered arrays in Chapter 4), you can look through the collection by looking at each element. Let's try this out, and then well examine how it works afterwards.

Try It Out – The Properties Collection

1 Open your editor of choice, and put the following lines into it:

```
<%
strConnect = "Driver={Microsoft Access Driver (*.mdb)};
DBQ=C:\Inetpub\wwwroot\BegASP\Code\Contact.mdb"
%>
```

Notice that we put the `<% ... %>` tags around this, to identify it as a server-side script. You'll want to change the `DBQ` part of this to point to the path where you put your Access database.

Save the file in `Inetpub\wwwroot\BegASP`, with the filename `DataStore.inc`.

> *You might be wondering about the suffix for this file, .inc. Although include files can have any name and suffix, the general standard is to use .inc or .asp for an include file.*

2 Create a new file, and type in the following HTML and script. Don't forget that this file can be obtained from the Wrox web site at `http://www.wrox.com/`, so if your typing is like mine you might prefer to download it instead of typing it in.

```
<HTML>

<!-- #INCLUDE FILE="DataStore.inc" -->

<HEAD>
<TITLE>ADO Connection Properties</TITLE>
</HEAD>
<BODY>
```

```
<TABLE BORDER=1>
<TR><TD>Property</TD><TD>Value</TD></TR>
<%
    Dim objConn        ' Connection object
    Dim objProp        ' Property object

    ' create the connection object
    Set objConn = Server.CreateObject ("ADODB.Connection")

    ' and open it
    objConn.Open strConnect

    ' loop through the properties
    For Each objProp In objConn.Properties
        Response.Write "<TR>" & _
            "<TD>" & objProp.Name & "</TD>" & _
            "<TD>" & objProp.Value & " </TD>" & _
            "</TR>"
    Next

    ' now close and clean up
    objConn.Close
    Set objConn = Nothing
%>
</TABLE>
</BODY>
</HTML>
```

Save this file in the same folder, calling it `ConnProps.asp`.

3 In your web browser, type the URL `http://my_server_name/BegASP/ConnProps.asp`.

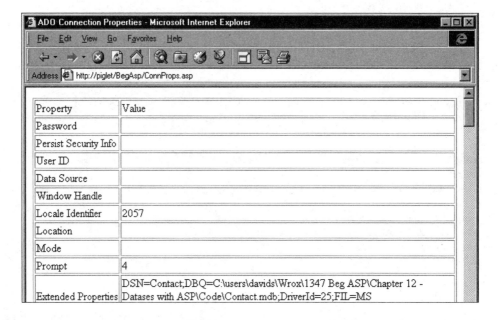

As you can see, there are a lot of properties in this collection, but there's no cause for alarm: you'll rarely use most of them.

How It Works

You've seen what this code does, so let's look at how it works in more detail.

First of all we include the data store file—this is exactly the same as shown earlier:

```
<!-- #INCLUDE FILE="DataStore.inc" -->
```

Now we create a table to show the properties and their values:

```
<TABLE BORDER=1>
<TR><TD>Property</TD><TD>Value</TD></TR>
```

Now the table header is created, we need to create the table body. For this, we loop through all of the properties using a **For Each** statement to look at each property. First, we declare a couple of variables: one for the connection object, and one for the property object.

```
<%
    Dim objConn          ' Connection object
    Dim objProp          ' Property object
```

Now we create the **Connection** object, and open it.

```
    ' create the connection object
    Set objConn = Server.CreateObject ("ADODB.Connection")

    ' and open it
    objConn.Open strConnect
```

Once the connection is open we can start looping through the connection. The **For Each** statement is perfect for collections as it sets the variable (in this case **objProp**) to each member of the collection in turn. Inside the loop we write the property **Name** and **Value** into cells in the table:

```
    ' loop through the properties
    For Each objProp In objConn.Properties
        Response.Write "<TR>" & _
            "<TD>" & objProp.Name & "</TD>" & _
            "<TD>" & objProp.Value & " </TD>" & _
            "</TR>"
    Next
```

Notice that we've included a non-break space here—the ** ** bit. This makes sure that a cell is actually filled with *something*, even if the property value is empty, and makes the table look better.

And finally we can close the connection and clean up.

```
      ' now close and clean up
      objConn.Close
      Set objConn = Nothing
  %>
  </TABLE>
  </BODY>
  </HTM
```

That's all there is to it. You'll find this technique of looping through a collection quite useful, and will see it again later.

You can use the **Properties** collection to find out what functionality is supported on a connection. For example, SQL Server allows you to have up to 4000 columns in a SELECT query, while Access allows 255. Admittedly this is unlikely to be a problem (and if it is, then you need to buy a SQL book!), but you could check the **Max Columns in Select** property to find this out.

To do this you don't need to loop through the whole collection, you can just access the element you need directly:

```
Response.Write "Cols = " & objConn.Properties ("Max Columns in Select")
```

This uses the same collection, but you are retrieving a Connection's property value using the property name.

The Connection Errors Collection

The **Errors** collection is much more useful than the **Properties** collection, as it contains all errors that have been created in response to a single failure. The words 'single failure' in that last sentence are are quite important, because when an ADO operation generates an error, the **Errors** collection is cleared before the new error details are inserted.

In a similar way to the **Properties** collection which contains **Property** objects, the **Errors** collection contains **Error** objects.

The **Error** object contains several properties that you'll need when looking at errors:

Property	Description
Number	The number of the error
Description	The description for the error
Source	Identifies the object that raised the error
SQLState	Holds the SQL error code
NativeError	Holds the database-specific error code

Using these properties, you'll be able to find out in more detail what error occured, so that this can be reported back to the user. Let's see how to do this.

Try It Out – The Errors Collection

1 Open up your editor, create a new file and add the following HTML and script:

```
<HTML>

<!-- #INCLUDE FILE="DataStore.inc" -->

<HEAD>
<TITLE>ADO Errors</TITLE>
</HEAD>
<BODY>

<%
    On Error Resume Next

    Dim objConn        ' Connection object
    Dim objProp        ' Property object
    Dim objError       ' Error object

    ' create the connection object
    Set objConn = Server.CreateObject ("ADODB.Connection")

    ' and open it
    objConn.Open strConnect

    ' now we can execute some SQL
    objConn.Execute "Select MissingColumn from MissingTable"

    ' Errors means the count will be greater than 0
    If objConn.Errors.Count > 0 Then

        ' loop through the errors
        For Each objError in objConn.Errors
            Response.Write "<TABLE>" & _
            "<TD>Error Property</TD>" & _
            "<TD>Contents</TD>" & _
            "<TR><TD>Number</TD><TD>" & _
                    objError.Number & "</TD></TR>" & _
            "<TR><TD>NativeError</TD><TD>" & _
                    objError.NativeError & "</TD></TR>" & _
            "<TR><TD>SQLState</TD><TD>" & _
                    objError.SQLState & "</TD></TR>" & _
            "<TR><TD>Source</TD><TD>" & _
                    objError.Source & "</TD></TR>" & _
            "<TR><TD>Description</TD><TD>" & _
                    objError.Description & "</TD></TR>" & _
            "</TABLE><P>"
        Next
    Else
```

417

```
        ' no errors
          Response.Write "There were no errors."
     End If

     ' now close and clean up
     objConn.Close
     Set objConn = Nothing
%>
</BODY>
</HTML>
```

2 Save the code in your `Inetpub\wwwroot\BegASP` directory, as `ConnErrs.asp`.

3 Type the URL into your browser, and view the page.

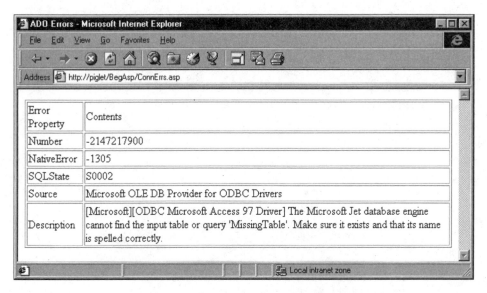

Error Property	Contents
Number	-2147217900
NativeError	-1305
SQLState	S0002
Source	Microsoft OLE DB Provider for ODBC Drivers
Description	[Microsoft][ODBC Microsoft Access 97 Driver] The Microsoft Jet database engine cannot find the input table or query 'MissingTable'. Make sure it exists and that its name is spelled correctly.

This is exactly what we expect to happen, because whilst the SQL statement we executed is correct SQL, it was looking for an invalid column in an invalid table.

How It Works

Once again we start with the include file, and give the `.asp` file a header:

```
<HTML>

<!-- #INCLUDE FILE="DataStore.inc" -->

<HEAD>
<TITLE>ADO Errors</TITLE>
</HEAD>
<BODY>
```

To ensure that the ASP script is not terminated when an error occurs, we need to use the **On Error** statement. This is similar to the one used in Visual Basic and VBA, but has less flexibility. All we can do is **Resume Next**, to continue processing at the next statement:

```
<%
    On Error Resume Next
```

Next we declare the variables. This time we declare a variable for the **Error** object:

```
        Dim objConn          ' Connection object
        Dim objProp          ' Property object
        Dim objError         ' Error object
```

Then we create the connection and open it:

```
        ' create the connection object
        Set objConn = Server.CreateObject ("ADODB.Connection")

        ' and open it
        objConn.Open strConnect
```

Then we can execute our SQL statement, with the known error. We haven't covered the **Execute** statement yet as this will be part of the next chapter, so we just using it here to force the error:

```
        ' now we can execute some SQL
        objConn.Execute "Select MissingColumn from MissingTable"
```

The **Count** property of the **Errors** collection tells us how many errors there have been, so we can test this before going into our error display section of code:

```
        ' Errors means the count will be greater than 0
        If objConn.Errors.Count > 0 Then
```

If there are errors, we can start looping through the **Errors** collection, using the same technique as we used on the **Properties** collection. We build up an HTML table containing all of the error information that we need to see:

```
            ' loop through the errors
            For Each objError in objConn.Errors
                Response.Write "<TABLE>" & _
                "<TD>Error Property</TD>" & _
                "<TD>Contents</TD>" & _
                "<TR><TD>Number</TD><TD>" & _
                        objError.Number & "</TD></TR>" & _
                "<TR><TD>NativeError</TD><TD>" & _
                        objError.NativeError & "</TD></TR>" & _
                "<TR><TD>SQLState</TD><TD>" & _
                        objError.SQLState & "</TD></TR>" & _
                "<TR><TD>Source</TD><TD>" & _
                        objError.Source & "</TD></TR>" & _
```

```
                    "<TR><TD>Description</TD><TD>" & _
                         objError.Description & "</TD></TR>" & _
                "</TABLE><P>"
          Next
```

If there are no errors, we can display a message that says so:

```
     Else
         ' no errors
          Response.Write "There were no errors."
     End If
```

Finally, we clean up and close the connection:

```
      ' now close and clean up
     objConn.Close
     Set objConn = Nothing
%>
</BODY>
</HTML>
```

That's all there is too it.

 One thing you could do is turn this error display into a separate include file of its own, which could then be included in any .asp file. It's a good practice to generalize and modularize code you're likely to use again and again—this makes it easier to maintain and debug larger applications. Anything that makes your life easier has got to be worth a go!

Try It Out – A Generic Error Routine

1 Start up your editor, and type in the code for the following include file:

```
<%
Sub CheckForErrors (objConn)

    ' Errors means the count will be greater than 0
    If objConn.Errors.Count > 0 Then

        ' loop through the errors
        For Each objError in objConn.Errors
            Response.Write "<TABLE>" & _
            "<TR><TD>Error Property</TD>" & _
            "<TD>Contents</TD></TR>" & _
            "<TR><TD>Number</TD><TD>" & _
                objError.Number & "</TD></TR>" & _
            "<TR><TD>NativeError</TD><TD>" & _
```

```
                    objError.NativeError & "</TD></TR>" & _
             "<TR><TD>SQLState</TD><TD>" & _
                    objError.SQLState & "</TD></TR>" & _
             "<TR><TD>Source</TD><TD>" & _
                    objError.Source & "</TD></TR>" & _
             "<TR><TD>Description</TD><TD>" & _
                    objError.Description & "</TD></TR>" & _
             "</TABLE><P>"
          Next
      End If

End Sub

%>
```

2 Save the code in the BegASP directory, with the name **Errors.asp**.

 Although this is an include file, we've used a .asp suffix to indicate that this contains ASP script that performs some action. Compare this to another include file that we have used recently, namely DataStore.inc: we use the .inc suffix in that case because the file just holds a variable. These files could easily have taken the same suffix, but I think it's good to differentiate between the two types of include files.

3 Now open up a new file, and type in the following:

```
<HTML>

<!-- #INCLUDE FILE="DataStore.inc" -->
<!-- #INCLUDE FILE="Errors.asp" -->

<HEAD>
<TITLE>ADO Errors</TITLE>
</HEAD>
<BODY>

<%
    On Error Resume Next

    Dim objConn        ' Connection object
    Dim objProp        ' Property object
    Dim objError       ' Error object

    ' create the connection object
    Set objConn = Server.CreateObject ("ADODB.Connection")

    ' and open it
```

```
        objConn.Open strConnect

        ' now we can execute some SQL
        objConn.Execute "Select MissingColumn from MissingTable"

        ' now check for errors
        CheckForErrors (objConn)

        ' now close and clean up
        objConn.Close
        Set objConn = Nothing
    %>
    </BODY>
    </HTML>
```

4 Save this in the same directory, with the name `UseErrors.asp`.

5 Call up the page `UseErrors.asp` from your browser. You'll see that this has the same result as before. Let's see how it works.

How It Works

Let first look at `Errors.asp`. Firstly, we define a sub-procedure, which has one argument, `objConn`. This will be used to hold the `Connection` object:

```
    <%
    Sub CheckForErrors (objConn)
```

Now we can check how many errors are in the collection:

```
        ' Errors means the count will be greater than 0
        If objConn.Errors.Count > 0 Then
```

If there are errors, create a table as before:

```
            ' loop through the errors
            For Each objError in objConn.Errors
            ...
            Next
```

That's all there is to it. Notice that the include file doesn't open the connection, and so it doesn't close the connection either: responsibility for this is taken by the calling routine.

The `UseErrors.asp` file is familiar too. The first thing you notice is that we include another file—the one you have just created, which houses the error routine.

```
    <HTML>

    <!-- #INCLUDE FILE="DataStore.inc" -->
    <!-- #INCLUDE FILE="Errors.asp" -->
```

```
<HEAD>
<TITLE>ADO Errors</TITLE>
</HEAD>
<BODY>

<%
    On Error Resume Next

    Dim objConn          ' Connection object
    Dim objProp          ' Property object
    Dim objError         ' Error object

    ' create the connection object
    Set objConn = Server.CreateObject ("ADODB.Connection")

    ' and open it
    objConn.Open strConnect

    ' now we can execute some SQL
    objConn.Execute "Select MissingColumn from MissingTable"
```

The code is the same up until this point, where we now call the new error routine, passing in our open connection:

```
    ' now check for errors
    CheckForErrors (objConn)

    ' now close and clean up
    objConn.Close
    Set objConn = Nothing
%>
</BODY>
</HTML>
```

Easy huh! You now have a simple generic error routine that you can use from any `.asp` file. This saves having to write it each time, and makes it easier to update.

Summary

We've covered quite a lot of ground in this chapter, and although we haven't really done a lot of database-type things, it's been important to get some of this groundwork covered. What we've looked at in this chapter is how to connect to a database, and what the connection gives us.

We've also looked at what ADO really means, and how it fits into the database strategy, and what OLE-DB will do for us in the future. Now it's time to look at how we get data from a data store, and that's where the next chapter comes in.

Expanding Data Access

In the previous chapter we spent a lot of time looking at the connection to the data store. While it's very useful, it isn't really very exciting, as what you really want to see is lots of data in your ASP pages. For that we need to expand our knowledge of ADO, so in this chapter we'll be:

- Looking at the ADO object model in more detail
- Examining what recordsets are and how we use them
- Using the **Command** object to send commands to the data store
- Revisiting the **Connection** object
- Getting more information about the recordset

This chapter is really going to get to the guts of data access within ASP. We'll be looking at how you can run queries and stored procedures, to both return and insert data. We'll also be looking at ways to build HTML tables automatically from a set of data.

The ADO Object Model

Let's have a look at that object model diagram again:

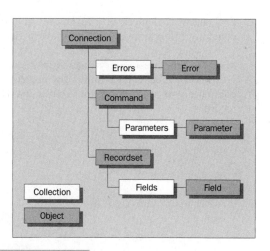

We've already looked at the `Errors` collection, so we'll skip that here, and we've seen the `Connection` object too. But, as we mentioned in the previous chapter, it looks like `Connection` is the main object and that `Command` and `Recordset` are dependent upon it. This is *not* the case—you will need some form of connection to get data to and from the data store, but you can create these 'on-the-fly'. And to make it doubly flexible, you can run queries directly from the `Connection` object too.

What is a Recordset?

If you've done any database work before you'll then know the answer to this one, but if you're new to some of this terminology then it shouldn't be too confusing. Quite simply, a **recordset** is a set of records—it really is that obvious. Databases store tables, and each table stores records. So a recordset is just some, or all, of those records.

A **record** is just a collection of related information. For example, if you are storing information about companies, you would probably want the following:

- Company Name
- Address
- Town
- State
- Zip Code
- Phone Number

Imagine a card file box full of company details. Each card is a record. If you reach into the box and grab a bunch of records, then you have a set of records—or a recordset.

Generally, a recordset is a set of related records. You don't often dip into the card file and pick out a bunch of random cards—you're usually interested in companies for a reason, perhaps all those in a particular state. When you create a recordset, you can define which records you are interested in.

Each individual piece of information in a record is termed a **field**. So in the example of the company information cards, we have a field called *Company Name*, a field called *Address*, etc.

A **key** is how we identify individual records. When you flick through your card file, how do you know when you've found the correct record? Probably because you know the name of the company you are looking for. This is the *key* piece of information with which you identify the record.

Connect String Differences

The samples in this chapter are written so that most will work against both SQL Server and Access database, although we are concentrating on using Access. The samples all use **strConnect** as the connect string.

The connect string is declared in **DataStore.inc**. The SQL Server one is:

```
strConnect = "Driver={SQL Server}; Server=YourServer; Database=YourDB;
UID=YourUID; PWD=YourPWD"
```

If you're going to use SQL Server data, you should change the following:

- ▶ *YourServer* to the name of your SQL Server
- ▶ *YourDB* to the name of your SQL Server database
- ▶ *YourUID* to your SQL Server logon name
- ▶ *YourPWD* to your SQL Server password

The Access connect string is:

```
strConnect = "Driver={Microsoft Access Driver (*.mdb)}; DBQ=YourDB"
```

You should change *YourDB* to the full pathname of your access database. If you're using the same set-up that we created in Chapter 13, then *YourDB* should be **C:\Inetpub\wwwroot\BegASP\Code\Contact.mdb**.

You can also use the DSN-based connection string, which is:

```
strConnect = "DSN=YourDSNName"
```

You should replace *YourDSNName* with the name of your DSN. In the last chapter we used a DSN called **Contact**, so this would give us a DSN of:

```
strConnect = "DSN=Contact"
```

For those samples that are not Access specific you can simply amend **DataStore.inc** file so that the appropriate connect string is commented out. (To comment out a line, simply place a single quote symbol, **'**, at the start of the line.) Hence, you can switch the samples from Access to SQL Server. This shows that, for the most part, ADO doesn't really care which database you are talking to.

The Recordset Object

We've already explained what recordsets are, and it follows that a **Recordset** object is the ASP object that we use to manipulate them. We've done some theory, so let's dive straight in and give it a try. We'll look at how it works afterwards, and then examine the **Recordset** object and some of the in more detail.

Try It Out – Creating a Recordset

1   Make sure you have created the **DataStore.inc** file as described previously. You can use the copy that we used in the examples in Chapter 13; it needs to be in the **Inetpub\wwwroot\BegASP** directory, with your other as your **.asp** files.

2   Download the file **adovbs.inc** from the Wrox web site, and place that in the same directory.

3   You'll also need to ensure that the **Contact.mdb** Access database is set up (see the previous section, and Chapter 13).

4   Create a new file, and put the following lines into it:

```
<HTML>

<!-- #INCLUDE FILE="DataStore.inc" -->
<!-- #INCLUDE FILE="adovbs.inc" -->

<HEAD>
<TITLE>ADO Recordset Object</TITLE>
</HEAD>
<BODY>

<%
    Dim objRec          ' recordset object

    ' create the recordset object
    Set objRec = Server.CreateObject ("ADODB.Recordset")

    ' now open it
    objRec.Open "Contact", strConnect, adOpenForwardOnly, _
                                    adLockReadOnly, adCmdTable

    ' now loop through the records
    While Not objRec.EOF
        Response.Write objRec("name") & ", "
        objRec.MoveNext
    Wend

    ' now close and clean up
    objRec.Close
    Set objRec = Nothing
%>

</BODY>
</HTML>
```

5 Save the file, in your **BegASP** directory, with the name **Recordset.asp**.

6 Load the page into your browser.

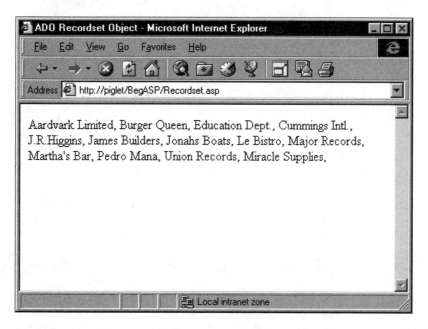

And *voila*—a list of every name in the table. Let's see how it works.

How It Works

We start with the familiar heading section, this time with the new include file. This will make the ADO constants available to the rest of our code. We'll be explaining these constants in a little while.

```
<HTML>

<!-- #INCLUDE FILE="DataStore.inc" -->
<!-- #INCLUDE FILE="adovbs.inc" -->

<HEAD>
<TITLE>ADO Recordset Object</TITLE>
</HEAD>
<BODY>
```

The next thing to do is declare our object variable

```
<%
    Dim objRec          ' recordset object
```

Now we can create the **Recordset** object. It's a part of the ADODB object model (notice that this is exactly the same method that we used when we created the **Connection** object):

```
' create the recordset object
Set objRec = Server.CreateObject ("ADODB.Recordset")
```

Once the object is created, we can open it:

```
' now open it
objRec.Open "Contact", strConnect, adOpenForwardOnly, _
                                  adLockReadOnly, adCmdTable
```

You can see that the **Open** method requires five parameters. The first is the source of the data—in this case it's the table **Contact**, whose data comes from the database file **Contact.mdb**. The second parameter is the connection string. Remember how we said that you didn't always need to create a **Connection** object? Well, this is one of those occasions. You'll see how we could have used one a little later.

The third and fourth parameters tell ADO what type of recordset to use. We'll be looking at these in detail in a page or two. The last parameter states that **Contact** is a table.

 You'll see how to use SQL and queries here later.

The recordset is now open, so we can step through the records. The **EOF** ("end-of-file") property tells us when we have gone past the last of the records in the recordset. While we're stepping through the recordset, the value of **EOF** is **Not True**; if we step past the last record then **EOF** will be set to **True**. Hence, we repeat the loop while **EOF** is **Not True**:

```
' now loop through the records
While Not objRec.EOF
```

Inside the loop we write out the field, **name**, and then move onto the next record:

```
        Response.Write objRec("name") & ", "
        objRec.MoveNext
    Wend
```

Finally we close the recordset:

```
    ' now close and clean up
    objRec.Close
    Set objRec = Nothing
%>

</BODY>
</HTML>
```

That's all there is to it, and this is a procedure you'll become familiar with during this chapter.

What are the Recordset Types?

You've seen that a recordset is a set of related records, and it's by means of a recordset that we can look at these records. However, what you are allowed to do with these records is defined by the **type** of the recordset. For example, if you are not going to change any data in a record, you can have a special recordset that doesn't let you change anything.

You're going to ask, "If I know I'm not going to change any records, why do I need to tell ADO this? Surely I could just make sure I don't make any changes?" Yes that's true, but telling ADO that you are not going to do any changes means that it can handle the recordset a little differently, and this can generally lead to better performance.

Recordset types are often called **cursor types**. This is nothing to do with the screen cursor, but is just another term for the type of recordset you will be using.

General Recordset Types

Let's have a look at the *general* recordset types, before we look at the specific ones for ADO.

▶ **Updateable and non-updateable recordsets.** These define whether or not you can update the data in your recordset. If your application is never going to change any data, then you should use *non-updateable* (or *read-only*) recordsets, because this allows the data provider to send the data to you and forget about it. It has no need to keep track of what you are doing, so this can give performance benefits.

▶ **Scrollable and non-scrollable recordsets.** These determine whether you can move backward through the recordset, onto previous records, or whether you are limited to only moving forwards. A *scrollable* recordset allows both backward and forward movement. Using a *non-scrollable* recordset can also give performance benefits, because the recordset doesn't have to keep track of the data once you've moved passed it, since by definition you can never go back to it.

▶ **Keyset and non-keyset recordsets.** Most tables in a database have a unique key of some kind, and this is the heart of a keyset recordset. When you request a *non-keyset* recordset you get all of the data back, but a *keyset* recordset just returns the unique keys, and only fetches the actual data when you request that record.

In fact, this is a generalization: in reality you'll probably find a set of records returned as well. The idea is that if all of the keys, plus a block of data, are returned then there is no delay in getting the first set of data. If you move to a key that is not within the current block, then another block of data is fetched. It's like going to a cookie shop and only buying one cookie at a time. Why not buy a batch of cookies, and then if you want some more later, you can buy another batch. The advantage of a keyset recordset is that the recordset only has to keep track of the keys, which are generally small, rather than a large amount of data.

▶ **Dynamic and static recordsets.** These determine which records are available in the recordset at a specific time. A *static* recordset contains only those records that were available when the recordset was created. A *dynamic* recordset only manages a *part* of the recordset. This means that if new records are added, deleted, or changed by other users while you are accessing the database they will become available when they scroll into the part of the recordset you are viewing. Back to the cookies—a bag of cookies is static.

You're never going to get more cookies in a bag than the number you originally bought (very unfair in my opinion). On the other hand, suppose you start at the counter and decide to have every type of cookie containing peanuts; then suddenly a tray of double-choc peanut crunch is added to the counter, then it's your lucky day! The recordset changes dynamically, in demand to the records you are actually managing at the time.

So it all boils down to how you see the records and how you move about the records. Let's look at the ADO recordset types.

ADO Recordset Types

There are four to deal with:

▶ **Forward Only:** This is the default type and is a non-scrollable recordset. This is often perfect in ASP code, because much of the time we are just building up a list of records, so we only ever need to start at the beginning record and move through each record in turn until we get to the end. We never need to move backwards again.

▶ **Static:** Similar to a forward only recordset, except that it is scrollable, so you can move back to previous records as well as moving forwards.

▶ **Dynamic:** The recordset is fully dynamic, and lets you see additions, changes and deletions that are made by other users. It's fully scrollable so you can move around the recordset any way you like.

▶ **Keyset:** Similar to the dynamic recordset, but you can't see records that other users add, although you *can* see changes to existing records. Any records that other users delete become inaccessible.

All you have to remember is what you actually want to *do* with your records. If you just want to step through them one at a time, making no changes, then a Forward-Only recordset is the one you need. If you want to scroll backwards too, but still don't want to make any changes, then you need a Static recordset. If you need to change the data then either a Forward-Only, a Dynamic or a Keyset recordset is required.

If you have a flick back to the line of code that creates the recordset you'll see where this was used:

```
objRec.Open "Contact", strConnect, adOpenForwardOnly, _
                              adLockReadOnly, adCmdTable
```

Here we have used a recordset type of **adOpenForwardOnly**. This tells us that we want to use a forward only recordset.

What is Locking?

We're all familiar with locking. Locking your front door stops the burglars walking off with your TV and video recorder. Locking your basement door stops your teenage children drinking your much-valued 1961 Chateaux Petrus! The same applies to records in a data store—locking prevents other people from changing them. There are four types of locking you can use:

- **Read-only**. The is the default, and no locking is performed since you can't change the data.

- **Pessimistic**. This is where you become very protective, and the record is locked as soon as you start editing it. This means that no one else can change the record until you release the lock.

- **Optimistic**. This is a more carefree attitude, where the records are only locked when you update them. This assumes that no one else will edit the record whilst you are editing it, so the lock is only placed whilst the record is actually being updated.

- **Optimistic Batch**. Batch update mode allows you to modify several records and then have them all updated at once, so this only locks each record as it is being updated.

Returning once again to our first example, you can see that we used this in the line that created the recordset:

```
objRec.Open "Contact", strConnect, adOpenForwardOnly, _
                            adLockReadOnly, adCmdTable
```

This tells us that we are using a read-only recordset, and we will not be changing any data.

ADO Constants

We just talked about the recordset types and locking, and there are certain times when you need to tell ADO which one of these you want to use, as shown in this code:

```
objRec.Open "Contact", strConnect, adOpenForwardOnly, _
                            adLockReadOnly, adCmdTable
```

The question you might have asked yourself is where these terms came from. We know what **adOpenForwardOnly** means, but why does it work?

It's a **constant**, which is defined in the include file, **adovbs.inc**. Each constant represents a specific numeric value. For example, **adovbs.inc** you'll find the four constants for the recordset type defined as follows:

```
Const adOpenForwardOnly = 0
Const adOpenKeyset = 1
Const adOpenDynamic = 2
Const adOpenStatic = 3
```

So why do we use constants? Well, consider the following two lines:

```
objRec.Open "Contact", strConnect, 0, 1, 2
```

and

```
objRec.Open "Contact", strConnect, adOpenForwardOnly, _
                            adLockReadOnly, adCmdTable
```

Now suppose your code has a bug in it. Ask yourself, "Which one of these lines is easier to read?" The answer is the second, because the constants actually *tell* you something. In the first line you have no idea what the arguments of **0**, **1**, or **2** mean, but by using constants you can quickly see what you are trying to achieve. So with the constants, when you need to refer to a keyset recordset you can just use **adOpenKeyset** instead of the number, which will make your code much easier to read.

When you install the NT Option Pack with IIS and the Data Access support, the file containing the recordset type constants is placed in **Program Files\Common Files\System\ADO** and is called **adovbs.inc**. This file is included in the samples from the Wrox web site, and to use it in the samples below you'll need to copy it into the directory in which you have your other **.asp** files. You might like to have a look at this file to see what it contains—don't change anything though! For the moment, don't worry about what these constants actually mean, as we'll explain them when we use them.

The Recordset Object in Detail

Now that you've seen how easy it can be to use a recordset, it makes sense to look into it a little more deeply. Let's start by looking at the syntax of the **Open** method:

```
recordset.Open Source, ActiveConnection, CursorType, LockType, Options
```

We briefly mentioned the arguments in the course of the example above; it's now time to examine them in more detail.

The Source Property

The **Source** is where the data comes from. In our first example, we used a table name; other valid sources could be a SQL statement, a stored procedure or query, or a **Command** object (more on that later). For example, all of these are valid:

```
objRec.Open "SELECT * FROM Contact", ...
```

```
objRec.Open "sp_contact"
```

```
objRec.Open "qryContact"
```

> *We'll be looking at stored procedures and queries a little later.*

You can also set the source by using the **Source** property of the **Recordset** object:

```
objRec.Source = "SELECT * FROM Contact"
```

In fact, by calling the **Open** method and specifying the *Source* parameter, you effectively fill the **Source** property indirectly.

The ActiveConnection Property

`ActiveConnection` identifies the data store connection. In our first example we used a connection string, but you could use a `Connection` object instead, like this:

```
Dim objConn
Dim objRec

Set objConn = Server.CreateObject ("ADODB.Connection")
Set objRec = Server.CreateObject ("ADODB.Recordset")

objConn.Open strConnect

objRec.Open "Contact", objConn, adOpenForwardOnly, adLockReadOnly,
adCmdTable
```

What's the advantage of doing it this way? Well, connecting to a data store is quite 'expensive'—it's a task that takes a long time. So if you need to use several recordsets, or one recordset run several times, it is best to only connect to the data store once, so use a `Connection` object.

On the other hand, if you are only running a single query once, then just use a connection string—this will create a connection for you. In fact, doing it this way allows you to derive the `Connection` object from the recordset, by using the `ActiveConnection` property:

```
Dim objConn
Dim objRec

Set objRec = Server.CreateObject ("ADODB.Recordset")

objRec.Open "Contact", strConn, adOpenForwardOnly, adLockReadOnly,
adCmdTable

Set objConn = objRec.ActiveConnection
```

> *Notice that this method doesn't require you to explicitly create the* `Connection` *object.*

You can probably gather that by using this code, the `ActiveConnection` property is filled in for you. Alternatively you can set it yourself:

```
objRec.ActiveConnection = strConnect
```

or

```
Set objRec.ActiveConnection = objConn
```

Although the two lines above appear to achieve the same thing, there is in fact a subtle difference. The first creates a new connection, because a connection string is being passed in. The second uses an existing `Connection` object, `objConn`, as the connection.

The CursorType Property

We've already discussed recordset types (cursors types), and the constants are fairly obvious, so we'll just recap that information here, showing what the constants are:

- **adOpenForwardOnly** gives you an updateable, non-scrollable recordset.
- **adOpenKeyset** gives you a scrollable keyset recordset.
- **adOpenDynamic** gives you a scrollable, fully dynamic recordset.
- **adOpenStatic** gives you a read only, scrollable recordset.

We've already seen how to pass this value as a parameter to the **Open** method. Alternatively, you can set the **CursorType** property like this:

```
objRec.CursorType = adOpenForwardOnly
```

The LockType Property

We've also discussed locking earlier in the chapter, so let's look just at the constants:

- **adLockReadOnly** gives a read only recordset, where no updating is allowed.
- **adLockPessimistic** gives an updateable recordset, that locks the records as soon as you start editing.
- **adLockOptimistic** gives an updateable recordset, where the lock is only placed just before you try and update the record.
- **adLockBatchOptimistic** gives optimistic locking for batch updates.

As you've probably guessed by now, you can also set the **LockType** property directly:

```
objRec.LockType = adLockReadOnly
```

The Options

Options specify how the **Source** property is interpreted, and can be one of the following values:

- **adCmdText** to indicate that **Source** holds command text, for example, a SQL command.
- **adCmdTable** to indicate that **Source** holds the name of a table.
- **adCmdStoredProc** to indicate that **Source** holds the name of a stored procedure or query.
- **adCmdUnknown** to indicate that **Source** holds an unknown type.

Unlike the other arguments the *Options* parameter doesn't map directly to a property of the **Recordset** object, but maps onto the **CommandText** property of the **Command** object. We'll be looking at this later.

EOF and BOF

We've already seen **EOF** in action in this chapter. You may well be familiar with these two properties, but you might not realize exactly what happens when you step past the end of a recordset.

If you move past the last record, **EOF** is set to **True** and the 'current record' is placed after the last record. You're going to ask, "How can that be, since there are no more records?" It's actually quite simple to understand with the aid of a diagram. Imagine that the boxes are records, and the gray area represents the current record pointer.

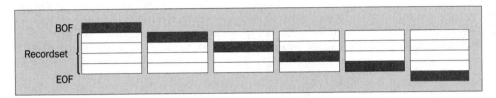

When we first open the recordset, the 'current record' is the first record, and as we move through the recordset (using **MoveNext**, perhaps) the current record moves too. Now, when we move past the last record we still have a 'current record' pointer, but it doesn't point to a valid record, because there isn't one there. Instead the **EOF** property is set to indicate that we have stepped passed the end of the recordset. The same process happens when moving backwards, except that it's the value of **BOF** that gets set to **True** instead.

If you open an empty recordset, then both **BOF** and **EOF** will be set to **True**.

Bookmarks

A bookmark is really pretty intuitive—it's a way of marking a place in a recordset. In fact it uniquely identifies a record in a recordset so you can always jump straight back to it. A bookmark is stored as a **variant** value, although you might not be able to view it, and you wouldn't want to anyway, since its value is only meaningful to ADO. There are several important facts· to note about bookmarks:

▶ Two bookmarks that point at the same record might have different values. This means that you can't compare bookmarks directly.

▶ If you create two recordsets from the same source, and set bookmarks on the same records, the bookmarks are not the same.

▶ Bookmarks are only available—when the datasource supports them—when using keyset and static recordsets.

The following section of code shows how you can use bookmarks:

```
Dim varBookmark

. . . ' code to create the Recordset object

varBookmark = objRec.Bookmark
```

```
. . . ' some processing of records

objRec.Bookmark = varBookmark
```

First, this creates a variant, **varBookmark**. Later, **varBookmark** is used to store the contents of the **Bookmark**. Later still, we set the recordset's **Bookmark** property back to the stored bookmark; this moves the record pointer back to the record that we saved proeviously. You'll see bookmarks in use when we look at the **Find** method.

Moving Through Records

In our first example, we saw seen how to step through a recordset using the **MoveNext** method. But what about other ways of moving? You probably won't be surprised to learn that there is a **MovePrevious** method, as well as **MoveFirst** and **MoveLast** (although the availability of these methods is dependent upon the recordset type). Since we haven't created any other cursor types, now is a good time to give it a go.

Try It Out – Moving Through Records

1 Be sure that you still have the files **DataStore.inc** and **adovbs.inc** in the directory **Inetpub\wwwroot\BegASP**, and the **Contact** database set up as we described in Chapter 13.

2 Open up your editor, create a new file, and enter the following:

```
<HTML>

<!-- #INCLUDE FILE="DataStore.inc" -->
<!-- #INCLUDE FILE="adovbs.inc" -->

<HEAD>
<TITLE>ADO Moving through records</TITLE>
</HEAD>
<BODY>

<%
    Dim objRec          ' recordset object

    ' create the recordset object
    Set objRec = Server.CreateObject ("ADODB.Recordset")

    ' now open it
    objRec.Open "Contact", strConnect, adOpenKeyset, _
        adLockReadOnly, adCmdTable

    ' now loop through the records
    While Not objRec.EOF
        Response.Write objRec("name") & ", "
```

```
        objRec.MoveNext
    Wend

    Response.Write "<P>"

    ' now go backwards
    objRec.Movelast
    While Not objRec.BOF
        Response.Write objRec("name") & ", "
        objRec.MovePrevious
    Wend

    ' now close and clean up
    objRec.Close
    Set objRec = Nothing
%>

</BODY>
</HTML>
```

3 Save the code in the **BegASP** directory, as **Moving.asp**.

4 Now open this file from your browser:

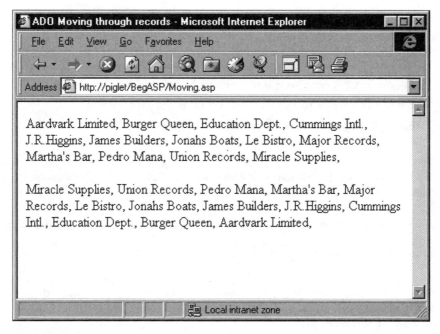

Not really a great surprise there. Let's see how this differs from **Recordset.asp**.

How It Works

You've probably noticed that most of the code is exactly the same as our first example, when we just stepped through the recordset forwards, so we'll only look at the differences.

As in the first example, we step through the recordset; when we pass the end, the **EOF** is set. This means that we have stepped passed the last record, and we no longer have a valid record pointer, so we need to move back to the last record:

```
objRec.Movelast
```

Now we are at the last record we can follow the same procedure, this time using the **MovePrevious** method to move to the previous record, and checking **BOF** to make sure we don't go beyond the beginning of the recordset:

```
While Not objRec.BOF
    Response.Write objRec("name") & ", "
    objRec.MovePrevious
Wend
```

Moving Directly

The last way of moving that we're going to look at is the **Move** method, which allows us to specify the number of records to move. The syntax for the move method is as follows:

objRecordset.Move *NumRecords, Start*

Here, *objRecordset* is the name of our recordset object. *NumRecords* is a parameter that specifies the number of records you wish to move, and *Start* is the point that you wish the move to start from. *Start* can be any one of the following:

- **adBookmarkCurrent** to use the current record as the start position
- **adBookmarkFirst** to use the first record as the start position
- **adBookmarkLast** to use the last record as the start position

FYI   These constants are all defined in the file adovbs.inc.

For example, to move three records further on from the current position you would use this:

```
objRec.Move 3, adBookmarkCurrent
```

FYI   If you don't specify the last parameter for the Move method, then it always defaults to adBookmarkCurrent.

To move backwards you just supply a negative value. So, moving back three records from the current position would be achieved like this:

```
objRec.Move -3, adBookmarkCurrent
```

If you attempt to move beyond the beginning or end of a recordset then **BOF** or **EOF** is set accordingly.

Finding Records

If you've looked at the ADO documentation that comes with the NT Option Pack, then you might be left wondering how to find records, because the **Find** method is not documented. The good news is that it is there, and it does work. However, it does not use indexes of any kind and is a full table scan, so with large recordsets both the **Find** method and the **Filter** method are slow. (We'll discuss the **Filter** method in the next section.)

The syntax for the **Find** method is:

*objRecordset.*Find   *Criteria,   SkipRecords,   SearchDirection,   Start*

We'll see the find method in action shortly, but first we'll explain what the arguments do. In fact, they're fairly straightforward:

- ▶ *Criteria* is a string that contains a set of comparisons that will be matched with the records to be retrieved.
- ▶ *SkipRecords* is the offset from the start position where the search should start (see also *Start*, below).
- ▶ *SearchDirection* can be set either to **adSearchForward** or **adSearchbackward**, to specify the direction to search in.
- ▶ *Start* is a bookmark that specifies the start position of the search. Then the parameter *SkipRecords* specifies the offset from this position.

Criteria is the most important argument here, and if you've done any SQL work you'll probably be familiar with the way you use it. The general form is shown below:

{*Recordset_field*} {*Comparison_operator*} {*Value*}

Here, *Recordset_field* is the name of the field in the recordset that you want to search against, *Comparison_operator* is the type of search, and *Value* is what you are looking for. *Comparison_operator* can be one of the following:

- ▶ **>**   to search for records greater than the value
- ▶ **<**   for records less than the value
- ▶ **=**   for records equal to the value
- ▶ **like**   for matching records

For example, you can search for "Le Bistro" in the **name** field, with the following line:

```
objRec.Find "name = 'Le Bistro'"
```

Notice that we've left out the last three arguments, since they are optional. If you do this, then the default is to start the search at the *current* record, and search *forwards* through the recordset.

In the example above, notice that we're searching for a string, `'Le Bistro'`: in this case, we must enclose the search string in single quotation marks. You don't need to do this for numeric values:

```
objRec.Find "Price = 34.95"
```

And when searching for dates, you should surround the date with **#** marks:

```
objRec.Find "Birthday = #10/23/98#"
```

When searching for strings you can also use **like** to specify matching records. So:

```
objRec.Find "name like 'b*'"
```

will find the next record where the field **name** starts with **b**. The ***** indicates that any number of characters can follow.

You might be wondering how to tell whether the record you're looking for has been found. It's quite simple: if no record is found, then **EOF** (or **BOF** if you're searching backwards) is set to **True**. Consequently, you must be aware of the fact that your current record will change, even if you can't find the record: so you might want to use a bookmark to keep a note of the current record.

Try It Out – Finding Records

1 Once again, we'll be using the files **DataStore.inc** and **adovbs.inc** and the **Contact** database, as we have done so far in this chapter.

2 Open your editor, create a new file and enter the following code:

```
<HTML>

<!-- #INCLUDE FILE="DataStore.inc" -->
<!-- #INCLUDE FILE="adovbs.inc" -->

<HEAD>
<TITLE>ADO Finding Records</TITLE>
</HEAD>
<BODY>

<%
    Dim objRec              ' recordset object
    Dim varBookmark         ' bookmark
```

```
    ' create the recordset object
    Set objRec = Server.CreateObject ("ADODB.Recordset")

    ' now open it
    objRec.Open "Contact", strConnect, adOpenKeyset, _
        adLockReadOnly, adCmdTable

    ' keep our current place
    Response.Write "Current Record: " & objRec("name") & "<BR>"
    varBookmark = objRec.Bookmark
    Response.Write "Looking for 'Le Bistro'<BR>"

    objRec.Find "name='Le Bistro'"
    If objRec.EOF Then
        Response.Write "Not Found: "
        objRec.Bookmark = varBookmark
    Else
        Response.Write "Found: "
    End If
    Response.Write "Current Record: " & objRec("name") & "<BR><P>"


    ' try again, this time an unknown record
    objRec.MoveFirst

    ' keep our current place
    Response.Write "Current Record: " & objRec("name") & "<BR>"
    varBookmark = objRec.Bookmark
    Response.Write "Looking for 'NoOneHereButUsChickens'<BR>"

    objRec.Find "name='NoOneHereButUsChickens'"

    If objRec.EOF Then
        Response.Write "Not Found: "
        objRec.Bookmark = varBookmark
    Else
        Response.Write "Found: "
    End If
    Response.Write "Current Record: " & objRec("name") & "<BR>"

    ' now close and clean up
    objRec.Close
    Set objRec = Nothing
%>

</BODY>
</HTML>
```

3 Save the code in your **BegASP** directory, calling it **Find.asp**.

4 Now open this file from your browser:

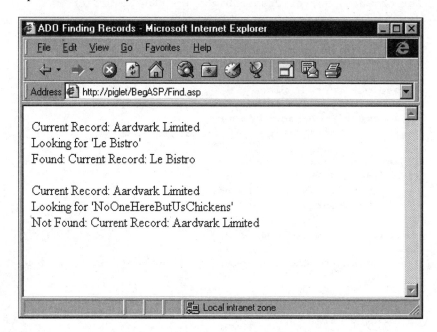

You can see that we start on the record for **Aardvark Limited**, and we search for **Le Bistro**. The first search succeeds—after this search, the current record is **Le Bistro**. The second search fails, because the record we are searching for doesn't exist, and we return back to our starting record.

How It Works

We only need to look at the first search, because the theory is the same for both searches. First, we write out what our current record is, and we set a bookmark to point to the current record:

```
Response.Write "Current Record: " & objRec("name") & "<BR>"
varBookmark = objRec.Bookmark
Response.Write "Looking for 'Le Bistro'<BR>"
```

Then we invoke the **Find** method looking for a record:

```
objRec.Find "name='Le Bistro'"
```

Following the search, we check the value of **EOF**: if it's **True**, then all records were searched fruitlessly, so we reset the current record back to the one saved in the bookmark, and output a line saying that the search term was not found. If **EOF** is **False**, then we simply inform the user that the search was successful:

```
If objRec.EOF Then
    Response.Write "Not Found: "
    objRec.Bookmark = varBookmark
Else
    Response.Write "Found: "
End If
```

We then display the current record:

```
Response.Write "Current Record: " & objRec("name") & "<BR><P>"
```

So finding records is quite easy, as long as we remember that if the record isn't found we might have to move ourselves back to the record from where we started.

Filtering Records

Finding records is very useful when you only have a few, unrelated records to look for, but what if you need to find a group of related records? You don't want to step through the recordset checking each record in turn, and it's quite impractical to use the **Find** method to find each one.

In this case you can **Filter** the recordset. This method restricts the records in the recordset by a certain criteria. For example:

```
objRec.Filter = "state = 'FL'"
```

Note the positioning of the single- and double-quotation marks again. This restricts the recordset to only those records where the state is **'FL'**.

You can also pass in an array of bookmarks, or one of the following constants:

▶ **adFilterNone** which removes the current filter and restores all records to the view.

▶ **adFilterPendingRecords** which shows only those records that have changed but have yet to be sent to the data store. This is only applicable in batch update mode (more on this later).

▶ **adFilterAffectedRecords** which shows only records affected by the last **Delete**, **Resync**, **UpdateBatch** or **CancelBatch** call. (We'll discuss these calls later in the chapter.)

▶ **adFilterFetchedRecords** which shows the records from the last call to retrieve records from the data store.

Let's have a look at an example.

Try It Out – Filtering Records

1 Check that the files **DataStore.inc** and **adovbs.inc** and the **Contact** database are set up, as for the other examples in this chapter.

2 Create a new file, and add the following code:

```
<HTML>

<!-- #INCLUDE FILE="DataStore.inc" -->
<!-- #INCLUDE FILE="adovbs.inc" -->
```

```
<HEAD>
<TITLE>Filtering Records</TITLE>
</HEAD>
<BODY>

<%
    Dim objRec          ' recordset object

    ' create the recordset object
    Set objRec = Server.CreateObject ("ADODB.Recordset")

    ' now open it
    objRec.Open "Contact", strConnect, adOpenStatic, _
        adLockReadOnly, adCmdTable

    ' now loop through the records
    Response.Write "All Contacts<BR>"
    While Not objRec.EOF
        Response.Write objRec("name") & ","
        objRec.MoveNext
    Wend

    ' only those contacts in Florida
    objRec.Filter = "state = 'FL'"

    ' now loop through the records
    Response.Write "<P>Contacts in Florida<BR>"
    While Not objRec.EOF
        Response.Write objRec("name") & ","
        objRec.MoveNext
    Wend

    ' now close and clean up
    objRec.Close
    Set objRec = Nothing
%>

</BODY>
</HTML>
```

3 Save the file in the `BegASP` directory as `Filter.asp`.

4 View the page from your browser.

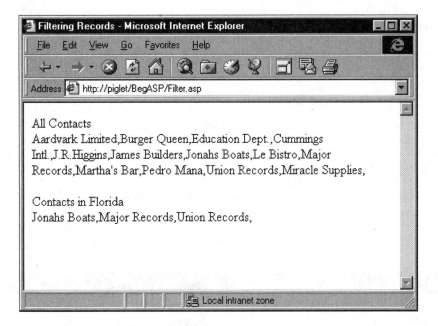

You can see that the filter has restricted the number of records in the recordset.

How It Works

At first we display all records, using the now familiar loop:

```
' now loop through the records
Response.Write "All Contacts<BR>"
While Not objRec.EOF
    Response.Write objRec("name") & ","
    objRec.MoveNext
Wend
```

Then we apply a filter, so we only show those contacts in Florida:

```
' only those contacts in Florida
objRec.Filter = "state = 'FL'"
```

This automatically reduces the number of records in the recordset and places the current record on the new first record. So we can then loop through the records again:

```
' now loop through the records
Response.Write "<P>Contacts in Florida<BR>"
While Not objRec.EOF
    Response.Write objRec("name") & ","
    objRec.MoveNext
Wend
```

The Fields Collection

So far we have looked at using just one field from a recordset. What if you want lots of fields, perhaps to build a table from the recordset? Well you could access each field like this:

```
objRec("Field1Name") & " " & objRec("Field2Name") & . . .
```

but this becomes tedious after a while. Point me at a programmer who wants to write the same code again and again, and I'll get my baseball bat out! We all want an easy life. So, let's introduce the `Fields` collection, which can skim *hours* off your development time (OK, I exaggerate a little, but you get the idea).

Unsurprisingly, the `Fields` collection contains an entry for each field in the current record. This means that you can look through the fields without knowing their names. Aha, now were talking. Let's use this to create a central reusable routine to create an HTML table from a recordset.

Try It Out – The Fields Collection

1 Check that the files `DataStore.inc` and `adovbs.inc` and the `Contact` database are set up, as for the other examples in this chapter.

2 The first thing to do is create the routine. We're going to put this in a separate file, so we can include it just like our other include files. Create a new file, and add the following code to it (don't worry about all the new stuff; we'll look at it after we've seen it working):

```
<%

Function RecToTable (objRec)

    Dim strT              ' table html string
    Dim fldF              ' current field object

    ' build the table header
    strT = "<TABLE BORDER=1>" & _
        "<TR ALIGN=CENTER>"

    ' each field as a table column name
    For Each fldF In objRec.Fields
        strT = strT & "<TD>" & fldF.Name & "</TD>"
    Next
    strT = strT & "</TR>"

    ' now build the rows
    intFields = objRec.Fields.Count - 1
    While Not objRec.EOF
        strT = strT & "<TR ALIGN=CENTER>"
```

```
        ' loop through the fields
        For Each fldF In objRec.Fields
            strT = strT & "<TD>" & fldF.Value & "</TD>"
        Next
        strT = strT & "</TR>"
        objRec.MoveNext
    Wend
    strT = strT & "</TABLE>"

    ' and finally return the table
    RecToTable = strT

End Function

%>
```

3 Save the code in the `BegASP` directory, in a file called `RecToTable.asp`.

4 Close `RecToTable.asp`, and start up a brand new file. Enter the following code:

```
<HTML>

<!-- #INCLUDE FILE="DataStore.inc" -->
<!-- #INCLUDE FILE="adovbs.inc" -->
<!-- #INCLUDE FILE="RecToTable.asp" -->

<HEAD>
<TITLE>ADO Fields Collection</TITLE>
</HEAD>
<BODY>

<%
    Dim objRec          ' recordset object

    ' create the recordset object
    Set objRec = Server.CreateObject ("ADODB.Recordset")

    ' now open it
    objRec.Open "Contact", strConnect, adOpenKeyset, _
        adLockReadOnly, adCmdTable

    ' now pass the recordset to the table function
    Response.Write RecToTable (objRec)

    ' now close and clean up
    objRec.Close
    Set objRec = Nothing
%>

</BODY>
</HTML>
```

5 Save this code in a file called `Fields.asp`.

6 Start up your browser, and view the page `Fields.asp`.

It's amazing, don't you think? Remember that this is actually produced by an include file, so you can include this in any ASP file where you need a table like this. Let's look at how it works.

How It Works

Let's look at `RecToTable.asp` first, since this is the one that does the work.

First we declare our function: the function will take a single argument, namely the recordset from which to build the table. It needs to be a function because we are going to build a string of the HTML tags that make up the table, and then return that string to the calling routine.

```
<%

Function RecToTable (objRec)
```

Next we declare a couple of variables. The first will hold the HTML tags that will make up the table, and the second will hold a `Field` object:

```
        Dim strT          ' table html string
        Dim fldF          ' current field object
```

Now we can really start. First we start building the string of tags for the table. This just starts by defining the table and the table header:

```
' build the table header
strT = "<TABLE BORDER=1>" & _
    "<TR ALIGN=CENTER>"
```

Now we need to build the header line:

```
' each field as a table column name
For Each fldF In objRec.Fields
    strT = strT & "<TD>" & fldF.Name & "</TD>"
Next
```

Remember how we looped through the **Properties** collection? Well, this is the same. We are looping through the **Fields** collection, and using **For Each** will set **fldF** to a **Field** object each time around the loop. The **Name** property of the **Field** just tells us what the field is called. So this code is adding the field names to the string, surrounding each one with the table cell start and end tags, like so:

```
<TD>ContactID</TD><TD>Name</TD>...
```

Once that loop has finished, we can terminate the table header.

```
strT = strT & "</TR>"
```

Now we've finished the header line we can start on the actual data. What we need to do is loop through the **Fields** for each row in the recordset, and this is going to go into the body of the HTML table. We can start looping through the records, using the same **While** loop as we've used before, checking for **EOF**:

```
While Not objRec.EOF
```

We are now in our first record: we need a row in the table, so we add the row tag:

```
strT = strT & "<TR ALIGN=CENTER>"
```

Now we are going to loop through the fields, adding each field as a cell in the table. We use the **Value** property of the **Field**, because this holds the actual field value:

```
' loop through the fields
For Each fldF In objRec.Fields
    strT = strT & "<TD>" & fldF.Value & "</TD>"
Next
```

That's all of the fields for one record, so we add the row terminator tag, and move onto the next record.

```
strT = strT & "</TR>"
objRec.MoveNext
```

And once the **While** loop has ended we terminate the table and return the string-of-tags bag to our calling routine:

```
    Wend
    strT = strT & "</TABLE>"

    ' and finally return the table
    RecToTable = strT

End Function

%>
```

So this is actually quite simple. We just loop through the records, and for each record loop through the fields. Now let's look at the calling routine, **Fields.asp**.

We have the usual include files, but this time we have the new ASP file we've just created. The creation of the recordset is exactly the same as we've seen before:

```
<HTML>

<!-- #INCLUDE FILE="DataStore.inc" -->
<!-- #INCLUDE FILE="adovbs.inc" -->
<!-- #INCLUDE FILE="RecToTable.asp" -->

<HEAD>
<TITLE>ADO Fields Collection</TITLE>
</HEAD>
<BODY>

<%
    Dim objRec          ' recordset object

    ' create the recordset object
    Set objRec = Server.CreateObject ("ADODB.Recordset")

    ' now open it
    objRec.Open "Contact", strConnect, adOpenKeyset, _
        adLockReadOnly, adCmdTable
```

Here's the new bit, where we write out the value that **RecToTable** returns. When we call **RecToTable**, we pass the recordset **objRec** that we've just created and it will convert this into the tags for an HTML table:

```
    ' now pass the recordset to the table function
    Response.Write RecToTable (objRec)
```

That's it. You can include **RecToTable.asp** in any file and use it to create a table.

FYI The sample files (on the Wrox web site) contain an extra file, RecToTable1.asp, which is much the same, but with the added bonus of formatting the values according to their types. So a currency value, for example, is formatted with the currency sign, etc.

Arrays of Rows

Another useful method is **GetRows**, which returns an array of the records and fields in a recordset. **GetRows** will return the number of rows you request, starting from the current row. Its syntax is:

```
varArrayname = objRecordset.GetRows (Rows, Start, Fields)
```

All of the arguments are optional, and if left off will return all rows, starting from the current row. If all rows are returned the record pointer is moved to the end of the recordset and **EOF** is set. If you want to restrict the number of rows you can enter the number in the *Rows* argument (or you can use the constant **adGetRowsRest** to return the rows remaining in the recordset).

Start is a bookmark (or one of the **adBookmark** constants shown earlier), that allows you to specify which record to start on.

Fields is the name, or number, of a field, and if specified only the values for the field are returned. This is quite useful if you want an array of just one field, the ID fields perhaps.

The array that **GetRows** returns is automatically dimensioned for you.

Try It Out – The GetRows Method

1 Check that the files **DataStore.inc** and **adovbs.inc** and the **Contact** database are set up, as for the other examples in this chapter.

2 Start up your editor, and enter the following code:

```
<HTML>

<!-- #INCLUDE FILE="DataStore.inc" -->
<!-- #INCLUDE FILE="adovbs.inc" -->

<HEAD>
<TITLE>ADO GetRows Method</TITLE>
</HEAD>
<BODY>

<%
    Dim objRec          ' recordset object
    Dim avarFields      ' array of fields
    Dim intRow          ' current row
    Dim intCol          ' current column
```

```
    ' create the recordset object
    Set objRec = Server.CreateObject ("ADODB.Recordset")

    ' now open it
    objRec.Open "Contact", strConnect, adOpenKeyset, _
        adLockReadOnly, adCmdTable

    ' get the data
    avarFields = objRec.GetRows

    ' loop through the array
    For intRow = 0 To UBound(avarFields, 2)
        For intCol = 0 To UBound(avarFields, 1)
            Response.Write avarFields(intCol, intRow) & ", "
        Next
        Response.Write "<BR>"
    Next

    ' now close and clean up
    objRec.Close
    Set objRec = Nothing
%>

</BODY>
</HTML>
```

3 Save the code in the **BegASP** directory, as **GetRows.asp**.

4 View the page from your browser:

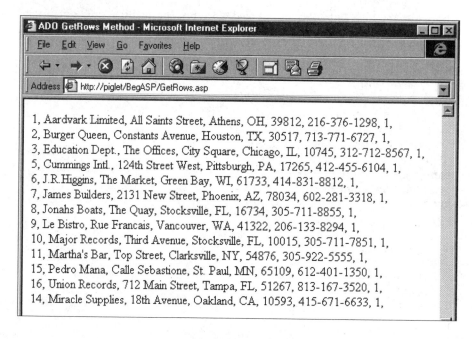

As you can see this just displays every field in every row.

How It Works

We'll skip past the header code; you're pretty familiar with that by now. We declare four variables next; the new ones here are one that will hold the array of data, and two for the loop counters.

```
<%
    Dim objRec          ' recordset object
    Dim avarFields      ' array of fields
    Dim intRow          ' current row
    Dim intCol          ' current column
```

The recordset is created as before:

```
    ' create the recordset object
    Set objRec = Server.CreateObject ("ADODB.Recordset")

    ' now open it
    objRec.Open "Contact", strConnect, adOpenKeyset, _
        adLockReadOnly, adCmdTable
```

And now we call the **GetRows** method. We're not passing in any arguments, so this will get *all* records for us:

```
    ' get the data
    avarFields = objRec.GetRows
```

And now the data is contained in the array, we can loop through both dimensions, printing out the values. We use **UBound** to find out how many elements there are in the array:

```
    ' loop through the array
    For intRow = 0 To UBound(avarFields, 2)
        For intCol = 0 To UBound(avarFields, 1)
            Response.Write avarFields(intCol, intRow) & ", "
        Next
        Response.Write "<BR>"
    Next
```

You might wonder why this wasn't used in **RecToTable** to create the HTML table, and there are two reasons. The first is that we wanted a table header with the names of the fields—**GetRows** just returns the data. The second is that the array takes up memory—since we already have the fields and values in the recordset, what's the point of copying them all to an array and then copying them out to the table? So in the previous example, we just created the table straight from the recordset.

When are the best occasions to use the **GetRows** method? Well, it's probably not a good idea to use it for large recordsets, but for small ones, or even small sets of data from a large recordset, it's fine.

The Command Object

The **Command** object is used for running processes against a data store. These can be commands that return recordsets, or they could be commands that don't return any values (for example, when you are inserting data). The **Command** object (let's call it **objCommand**) is created the same way as the **Connection** and **Recordset** objects:

```
Set objCommand = Server.CreateObject ("ADODB.Command")
```

To run a command you use this syntax:

```
objCommand.Execute RecordsAffected, Parameters, Options
```

All three arguments are optional and can be omitted. Let's have a look at them.

This is the first instance of an ADO object that returns something back to you in one of the parameters. *RecordsAffected* is for action queries (those that insert or update data) and will return the number of records that were affected by the query.

Parameters hold an array of parameters to be passed to the command. This allows you to write generic commands and pass in only the information that changes. We'll be looking at this in more detail later in the chapter, when we look at stored procedures and queries.

Options is the same as the *Options* argument in the **Recordset.Open** method, specifying the type of command being run.

One thing you might have noticed is that there's nothing in the **Execute** method that specifies the command to run. Well spotted. For that you need the **CommandText** property:

```
objCommand.CommandText = "Contact"
objCommand.Execute , , adCmdTable
```

Here we set the **CommandText** to the table, **Contact**, and then **Execute** the command. Notice that the first two arguments have been omitted (you still need the commas even if leaving out the arguments), but that we do specify the **CommandType**. Instead of the two lines above, we could have done this by using the **CommandType** property, like this:

```
objCommand.CommandText = "Contact"
objCommand.CommandType = adCmdTable
objCommand.Execute
```

There's also been no mention of the connection: so how does the command know which data store to use? At this stage it doesn't, so you need to fill in the **ActiveConnection** property as well. This can be a **Connection** object or a connection string:

```
objCommand.ActiveConnection = strConnect
objCommand.CommandText = "Contact"
objCommand.CommandType = adCmdTable
objCommand.Execute
```

The command can also return a recordset, so the four lines above could be:

```
objCommand.ActiveConnection = strConnect
objCommand.CommandText = "Contact"
objCommand.CommandType = adCmdTable
Set objRec = objCommand.Execute
```

This makes far more sense, given that the code is just returning the **Contact** table.

Try It Out – The Command Object

1 Check that the files **DataStore.inc** and **adovbs.inc** and the **Contact** database are set up, as for the other examples in this chapter.

2 In your editor, create a new file, and enter the following code:

```
<HTML>

<!-- #INCLUDE FILE="DataStore.inc" -->
<!-- #INCLUDE FILE="adovbs.inc" -->

<HEAD>
<TITLE>ADO Command Object</TITLE>
</HEAD>
<BODY>

<%
    Dim objRec              ' recordset object
    Dim objCommand          ' command object

    ' create the objects
    Set objCommand = Server.CreateObject ("ADODB.Command")
    Set objRec = Server.CreateObject ("ADODB.Recordset")

    ' fill in the command properties
    objCommand.ActiveConnection = strConnect
    objCommand.CommandText = "Contact"
    objCommand.CommandType = adCmdTable

    ' now open it
    Set objRec = objCommand.Execute

    ' now loop through the records
    While Not objRec.EOF
        Response.Write objRec("name") & ", "
        objRec.MoveNext
    Wend
```

```
        ' now close and clean up
        objRec.Close
        Set objRec = Nothing
%>


</BODY>
</HTML>
```

3 Save the file in your **BegASP** directory, as **Command.asp**, and view the page in your browser:

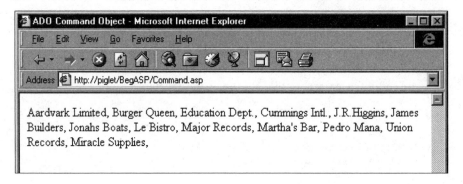

As you can see, this just performs the same task as the recordset **Open** method. In fact you can mix the two together, because the *Source* argument of the **Open** method can be a **Command** object:

```
objCommand.ActiveConnection = strConnect
objCommand.CommandText = "Contact"
objCommand.CommandType = adCmdTable
objRec.Open objCommand
```

This sort of flexibility between the objects is one of the strengths of the new object model. You're not dependent upon creating objects in a set order, or even using specific objects for specific tasks. It's a mix'n'match world. But is it useful? Yes it is, because it saves you having to create different objects. If you want to run two commands, one an action query that doesn't return any records and one that returns a recordset, you can use the same object—there's no need to create two objects just because you want to perform two tasks.

Let's give an action command a go...

Try It Out - An Action Command

1 Check that the files **DataStore.inc** and **adovbs.inc** and the **Contact** database are set up, as for the other examples in this chapter.

2 Open your editor, create a new file and add the following code:

```
<HTML>

<!-- #INCLUDE FILE="DataStore.inc" -->
<!-- #INCLUDE FILE="adovbs.inc" -->

<HEAD>
<TITLE>ADO Command Object - Action Query</TITLE>
</HEAD>
<BODY>

<%
    Dim objCommand          ' command object
    Dim intRecords          ' number of records affected

    ' create the object
    Set objCommand = Server.CreateObject ("ADODB.Command")

    ' fill in the command properties
    objCommand.ActiveConnection = strConnect
    objCommand.CommandType = adCmdText

    ' now run it
    objCommand.CommandText = "UPDATE Contact SET Name = Name"
    objCommand.Execute intRecords
    Response.Write "'UPDATE Contact SET Name = Name' updated " & _
                intRecords & " records<P>"

    ' and again with a different command
    objCommand.CommandText = "UPDATE Contact SET Name = Name " & _
                            " WHERE state = 'CA'"
    objCommand.Execute intRecords
    Response.Write "'UPDATE Contact SET Name = Name " & _
                "<BR>WHERE state = 'CA' updated " & _
                intRecords & " records<P>"

    ' finally clean up
    Set objCommand = Nothing
%>

</BODY>
</HTML>
```

459

3 Save the file as `Action.asp`; start up your browser and view the page:

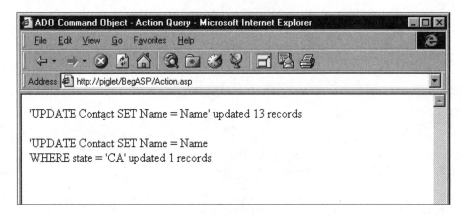

As you can see the first update query updated every record in the table, which is correct since there was no restriction on the query. The second query had a **WHERE** clause, so it only update one record—again correct.

How It Works

We have the usual header to start with. Next come the variable declarations. There's one for the command object, and one for the number of records that were affected by the command:

```
Dim objCommand        ' command object
Dim intRecords        ' number of records affected
```

Then we create the **Command** object and set the connection and type properties:

```
' create the object
Set objCommand = Server.CreateObject ("ADODB.Command")

' fill in the command properties
objCommand.ActiveConnection = strConnect
objCommand.CommandType = adCmdText
```

And now we can run the command:

```
' now run it
objCommand.CommandText = "UPDATE Contact SET Name = Name"
objCommand.Execute intRecords
Response.Write "'UPDATE Contact SET Name = Name' updated " & _
                intRecords & " records<P>"
```

This just runs a SQL **UPDATE** statement, which has no real effect because it sets the value of a field to the value it's already got. However, it is updating records, and when we **Execute** the command the number of records will be passed back to us in `intRecords`. We then use `Response.Write` to display the number of records we changed.

The second time, we add a **WHERE** clause to the SQL statement, so it will only affect one record. We use the same **Execute** and then display the number of records changed:

```
' and again with a different command
objCommand.CommandText = "UPDATE Contact SET Name = Name " & _
                            " WHERE state = 'CA'"
objCommand.Execute intRecords
Response.Write "'UPDATE Contact SET Name = Name " & _
                "<BR>WHERE state = 'CA' updated " & _
                intRecords & " records<P>"
```

So this gives you a good way to double check your actions. For example, if you run a SQL command that inserts a single record, and **intRecords** comes back as 0, you can probably guess that something has gone wrong.

The Connection Object (Reprise)

Yes, the **Connection** object lives again. Just when you thought you'd seen the end of it, back it comes like a bounced check. Well we shouldn't think like that, because there's one aspect of the **Connection** object that we used in the previous chapter but didn't explain. That's right, it's the **Execute** method. We deliberately left it until now, because by now you have a good idea of what a recordset is and how it can be used, and it makes it much easier to explain certain bits of the **Execute** method.

The full syntax for the **Execute** method is:

*objConnection.***Execute** *CommandText, RecordsAffected, Options*

or, if the command returns records:

Set *objRecordset = objConnection.***Execute** *CommandText, RecordsAffected, Options*

So in fact, we don't really need to revisit this, as this works in exactly the same way as the **Execute** method of the **Command** object. We reintroduced it here to show that flexibility again—the mix'n'match objects.

> *Although these work the same way, there is in fact a difference. The **Command** object must be used if SQL statements are to be prepared or if parameters are to be used. A **prepared** SQL statement is where you pass in the actual SQL statement, and it is compiled into a form ready to run—this is useful if the SQL is to be run several times. Also, command objects are not always supported by all data sources, so when they aren't, SQL statements can be executed (almost) as efficiently with **objConnection.Execute**.*

Using Queries or Stored Procedures

You've seen some examples of recordsets that were created from tables or from a SQL query, and you've seen that one of those SQL queries is rather unwieldy. Wouldn't it be nice if you could name these queries and just use that name in your ASP code? Well, yes it would, and that's exactly what **stored procedures** and **queries** are—ready to run SQL statements, that the SQL database has made ready for execution. There's a few good reasons to use stored procedures:

 They make your code more readable

They are quicker, since they are stored in a form which is faster to run than straight SQL

They can be reused by many ASP pages

> **FYI**
>
> Although we are concentrating on Access here, we've mentioned stored procedures because they are very similar in nature to Access queries. If you are not familier with SQL Server then don't worry about not understanding the odd line or two—we've covered both for completeness.

The use of queries in ASP is much the same as the samples you've already seen. For example, to run a **Command** using a stored procedure you could do this:

```
objCommand.ActiveConnection = strConnect
objCommand.CommandText = "usp_NameAndState"
objCommand.CommandType = adCmdStoredProc

Set objRec = objCommand.Execute
```

Notice that the **CommandType** has changed to reflect the fact that we are now using a stored procedure rather than a table; other than that, the command structure is just the same as we've seen previously.

For an Access query, the method is exactly the same. You just use the name of an existing Access query. In fact, at this level there is no difference between an Access query and a SQL Server stored procedure.

Parameters

You might think that using stored procedures gives you less flexibility because you can't customize them as easily, but this is where the **Parameters** collection comes in. Parameters allow you to pass values into and out of stored procedures, in just the same way you pass parameters to functions. So they are a way of writing generic queries, but with the added bonus of having user-supplied information.

In Access you can turn a standard query into a parameter-based query by supplying a value in the Criteria field for the column you wish the parameter to apply to:

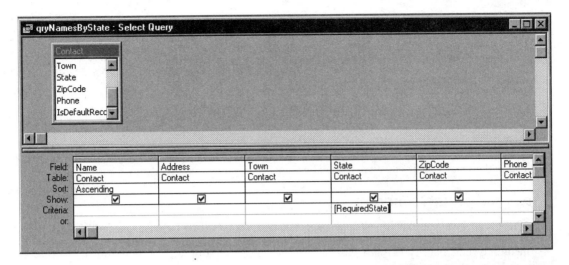

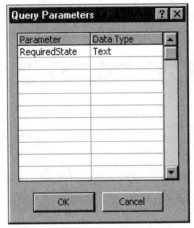

You can also add this to the Parameters for the query (select **Parameters** from the **Query** menu), which allows you to add the parameter name and specify the type:

This isn't required but it does allow Access to perform the correct conversion of types where necessary.

For a SQL Server stored procedure, you create the procedure in the normal way, using SQL statements, but add the parameters to the declaration. For example, the **usp_NamesByState** stored procedure in the **Samples** database is declared like this:

```
CREATE PROCEDURE usp_NamesByState
    @State char(2)
AS
    SELECT    Name, Address, Town, State, ZipCode, Phone
    FROM      Contact
    WHERE     State = @State
    ORDER BY Name
```

Here the parameter is **@State** (all SQL Server parameters are preceded by the **@** sign) and is a character string or length 2.

This stored procedure file can be downloaded from the sample site—it's in the `.contact.sql` *file.*

If you try to run a query that expects parameters without passing any in you'll get this type of message (this one is from an Access query):

Microsoft OLE DB Provider for ODBC Drivers error '80040e10'
[Microsoft][ODBC Microsoft Access 97 Driver] Too few parameters. Expected 1.
/wrox/1347 Beg ASP/Chapter 14 - Expanding Data Access/Code/AccQueryParms.asp, line 20

This quite clearly tells you that it is expecting a parameter, and you didn't supply one.

The Parameters Collection

So how do you pass parameters into a query that expects them? It's simple: you use the `Parameters` collection. This contains a list of all parameters that you wish to pass into a query, including their data types, and whether they are used to supply data or return it.

Here's a couple of examples. First, we'll create one that uses an Access query, and then we'll create on that uses a SQL server query.

Try It Out – The Parameters Collection and Access

1 Check that the files `DataStore.inc` and `adovbs.inc` and the `Contact` database are set up, as for the other examples in this chapter.

2 In your editor, create a new file and add the following code:

```
<HTML>

<!-- #INCLUDE FILE="DataStore.inc" -->
<!-- #INCLUDE FILE="adovbs.inc" -->

<HEAD>
<TITLE>Access Parameter Query</TITLE>
</HEAD>
<BODY>

<%
    Dim objRec              ' recordset object
    Dim objCommand          ' command object
    Dim objParameter        ' parameter object

    ' create the objects
    Set objCommand = Server.CreateObject ("ADODB.Command")
    Set objRec = Server.CreateObject ("ADODB.Recordset")
```

```
    ' fill in the command properties
    objCommand.ActiveConnection = strConnect
    objCommand.CommandText = "qryNamesByState"
    objCommand.CommandType = adCmdStoredProc

    ' now the parameters
    Set objParameter = objCommand.CreateParameter ("RequiredState",
adChar, _
            adParamInput, 2)
    objCommand.Parameters.Append objParameter

    objCommand.Parameters("RequiredState") = "FL"

    ' now open it
    Set objRec = objCommand.Execute

    ' now loop through the records
    While Not objRec.EOF
        Response.Write    objRec("Name") & ", " & _
                objRec("Address") & ", " & _
                objRec("State") & ", " & _
                objRec("ZipCode") & ", "& _
                objRec("Phone") & "<BR>"
        objRec.MoveNext
    Wend

    ' now close and clean up
    objRec.Close
    Set objRec = Nothing
    Set objCommand = Nothing
    Set objParameter = Nothing
%>

</BODY>
</HTML>
```

3 Save the code in your **BegASP** directory, in a file called **AccQueryParms.asp**.

4 View the page from your browser:

Notice that this only shows those contacts in Florida. We'll explain the structure of the code in a moment. First, we'll try another one, this time using SQL Server.

Try It Out – The Parameters Collection and SQL Server

1 In your editor, create a new file and add the following code:

```
<HTML>

<!-- #INCLUDE FILE="DataStore.inc" -->
<!-- #INCLUDE FILE="adovbs.inc" -->

<HEAD>
<TITLE> ADO Parameters Collection</TITLE>
</HEAD>
<BODY>

<%
    Dim objRec              ' recordset object
    Dim objCommand          ' command object
    Dim objParameter        ' parameter object

    ' create the objects
    Set objCommand = Server.CreateObject ("ADODB.Command")
    Set objRec = Server.CreateObject ("ADODB.Recordset")

    ' fill in the command properties
    objCommand.ActiveConnection = strConnect
    objCommand.CommandText = "usp_NamesByState"
    objCommand.CommandType = adCmdStoredProc

    ' now the parameters
    Set objParameter = objCommand.CreateParameter ("@State", adChar, _
                            adParamInput, 2)
    objCommand.Parameters.Append objParameter

    objCommand.Parameters("@State") = "FL"

    ' now open it
    Set objRec = objCommand.Execute

    ' now loop through the records
    While Not objRec.EOF
        Response.Write objRec("name") & ", "
        objRec.MoveNext
    Wend

    ' now close and clean up
    objRec.Close
```

```
    Set objRec = Nothing
    Set objCommand = Nothing
    Set objParameter = Nothing
%>


</BODY>
</HTML>
```

2 Save the code in the **BegASP** directory, with the name **StoredProcParms.asp**.

3 View the page from your browser:

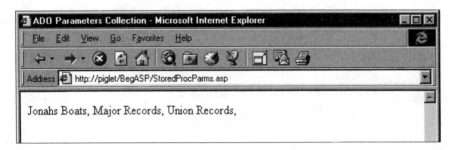

You might like to try changing the parameter value from **FL** to **CA**, just to prove that it returns a different set of records.

How It Works

The code in this explanation corresponds to the SQL Server example. The structure of the Access example works in much the same way.

There's no change to the header, so we'll just skip that, and jump straight into the code. Firstly we have the variables to store the object:

```
Dim objRec              ' recordset object
Dim objCommand          ' command object
Dim objParameter        ' parameter object
```

Then we create our **Command** and **Recordset** objects, and set the properties for the command:

```
' create the objects
Set objCommand = Server.CreateObject ("ADODB.Command")
Set objRec = Server.CreateObject ("ADODB.Recordset")

' fill in the command properties
objCommand.ActiveConnection = strConnect
objCommand.CommandText = "usp_NamesByState"
objCommand.CommandType = adCmdStoredProc
```

And now we create the parameter. We'll look at the syntax of this in more detail in a moment.

```
' now the parameters
Set objParameter = objCommand.CreateParameter ("@State", adChar, _
                         adParamInput, 2)
```

Once the parameter is created we can **Append** it to the **Parameters** collection:

```
objCommand.Parameters.Append objParameter
```

And then we can set the actual value of the parameter:

```
objCommand.Parameters("@State") = "FL"
```

We then open the recordset as normal and display the records:

```
' now open it
Set objRec = objCommand.Execute

' now loop through the records
While Not objRec.EOF
    Response.Write objRec("name") & ", "
    objRec.MoveNext
Wend
```

Finally, we can clean up:

```
' now close and clean up
objRec.Close
Set objRec = Nothing
Set objCommand = Nothing
Set objParameter = Nothing
```

Creating Parameters

Let's look at that **CreateParameter** method in more detail. It can take five arguments:

- ▶ *Name*, which is the name of the parameter, as defined in the query or stored procedure.
- ▶ *Type*, to define the data type of the parameter. A full list of types is contained in the ADO constants file, **adovbs.inc**.
- ▶ *Direction*, to specify whether we are sending data to the procedure, getting data from the procedure, or both.
- ▶ *Size*, to specify the maximum length of the parameter value. This is most useful for text parameters.
- ▶ *Value*, to specify the value of the parameter.

So the syntax of the method call looks like this:

```
Set obj = objCommand.CreateParameter(Name, Type, Direction, Size, Value)
```

Since these arguments are optional, you can also choose to create the parameter and then set the properties:

```
Set objParameter = objCommand.CreateParameter
objParameter.Name = "@state"
objParameter.Type = adChar
objParameter.Size = 2
objParameter.Direction = adInput
objParameter.Value = 100
```

You can also omit the whole step of creating the parameter on it's own by this syntax:

```
objCommand.Parameters.Append objCommand.CreateParameter ("@state", _
                                    adChar, adInput, 2, "FL")
```

Output Parameters

SQL Server stored procedures have the ability to return values as well as performing actions. For example, using the `Contact` database, suppose you want a count of all contacts that live in a particular state. You could easily do this with the following SQL code:

```
CREATE PROCEDURE usp_ContactInState
    @State  varchar(2)
AS
SELECT COUNT(*)
FROM    Contact
WHERE   state=@State
```

and this would return a recordset containing just one column and one row, which would be the value you are after. You could call this by creating a procedure and passing in the state that you are interested in. But what if you didn't want the bother of creating a recordset and getting the value? You could modify the procedure as follows:

```
CREATE PROCEDURE usp_ContactInState
    @State  varchar(2),
    @Number int OUTPUT
AS
SELECT @Number = COUNT(*)
FROM    Contact
WHERE   state=@State
```

The second parameter here is an `OUTPUT` parameter, which means we can return a value in it. Our ASP code to call this could be like this:

```
Dim intNumber

. . . ' code to create command object

objCommand.Parameters.Append objCommand.CreateParameter ("@State", _
                                    adVarChar, adParamInput, 2, "FL")
objCommand.Parameters.Append objCommand.CreateParameter ("@Number", _
                                    adInteger, adParamOutput)
```

469

```
objCommand.Execute

intNumber = objCommand.Parameters("@Number")
```

Here the second parameter is given a *Direction* argument of `adParamOutput`, to match the `OUTPUT` parameter of the stored procedure. You can see we're not giving it a value like we do with the input parameter. After the command has been executed the `@Number` parameter in the parameters collection will hold the value returned from the stored procedure.

Return Values

Stored procedures can have a return value as well as output parameters, and this value needs to be handled in a similar way. Return values are always the *first-named* parameter (i.e. the zero parameter—parameter lists are zero-based) in the parameters collection, and have a different `Direction`:

```
objCommand.CreateParameter("Return", adVarChar, adParamReturnValue, 8)
```

This shows a return value that is a character string of eight characters. You must append a return value parameter first, before you append any other parameters. Once the command has run you can access this parameter like any other:

```
strReturn = objCommand.Parameters("Return")
```

or

```
strReturn = objCommand.Parameters(0)
```

Asking for the Parameters

If you don't want to go to the bother of adding parameters for a parameterized query, you can use the `Refresh` method to tell ADO to query the data provider. For example:

```
objCommand.Parameters.Refresh
```

ADO then contacts the data provider and fills in the parameters collection for you. You can then just add the values and execute the command. For example:

```
objCommand.Parameters.Refresh

objCommand.Parameters ("param1").Value = "param1 value"
```

This allows you to concentrate on the actual code rather than getting bogged down by the details of the parameters. This helps if you change the stored procedure as you'll need to do less changes to your ASP code. It's also extremely useful if you are having problems getting your types and sizes correct. If you find you are getting a lot of errors in your parameters, you can just change your code to do a refresh and then print out the types and values.

One thing to remember when using `Refresh` is that it makes a trip to the data store to extract the parameter information, which obviously introduces a delay. You may consider it worthwhile appending the parameters manually if you think speed is a problem.

Modifying Data

Having covered a myriad of ways of getting data out of data stores, the last topic to look at is how to change data and to add new data. There are two major ways of doing this, one of which you've already covered—using parameter queries. If you can't see how this could be done, have a look at the following Access query:

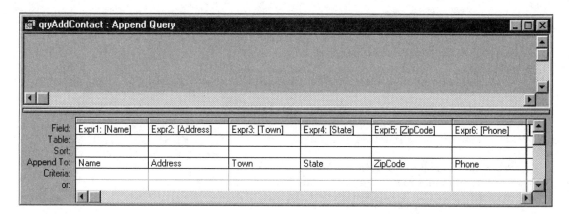

This is an **Append** query that will add a record into the **Contact** table. All of the values to **Append** are supplied as parameters. The following shows a SQL Server stored procedure to do the same thing:

```
CREATE PROCEDURE usp_AddContact
    @Name      varchar(50),
    @Address   varchar(255),
    @Town      varchar(50),
    @State     char(2),
    @ZipCode   varchar(25),
    @Phone     varchar(25)
AS
    INSERT INTO Contact (Name, Address, Town, State, ZipCode, Phone)
    VALUES (@Name, @Address, @Town, @State, @ZipCode, @Phone)
```

This will add a new entry into the **Contact** table using the values supplied in the stored procedures parameters. You can simply add new records like this:

```
objCommand.CommandText = "qryAddContact"
objCommand.ActiveConnection = strConnect
objCommand.CommandType = adCmdStoredProc

Set objParameter = objCommand.CreateParameter ("Name", adChar, _
                              adParamInput, 255, "Janine Lloyd")
objCommand.Parameters.Append objParameter

Set objParameter = objCommand.CreateParameter ("Address", adChar, _
                              adParamInput, 255, "24 Eastcote Road")
objCommand.Parameters.Append objParameter
```

471

```
    Set objParameter = objCommand.CreateParameter ("Town", adChar, _
                                   adParamInput, 255, "Palm Springs")
    objCommand.Parameters.Append objParameter

    Set objParameter = objCommand.CreateParameter ("State", adChar, _
                                   adParamInput, 255, "CA")
    objCommand.Parameters.Append objParameter

    Set objParameter = objCommand.CreateParameter ("ZipCode", adChar, _
                                   adParamInput, 255, "13245")
    objCommand.Parameters.Append objParameter

    Set objParameter = objCommand.CreateParameter ("Phone", adChar, _
                                   adParamInput, 255, "132 546 5766")
    objCommand.Parameters.Append objParameter

    objCommand.Execute intRecords

    If intRecords = 1 Then
        Response.Write "Record added sucessfully"
    End If
```

This is pretty simple. It uses commands you're already familiar with, and it's also extremely practical. If all you are doing is adding records then this is the best method to use, since you don't have the overhead of creating a recordset. It's also good for updating data by using an **Update** query (or **UPDATE** statements in a SQL Server stored procedure).

Updating Data Using a Recordset

Using action queries might be a good way of inserting and updating records if that's all you want to do, but what if you have a recordset and you want to change data? It seems silly to run an **Action** query when you've already got the data. So this is where the **AddNew** and **Update** statements come in.

Try It Out – Adding New Records

1 Check that the files **DataStore.inc** and **adovbs.inc** and the **Contact** database are set up, as for the other examples in this chapter.

2 In your editor, create a new file and add the following code:

```
<HTML>

<!-- #INCLUDE FILE="DataStore.inc" -->
<!-- #INCLUDE FILE="adovbs.inc" -->

<HEAD>
<TITLE>Adding new records</TITLE>
```

```
</HEAD>
<BODY>

<%
    Dim objRec          ' recordset object

    ' create the recordset object
    Set objRec = Server.CreateObject ("ADODB.Recordset")

    ' now open it
    objRec.Open "Contact", strConnect, adOpenStatic, _
        adLockOptimistic, adCmdTable

    ' add the new records
    objRec.AddNew
    objRec("Name") = "New Name"
    objRec("Address") = " 23 Stanington Drive "
    objRec.Update

    ' now find it, just to prove it is there
    objRec.Find "Name = 'New Name'"
    If objRec.EOF Then
        Response.Write "Record not found"
    Else
        Response.Write "Sucessfully added 'New Name'<BR>"
        Response.Write "Address is '" & objRec("Address") & "'"
    End If

    ' now close and clean up
    objRec.Close
    Set objRec = Nothing
%>

</BODY>
</HTML>
```

Note that this connects to the Access database. To connect it to SQL Server just amend the **DataStore.inc** as we described at the start of the chapter.

3 Save the file in your **BegASP** directory, with the name **AddNew.asp**.

4 Open your browser and view the page:

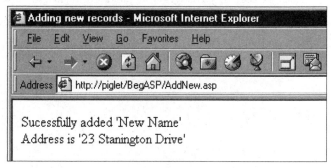

How It Works

As usual we start with a variable for the **Recordset** object, and then create the object:

```
Dim objRec          ' recordset object

' create the recordset object
Set objRec = Server.CreateObject ("ADODB.Recordset")
```

Then we open the recordset. Notice that this is a static recordset with optimistic locking. All our other recordsets have been read-only, but we can't have that if we are updating the data:

```
' now open it
objRec.Open "Contact", strConnect, adOpenStatic, _
    adLockOptimistic, adCmdTable
```

Now we can add the data. The **AddNew** method creates a new, empty record for us to fill, so we set the fields to their required values:

```
' add the new records
objRec.AddNew
objRec("Name") = "New Name"
objRec("Address") = " 23 Stanington Drive "
```

And then we call the **Update** method, which will write the data back to the data source.

```
objRec.Update
```

And finally we just have a look for the data we've just added, just to prove it really is there:

```
' now find it, just to prove it is there
objRec.Find "Name = 'New Name'"
If objRec.EOF Then
    Response.Write "Record not found"
Else
    Response.Write "Sucessfully added 'New Name'<BR>"
    Response.Write "Address is '" & objRec("Address") & "'"
End If
```

Updating Existing Data

This is almost exactly the same procedure as adding new records, except that you don't issue an **AddNew** call. Any changes you make apply to the current record:

```
objRec("Field").Value = "New_Value"
objRec.Update
```

This sets the new value of **Field** to *New_Value*.

Canceling mistakes

If you have made some changes to a record, and then realize that you don't want to keep these changes, you can simply call the `CancelUpdate` method. This works for both new records and changes to existing records, as long as `Update` has not been called:

```
objRec.AddNew
objRec("Field").Value = "New_Value"
objRec.CancelUpdate
```

Following these lines of code, the recordset will be in the state it was before you issued the `AddNew`.

Batch Updates

The last method of updating records is in **batch update** mode. This allows you to do multiple changes to the recordset, and then send all of those changes back to the data store in one go. For batch update mode you need to set the `LockType` property to be `adLockBatchOptimistic`. For example:

```
objRec.Open "Contact", strConnect, adOpenStatic, _
                              adLockBatchOptimistic, asCmdTable
```

You can then make several changes and then call the `UpdateBatch` method, optionally passing a single argument, which can be one of:

▶ `adAffectCurrent`, for the update to only write changes for the current record.

▶ `adAffectGroup` for the update to only write records the match the current `Filter` property.

▶ `adAffectAll` for the update to write all pending changes. This is the default value.

This would enable you do have some code like this:

```
objRec.Open "Contact", strConnect, adOpenStatic, _
                              adLockBatchOptimistic, asCmdTable

objRec("Field").Value = "New_Value"
objRec.MoveNext
objRec("Field").Value = "New_Value"
objRec.UpdateBatch adAffectAll
```

There's also a get-out clause, just in case you've made a mistake or don't need the changes:

```
objRec.CancelBatch adAffectAll
```

Like `Update`, the parameter is optional and can be one of the values described.

Deleting Records

Finally, we come to **deleting** records. You probably won't be surprised to learn that there is a `Delete` method for the recordset:

```
objRec.Delete
```

which deletes the current record. You can also use an argument of **adAffectCurrent** to delete only the current record, or **adAffectGroup** to delete all records that satisfy the current **Filter**.

The record is deleted immediately unless you are in batch update mode, in which case the `Delete` requests remain pending until you call the **UpdateBatch** method. If you've deleted records, you can filter the recordset using **adFilterPendingRecords** to show only the records that have been deleted.

Combined Example

This example uses several techniques introduced during the book to show how you can customize data access so that the user has a great deal of control over what is seen. All of the examples we have seen have shown recordsets that were hard coded—the user had no control over them. This isn't really a great technique for interactive web sites, so let's look at how we can cure this problem.

We are still going to use the Contact table in the Access database, but instead of showing all of the fields the user is going to select which ones they would like to see. We'll build up a SQL **SELECT** statement and create a table of their records.

Try It Out - A Customized Recordset

1 Check that the files **DataStore.inc** and **adovbs.inc** and the **Contact** database are set up, as for the other examples in this chapter. Ensure that the include file, **RecToTable.asp**, is also contained in your **BegASP** directory (we created this file earlier in the chapter).

2 In your editor, create a new file and add the following code:

```
<HTML>

<!-- #INCLUDE FILE="adovbs.inc" -->
<!-- #INCLUDE FILE="DataStore.inc" -->
<!-- #INCLUDE FILE="RecToTable.asp" -->

<HEAD>
<TITLE>Find Contacts</TITLE>
</HEAD>
<BODY>
```

```
<%
    Dim strSQL          ' SQL String
    Dim objRec          ' Recordset object
    Dim objField        ' Field object
    Dim intCount        ' number of fields selected
    Dim vbQuote         ' quote character
    Dim vbCR            ' carriage return


    ' set the constants
    vbQuote = Chr(34)
    vbCR = Chr(13)


    ' check whether we have selected a state or not
    If Request.Form("Field").Count > 0 Then

        ' we have a state, therefore show contacts for selected state

        ' find out which fields are to be selected
        strSQL = ""
        For intCount = 1 to Request.Form("Field").Count
            strSQL = strSQL & Request.Form("Field")(intCount) & ", "
        Next

        ' strip off the trailing comma and space added in the loop
        strSQL = Left(strSQL, Len(strSQL) - 2)

        strSQL = "SELECT " & strSQL & " FROM Contact"

        ' only add a where clause if they requested a state
        If Request.Form("State") <> "" Then
            strSQL = strSQL & " WHERE State = '" & Request.Form("State")
& "'"
        End If

        ' create the recordset
        Set objRec = Server.CreateObject ("ADODB.Recordset")

        objRec.Open strSQL, strConnect, adOpenForwardOnly, _
                adLockReadOnly, adCmdText

        ' write a table of the recordset
        Response.Write RecToTable (objRec)

        ' clean up
        objRec.Close
        Set objRec = Nothing
%>

<%
    Else
%>
```

```
        <FORM NAME=ContactInfo ACTION="ContactsInState.asp"
METHOD="POST">
        <H2>Find Contacts by State</H2>
        Enter the State to find:
        <INPUT TYPE=TEXT NAME="State">
        <P>
        Please select which fields you would like:<P>
<%

        ' create a recordset on the Contacts
        Set objRec = Server.CreateObject ("ADODB.Recordset")

        objRec.Open "Contact", strConnect, adOpenForwardOnly, _
            adLockReadOnly, adCmdTable

        ' create a checkbox in the form for each field in the recordset
        For Each objField in objRec.Fields
            Response.Write "<INPUT TYPE=CHECKBOX NAME=" & _
                vbQuot & "Field" & vbQuot & _
                " VALUE=" & _
                vbQuot & objField.Name & vbQuot & _
                ">" & objField.Name & "<BR>" & vbCR
        Next

        ' clean up
        objRec.Close
        Set objRec = Nothing
%>


        <INPUT TYPE=SUBMIT VALUE="Find">
        <INPUT TYPE=RESET VALUE="Clear">
        </FORM>

<%
    End If
%>

</BODY>
</HTML>
```

3 Save this in your **BegASP** directory, with the name **ContactsInState.asp**.

4 Now call up this page in your browser.

This shows the first part of the form. You can see that there is a text box to allow the user to select a state, and each field in the `Contact` table has a check box, to allow you to select whether you want this field to be shown.

5 Select a state (FL is in the `Contact` table, or you can leave it blank for all states).

6 Select the check boxes next to the fields you wish to see, and click the Find button.

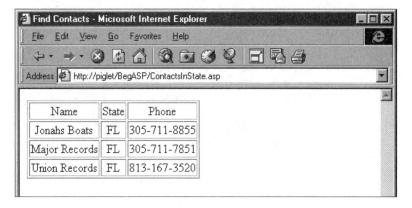

And there we have it. I only selected three fields, and it's shown them. Pretty cool eh? And pretty simple too.

How It Works

The ASP code in this example is in two parts. The first part creates the list of fields to select, and the second looks at those fields and produces the table. We've used a single ASP file that has a big **If** statement in it, checking which part we are in. So the outline of what we are doing is this:

```
Check the Form to see if any checkboxes are selected
If no checkboxes are selected then
        Create the check boxes
        Allow user to Submit request
Else
        Check which checkboxes were selected
        Build a SQL query string
        Create a recordset
        Display the fields
End If
```

How do you know if any checkboxes are selected? It's simple. They will be part of a **Form** object, and if they all have the same name, then the **Count** property of the **Form** object will contain the number selected:

```
If Request.Form("Field").Count > 0 Then
```

So we can use this statement to switch between our two modes of operation. Let's first look at what happens if no checkboxes are selected, where we create the check boxes.

The first thing we do is create the recordset—it's just a normal recordset based upon the **Contact** table:

```
' create a recordset on the Contacts
Set objRec = Server.CreateObject ("ADODB.Recordset")

objRec.Open "Contact", strConnect, adOpenForwardOnly, _
    adLockReadOnly, adCmdTable
```

Now we can loop through the **Fields** collection—remember this contains a list of all fields in the recordset:

```
' create a checkbox in the form for each field in the recordset
For Each objField in objRec.Fields
    Response.Write "<INPUT TYPE=CHECKBOX NAME=" & _
        vbQuot & "Field" & vbQuot & _
        " VALUE=" & _
        vbQuot & objField.Name & vbQuot & _
        ">" & objField.Name & "<BR>" & vbCR
Next
```

In here you'll find the HTML code for creating a checkbox:

```
<INPUT TYPE=CHECKBOX NAME="CheckBoxName"
VALUE="CheckBoxValue">DisplayText
```

Since we want to process these fields as one, we name all of them the same—**Field**. The *CheckBoxValue* and *DisplayText* are both specified as the name of the field, since we are going to use the **Form** object later to extract these. This will give us a set of checkboxes like this:

```
<INPUT TYPE=CHECKBOX NAME=Field VALUE=Name>Name<BR>
<INPUT TYPE=CHECKBOX NAME=Field VALUE=Address>Address<BR>
```

So by the time the user sees the screen, we have the following:

▶ A text box for the state

▶ A check box for each field

▶ A **Submit** button

▶ A **Clear** button

The **Submit** button is defined as:

```
<FORM NAME=ContactInfo ACTION="ContactsInState.asp" METHOD="POST">
```

so we are calling the same ASP file, using the **POST** action. When the user clicks the Submit button, the second part of the code is run (assuming a check box is selected).

The **Count** property of the **Form** object tells us how many checkboxes have been selected, so we can loop through the **Form** collection building a string of each field name—this corresponds to the **VALUE** property of the checkbox:

```
' find out which fields are to be selected
strSQL = ""
For intCount = 1 to Request.Form("Field").Count
    strSQL = strSQL & Request.Form("Field")(intCount) & ", "
Next
```

We then strip of the trailing comma that the loop added:

```
' strip off the trailing comma and space added in the loop
strSQL = Left(strSQL, Len(strSQL) - 2)
```

Then we add the table name:

```
strSQL = "SELECT " & strSQL & " FROM Contact"
```

Finally we see whether a **State** was entered, and if it was add a **WHERE** clause:

```
' only add a where clause if they requested a state
If Request.Form("State") <> "" Then
    strSQL = strSQL & " WHERE State = '" & Request.Form("State")
& "'"
    End If
```

At this stage we have a full SQL string. The number of columns selected will depend upon those selected by the user, so we create a recordset based upon this SQL string:

```
' create the recordset
Set objRec = Server.CreateObject ("ADODB.Recordset")

objRec.Open strSQL, strConnect, adOpenForwardOnly, _
          adLockReadOnly, adCmdText
```

And finally we use the `RecToTable` function (that we created earlier) to display a table of the recordset:

```
' write a table of the recordset
Response.Write RecToTable (objRec)
```

That's really all there is to it. You can see that with two small sections of ASP code you have a very flexible form, that gives the user a great deal of control over what they see.

Summary

This chapter has covered an awful lot of ground, looking at the most important aspects of ADO, such as creating recordsets and moving around the records, as well as how to modify the data. You've seen that the `Recordset` is really the heart of ADO, with the `Command` and `Connection` objects being just a way to run commands, or generate recordsets. Obviously there is more to these objects, but this is one of their main tasks.

As you use ASP more you'll probably discover you are doing two main tasks with ADO:

▶ Generating dynamic pages from recordsets. You can actually create a web site that is almost entirely data bound, having only a few ASP pages, and all of the data generated from a data store. Updating the site simply becomes a matter of updating the database. Much of the Wrox Press web site is generated in this way.

▶ Adding new data in response to user information. An example of this is the 'guest book' type of page, where an HTML form requests information from the user and this is added to a database. We use this technique for the Addendum pages, where you can inform us of any errors in our books.

Obviously you won't be limited to these two tasks, but you'll find that they can take a lot of maintenance effort out of your site.

Writing an Application

We have now reached the end of our journey through the world of Active Server Pages, and we have seen many different aspects of what Active Server Pages can bring to web pages. Each of the previous chapters has looked at a different part of the system. With all of that preliminary learning accomplished, we can now set out and write a whole application using Active Server Pages.

This application will leverage many of the different functions that we have looked at in this book. Some of the functions we will be using are:

- Client-side scripting using JavaScript
- Server-side scripting using VBScript
- The **Request** and **Response** objects to communicate with the web client
- The **Session** object to manage a user session
- Active Data Objects (ADO) to manipulate information in a database

By using all of these functions in a single application, we will be able to see how they interact with each other in a 'real-life' environment. While this chapter won't explain every single line of code in detail, it *will* provide you with sufficient information to let you implement this application as-is, or modify it to suit your needs. Alternatively, you can use it as a set of guidelines to write your own applications.

WROX Classifieds

The emergence of the Internet as a worldwide standard for communicating information has opened up a number of new business opportunities. One of these opportunities is the area known as Electronic Commerce: the Internet is able to take the place of a traditional bricks-and-mortar store. For very little overhead, people are now able to sell their products electronically. The Internet has enabled the buyer and the seller to be brought together in a virtual (rather than a physical) manner.

An example of commerce between two people is the traditional newspaper classified ads. These allow people to list items that they wish to sell, and then provide a means (usually a telephone number) by which a prospective buyer can contact them. Since this is a way of bringing a buyer and seller together, we can probably come up with a way to use the Internet to make the interaction better.

With a newspaper classified, the downstream flow of information (from seller to buyer) uses a different method from the upstream (buyer to seller) flow. Downstream, the information flows on paper. Upstream, the information is relayed via the telephone or in person. By using the Internet to provide a solution, both the upstream and downstream communications can be accomplished using the same method—a web browser.

In our example, we will be looking at a web-based classified ad system. This system will allow users to:

> View items for sale

> Bid on an item they wish to purchase

> List items that they wish to sell

The Internet classified ad system provides certain advantages to the seller over traditional printed classifieds:

> The seller can add items for sale and have them immediately accessible to potential buyers. That is, they don't have to wait for the newspaper to be printed.

> The responses from the potential buyers are held by the system rather than passed directly back to the seller. This means that the seller doesn't have to be available to respond 24 hours a day.

> The seller can dynamically adjust the price based on the response that an item receives.

The Internet classified ad system also provides advantages for the buyer:

> They can see the level of interest in an item before determining the price they are willing to pay.

> They are advised whether they have offered the highest bid for a product.

> They can have access to items for sale from different geographic regions, due to the global nature of the Internet.

We will be building our application in a set of stages. Each of these stages will build on the previous ones, and will add an additional piece of functionality to the application. The sequence for building this application is:

> Database setup

> Home page construction

> User registration and login

> Adding items for sale

- Browsing items for sale
- Bidding for an item
- Accepting a bid

To get us started, we will look at how to set up the database tables that will support the Internet classified ad system. Our application will use a Microsoft Access database to store all of its information: this choice combines Access's ease of database construction with the future scalability to a server-based database system such as SQL Server.

For the purposes of building this application, we will be assuming that you have Microsoft Access available as a database platform. The database and its supporting files are all available on this book's segment of the Wrox website, at **http://www.wrox.com**, and can be downloaded. The next section will deal with how to use Access to create the database.

Database Setup

As with all applications that store information and allow retrieval of that information, some form of data storage is needed. This data storage can be memory-based, text file-based, custom file format-based, or relational database-based. In any case, the *physical* storage of the information is complemented by a 'theoretical' description of the way the information is *logically* stored. This is known as the **data model**. Below is a picture of the data model for our Internet classified ad application.

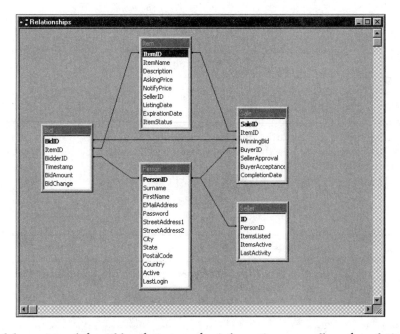

A data model consists of the tables that store the information, as well as the relationships that these tables have with each other. Let's look at the different data tables in our application and see what types of information are stored in each.

Person Table

The Person table is used to store information about each user that is accessing the system. This information includes the user's name and address, as well as their e-mail address. Their e-mail address, along with a password that is also stored in this table, is used to provide login functionality to the system.

The structure of the Person table is:

Field Name	Data Type	Description
PersonID	Long	System-generated unique identifier
Surname	Text	User's last name *(required)*
FirstName	Text	User's first name *(required)*
EmailAddress	Text	User's e-mail address—used for Login *(required)*
Password	Text	User defined password—used for Login *(required)*
StreetAddress1	Text	
StreetAddress2	Text	
City	Text	
State	Text	
PostalCode	Text	
Country	Text	
Active	Boolean	Flag indicating that the user is an active user
LastLogin	Date/Time	Date and time of the last time this user logged into the application

Seller Table

The Seller table is used to store additional information about a person, once they become a seller. This information is primarily statistical, detailing the numbers of items that the seller currently has for sale, as well as the total number of items that they have *ever* listed. This table is associated directly with the Person table, where each user defined in the Person table can have either zero or one seller record, indicating whether or not they are a seller.

The structure of the Seller table is:

Field Name	Data Type	Description
ID	Long	System-generated unique identifier
PersonID	Long	Foreign key to relate this record to the corresponding Person table record
ItemsListed	Text	Total number of items that this user has ever listed for sale
ItemsActive	Text	Number of items that are currently for sale
LastActivity	Date/Time	Date and time of the last time this seller changed the items they have for sale

We noted above that there is an association between the Person and Seller tables. This association is defined using keys.

What is a Key?

In our database environment, we need to be able to retrieve the exact records we're after, and be confident that they are definitely the right ones. To help us do this, we use **keys**. A key is a field—or set of fields—that uniquely identifies a particular record in the table. The way in which we set up the keys in our tables determines the uniqueness of records, and also allows us to link these records to records in other tables.

The relationship from one table to another table is defined using a **foreign key**. A foreign key is a way of referencing a unique record in another table. In our Seller table, we have the PersonID field, which refers (via the PersonID field in the Person table) to a record describing a unique individual. So the Seller table's PersonID is a foreign key for the Person table.

Item Table

Now that we have defined the users and the sellers in the application, we need a place to store the goods that are being sold. These are stored in the Item table. The Item table holds descriptive information about the item for sale, the pricing information, and some 'current status' information as well.

The structure of the Item table is:

Field Name	Data Type	Description
ItemID	Long	System-generated unique identifier
ItemName	Text	Descriptive name of the item
Description	Memo	Text description of the item
AskingPrice	Currency	Price that the seller desires
NotifyPrice	Currency	Price level at which the seller should be notified
SellerID	Long	Foreign key indicating the seller of the item
ListingDate	Date/Time	Date and time that the item was listed for sale
ExpirationDate	Date/Time	Date and time that the item will no longer be for sale
ItemStatus	Text	Current item status—can be blank, Pending, or Sold

Bid Table

When a potential buyer finds an item they are interested in, they will place a bid on that item. A bid is an intention to buy an item at a specified price. This bid price must be higher than any previous bid prices for the same item. The bid information is stored so that the seller can review the interest in the item they are selling.

The structure of the Bid table is:

Field Name	Data Type	Description
BidID	Long	System-generated unique identifier
ItemID	Long	Foreign key indicating the item being bid on
BidderID	Long	Foreign key indicating the person bidding on the item
Timestamp	Date/Time	Date and time that the bid was submitted
BidAmount	Currency	Amount that the buyer is willing to pay for the item
BidChange	Currency	Difference between current bid and previous bid

Sale Table

The seller of an item is able to review the various bids that have been made on that item. When the seller finds an acceptable bid, they can accept that bid. This will begin the actual sale process. In the sale process, the information about the winning bid is recorded in the **Sale** table. The sale is considered 'pending' until the potential buyer acknowledges the successful purchase of the item.

The structure of the **Sale** table is:

Field Name	Data Type	Description
SaleID	Long	System-generated unique identifier
ItemID	Long	Foreign key indicating the item being bid on
WinningBid	Currency	Final selling price of the item
BuyerID	Long	Foreign key indicating the successful buyer of the item
SellerApproval	Boolean	Indicates that the seller has approved the sale
BuyerAcceptance	Boolean	Indicates that the buyer has accepted the sale
CompletionDate	Date/Time	Date and time that the sale was completed

Try It Out – Creating the Database

1 The first step will be to create the database in Access. First, start up Microsoft Access from your Start menu. To create the database, select **File | New Database** from the toolbar.

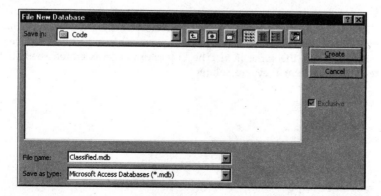

Choose a location for your database: In this example, we've chosen the directory **Inetpub\wwwroot\BegASP\Code**. Type in the name of your database: here, we've called it **Classified**.

2 Now that our database exists, we can start to build it up. First, we'll create the Person table. To create the new table, click on the New button, and select Design View to create the new table. Then hit OK.

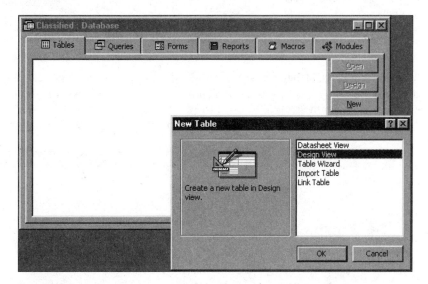

3 Now, we can begin setting up the fields in our database. Add the fields and set their data types so that it looks like this:

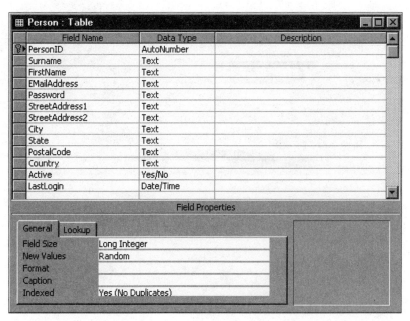

FYI   Note that filling in the **Description** column is optional.

4 In order to enforce the uniqueness of records within this table, we'll create a **primary key**. To do this, select the PersonID field, and press the Primary Key icon in the toolbar:

This will ensure that for every record in this table, the PersonID field contains a unique value.

5 There are a number of fields that store *optional* information: these are the StreetAddress1, StreetAddress2, City, State, PostalCode and Country fields. We need to ensure that these will allow zero-length strings. To do this, select each of these fields in turn, then left-click on the Allow Zero Length field, and select Yes in the resulting dropdown menu.

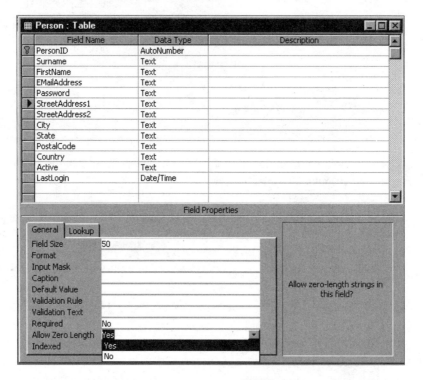

6 Finally, save the table by pressing the Save icon, , and naming the table Person.

7 Next, we'll create the Seller table. In order to create the Seller table—and indeed all the remaining tables—we essentially repeat the procedure outlined in steps 2 through 6. To recap, these steps are:

▶ Create a new table in Design Mode

▶ Add the fields and set their types

▶ Set the primary key

▶ Save the table

For the Seller table, add the fields shown here:

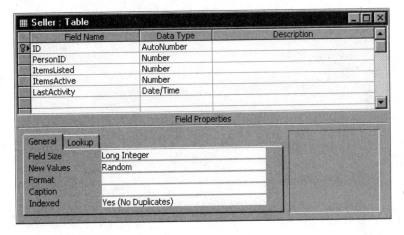

Set the ID field as the primary key, and save the table with the name Seller.

8 Next, create the Item table. For the Item table, add the fields as shown here:

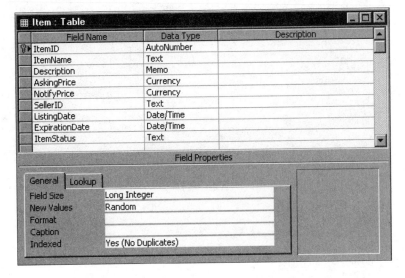

Set the ItemID field as the primary key and save the table as the Item table.

9 Create the Bid table. For the Bid table, add the fields as shown here:

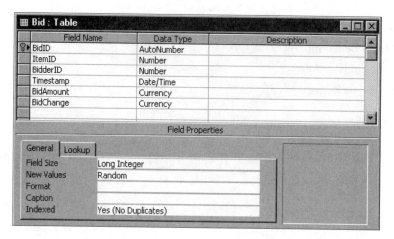

Set the BidID field as the primary key, and save the table using the name Bid.

10 While setting up the Bid table, highlight the Timestamp field; then, in the Default Value box, insert **Now()**.

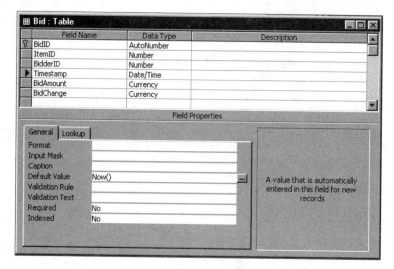

11 Finally, create the Sale table, with fields as shown here:

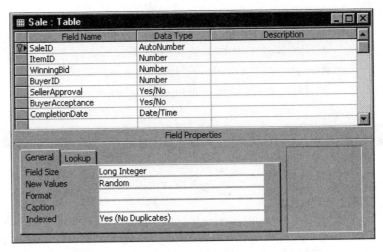

Set the SaleID field as the primary key, and save the table as the Sale table.

How It Works

In this example, we have created the tables that are needed to store the information for our classified ads application. We have created primary keys for each table: this is intended to help ensure that the data held is consistent. The primary keys also allow relationships to be set up between the tables, which allows us to mimic our data model.

Notice that in each table, the data type of the primary key is AutoNumber. This is a special type of database field. The user accessing the table is not allowed to put a value into this field. Rather, the *system* will generate the value for each new record. By making this the primary key, we can be sure that the value stored here will *always* be unique. By choosing to create these new values as Random (see the New Values field in the screenshots above), we ensure that if the data is ever copied to another database, there would no problems with conflicting keys.

Setting up the DSN

When we come to write the code for our application, we'll need to refer to our database via an ODBC System DSN. Back at the very beginning of Chapter 13, we gave a set of instructions for using the ODBC Control Panel applet to set up a DSN for the `Contact.mdb` database.

By following those instructions, you should be able to create a DSN for our new `Classified.mdb` database. Just set the Data Source Name to Classified; insert a suitable Description; and use Select to insert the location of the database.

The Home Page

With our database created, the next step is to create the pages that make up the application. The first page that we will create is the starting point of the application—the home page.

The home page of the application is responsible for welcoming the user to the application, providing some information about what the application is for, and displaying the top-level menu selections for the user.

From our application's home page, the user will be able to:

◗ Browse the items that are for sale

◗ Log into the system (if they are a registered user)

◗ Register with the system (if they are a *new* user)

Try It Out – Creating the Home Page

1 Using your favored web page editor, or NotePad, create a new ASP file.

2 Enter the following code into your editor. If you want, you can download this file, as well as all of the other files in this example, from the WROX web site at `http://rapid.wrox.co.uk/books/1347`.

```
<% Session.Abandon %>
<!DOCTYPE HTML PUBLIC "-//W3C//DTD HTML 3.2 Final//EN">
<BASEFONT FACE="Comic Sans MS" COLOR="DarkBlue">
<HTML>
<HEAD>
<TITLE>WROX Classifieds</TITLE>
</HEAD>

<BODY BGCOLOR="#FFFF80">
<CENTER><H1>WROX Classifieds<BR>Main Menu</H1>
</CENTER>

<P>Thank you for visiting the WROX Classifieds Site.  We offer you the
opportunity to:
<UL>
<LI>Browse for items for sale
<LI>Bid on items for sale
<LI>List your own items for sale
</UL>
<P>Feel free to browse our listings.  You don't need to register to do
that.  If you want to bid on an item, or sell some yourself, we will ask
you to register with us.
<HR>
<TABLE BORDER=0 WIDTH=100%>
<TR ALIGN=CENTER>
<TD WIDTH=33%><A HREF="browse.asp">Browse the listings</A></TD>
<TD WIDTH=33%><A HREF="login.asp">Login</A></TD>
<TD WIDTH=33%><A HREF="register.asp">I'm a new user</A></TD>
</TR></TABLE>

</BODY>
</HTML>
```

3 Save the file as `default.asp`. Save the file to your usual `BegASP` directory so that the ASP script will be processed correctly.

4 View the page in your web browser:

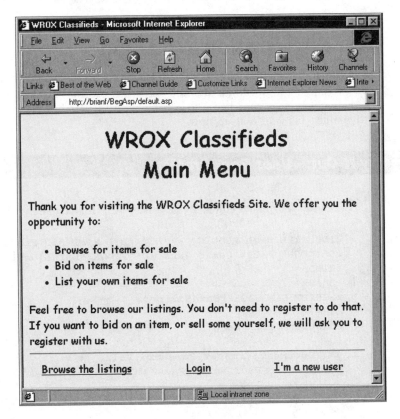

How It Works

As you can see, this is a pretty plain vanilla web page. The function of this page is twofold. First, to present the user with information about what can be done at this site, and second, to give them the navigation controls needed to begin using the system.

When you look at the page, you'll notice that it is mostly straight HTML. There is only one piece of ASP script in it:

```
<% Session.Abandon %>
```

This is the initial line of the file, so it's the first statement processed by ASP when a user makes their inaugural visit to the site. This initializes the settings ready for the user's new WROX session to start.

Throughout the site, we will be using session-level variables to store information about the current user. To be on the safe side, we want to reset all of these variables when the user first enters the site. This could prove useful if the application is called up from a public access terminal, where multiple users could be getting in to the site from the same browser. The **Abandon** method of the **Session** object will terminate any current user session, thus automatically resetting any session-level variables.

We have placed the navigation controls at the bottom of the page. These controls are simply hyperlinked text that will take the user to the appropriate page for each menu selection. Each of these pages will be covered in detail later in the chapter.

User Registration and Login

As the user arrives at the site for the first time, there are two functions that they can perform. They can choose to browse the sale items list, by choosing the "Browse the listings" hyperlink. Alternatively, they can choose to register with the site by selecting the "I'm a new user" hyperlink. Let's set that up now.

Try It Out – User Registration

1. Using your usual editor, create a new ASP file containing the following code:

```
<!DOCTYPE HTML PUBLIC "-//W3C//DTD HTML 3.2 Final//EN">
<BASEFONT FACE="Comic Sans MS" COLOR="DarkBlue">
<HTML>
<HEAD>
<SCRIPT LANGUAGE="JavaScript">
<!--
function VerifyData()
{
If (Document.FrmUser.Password.Value !=
document.frmUser.VerifyPassword.value)
{
        alert ("Your passwords do not match - please reenter");
        Return False;
}
Else
        Return True;
}
-->
</SCRIPT>

<TITLE>WROX Classifieds - User Registration</TITLE>
</HEAD>

<BODY BGCOLOR="#FFFF80">
<CENTER><H1>WROX Classifieds<BR>
<% If Request("Update") = "1" Then %>
Update
<% Else %>
New
<% End If %>
 User Registration</H1></CENTER>
<P>
```

```
<% If Request("NotFound") = "1" Then %>
<I>We were unable to locate your information. Please take the time to
register again.</I><P>
<% End If %>

<% If Request("Update") = "1" Then %>
Please change your registration information as listed below<P>
<% Else  %>
In order to bid or list items for sale, you will need to be registered
with our system.  Please take a few minutes to enter the information
below.  Once you have done that, you will have full access to the system.
<% End If %>

<FORM ACTION="AddUser.asp" NAME="frmUser" METHOD="POST" onSubmit="return
VerifyData()">
<TABLE BORDER=0>

<TR><TD width=20% rowspan=11> </TD>
<TD>E-Mail Address:</TD>
<TD><INPUT TYPE="Text" NAME="email" VALUE="<%= Session("EMailAddress")
%>" SIZE="40"></TD>
</TR>

<TR>
<TD>First Name:</TD>
<TD><INPUT TYPE="Text" NAME="FirstName" VALUE="<%= Session("FirstName")
%>" SIZE="40"></TD>
</TR>

<TR>
<TD>Last Name:</TD>
<TD><INPUT TYPE="Text" NAME="LastName" VALUE="<%= Session("Surname") %>"
SIZE="40"></TD>
</TR>

<TR>
<TD>Address:</TD>
<TD><INPUT TYPE="Text" NAME="Address1" VALUE="<%=
Session("StreetAddress1") %>" SIZE="40"></TD>
</TR>

<TR>
<TD></TD>
<TD><INPUT TYPE="Text" NAME="Address2" VALUE="<%=
Session("StreetAddress2") %>" SIZE="40"></TD>
</TR>

<TR>
<TD>City:</TD>
<TD><INPUT TYPE="Text" NAME="City" VALUE="<%= Session("City") %>"
SIZE="40"></TD>
</TR>
```

499

```
<TR>
<TD>State:</TD>
<TD><INPUT TYPE="Text" NAME="State" VALUE="<%= Session("State") %>"
SIZE="40"></TD>
</TR>

<TR>
<TD>Postal Code:</TD>
<TD><INPUT TYPE="Text" NAME="PostalCode" VALUE="<%= Session("PostalCode")
%>" SIZE="40"></TD>
</TR>

<TR>
<TD>Country:</TD>
<TD><INPUT TYPE="Text" NAME="Country" VALUE="<%= Session("Country") %>"
SIZE="40"></TD>
</TR>

<TR>
<TD> <P>Password:</TD>
<TD valign=bottom><INPUT TYPE="Password" NAME="Password" VALUE="<%=
Session("Password") %>" SIZE="40"></TD>
</TR>

<TR>
<TD>Verify Password:</TD>
<TD><INPUT TYPE="Password" NAME="VerifyPassword" SIZE="40"></TD>
</TR>

<TR>
<TD></TD>
<TD align=center colspan=2><BR><INPUT TYPE="Submit" VALUE="Submit
Registration">  <INPUT TYPE="RESET"></TD>
</TR>
</TABLE>
</FORM>

<HR>
<TABLE BORDER=0 WIDTH=100%>
<TR ALIGN=CENTER>
<TD WIDTH=33%><A HREF="browse.asp">Browse the listings</A></TD>
<TD WIDTH=33%><A HREF="login.asp">Login</A></TD>
<TD WIDTH=33%>I'm a new user</TD>
</TR></TABLE>

</BODY>
</HTML>
```

2 Save the file as **register.asp** in your **BegASP** directory.

3 Create a new file in your editor and enter the following code:

```
<!--#include file="Chap15DB.inc"-->
<%
Dim rsUsers
Set rsUsers = Server.CreateObject("ADODB.Recordset")
rsUsers.Open "Person", db, adOpenForwardOnly, adLockOptimistic,
adCmdTable
rsUsers.Filter = "EMailAddress = '" & Request.Form("email") & "'"
if rsUsers.EOF then
 rsUsers.AddNew
end if
rsUsers("Surname") = Request.Form("LastName")
rsUsers("FirstName") = Request.Form("FirstName")
rsUsers("EMailAddress") = Request.Form("email")
rsUsers("Password") = Request.Form("password")
rsUsers("StreetAddress1") = Request.Form("Address1")
rsUsers("StreetAddress2") = Request.Form("Address2")
rsUsers("City") = Request.Form("City")
rsUsers("State") = Request.Form("State")
rsUsers("PostalCode") = Request.Form("PostalCode")
rsUsers("Country") = Request.Form("Country")
rsUsers("Active") = True
rsUsers("LastLogin") = Now
rsUsers.Update
Dim strName, value
For Each sField In rsUsers.Fields
 strName = sField.Name
 value = sField.value
 Session(strName) = value
Next
Session("bValidUser") = True
Response.Redirect "registeredMenu.asp"
%>
```

4 Save this file as `addUser.asp`.

5 Now we'll create the include file that was called from the file above. Create another file in your editor and enter the following code:

```
<!-- #Include file="adovbs.inc" -->
<%
Dim db
Set db = Server.CreateObject("ADODB.Connection")
db.Open "Classified"

If Session("bValidUser") = True and Session("PersonID") = "" Then
Dim rsPersonIDCheck
Set rsPersonIDCheck = Server.CreateObject("ADODB.Recordset")
```

```
Dim strSQL
strSQL = "SELECT PersonID FROM Person WHERE EMailAddress = '" &
Session("EMailAddress") & "';"
rsPersonIDCheck.Open strSQL, db
If rsPersonIDCheck.EOF Then
        Session("bValidUser") = False
Else
        Session("PersonID") = rsPersonIDCheck("PersonID")
End If
rsPersonIDCheck.Close
End If
%>
```

6 Save this file as **Chap15DB.inc**.

7 Note that **Chap15DB.inc** itself uses the file **adovbs.inc** as an include file. This file is supplied with the other samples for this book: you'll need to check that this file is contained in the same directory as your other **.asp** files.

8 From the home page, click on the I'm a new user hyperlink to view the registration page. Don't press the Submit button, as we have not added the page to handle that yet.

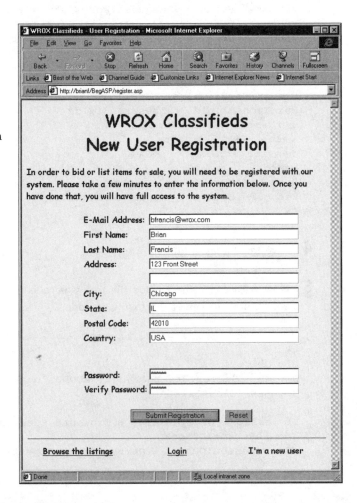

How It Works

There's quite a lot to get through here. Here goes.

In this example, the user is presented with a form to submit information. When they have entered the information and pressed the Submit Registration button, a client-side script is run to ensure that the passwords match. The information is then submitted to an ASP script that will perform the database updates. Once that script has completed, the user will be automatically redirected to another page.

In looking at the **register.asp** file, the first interesting piece of code is the client-side script section. We will be using JavaScript for our client-side validation routines. This will allow the page to be accessed by the widest range of browsers.

```
<SCRIPT LANGUAGE="JavaScript">
<!--
function VerifyData()
{
If (Document.FrmUser.Password.Value !=
document.frmUser.VerifyPassword.value)
{
        alert ("Your passwords do not match - please reenter");
        Return False;
}
Else
        Return True;
}
-->
</SCRIPT>
```

The purpose of this script is to compare the values that the user entered in the Password and Verify Password fields on the form. To ensure that the user entered the password that they intended, the system requires that they enter it twice. Rather than have the *server* validate that the entries are the same, we will perform the check at the client. If they match, then the processing continues. If they don't, then a message box is shown to the user, and they are given a chance to change their entries.

This function is called by adding a parameter to the **<FORM>** tag:

```
<FORM ACTION="AddUser.asp" NAME="frmUser" METHOD="POST" onSubmit="return
VerifyData()">
```

The **onSubmit** parameter is used to identify the client-side function that will be called when the user submits the form. In our case, this function is **VerifyData()**, which will return a result of either **True** or **False**. If the function determines that the form is acceptable, then **True** is returned. If the form should *not* be submitted, then **False** is returned.

As well as being used for new user registration, this page will also allow *existing* users to modify their information. This means that there are two possible parameters that can be passed to this page. One calls the function for a new registration, and the other calls the function for modifying an existing user's data. The display text for each of these procedures is different, and is controlled by what the page is currently being used for:

```
<% If Request("Update") = "1" Then %>
 Please change your registration information as listed below<P>
<% Else %>
 In order to bid or list items for sale, you will need to be registered
with our system.  Please take a few minutes to enter the information
below.  Once you have done that, you will have full access to the system.
<% End If %>
```

If the query string parameter called `Update` has a value of 1 (True), then we know that the user is trying to change their existing information. You will see in later pages how this is used. In this case, their page prompt will be "Update User Registration" instead of "New User Registration".

In addition to updating existing user data, the page can also be called by the `addUser.asp` script if there is an error in the information that the user entered. In this case, a query string parameter `NotFound` with a value of 1 indicates that there was a problem registering a user; the prompt that the user sees is controlled by this parameter:

```
<% If Request("NotFound") = "1" Then %>
 <I>We were unable to locate your information. Please take the time to
register again.</I><P>
<% End If %>
```

If we're using the form to update existing information, then we need to load the current information into the form, to show the user's 'initial values'. In our application, all of the current user's information is stored in session-level variables. Hence, it is a simple matter of retrieving the information for each of the fields from its corresponding session-level variable:

```
<TR><TD width=20% rowspan=11> </TD>
<TD>E-Mail Address:</TD>
<TD><INPUT TYPE="Text" NAME="email" VALUE="<%= Session("EMailAddress")
%>" SIZE="40"></TD>
</TR>

<TR>
<TD>First Name:</TD>
<TD><INPUT TYPE="Text" NAME="FirstName" VALUE="<%= Session("FirstName")
%>" SIZE="40"></TD>
</TR>
. . .
```

In the case of a new user, the session-level variables will be 'undefined', and consequently will have no values—so they will just return blank strings.

> *You may remember this very nice feature: Many other languages generate an error if an attempt is made to access an undefined variable. In VBScript and ASP, a blank string is returned, avoiding giving the user a nasty error message.*

The only field that is not dealt with in this way is the **Password** verification field. We want to force the user to type in their password at least once, in order to verify their identity. Hence, we *don't* associate a default value with the **Password** verification field:

```
<TR>
<TD> <P>Password:</TD>
<TD valign=bottom><INPUT TYPE="Password" NAME="Password" VALUE="<%=
Session("Password") %>" SIZE="40"></TD>
</TR>

<TR>
<TD>Verify Password:</TD>
<TD><INPUT TYPE="Password" NAME="VerifyPassword" SIZE="40"></TD>
</TR>
```

When the user submits the form, and the form is accepted (that is, their password values match), processing is then passed to the **addUser.asp** file. This file is a bit different from most ASP script files, in that it has no user interface. The sole function of the file is to take the information submitted by the form in the **register.asp** file, and put those values into the database. Based on the results of these database functions, the browser is directed to another page, where the user continues with the application. Let's look at **addUser.asp**.

The first line of the **adduser.asp** file is a server-side include directive:

```
<!--#include file="Chap15DB.inc"-->
```

This directive will instruct the ASP script processor to load the file named **Chap15DB.inc** and process its contents as if it were part of the **adduser.asp** file. This server-side include file is used to encapsulate the data access connection information into one file.

The first line of the **Chap15DB.inc** file is another server-side include directive. In this case, the included file is **adovbs.inc**:

```
<!-- #Include file="adovbs.inc" -->
```

As we discussed in Chapter 14, this contains all of the named parameters for the ADODB objects. This will allow us to use the more readable names, such as **adCmdText**, instead of numeric values.

The **Chap15DB.inc** file is used to perform two functions. The first declares a variable that will hold the database connection and then creates and opens that connection:

```
Dim db
Set db = Server.CreateObject("ADODB.Connection")
db.Open "Classified"
```

This code references the database **Classified.mdb** that we created in the previous 'Try It Out'. The reference is made by the ODBC System DSN, **Classified**, that was set up using the ODBC Control Panel applet (the procedure for this was originally described at the beginning of Chapter 13). By putting this information into a server-side include file, as we have done here, we can easily replace **Classified** with a different database DSN later on, if necessary.

The second function of `Chap15DB.inc` is to retrieve the current user's `PersonID` value from the Person table. When a new user is added to the system, there is no easy way to determine the value of the system-generated primary key—and yet this value will be needed throughout the application. Now, the `Chap15DB.inc` file will be a part of any ASP script that performs database access, so it's a convenient place to ensure that we have this value:

```
Dim rsPersonIDCheck
Set rsPersonIDCheck = Server.CreateObject("ADODB.Recordset")
```

If this value is not present, then we will retrieve it from the Person table. This is done by querying the database for the information that we need. The results of the query will be returned as a recordset—so first we need to *create* the recordset:

```
strSQL = "SELECT PersonID FROM Person WHERE EMailAddress = '" &
Session("EMailAddress") & "';"
rsPersonIDCheck.Open strSQL, db
```

The SQL query will be written such that it retrieves only the necessary value, rather than the entire record. The **WHERE** clause tells the SQL query the e-mail address of the user in question. Then the query goes in search of the user's `PersonID` value:

```
If rsPersonIDCheck.EOF Then
        Session("bValidUser") = False
Else
        Session("PersonID") = rsPersonIDCheck("PersonID")
End If
```

If there is no information in the database for the given e-mail address, then the current user is logged out by setting the session-level variable **bValidUser** to **False**. Otherwise, the **PersonID** value is stored in a session-level variable called **PersonID**.

Once the database has been opened, and we have ensured that the current user has all of the necessary information stored in session-level variables, we can get back to adding a new user to the system, in **newUser.asp**. To handle the interaction with the Person table, we will use another recordset object:

```
Dim rsUsers
Set rsUsers = Server.CreateObject("ADODB.Recordset")
rsUsers.Open "Person", db, adOpenForwardOnly, adLockOptimistic,
adCmdTable
rsUsers.Filter = "EMailAddress = '" & Request.Form("email") & "'"
if rsUsers.EOF then
 rsUsers.AddNew
 end if
```

In this case, the recordset will be populated with the contents of a table rather than the results of a query. We also add the **adLockOptimistic** parameter to the **Open** method of the recordset, which will allow us to write information into the table.

A filter is set to retrieve all of the records with an e-mail address that matches the value submitted by the form. If there are no records that match, then we know that we have a new user, and the **AddNew** method of the **Recordset** object is called to create a new blank record ready for data.

Next, we retrieve all the values for the fields of the recordset:

```
rsUsers("Surname") = Request.Form("LastName")
rsUsers("FirstName") = Request.Form("FirstName")
rsUsers("EMailAddress") = Request.Form("email")
rsUsers("Password") = Request.Form("password")
rsUsers("StreetAddress1") = Request.Form("Address1")
rsUsers("StreetAddress2") = Request.Form("Address2")
rsUsers("City") = Request.Form("City")
rsUsers("State") = Request.Form("State")
rsUsers("PostalCode") = Request.Form("PostalCode")
rsUsers("Country") = Request.Form("Country")
rsUsers("Active") = True
rsUsers("LastLogin") = Now
```

The values are passed in from the form and copied to the appropriate fields in the recordset. If we're updating an existing record, then the new values simply overwrite any existing data. Otherwise, the data is written to the new user's record. Once all of the information has been added, the data is written to the database by using the **Update** method of the recordset object.

```
rsUsers.Update
```

The next step is to write all of the information from the recordset into session-level variables. There is no single method that will automatically perform this copy. We could have written a series of statements that copied each field from the recordset to the session-level variable, but that would have been pretty tedious. Instead, we utilize one of the collections of the recordset object—the **Fields** collection—that contains all of the individual **Field** objects in the recordset:

```
Dim strName, value
For Each sField In rsUsers.Fields
 strName = sField.Name
 value = sField.value
 Session(strName) = value
Next
Session("bValidUser") = True
```

We use the **For...Each** statement to iterate through each member of the collection. We retrieve the name and value of each **Field** object. Then we can create a corresponding session-level variable that has the same name as the **Field** object, and assign it the same value.

Then, since the user has successfully been registered, we set the **bValidUser** session-level variable to True.

Finally, we instruct the client browser to load the **registeredMenu.asp** page automatically. This will present a registered user's home page to our newly registered user.

```
Response.Redirect "registeredMenu.asp"
```

The Login Screen

Any registered user who visits the site should not have to go through the registration process
again. To allow previously registered users to identify themselves, we will present a login screen.

1 Create a new ASP file and key in the following code:

```
<!DOCTYPE HTML PUBLIC "-//W3C//DTD HTML 3.2 Final//EN">
<BASEFONT FACE="Comic Sans MS" COLOR="DarkBlue">
<HTML>
<HEAD>
<TITLE>WROX Classifieds - Login</TITLE>
</HEAD>

<BODY BGCOLOR="#FFFF80">
<CENTER><H1>WROX Classifieds<BR>Login</H1></CENTER>
<P>
<% If Request("Again") = "1" Then
 If Request("BadPW") = "True" Then %>
        Invalid Password<BR>
<%      Else  %>
        E-Mail Address not found.  Try again<BR>
<% End If %>
<% End If %>
Please enter your e-mail address and password to login to the system.
<FORM ACTION="CheckLogin.asp<% If Request("Again") = "1" then
%>?Again=1<% End If %>" METHOD="POST">
<TABLE BORDER=0>
<TR><TD>E-Mail Address:</TD>
<TD><INPUT TYPE="Text" NAME="email" <% If Request("Again") = "1" Then %>
VALUE="<%= Session("EMailAddress") %>"<% End If %> SIZE="40"></TD>
</TR>
<TR><TD>Password:</TD>
<TD><INPUT TYPE="Password" NAME="Password" SIZE="40"></TD>
</TR>
<TR><TD></TD>
<TD align=center><INPUT TYPE="Submit" VALUE="Login">  <INPUT
TYPE="RESET">
</TD></TR>
</TABLE>
</FORM>

<HR>
<TABLE BORDER=0 WIDTH=100%>
<TR ALIGN=CENTER>
<TD WIDTH=33%><A HREF="browse.asp">Browse the listings</A></TD>
<TD WIDTH=33%>Login</TD>
```

```
<TD WIDTH=33%><A HREF="register.asp">I'm a new user</A></TD>
</TR></TABLE>

</BODY>
</HTML>
```

2 Save the file as `login.asp`. in your `BegASP` directory.

3 Create another new ASP file using your editor and enter the following code:

```
<!--#include file="Chap15DB.inc"-->
<%
Dim strEMail, strPassword
strEMail = Request("EMail")
strPassword = Request("Password")

Dim rsUsers
Dim sql
Set rsUsers = Server.CreateObject("ADODB.Recordset")
sql = "SELECT * FROM Person WHERE EMailAddress = '" & strEMail & "';"
rsUsers.Open sql, db

If Not rsUsers.EOF Then
If UCase(rsUsers("Password")) = UCase(strPassword) Then
        Dim strName, value
        For Each sField In rsUsers.Fields
                strName = sField.Name
                value = sField.value
                Session(strName) = value
        Next
        Session("bValidUser") = True
        Response.Redirect "registeredMenu.asp"
Else
        Session("EMailAddress") = Request("EMail")
        If Request("Again") = "1" Then
                Response.Redirect "register.asp"
        Else
                Response.Redirect "login.asp?Again=1&BadPW=True"
        End If
End If
Else
Session("EMailAddress") = Request("EMail")
If Request("Again") = "1" Then
        Response.Redirect "register.asp?NotFound=1"
Else
        Response.Redirect "login.asp?Again=1"
End If
End If
%>
```

4 Save the file as `CheckLogin.asp` in your `BegASP` directory.

5 Create another ASP file and key in the following code:

```
<%
If Session("PersonID") = "" Then
Response.Redirect "login.asp"
End If
%>

<!DOCTYPE HTML PUBLIC "-//W3C//DTD HTML 3.2 Final//EN">
<BASEFONT FACE="Comic Sans MS" COLOR="DarkBlue">
<HTML>
<HEAD>
<TITLE>WROX Classifieds</TITLE>
</HEAD>

<BODY BGCOLOR="#FFFF80">
<CENTER><H1>WROX Classifieds<BR>Registered User Menu</H1>
<H3>Welcome <%= Session("FirstName") & " " & Session("Surname") %></H1>
</CENTER>
<P>Thank you for visiting the WROX Classifieds Site.  We offer you the
opportunity to:
<UL>
<LI>Browse for items for sale
<LI>Bid on items for sale
<LI>List your own items for sale
</UL>
<HR>
<TABLE BORDER=0 WIDTH=100%>
<TR ALIGN=CENTER>
<TD WIDTH=33%><A HREF="browse.asp">Browse the listings</A></TD>
<TD WIDTH=33%><A HREF="ForSale.asp">List/Edit Sale Items</a></TD>
<TD WIDTH=33%><A HREF="register.asp?update=1">Edit Registration Info</
A></TD>
</TR></TABLE>

</BODY>
</HTML>
```

6 Save the file as `registeredMenu.asp` in the `BegASP` directory.

7 From the home page, click on the Login hyperlink to view the login page.

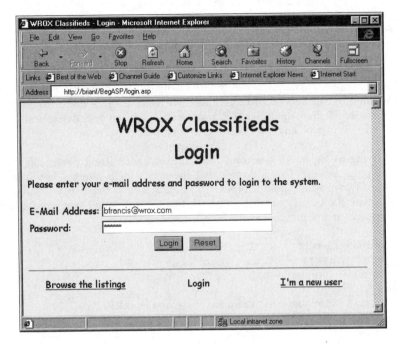

8 After you enter your information, click on the Login button. You will then be taken to the registered user's home page.

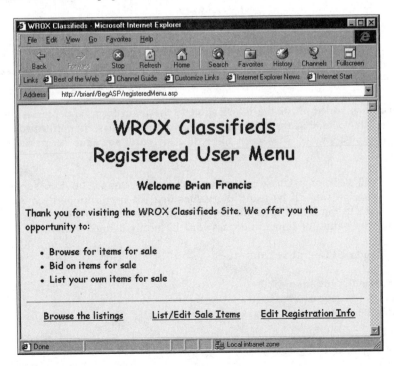

How It Works

When a previously registered user wants access to the system, we need to present them with an opportunity to enter their e-mail address and password. This is done by using a `<FORM>` on a page. With some web servers, the user registration can be accomplished with the web server itself. In our example, we will be performing the validation ourselves.

Just like the `register.asp` page, the `login.asp` page is a multi-use page. When a user is entering an e-mail address and password, there are instances where the information they enter cannot be validated by the server. In those cases, we want to give the users another chance to enter the information. Rather than creating a separate page, we will dynamically create the login page based on the results of any previous login attempt.

If the user is trying to log in for a second time, then a query string parameter named `Again` is attached to the page request. This indicates that the user's login attempt has failed for some reason. There are two possible failure types. The first is where the e-mail address is *not* found; the second is where the e-mail address *is* found, but the submitted password does not match the password stored in the database:

```
<% If Request("Again") = "1" Then
If Request("BadPW") = "True" Then %>
        Invalid Password<BR>
<% Else   %>
        E-Mail Address not found.  Try again<BR>
<% End If %>
<% End If %>
```

When the user is asked to enter their login information again, we will go ahead and set the initial displayed values to the values that were submitted originally. This gives the user a visual clue as to the information they entered previously:

```
<TR><TD>E-Mail Address:</TD>
<TD><INPUT TYPE="Text" NAME="email" <% If Request("Again") = "1" Then %>
VALUE="<%= Session("EMailAddress") %>"<% End If %> SIZE="40"></TD>
</TR>
```

When the user has added all of the information to the login form, and presses the Submit button, the task of validating the information against the database is performed by the `CheckLogin.asp` script file. This script file is like the `addUser.asp` script file in that it has no user interface.

Since this file will perform database access, we include the `Chap15DB.inc` server-side include file. Within the script, we will be using the values that the user supplied for e-mail address and password. To add to the legibility of the text, and to increase the performance of the script, we will be storing the values of Email and password in locally-defined variables:

```
<!--#include file="Chap15DB.inc"-->
<%
Dim strEMail, strPassword
strEMail = Request("EMail")
strPassword = Request("Password")
```

We will be using a SQL query to return all of the **Person** records whose e-mail address matches the one supplied by the user. The results of this SQL query will be stored in a recordset for later investigation:

```
Set rsUsers = Server.CreateObject("ADODB.Recordset")
sql = "SELECT * FROM Person WHERE EMailAddress = '" & strEMail & "';"
rsUsers.Open sql, db
```

We first check to see if the SQL query returned any records to the recordset. If a record does exist, then we know that at least the email address submitted by the user matches one in the database. The next step is to compare the passwords. In our application, passwords are not case sensitive. To compare the password from the database with the one submitted by the user, we force both to all uppercase before performing the comparison:

```
If Not rsUsers.EOF Then
  If UCase(rsUsers("Password")) = UCase(strPassword) Then
```

If the passwords do match, then we have a valid user. We will borrow the code from the **addUser.asp** file that copies the contents of the current record in a recordset into session-level variables. In fact, all of this code here is very similar to the code found in **addUser.asp**: after the session-level variables are created, the **bValidUser** flag is set and the client is redirected to the Registered User home page:

```
        Dim strName, value
        For Each sField In rsUsers.Fields
                strName = sField.Name
                value = sField.value
                Session(strName) = value
        Next
        Session("bValidUser") = True
        Response.Redirect "registeredMenu.asp"
```

If the e-mail addresses match, but the passwords do not, then we will need to send the user back to the login page to try again. The query string is set to indicate a bad password, so that the login page can display the appropriate prompt:

```
    Else
        Session("EMailAddress") = Request("EMail")
        If Request("Again") = "1" Then
                Response.Redirect "register.asp"
        Else
                Response.Redirect "login.asp?Again=1&BadPW=True"
        End If
    End If
```

Finally, if the e-mail address cannot be found, then the user is given one more chance to enter the correct login. If—on the second chance—the e-mail address still cannot be found, then the user is sent to the registration page and asked to register as a new user:

```
  Else
  Session("EMailAddress") = Request("EMail")
  If Request("Again") = "1" Then
        Response.Redirect "register.asp?NotFound=1"
  Else
        Response.Redirect "login.asp?Again=1"
  End If
  End If
  %>
```

Once a user is successfully registered with the system, they are sent to the **Registered User** home page. This page provides a different set of navigational tools, and displays a personalized greeting to the user. Later in this chapter, we will add to the registered user's home page to provide additional information.

Since this page is for registered users only, we will check to see if they have been properly registered. If they have not, then their browser will be redirected to the login page so that they may log in to the system:

```
<%
If Session("PersonID") = "" Then
 Response.Redirect "login.asp"
End If
%>
```

To provide a personalized greeting to the user, we will be displaying their name in a welcome message. Since all of the user information is stored as session-level variables, there is no need to perform any database access to retrieve this information. It can simply be retrieved from the appropriate session-level variables:

```
<CENTER><H1>WROX Classifieds<BR>Registered User Menu</H1>
<H3>Welcome <%= Session("FirstName") & " " & Session("Surname") %></H1>
</CENTER>
```

Now that the user has become a registered user of the site, and can successfully log in to it, the next step is to start listing items that they have for sale.

Adding Items for Sale

Any registered user of this site is able to list items for sale. When listing an item for sale, the user is asked to provide some information about it. Some of this information will be displayed to potential buyers, and some is used internally in the system. The information involved for each sale item is:

- A descriptive name for the item
- A long description of the item
- The price you desire for the item
- The price at which the system should notify you
- The date after which the item will no longer be for sale

There is more to managing the 'for sale' items than simply adding items to a list. There also needs to be some mechanism for editing and removing these items. We'll cover these interfaces in the following Try-It-Out.

Try It Out – Displaying Items User Has for Sale

1 Using your preferred editor, create a new ASP file; enter the following code into your editor:

```
<!--#include file="Chap15DB.inc"-->
<%
If Session("PersonID") = "" Then
Response.Redirect "login.asp"
End If
%>

<!DOCTYPE HTML PUBLIC "-//W3C//DTD HTML 3.2 Final//EN">
<BASEFONT FACE="Comic Sans MS" COLOR="DarkBlue">
<HTML>
<HEAD>
<TITLE>WROX Classifieds</TITLE>
</HEAD>

<BODY BGCOLOR="#FFFF80">
<CENTER>
<H1>WROX Classifieds<BR>Selling Items</H1>
<H3>Welcome <%= Session("FirstName") & " " & Session("Surname") %></H1>
</CENTER>

<P>You currently have the following items for sale:</P>
<%
Dim rsItems
Set rsItems = Server.CreateObject("ADODB.Recordset")
rsItems.Filter = "SellerID = " & Session("PersonID")
rsItems.Open "Item", db
If Not rsItems.EOF Then
%>

<TABLE BORDER="1" CELLSPACING="3" CELLPADDING="3">
<TR><TH>Item ID<BR><FONT SIZE="-1">Click to Edit</FONT></TH>
<TH>Name</TH>
<TH>Asking Price</TH>
<TH>Listing Date</TH>
<TH>Current Bid</TH>
<TH>Bid Time</TH></TR>
<%
Do While Not rsItems.EOF
Response.Write "<TR ALIGN=CENTER><TD>"
Response.Write "<A HREF=""item.asp?Action=Edit&Item=" & rsItems("ItemID")
& """>"
```

```
Response.Write rsItems("ItemID")
Response.Write "</A></TD><TD>"
Response.Write rsItems("ItemName")
Response.Write "</TD><TD>"
Response.Write FormatCurrency(rsItems("AskingPrice"))
Response.Write "</TD><TD>"
Response.Write FormatDateTime(rsItems("ListingDate"),2)
Response.Write "</TD><TD>"
rsItems.MoveNext
Loop
rsItems.Close
%>
</TABLE>

<%
Else
%>
<P><H2>No items currently for sale</H2></P>
<%
End If
%>
<HR>
<TABLE BORDER=0 WIDTH=100%>
<TR ALIGN=CENTER>
<TD WIDTH=33%><A HREF="browse.asp">Browse the listings</A></TD>
<TD WIDTH=33%><A HREF="item.asp?Action=AddNew">Add Sale Items</A></TD>
<TD WIDTH=33%><A HREF="register.asp?update=1">Edit Registration Info
</A></TD>
</TR>
</TABLE>

</BODY>
</HTML>
```

2 Save the file as **ForSale.asp** in your **BegASP** directory.

3 From the Registered Users home page (**registeredMenu.asp**), click on the List/Edit Sale Items hyperlink to view the 'Items for Sale' page.

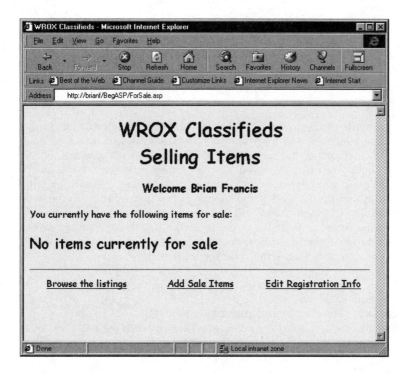

How It Works

This page is used to display the items that the logged-in user currently has for sale. This information is retrieved by querying the Item table for all records where the `SellerID` field is the ID of the current user. The information is then displayed in a table for the user to see.

Since this page will be performing database queries, we will include the `Chap15DB.inc` file, which contains the connection information to the database. Since this page only has relevance to a registered user, we must first check whether or not the user is already registered—if they are not, then we redirect them to the login page:

```
<!--#include file="Chap15DB.inc"-->
<%
If Session("PersonID") = "" Then
 Response.Redirect "login.asp"
End If
%>
```

To retrieve the listing of the items for sale, we will create a recordset. This recordset will be built using the contents of the Item table. We'll fill it *only* with the records for the current user; to achieve this we apply a filter. A filter is very similar to the **WHERE** clause in a SQL statement. In our case, we are telling the recordset to display *only* those Item records for which the value of the `SellerID` field is equal to the `PersonID` of the current user, which is stored in a session-level variable. We then check to see if there are any records that match the filter:

```
Dim rsItems
Set rsItems = Server.CreateObject("ADODB.Recordset")
rsItems.Filter = "SellerID = " & Session("PersonID")
rsItems.Open "Item", db
If Not rsItems.EOF Then
%>
```

If there are records that match our filter, we will display the information to the user in a table. The `Do...While` statement will loop through all of the rows of the table. Each row of the table corresponds to one record in the recordset. The first column will contain the item ID. This will also be a hyperlink: when clicked, it will display a page that enables the user to edit this item's information. Since the `AskingPrice` field is a currency value, we will use the `FormatCurrency` function to give it the proper formatting. In addition, with the `ListingDate` field, the `FormatDateTime` function will present the date in its short format. When all the information for the record is placed into the table, we use the `MoveNext` method of the recordset object to move on to the next record. Once we have gone through all of the records, we can close the recordset. Here's the code for all that:

```
<%
Do While Not rsItems.EOF
Response.Write "<TR ALIGN=CENTER><TD>"
Response.Write "<A HREF=""item.asp?Action=Edit&Item=" & rsItems("ItemID")
& """>"
Response.Write rsItems("ItemID")
Response.Write "</A></TD><TD>"
Response.Write rsItems("ItemName")
Response.Write "</TD><TD>"
Response.Write FormatCurrency(rsItems("AskingPrice"))
Response.Write "</TD><TD>"
Response.Write FormatDateTime(rsItems("ListingDate"),2)
Response.Write "</TD><TD>"
rsItems.MoveNext
Loop
rsItems.Close
%>
```

We present a set of navigation controls across the bottom of the page. There's a new control on this page that allows the user to add a new sale item:

```
<TABLE BORDER=0 WIDTH=100%>
<TR ALIGN=CENTER>
<TD WIDTH=33%><A HREF="browse.asp">Browse the listings</A></TD>
<TD WIDTH=33%><A HREF="item.asp?Action=AddNew">Add Sale Items</A></TD>
<TD WIDTH=33%><A HREF="register.asp?update=1">Edit Registration Info
</A></TD>
</TR>
</TABLE>
```

Adding and Editing Items

Now, we'll look at how this page is constructed.

Try It Out – Adding and Editing Items

1 Create a new ASP file with your editor and key in the following code:

```
<!--#include file="Chap15DB.inc"-->
<!DOCTYPE HTML PUBLIC "-//W3C//DTD HTML 3.2 Final//EN">
<BASEFONT FACE="Comic Sans MS" COLOR="DarkBlue">
<HTML>
<HEAD>
<TITLE>WROX Classifieds - Item for Sale</TITLE>
</HEAD>

<BODY BGCOLOR="#FFFF80">
<%
Dim bNew
Select Case Request.QueryString("Action")
Case "AddNew"
bNew = True
%>

<CENTER><H1>WROX Classifieds<BR>Add New Sale Item</H1></CENTER>
<P>
Please add the following information for the item you have for sale.
<FORM ACTION="AddItem.asp" METHOD="POST">
<INPUT TYPE="Hidden" NAME="ItemID" VALUE="">

<%
Case "Edit"
Dim rsItem, sql
Set rsItem = Server.CreateObject("ADODB.Recordset")
sql = "SELECT * FROM Item WHERE ItemID = " & Request("Item") & ";"
rsItem.Open sql, db, adOpenForwardOnly, adLockOptimistic, adCmdText
bNew = False
%>
<CENTER><H1>WROX Classifieds<BR>Edit Sale Item</H1></CENTER>
<P>
Please edit the information for this item currently for sale.
<FORM ACTION="addItem.asp" METHOD="POST">
<INPUT TYPE="Hidden" NAME="ItemID" VALUE="<%= Request("Item") %>">
<% End Select %>

<TABLE BORDER=0>
<TR>
<TD WIDTH=20% ROWSPAN=11> </TD>
<TD>Item Name:</TD>
```

```
<TD><INPUT TYPE="Text" NAME="ItemName" VALUE="<% If Not bNew Then
Response.Write rsItem("ItemName") End If %>" SIZE="40" MAXLENGTH="75">
</TD>
</TR>
<TR>
 <TD>Description:</TD>
 <TD><TEXTAREA NAME="Description" COLS="40" ROWS="3" WRAP="VIRTUAL"><% If
Not bNew Then Response.Write rsItem("Description") End If %></TEXTAREA>
</TD>
</TR>
<TR>
 <TD>Asking Price:</TD>
 <TD><INPUT TYPE="Text" NAME="AskingPrice" VALUE="<% If Not bNew Then
Response.Write rsItem("AskingPrice") End If %>" SIZE="40"></TD>
</TR>
<TR>
 <TD>Notify Price:</TD>
 <TD><INPUT TYPE="Text" NAME="NotifyPrice" VALUE="<% if Not bNew then
Response.Write rsItem("NotifyPrice") end if %>" SIZE="40"></TD>
</TR>
<TR>
 <TD>Sale Expiration Date:</TD>
 <TD><INPUT TYPE="Text" NAME="ExpirationDate" VALUE="<% if Not bNew then
Response.Write FormatDateTime(rsItem("ExpirationDate"),2) end if %>"
SIZE="40"></TD>
</TR>
<TR>
 <TD></TD>
 <TD ALIGN=CENTER COLSPAN=2><BR><% If Not bNew Then %><INPUT TYPE="Submit"
NAME="Delete" VALUE="Delete Item"><% End If %>  <INPUT
TYPE="Submit" VALUE="<% If bNew then %>Add New Item<% Else %>Update
Item<% End If %>">  <INPUT TYPE="RESET"></TD>
</TR>
</TABLE>

</FORM>

<HR>
<TABLE BORDER=0 WIDTH=100%>
<TR ALIGN=CENTER>
<TD WIDTH=33%><A HREF="browse.asp">Browse the listings</A></TD>
<TD WIDTH=33%>Add Sale Items</TD>
<TD WIDTH=33%><A HREF="register.asp?update=1">Edit Registration Info
</A></TD>
</TR>
</TABLE>

</BODY>
</HTML>
```

2 Save the file as `Item.asp`, in your `BegASP` directory.

3 Create another blank file in your editor and enter the following code:

```
<!--#include file="Chap15DB.inc"-->
<%
Dim rsItem
Dim bNew
Set rsItem = Server.CreateObject("ADODB.Recordset")
rsItem.Open "Item", db, adOpenForwardOnly, adLockOptimistic, adCmdTable
If Request.Form("Delete") <> "" Then
rsItem.Filter = "ItemID = " & Request("ItemID")
If Not rsItem.EOF Then rsItem.Delete
rsItem.Close
Else
If Request("ItemID") = "" Then
        bNew = True
        rsItem.AddNew
Else
        rsItem.Filter = "ItemID = " & Request("ItemID")
        bNew = False
End If
rsItem("ItemName") = Request.Form("ItemName")
rsItem("Description") = Request.Form("Description")
rsItem("AskingPrice") = Request.Form("AskingPrice")
rsItem("NotifyPrice") = Request.Form("NotifyPrice")
rsItem("SellerID") = Session("PersonID")
rsItem("ItemStatus") = "Active"
If bNew = True Then
        rsItem("ListingDate") = Now
End If
If Left(Request.Form("ExpirationDate"),1) = "+" then
        Dim dDelta
        dDelta =
Mid(Request.Form("ExpirationDate"),2,len(Request.Form("ExpirationDate")))
        rsItem("ExpirationDate") = DateAdd("d", dDelta, Now)
Else
        rsItem("ExpirationDate") = Request.Form("ExpirationDate")
End If
rsItem.Update

If bNew Then
        Dim rsSeller
        Set rsSeller = Server.CreateObject("ADODB.Recordset")
        rsSeller.Open "Seller", db, adOpenForwardOnly, adLockOptimistic,
adCmdTable
        rsSeller.Filter = "PersonID = " & Session("PersonID")
        If rsSeller.EOF Then
                rsSeller.AddNew
                rsSeller("PersonID") = Session("PersonID")
```

```
                  rsSeller("ItemsListed") = 0
                  rsSeller("ItemsActive") = 0
            End If
         rsSeller("ItemsListed") = rsSeller("ItemsListed") + 1
         rsSeller("ItemsActive") = rsSeller("ItemsActive") + 1
         rsSeller("LastActivity") = Now
         rsSeller.Update
         rsSeller.Close
   End If
   End If
   Response.Redirect "ForSale.asp"
   %>
```

4 Save the file as **addItem.asp**, in your **BegASP** directory.

5 Go back to your browser. From the 'Selling Items' page (**ForSale.asp**), click on the Add New Item button, and insert sale details for some item that you wish to sell:

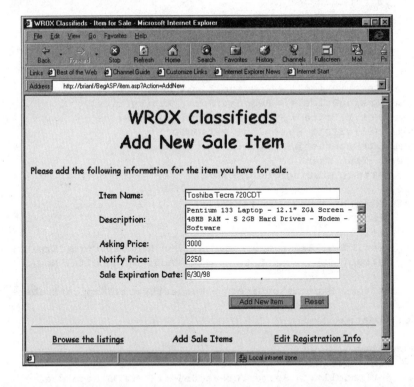

6 Now click on Add New Item. This will return you to the 'Selling Items' page

(`ForSale.asp`), which now sumarizes the items that you have for sale.

7 Click on the ItemID of an item that you wish to edit (there's only one here at the moment). Alternatively, click on the Add Sale Items hyperlink at the bottom to add more new entries.

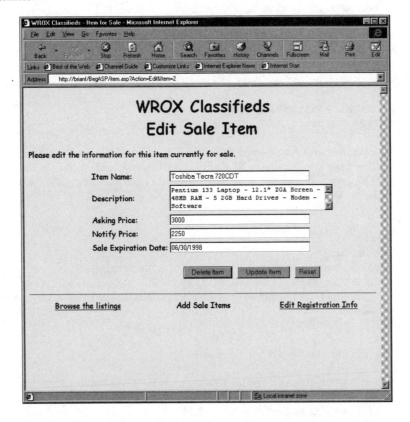

How It Works

The `item.asp` page is used both for adding new sale items and editing existing sale items. At any given time, the query string variable called `Action` indicates the particular function that the page is performing.

The `Select Case` statement is used to evaluate the value of the `Action` variable, and consequently select the appropriate code block to execute. If the value of `Action` is `AddNew`, then this form is being used to add a new sale item:

```
Dim bNew
Select Case Request.QueryString("Action")
Case "AddNew"
bNew = True
%>
```

In this case, the header information on the page indicates to the user that they are adding a *new* item. Notice that this is done as straight HTML, inside of the ASP page. You need to remember that the flow control statements like `Select Case` and `If Then` affect both script and HTML. This HTML code outputs our header within the `Select Case` statement; it is only displayed when the user is adding a new item:

```
<CENTER><H1>WROX Classifieds<BR>Add New Sale Item</H1></CENTER>
<P>
Please add the following information for the item you have for sale.
```

After the header, the page displays a `FORM` that allows the user to add (or edit) item information. When the user has entered the information, the form will be submitted and processed by the `AddItem.asp` file. In this case, since the user is adding a *new* item, the item's ID is still to be determined, so we pass a blank value to the `AddItem.asp` script:

```
<FORM ACTION="AddItem.asp" METHOD="POST">
<INPUT TYPE="Hidden" NAME="ItemID" VALUE="">
```

In the second case, the user has elected to edit an *existing* sale item. We first need to retrieve the item's information from the database. To do this, we use a recordset that is created from the results of an SQL query. This query will return records from the Item table where the value of ItemID is the same as the one we want to edit:

```
<%
Case "Edit"
Dim rsItem, sql
Set rsItem = Server.CreateObject("ADODB.Recordset")
sql = "SELECT * FROM Item WHERE ItemID = " & Request("Item") & ";"
rsItem.Open sql, db, adOpenForwardOnly, adLockOptimistic, adCmdText
bNew = False
%>
```

We display the appropriate header on the page:

```
<CENTER><H1>WROX Classifieds<BR>Edit Sale Item</H1></CENTER>
<P>
Please edit the information for this item currently for sale.
```

We use the same ASP script, `addItem.asp`, to handle the editing of an item along with the addition of an item. Since we are editing an item, we need to pass its `itemID` to the script for processing. This is done using a hidden `FORM INPUT` field:

```
<FORM ACTION="addItem.asp" METHOD="POST">
<INPUT TYPE="Hidden" NAME="ItemID" VALUE="<%= Request("Item") %>">
<% End Select %>
```

Next, we build the form to allow the user to modify the information about the item. The form is laid out in a table so that we have nice formatting. The form is used both for editing and for new entry; in the case of editing, we need to display the existing information in the corresponding field:

```
<TABLE BORDER=0>
<TR>
<TD WIDTH=20% ROWSPAN=11> </TD>
 <TD>Item Name:</TD>
 <TD><INPUT TYPE="Text" NAME="ItemName" VALUE="<% If Not bNew Then
Response.Write rsItem("ItemName") End If %>" SIZE="40" MAXLENGTH="75">
</TD>
</TR>
<TR>
 <TD>Description:</TD>
 <TD><TEXTAREA NAME="Description" COLS="40" ROWS="3" WRAP="VIRTUAL">
<% If Not bNew Then Response.Write rsItem("Description") End If %>
</TEXTAREA></TD>
</TR>
```

You may have noticed that, at the beginning of the script, we set a variable called **bNew** to indicate whether the user is adding a new item. In each **FORM** element, we check its value; if it is **False**, then the user is editing an existing record. If this is the case, then we can take the value that was contained in the database and display it in the form using the **VALUE** property of the **INPUT** element. For the **Description** field, since we are using a **TEXTAREA** element, the existing data goes in between the **<TEXTAREA></TEXTAREA>** tags.

When the form is complete, we give the user three options:

```
<TD ALIGN=CENTER COLSPAN=2><BR><% If Not bNew Then %><INPUT TYPE="Submit"
NAME="Delete" VALUE="Delete Item"><% End If %>  <INPUT
TYPE="Submit" VALUE="<% If bNew then %>Add New Item<% Else %>Update
Item<% End If %>">  <INPUT TYPE="RESET"></TD>
</TR>
</TABLE>
```

First, they can reset the information in the form and start over. Second, they can choose to submit the information on the form. Again, we are using the value of the **bNew** variable to change the label on the Submit button. This demonstrates one of the greatest strengths of Active Server Pages—the ability to dynamically change the presentation of information based on the content and the context.

Lastly, the user can choose to delete the item from the database. Since this is only relevant when the user is editing an existing item, this button is only displayed when the value of **bNew** is **False**. In addition to having a **VALUE** parameter, which controls the button caption, the Delete button also has a **NAME** parameter. In a moment, we'll see how this is used in the **addItem.asp** file to determine which of the buttons was clicked by the user.

That's it for the **Item.asp** code. Let's look at **addItem.asp** now.

In the **addItem.asp** file, we will be interacting with the Item table by using a recordset that is populated with the contents of the table. Since we will be changing the information in the table, we need to set the locking parameter to **adLockOptimistic**. This will allow us to change the information in the table:

```
Dim rsItem
Dim bNew
Set rsItem = Server.CreateObject("ADODB.Recordset")
rsItem.Open "Item", db, adOpenForwardOnly, adLockOptimistic, adCmdTable
```

We first check to see whether the user selected the Delete button on the **Item.asp** page. If so, the contents of the **NAME** parameter from that button will be placed in the **Delete** element of the **Form** collection. We know that if there is any value present, then the user wishes to delete this item. To perform the deletion, we set a **Filter** on the recordset so that only the record that matches the **ItemID** is present. Although there should be one and only one record present after the filter is applied, we perform a check to make sure that a record is present before issuing the **Delete** method to remove the record. Once that has been completed, we can close the recordset:

```
If Request.Form("Delete") <> "" Then
    rsItem.Filter = "ItemID = " & Request("ItemID")
    If Not rsItem.EOF Then rsItem.Delete
    rsItem.Close
```

Having completed the deletion, we now need to check whether the user is adding a new item, or editing an existing one. This is determined by the value supplied in the ItemID element of the **Request**:

```
Else
    If Request("ItemID") = "" Then
        bNew = True
        rsItem.AddNew
    Else
        rsItem.Filter = "ItemID = " & Request("ItemID")
        bNew = False
    End If
```

If the user is adding a new item, then we call the **AddNew** method of the recordset to prepare a new item of information. If we are editing an existing item, then we set the **Filter** property so that the recordset contains only the item we are interested in.

> *Notice that we don't specify the **Request** object collection as the place to look for the **ItemID** value. This is being done simply to show a programmer's shortcut. As we saw in Chapter 7, if the collection is not specified when accessing an item, then the collections are searched in this order: **QueryString**, **Form**, **Cookies**, **ClientCertificate**, **ServerVariables**. If the name appears in multiple collections, then the first collection that it appears in will be the one whose value is returned.*

We can now update all of the fields of the recordset. Since we have preloaded the form fields with the existing data, we don't have to worry about updating fields that the user did not want to change. The **ListingDate** field should only be updated if this is a new record, so we again use the **bNew** variable to indicate that:

```
rsItem("ItemName") = Request.Form("ItemName")
rsItem("Description") = Request.Form("Description")
rsItem("AskingPrice") = Request.Form("AskingPrice")
rsItem("NotifyPrice") = Request.Form("NotifyPrice")
```

```
    rsItem("SellerID") = Session("PersonID")
    rsItem("ItemStatus") = "Active"
    If bNew = True Then
            rsItem("ListingDate") = Now
    End If
    If Left(Request.Form("ExpirationDate"),1) = "+" then
            Dim dDelta
            dDelta =
  Mid(Request.Form("ExpirationDate"),2,len(Request.Form("ExpirationDate")))
            rsItem("ExpirationDate") = DateAdd("d", dDelta, Now)
    Else
            rsItem("ExpirationDate") = Request.Form("ExpirationDate")
    End If
    rsItem.Update
```

A nice user interface feature that we support here is the ability to enter the sale expiration date as a number of days. This means that if the user wants the sale period for an item to be three weeks, then they simply enter +21, and the system will figure out what the expiration date should be. We use the **DateAdd** method to compute this; we add the number of days specified by the user to today's date. Once all of the changes have been made, the **Update** method of the recordset is called and the changes are written to the database.

When we are adding a new item for sale, we also need to update the **Seller** table. This table contains statistical information about an individual seller. To update this information, we will use a recordset that is based on the contents of the **Seller** table. Once the recordset is opened, we set a **Filter** on it to only display the record for the current user. If this filter returns an empty recordset, we know that we need to add a new record to the **Seller** table:

```
    If bNew Then
            Dim rsSeller
            Set rsSeller = Server.CreateObject("ADODB.Recordset")
            rsSeller.Open "Seller", db, adOpenForwardOnly, adLockOptimistic,
    adCmdTable
            rsSeller.Filter = "PersonID = " & Session("PersonID")
            If rsSeller.EOF Then
                    rsSeller.AddNew
                    rsSeller("PersonID") = Session("PersonID")
                    rsSeller("ItemsListed") = 0
                    rsSeller("ItemsActive") = 0
            End If
            rsSeller("ItemsListed") = rsSeller("ItemsListed") + 1
            rsSeller("ItemsActive") = rsSeller("ItemsActive") + 1
            rsSeller("LastActivity") = Now
            rsSeller.Update
            rsSeller.Close
    End If
```

To do this, we call the **AddNew** method, and then update the information in the record. We will be initializing the **ItemsListed** and **ItemsActive** fields to 0. Since the user has just added another item for sale, we can add one to the values of both the **ItemsListed** and **ItemsActive** fields. When we added the new record, this is why we initialized the values to 0.

If there had been a non-numeric value present before we initialized it, then adding 1 to it would have generated an error. Finally, we set the `LastActivity` field to today, then update and close the recordset.

Once all of the information has been updated in the database, we will redirect the browser back to the `ForSale.asp` page:

```
Response.Redirect "ForSale.asp"
%>
```

Since that page is dynamically generated, it will display the new or updated item information in its table.

Browsing Items for Sale

Now that you have entered items for sale into the system, the next step is to *browse* the items that are for sale. Our system provides a very simple interface for doing this. All of the items are merely presented in a list. This leaves the door open for later enhancement, such as providing other ways of viewing the items that are for sale.

Try It Out – Browsing the Items for Sale

1 Activate your web page editor and key up the following code:

```
<!--#include file="Chap15DB.inc"-->
<!DOCTYPE HTML PUBLIC "-//W3C//DTD HTML 3.2 Final//EN">
<BASEFONT FACE="Comic Sans MS" COLOR="DarkBlue">
<HTML>
<HEAD>
<TITLE>WROX Classifieds</TITLE>
</HEAD>

<BODY BGCOLOR="#FFFF80">
<CENTER><H1>WROX Classifieds<BR>Items for sale</H1>
<% If Session("PersonID") <> "" Then %>
 <H3>Welcome <%= Session("FirstName") & " " & Session("Surname") %></H3>
<% End If %>
</CENTER>
<P>These items are currently for sale:</P>
<%
Dim rsItems, sql
sql = "SELECT * FROM Item WHERE ExpirationDate > #" &
FormatDateTime(Now,2) & "# AND ItemStatus = 'Active';"

Set rsItems = Server.CreateObject("ADODB.Recordset")
rsItems.Open sql, db
```

```
If Not rsItems.EOF Then%>
<TABLE BORDER="1" CELLSPACING="3" CELLPADDING="3">
<TR><TH>Item ID<% If Session("PersonID") <> "" Then %><BR>
Click to Bid
<%
End If %></TH>
<TH>Name</TH><TH>Asking Price</TH><TH>Listing Date</TH>
<TH>Current Bid</TH><TH>Bid Time</TH></TR>
<%
Do While Not rsItems.EOF
        Response.Write "<TR align=center><TD>"
        If Session("PersonID") <> "" Then
                Response.Write "<A HREF=""bid.asp?Item=" &
rsItems("ItemID") & """>"
        End If
        Response.Write rsItems("ItemID")
        If Session("PersonID") <> "" then
                Response.Write "</A>"
        End If
        Response.Write "</TD><TD>"
        Response.Write rsItems("ItemName")
        Response.Write "</TD><TD>"
        Response.Write FormatCurrency(rsItems("AskingPrice"))
        Response.Write "</TD><TD>"
        Response.Write FormatDateTime(rsItems("ListingDate"),2)
        Response.Write "</TD>"
        Response.Write "</TR>"
        rsItems.MoveNext
Loop
rsItems.Close
%>
</TABLE>

<%
Else%>
<H2>No Items currently for sale</H2>
<%
End If%>

<P>
<HR>
<TABLE BORDER=0 WIDTH=100%>
<TR ALIGN=CENTER>
<% If Session("PersonID") <> "" then %>
<TD WIDTH=33%>Browse the listings</TD>
<TD WIDTH=33%><A HREF="ForSale.asp">List/Edit Sale Items</A></TD>
<TD WIDTH=33%><A HREF="register.asp?update=1">Edit Registration Info
</A></TD>
</TR>
</TABLE>
<% Else  %>
```

```
<TD WIDTH=33%>Browse the listings</TD>
<TD WIDTH=33%><A HREF="login.asp">Login</A></TD>
<TD WIDTH=33%><A HREF="register.asp">I'm a new user</A></TD>
</TR>
</TABLE>
<% End If %>

</BODY>
</HTML>
```

2 Save the file as **Browse.asp** in the **BegASP** directory.

3 From the Selling Items page (**ForSale.asp**), click on Browse the listings.

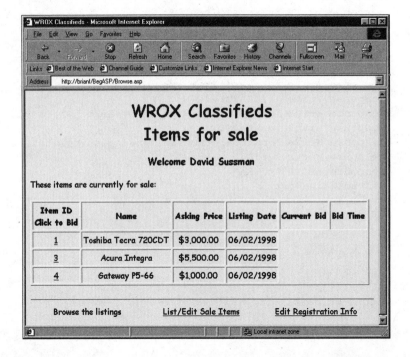

 FYI I've also created another user who is selling other items. They're displayed in the screen above.

How It Works

The method for displaying the items for sale is very similar to the method used for the List/Edit Sale Items page. The primary difference is that this page will display *all* items for sale by all users, while the List/Edit Sale Items page displays *only* those items being sold by the current user.

530

This page can be displayed for users who are registered with the system and for users who have not registered. If the user has registered, then we want to give some visual indication that the system recognizes who they are.

By checking the value of the session-level variable **PersonID**, we can determine if we have a currently logged-in user. If this is a registered user, then we will display their first name and surname just below the title of the page:

```
<% If Session("PersonID") <> "" Then %>
<H3>Welcome <%= Session("FirstName") & " " & Session("Surname") %></H3>
<% End If %>
```

As we have shown before, all of the information about the user is stored in session-level variables, so retrieving it is quick and easy.

We will be using a recordset to store all of the items that are currently for sale. This recordset is populated from the results of a SQL query:

```
Dim rsItems, sql
sql = "SELECT * FROM Item WHERE ExpirationDate > #" &
FormatDateTime(Now,2) & "# AND ItemStatus = 'Active';"

Set rsItems = Server.CreateObject("ADODB.Recordset")
rsItems.Open sql, db
```

This query will retrieve all of the records from the Item table that have an **ItemStatus** value of **Active**, and whose Expiration Date has not yet passed. We can check the **EOF** property of the new recordset to determine if there are any items for sale:

```
If Not rsItems.EOF Then%>
```

If the database contains items for sale, we loop through each record in the recordset and display the information about each item in a table, one row per item. We create a hyperlink around the Item ID—this allows a user to bid on that item. Since this page can be seen by both registered and non-registered users, we need only show this hyperlink if this is a registered user. Again, we will check the value contained in the session-level variable PersonID to see if the current user is registered. Other than that, the display is very similar to the display used in the List/Edit Sale Items page:

```
<%
Do While Not rsItems.EOF
        Response.Write "<TR align=center><TD>"
        If Session("PersonID") <> "" Then
                Response.Write "<A HREF=""bid.asp?Item=" &
rsItems("ItemID") & """>"
        End If
        Response.Write rsItems("ItemID")
        If Session("PersonID") <> "" then
                Response.Write "</A>"
        End If
        Response.Write "</TD><TD>"
```

```
            Response.Write rsItems("ItemName")
            Response.Write "</TD><TD>"
            Response.Write FormatCurrency(rsItems("AskingPrice"))
            Response.Write "</TD><TD>"
            Response.Write FormatDateTime(rsItems("ListingDate"),2)
            Response.Write "</TD>"
            Response.Write "</TR>"
            rsItems.MoveNext
    Loop
    rsItems.Close
    %>
```

If the recordset that our query created is empty, then we can display a message to the user indicating that there are no items currently for sale:

```
<%
Else%>
<H2>No Items currently for sale</H2>
<%
End If%>
```

In the screenshot of the page, you may have noticed the Current Bid and Bid Time columns. These are used to display any current bid information about each item. Next, we'll talk about how to bid for an item—after that, we'll return to this page and show you how to display the bid information.

Bidding for an Item

The user browses the list of items for sale, and selects an item that they are interested in. Then they can place a bid on that item. To place a bid on an item, the user will select the hyperlinked ItemID of the item they wish to bid on. This will take them to a page where they can enter their bid.

Try It Out – Bidding for an Item

1 Using your favorite web page editor, create a new ASP file.

2 Type in the following:

```
<!--#include file="Chap15DB.inc"-->
<!DOCTYPE HTML PUBLIC "-//W3C//DTD HTML 3.2 Final//EN">
<BASEFONT FACE="Comic Sans MS" COLOR="DarkBlue">
<HTML>
<HEAD>
<TITLE>WROX Classifieds - Item Bid</TITLE>
</HEAD>
```

```
<BODY BGCOLOR="#FFFF80">
<%
Dim rsItem, sql, itemName, Description
Set rsItem = Server.CreateObject("ADODB.Recordset")
sql = "SELECT * FROM Item WHERE ItemID =" & Request("Item")
rsItem.Open sql, db
itemName = rsItem("ItemName")
Description = rsItem("Description")
rsItem.Close

Dim rsBids
Set rsBids = Server.CreateObject("ADODB.Recordset")
sql = "SELECT * FROM Bid WHERE ItemID =" & Request("Item") & " ORDER BY
TimeStamp DESC;"
rsBids.Open sql, db
%>

<CENTER><H1>WROX Classifieds<BR>Bidding for <%= ItemName %></H1></CENTER>
<P>
<%
Dim highBid
highBid = 0
If rsBids.EOF Then%>
No Bids Currently Placed
<%
Else%>
Bid History (Newest to Oldest)
<TABLE BORDER="2" CELLSPACING="3" CELLPADDING="3">
<TR><TH>Bidder ID</TH>
<TH>Timestamp</TH>
<TH>Amount Bid</TH>
<TH>Last Change</TH></TR>
<%
Do While Not rsBids.EOF %>
        <TR><TD><%= rsBids("BidderID") %></TD>
        <TD><%= rsBids("Timestamp") %></TD>
        <TD ALIGN=RIGHT><%= FormatCurrency(rsBids("BidAmount")) %></TD>
        <TD ALIGN=RIGHT><%= FormatCurrency(rsBids("BidChange")) %></TD>
        </TR>
<%
        If highBid = 0 Then highBid = rsBids("BidAmount")
        rsBids.MoveNext
Loop
rsBids.Close
%>
</TABLE>
<% End If %>

<FORM NAME="frmBid" ACTION="AddBid.asp" METHOD="POST" onSubmit="return
VerifyData()">
<INPUT TYPE="Hidden" NAME="ItemID" VALUE="<%= Request("Item") %>">
```

533

```
<P>
<TABLE WIDTH="70%" BORDER="0" CELLPADDING=5>
<TR>
 <TD WIDTH=20% ROWSPAN=11> </TD><TD WIDTH=15%>Item Name:</TD>
 <TD><%= ItemName %></TD>
</TR>
<TR>
 <TD></TD>
 <TD><%= Description %></TD>
</TR>
<TR>
 <TD>Bid:</TD>
 <TD><INPUT TYPE="Text" NAME="Bid" SIZE="40"></TD>
</TR>
<TR>
 <TD></TD>
 <TD ALIGN=CENTER COLSPAN=2><BR><INPUT TYPE="Submit" VALUE="Bid on
Item">  <INPUT TYPE="RESET"></TD>
</TR>
</TABLE>
</FORM>

<HR>
<TABLE BORDER=0 WIDTH=100%>
<TR ALIGN=CENTER>
<TD WIDTH=33%><A HREF="browse.asp">Browse the listings</A></TD>
<TD WIDTH=33%>Add Sale Items</TD>
<TD WIDTH=33%><A HREF="register.asp?update=1">Edit Registration Info
</A></TD></TR>
</TABLE>

</BODY>
<SCRIPT language="JavaScript">
<!--
function VerifyData()
{
 if (document.frmBid.Bid.value <= <%= highBid %>)
 {
       alert ("You must bid higher than the previous bid of <%=
FormatCurrency(highBid) %>.");
       return false;
 }
 else
       return true;
}
-->
</SCRIPT>

</HTML>
```

3 In the `BegASP` directory, save the file as `Bid.asp`.

4 Create another blank file in your editor and enter the following code:

```
<!--#include file="Chap15DB.inc"-->
<%
Dim oCmd, rsHighBid, sql, highBid

Set oCmd = Server.CreateObject("ADODB.Command")
Set oCmd.ActiveConnection = db
sql = "SELECT Max(BidAmount) AS MaxBidAmount FROM Bid WHERE ItemID = " &
Request("ItemID") & ";"
oCmd.CommandType = adCmdText
oCmd.CommandText = sql
set rsHighBid = oCmd.Execute

If IsNull( rsHighBid("MaxBidAmount") ) Then
highBid = 0
Else
highBid = rsHighBid("MaxBidAmount")
End If
rsHighBid.Close

Dim rsBid
Set rsBid = Server.CreateObject("ADODB.Recordset")
rsBid.Open "Bid", db, adOpenForwardOnly, adLockOptimistic, adCmdTable
rsBid.AddNew
rsBid("ItemID") = Request.Form("ItemID")
rsBid("BidderID") = Session("PersonID")
rsBid("BidAmount") = CCur(Request.Form("Bid"))
rsBid("BidChange") = CCur(Request.Form("Bid")) - highBid

rsBid.Update
Response.Redirect "browse.asp"
%>
```

5 Save the file as `AddBid.asp` in the `BegASP` directory.

6 From the Browse page, click on the ItemID of an item that you want to bid on.

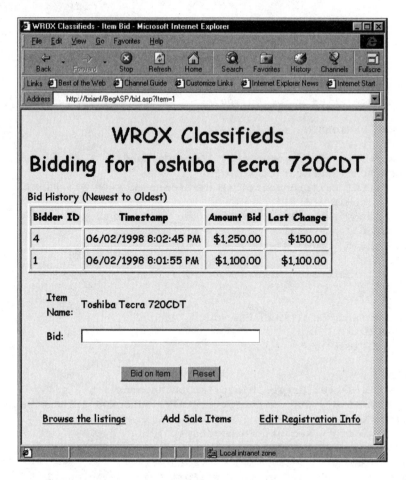

I've added a couple of 'previous bids' here, so you can see what they look like. The first time you make a bid, you'll receive the message "No bids currently placed" instead of the 'Bid History' table.

How It Works

There are two parts to the page for bidding on an item. First, there is a listing of all of the current bids on the item. Second, there is a form that allows you to place your own bid on the item.

The first step is to retrieve the descriptive information about the item. This information is stored in the Item table. We use a recordset that is populated by a SQL query to retrieve the information, and we store the values of the item's name and description in local variables for later use:

```
Dim rsItem, sql, itemName, Description
Set rsItem = Server.CreateObject("ADODB.Recordset")
sql = "SELECT * FROM Item WHERE ItemID =" & Request("Item")
rsItem.Open sql, db
```

```
itemName = rsItem("ItemName")
Description = rsItem("Description")
```

Since we have done all that we need to do with the item recordset, we can go ahead and close it:

```
rsItem.Close
```

Next, we will turn our attention to building the listing of the previous bids for the item we are bidding on. The information about bids is stored in the **Bid** table. We will retrieve all of the bids for the current item by using a SQL query, and store the results in a recordset. The SQL query will select all of the Bid records where the **ItemID** of the bid matches the **ItemID** of the item we are bidding on:

```
Dim rsBids
Set rsBids = Server.CreateObject("ADODB.Recordset")
sql = "SELECT * FROM Bid WHERE ItemID =" & Request("Item") & " ORDER BY
TimeStamp DESC;"
rsBids.Open sql, db
```

We also use the **ORDER BY** clause of the SQL statement to arrange the bids according to the time that they were placed. Since we want to see the bids in reverse order—that is, from newest to oldest—we add the **DESC** modifier to the **ORDER BY** clause.

One of the pieces of information that we need from the bid information is the amount of the highest bid. We know that each bid placed must be higher than the previous bid placed. Therefore, the last bid to be placed will also have the highest amount. Since we have retrieved our records in reverse time order, the first record we retrieve will also be the highest bidder. The amount of the highest bid will be placed in the local variable **highBid**:

```
<%
Dim highBid
highBid = 0
If rsBids.EOF Then%>
No Bids Currently Placed
```

We loop through all of the bids and display their information on a row in the table:

```
<%
Do While Not rsBids.EOF %>
        <TR><TD><%= rsBids("BidderID") %></TD>
        <TD><%= rsBids("Timestamp") %></TD>
        <TD ALIGN=RIGHT><%= FormatCurrency(rsBids("BidAmount")) %></TD>
        <TD ALIGN=RIGHT><%= FormatCurrency(rsBids("BidChange")) %></TD>
        </TR>
<%
        If highBid = 0 Then highBid = rsBids("BidAmount")
        rsBids.MoveNext
Loop
rsBids.Close
%>
```

To display the amount of each bid and the change since the last bid in a currency format, we use the **FormatCurrency** function to properly format the string. The variable storing the highest bid is initialized to zero. We know that in the first iteration of the loop its value will still be 0. By checking for this, we can assign the amount of the first bid in the list as the high bid amount. All subsequent times through the loop, the value of **highBid** will be something other than 0, so the value will not be changed.

Once all of the previous bid information has been displayed, we can display the form, to let the user enter the amount that they wish to bid. This form will send its contents to the **AddBid.asp** script file for processing:

```
<FORM NAME="frmBid" ACTION="AddBid.asp" METHOD="POST" onSubmit="return
VerifyData()">
<INPUT TYPE="Hidden" NAME="ItemID" VALUE="<%= Request("Item") %>">
```

In this example, we also want to do some client-side validation of the information that is being submitted. To do this, we have added an **onSubmit** parameter to the **<FORM>** tag. This parameter will tell the browser to run the **VerifyData()** method when the form submit button is pressed, but before the form is actually submitted.

The **VerifyData()** function is called when the user presses the Submit button to submit their bid for the item. It is important to ensure that any bid being submitted is higher than any previous bid. To check this without involving a round trip to the server, we use a client-side validation routine: we check to see whether the bid that the user just entered is higher than the previous high bid. If it is, then the form will continue to be submitted. If the bid is lower, then the form will not be submitted and an error message box will be displayed for the user:

```
<SCRIPT language="JavaScript">
<!--
function VerifyData()
{
if (document.frmBid.Bid.value <= <%= highBid %>)
{
        alert ("You must bid higher than the previous bid of <%=
FormatCurrency(highBid) %>.");
        return false;
}
else
        return true;
}
-->
</SCRIPT>
```

When the form is finally submitted for processing, the processing is performed by the **addBid.asp** script file. This is another of our interface-less files. All that it is responsible for is adding the bid information to the database, then sending the user off to another page.

The first step in the **addBid.asp** script is to determine the item's previous high bid. To do this, we use the **Command** object. The **Command** object is another ADO object like the recordset object. We use it to execute a SQL statement to create a recordset:

```
<%
Dim oCmd, rsHighBid, sql, highBid

Set oCmd = Server.CreateObject("ADODB.Command")
Set oCmd.ActiveConnection = db
sql = "SELECT Max(BidAmount) AS MaxBidAmount FROM Bid WHERE ItemID = " &
Request("ItemID") & ";"
oCmd.CommandType = adCmdText
oCmd.CommandText = sql
set rsHighBid = oCmd.Execute
```

While we could have just as easily used a recordset object here, you will see in a later example how this is done.

The `Command` object has three parameters, that must be set before it can function properly. First, the `ActiveConnection` property should reference the same connection object, `db`, which we have used with all of our recordsets. Second, since we will be using a SQL query to retrieve information, we need to set the `CommandType` property to `adCmdText`. This tells the `Command` object that we will be passing a text command, rather than a table name, for it to process. Finally, we need to set the `CommandText` property to the SQL statement that we have created.

Our SQL statement will be used to perform calculations along with retrieving information from the Bid table. Since we're only interested in the time and value of the previous high bid, we can use the `Max()` function inside of the SQL statement. This function will go through all of the records that match the `WHERE` clause, and return only the record that has the highest value.

> We have also added an `AS` statement to the SQL query, which renames the results of the
> `Max()` functions. If we don't do this, then we would have to access the field as
> `Max(BidAmount)` which is a little confusing.

Since we are performing a calculation in our SQL query, there will always be a result returned. This means that we cannot use the `EOF` property to determine whether or not any information is present. Instead, we must check whether each value is Null. A Null value implies that there are no previous bids; and therefore the high bid is 0:

```
If IsNull( rsHighBid("MaxBidAmount") ) Then
highBid = 0
Else
highBid = rsHighBid("MaxBidAmount")
End If
```

Once we have retrieved the high bid information, we can close this recordset.

```
rsHighBid.Close
```

Next, we can add the new bid to the Bid table. This will be done using a recordset that represents the table. We will open it using the `adLockOptimistic` parameter, so that we can write the new bid to the table. The value of the `BidChange` field is calculated by subtracting the previous high bid from the new bid. Once all of the data has been entered, the `Update` method is called to write the changes to the database:

```
Dim rsBid
Set rsBid = Server.CreateObject("ADODB.Recordset")
rsBid.Open "Bid", db, adOpenForwardOnly, adLockOptimistic, adCmdTable
rsBid.AddNew
rsBid("ItemID") = Request.Form("ItemID")
rsBid("BidderID") = Session("PersonID")
rsBid("BidAmount") = CCur(Request.Form("Bid"))
rsBid("BidChange") = CCur(Request.Form("Bid")) - highBid

rsBid.Update
```

Finally, the user is redirected back to the **browse** page:

```
Response.Redirect "browse.asp"
```

Now that we know how to retrieve bid information from the database, we can go back to some of the previous screens and add in the code to display the bid history.

Try It Out – Add the Bid History Display

We will be adding bid history information to the Browse and Item pages. We will also be adding some additional code to the item deletion script that is found in the **addItem.asp** page.

1 Using your chosen editor, open the **browse.asp** file.

2 Add the following highlighted fragments into the body of the **browse.asp** file:

```
If Not rsItems.EOF Then%>
<TABLE BORDER="1" CELLSPACING="3" CELLPADDING="3">
<TR><TH>Item ID<% If Session("PersonID") <> "" Then %><BR>
Click to Bid
<%
End If %></TH>
<TH>Name</TH><TH>Asking Price</TH><TH>Listing Date</TH>
<TH>Current Bid</TH><TH>Bid Time</TH></TR>
<%
Dim oCmd, rsBid
Set oCmd = Server.CreateObject("ADODB.Command")
Set oCmd.ActiveConnection = db
sql = "SELECT Max(BidAmount) AS MaxBidAmount, Max(TimeStamp) as
LastBidTime FROM Bid"
oCmd.CommandType = adCmdText
Do While Not rsItems.EOF
        Response.Write "<TR align=center><TD>"
        If Session("PersonID") <> "" Then
                Response.Write "<A HREF=""bid.asp?Item=" &
rsItems("ItemID") & """>"
```

```
          End If
          Response.Write rsItems("ItemID")
          If Session("PersonID") <> "" then
                  Response.Write "</A>"
          End If
          Response.Write "</TD><TD>"
          Response.Write rsItems("ItemName")
          Response.Write "</TD><TD>"
          Response.Write FormatCurrency(rsItems("AskingPrice"))
          Response.Write "</TD><TD>"
          Response.Write FormatDateTime(rsItems("ListingDate"),2)
          Response.Write "</TD>"
          oCmd.CommandText = sql & " WHERE ItemID = " & rsItems("ItemID") &
";"

          Set rsBid = oCmd.Execute
          If IsNull( rsBid("MaxBidAmount") ) Then
                  Response.Write "<TD colspan=2><FONT SIZE=""-1"">No bids
placed</FONT></TD></TR>"
          Else
                  Response.Write "<TD>" &
FormatCurrency(rsBid("MaxBidAmount"))
                  Response.Write "</TD><TD>"
                  Response.Write rsBid("LastBidTime")

                  Response.Write "</TD>"
                  Dim sql2, rsHighBidder
                  sql2 = "SELECT BidderID FROM Bid WHERE ItemID = " &
rsItems("ItemID") & " ORDER BY TimeStamp DESC"
                  oCmd.CommandType = adCmdText
                  oCmd.CommandText = sql2
                  Set rsHighBidder = oCmd.Execute
                  If rsHighBidder("BidderID") = Session("PersonID") Then
                          Response.Write "<TD><FONT size=""-1""
COLOR=""Red"">Current High Bidder</FONT></TD>"
                          rsHighBidder.Close
                  End If
                  Response.Write "</TR>"
          End If
          rsBid.Close
          rsItems.MoveNext
Loop
rsItems.Close
%>
</TABLE>
```

3 Save these changes to the **browse.asp** file.

4 Click on the Browse the listings hyperlink to view the new browse page.

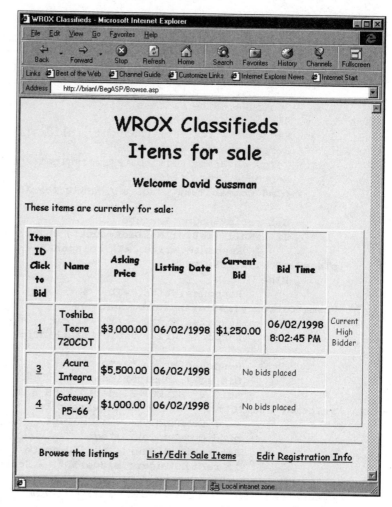

5 Next, open the **ForSale.asp** file in your editor.

6 Insert the following code snippets into the body of the **ForSale.asp** file:

```
<TABLE BORDER="1" CELLSPACING="3" CELLPADDING="3">
<TR><TH>Item ID<BR><FONT SIZE="-1">Click to Edit</FONT></TH>
<TH>Name</TH>
<TH>Asking Price</TH>
<TH>Listing Date</TH>
<TH>Current Bid</TH>
<TH>Bid Time</TH></TR>
<%
Dim oCmd, rsBid
Set oCmd = Server.CreateObject("ADODB.Command")
Set oCmd.ActiveConnection = db
sql = "SELECT Max(BidAmount) AS MaxBidAmount, Max(TimeStamp) as
```

```
LastBidTime FROM Bid"
oCmd.CommandType = adCmdText

Do While Not rsItems.EOF
Response.Write "<TR ALIGN=CENTER><TD>"
Response.Write "<A HREF=""item.asp?Action=Edit&Item=" & rsItems("ItemID")
& """>"
Response.Write rsItems("ItemID")
Response.Write "</A></TD><TD>"
Response.Write rsItems("ItemName")
Response.Write "</TD><TD>"
Response.Write FormatCurrency(rsItems("AskingPrice"))
Response.Write "</TD><TD>"
Response.Write FormatDateTime(rsItems("ListingDate"),2)
Response.Write "</TD><TD>"
oCmd.CommandText = sql & " WHERE ItemID = " & rsItems("ItemID") & ";"
Set rsBid = oCmd.Execute
If IsNull( rsBid("MaxBidAmount") ) Then
        Response.Write "</TD><TD></TD></TR>"
Else
        Response.Write FormatCurrency(rsBid("MaxBidAmount"))
        Response.Write "</TD><TD>"
        Response.Write rsBid("LastBidTime")
        Response.Write "</TD></TR>"
End If
rsBid.Close
rsItems.MoveNext
Loop
rsItems.Close
%>
</TABLE>
```

7 Save these changes to the **ForSale.asp** file.

8 Click on the List/Edit Sale Items hyperlink to view the changes to the page.

543

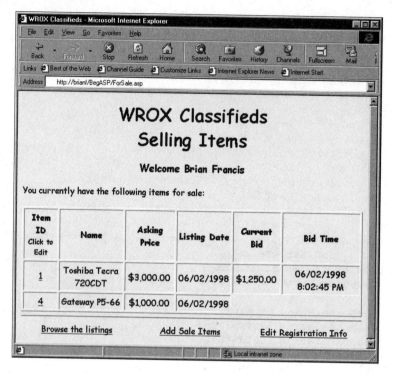

9 Using your favorite web page editor, open the `addItem.asp` file and add the following highlighted code:

```
If Request.Form("Delete") <> "" Then
rsItem.Filter = "ItemID = " & Request("ItemID")
If Not rsItem.EOF Then rsItem.Delete
rsItem.Close
Dim rsBids, sql
Set rsBids = Server.CreateObject("ADODB.Recordset")
sql = "DELETE FROM Bid WHERE ItemID = " & Request("ItemID")
rsBids.Open sql, db, adOpenForwardOnly, adLockOptimistic, adCmdText
Else
```

10 Save these changes to the `addItem.asp` file.

How It Works

Now that we know how to retrieve information about bids from the database, it is relatively simple to add that information wherever we display information about items. In the Browse the Listings page, we will be adding two pieces of information concerning bids.

For each item, we will display the time and value of the last bid. For each item for which the current user is the high bidder, we will provide a visual indicator of that status.

The first thing that we need to do is to prepare our `Command` object. This object will be used repeatedly, with each item to retrieve the last bid and timestamp for each item. Since the `SELECT` and `FROM` portions of the SQL statement will remain the same, we will store those in a local variable:

```
Dim oCmd, rsBid
Set oCmd = Server.CreateObject("ADODB.Command")
Set oCmd.ActiveConnection = db
sql = "SELECT Max(BidAmount) AS MaxBidAmount, Max(TimeStamp) as
LastBidTime FROM Bid"
oCmd.CommandType = adCmdText
```

Since we're looping through each item in the database and displaying its information in the table, we also want to display the bid information. By storing the `SELECT` and `FROM` clauses of the SQL statement in a local variable, all we have to do is add the `WHERE` clause that corresponds to the individual item that we are at right now:

```
        oCmd.CommandText = sql & " WHERE ItemID = " & rsItems("ItemID") &
";"
        Set rsBid = oCmd.Execute
```

Since we are retrieving computed information, rather than information from a record itself, the recordset will always have exactly one record in it. If the value of `MaxBidAmount` is not null, then we know that we have a previous bid, and we can display the amount along with the timestamp for the user:

```
        If IsNull( rsBid("MaxBidAmount") ) Then
                Response.Write "<TD colspan=2><FONT SIZE=""-1"">No bids
placed</FONT></TD></TR>"
        Else
                Response.Write "<TD>" &
FormatCurrency(rsBid("MaxBidAmount"))
                Response.Write "</TD><TD>"
                Response.Write rsBid("LastBidTime")

                Response.Write "</TD>"
```

Next, we want to determine whether it's the current user that placed the current highest bid. While it would be nice to use a single SQL query to retrieve both the high bid amount and the high bid `PersonID`, the use of the `Max()` function does not permit that. We do benefit from the reuse of the `Command` object, and we just create a new SQL query to retrieve the `BidderID` from the bid record containing the latest bid for this item. If this `BidderID` value matches the `PersonID` value that is stored in a session-level variable, then we know that the current user is also the high bidder, and can display a message stating so:

```
                Dim sql2, rsHighBidder
                sql2 = "SELECT BidderID FROM Bid WHERE ItemID = " &
        rsItems("ItemID") & " ORDER BY TimeStamp DESC"
                oCmd.CommandType = adCmdText
                oCmd.CommandText = sql2
                Set rsHighBidder = oCmd.Execute
```

```
                    If rsHighBidder("BidderID") = Session("PersonID") Then
                          Response.Write "<TD><FONT size=""-1""
     COLOR=""Red"">Current High Bidder</FONT></TD>"
                          rsHighBidder.Close
                    End If
                    Response.Write "</TR>"
```

Next, we can move to the **ForSale.asp** script file and add the display of bid information to that page. As we have done before, we will be using the **Command** object to select the highest bidder from each item in the list:

```
Dim oCmd, rsBid
Set oCmd = Server.CreateObject("ADODB.Command")
Set oCmd.ActiveConnection = db
sql = "SELECT Max(BidAmount) AS MaxBidAmount, Max(TimeStamp) as
LastBidTime FROM Bid"
oCmd.CommandType = adCmdText
```

For each item that is retrieved, we will create a SQL query that will return the highest bid amount along with its timestamp. If a bid has been placed on the item, this information is displayed for the user. Since the **MaxBidAmount** value is a currency, we will use the **FormatCurrency** function to provide the proper formatting:

```
oCmd.CommandText = sql & " WHERE ItemID = " & rsItems("ItemID") & ";"
Set rsBid = oCmd.Execute
If IsNull( rsBid("MaxBidAmount") ) Then
        Response.Write "</TD><TD></TD></TR>"
Else
        Response.Write FormatCurrency(rsBid("MaxBidAmount"))
        Response.Write "</TD><TD>"
        Response.Write rsBid("LastBidTime")
        Response.Write "</TD></TR>"
End If
rsBid.Close
```

Finally, we need to look at one part of the **addItem.asp** script file. If you remember, this script was used for adding new items, editing existing items, as well as deleting items. When we delete an item, we also want to clean up all of the bids that are associated with that item.

To do this, we will be using a recordset object to issue a SQL query. This SQL query is a bit different from those that we have seen before. Instead of using a **SELECT** statement to retrieve information from a table, we will be using a **DELETE** statement:

```
Dim rsBids, sql
Set rsBids = Server.CreateObject("ADODB.Recordset")
sql = "DELETE FROM Bid WHERE ItemID = " & Request("ItemID")
rsBids.Open sql, db, adOpenForwardOnly, adLockOptimistic, adCmdText
```

This will cause all of the records in the Bid table that match the **WHERE** clause to be deleted. Our **WHERE** clause will identify all of the bids that have been made on the item we are deleting. When a **DELETE** SQL query is used to open a recordset, the deletion is carried out, and then the recordset is automatically closed.

Accepting a Bid

The last function in our classified ads system will allow the seller to accept a buyer's bid. When this happens, the buyer is notified, and can accept (or reject) the deal at that point. When the deal is accepted by both parties, the information is logged to the database.

Try It Out – Accepting a Bid

1 Open the `Item.asp` file.

2 Add the following highlighted code, between the end `</TABLE>` and end `</FORM>` tags:

```
</TR>
</TABLE>
<%
If Request.QueryString("Action") = "Edit" then
Dim rsBids
Set rsBids = Server.CreateObject("ADODB.Recordset")
sql = "SELECT * FROM Bid WHERE ItemID =" & Request("Item") & " ORDER BY
TimeStamp DESC;"
rsBids.Open sql, db
%>
<HR>
<P>
<% If rsBids.EOF Then %>
        No Bids Currently Placed
<% Else %>
        Bid History (Newest to Oldest)<P>
        <DD><TABLE BORDER="2" CELLSPACING="3" CELLPADDING="3">
        <TR>
        <TH>Bidder ID</TH><TH>Timestamp</TH><TH>Amount Bid</TH><TH>Last
Change</TH></TR>
<%
        Dim bFirst
        bFirst = True
        Do While Not rsBids.EOF
%>
                <TR><TD><%= rsBids("BidderID") %></TD>
                <TD><%= rsBids("Timestamp") %></TD>
                <TD ALIGN=RIGHT><%= FormatCurrency(rsBids("BidAmount"))
%></TD>
                <TD ALIGN=RIGHT><%= FormatCurrency(rsBids("BidChange"))
%></TD>
                <% If bFirst Then %>
                        <TD ALIGN=RIGHT><A HREF="SellItem.asp?Item=<%=
Request("Item") %>&BidID=<%= rsBids("BidID") %>">Click to sell to this
bidder</A></TD>
                <%
```

```
                    bFirst=False
            End If%>
        </TR>
        <%rsBids.MoveNext
loop
rsBids.Close%>
</TABLE>
<% End If %>
<% End If %>
```

```
</FORM>
```

3 Don't forget to save your changes to this file, with the same filename. From the Selling Items page, click on the ID of an item that has a current bid on it.

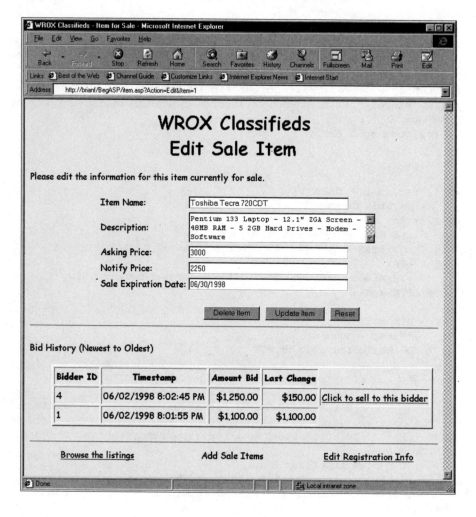

4 Now, create a new ASP file and enter the following code:

```
<!--#include file="Chap15DB.inc"-->
<!DOCTYPE HTML PUBLIC "-//W3C//DTD HTML 3.2 Final//EN">
<BASEFONT FACE="Comic Sans MS" COLOR="DarkBlue">
<HTML>
<HEAD>
<TITLE>WROX Classifieds - Item Sale</TITLE>
</HEAD>

<BODY BGCOLOR="#FFFF80">
<CENTER><H1>WROX Classifieds<BR>Item Sale</H1></CENTER>
<P>
<%
Dim rsBid, sql
Set rsBid = Server.CreateObject("ADODB.Recordset")
sql = "SELECT BidderID, FirstName, Surname, EMailAddress, BidAmount,
ItemName, AskingPrice FROM Person INNER JOIN (Item INNER JOIN Bid ON
Item.ItemID = Bid.ItemID) ON Person.PersonID = Bid.BidderID WHERE
(((Bid.BidID)=" & Request.QueryString("BidID") & "));"

rsBid.Open sql, db, adOpenForwardOnly, adLockOptimistic, adCmdText

%>
<TABLE BORDER=0>
<TR>
<TD WIDTH=20% ROWSPAN=11> </TD>
<TD>Item Name:</TD>
<TD><FONT COLOR="Blue"><%= rsBid("ItemName") %></TD>
</TR>

<TR>
<TD>Asking Price:</TD>
<TD><FONT COLOR="Blue"><%= FormatCurrency(rsBid("AskingPrice")) %>
</FONT></TD>
</TR>

<TR>
<TD>Bid Amount:</TD>
<TD><FONT COLOR="Blue"><%= FormatCurrency(rsBid("BidAmount")) %></TD>
</TR>

<TR><TD>Bidder:</TD>
<TD><FONT COLOR="Blue"><FONT COLOR="Blue"><%= rsBid("FirstName") & " " &
rsBid("Surname") %></TD>
</TR>

<TR>
<TD>E-Mail:</TD>
<TD><FONT COLOR="Blue"><%= rsBid("EMailAddress") %></TD>
</TR>
```

```
</TABLE>
<%
Dim oCmd
Set oCmd = Server.CreateObject("ADODB.Command")
sql = "UPDATE Item SET ItemStatus = 'Pending' WHERE (((Item.ItemID)=" &
Request.QueryString("Item") & "));"
oCmd.CommandText = sql
oCmd.CommandType = adCmdText
Set oCmd.ActiveConnection = db
oCmd.Execute

sql = "INSERT INTO Sale (ItemID, BuyerID, WinningBid, SellerApproval)
VALUES (" & Request.QueryString("Item") & ", " & rsBid("BidderID") & ", "
& rsBid("BidAmount") & ", Yes);"
oCmd.CommandText = sql
oCmd.Execute
%>

<P>
<CENTER>Sale Completed - The purchaser will now be notified</CENTER>
<HR>
<P>

<HR>
<TABLE BORDER=0 WIDTH=100%>
<TR ALIGN=CENTER>
<TD WIDTH=33%><A HREF="browse.asp">Browse the listings</A></TD>
<TD WIDTH=33%>Add Sale Items</TD>
<TD WIDTH=33%><A HREF="register.asp?update=1">Edit Registration Info
</A></TD>
</TR>
</TABLE>

</BODY>
</HTML>
```

5 Save the file as `SellItem.asp` in the `BegASP` directory.

6 Click on the Click to
Sell to this Bidder
hyperlink to begin the
sale process.

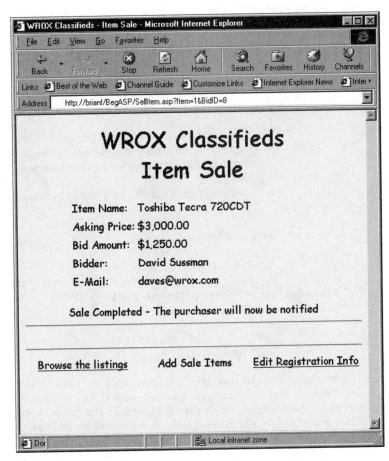

How It Works

To begin the sales process, we need to add the listing of bids to the item page. We do this in much the same way that we added these listings to previous pages. The primary difference here is that we'll retrieve *all* the bids, not just the highest.

To retrieve the bids from the database, we use a SQL query to generate a recordset. This query will return all of the bids for the current item and sort the bids from newest to oldest:

```
<%
If Request.QueryString("Action") = "Edit" then
Dim rsBids
Set rsBids = Server.CreateObject("ADODB.Recordset")
sql = "SELECT * FROM Bid WHERE ItemID =" & Request("Item") & " ORDER BY
TimeStamp DESC;"
rsBids.Open sql, db
%>
```

These bids will be displayed in a table, with each row corresponding to one bid. Before we go through the list of bids, we will create a local variable called `bFirst` and set it to `True`:

```
<%
        Dim bFirst
        bFirst = True
        Do While Not rsBids.EOF
%>
```

This will be used to signify the first time through the loop. Now we set the table headers:

```
        <TR><TD><%= rsBids("BidderID") %></TD>
        <TD><%= rsBids("Timestamp") %></TD>
        <TD ALIGN=RIGHT><%= FormatCurrency(rsBids("BidAmount"))
%></TD>
        <TD ALIGN=RIGHT><%= FormatCurrency(rsBids("BidChange"))
%></TD>
```

Then we use a loop to set the table contents:

```
        <% If bFirst Then %>
                <TD ALIGN=RIGHT><A HREF="SellItem.asp?Item=<%=
Request("Item") %>&BidID=<%= rsBids("BidID") %>">Click to sell to this
bidder</A></TD>
        <%
                bFirst=False
        End If%>
```

The first time through this loop, we know that the bid is the high bidder. If the seller wishes to sell the item, then they can sell it to the person that has submitted the highest bid. When the **bFirst** value is **True** we display a hyperlink: the seller clicks on this link to sell the item. After the hyperlink has been displayed, the value of **bFirst** is set to **False**; hence, the 'sell' hyperlink is displayed on one line only.

When the Click to sell to this bidder link is clicked, the **SellItem.asp** page is displayed. This page will display information about the sale as well as update the database tables.

To retrieve the information to be displayed on this page, we need to get data from three different tables:

▶ The Bid table has the ID of the winning bidder, as well as the amount that they bid.

▶ The Item table has the name of the item along with the asking price of the item.

▶ The Person table has the first name, surname, and e-mail address of the buyer.

To retrieve all of this information at once, we will be creating a SQL statement, known as a **JOIN**:

```
<%
Dim rsBid, sql
Set rsBid = Server.CreateObject("ADODB.Recordset")
sql = "SELECT BidderID, FirstName, Surname, EMailAddress, BidAmount,
ItemName, AskingPrice FROM Person INNER JOIN (Item INNER JOIN Bid ON
```

```
Item.ItemID = Bid.ItemID) ON Person.PersonID = Bid.BidderID WHERE
(((Bid.BidID)=" & Request.QueryString("BidID") & "));"

rsBid.Open sql, db, adOpenForwardOnly, adLockOptimistic, adCmdText

%>
```

At the beginning of this chapter, you may recall that we discussed primary keys and foreign keys. Well, this is where we use them. The Bid table contains foreign keys for both the Item and the Person table. To create the join, we use the value of these foreign keys to pull information from the other tables.

To better examine how this SQL statement works, let's break it down into pieces. The first piece is the **WHERE** clause:

```
sql = "SELECT BidderID, FirstName, Surname, EMailAddress, BidAmount,
ItemName, AskingPrice FROM Person INNER JOIN (Item INNER JOIN Bid ON
Item.ItemID = Bid.ItemID) ON Person.PersonID = Bid. WHERE (((Bid.BidID)="
& Request.QueryString("BidID") & "));"
```

This will retrieve every record from the Bid table, whose **BidID** value is equal to the value passed into this page in the query string. Since the **BidID** is a primary key of the Bid table, this **WHERE** clause can only return at most one record.

Next, we will look at the **SELECT** portion of the SQL statement:

```
sql = "SELECT BidderID, FirstName, Surname, EMailAddress, BidAmount,
ItemName, AskingPrice FROM Person INNER JOIN (Item INNER JOIN Bid ON
Item.ItemID = Bid.ItemID) ON Person.PersonID = Bid.BidderID WHERE
(((Bid.BidID)=" & Request.QueryString("BidID") & "));"
```

The **SELECT** statement is the same as other select statements except in one detail: namely, that the fields that we have named are coming from *different* tables. The **BidderID** and **BidAmount** fields are in the Bid table, while **FirstName**, **Surname**, and **EmailAddress** are from Person, and **ItemName** and **AskingPrice** are from Item.

It is in the **FROM** clause that the tables are tied together:

```
sql = "SELECT BidderID, FirstName, Surname, EMailAddress, BidAmount,
ItemName, AskingPrice FROM Person INNER JOIN (Item INNER JOIN Bid ON
Item.ItemID = Bid.ItemID) ON Person.PersonID = Bid.BidderID WHERE
(((Bid.BidID)=" & Request.QueryString("BidID") & "));"
```

Starting from the inside, we have joined Item and Bid together using an **INNER JOIN** for those records where the value of **ItemID** in the Item table matches the value of **ItemID** in the Bid table. An **INNER JOIN** means that we will retrieve only the records that match on both sides. Then, moving outward, we join the results of the first join with the Person table, where the **PersonID** in the Person table matches the **BidderID** in the Bid table. All of these records will be combined together and returned as a single recordset.

After displaying the information for the seller, we can then update the database tables to begin recording the sale. We use a **Command** object to interact with the database:

```
Dim oCmd
Set oCmd = Server.CreateObject("ADODB.Command")
```

This interaction will be in the form of SQL statements. So far in this chapter, we have looked at **SELECT** and **DELETE** SQL statements. Now, we will be introducing two others. Here's the first:

```
sql = "UPDATE Item SET ItemStatus = 'Pending' WHERE (((Item.ItemID)=" &
Request.QueryString("Item") & "));"
oCmd.CommandText = sql
oCmd.CommandType = adCmdText
Set oCmd.ActiveConnection = db
oCmd.Execute
```

The **UPDATE** SQL statement is used to change the value of fields in an existing record. In our example, we will be changing the **ItemStatus** field to a value of **Pending**, in the record that corresponds to the item we are selling. In this case, we are only updating one record.

> *Using the **UPDATE** statement is probably overkill—we could have just used a recordset. But, for updating multiple records at once, nothing can beat the **UPDATE** statement.*

Here's the second new SQL statement:

```
sql = "INSERT INTO Sale (ItemID, BuyerID, WinningBid, SellerApproval)
VALUES (" & Request.QueryString("Item") & ", " & rsBid("BidderID") & ", "
& rsBid("BidAmount") & ", Yes);"
oCmd.CommandText = sql
oCmd.Execute
```

The **INSERT** SQL statement is used to add new records to an existing table. This is very similar to opening a recordset and then using the **AddNew** method. Again, either method could be used in this case. We just wanted to look at something new. The **INSERT** statement has three separate parts:

- ▶ **The target table:** First, we have to identify into which table you want to insert the record. In this example, we will be adding a record to the Sale table.

- ▶ **The target fields:** Second, we list the fields that we will be adding data to. By default, you add data to all the fields. In this case, we only want to add data to a few fields, so we list them enclosed in parentheses, following the name of the table.

- ▶ **The values to insert.** Finally, we identify the actual values that will be inserted into the fields that we specified. These values need to be in the same physical order as the list of fields that we stated previously.

When the SQL statement is executed using the **Command** object, a new record will be created, and the values that we have listed will be added to the fields that we have specified.

Notifiying the Bidder

Now that all of the database tables have been updated, there's just one last step: to notify the buyer that their bid has been accepted.

Try It Out – Notifying the Buyer

1 Using your most trusted editor, open the `registeredMenu.asp` file.

2 Add the following highlighted line at the very beginning of `registeredMenu.asp`:

```
<!--#include file="Chap15DB.inc"-->
<%
If Session("PersonID") = "" Then
Response.Redirect "login.asp"
End If
%>
```

3 Also, add the following highlighted code to the body of `registeredMenu.asp`:

```
<UL>
<LI>Browse for items for sale
<LI>Bid on items for sale
<LI>List your own items for sale
</UL>
<%
Dim rsPendingSales, sql
Set rsPendingSales = Server.CreateObject("ADODB.Recordset")
sql = "SELECT SaleID, WinningBid, ItemName FROM Sale INNER JOIN Item ON
Sale.ItemID = Item.ItemID WHERE BuyerID=" & Session("PersonID") & " AND
BuyerAcceptance=FALSE;"

rsPendingSales.Open sql, db
If Not rsPendingSales.EOF Then
Response.Write "You have placed the winning bid on these items:<P>"
Response.Write "<DD><TABLE CELLPADDING=3 BORDER=1>"
Response.Write "<TR><TH>Item Name<BR><FONT SIZE=-1>Click to Purchase</
FONT></TH><TH>Winning Bid</TH></TR>"
Do While Not rsPendingSales.EOF
        Response.Write "<TR><TD align=center><A
HREF=""approvePurchase.asp?SaleID=" & rsPendingSales("SaleID") & """>"
        Response.Write rsPendingSales("ItemName")
        Response.Write "</TD><TD ALIGN=RIGHT>"
        Response.Write FormatCurrency(rsPendingSales("WinningBid"))
        Response.Write "</TD></TR>"
        rsPendingSales.MoveNext
```

```
loop
Response.Write "</TABLE><P></DD>"
End If
%>
<HR>
```

4 Now save the changes that you've made to `registeredMenu.asp`.

5 View the Registered User Home page by logging into the system again.

6 Open your editor and create a new ASP file.

7 Type in the following code:

```
<!--#include file="Chap15DB.inc"-->
<%
Dim rsSale, ItemID
Set rsSale = Server.CreateObject("ADODB.Recordset")
rsSale.Open "Sale", db, adOpenForwardOnly, adLockOptimistic, adCmdTable

rsSale.Filter = "SaleID = " & Request("SaleID")
```

```
rsSale("BuyerAcceptance") = True
rsSale("CompletionDate") = Now
ItemID = rsSale("ItemID")
rsSale.Update
rsSale.Close

Dim oCmd
Set oCmd = Server.CreateObject("ADODB.Command")
sql = "UPDATE Item SET ItemStatus = 'Sold' WHERE (((Item.ItemID)=" &
ItemID & "));"
oCmd.CommandText = sql
oCmd.CommandType = adCmdText
Set oCmd.ActiveConnection = db
oCmd.Execute

Response.Redirect "registeredMenu.asp"
%>
```

8 Save the file as `approvePurchase.asp` in your `BegASP` directory.

How It Works

The Registered Users home page is displayed when a user logs into the system. This is an excellent time to notify them that their bid for an item has been accepted. To do this, we will check the Sale table to see if there are any pending sales associated with the current user.

To determine whether there are any pending sales, we use a SQL query to generate a recordset. This SQL query will pull information from both the Sale table as well as the Item table:

```
<%
Dim rsPendingSales, sql
Set rsPendingSales = Server.CreateObject("ADODB.Recordset")
sql = "SELECT SaleID, WinningBid, ItemName FROM Sale INNER JOIN Item ON
Sale.ItemID = Item.ItemID WHERE BuyerID=" & Session("PersonID") & " AND
BuyerAcceptance=FALSE;"

rsPendingSales.Open sql, db
```

Again, we use a `JOIN` to pull information from the two tables. We join the Sale table to the Item table using the `ItemID` field that exists in each table. We retrieve only the Sale records that have a `BuyerID` matching the current user, and do not have a `True` value in the `BuyerAcceptance` field.

If there are pending sales for this user, then they are displayed in a table. The name of the item is also displayed as a hyperlink—the user can click on the hyperlink to indicate that they approve the purchase of the item. This hyperlink will load the `approvePurchase.asp` script:

```
If Not rsPendingSales.EOF Then
Response.Write "You have placed the winning bid on these items:<P>"
Response.Write "<DD><TABLE CELLPADDING=3 BORDER=1>"
Response.Write "<TR><TH>Item Name<BR><FONT SIZE=-1>Click to Purchase</
```

```
      FONT></TH><TH>Winning Bid</TH></TR>"
      Do While Not rsPendingSales.EOF
            Response.Write "<TR><TD align=center><A
      HREF=""approvePurchase.asp?SaleID=" & rsPendingSales("SaleID") & """>"
            Response.Write rsPendingSales("ItemName")
            Response.Write "</TD><TD ALIGN=RIGHT>"
            Response.Write FormatCurrency(rsPendingSales("WinningBid"))
            Response.Write "</TD></TR>"
            rsPendingSales.MoveNext
      loop
      Response.Write "</TABLE><P></DD>"
      End If
```

The `approvePurchase.asp` script file is used to update the information in the Sale table record. This update will be done using a `Recordset` object. The specific Sale record that we are interested in will be retrieved by setting a `Filter` on the recordset:

```
<!--#include file="Chap15DB.inc"-->
<%
Dim rsSale, ItemID
Set rsSale = Server.CreateObject("ADODB.Recordset")
rsSale.Open "Sale", db, adOpenForwardOnly, adLockOptimistic, adCmdTable

rsSale.Filter = "SaleID = " & Request("SaleID")
```

With the record that we want to change as the current record, we can set the `BuyerAcceptance` field to `True` and set the sale `CompletionDate` to the current date time. In order to update the Item table, we need to grab the `ItemID` associated with the sale and store it temporarily in a local variable:

```
rsSale("BuyerAcceptance") = True
rsSale("CompletionDate") = Now
ItemID = rsSale("ItemID")
```

Once the fields are updated, we can write the changes to the database and then close the recordset:

```
rsSale.Update
rsSale.Close
```

The last step is to update the `ItemStatus` field in the Item table:

```
Dim oCmd
Set oCmd = Server.CreateObject("ADODB.Command")
sql = "UPDATE Item SET ItemStatus = 'Sold' WHERE (((Item.ItemID)=" &
ItemID & "));"
oCmd.CommandText = sql
oCmd.CommandType = adCmdText
Set oCmd.ActiveConnection = db
oCmd.Execute

Response.Redirect "registeredMenu.asp"
%>
```

We will leverage the code from the `SellItem.asp` script file that we used to change the `ItemStatus` to `"Pending"`. We need to make two further changes. First, we need to update the `ItemStatus` field to `"Sold"`. Second, we need to use the `ItemID` value that we just stored in a local variable. Once the `ItemStatus` field has been updated, we can send the user back to the Registered Users home page. This page is dynamically created, so if there are other pending sales, they will be displayed for the user.

Next Steps

This application has merely scratched the surface of what an online classified ad system can do. There are a number of ways in which it can be extended and enhanced to provide better functionality. For example, you could:

▶ Add a category field to the Item table. This would let the seller categorize their items better, and also opens possibilities for different ways of browsing, instead of a straight list of items.

▶ Create a bid status window that the seller can leave open on their desktop. Ideally, this would be refreshed periodically, to show the current bid on items they have for sale.

▶ Add support for richer information about the items, such as pictures, links to other sites, and reviews from buyers.

▶ Extend the database to support multiple quantities of the same item being sold. For example, if you had 10 computers to sell, you could enter them as a single item with a quantity of 10, rather than 10 separate items.

As your web site grows in popularity and generates increasing traffic, you can begin to think about migrating to a Windows NT Server platform. This migration will allow you to:

▶ Upsize the database from Access to SQL Server. With SQL Server, you get the benefits of a true database server, along with the increased performance that it affords.

▶ Utilize the Collaborative Data Objects support on NT Server to allow the server to automatically generate e-mail messages that can be sent to users of the system.

▶ Utilize the scalability of Microsoft Transaction Server and create custom components that perform the application functionality with much better performance.

While all of these topics are beyond the scope of this book, there is an excellent reference that will cover all of these topics and more. If you are interested, take a look at the new Professional Active Server Pages 2.0 book (ISBN 1-861001-26-6) from WROX.

Summary

In this chapter, we have built a working application using Active Server Pages. Spread throughout the application, we have used features such as:

▶ Client-side scripting using JavaScript to validate passwords and proper bid amounts.

▶ Server-side scripting using VBScript that presents a custom presentation to different users.

▶ The **Request** and **Response** objects that allow us communicate with the web client and pass information back and forth.

▶ The **Session** object to manage a user session that tracks a user through the application and holds all of their pertinent information.

▶ ActiveX Data Objects (ADO) to manipulate the information in our Classified Ads database.

We have now reached the end of your journey through an introduction to Active Server Pages, and we trust that you come away from this with a better understanding of the power that ASP provides your web applications. ASP can be used for simple dynamic pages, or for retrieving information from a database. As you learn more about it, you can begin to envision applications that integrate all aspects of its functionality, and provide a compelling application for your users. With the foundation that has been laid in this book, you should be well on your way to creating dynamic web sites using Active Server Pages. You can find further support in the form of *Professional Active Server Pages 2.0* (ISBN 1-861001-26-6) or *Professional Active Server Pages Techniques for Webmasters* (ISBN 1-861001-79-7), which are both published by Wrox Press.

The VBScript Language

This appendix is intended as a quick reference and guide to using VBScript. It is not a tutorial, rather a summary of the language's features, and if you need more information, refer back to Chapters 3-6, where we look at writing VBScript.

Array Handling

Dim—declares an array variable. This can be static with a defined number of elements or dynamic and can have up to 60 dimensions
ReDim—used to change the size of an array variable which has been declared as dynamic.
Preserve—keyword used to preserve the contents of an array being resized. If you need to use this then you can only re-dimension the rightmost index of the array.

```
Dim strEmployees ()
ReDim strEmployees (9,1)

strEmployees (9,1) = "Phil"

ReDim strEmployees (9,2)              'loses the contents of element (9,1)
strEmployees (9,2) = "Paul"

ReDim Preserve strEmployees (9,3)   'preserves the contents of (9,2)
strEmployees (9,3) = "Smith"
```

LBound– returns the smallest subscript for the dimension of an array. Note that arrays always start from the subscript zero so this function will always return the value zero.
UBound—used to determine the size of an array.

```
Dim strCustomers (10, 5)
intSizeFirst = UBound (strCustomers, 1)       'returns SizeFirst = 10
intSizeSecond = UBound (strCustomers, 2)      'returns SizeSecond = 5
```

> *The actual number of elements is always one greater than the value returned by UBound because the array starts from zero.*

Assignments

Let—used to assign values to variables (optional).
Set—used to assign an object reference to a variable.

```
Let intNumberOfDays = 365

Set txtMyTextBox = txtcontrol
txtMyTextBox.Value = "Hello World"
```

Constants

Empty—an empty variable is one that has been created but not yet assigned a value.
Nothing—used to remove an object reference.

```
Set txtMyTextBox = txtATextBox        'assigns object reference
Set txtMyTextBox = Nothing            'removes object reference
```

Null—indicates that a variable is not valid. Note that this isn't the same as **Empty**.
True—indicates that an expression is true. Has numerical value –1.
False—indicates that an expression is false. Has numerical value 0.

Error constant

Constant	Value
vbObjectError	&h80040000

System Color constants

Constant	Value	Description
vbBlack	&h00	Black
vbRed	&hFF	Red
vbGreen	&hFF00	Green
vbYellow	&hFFFF	Yellow
vbBlue	&hFF0000	Blue
vbMagenta	&hFF00FF	Magenta
vbCyan	&hFFFF00	Cyan
vbWhite	&hFFFFFF	White

Comparison constants

Constant	Value	Description
vbBinaryCompare	0	Perform a binary comparison.
vbTextCompare	1	Perform a textual comparison.
vbDatabaseCompare	2	Perform a comparison based upon information in the database where the comparison is to be performed.

Date and Time constants

Constant	Value	Description
vbSunday	1	Sunday
vbMonday	2	Monday
vbTuesday	3	Tuesday
vbWednesday	4	Wednesday
vbThursday	5	Thursday
vbFriday	6	Friday
vbSaturday	7	Saturday
vbFirstJan1	1	Use the week in which January 1 occurs (default).
vbFirstFourDays	2	Use the first week that has at least four days in the new year.
vbFirstFullWeek	3	Use the first full week of the year.
vbUseSystem	0	Use the format in the regional settings for the computer.
vbUseSystemDayOfWeek	0	Use the day in the system settings for the first weekday.

Date Format constants

Constant	Value	Description
vbGeneralDate	0	Display a date and/or time in the format set in the system settings. For real numbers display a date and time. For integer numbers display only a date. For numbers less than 1, display time only.
vbLongDate	1	Display a date using the long date format specified in the computers regional settings.
vbShortDate	2	Display a date using the short date format specified in the computers regional settings.
vbLongTime	3	Display a time using the long time format specified in the computers regional settings.
vbShortTime	4	Display a time using the short time format specified in the computers regional settings.

File Input/Output constants

Constant	Value	Description
ForReading	1	Open a file for reading only.
ForWriting	2	Open a file for writing. If a file with the same name exists, its previous one is overwritten.
ForAppending	8	Open a file and write at the end of the file.

String constants

Constant	Value	Description
vbCr	Chr(13)	Carriage return only
vbCrLf	Chr(13) & Chr(10)	Carriage return and linefeed (Newline)
vbLf	Chr(10)	Line feed only
vbNewLine	-	Newline character as appropriate to a specific platform
vbNullChar	Chr(0)	Character having the value 0
vbNullString	-	String having the value zero (not just an empty string)
vbTab	Chr(9)	Horizontal tab

Tristate constants

Constant	Value	Description
TristateTrue	-1	True
TristateFalse	0	False
TristateUseDefault	-2	Use default setting

VarType constants

This summarizes the different variable types you can use in VBScript. Remember that if you don't specify a variable type, your variables will automatically be treated as variants. (See Chapter 4 for further details).

Constant	Value	Description
vbEmpty	0	Un-initialized (default)
vbNull	1	Contains no valid data
vbInteger	2	Integer subtype
vbLong	3	Long subtype

Constant	Value	Description
vbSingle	4	Single subtype
vbDouble	5	Double subtype
vbCurrency	6	Currency subtype
vbDate	7	Date subtype
vbString	8	String subtype
vbObject	9	Object
vbError	10	Error subtype
vbBoolean	11	Boolean subtype
vbVariant	12	Variant (used only for arrays of variants)
vbDataObject	13	Data access object
vbDecimal	14	Decimal subtype
vbByte	17	Byte subtype
vbArray	8192	Array

Control Flow

For...Next—executes a block of code a specified number of times.

```
Dim intSalary (10)
For intCounter = 0 to 10
   intSalary (intCounter) = 20000
Next
```

For Each...Next Statement—repeats a block of code for each element in an array or collection.

```
For Each Item In Request.QueryString("MyControl")
  Response.Write Item & "<BR>"
Next
```

Do...Loop—executes a block of code while a condition is true or until a condition becomes true.

```
Do While strDayOfWeek <> "Saturday" And strDayOfWeek <> "Sunday"
   MsgBox ("Get Up! Time for work")
   ...
Loop
```

```
Do
   MsgBox ("Get Up! Time for work")
   ...
Loop Until strDayOfWeek = "Saturday" Or strDayOfWeek = "Sunday"
```

If...Then...Else—used to run various blocks of code depending on conditions.

```
If intAge < 20 Then
    MsgBox ("You're just a slip of a thing!")
ElseIf intAge < 40 Then
    MsgBox ("You're in your prime!")
Else
    MsgBox ("You're older and wiser")
End If
```

Select Case—used to replace **If...Then...Else** statements where there are many conditions.

```
Select Case intAge
Case 21,22,23,24,25,26
    MsgBox ("You're in your prime")
Case 40
    MsgBox ("You're fulfilling your dreams")
Case 65
    MsgBox ("Time for a new challenge")
End Select
```

Note that **Select Case** can only be used with precise conditions and not with a range of conditions.

While...Wend—executes a block of code while a condition is true.

```
While strDayOfWeek <> "Saturday" AND strDayOfWeek <> "Sunday"
    MsgBox ("Get Up! Time for work")
    ...
Wend
```

Functions

VBScript contains several functions that can be used to manipulate and examine variables. These have been subdivided into the general categories of:

- Conversion Functions
- Date/Time Functions
- Math Functions
- Object Management Functions
- Script Engine Identification Functions
- String Functions
- Variable Testing Functions

For a full description of each function, and the parameters it requires, see the VBScript Help file. This is installed by default in your **Docs/ASPDocs/VBS/VBScript** subfolder of your IIS installation directory.

Conversion Functions

These functions are used to convert values in variables between different types:

Function	Description
Asc	Returns the numeric ANSI code number of the first character in a string.
AscB	As above, but provided for use with byte data contained in a string. Returns result from the first byte only.
AscW	As above, but provided for Unicode characters. Returns the `Wide` character code, avoiding the conversion from Unicode to ANSI.
Chr	Returns a string made up of the ANSI character matching the number supplied.
ChrB	As above, but provided for use with byte data contained in a string. Always returns a single byte.
ChrW	As above, but provided for Unicode characters. Its argument is a `Wide` character code, thereby avoiding the conversion from ANSI to Unicode.
CBool	Returns the argument value converted to a `Variant` of subtype `Boolean`.
CByte	Returns the argument value converted to a `Variant` of subtype `Byte`.
CDate	Returns the argument value converted to a `Variant` of subtype `Date`.
CDbl	Returns the argument value converted to a `Variant` of subtype `Double`.
CInt	Returns the argument value converted to a `Variant` of subtype `Integer`.
CLng	Returns the argument value converted to a `Variant` of subtype `Long`.
CSng	Returns the argument value converted to a `Variant` of subtype `Single`.
CStr	Returns the argument value converted to a `Variant` of subtype `String`.
Fix	Returns the integer (whole) part of a number.
Hex	Returns a string representing the hexadecimal value of a number.
Int	Returns the integer (whole) portion of a number.
Oct	Returns a string representing the octal value of a number.
Round	Returns a number rounded to a specified number of decimal places.
Sgn	Returns an integer indicating the sign of a number.

Date/Time Functions

These functions return date or time values from the computer's system clock, or manipulate existing values:

Function	Description
Date	Returns the current system date.
DateAdd	Returns a date to which a specified time interval has been added.
DateDiff	Returns the number of days, weeks, or years between two dates.

Function	Description
DatePart	Returns just the day, month or year of a given date.
DateSerial	Returns a Variant of subtype Date for a specified year, month, and day.
DateValue	Returns a Variant of subtype Date.
Day	Returns a number between 1 and 31 representing the day of the month.
Hour	Returns a number between 0 and 23 representing the hour of the day.
Minute	Returns a number between 0 and 59 representing the minute of the hour.
Month	Returns a number between 1 and 12 representing the month of the year.
MonthName	Returns the name of the specified month as a string.
Now	Returns the current date and time.
Second	Returns a number between 0 and 59 representing the second of the minute.
Time	Returns a Variant of subtype Date indicating the current system time.
TimeSerial	Returns a Variant of subtype Date for a specific hour, minute, and second.
TimeValue	Returns a Variant of subtype Date containing the time.
Weekday	Returns a number representing the day of the week.
WeekdayName	Returns the name of the specified day of the week as a string.
Year	Returns a number representing the year.

Math Functions

These functions perform mathematical operations on variables containing numerical values:

Function	Description
Atn	Returns the arctangent of a number.
Cos	Returns the cosine of an angle.
Exp	Returns e (the base of natural logarithms) raised to a power.
Log	Returns the natural logarithm of a number.
Randomize	Initializes the random-number generator.
Rnd	Returns a random number.
Sin	Returns the sine of an angle.
Sqr	Returns the square root of a number.
Tan	Returns the tangent of an angle.

Object Management Functions

These functions are used to manipulate objects, where applicable:

Function	Description
`CreateObject`	Creates and returns a reference to an ActiveX or OLE Automation object.
`GetObject`	Returns a reference to an ActiveX or OLE Automation object.
`LoadPicture`	Returns a picture object.

Script Engine Identification

These functions return the version of the scripting engine:

Function	Description
`ScriptEngine`	A string containing the major, minor, and build version numbers of the scripting engine.
`ScriptEngineMajorVersion`	The major version of the scripting engine, as a number.
`ScriptEngineMinorVersion`	The minor version of the scripting engine, as a number.
`ScriptEngineBuildVersion`	The build version of the scripting engine, as a number.

String Functions

These functions are used to manipulate string values in variables:

Function	Description
`Filter`	Returns an array from a string array, based on specified filter criteria.
`FormatCurrency`	Returns a string formatted as currency value.
`FormatDateTime`	Returns a string formatted as a date or time.
`FormatNumber`	Returns a string formatted as a number.
`FormatPercent`	Returns a string formatted as a percentage.
`InStr`	Returns the position of the first occurrence of one string within another.
`InStrB`	As above, but provided for use with byte data contained in a string. Returns the byte position instead of the character position.
`InstrRev`	As `InStr`, but starts from the end of the string.
`Join`	Returns a string created by joining the strings contained in an array.
`LCase`	Returns a string that has been converted to lowercase.
`Left`	Returns a specified number of characters from the left end of a string.
`LeftB`	As above, but provided for use with byte data contained in a string. Uses that number of bytes instead of that number of characters.

Function	Description
Len	Returns the length of a string or the number of bytes needed for a variable.
LenB	As above, but is provided for use with byte data contained in a string. Returns the number of bytes in the string instead of characters.
LTrim	Returns a copy of a string without leading spaces.
Mid	Returns a specified number of characters from a string.
MidB	As above, but provided for use with byte data contained in a string. Uses that numbers of bytes instead of that number of characters.
Replace	Returns a string in which a specified substring has been replaced with another substring a specified number of times.
Right	Returns a specified number of characters from the right end of a string.
RightB	As above, but provided for use with byte data contained in a string. Uses that number of bytes instead of that number of characters.
RTrim	Returns a copy of a string without trailing spaces.
Space	Returns a string consisting of the specified number of spaces.
Split	Returns a one-dimensional array of a specified number of substrings.
StrComp	Returns a value indicating the result of a string comparison.
String	Returns a string of the length specified made up of a repeating character.
StrReverse	Returns a string in which the character order of a string is reversed.
Trim	Returns a copy of a string without leading or trailing spaces.
UCase	Returns a string that has been converted to uppercase.

Variable Testing Functions

These functions are used to determine the type of information stored in a variable:

Function	Description
IsArray	Returns a **Boolean** value indicating whether a variable is an array.
IsDate	Returns a **Boolean** value indicating whether an expression can be converted to a date.
IsEmpty	Returns a **Boolean** value indicating whether a variable has been initialized.
IsNull	Returns a **Boolean** value indicating whether an expression contains no valid data
IsNumeric	Returns a **Boolean** value indicating whether an expression can be evaluated as a number.
IsObject	Returns a **Boolean** value indicating whether an expression references a valid ActiveX or OLE Automation object.
TypeName	Returns the subtype of a variable.
VarType	Returns a number indicating the subtype of a variable.

Variable Declarations

`Dim`—declares a variable.

Error Handling

`On Error Resume Next`—indicates that if an error occurs, control should continue at the next statement.
`Err`—this is the error object that provides information about run-time errors.

Error handling is very limited in VBScript and the `Err` object must be tested explicitly to determine if an error has occurred.

Input/Output

This consists of **Msgbox** for output and **InputBox** for input:

MsgBox

This displays a message, and can return a value indicating which button was clicked.

```
MsgBox "Hello There",20,"Hello Message","c:\windows\MyHelp.hlp",123
```

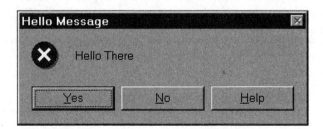

The parameters are:
`"Hello There"`—this contains the text of the message and is obligatory.
`20`— this determines which icon and buttons appear on the message box.
`"Hello Message"`—this contains the text that will appear as the title of the message box.
`"c:\windows\MyHelp.hlp"`—this adds a Help button to the message box and determines the help file that is opened if the button is clicked.
`123`—this is a reference to the particular help topic that will be displayed if the Help button is clicked.

573

The value of the icon and buttons parameter is determined using the following tables:

Constant	Value	Buttons
vbOKOnly	0	OK
vbOKCancel	1	OK Cancel
vbAbortRetryIngnore	2	Abort Retry Ignore
vbYesNoCancel	3	Yes No Cancel
vbYesNo	4	Yes No
vbRetryCancel	5	Retry Cancel
vbDefaultButton1	0	The first button from the left is the default.
vbDefaultButton2	256	The second button from the left is the default.
vbDefaultButton3	512	The third button from the left is the default.
vbDefaultButton4	768	The fourth button from the left is the default.

Constant	Value	Description	Icon
vbCritical	16	Critical Message	
vbQuestion	32	Questioning Message	
vbExclamation	48	Warning Message	
vbInformation	64	Informational Message	

Constant	Value	Description
vbApplicationModal	0	Just the application stops until user clicks a button.
vbSystemModal	4096	Whole system stops until user clicks a button.

To specify which buttons and icon are displayed you simply add the relevant values. So, in our example we add together 4 + 256 + 16 + 4096 to display the Yes and No buttons, with No as the default, with the **Critical** icon, and the user being unable to use any application, besides this one, when the message box is displayed.

You can determine which button the user clicked by assigning the return code of the **MsgBox** function to a variable:

```
intButtonClicked = MsgBox ("Hello There",35,"Hello Message")
```

Notice that brackets enclose the **MsgBox** parameters when used in this format. The following table determines the value assigned to the variable **intButtonClicked**:

Constant	Value	Button Clicked
vbOK	1	OK
vbCancel	2	Cancel
vbAbort	3	Abort
vbRetry	4	Retry
vbIgnore	5	Ignore
vbYes	6	Yes
vbNo	7	No

InputBox

This accepts text entry from the user and returns it as a string.

```
strTextEntered = InputBox ("Please enter your name","Login","John
Smith",500,500)
```

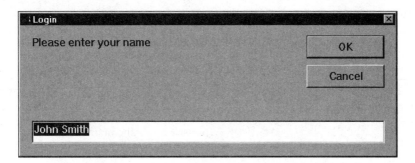

"Please enter your name"–this is the prompt displayed in the input box.
"Login"– this is the text displayed as the title of the input box.
"John Smith"– this is the default value displayed in the input box.
500—specifies the x position of the input box.
500—specifies the y position of the input box.

As with the **MsgBox** function, you can also specify a help file and topic to add a Help button to the input box.

Procedures

`Call`—optional method of calling a subroutine.
`Function`—used to declare a function.
`Sub`—used to declare a subroutine.

Other Keywords

`Rem`—old style method of adding comments to code.
`Option Explicit`—forces you to declare a variable before it can be used.

Visual Basic Run-time Error Codes

The following error codes also apply to VBA code, and many will not be appropriate to an application built completely around VBScript. Nevertheless, this summary table should help with debugging and error handling in your code.

Code	Description	Code	Description
3	Return without GoSub	52	Bad file name or number
5	Invalid procedure call	53	File not found
6	Overflow	54	Bad file mode
7	Out of memory	55	File already open
9	Subscript out of range	57	Device I/O error
10	This array is fixed or temporarily locked	58	File already exists
		59	Bad record length
11	Division by zero	61	Disk full
13	Type mismatch	62	Input past end of file
14	Out of string space	63	Bad record number
16	Expression too complex	67	Too many files
17	Can't perform requested operation	68	Device unavailable
18	User interrupt occurred	70	Permission denied
20	Resume without error	71	Disk not ready
28	Out of stack space	74	Can't rename with different drive
35	Sub or Function not defined	75	Path/File access error
47	Too many DLL application clients	76	Path not found
48	Error in loading DLL	322	Can't create necessary temporary file
49	Bad DLL calling convention	325	Invalid format in resource file
51	Internal error	380	Invalid property value

Code	Description	Code	Description
423	Property or method not found	1002	Syntax error
424	Object required	1003	Expected ':'
429	OLE Automation server can't create object	1004	Expected ';'
430	Class doesn't support OLE Automation	1005	Expected '('
432	File name or class name not found during OLE Automation operation	1006	Expected ')'
438	Object doesn't support this property or method	1007	Expected ']'
		1008	Expected '{'
440	OLE Automation error	1009	Expected '}'
442	Connection to type library or object library for remote process has been lost. Press OK for dialog to remove reference.	1010	Expected identifier
		1011	Expected '='
		1012	Expected 'If'
		1013	Expected 'To'
443	OLE Automation object does not have a default value	1014	Expected 'End'
		1015	Expected 'Function'
445	Object doesn't support this action	1016	Expected 'Sub'
446	Object doesn't support named arguments	1017	Expected 'Then'
		1018	Expected 'Wend'
447	Object doesn't support current locale setting	1019	Expected 'Loop'
		1020	Expected 'Next'
448	Named argument not found	1021	Expected 'Case'
449	Argument not optional	1022	Expected 'Select'
450	Wrong number of arguments or invalid property assignment	1023	Expected expression
		1024	Expected statement
451	Object not a collection	1025	Expected end of statement
452	Invalid ordinal	1026	Expected integer constant
453	Specified DLL function not found	1027	Expected 'While' or 'Until'
454	Code resource not found	1028	Expected 'While', 'Until' or end of statement
455	Code resource lock error		
457	This key is already associated with an element of this collection	1029	Too many locals or arguments
		1030	Identifier too long
458	Variable uses an OLE Automation type not supported in Visual Basic	1031	Invalid number
		1032	Invalid character
481	Invalid picture	1033	Un-terminated string constant
500	Variable is undefined	1034	Un-terminated comment
501	Cannot assign to variable	1035	Nested comment
1001	Out of memory		

Code	Description	Code	Description
1036	'Me' cannot be used outside of a procedure	1040	Invalid 'for' loop control variable
		1041	Variable redefinition
1037	Invalid use of 'Me' keyword	1042	Must be first statement on the line
1038	'loop' without 'do'	1043	Cannot assign to non-ByVal argument
1039	Invalid 'exit' statement		

For more information about VBScript, visit Microsoft's VBScript site at:

```
http://www.microsoft.com/vbscript/us/techinfo/vbsdocs.htm
```

and for a complete Wrox tutorial on VBScript, take a look at Instant VBScript, ISBN 1-861000-44-8, by Alex Homer and Darren Gill

Active Server Pages Object Model

This appendix offers a handy reference to the Active Server Pages Object Model, and in each case provides the properties, methods and events for the object, along with their collections. For more information, please turn to the indicated chapter for each object. The two Active Server Components that we dealt with in depth in Chapter 10, **AdRotator** and Content Linker (**NextLink**) are also included here, after the **Server** object.

Request Object

The **Request** object is one of the central objects in the Active Server Pages object model, and is vital for controlling how the user sends information to the server. Using the **Request** object, the server can obtain information about what the user wants, and manipulate this within ASP. We covered the **Request** object thoroughly in Chapter 7.

Collections	Description
ClientCertificate	Client certificate values sent from the browser. Read Only.
Cookies	Values of cookies sent from the browser. Read Only.
Form	Values of form elements sent from the browser. Read Only.
QueryString	Values of variables in the HTTP query string. Read Only.
ServerVariables	Values of the HTTP and environment variables. Read Only.

Property	Description
TotalBytes	Specifies the number of bytes the client is sending in the body of the request. Read Only.

Method	Description
BinaryRead	Used to retrieve data sent to the server as part of the POST request

Response Object

As we discussed in detail in Chapter 8, the **Response** object is used to send the server's output to the client. In this sense, the **Response** object is the counterpart to the **Request** object: the **Request** object gathers information from both the client and the server, and the **Response** object sends, or resends, the information to the client by writing to the HTTP data stream.

Collections	Description
Cookies	Values of all the cookies to send to the browser.

Properties	Description
Buffer	Indicates whether to buffer the page until complete.
CacheControl	Determines whether proxy servers are able to cache the output generated by ASP.
Charset	Appends the name of the character set to the content-type header
ContentType	HTTP content type (i.e. **"Text/HTML"**) for the response.
Expires	Length of time before a page cached on a browser expires.
ExpiresAbsolute	Date and time when a page cached on a browser expires.
IsClientConnected	Indicates whether the client has disconnected from the server
PICS	Adds the value of a PICS label to the pics-label field of the response header.
Status	Value of the HTTP status line returned by the server.

Methods	Description
AddHeader	Adds or changes a value in the HTML header.
AppendToLog	Adds text to the web server log entry for this request.
BinaryWrite	Sends text to the browser without character-set conversion.
Clear	Erases any buffered HTML output.
End	Stops processing the page and returns the current result.
Flush	Sends buffered output immediately.
Redirect	Instructs the browser to connect to a different URL.
Write	Writes a variable to the current page as a string.

The remaining **Response** interface elements can be divided into groups, like this:

Response Items	Description
`Write,BinaryWrite`	Inserts information into a page.
`Cookies`	Sends cookies to the browser.
`Redirect`	Redirects the browser.
`Buffer,Flush,Clear,End`	Buffers the page as it is created.
`Expires, ExpiresAbsolute, ContentType, AddHeader, Status, CacheContol, PICS, Charset`	Sets the properties of a page.
`IsClientConnected`	Checks the client connection

Application Object

Each Application has its own **Application** Object. This object stores variables and objects for application-scope usage. It also stores information about any currently active sessions. For further details, please consult Chapter 9.

Collections	Description
`Contents`	Contains all of the items added to the application through script commands
`StaticObjects`	Contains all of the objects added to the application with the `<OBJECT>` tag

Method	Description
`Lock`	Prevents other clients from modifying application properties.
`Unlock`	Allows other clients to modify application properties.

Events	Description
`OnStart`	Occurs when a page in the application is first referenced.
`OnEnd`	Occurs when the application ends, i.e. when the web server is stopped.

Session Object

The **Session** Object, like the **Application** Object, is covered in Chapter 9. It is used to keep track of an individual browser as it navigates through your web site.

Collections	Description
Contents	Contains all of the items added to the Session through script commands.
StaticObjects	Contains all of the objects added to the Session with the **<OBJECT>** tag.

Method	Description
Abandon	Destroys a **Session** object and releases its resources.

Properties	Description
CodePage	Sets the codepage that will be used for symbol mapping
LCID	Sets the locale identifier
SessionID	Returns the session identification for this user
Timeout	Sets the timeout period for the session state for this application, in minutes.

Events	Description
OnStart	Occurs when the server creates a new session
OnEnd	Occurs when a session is abandoned or times out.

Server Object

The **Server** Object is covered in Chapter 10—Active Server Components. Its main use is to create components.

Property	Description
ScriptTimeout	Length of time a script can run before an error occurs.

Methods	Description
CreateObject	Creates an instance of an object or server component.
HTMLEncode	Applies HTML encoding to the specified string.
MapPath	Converts a virtual path into a physical path.
URLEncode	Applies URL encoding including escape chars to a string.

The Ad Rotator Component

The **AdRotator** Component is covered in Chapter 10. It allows you to rotate through a fixed list of advert banners, changing the displayed advert each time the page is referenced from a browser.

Method	Description
GetAdvertisement	Gets details of the next advertisement and formats it as HTML.

Property	Description
Border	Size of the border around the advertisement.
Clickable	Defines whether the advertisement is a hyperlink.
TargetFrame	Name of the frame in which to display the advertisement.

The Content Linking Component

The Content Linker (called **NextList** in code) is used to establish a set route through your ASP pages; the **list** file provides the itinerary a browser will take through the website.

Method	Description
GetListCount	Number of items in the file **list**.
GetListIndex	Index of the current page in the file **list**.
GetNextURL	URL of the next page in the file **list**.
GetNextDescription	Description of the next page in the file **list**.
GetPreviousURL	URL of the previous page in the file **list**.
GetPreviousDescription	Description of previous page in the file **list**.
GetNthURL	URL of the nth page in the file **list**.
GetNthDescription	Description of the nth page in the file **list**.

Scripting Object Methods and Properties

This is a reference summary for the Scripting Objects we covered in Chapter 11, as well as the objects from the **FileSystemObject** object hierarchy. Please refer to that chapter for detailed information.

The Dictionary Object

The **Dictionary** object stores information. You can attach a key word to each piece of information. Later, when you want to retrieve the information, all you do is provide the dictionary with the key word, and it will return the information you have stored there.

Method	Description
Add	Adds the key/item pair to the **Dictionary**.
Exists	**True** if the specified key exists, **False** if it does not.
Items	Returns an array containing all the items in a **Dictionary** object.
Keys	Returns an array containing all the keys in a **Dictionary** object.
Remove	Removes a single key/item pair.
RemoveAll	Removes all the key/item pairs.

Property	Description
CompareMode	Sets or returns the string comparison mode for the keys. Unavailable in JScript.
Count	Read-only. Returns the number of key/item pairs in the **Dictionary**.
Item	Sets or returns the value of the item for the specified key.
Key	Sets or returns the value of a key.

The FileSystemObject Object

With the `FileSystemObject` object, you can access the file system of the web serve to manipulate files, folders and directory paths, as well as get general information.

Method	Description
`CreateTextFile`	Creates a file and returns a `TextStream` object to access the file.
`OpenTextFile`	Opens a file and returns a `TextStream` object to access the file.

All the methods of `FileSystemObject` can be divided into several categories as shown in the following table:

Category	Methods
File Manipulation	`CopyFile, CreateTextFile, DeleteFile, FileExists, MoveFile, OpenTextFile`
Folder Manipulation	`CopyFolder, CreateFolder, DeleteFolder, FolderExists, MoveFolder`
Path Manipulation	`BuildPath`
Information	`GetAbsolutePathName, GetBaseName, GetDrive, GetDriveName, GetExtensionName, GetFile, GetFileName, GetFolder, GetParentFolderName, GetSpecialFolder, GetTempName`

The TextStream Object

The `TextStream` object allows you access the contents of a file as a text file.

Method	Description
`Close`	Closes an open file.
`Read`	Reads characters from a file.
`ReadAll`	Reads an entire file as a single string.
`ReadLine`	Reads a line from a file as a string.
`Skip`	Skips and discards characters when reading a file.
`SkipLine`	Skips and discards the next line when reading a file.
`Write`	Writes a string to a file.
`WriteLine`	Writes a string (optional) and a newline character to a file.
`WriteBlankLines`	Writes newline characters to a file.

Property	Description
AtEndOfLine	**True** if the file pointer is at the end of a line in a file.
AtEndOfStream	**True** if the file pointer is at the end of a file.
Column	Returns the column number of the current character in a file.
Line	Returns the current line number in a file. Both start at **1**.

The FileSystemObject object hierarchy

Below, we have included summary tables detailing the properties methods and events of the objects in the **FileSystemObject** hierarchy, **Drive**, **File** and **Folder**.

Drive Object

Property	Description
AvailableSpace	Returns the amount of space available on specified drive.
DriveLetter	Returns the drive letter for the specified drive.
DriveType	Returns the value indicating the type of specified drive. Can have one of the following values: 0 = Unknown 1 = Removable 2 = Fixed 3 = Network 4 = CD-ROM 5 = RAM Disk
FileSystem	Returns the type of file system for the specified drive. Return types include *FAT*, *NTFS* and *CDFS*.
FreeSpace	Returns the amount of free space available on specified drive.
IsReady	Returns a boolean value indicating if drive is ready (true) or not (false)
Path	Returns the path for specified drive.
RootFolder	Returns the **Folder** object representing the root folder of the specified drive.
SerialNumber	Returns a decimal serial number used to uniquely identify a disk volume.
ShareName	Returns the network share name for the specified drive.
TotalSize	Returns the total space (in bytes) of the specified drive.
VolumeName	Returns the volume name of the specified drive.

Folder Object

Property	Description
Attributes	Sets or returns the attributes of the folder. Can be combination of the following values: 0 = Normal 1 = ReadOnly 2 = Hidden 4 = System 8 = Volume 16 = Directory 32 = Archive 64 = Alias 128 = Compressed
DateCreated	Returns the date and time when the specified folder was created
DateLastAccessed	Returns the date and time when the specified folder was last accessed
DateLastModified	Returns the date and time when the specified folder was last modified
Drive	Returns the drive letter of the drive on which the specified folder resides
IsRootFolder	Returns boolean value indicating if the specified folder is the root folder (true) or not (false)
Name	Sets or returns the name of the specified folder
ParentFolder	Returns the **Folder** object for the parent of the specified folder
Path	Returns the path for the specified folder
ShortName	Returns the 8.3 version of folder name
ShortPath	Returns the 8.3 version of folder path
Size	Returns the size of all files and subfolders contained in the folder
SubFolders	Returns a **Folders** collection consisting of all folders contained in a specified folder

Method	Description
Copy	Copies the specified folder from one location to another
Delete	Deletes a specified folder
Move	Moves a specified folder from one location to another

File Object

Property	Description
Attributes	Sets or returns the attributes of file. See description of **Folder** object above
DateCreated	Returns the date and time that the specified file was created
DateLastAccessed	Returns the date and time that the specified file was last accessed
DateLastModified	Returns the date and time that the specified file was last modified
Drive	Returns the drive letter of the drive on which the specified file resides
Name	Sets or returns the name of the specified file
ParentFolder	Returns the **Folder** object for the parent of the specified file
Path	Returns the path for specified file
ShortName	Returns the 8.3 version of file name
ShortPath	Returns the 8.3 version of file path
Size	Returns the size of the file
Type	Returns information about the type of a file

Method	Description
Copy	Copies the specified file from one location to another
Delete	Deletes a specified file
Move	Moves a specified file from one location to another

HTTP 1.1 Error Codes

This appendix lists the client and server error codes with default explanations, provided by Microsoft Internet Information Server; they are included in case you run into errors as you experiment with ASP.

Error Code	Short Text	Explanation
400	Bad Request	Due to malformed syntax, the request could not be understood by the server. The client should not repeat the request without modifications.
401.1	Unauthorized: Logon Failed	This error indicates that the credentials passed to the server do not match the credentials required to log on to the server. Please contact the Web server's administrator to verify that you have permission to access the requested resource.
401.2	Unauthorized: Logon Failed due to server configuration	This error indicates that the credentials passed to the server do not match the credentials required to log on to the server. This is usually caused by not sending the proper WWW-Authenticate header field. Please contact the Web server's administrator to verify that you have permission to access to requested resource.
401.3	Unauthorized: Unauthorized due to ACL on resource	This error indicates that the credentials passed by the client do not have access to the particular resource on the server. This resource could be either the page or file listed in the address line of the client, or it could be another file on the server that is needed to process the file listed on the address line of the client. Please make a note of the entire address you were trying to access and then contact the Web server's administrator to verify that you have permission to access the requested resource.

Error Code	Short Text	Explanation
401.4	Unauthorized: Authorization failed by filter	This error indicates that the Web server has a filter program installed to verify users connecting to the server. The authentication used to connect to the server was denied access by this filter program. Please make a note of the entire address you were trying to access and then contact the Web server's administrator to verify that you have permission to access the requested resource.
401.5	Unauthorized: Authorization failed by ISAPI/CGI app	This error indicates that the address on the Web server you attempted to use has an ISAPI or CGI program installed that verifies user credentials before proceeding. The authentication used to connect to the server was denied access by this program. Please make a note of the entire address you were trying to access and then contact the Web server's administrator to verify that you have permission to access the requested resource.
403.1	Forbidden: Execute Access Forbidden	This error can be caused if you try to execute a CGI, ISAPI, or other executable program from a directory that does not allow programs to be executed. Please contact the Web server's administrator if the problem persists.
403.2	Forbidden: Read Access Forbidden	This error can be caused if there is no default page available and directory browsing has not been enabled for the directory, or if you are trying to display an HTML page that resides in a directory marked for Execute or Script permissions only. Please contact the Web server's administrator if the problem persists.
403.3	Forbidden: Write Access Forbidden	This error can be caused if you attempt to upload to, or modify a file in, a directory that does not allow Write access. Please contact the Web server's administrator if the problem persists.
403.4	Forbidden: SSL required	This error indicates that the page you are trying to access is secured with Secure Sockets Layer (SSL). In order to view it, you need to enable SSL by typing "https://" at the beginning of the address you are attempting to reach. Please contact the Web server's administrator if the problem persists.
403.5	Forbidden: SSL 128 required	This error message indicates that the resource you are trying to access is secured with a 128-bit version of Secure Sockets Layer (SSL). In order to view this resource, you need a browser that supports this level of SSL. Please confirm that your browser supports 128-bit SSL security. If it does, then contact the Web server's administrator and report the problem.
403.6	Forbidden: IP address rejected	This error is caused when the server has a list of IP addresses that are not allowed to access the site, and the IP address you are using is in this list. Please contact the Web server's administrator if the problem persists.

Error Code	Short Text	Explanation
403.7	Forbidden: Client certificate required	This error occurs when the resource you are attempting to access requires your browser to have a client Secure Sockets Layer (SSL) certificate that the server recognizes. This is used for authenticating you as a valid user of the resource. Please contact the Web server's administrator to obtain a valid client certificate.
403.8	Forbidden: Site access denied	This error can be caused if the Web server is not servicing requests, or if you do not have permission to connect to the site. Please contact the Web server's administrator.
403.9	Access Forbidden: Too many users are connected	This error can be caused if the Web server is busy and cannot process your request due to heavy traffic. Please try to connect again later. Please contact the Web server's administrator if the problem persists.
403.10	Access Forbidden: Invalid Configuration	There is a configuration problem on the Web server at this time. Please contact the Web server's administrator if the problem persists.
403.11	Access Forbidden: Password Change	This error can be caused if the user has entered the wrong password during authentication. Please refresh the page and try again. Please contact the Web server's administrator if the problem persists.
403.12	Access Forbidden: Mapper Denied Access	Your client certificate map has been denied access to this Web site. Please contact the site administrator to establish client certificate permissions. You can also change your client certificate and retry, if appropriate.
404	Not Found	The Web server cannot find the file or script you asked for. Please check the URL to ensure that the path is correct. Please contact the server's administrator if this problem persists.
405	Method Not Allowed	The method specified in the Request Line is not allowed for the resource identified by the request. Please ensure that you have the proper MIME type set up for the resource you are requesting. Please contact the server's administrator if this problem persists.
406	Not Acceptable	The resource identified by the request can only generate response entities that have content characteristics that are "not acceptable" according to the Accept headers sent in the request. Please contact the server's administrator if this problem persists.
407	Proxy Authentication Required	You must authenticate with a proxy server before this request can be serviced. Please log on to your proxy server, and then try again. Please contact the Web server's administrator if this problem persists.

Error Code	Short Text	Explanation
412	Precondition Failed	The precondition given in one or more of the Request-header fields evaluated to FALSE when it was tested on the server. The client placed preconditions on the current resource meta-information (header field data) to prevent the requested method from being applied to a resource other than the one intended. Please contact the Web server's administrator if the problem persists.
414	Request-URI Too Long	The server is refusing to service the request because the Request-URI is too long. This rare condition is likely to occur only in the following situations: A client has improperly converted a POST request to a GET request with long query information. A client has encountered a redirection problem (for example, a redirected URL prefix that points to a suffix of itself). The server is under attack by a client attempting to exploit security holes present in some servers using fixed-length buffers for reading or manipulating the Request-URI. Please contact the Web server's administrator if this problem persists.
500	Internal Server Error	The Web server is incapable of performing the request. Please try your request again later. Please contact the Web server's administrator if this problem persists.
501	Not Implemented	The Web server does not support the functionality required to fulfill the request. Please check your URL for errors, and contact the Web server's administrator if the problem persists.
502	Bad Gateway	The server, while acting as a gateway or proxy, received an invalid response from the upstream server it accessed in attempting to fulfill the request. Please contact the Web server's administrator if the problem persists.

Please note that Server error message files are placed in HELP \ COMMON *folder of* *Windows or Windows NT.*

Useful References and URLs

Here are the URLs of some great ASP pages.

Online tutorials and evening classes, some great discussion of `global.asa` problems, a large free components directory, some sample applications plus much more can be found at:

`http://www.activeserverpages.com`

In depth articles on programming IIS, ASP and ADSI can be found at:

`http://www.15seconds.com`

One man's deep obsession with ASP has put together an awesome compendium of script libraries, tutorials, components, ASP related articles, lists of consultants, newsgroups and mailing lists. Find them in:

`http://www.asphole.com`

Columns, references and a whole lot of useful links can be found at:

`http://www.aspalliance.com`

Mentioned earlier in this book, Steve Genusa works day and night on component designs to ensure that ASP developers can tackle any task without having to wait 6 months to a year for a specific component. The fruits off his labor can be enjoyed at:

`http://www.serverobjects.com`

Manohar Kamath's site is devoted to various Internet technologies, specifically those that fall under the umbrella of Microsoft's Active technologies. It covers ASP from a business/technology angle. Check it out at:

`http://www.kamath.com`

Other Useful URLs

You can also get free components and other ASP related information from:

```
http://homepages.id.ibs.se/henrik/aspfaq/
http://www.tarsus.com
```

Glossary of Terms and Acronyms

As you're no doubt aware, the number of acronyms in current use increases at an astonishing rate. This is by no means a complete glossary, simply an attempt to provide translations for the most widely used acronyms. A full and up-to-date glossary is available from the Resource Tools page of our website, accessible from the Resources link on our home page, `http://rapid.wrox.co.uk`

A

ACID   **Data transaction properties**. For a transaction to be considered valid, it must be Atomic, Consistent, Isolated and Durable - hence the acronym.

ACL   **Access Control List**. Internal object used by Windows NT to store user permissions for an individual resource, such as a disk file or directory.

ADC   **Advanced Data Connector**. An Active Server Component, usually referred to as the Data Access Component, which can provide the interface between a script and a data source.

ADO   **ActiveX Data Objects**. A series of ActiveX objects that are the preferred way to provide data access capabilities to any kind of data store, such as relational databases, message stores, etc.

ADS   **Active Directory Services**. A network-centric repository for all kinds of information about all the resources on the network and connected networks. New in Windows NT5.

ADSI   **Active Directory Service Interface**. The **API** for the Microsoft Active Directory Service. Allows programmers to read and manipulate the contents of the directory in code.

ANSI   **American National Standards Institute**. A standards body that provides definitions on computing topics such as programming languages and character sets.

API   **Application Programming Interface**. A series of functions exposed by an application or operating system that allow programmers to access and use the services it provides.

ARP   **Address Resolution Protocol**. A high-level network protocol running over **TCP/IP** that identifies network hardware addresses on a **LAN** given an **IP** address.

ASCII   **American Standard Code for Information Interchange**. A standard definition for character sets. Limited to 255 characters and slowly being superseded by Unicode, which uses 2 bytes per character and can store all types of foreign characters.

ASP   **Active Server Pages**. A Microsoft server-based scripting language that combines **HTML** and script code into a single file. Can be used create all kinds of dynamic pages.

ATM   **Asynchronous Transfer Mode**. A communication protocol designed to offer much higher data transmission speeds over existing networks than traditional methods such as Ethernet.

B

BDC	**Backup Domain Controller**. A Windows NT Server installation that holds a read-only backup copy of security and other information for a network domain. Can authenticate users, and be promoted to a **PDC** in case of failure of the primary machine.
BSC	**Backup Site Controller**. A server within a Microsoft Message Queue Server site. It stores a backup copy of the part of the **MSMQ** Information Store database that applies to the site in case the **PSC** should fail.

C

CA	**Certificate Authority**. A (usually) well known and trusted third party that issues certificates for encryption and verification use. Examples are Verisign and Thawte Consulting.
CDF	**Channel Definition Format**. A Microsoft specialized implementation of **XML**, used to define channels in Internet Explorer 4+ and Windows 98.
Certificate	**A form of identification for secure communication**. Certificates are used to pass public encryption keys between applications, and to verify the certificate holder. Used for secure communication with **HTTPS** and by **MSMQ**.
CGI	**Common Gateway Interface**. A standardized interface exposed by most Web servers. Allows script and executable programs to access the user requests and server responses in order to create dynamic pages.
CIFS	**Common Internet File System**. An open and cross-platform mechanism for clients to request files over a network. Based on the **SMB** protocol widely used by PCs and workstations on a variety of operating systems.
COM	**Component Object Model**. The Microsoft open standard that defines how components communicate. Currently being extended as COM+, which adds extra features that make building component interfaces easier.
CORBA	**Common Object Request Broker Architecture**. A standard for integration and communication between components. Generally UNIX-based, and supported by Sun, Netscape, IBM, etc.
Corpus	**Index Server document collection**. The set of documents, files and other resources that are indexed by Microsoft Index Server or other indexing service.
CRL	**Certificate Revocation List**. A list of certificates that are no longer valid. Maintained and published by the **CA** that originally issued these certificates.
Crossware	**Netscape development environment**. A design methodology that defines how applications can be built so that they can run both over an internal network, and out to external partners over the Internet.
CryptoAPI	**Cryptographic Application Programming Interface**. A Microsoft **API** that provides services for authentication, encoding and encryption in Windows 32-bit applications.
CSP	**Cryptographic Service Provider**. A code module that integrates with the **CryptoAPI** to perform the authentication, encoding and encryption. Often created by **ISV**s.
CSS1	**Cascading Style Sheets (Level 1)**. The W3C-approved way to specify text formatting and layout in a Web page. Currently being expanded to **CSS2**. Several style sheets can be linked to a Web page, or the style information embedded within the page.

D

Daemon   **Background network program**. A software application or service that runs continually within a network node to handle any of a range of tasks such as directing mail or routing data.

DAO   **Data Access Objects**. A Microsoft data access technology with a complex multi-level object model, introduced for use with MS Access and Office. Now superseded by **ADO**.

DBMS   **Database Management System**. A program or environment that stores, manages and retrieves data, for example SQL Server, Oracle, DB2, etc. Usually a relational database system.

DCOM   **Distributed Component Object Model**. The implementation of **COM** that allows components to communicate over a network connection, rather than being limited to the same machine.

DES   **Data Encryption Standard**. A standard that protects passwords from being read and then used again on the same a network to obtain unofficial access.

DHCP   **Dynamic Host Configuration Protocol**. A protocol under which a client can contact a server to obtain a valid IP network address for its own use, rather than using one hard-wired into the client. Useful on large networks to prevent **IP** address conflicts.

DHTML   **Dynamic HTML**. The overall moniker for the ability of the latest generation of browsers to change the contents of a Web page using script code, while it is loaded.

DLL   **Dynamic Link Library**. A software component or library of functions stored as a disk file in a special format. Used by other applications that require these functions.

DNA   **Distributed interNet Applications Architecture**. A methodology for three-tier application design using components that communicate via **COM** and **DCOM**. Also a broad marketing term for the combination of the different services offered by Windows NT.

DNS   **Domain Name System**. Also refers to a Domain Name Server. Translates a text **URL** (such as `http://rapid.wrox.co.uk`) into the equivalent **IP** address (`194.73.51.228`).

DOM   **Document Object Model**. A standard definition of the structure and content of a Web page when displayed in a browser or other user agent. Used in scripting to manipulate the contents of the document.

DSN   **Data Source Name**. A specification of all the information required to connect to and access a data store. Used with **ODBC**, and can also be stored as a file on disk (File **DSN**) or with system-wide access (System **DSN**).

DTC   **Distributed Transaction Coordinator**. A software component that manages changes to a data source under control of a transaction manager. Allows updates to be rolled back if the transaction needs to be aborted, leaving the data store unchanged.

DTD   **Document Type Definition**. A set of rules that define how the rules of **SGML** are applied to a particular markup language.

E

ECMA   **European Computer Manufacturers Association**. A standards body that manages and ratifies proposals for computer technologies. Issues the open standard for the scripting language ECMAScript, which is based on JavaScript and JScript.

F

FAT   **File Allocation Table**. The original MS-DOS format for disks. Has no built-in security, and imposes restrictions on the way files are physically stored. The limited number of allocation units it supports means that it is inefficient on large disks.

FAT32   **32-bit File Allocation Table**. An upgraded version of **FAT** introduced with the Windows 95 OSR2 update. Can handle more allocation units on large disks, with corresponding reduction in cluster size, to provide more efficient file storage.

Firewall   **Network security component**. A software component that acts as a filter restricting specific types of network packets from passing from one network to another. Often used between a **LAN** and the Internet.

FTP   **File Transfer Protocol**. A standard Internet protocol for transfering files between machines. Generally faster and more efficient than email or **HTTP**.

G

GIF   **Graphics Interchange Format**. A format for graphics and images that compresses the content to provide efficient transmission over a network. Developed by CompuServe and now in common use on the Internet.

GINA   **Password filter component**. A software component that can be added to Windows NT to perform extra checking on user passwords as they are changed, ensuring they are strong enough to meet security requirements.

Gopher   **Internet search and retrieve protocol**. A protocol designed to allow clients to search for, retrieve and display documents over the Internet. Generally superseded by the Web, and no longer in common use.

GUID   **Globally Unique Identifier**. A 128-bit number that is generated automatically and used to refer to a resource, component, directory entry or any other type of object. Guaranteed to be unique.

H

HTML   **Hypertext Markup Language**. The language of the Web. A way of inserting tags (elements and attributes) into a text page to add formatting, rich content, and other information.

HTTP   **Hypertext Transfer Protocol**. A protocol running over **IP** and designed for the World Wide Web. Provides packaging of information that can contain instruction headers and other data about the content.

HTTPS   **Hypertext Transfer Protocol Secure**. The secure version of **HTTP** using certificates that can uniquely identify the server and client, and encrypt all communication between them.

I

ICMP   **Internet Control Message Protocol**. An extension to **IP** that permits extra control, test and error messages to be incorporated into the packet stream.

IDC   **Internet Database Connector**. A Microsoft server-based scripting language for linking **ODBC** data sources to a Web server, so as to create dynamic pages based on a database.

IE   **Internet Explorer**. Microsoft's Web browser. What more can you say?

I

IETF   **Internet Engineering Task Force**. A large multi-vendor international group of engineers, operators, vendors and researchers that defines, proposes and ratifies technical standards for the Internet.

IIOP   **Internet Inter-Orb Protocol**. A standard, like **CORBA**, for communication between Java-based components such as JavaBeans. Allows components to communicate over the Internet in a Crossware application.

IIS   **Internet Information Server**. The Web server software included with Microsoft Windows NT. Supports applications that use **CGI**, **ASP**, **IDC** and **ISAPI**; and interfaces with Windows NT and other services running on the server machine.

IP   **Internet Protocol**. The low-level part of the **TCP/IP** protocol. **IP** assembles the **TCP** packets, adds address information, and despatches them over the network.

IPX/SPX   **Novell NetWare network protocol**. A network protocol developed by Novell to allow servers to provide an easily navigable network structure, and to share network resources.

ISAPI   **Internet Server Application Programming Interface**. A broadly standardized interface that allows server-side programs to create dynamic Web pages, in a similar way to **CGI**.

ISDN   **Integrated Services Digital Network**. A technology for combining voice and data in separate streams over a standard PSTN phone line to provide higher speeds, increased capacity and multiple channels.

ISO   **International Standards Organization**. A world-wide group of standards bodies that create international standards, including information technology related areas.

ISP   **Internet Service Provider**. An agency or company that provides a connection to the Internet, usually as a leased line or a dial-up link.

ISV   **Independent Software Vendor**. Term used to describe companies that produce software or components for use with other companies operating systems or technologies.

ITU   **International Telecommunications Union**. An international body that defines the standards for modems and low level transmission of data, typically over public networks like the PSTN.

J

JavaBean   **Java software component**. A software component, built in Java, that implements a control or provides a series of functions for use within another application.

JDBC   **Java Database Connectivity**. A software interface layer that allows Java applications and components to access data stores via **ODBC**.

JDK   **Java Development Kit**. A set of documentation, samples and tools that provide programmers with the information required when creating Java applications and components.

JIT   **Just In Time**. An acronym applied to several technologies to indicate that a process, such as compilation of byte code, is carried out just before it is required by an application.

JPEG   **Joint Photographic Experts Group**. A body that designed and promotes the **JPEG** (**JPG**) graphics format, which combines high color depth with small file size for photographic still images by using a lossy compression scheme.

K

Kerberos   **Network security protocol**. A security technology that has been under development in academic institutes for some time. Windows NT 5 uses this, replacing the existing **LAN** Manager based security methods in NT 3.5 and NT 4.

L

LAN   **Local Area Network**. A series of machines in close proximity, usually in the same building, connected together. Uses any of a range of common network protocols, often referred to as Ethernet.

LDAP   **Lightweight Directory Access Protocol**. An Internet standard used to access directory information on remote servers. Uses less resources than the traditional **X.500** protocol.

Locale   **Language and locality information**. A text string such as "en-us" that accurately identifies a language and locality to allow programs to use language-specific formatting and processes. Can also be identified by a number called the LocaleID.

M

MAPI   **Mail (or Message) Application Programming Interface**. The Microsoft standard application programming interface for email software. Allows programs to read, create, send and manipulate stored messages.

MDA   **Message Digest Algorithm**. A software algorithm that creates a digest for a message or other stream of data. The digest is unique, and the original data cannot be recreated from it. Generally specified as MD2, MD4, MD5, etc.

MDAC   **Microsoft Data Access Components**. A series of component objects that provide data access services such as **ADO** to Windows applications.

MIME   **Multipurpose (or Multimedia) Internet Mail Extension**. Defines the content type of a document, file or message attachment, for example "image/mpeg" or "text/plain".

MPEG   **Motion Pictures Expert Group**. A body that designed and promotes the **MPEG** (**MPG**) moving graphics format, which combines high color depth with small file size for photographic moving images by using a lossy compression scheme.

MQIS   **Message Queue Information Store**. The central repository of information about an **MSMQ** enterprise, stored on the **PEC** and distributed to each site via the **PSCs** and **BSCs**.

MSMQ   **Microsoft Message Queue Server**. A Windows NT service that provides robust and secure transmission of messages between servers, which can be on different connected networks.

MTS   **Microsoft Transaction Server**. A Windows NT service that acts as both an object broker for components and as a distributed transaction manager. The basis for most **DNA** applications that require data access.

N

Namespace   **A name resolution area**. The bounded area within which a named object can be resolved. Examples are a subtree in a directory service, or a class within a component.

NDS   **Novell Directory Service**. Novell's implementation of a network-centric directory service. Has been available for some time, and is in common use on large NetWare networks. Supported by Windows NT.

NetBEUI   **Networking protocol**. The native protocol that forms the basis for Microsoft Networking in Windows environments.

N

NetBIOS	**Networking protocol**. A widely accepted and implemented standard for networking in a **LAN** environment.
NIC	**Network Interface Card**. The hardware providing the connection between a computer or peripheral and the network. Usually a plug-in card with sockets for a range of cable connector types.
NNTP	**Network News Transfer Protocol**. A protocol that transports news messages to special servers and client software over the Internet. Provides cross referencing, expiration, and search and retrieval facilities.
NOS	**Network Operating System**. A generic term for the protocol and software that provides communication services over a network. Examples are **NetBIOS**, **TCP/IP**, etc.
NTFS	**NT File System**. The Windows NT native disk format. Provides an efficient data storage format, and allows a range of security settings to be applied to individual files and directories.
NTLM	**NT LAN Manager authentication**. The protocol normally referred to as Challenge/Response that Windows NT uses to pass authentication information between the client and server when logging on.

O

OCX	**OLE Control Extension**. A software component stored as a disk file in a special format for use by other applications. Similar to a **DLL**, but generally offers a single function to create an object or control.
ODBC	**Open Database Connectivity**. An open standard originally developed by Microsoft to allow transparent data access to all kinds of data stores such as relational databases. Drivers are manufactured by third parties to suit their own data store.
ODSI	**Open Directory Services Interface**. A set of industry-standard functions that can be implemented by a directory service, such as **LDAP** and **ADS**, to allow other applications to access the directory content.
OLAP	**On-line Analytical Processing**. A data store (or data warehouse) holding data in a multi-dimensional fashion. Often used for decision support and other commercial enquiry systems.
OLE	**Object Linking and Embedding**. The fore-runner to ActiveX. Uses COM to let components communicate, and allows applications to use the services of other applications as though they were just components.
OLE DB	**Object Linking and Embedding Database**. The new standard data access programming interface from Microsoft that is designed to replace **ODBC**, and provide wider coverage of different types of data stores.
OLTP	**On-line Transaction Processing**. The technique of performing order or information processing in real time, rather than storing the transactions for executaion as a batch at a later time.
OMG	**Object Management Group**. An alliance of vendors formed to define and promote the **CORBA** object spcification. Prominent members are Sun, Netscape and IBM.
ONE	**Open Network Environment**. A Netscape development environment based on open standards that makes it easy to build, deploy and run applications over the Internet. See also **Crossware**.
OSF	**Open Software Federation**. A multi-vendor body that defines and promotes open standards for Unix-based operating systems and software.

P

Package	**Group of MTS components**. A set of related components installed into **MTS** that are defined and used together in an application. The package defines the security trust boundary for the component group.
PASSFILT	**Password filter component.** An interchangeable software component within Windows NT that performs checking on user passwords as they are entered, ensuring they are strong enough to meet security requirements.
PDC	**Primary Domain Controller**. The Windows NT server installation that holds the central security and other information for the entire network domain.
PEC	**Primary Enterprise Controller**. The server that is at the root of Microsoft Message Queue Server enterprise. It stores the complete **MSMQ** Information Store database.
Perl	**Practical Extraction and Reporting Language**. A scripting language used with the first Web applications. Runs on the server and can create dynamic pages via the **CGI**.
PFX	**Personal Information Exchange**. A protocol that can safely and securely transfer the contents of a **PStore** from one location to another.
PGP	**Pretty Good Privacy**. An independently developed encryption application that uses public keys to allow secure transmission of messages.
PING	**Packet Internet Grouper**. A diagnostic utility program that uses **ICMP** to request messages from a remote server to check that it is available and can respond.
PKCS	**Public Key Cryptography Standard**. A generic term used to describe the various available types of public key encryption standards such as **DES**, **RSA**, etc.
PNG	**Portable Network Graphics**. A format for graphics and images that compresses the content to provide efficient transmission over a network. Developed by W3C, but not yet in commmon use.
POP3	**Post Office Protocol**. An Internet protocol designed to transmit email messages and attachments between mail servers. Offers extra features over the earlier **SMTP** protocol.
PPP	**Point-to-Point Protocol**. An industry-wide standard protocol that defines how packets are exchanged over the Internet, particularly via a modem.
PPTP	**Point-To-Point Tunneling Protocol**. A protocol that allows native network services such as **NetBEUI** and **IPX** to be used to create a secure and reliable connection over the Internet.
Proxy	**Software connection component**. A software program or service (as in proxy server) that acts as an intermediate gateway and connects two processes or users. In the case of a proxy server, it can also filter the network packets.
PSC	**Primary Site Controller**. A server that is at the root of Microsoft Message Queue Server site. It stores a copy of the part of an **MSMQ** Information Store database that applies to the site.
PStore	**Protected Information Store**. A Windows NT technology that provides a secure store for personal and security information about the network users. Can contain certificates, credit card details, personal information, etc.
PTT	**Private Telecommunications Technology**. A certificate-based protocol, similar to **SSL**, which can provide more robust and secure authentication and encryption over a network.

R

RAS   **Remote Access Service**. A Windows technology that allows dial-up users to connect to a network (over a phone line or the Internet, for example) and access the resources on the network as though they were a local user.

RDO   **Remote Data Objects**. A Microsoft remote data access technology with a complex multi-level object model, introduced for use with programming languages like Visual Basic. Now superseded by **ADO**.

RDS   **Remote Data Service**. A Microsoft technology that provides a persistent and automatic method for caching data from a server-side data source on the client, for use in a Web page or other application.

Role   **Transaction Server security context**. Roles are used to define the user accounts that can execute a component running under **MTS**. They simplify security management in **DNA**-based applications.

RPC   **Remote Procedure Call**. A standard defined by the Open Software Foundation that allows one process to execute methods defined by another process, either on the same machine or across a network.

RSA   **Public key cryptography method**. A standard type of encryption technique designed by Rivest, Shamir and Adleman for securing data passing over a network or between components.

S

S/MIME   **Secure Multipurpose Internet Mail Extension**. A version of **MIME** that allows the contents of the message and attachments to be digitally signed and encrypted, using standard public key ciphers, hash functions and certificates.

SChannel   **Secure Channel**. A security service provider module that sits on top of the Microsoft **CryptoAPI**, and implements the public key encryption between a client and the server.

SDK   **Software Development Kit**. A set of documentation, samples and tools that provide programmers with the information required to work with a technology - for example the **IE4 SDK** for Internet Explorer 4.

SET   **Secure Electronic Transaction**. A protocol for implementing secure electronic transactions over the Internet. Particularly aimed at financial institutions for handling credit card and related information.

SGML   **Standard Generalized Markup Language**. A root language for the formal definition of other markup languages, and not directly used for programming. Designed to provide portability and flexibility between markup languages based on it.

SHA   **Secure Hash Algorithm**. A software algorithm that creates a digest for a message or other stream of data. The digest is unique, and the original data cannot be recreated from it.

SID   **Security Identifier**. A non-volatile hidden **GUID** that identifies a user account in Windows NT. When accounts are deleted and recreated, a new **SID** is applied to them. The **SID** is passed between applications running under NT, instead of the username.

SMB   **Server Message Block**. A protocol used in Windows Networking to provide network-wide access to files and printers.

SMTP   **Simple Mail Transfer Protocol**. The first email transfer protocol for the Internet. Still used to transmit simple mail messages, but slowly being replaced by **POP3**.

SNA   **System Network Architecture**. A standard communication framework developed by IBM to allow communication between different models of computer, including minicomputers and mainframes.

S

SNMP	**Simple Network Management Protocol**. A standard for remote management of devices such as routers and other services over a **TCP/IP** network. Also provides monitoring services for a network.
SQL	**Structured Query Language**. A standard language for accessing data in relational databases. **ANSI** provide a base definition but many vendors have added extra proprietary features and extensions.
SSI	**Server-side Include**. An instruction within a Web page or script that causes the Web server to execute a program, or insert a file or other information into the **HTML** stream sent to the client.
SSL	**Secure Sockets Layer**. A technology originally developed by Netscape to provide client and server verification, and secure communication between a Web browser and server. Uses public key and secret key encryption.
SSP	**Security Support Provider**. A software library that manages a set of security functions. Multiple **SSP**s can be installed, each from a different vendor if required. See **SSPI**.
SSPI	**Security Service Provider Interface**. A standard programming interface specification that allows applications to query any SSP and use its services. Example **SSP**s are **Kerberos**, **NTLM**, and **SSL**.
Stub	**Software connection component**. A software component within an application that links to a corresponding proxy elsewhere, and handles the communication of data between them. May be running in a separate environment from the proxy, or just on a different execution thread.

T

TAPI	**Telecommunications Application Programming Interface**. A set of standard programming functions that can be implemented by applications that interface with telecommunications equipment, i.e. telephones, exchanges, fax machines, voice mail, etc.
TCO	**Total Cost of Ownership**. The cost, generally far exceeding original purchase price, of a computer system. Includes such things as training, maintenance, support, consumables, etc.
TCP	**Transport Control Protocol**. The high-level part of the **TCP/IP** protocol. **TCP** creates the data packets and passes them to **IP** for transmission over the network. It is also responsible for marshalling and sorting received packets, and basic packet error detection.
TCP/IP	**Transport Control Protocol/Internet Protocol**. The base protocol of the Internet, also used on internal networks and Intranets. Passes data in routable packets between servers, and supports high-level protocols like **HTTP**, **FTP**, etc.
TDC	**Tabular Data Control**. An ActiveX control, part of the **MDAC** Universal Data Access components package, that provides client-side access and caching over **HTTP** for data stored in text format.
TLA	**Three Letter Acronym**. A recursive definition designed to make fun of the way the industry tends to name its products and services.
TRID	**OLE Transaction Identifier**. A unique identifier (**GUID**) for a transaction process that is executing against an **OLE** Transactions resource manager.
TSQL	**Transact SQL**. A set of extensions to **SQL** implemented in MS SQL Server, which allow (amongst other things) more complex queries to be created and compiled as stored procedures within the database.

U

UDA   **Universal Data Access.** Microsoft term describing a concept of using one data access technology with all enterprise data sources. Based on **ADO** and **OLE DB**. See also **MDAC.**

UNC   **Uniform Naming Convention.** A combination of server name and resource path and name which identifies a resource on a local or wide-area network. Common **UNCs** start with the double-backslash, such as `\\sunspot\C\documents\myfile.doc.`

URL   **Universal Resource Locator.** A combination of a protocol, host name, (optional) port, path and resource name. Uniquely identifies a resource on the Internet. For example `http://www.wrox.com:8080/books/index.htm.`

V

VB   **Visual Basic.** Microsoft's entry-level programming language and environment for Windows programming, including building components and specialist applications.

VBA   **Visual Basic for Applications.** Microsoft's version of Visual Basic that is designed to be used as a replacement and extension of macros in applications, rather than as a stand-alone programming language.

VJS   **Visual JavaScript.** A Netscape tool for rapid crossware development, providing an array of components and services together with an **HTML** page designer.

VRML   **Virtual Reality Modelling Language.** A strandardized programming language that allows moving 3D-style effects to be created within **HTML** applications.

W

W3C   **World Wide Web Consortium.** The main body responsible for managing and ratifying standards for the Internet, especially the World Wide Web (WWW).

WAM   **Web Application Manager.** A sub-system component of **IIS** that is used to control applications that run in a separate area of memory (i.e. out of process) from the Web server.

WAN   **Wide Area Network.** A series of machines or networks that are outside the limits of normal network cable length limits. Usually connection is via phone lines or fibre optic cables, radio or satellite links, or the Internet.

WINS   **Windows Internet Name Service.** A protocol and corresponding service that maps textual addresses to the equivalent **IP** address in Windows-based networks. See also **DNS.**

WinSock **Windows Sockets.** The software component that forms the connection to an **IP**-based network, and handles the transfer of data from the machine onto and off the network at the lowest level.

WOSA   **Windows Open System Architecture.** A range of **API**s that allow programmers to access various Windows technologies in a uniform and standard way. Includes specifications for **ODBC**, **MAPI**, and **TAPI.**

X

X.500   **Directory access protocol**. The high-level specification and interface definition for directory access. Generally used in commercial mainframe environments.

X.509   **Certificate format standard.** The principal standard format definition for certificates that are used to provide encryption and authentication.

XA   **X/Open transaction interface**. The X/Open organization defined standard for communication between transaction managers and resource managers in a two-phase commit distributed transaction system.

XATM   **XA Transaction Manager**. A component included in **MTS** that allows transactions against data stores which use the **XA** interface to be integrated into **MTS** transactions.

XID   **XA Transaction Identifier**. A unique identifier for a transaction process that is executing against an **XA** resource manager.

XML   **Extensible Markup Language**. A new markup language based on **SGML**, and designed to remove the limitation imposed by **HTML**. Allows a page to contain a definition and execution plan for the elements, and well as their content.

XSL   **Extensible Stylesheet Language**. A specialist development of **XML** designed to provide flexible ways of adding style, display and layout information to a document.

Z

ZAW   **Zero Administration for Windows**. A Microsoft initiative incorporated into NT5 which provides ways to reduce the Total Cost of Ownership in networked environments by providing automatic software installation and fixes, and other features.

Support and Errata

One of the most irritating things about any programming book can be when you find that bit of code you've just spent an hour typing simply doesn't work. You check it a hundred times to see if you've set it up correctly and then you notice the spelling mistake in the variable name on the book page. Grrr! Of course, you can blame the authors for not taking enough care or testing the code thoroughly, the editors for not doing their job properly, or the proofreaders for not being eagle-eyed enough, but this doesn't get around the fact that mistakes do happen.

We try hard to ensure no mistakes sneak out into the real world, but we can't promise that this book is 100% error free. What we can do is offer the next best thing by providing you with immediate support and feedback from experts who have worked on the book and try to ensure that future editions eliminate these gremlins. The following section will take you step by step through the process of posting errata to our web site to get that help. The sections that follow, therefore, are:

- Wrox Developers Membership
- Finding a list of existing errata on the web site
- Adding your own errata to the existing list
- What happens to your errata once you've posted it (why doesn't it appear immediately?)

There is also a section covering how to e-mail a question for technical support. This comprises:

- What your e-mail should include
- What happens to your e-mail once it has been received by us

So that you only need view information relevant to yourself, we ask that you register as a Wrox Developer Member. This is a quick and easy process, that will save you time in the long-run. If you are already a member, just update membership to include this book.

Wrox Developer's Membership

To get your FREE Wrox Developer's Membership click on Membership in the navigation bar of our home site

www.wrox.com.

This is shown in the following screen shot:

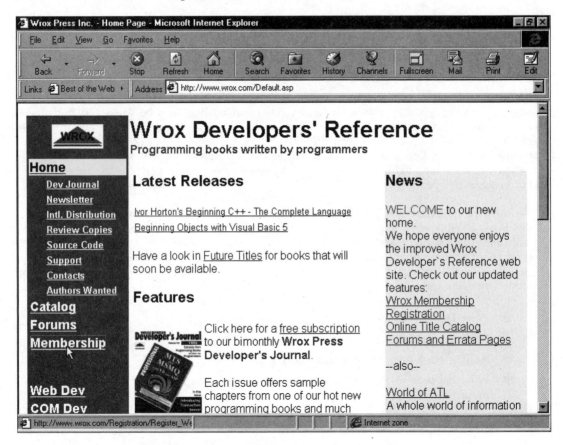

Then, on the next screen (not shown), click on New User. This will display a form. Fill in the details on the form and submit the details using the submit button at the bottom. Before you can say 'The best read books come in Wrox Red' you will get the following screen:

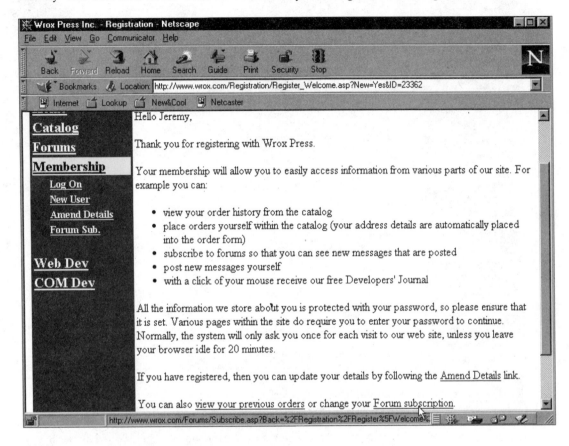

Finding an Errata on the Web Site.

Before you send in a query, you might be able to save time by finding the answer to your problem on our web site: `http:\\www.wrox.com`.

Each book we publish has its own page and its own eratta sheet. You can get to any book's page by clicking on support from the left hand side navigation bar.

From this page you can locate any books errata page on our site. Select your book from the pop-up menu and click on it.

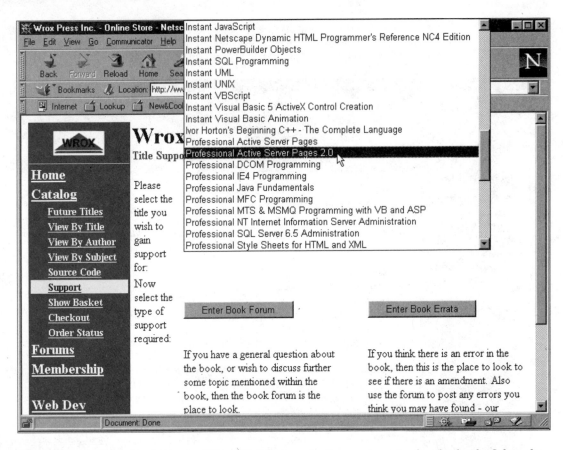

Then click on **Enter Book Errata**. This will take you to the errata page for the book. Select the criteria by which you want to view the errata, and click the **apply criteria** button. This will provide you with links to specific errata. For an initial search, you are advised to view the errata by page numbers. If you have looked for an error previously, then you may wish to limit your search using dates. We update these pages daily to ensure that you have the latest information on bugs and errors.

Adding an Errata to the Sheet Yourself

It's always possible that you may find your error is not listed, in which case you can enter details of the fault yourself. It might be anything from a spelling mistake to a faulty piece of code in the book. Sometimes you'll find useful hints that aren't really errors on the listing. By entering errata you may save another reader hours of frustration, and of course, you will be helping us provide even higher quality information. We're very grateful for this sort of advice and feedback. You can enter errata using the 'ask a question' of our editors link at the bottom of the errata page. Click on this link and you will get a form on which to post your message.

Fill in the subject box, and then type your message in the space provided on the form. Once you have done this, click on the Post Now button at the bottom of the page. The message will be forwarded to our editors. They'll then test your submission and check that the error exists, and that the suggestions you make are valid. Then your submission, together with a solution, is posted on the site for public consumption. Obviously this stage of the process can take a day or two, but we will endeavor to get a fix up sooner than that.

E-mail Support

If you wish to directly query a problem in the book with an expert who knows the book in detail then e-mail **support@wrox.com**, with the title of the book and the last four numbers of the ISBN in the subject field of the e-mail. A typical e-mail should include the following things:

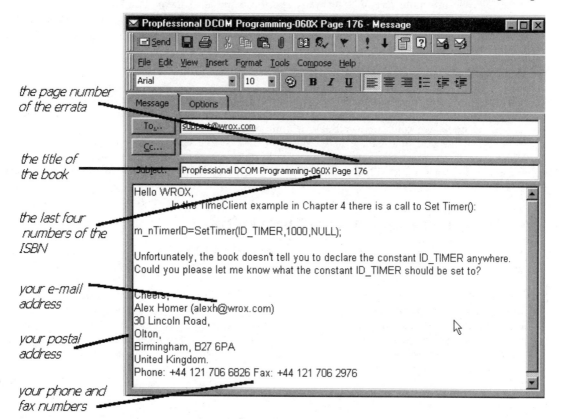

the page number of the errata

the title of the book

the last four numbers of the ISBN

your e-mail address

your postal address

your phone and fax numbers

We won't send you junk mail. We need the details to save your time and ours. If we need to replace a disk or CD we'll be able to get it to you straight away. When you send an e-mail it will go through the following chain of support:

Customer Support

Your message is delivered to one of our customer support staff who are the first people to read it. They have files on most frequently asked questions and will answer anything general immediately. They answer general questions about the book and the web site.

Editorial

Deeper queries are forwarded to the technical editor responsible for that book. They have experience with the programming language or particular product and are able to answer detailed technical questions on the subject. Once an issue has been resolved, the editor can post the errata to the web site.

The Authors

Finally, in the unlikely event that the editor can't answer your problem, s/he will forward the request to the author. We try to protect the author from any distractions from writing. However, we are quite happy to forward specific requests to them. All Wrox authors help with the support on their books. They'll mail the customer and the editor with their response, and again all readers should benefit.

What we can't answer

Obviously with an ever growing range of books and an ever-changing technology base, there is an increasing volume of data requiring support. While we endeavor to answer all questions about the book, we can't answer bugs in your own programs that you've adapted from our code. So, while you might have loved the help desk systems in our Active Server Pages book, don't expect too much sympathy if you cripple your company with a live adaptation you customized from Chapter 12. But do tell us if you're especially pleased with the routine you developed with our help.

How to tell us exactly what you think

We understand that errors can destroy the enjoyment of a book and can cause many wasted and frustrated hours, so we seek to minimize the distress that they can cause.

You might just wish to tell us how much you liked or loathed the book in question. Or you might have ideas about how this whole process could be improved. In which case you should e-mail `feedback@wrox.com`. You'll always find a sympathetic ear, no matter what the problem is. Above all you should remember that we do care about what you have to say and we will do our utmost to act upon it.

Beginning
Active Server Pages 2.0

Symbols

K

Key method, Dictionary object 339
keys
 ClientCertificate collection 228
 cookies 285, 288
 cookies collection 226
 databases
  definition of 489
  foreign keys 489, 553
  primary keys 492, 495, 553
 definition of 426
 Dictionary object
  changing 339
  name/value pairs 336
  value of, changing 338
 ServerVariable name, storing with 216
Keys method, Dictionary object 341
keyset recordsets 431
 ADO 432

L

LANGUAGE attribute
 <% and %> tags 54
 script tags 50
LCID property, Session object 274
Left function, definition of 116
Len function, definition of 116
less than (<) operator 105
less than or equal to (<=) operator 105
lifetime
 global variables 125
 local variables 123
line breaks

 tags 84
 source code, adding 360
lines, definition of 137
list boxes, multi-select 256
LiveScript 14

local variables
 creating 123
 definition of 122
 lifetime of 123
locale identifiers 274
Lock method, Application object 264, 266, 283
locking
 constants 436
 definition of 432
 optimistic 433, 525, 539
 pessimistic 433
 read-only 433
LockType property 475
 Recordset property 436
log files, creating 361, 363
logical operators, definition of 106
login screen
 creating 508, 512
 failed login attempts 512
login verification 503
long type, definition of 100
loops
 array contents, displaying with 130
 looping controls
  definition of 136, 138, 140
  Do While 138, 150, 156
  examples 139
  For Each 507
  For Each ... Next 156
  For ... Next 138, 150
 string manipulation, loops for 121
 infinite 157
LTrim function, definition of 118

numeric subtypes 99
bytes 100
double 100
integers 100
long type 100
single type 100

O

object models
ActiveX Data Objects (ADO) 409
definition of 193
FileSystemObject object, object model of 342
instances, creating from 296
road map, object models as 198
object subtype, definition of 102
<OBJECT> tag 14
object-oriented programming, definition of 176
ObjectContext object 36, 194
definition of 198
objects 15, 35, 175
Active Server objects 36
built-in objects 194
definition of 176
events
events generated by 181
firing 182
instances of 177
interfaces 183
methods of 178
calling object methods 189
ObjectContext 198
Page level objects 196
programmatic objects 183
programming with objects 183
properties of 177
altering 185
setting 185
Request 196
Response 197

OLE-DB
ActiveX Data Objects 408
definition of 407
Open DataBase Connectivity (ODBC) vs. 410
On Error 383, 384
Open DataBase Connectivity (ODBC)
definition of 406
OLE-DB vs. 410
Open method
Connection object 405, 412
Recordset object 430, 434, 506
OpenAsTextStream method
File object 355
TextStream object 358
parameters 358
opening tags 45
OpenTextFile method, FileSystemObject object 355, 363
operating systems, detection of 223
operators
arithmetic 104
comparison 105
logical 106
optimistic locking 433, 525, 539
Option Explicit
debugging and 372, 393
debugging programs with 108
placement of 108
< or >, displaying 360
OR operator 106
ORDER BY clause 537
order of calculation, indicating with brackets 110
order of execution 56
changing 135
example testing 58
JScript example testing 59
output buffer, controlling 239
output parameters 469

P

V

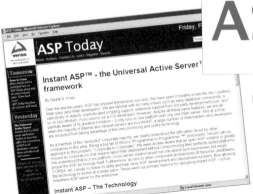

ASP Today
www.asptoday.com

It's not easy keeping up to date with what's hot and what's not in the ever-changing world of internet development. Even if you stick to one narrow topic like ASP, trawling through the mailing lists each day and finding new and better code is still a twenty-four-seven job. Which is where we come in.

You already know Wrox Press from its series of titles on ASP and its associated technologies. We realise that we can't bring out a book everyday to keep you all up to date, so from March 1, we're starting a brand new website at www.asptoday.com which will do all the hard work for you. Every week you'll find new tips, tricks and techniques for you to try out and test in your development, covering ASP components, ADO, RDS, ADSI, CDO, Security, Site Design, BackOffice, XML and more. Look out also for bug alerts when they're found and fixes when they're available.

We hope that you won't be shy in telling us what you think of the site and the content we put on it either. If you like what you'll see, we'll carry on as we are, but if you think we're missing something, then we'll address it accordingly. If you've got something to write, then do so and we'll include it. We're hoping our site will become a global effort by and for the entire ASP community.

In anticipation,
Dan Maharry, ASPToday.com

Beginning Active Server Pages 2.0 - Registration Card

Name _____

Address _____

_____

_____

City _____ State/Region _____

Country _____ Postcode/Zip _____

E-mail _____

Occupation _____

How did you hear about this book? _____

☐ Book review (name) _____

☐ Advertisement (name) _____

☐ Recommendation _____

☐ Catalog _____

☐ Other _____

Where did you buy this book? _____

☐ Bookstore (name) _____ City _____

☐ Computer Store (name) _____

☐ Mail Order _____

☐ Other _____

What influenced you in the purchase of this book?

☐ Cover Design

☐ Contents

☐ Other (please specify) _____

How did you rate the overall contents of this book?

☐ Excellent   ☐ Good

☐ Average   ☐ Poor

What did you find most useful about this book? _____

What did you find least useful about this book? _____

Please add any additional comments. _____

What other subjects will you buy a computer book on soon? _____

What is the best computer book you have used this year? _____

Note: This information will only be used to keep you updated about new Wrox Press titles and will not be used for any other purpose or passed to any other third party.

Check here if you DO NOT want to receive support for this book ▮

WROX PRESS INC.

Wrox writes books for you. Any suggestions, or
ideas about how you want information given in
your ideal book will be studied by our team.
Your comments are always valued at Wrox.

Free phone in USA 800-USE-WROX
Fax (312) 893 8001

UK Tel. (0121) 687 4100   Fax   (0121) 687 4101

Computer Book Publishers

NB. If you post the bounce back card below in the UK, please send it to:
Wrox Press Ltd., Arden House, 1102 Warwick Road, Acocks Green,
Birmingham. B27 6BH. UK.

NO POSTAGE
NECESSARY
IF MAILED
IN THE
UNITED STATES

BUSINESS REPLY MAIL
FIRST CLASS MAIL   PERMIT#64   CHICAGO, IL

POSTAGE WILL BE PAID BY ADDRESSEE

WROX PRESS INC.
29 S. LA SALLE ST.
SUITE 520
CHICAGO IL 60603-USA